PENGUIN CLASSICS

THE ARTHASHASTRA

L.N. Rangarajan graduated from the University of Madras with an M.Sc in experimental physics. He joined the Indian Foreign Service in 1956 and has been Ambassador to Greece, Sudan, Tunisia, Norway and Iceland.

A political economist with a special interest in conflict limitation and negotiation, he has contributed articles on political economy to several journals. His previous publications include: *Commodity Conflict: The Political Economy of International Commodity Negotiations* and *The Limitation of Conflict: A Theory of Bargaining and Negotiation*.

L.N. Rangarajan is married to a musician and has two sons.

KAUTILYA

THE ARTHASHASTRA

EDITED, REARRANGED,
TRANSLATED AND INTRODUCED
BY
L.N. RANGARAJAN

PENGUIN BOOKS
An imprint of Penguin Random House

PENGUIN BOOKS

USA | Canada | UK | Ireland | Australia
New Zealand | India | South Africa | China

Penguin Books is part of the Penguin Random House group of companies
whose addresses can be found at global.penguinrandomhouse.com

Published by Penguin Random House India Pvt. Ltd
4th Floor, Capital Tower 1, MG Road,
Gurugram 122 002, Haryana, India

Penguin
Random House
India

First published by Penguin Books India 1992

Copyright © L.N. Rangarajan 1987

All rights reserved

75 74 73 72

ISBN 9780140446036

Printed at Replika Press Pvt. Ltd, India

AUTHOR'S NOTE

o <u>Arabic numerals</u> indicate the number of the verse. For example, {1.1.1} Book 1, Chapter 1, verse number 1. Verse numbers are as in Kangle, *The Kautiliya Arthashastra*, Part I (text) and Part II (translation), second edition; University of Bombay 1969.

o <u>Roman numerals</u> indicate a reference to the Part and Section in this translation. I (i)Part 1, Section 1.

o <u>Square brackets</u> [] enclose translator's additions and comments.

o <u>Double braces</u> {} enclose verse numbers.

o <u>Parentheses</u> () are used normally. In the translation, material within parantheses is that found in the text.

o <u>Sanskrit words</u> are in italics; diacritical marks are not used.

CONTENTS

PREFACE

Both Kautilya the preceptor and his masterwork the *Arthashastra* are much misunderstood. Popularly known as Chanakya, he is maligned and often ridiculed as a teacher of unethical, not to say immoral, practices and as an advocate of the theory that 'the ends justify the means'. 'Chanakyan' has entered Indian vocabulary as the equivalent of 'Machiavellian'. Most people know little of what Kautilya actually said in the *Arthashastra*. The only thing they can recall is the '*mandala*' theory, based on the principles: 'Every neighbouring state is an enemy and the enemy's enemy is a friend.'

This popular view is not only simplistic but untrue. Only scholars of ancient Indian history are aware of the range and depth of the *Arthashastra*. It is a pioneering work on statecraft in all its aspects, written at least one thousand five hundred years ago. Unfortunately, the greatness of Kautilya remains unappreciated for want of a modern translation. The main objective of this translation is to make it as simple and modern as possible, avoiding intricate constructions and archaisms, thereby making it easily understood by the educated lay reader. For reasons explained in greater detail in the Introduction, the order of verses in the original text is not strictly followed in this translation; some rearrangement and regrouping by topic has been made. A lengthy Introduction and a description of the Kautilyan state and society have become necessary in order to satisfy scholars and provide the necessary background for others.

This translation is made by a political economist in the belief that the precepts of Kautilya on the social, political and economic structure of the ideal state are relevant even today. It is not for me to say whether I have succeeded. I shall be grateful for all corrections, comments and suggestions for improvement, from scholars and laymen alike.

Dharma Kumar has been a source of constant encouragement to me in this book, as she has been with all my other books. I am grateful to my wife, Joyce and my son Gautam for carefully reading through the manuscript, correcting infelicities of language, eliminating confusion in translation and, on the whole, making it more comprehensible. They also proof-read the typeset manuscript. I am also grateful to Gautam and my elder son, Vijay, for help in word processing, typesetting and drawing the diagrams.

Thanks are also due to the Government of India for permitting me to use the Embassy computers for word processing.

I am grateful to Olav F. Knudsen, the Director of the Norwegian Foreign Policy Institute, (NUPI), and his colleagues Jorgen Lochen and Ole Dahl-Gulliksen, for their assistance in printing out the typeset manuscript.

I also thank David Davidar and his colleagues for their cooperation.

Above all, I am beholden to the pioneers, Dr. Kangle and Dr. Shamasastry, to whom this new translation is, in all humility, dedicated. I need not add that I alone bear the responsibility for any shortcomings.

Oslo, Summer solstice, 1990 ·   L.N. Rangarajan

प्रजासुखे सुखं राज्ञः प्रजानां च हिते हितम्।
नात्मप्रियं हितं राज्ञः प्रजानां तु प्रियं हितम्।।

In the happiness of his subjects lies the king's happiness; in their welfare his welfare. He shall not consider as good only that which pleases him but treat as beneficial to him whatever pleases his subjects. {1.19.34}

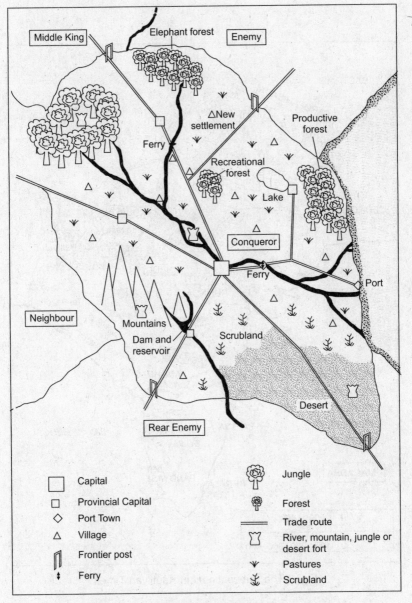

Fig. 1 A Hypothetical Kautilyan State

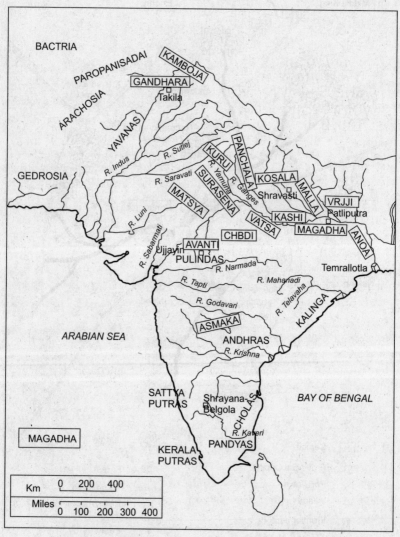

Fig. 2 The Subcontinent in Kautilyan Times

INTRODUCTION

From time immemorial, the great aims of human endeavour (the *purusharthas*) have been classified in India as being four:- *dharma, artha, kama* and *moksha*, roughly translated as moral behaviour, wealth, worldly pleasures and salvation. Of these, *moksha* has always been held, unanimously and unambiguously, to be the highest ideal to which a human being can aspire. It is not easy to define *moksha;* it is, basically, self-realization through liberation—the liberation from earthly bondage by realizing the divine in the human, the spiritual in the physical and the *Atman* or soul in the mind–body complex. It is the final beatific and timeless state of the enfranchised soul, and it is not possible to achieve it by mere mental processes or literary thought.[1] However, the pursuit of the three objectives—*dharma, artha* and *kama*—can contribute to the attainment of *moksha.*

Of the three objectives capable of being studied and practised, *dharma* has always occupied the premier place. *Dharma* not only signifies an absolute and immutable concept of righteousness but also includes the idea of duty which every human being owes to oneself, to one's ancestors, to society as a whole and to universal order. *Dharma* is law in its widest sense—spiritual, moral, ethical and temporal. Every individual, whether the ruler or the ruled, is governed by his or her own *dharma*. To the extent that society respected *dharma*, society protected itself; to the extent society offended it, society undermined itself. The literature on the *Dharmashastras*, both the original scriptures and the commentaries thereon, is very extensive. The definitive modern study is, of course, the magnificent five-volume 'History of the *Dharmashastra*' by Dr. P.V. Kane. For our present purposes, we need only observe that everything in Indian polity—the rights and duties of rulers, ministers, priests and people—is governed by the concept of *dharma*.

THE RANGE OF *ARTHASHASTRAS*

Artha follows *dharma*. As used in *Arthashastras* generally and by Kautilya, the last and greatest master of the science, *artha* has a much wider significance than merely 'wealth'. The material well-being of individuals is a part of it. As Kautilya says in the concluding section of his book: 'The source of the livelihood of men is wealth'. He then draws the corollary that the wealth of a nation is both the territory of the state and its inhabitants who may follow a variety of occupations {15.1.1}. The state or government has a crucial role to play in maintaining the material well-being of the nation and its people. Therefore, an important part of *Arthashastras* is 'the science of economics', including starting productive enterprises, taxation, revenue collection, budget and accounts.

The aim of pursuing successful economic policies, particularly through productive enterprises, is also to increase the revenues of the state and appropriate the surpluses for the state treasury. *Kosha* (treasury) is an essential constituent of the state, 'A King with a depleted treasury eats into the very vitality of the citizens and the country' says Kautilya {2.1.16}. At the same time, a King who impoverishes his own people or angers them by unjust exactions will also lose their loyalty {7.5.27}. A balance has to be maintained between the welfare of the people and augmenting the resources of the state.

This presupposes two things—maintenance of law and order and an adequate administrative machinery. In this context, maintaining law and order involves not only the detection and punishment of criminals (as in Book 4 of the text on 'The removal of thorns', i.e., anti-social elements) but also upholding the fabric of society. The state has a responsibility for ensuring the observance of laws concerning relations between husbands and wives, inheritance, the rights of women, servants and slaves, contracts and similar civil matters. Further, there have to be laws to avoid losses to the state treasury and to prevent embezzlement or misuse of power by servants of the state. Therefore an integral part of *Arthashastra* is *dandaniti*, the enforcement of laws by a voluminous and comprehensive set of fines and punishments.

Dandaniti, the science of law enforcement, is the name given in the *Mahabharata* to the mythical original work of this kind, said to have been handed down by *Brahma* himself at the time of creation.[2] *Danda*, meaning rod or staff, stands for the sceptre wielded by rulers; it also has many other meanings. For example, the army is called *danda*. It is also one of the four methods of dispute settlement and connotes the use of force. *Kosadanda* (the treasury and the army) is an expression which occurs often to indicate the combined economic power and military might of a state. *Danda* thus covers all aspects of the coercive power of a state. Where it means punishment, it has to be understood as just punishment. For: 'A king meting out unjust punishment is hated by the people he terrorises while one who is too lenient is held in contempt; whoever imposes just and deserved punishment is respected and honoured {1.4.7-10}.

The extensive responsibilities of the state for promoting economic well-being and preserving law and order demand an equally extensive administrative machinery. Any text on *Arthashastra* has to contain details of the organization of the civil service as well as the duties and responsibilities of individual officials.

A ruler's duties in the internal administration of the country are three-fold: *raksha* or protection of the state from external aggression, *palana* or maintenance of law and order within the state, and *yogakshema* or safeguarding the welfare of the people.

The prosperity of the state and its inhabitants cannot be maintained unless new territory is acquired by settlement of virgin lands, by alliance or by conquest. In a political environment which had many kings, any one of them resting content with his own territory was likely to fall prey to the expansionist ambitions of another. How to deal with other kings by using peaceful or warlike methods is the foreign policy aspect of *Arthashastra*. Since conquest is the most important method of acquisition (*labha*) of new territory, preparing for and waging war also becomes an integral part of the science.

Artha is an all-embracing word with a variety of meanings. In {1.7.6-7}, it is used in the sense of material well-being; in {15.1.1}, livelihood; in {1.4.3}, economically productive activity, particularly in agriculture, cattle rearing and trade; and, in general, wealth as in the '*Wealth of Nations*'. *Arthashastra* is thus 'the science of politics' as it is used in {1.1.1} or {1.4.3}. It is the art of government in its widest sense. The subjects covered include: administration; law, order and justice; taxation, revenue and expenditure; foreign policy; defence and war. Its three objectives follow one from the other: promotion of the welfare of the subjects leads to acquisition of wealth which, in turn, makes it possible to enlarge the territory by conquest.

It is true that many areas covered by the *Arthashastras* are also included in the *Dharmashastras*. There is, however, a crucial difference between the two. The *Dharmashastras* address themselves to the individual, teaching him his *dharma*, and regard deviations from it as sins to be expiated by ritual. The *Arthashastras* are addressed to rulers and regard transgressions of law as crimes to be punished by the state.

THE ORIGIN OF *ARTHASHASTRAS*

Kautilya was not the originator of the science. He himself acknowledges that his work is based on similar treatises of the past. There are in all one hundred and twelve places in the text where a number of earlier authorities and opinions held by them are mentioned. Five different schools of thought—those of Brihaspati, Ushanas, Prachetasa Manu,[3] Parasara and Ambhi—are referred to, often because Kautilya disagrees with the advice given by them. Some individual teachers of high repute, like Vishalaksha and Bharadwaja, are also quoted. From a number of quotations and references in later works, we know that there were at least four distinct schools and thirteen individual teachers of *Arthashastra* before Kautilya. (See Notes on Translation No.1). Unfortunately, all the earlier works are lost and Kautilya's is the earliest text that has come down to us.

The study of economics, the art of government and foreign policy is thus very old; the development of the science in India, according to some scholars, may have started around 650 B.C. One reason for the disappearance of the extensive early literature could well be that Kautilya's masterly treatise superseded them and made them redundant.

KAUTILYA—THE LEGEND

Who was Kautilya, this mastermind, who could write a definitive treatise on economics and government, at a time when large parts of the world were steeped in intellectual darkness? All sources of Indian tradition—Brahmanical, Buddhist and Jain—agree that Kautilya (also referred to as Vishnugupta in a stanza traditionally included at the end of the work) destroyed the Nanda dynasty and installed Chandragupta Maurya on the throne of Magadha.[4] The name 'Kautilya' denotes that he is of the *kutila gotra*;[5] 'Chanakya' shows him to be the son of Chanaka and 'Vishnugupta' was his personal name.

Except for one incident, little is known about his early life. One legend has it that he was a Kerala Brahmin, impoverished, lean and unprepossessing, who somehow found himself in the court of the Nanda king at Pataliputra. Another is that he was a North Indian Brahmin, born and educated in the famous University town of Taxila, who came to Pataliputra to win laurels in philosophic disputation. Kautilya, says one Buddhist source, 'was known for his proficiency in the three *Vedas*, in the *mantras*, skill in stratagem, dexterity in intrigue and policy, but also for his physical ugliness, disgusting complexion, deformity of legs and other limbs.'[6] According to Buddhist and Jain traditions, his parents noticed that Kautilya was born with a full set of teeth, a mark of a future king. They had the teeth removed (making him uglier) because either the father or the mother did not want him to become a king. He became a king-maker instead.

Dhana-Nanda (the Nanda of great wealth), the king to whose court Kautilya came, was known to be not only base-born but miserly. Curtius reports that Porus, who defeated Alexander, wrote to him that the Nanda king 'was not merely a man originally of no distinction, but even of the very meanest condition. His father was in fact a barber.'[7] The father became the lover of the queen of the country, assassinated the king and, while acting as a guardian to the royal children, had them put to death. On top of his ignoble origins, Dhana-Nanda was also hated by his subjects for his avarice. This arrogant king insulted Kautilya who had come to Pataliputra to display his knowledge, ordering him to leave a feast after he had started eating. The incensed Kautilya vowed not to tie his forelock knot again until he had destroyed the Nanda dynasty root and branch. He wandered disguised as an ascetic searching for a suitable person who would help him to achieve his objective.

He came upon the boy Chandragupta, of royal line but fostered by a cowherd, playing with his companions on the village grounds. The boy was acting the role of a king, dispensing justice and giving orders to his 'ministers'. On the ascetic beseeching him for alms, the 'king' grandly gave away a herd of someone else's cows! Kautilya was so impressed with the boy's leadership qualities that he bought the boy then and there for a thousand *panas*, took him to Taxila and gave him an education fit for a future king.

Together Kautilya and Chandragupta set about attacking the Nanda kingdom only to meet with failure at first. Legend has it that the right tactics for destroying a powerful kingdom came to them when they saw a woman with whom they had taken shelter scolding her son 'You are just like Chandragupta!' because he had got his fingers burnt by starting to eat from the centre of a hot dish. They changed their tactics and began the conquest from the frontiers. Chandragupta then entered into an alliance with the King of a mountain kingdom. Though the young Maurya and his supporters were inferior in armed strength, they began by harassing the outlying areas. Garrisons were stationed in each conquered state to prevent a revolt behind them.

One story about the conquest is that when Chandragupta failed to conquer a town he was besieging, Kautilya entered it disguised as a beggar and predicted that the siege would be lifted if the people removed the idols from a temple. The gullible population did so and the besiegers pretended to withdraw. When the citizens were celebrating their supposed liberty, the attackers returned to take them by surprise.

Gradually Chandragupta converged towards Pataliputra, besieged it, drove out Dhana-Nanda and was installed as the King of Magadha.

Kautilya then retired from active life and reflected on all that he had learnt. Having found earlier works on statecraft unsatisfactory in many respects, he composed his own definitive work.

The traditional legend is, of course, not an accurate historical record. Nevertheless, the stories are not without point. Kautilya's *Arthashastra* is a practical work which could have been written only by one who had implemented the tactics which he preached. How to form alliances, how to attack a powerful king, how to deal with revolts in the rear, what tricks to play on gullible people—there is plenty of evidence in the text to indicate that the author was giving real-life answers to every conceivable hypothetical situation.

KAUTILYA—THE AUTHOR

Notwithstanding the weight of Indian tradition, some scholars have expressed doubts about the authorship of what we now know as Kautilya's *Arthashastra* and the date of its composition. Was the author really a historical person who helped Chandragupta become the King of Magadha? This question is important for assigning a date to the work.

A variety of arguments have been advanced to ascribe to the work a date later than the first Maurya Emperor. These include a comparison of the society as described in the work with those in the *Smritis* of Manu and Yagnavalkya, a comparison of the technical information in it with that in other *shastras* (e.g. chemistry, gemmology or the Shilpashastra, the science of architecture), the knowledge of metals or the nature of weaponry described in it, the training of horses or elephants and the rules on composition of edicts. It is not possible to go into the details of all the arguments and counter-arguments in this brief Introduction. Prof. Kangle has analysed these exhaustively in over fifty pages in his 'Study'[8] We may refer to only two. First, is there any confirmation from non-Indian sources, particularly Greek ones, for the existence of Kautilya in Chandragupta's time? If it were available, Kautilya can be given a firm historical date. The second is whether Kautilya, the teacher, actually wrote the work or whether it is a compilation by him or his disciples. We choose this second question because a recent thesis (1968) by T.R. Trautmann,[9] written after Kangle's Study was published, has concluded that 'Kautilya's *Arthashastra*, while composed by a single person, has no one creator'. Since completing this book, I have come to know that at a workshop convened by the Indian Council for Historical Research, it was concluded that the *Arthashastra* was a compilation made by a scholar, Kautilya, in 150 A.D. Prof. Trautmann is reported to have said that 'Chanakya did not have a name called Kautilya'.[10]

There is, however, no doubt that Chandragupta Maurya ascended the throne around 321 B.C. One argument for doubting the existence of Kautilya is that Megasthenes, who was Ambassador of Seleucos at the Court of Chandragupta, does not mention Kautilya by name. However, the 'Indika' of Megasthenes is not available in its entirety but only in a few fragments in the writings of later Greek historians; the fact that in the few extracts that we have Kautilya is not mentioned cannot lead to the presumption that this was so in the whole work. In any case, Megasthenes is not a reliable witness; stories of mythical animals and tribal people with such large ears that they could wrap themselves in them like blankets are mixed with precise descriptions of the length of roads or width of moats. 'Indika' is a mixture of fact and fable, history and hearsay. The absence of a reference to Kautilya in the meagre information available from sources contemporaneous with Chandragupta neither proves nor disproves his existence.

Some scholars, while acknowledging that there might have been a teacher of the *Arthashastra*, consider the text to be a compilation by later disciples. For example, Trautmann has done what purports to be a statistical analysis of the text, to 'prove' that different books of the text were written by different people at different times. The exercise stands on the flimsy theoretical ground that authorship can be proved by analysing the frequency of 'mundane high frequency function words. Trautmann's analysis is based on counting words such as 'and', 'then', 'also', 'hence', etc. There is little credible evidence to prove this assertion is applicable to all languages, particularly to Sanskrit which had not yet become set in Paninian grammar. Prof. Kangle has tackled the point about 'composition' as opposed to 'creation' thus: 'Even if we assume that some later members of the school 'composed' a text for study, this would not differ materially and even verbally from what was known to be the teaching of the founder. "Composition" of a text had a different connotation in ancient India with a persistent tradition of oral transmission from what it means in modern times.'[11] Kautilya himself has made it clear that there were other *Arthashastras* before his and that his work is a refined and improved treatise. It is, therefore, not surprising if parts of the treatise reproduce earlier versions; this is particularly true of the 380 *shlokas* or verse stanzas, mostly found at the end of chapters. But Kautilya's treatise is not a mere compilation; there is enough evidence to prove that he brought an original mind to bear on all aspects of the *shastra*, to the extent of clearly mentioning the schools with which he disagreed and why he disagreed with them. Some of the books have no references to earlier works and some very few;

for example, the long Book 2 on Administration has only two references. On the other hand, Book 7 on Foreign Policy cites earlier teachers many times. It is not unreasonable to conclude that this is due to Kautilya modifying earlier teachings, particularly on subjects like relations between states, on the basis of his own wisdom and practical experience.

A careful reading of the complete text will show that it is an integral whole. Definitions and special terms explained in one place are picked up and used in the same sense elsewhere. There is a uniformity of style. The techniques of logical analysis are similar throughout the work. There is a consistency in the use of arithmetical permutations and combinations. No doubt there are a few contradictions; but these are surprisingly few considering the length of the work and its antiquity. They are either the result of left-overs from earlier works or due to interpolations. After a comprehensive examination of all points of view, Prof. Kangle has concluded that 'there is no convincing reason why this work should not be regarded as the work of Kautilya who helped Chandragupta to come to power in Magadha'.[12] In doing so, he has cited H. Jacobi: 'Without weighty grounds, we must not push aside unanimous Indian tradition; else one practises scepticism, not criticism'.[13]

Those who question the ascription of the 4th century B.C. as the date of the work place it not later than 150 A.D. Establishing a convincing date is, no doubt, important to scholars. However, Kautilya's greatness is in no way diminished if we choose any date between 1850 and 2300 years ago. The work is of great antiquity. Kautilya was clearly a pioneer of the art of statecraft, a brilliant intellectual and a teacher whose precepts have enduring validity.

THE TEXT, COMMENTARIES AND TRANSLATIONS

Kautilya's *Arthashastra* had never been forgotten in India and is often mentioned in later literature, sometimes eulogistically and sometimes derisively. But the text itself was not available in modern times until, dramatically, a full text on palm leaf in the *grantha* script, along with a fragment of an old commentary by Bhattasvamin, came into the hands of Dr. R. Shamasastry of Mysore in 1904. He published not only the text (1909) and an English translation (1915) but also an Index Verborum in three volumes listing the occurrence of every word in the text.[14] Subsequently another original manuscript and some fragments, in a variety of scripts, were discovered as well as old commentaries of the text. In addition to Dr. Shamasastry's translation, there is an edition of the text with a complete Sanskrit commentary by T. Ganapati Sastri, a German translation with voluminous notes by J.J. Meyer, a Russian translation and translations in many Indian languages.

Dr. R.P. Kangle of the University of Bombay devoted many years of painstaking erudition and scholarship to comparing the various texts and translations. His monumental three-volume edition of the *Arthashastra* was first published between 1960 and 1965. The set contains: (i) a definitive critically edited text with precise numbering of the *sutras* and verses, (ii) an English translation with detailed notes which take into account all other translations and (iii) an exhaustive study.

All students of the *Arthashastra* owe a great debt to Dr. Shamasastry and Dr. R.P. Kangle. That is why I have dedicated this new translation, in all humility, to these two great scholars.

The text contains fifteen *adhikaranas* or Books. The first chapter of Book 1 is a detailed table of contents and in one verse {1.1.18}, states that the text has 150 chapters, 180 *prakaranas* and six thousand verses in all. A *prakarana* is a section devoted to a specific topic; the number of chapters is not the same as the number of sections because sometimes a chapter deals with more than one topic and sometimes a topic is spread over more than one chapter. In Shamasastry's text, the *sutras* are divided by appropriate stops but are not numbered. Every *sutra* and *shloka* is clearly numbered in Kangle's text and translation and we shall follow the same system.

The *Arthashastra* is mainly in prose of the *sutra* form, with only 380 *shlokas*. Though *sutra* can be translated as 'maxim', we shall refer, for the sake of convenience, to both *sutra* and *shloka* as 'verse' in this translation. The actual number of verses (*sutras* and *shlokas*) in Kangle's edition is 5348. The fact that the text does not contain 6000 verses as claimed in {1.1.18} has led to the speculation that a part, about one-ninth of the present length, may have been lost over the centuries. Kangle's analysis[15] establishes that this is quite unlikely. In fact, it is more likely that some verses might have entered into the text due to scribal error from marginal glosses by commentators; these number 35 in all. The figure of 6000 is an approximation, not meant to be an exact count.

Barring any new discoveries, the text, as we now have it, can be taken to be as complete and as faithful a rendering of the original as is possible for a work of this antiquity.

Since, for reasons explained below, the verses are arranged in this translation in an order different from that of the original text, it may be useful to have a brief indication of the contents of the different Books. The following summary is an extract from Kangle's 'Study'.[16]

After a brief introduction setting the *Arthashastra* in the context of other sciences, Book 1 deals with the King—his training, the appointment of ministers and other officers of the state, the daily routine to be followed by the ruler and his safety and security. Book 2 describes the duties of the various executive officers of the state and gives a full picture of state activities in agriculture, mining, leisure activities and so on. Book 3, which is concerned with law and the administration of justice, reproduces a complete code of law. Book 4 deals with the suppression of crime and includes sections on detection of crime, control over merchants and artisans, torture and capital punishment. Book 5 is a miscellaneous collection of topics including the salary scales of officials.

Book 6 is very short, containing only two chapters, but both are important, since they set out the theoretical basis for the whole work. The first chapter sets out the theory of the constituent elements of a state and the second the theory of foreign policy.

Book 7 contains an exhaustive discussion on the way in which each of the six methods of foreign policy may be used in various situations that are likely to arise in the conduct of foreign policy. Book 8 is concerned with *vyasanas*, usually translated as calamities, which may affect adversely the efficient functioning of the various constituent elements. Book 9 deals with preparations for war and includes topics such as: the different kinds of troops that could be mobilised, the proper conditions for starting an expedition and the dangers to be guarded against before starting. Book 10 is concerned with fighting and describes the main battle camp, types of battle arrays and different modes of fighting. Book 11 has only one chapter and describes how a conqueror should tackle oligarchies governed by a group of chiefs instead of a single king. Book 12 shows how a weak king, when threatened by a stronger king, should frustrate the latter's designs and ultimately overcome him. Book 13 is concerned with the conquest of the enemy's fort by subterfuge or by fighting. It also describes how the conquered territories should be ruled.

Book 14 deals with secret and occult practices, and the last Book describes the methodology and the logical techniques used in the work. Though the placement of some books and some chapters may not seem strictly logical, it can be said that, by and large, the first five books deal with internal administration and the last eight on a state's relations with its neighbours.

WHY A NEW TRANSLATION?

Though Shamasastry's and Kangle's translations are widely available, there are a number of reasons for my venturing to make a new one.

1. The last (third) edition revised by Shamasastry himself was published in 1929 and is thus over sixty years old. Since then, manuscripts have been discovered and much work has been done by scholars, both Indian and foreign, on fathoming the meaning. Though Shamasastry has cross-referenced his edition of the text with his translation by page number, it is difficult to establish a precise correspondence, verse by verse, between text and translation. The translation itself is somewhat archaic; for example, he uses 'amercement' to indicate a (monetary) fine.

2. Dr. Kangle's translation, Part II of his work, is thorough and takes note of every possible variation of the text and every alternative suggested by others for the translation. However, this has resulted in voluminous footnotes, almost half of every page, making it more a work for scholars than for the average reader who only wants to understand Kautilya.

3. All translations into English or other foreign languages have been made by Indologists and Sanskrit scholars who were concerned with preserving literary exactness with the result that comprehensibility has been sacrificed for fidelity to the text. A few examples {2.6.23, 2.7.19, 2.14.2, 2.23.5, and 4.2.24} from Kangle's translation are shown below with the present translation for comparison:

Kangle's translation	This translation
Current (expenditure), that arising out of current gain (and)—this is (four-fold) expenditure.	Actual expenditure shall be shown under the headings (i) budgeted day-to-day expenditure, (ii) unbudgeted day-to-day expenditure and (iii) foreseen periodic expenditure (fortnightly, monthly or annual).
And he should make the superintendent pay eight-fold whatever may increase the balance over the total of income (as shown) on the page inside (the account books) or whatever the (officer) may cause to decrease (from the balance) because of (the inflation of) expenditure.	In case audit discovers a discrepancy which has the effect of either proving a higher actual income or a lower actual expenditure, the official responsible shall pay a penalty of eight times the discrepancy.

They should do the work with the time and the (nature of the) work stipulated, without stipulation as to time when there is the excuse of the (nature of the work).

[Artisans and craftsmen] shall complete the work agreed upon within the stipulated time; if the work to be done is of a special nature, no time limit need be stipulated.

What falls in between the purchaser and the seller becomes different from what is received.

Merchants shall not count the brokerage paid to middle-men as part of their costs [in calculating their profit margins].

If a (woman) after receiving the wage does not carry out the work, he should make her forfeit the tongs formed by the thumb (and the middle finger) also those who have misappropriated or stolen and then run away.

Cutting off the thumb and a finger is the punishment for women who (i) having taken their wages do not return the finished work, (ii) misappropriate or steal the material supplied or (iii) run away with the raw material supplied to them.

In some verses, a literal translation creates confusion; for instance, in Kangle's translation of {7.13.21}, given below, we do not know who is the 'enemy' in the four places where the word is employed. 'In case they have come after obtaining a gain, that attacker in the rear, whose enemy is weaker in point of gain or power, overreaches, or in case the enemy against whom (his enemy) had marched might do harm to the enemy in battle.'

Very long verses, such as those describing forty ways of embezzlement by government servants {2.8.21} or on the reasons for a king taking shelter in a fort {7.15.12} are particularly difficult to understand if written as one long unbroken sentence occupying a page.

4. It is well known that the Arthashastra is full of tedious lists such as the lists of salts, sugars and vinegars in {2.15}; types of loss from milling different kinds of rice in {2.15.15}; rations for horses and elephants in {2.31.13-15}; and types of gold from different regions {2.13.3}. Simply following the textual order leads to the breaking up of Kautilya's reasoning and inhibits the understanding of his politico-eccnomic logic. He himself had, no doubt, to list all such specialized knowledge because he was writing a teaching manual which had to be learnt by rote. Not all Kautilya's lists or classifications are puerile or useless; nevertheless, the order of an orally transmitted instruction manual is not the order which we would use today.

5. It is difficult, by reading the existing translations, to get a comprehensive idea of Kautilya's teachings on any given subject. Kangle in his 'Study' has brought these together under different headings: Economy, Administration, Defence, External Affairs, etc. But the 'Study' presupposes a thorough knowledge of the text and one has to often refer to the actual translation in a different volume.

6. Every scholar has his own perspective, not to say prejudices. For example, there is a passage in the *Arthashastra* dealing extensively with the King's advisers and councillors; Radha Kumud Mookerji interprets *mantri* (councillor) as Prime Minister[17] while R.C. Majumdar equates the *mantriparishad* (council of ministers) to the Privy Council of Great Britain.[18] On the other hand, Jayaswal sees in the text 'assemblies of the people and the country' which the King could not overrule and to which the King had to submit all proposals for raising revenue; K.P. Jayaswal sees a constitutional monarchy with a powerful Parliament.[19] On the whole, it is difficult to avoid the conclusion that those who wanted to see democracy as a form of government in ancient India saw it in the *Arthashastra*, just as those who saw only autocratic monarchy also saw it there. Analogies with modern political systems are useful if they help to illuminate the meaning of the text; but this should not be carried to the extent of imputing to Kautilyan times systems, institutions and organizations which did not exist then. While scholars are entitled to speculate, translators have to be more careful.

7. An interesting phenomenon common to all Indian translators is their strenuous denial that Kautilya gave any special status to Brahmins. For example, Kangle says in his Study: 'The text does not, as a rule, show such partiality to Brahmins as such.'[20] Shamasastry: 'Undue partiality to Brahmins ...(is) assigned no prominence in the *Arthashastra*.'[21] Discussing the verse about using women to entice and betray a chief of an oligarchy Kangle says: 'It is extremely doubtful if the women folk of any Brahmin community were engaged in the sort of work expected of them'.[22] In the next chapter, on the social and economic aspects of the Kautilyan state, I have given a list of all the verses where special privileges are mentioned; these range from immunity from torture and the death sentence to free travel on the ferries!

8. Similar reticence is shown for reasons of puritanism. Some translators are unwilling to face the fact that a virgin could be deflowered by a woman or could do so herself. {4.12.20, 21}.

9. Lastly, there are a number of places where previous translators have disagreed with each other totally. There are many such instances and some of them quite major. Examples are 7.3.23, 32 and 7.4.8.

To summarise, presently available translations suffer from archaic expressions, voluminous footnotes, incomprehensible literalness, muddling of the text with tedious facts, difficulty in understanding a topic scattered in different places, divergence of opinion and personal prejudices or predilections. I do not imply that the earlier translations should be condemned as useless; not at all. It is the painstaking scholarship of Kangle and Shamasastry that makes it possible for those like me to do a new translation. It is on the shoulders of these giants that I stand.

POINTS ABOUT THIS TRANSLATION

Improving clarity has meant studying every one of the over five thousand verses, comparing existing translations, taking note of suggested alternatives and then putting the meaning into modern English. Sometimes, a judgment has had to be made about which translation is to be preferred. In preferring one version to another, a guiding principle has been to maintain consistency; subject only to the exigencies of the context, the same word in the original has been translated the same way throughout. For example, *atavi* is always translated as jungle and *vana* as forest, though other translators have used these interchangeably. Consistency cannot, however, be slavishly followed; the word *artha* itself has to be given one of its many meanings, depending on the context.

We must, however, remember that, since the *Arthashastra* is a specialised text, some words have meanings peculiar only to this science. For example, *yoga* has the meaning in Books 12 and 13 of a trick or stratagem; *upanishad*, in Book 14, means a magical or occult trick; *vyasana*, always translated as a calamity, has the special meaning of any adversity that renders one of the constituents of the state less effective; *yatra* and *yana* are often used to describe a military expedition. *Abhityakta* is another special term used for a condemned man sent on a nefarious errand, his own fate being irrelevant {e.g. 9.3.38; 9.6.29}. See Notes on Translation No.2.

In a few cases, I have adopted a terminology quite different from those of earlier translators. A tax, frequently mentioned in the *Arthashastra*, is *vyaji*. From the context, it seems to have been applied both as a sales tax and a purchase tax. On balance, it is better to translate it as a transaction tax, i.e. a tax automatically levied when the state bought or sold goods. This is borne out by the precise description of balances and measures capable of automatically levying the tax. In Book 2 on the organization of the state administration, thirty-two officials are given the title *adhyaksha*. Though they are all heads of departments, they may belong to different grades just as today the seniority of a head of department may depend on the size or importance of his department. Previous translators have used different expressions for each one; indeed, there is a bewildering multiplicity of nomenclature. In order to bring out the point that any *adhyaksha* was a head of department, I have added the word 'chief' as in Chief Commissioner of Customs, Chief Controller of State Trading or Chief Protector of Animals. Clearly, there were some officials (the Samahartr and the Samnidhatr, in particular) who were of a higher rank than the *adhyakshas*; they have been given special names. Other changes worth mentioning pertain to duties of the village headman; labour law and the law on slavery and assault; appropriate explanations are given in Appendix 15 'Notes on Translation'.

Clarity can also be improved by the judicious use of tables and diagrams. A long description of how towns were laid out or forts constructed is less meaningful than its pictorial representation. I have, therefore, not translated verbally such passages (which include layout of camps and details of construction of elephant and horse stables) but replaced them by diagrams. There are 43 maps, figures and diagrams. Tables have been used to show schematically the similarities in the forty ways of embezzlement by government servants or unequal treaties. All fines and punishments, of which there are a great number, are depicted in a consistent tabular form.

Other changes made for improving clarity are: (i) breaking up long verses into shorter sentences, (ii) setting them out in different lines and numbered sub-sections and (iii) putting, with rare exceptions, such as {7.14}, direct speech into indirect speech.

In order to make the translation more readable, it is often necessary to add a few words to improve continuity or to amplify. These additions have all been put in square brackets [...] so that the reader may be aware of what has been added by this translator.

For the convenience of the reader, I have added a special section in Part I explaining the short-hand expressions used by Kautilya throughout for commodities and for the four methods of dispute settlement (*sama, dana, bheda* and *danda*). I have also included an indication of the value of money (*pana*) in the *Arthashastra*.

I do not claim that I have succeeded in translating every verse satisfactorily. Some, like {7.13.38} and {7.6.35,36} are incomprehensible; the attempt made here to give them meaning can, at best, be only an educated guess.

Two special usages are worth mentioning. Following Prabhati Mukherjee, I have used the word *varna* as such because of the tendency to confuse the words *varna* and *jati* and translate them both indiscriminately as 'caste'. *Varna* here means strictly the four-fold division of Hindu society. I have also used the term 'Arya' to denote the four *varnas* because of the degradation to which the word 'Aryan' has been subjected to in modern European history.[23]

REARRANGEMENT

The major difference between this translation and earlier ones is, of course, the rearrangement of verses in an order different from the original Sanskrit text. I should explain why I found it necessary to do so.

The original has an admirable logic of its own in the order of presentation of the topics. In the oral tradition, when all texts had to be memorized, it was necessary to learn the duties of the Chief Controller of Crown Lands, along with all the details about agriculture—rainfall, soil, types of crops, use of labour, etc. Nowadays, we will find it easier to understand the text if the part relating to the administrative structure of government is separated from topics concerning land tenure, revenue system or control over trade.

Another reason for rearranging the text is that Kautilya has sometimes lumped together miscellaneous topics in the same Book. For instance, there is no reason why the salaries of administrative officials should have been put in {5.3}, while the other five chapters deal with secret conduct. It is more logical, and more succinct, to indicate the salary of each official along with his duties and responsibilities and to append a table of salaries to explain the hierarchy. Likewise, it is better to add the duties of the Chief Controller of Private Trade given in Book 4 on criminal law to the section on the duties of heads of departments.

I have mentioned earlier that there are 380 *shlokas* in the Sanskrit text. These are usually found at the end of chapters and, most probably, have been incorporated from the *Arthashastras* of earlier teachers. They are usually pithy and epigrammatic, encapsulating admirably the thrust of a topic. Wherever appropriate, I have placed them at the beginning of each topic; some have been used on the title pages of different Parts.

Rearrangement also makes it possible to deal with the various lists and classifications. I have compressed such lists (weights and measures, rations, recipes for alcoholic beverages, weaponry etc.) and given them in the Appendices. For ease of reference, I have also added an Appendix on the commodities mentioned in the text. Some lists have, however, been retained in their proper places, because they are an integral part required for understanding what follows them. The classification of states

{6.2.13-23}, those likely to become traitors {1.14.2-5}, contrivances and tricks for killing an enemy {12.4.22-28; 12.5.1-8}, and some battle formations {10.6} are examples of such useful lists.

In the process of modernizing and regrouping, I found that some verses can be omitted without affecting the meaning. For example, there are tautological definitions: 'lending at interest of goods from the treasury is lending' {2.8.7} or the verse which follows: 'trading in state commodities is trading'. There are superfluous statements: 'Thus ends the law governing slaves' {3.1.25}; or 'Hereafter are explained measurements of time' {2.20.36}. I have instead used topic headings and sub-headings to avoid repetition and improve readability. I must emphasize that all explanatory headings are my additions.

A major omission is Book 14, dealing with secret and occult practices. Most of it is untranslatable, since we cannot guess at the meaning of the various herbs, plants and occult material listed in it. In any case, we find it hard to believe, in this day and age, that a 'mixture of the lizard and the house-lizard causes leprosy' {14.1.20}! We can take it for granted that society in Kautilyan times believed in magic and occult practices and need not burden this translation with incomprehensible minutiae. In any case, the genuineness of Book 14 has been questioned; some scholars, though not Dr. Kangle, think that this could be an interpolation.[24]

Though punishment—*danda*—plays an important part in maintaining social order, the text often indicates the nature of the transgression only indirectly by specifying the punishment for it. For the sake of clarity and consistency, I have regrouped all fines and punishments at the end of each topic and mentioned the transgression separately. Incidentally, this helps to separate the law on what should not be done from the penalty for breaking it.

The work involved in regrouping has enabled me to add a new section. So far as I am aware, there is no article or study which gives a complete picture of how the Kautilyan state obtained its revenue; in section ii of Part V I have collated all relevant information under 'Sources of Revenue'.

I am not listing here all such rearrangements; sometimes only individual verses are affected by transposition and sometimes long passages and even chapters. At the beginning of each section, I have indicated the nature of the regrouping and the reasons for it.

I do not claim that the rearrangement made in this translation is the perfect way of doing it, or even the only way. There has been one other attempt by a compiler, selecting from existing translations, to rearrange the part of the text relating to law, justice and jurisprudence.[25] Any suggestions for improvement will be gratefully received.

This translation is meant to be read as a continuous narrative. The few footnotes are meant mainly for cross-reference and, sometimes, for clarification. To help those readers who may want to refer to the original text, verse numbers are shown throughout the translation, wherever the order departs from the original, within double braces {Book. Chapter. Verse number}. The reference is always to Kangle, Parts I and II. In addition, there is a verse index which shows by textual order where a given verse may be found in the translation.

ON UNDERSTANDING KAUTILYA

There are two ways, both valid, of looking at Kautilya's *Arthashastra*. The historian sees it as a valuable document which throws light on the state and society in India at that time, whether it be 300 BC or 150 AD. The second way, which this translation emphasizes, is to regard Kautilya as a great preceptor of statecraft, whose teachings have a universal validity.

The historical aspect is the one that has till now been accorded prominence by scholars. The twelve-page bibliography in Aradhana Parmar's book[26] is an indication of the number of Indian and foreign scholars who have drawn conclusions relevant to Indian history. Radha Kumud Mookerjee's 'Chandragupta Maurya and His Times' has a valuable comparison of the information in the *Arthashastra* with the accounts given by ancient Greek historians.

We must not, however, assume that the picture of India given in the *Arthashastra* is true for all periods of ancient Indian history. Though Kautilya wrote long after the time of Buddha, who died in 486 BC, the state of society portrayed in the *Arthashastra* is, in the main, pre-Buddhistic. On the other hand, the norms under which Hindu society has functioned for the last two millenia are those of the *Smritis*; the earliest and most important of these, the *Manusmriti*[27] was codified sometime in the first two centuries AD. The *Smritis* depict the ideal Hindu society as reconstructed and reformed after the influence of Buddhism had begun to decline in India. Owing partly to the influence of the highly moral and compassionate teachings of the Buddha and partly to the precepts of the Vedanta of reformed Brahmanism, a number of practices and customs which existed in Kautilya's time had disappeared by the time of the *Smritis*.

The social customs that existed in Kautilya's times but went out of practice a few centuries later are quite significant. In Kautilyan times, a husband and wife could divorce each other on grounds of mutual incompatibility. Widows could remarry; so could women whose husbands had been abroad for a long time. Eating meat or drinking or taking up arms were not prohibited for Brahmins. More reliance was placed on occult and secret practices.

It is not merely the norms of Indian society which changed and evolved over the millenia. The knowledge of gems and jewellery, the state of the art of metallurgy, the weapons and armour used, the way horses and elephants were trained—all these were different at different periods. In fact, it is the comparison of the data in the *Arthashastra* with that in other works and the question of who borrowed from whom that prompts scholars to ascribe different dates to the *Arthashastra* itself.

The caution about not extrapolating is particularly important on matters relating to the economy. The *Arthashastra*, naturally, has a lot of detailed information on the economy of a state, methods of raising revenue and budgeting. These details, which are logically interconnected, have to be read in the context of the aims of the King and the state as described by Kautilya.

I have, therefore, added a special section, following this Introduction, giving an outline of the Kautilyan state, the society and the economy, so that the translation can be placed in the appropriate context.

KAUTILYA, THE TEACHER

I would not have embarked on this new translation were I not convinced that Kautilya's precepts are of universal applicability. His counsels on the relationship between the ruler and the ruled, on the role of the state for maintaining the wealth of the nation and the welfare of the people, on the relations between neighbouring states, on alliances and on the conduct of foreign policy based on the relative strengths of the participants are as applicable today as they were in his day. To the extent our society is significantly different from his, to that extent some of the Kautilyan precepts have become irrelevant to us. Hence, these aspects also have to be understood in the context of the state and society described in the next chapter.

If we are to comprehend clearly Kautilya's teachings and apply them judiciously to the modern world, we also have to be aware of the essential characteristics of the work. The treatise is about an ideal state—not that such a state actually ever existed or is even likely to exist now or in the future. To the extent any of the six constituent elements of a state—the ruler, the ministers, the urban and the rural population, the economic power and the military might—differ from the ideals Kautilya has set out, to that extent the advice given by him has to be modified.

The *Arthashastra* is essentially a treatise on the art of government and is, by nature, instructional. It seeks to instruct all kings and is meant to be useful at all times wherever *dharma* is held to be pre-eminent. Because it is instructional, its basis is the practice of government. We will not find in it a theoretical discussion about why there should be a state at all or, if there is to be one, what kind of state is the best. For Kautilya, the existence of the state and the king are axioms. In fact, 'the King and his rule encapsulate all the constituents of the state' {8.2.1}. Kautilya's special contributions to the theoretical analysis of the functioning of a state are two. These are: (i) analysis of aspects of internal administration in terms of the six constituent elements of the state and (ii) analysis of the relations between states in terms of the theory of the circle of states. The two chapters of Book 6 are used to set out these theoretical concepts and define the terms used in their development. The rest of the treatise is a Manual of Instruction for kings and officers of the state.

There are three distinct parts in this manual. The Manual of Administration describes the organization of the apparatus of the state and prescribes the duties and responsibilities of every key official, either for maintaining order or for collecting revenue. There are, naturally, parts devoted to budgetary control, enforcement of civil service discipline and the public's civic resonsibility. The Code of Law and Justice covers both civil and criminal law and is, basically, a Penal Code; the extensive and graded penalties and fines prescribed in it have the twin aims of deterring transgressions and collecting revenue for the state. The third part is a Manual of Foreign Policy, the primary aim of which is acquisition of territory by conquest. The three manuals correspond to the three objectives of the state—wealth, justice and expansion. A stable and prosperous state, which only a just administration can secure, is a prerequisite for accumulation of wealth which is then used to augment the territory.

A fourth topic which runs throughout the treatise, in both the internal and foreign policy sections, is the use of an elaborate secret service mechanism.

As a textbook intended for practitioners of statecraft, Kautilya does not simply lay down a rule but modifies it every time to suit the action to the conditions prevailing. This comprehensive treatment sometimes becomes complex and tiresome, as in {12.4} and {12.5}, describing every possible method of killing an aggressor. In being so comprehensive Kautilya only follows his own advice that every situation ought to be analysed thoroughly before an action plan is formulated; good counsel and good judgment are more important than power and might.

The analyses are pursued with impeccable logic. For instance, Book 12 is devoted to examining the situation of the weak king. Kautilya does not assume that the conqueror will always be stronger than his enemy or that he will always win. Since setbacks were bound to occur, there is advice on how to overcome them.

One example of laying down a general principle and the prescribing modifications to it depending on the actual situation is in {7.7} on bargaining power. The general rule is that the payment to be made by one king for the use of the troops of another shall depend on the relative power equation between the two; this 'payment according to power' formula is then modified to suit every contingency.

Similar comprehensive logic is used to analyse all possible variations of when to attack an enemy in the rear {7.13} or provoking dissension among members of an oligarchy {11.1.34-39}. Often, the order of preference is clearly laid down (do A, if A is not possible then B, and so on). An example is the choice of kings whose protection a king may seek {7.15.1-8}. We only have to read Book 9 on mobilisation for a military campaign, particularly {9.1.26-33} on the interrelationship between power, place and time, to see the power of deductive logic in Kautilya's thinking.

There are many examples of Kautilya's ability to provide for every contingency. He recommends that the forces for the defence of the city should be placed under a number of chiefs, to avoid the possibility of a single chief usurping power in the king's absence {2.4.29,30}. A secret treasury shall be built in a remote area, using prisoners condemned to death {2.5.4}. The sentence was presumably carried out after the work was done, so that none but the king knew where the secret treasury to be used in times of emergency was located. Kautilya's attention to detail is shown by his instructions to install rain gauges {2.5.7}, what to do with the gleanings from Crown lands after the harvest {2.24.30} or the tricks which goldsmiths use to steal their customer's gold {2.14}. It is not necessary to multiply examples, the reader will discover many more in the text.

In spite of its patently didactic character and its declared twin aims of practical utility and analytical comprehensiveness, many commentators have chosen to read different things into the *Arthashastra*. I have given earlier some examples of the tendency to read modern forms of government into it. Noting the extensive control over the economy exercised by the state, B. Breloer[28] has drawn the conclusion that the *Arthashastra* presupposes economic planning by the state, almost giving the impression that Kautilya had thought of a modern planned economy. There is no need to impute this degree of clairvoyance to Kautilya. Russian commentators like V.I. Kalyanov see the *Arthashastra* in the light of the division, based on Marxist principle, of the periods of Indian history.

They place the text in the period of transition between 'the decay of a slave owning society' and 'the rise of early feudalism'.[29]

Among scholars, there are two extreme points of view and many shades in between. One extreme is to deny that Kautilya said anything useful at all. An example is A.B. Keith's observation: 'It is a very misplaced patriotism which asks us to admire the *Arthashastra* as representing the fine flower of Indian political thought. It would, indeed be melancholy if this were the best that India could show against the *Republic* of Plato or the *Politics* of Aristotle.'[30]

The other extreme is to hold that Kautilya was a lone genius and other thinkers were worthless. For example, Parmar says: '(Kautilya is) not merely a preserver of old political ideas but a creator of new ones. He is impatient with the existing unsystematic and chaotic theories of polity and removes the cobweb in political thinking through his incisive logic and firm grasp of the realities of statecraft.'[31] Since the texts of *Arthashatras* by teachers before Kautilya are all lost and all we have are a few bits quoted by Kautilya only to contradict them, there is no reason to jump to the conclusion that the previous teachings were all unsystematic, chaotic and full of cobwebs.

Comparisons of Kautilya with people who lived much later are also quite common, the most ridiculous one with Bismarck. A more usual comparison is with Machiavelli, the author of *The Prince*. This annoys many Indians who believe that, because Kautilya lived many centuries before Machiavelli, it is the latter who should be compared with the former. We need not see anything sinister in such a comparison. People can only compare the unknown with the known; most foreigners know something of Machiavelli and precious little of Kautilya. A more important point is that the sobriquet of 'Indian Machiavelli' given to Kautilya is unfair to both. This is not the place to go into the details of the lamentable misapprehension of the significance of Machiavelli's work even in the Western world. If Kautilya and Machiavelli thoughts have similarities, it only shows that the nature of people and princes has changed little over the two millenia which separates them.

I will now explain why the condemnation of Kautilya as an unethical teacher is based on ignorance of his work. His is always a sane, moderate and balanced view. He placed great emphasis on the welfare of the people. His practical advice is rooted in *dharma*. But, as a teacher of practical statecraft, he advocated unethical methods in the furtherance of national interest.

Whenever Kautilya quotes the advice of an earlier and then offers his own, his is the saner and more moderate view. All teachers before him seem to have considered a prince a danger to the king from the moment of his birth. Only Kautilya emphasizes the need for bringing up the prince properly and to train him to be a successor. One teacher, in fact, recommends that the prince should be tempted by secret agents to revolt against his father but Kautilya says that there is no greater sin than poisoning an innocent mind by temptation {1.17.30-37}. Likewise, the king should not make himself or his queen the target in testing the probity of ministers. 'He shall not corrupt the uncorrupted; that would be like adding poison to water.' {1.10.17-22}

Kautilya always qualifies his suggestions or advice with the injunction to modify it according to circumstances. Phrases like 'according to conditions' occur often whether in connection with the location of the divisional headquarters {2.3.3}, the number of advisers {1.15.41} or the number of ministers {1.15.50}. The punishment prescribed for passing urine or faeces in public places is mitigated if the person did so due to illness, medication or fear {2.36.29}. The rules about sanitation in private dwellings in the city were relaxed during childbirth {3.8.6}]. Reduced punishments could be awarded for some offences if there were mitigating circumstances such as mistake, intoxication or temporary insanity {3.18.5; 3.19.4}.

Kautilya does not trust traders, believing that they are always ready to make money at the cost of the consumer. But even they are entitled to state assistance when they lose their goods through no fault of their own {4.2.32}. In the administration of justice, Kautilya warns not to take a mere confession, without corroborative proof, of having committed a theft or burglary as proof of guilt; such confessions may be due to fear of being tortured {4.8.11}.

Kautilya does not advocate that all those who stand in the conqueror's way should be attacked indiscriminately. 'The king who attacks a righteous ruler will be hated by his own people and others. Conversely, one who attacks an unrighteous ruler will be liked by all.' {7.3.12} When there was a choice between attacking a strong but unjust king and a weak and just one, Kautilya advises that the unjust king should be attacked even though he would be a stronger adversary; for, 'the subjects of the just king will not only come to his help . . . but follow him till death.' {7.5.16-18} Chiefs of oligarchies are advised to endear themselves to their subjects by just behaviour {11.1.56}. Just behaviour by the rulers towards the ruled was, thus, of universal application.

The best example of Kautilya's concern for fairness is his advice on how to treat conquered territory. 'The conqueror shall substitute his virtues for the defeated enemy's vices and where the enemy was good, he shall be twice as good...He shall follow policies which are pleasing and beneficial to the constituents by acting according to his *dharma* and by granting favours and tax exemptions, giving gifts and bestowing honours....He shall adopt the way of life, dress, language and customs of the people and show the same devotion to the gods of territory and participate in the people's festivals and amusements...He shall please the chiefs of the towns, country, castes and guilds...The ill, the helpless and the distressed shall be helped...The slaughter of animals shall be prohibited on specified days...' Verses {13.5.3-15} are in themselves a charter of just administration.

While saying that disloyal subject kings should be put to death, Kautilya also says: 'The conqueror shall not covet the slain king's land, wealth, sons or wives but give the members of the family their appropriate positions.' {7.16.26,27}

The notoriety which Kautilya has acquired as an advocate of immoral and unethical policies is unjust because he always adds qualifications when he recommends such policies. These were either required because the interests of the state demanded it or because the persons against whom these were directed were enemies of the state {5.2.69}. These methods were not to be used against those who were neither evil nor treacherous. Kautilya only made explicit, without hypocrisy, what nation states, ancient and modern, have always practised.

Verse {1.19.34}, given as the epigraph to this translation, summarises Kautilya's concept of welfare of the subjects. The number of verses dealing with not only people's welfare but also animal welfare are many. A section in the next chapter is devoted to showing where to find all the verses on welfare. Suffice it to say that Kautilya precisely identifies those who need the protection of the state and prescribes remedies ranging from free transport on ferries to protection during battles.

The *Arthashastra* is a mixture of both what we applaud today and what we consider to be reprehensible. Kautilya has a great deal to say about civic responsibility; the obligation of every householder to take precautions against fire is mentioned; so is a prohibition on cutting trees in public parks. Consumer protection and vigilance against exploitation of the people by government servants are aspects which we consider good. Equally, some of Kautilya's suggestions will be seen by us as unethical. For example, he suggests the idea of two kinds of touchstones—one which overestimates the quality of the gold sold to the public and the other which underestimates the quality when bought {2.13.22-24}. The extensive use of the secret service is, in principle, unethical. In this translation, all material relevant to the constitution and operation of the secret services has been brought together in Part IX. The innumerable unsavoury methods are there for all to see.

Kautilya did take a cynical view of humanity and his teachings are based on the principle that no one can be trusted. For example, a wife who shows excessive grief at the violent death of her husband should be suspected of having murdered him {4.7.14}. This cynicism also prompts Kautilya to give practical advice. When a prince is too young to ascend the throne on the death of his father and is being trained to be king, a Regent rules on his behalf. 'A poor but handsome man of the same family should be kept near the mother lest her mind wavers and she takes on a lover who may become a danger to the state and the young prince' {5.6.41}.

While Kautilya has no compunction about exploiting the gullibility of the people, he himself had no belief in magic or the occult. Most of his phenomena are tricks which he tells us how to perform; poisons and stupefying chemicals are frequently mentioned. Kautilya did not even believe in astrology. 'Wealth will slip away from that childish man who constantly consults the stars. The only guiding star of wealth is itself; what can the stars of the sky do?' {9.4.26}

THE RELEVANCE OF KAUTILYA

Is Kautilya relevant to the twentieth century? I would not have attempted this new translation for the general reader were I not convinced that he is. In so far as the nature of human beings remains the same and states behave as they always have done, he is relevant. In its detail, whether on the Code of Penalties or on battle formations, the *Arthashastra* may only be of historical interest. But, when he discusses the economy, just administration or relations between states, we can learn from his wisdom. I shall cite a few examples.

When Kautilya talks of *kulasamghas*—clan oligarchies—we can see similarities to the rule, by a collection of Princes, of modern Saudi Arabia {11.1}. When he suggests that the death of a king should be kept secret until a series of measures had been taken to protect the kingdom, we note that it was practised until recently in the Soviet Union {5.6.1-22}. Kautilya gives a list of methods of imposing an unwelcome additional tax burden on people in times of adversity; one suggestion is that secret agents should start the fund-raising by putting a high figure against their own names. These days Presidents and Prime Ministers start off public collections with large personal subscriptions. Kautilya accords the *purohita* a very high place; though his official functions were restricted to religion and ritual, he exercised great personal influence over the king as the sacrificer and magician. Many present-day Indian politicians are reported to be influenced by such personal 'sacrificers and magicians'. Kautilya describes many secret methods by which a foreign ruler may be killed; he would not have been surprised about the attempts of the United States to kill Fidel Castro with an exploding cigar or about the arguments whether a CIA-supported coup could end in the 'accidental' death of the foreign ruler. The *Arthashastra* recommends apparently immoral means against traitors and enemies of the state and distinctly adds that such means are not to be used against law-abiding subjects. What are the limits to the methods that a state may use against terrorists who kill innocents is a matter of continuing debate in all civilized countries.

Finally, I can do no better than to quote the following from Dr. Kangle's 'Study' to show the relevance of Kautilya to the twentieth century.[32]

'We have still the same distrust of one nation by another, the same pursuit of its own interest by every nation tempered only by considerations of expediency, the same effort to secure alliances with the same disregard of them in self-interest, the same kind of intelligence service maintained by one nation in the territory of another which we find referred to in the *Arthashastra*....It is difficult to see how rivalry and the struggle for supremacy between the nations can be avoided and the teaching of this shastra which is based on these basic facts rendered altogether superfluous until some sort of a one-world government or an effective supra-national authority is established....But until that happens, the teachings of this *sastra* would in actual practice be followed by nations, though it may be unknown to them and though it may be openly condemned by those that know it.'

To conclude, the purpose of this Introduction has been to justify my contention that the popular image of Kautilya is not only simplistic but due to ignorance of what he actually wrote. The purpose is not to whitewash him. We need not try to explain away his cynical view of humanity, the special status given by him to Brahmins, his preference for a noble royal line, his inclusion of torture as a method of criminal investigation or his use of the secret service. But we need to balance these with his moderation, his insistence on a just administration, his knowledge of economics, his comprehensive attention to detail, his impeccable powers of logic and analysis and, most of all, his emphasis on people's welfare. Kautilya is so great that he does not need us to extol or exculpate him. He can speak for himself. This translation, therefore, gives the readers an opportunity to listen to Kautilya as he spoke.

THE KAUTILYAN STATE AND SOCIETY

The scope of this chapter is limited to two purposes—firstly, to set the stage for a better understanding of the translation and secondly, to enable the reader to trace the verses in this translation dealing with a specific subject, especially those not usually found in other studies. In this sense, it is more a road map than a comprehensive commentary. The aim is neither to provide a detailed summary of the text as a whole nor to make a comparison of Kautilya's views with those in the *Dharmashastras*, *nitishastras*, or other texts. For such comparative studies, the reader is referred to the works listed in the Bibliography; Kangle's 'Study' is particularly recommended.

In the various Parts of this translation, all verses concerning topics such as the King, the Administrative Structure, Budget and Accounts, Law and Justice, Foreign Policy or War, have been brought together. Hence, the following description of the Kautilyan state and society covers only those aspects which straddle different Parts. The explanatory introductions to each Part supplement this chapter. Since foreign policy is not touched upon in this chapter, the attention of the reader is particularly invited to the introduction to Part X.

In order to understand better the nature of the kingdoms in the *Arthashastra*, the first section of this chapter contains a brief description of the natural features of an imaginary Kautilyan country (see end-paper).

Kautilyan society is covered in the next section starting with the structure of the society and the complex *varna* and outcast system. It is also important to note aspects of the daily life of the people, particularly how they lived in the towns and villages, what they ate and drank, how they spent their leisure and what part religion played in their lives. Since the status of women in Kautilyan society is a topic which has been somewhat neglected in the studies on the *Arthashastra*, the last sub-section brings together all the major areas dealing with women, including their livelihood and their rights.

Though economics is an important part of the *Arthashastra*, it is difficult to form a clear idea of the economic system, since Kautilya's ordering of topics is so different. The relative importance between state and private economic activities, land use, agriculture in its technical as well as revenue aspects, animal husbandry, mining and manufacturing, labour and employment and trade are covered in the third section.

I have stressed in the Introduction how Kautilya's repeated emphasis on welfare has been ignored or misinterpreted. The last section is, therefore, devoted to a compilation of the verses on welfare of the people and animal welfare.

I reiterate that the verses are mentioned here only as references and that every verse relating to a topic is not listed here. While, for the sake of readability, a brief indication of the general tenor of the verses is given, the actual translation will need to be consulted to find out what exactly Kautilya said. The location of any verse can be ascertained from the verse index.

THE COUNTRY

How big was the Kautilyan country? During the period to which a date can be ascribed to the *Arthashastra*, i.e., between the 4th century BC and 150 AD, there were only two empires, the Nanda and the Mauryan. In fact, Chandragupta Maurya was the first conqueror to join together the Indus valley and the Gangetic plain in one vast empire. Before the empires arose and after their disintegration, the political map of the subcontinent showed not more than six large kingdoms in the Gangetic plain, various republics in the predominantly hilly areas in the west and the north and a number of smaller kingdoms whose relative independence must have varied with the power of a large neighbour. The *Arthashastra* also discusses foreign policy in terms of four powerful kingdoms—the conqueror's own (for example, *Magadha*, the present-day southern Bihar), the enemy's (say, *Kashi*) and the Middle and Neutral kingdoms (*Koshala* or *Vriji*).[1] The sixteen *mahajanapadas* (great races or nations states) before 600 BC, the subcontinent in Mauryan times, and the situation after its break-up are shown in the end-paper map.[2]

A hypothetical Kautilyan country was a compact unit ruled by a king or, in some cases, an oligarchy of chiefs. Kautilya envisages a variety of natural features—mountains, valleys, plains, deserts, jungles, lakes and rivers—though in practice all these may not be found in every country. The frontier regions were either mountainous or jungles inhabited by tribes which were not completely under the control of the king. The frontier was protected by forts {2.3.1} especially on trade routes to other countries. References to ships and trade by sea {2.28.7-12} show that some countries had a sea coast.

The main city, in the central part of the country, was located near a perennial water source, and well laid out and fortified {2.3.3-5}. There were at least four other towns functioning as the headquarters of the provinces into which the country was divided {2.1.4}.

The *janapada* or countryside consisted of villages with clearly marked boundaries {2.1.3, 3.9.10-14}; pasture lands lay between villages on land not suitable for agriculture {2.34.6}. Roads of different widths, depending on the nature of the traffic, connected not only the towns and villages but also the country with its neighbours {2.4.1-5}. Rivers and lakes had dams and embankments impounding water for agriculture {2.1.20-23}.

There were three kinds of useful forests, different from the untamed jungles. These were (i) forests for recreational use like hunting {2.2.3,4}; (ii) economically useful ones for collecting forest produce like timber {2.2.5} and (iii) nearer the frontier, elephant forests, where wild elephants could be captured {2.2.6-16}. Special areas were allocated in the forests for ascetics and the schools of Brahmins learned in the Vedas {2.2.2}.

Plenty of land was available for settlement {2.1.1-4}, indicating a fairly low density of population and many uninhabited tracts.

THE KAUTILYAN SOCIETY

ARYAS AND NON-ARYAS

Society was clearly divided into two—*Aryas* of the four *varnas* and non-Aryas, i.e. those outside the pale. An *Arya* could never be treated as a slave {3.13.4} though he could pledge himself and his family in times of disaster. Detailed regulations have been prescribed for such pledging and redemption {3.13.5-8}. An *Arya* captured in war could be released on payment of half the ransom demanded for others {3.13.9}.

Posing as an Arya in a drinking hall was forbidden {2.25.15}; on the other hand, an *Arya* was expected to conduct himself with dignity even in drinking halls {2.25.3}.

The sub-groups within the *Arya* and the non-*Arya* populations are dealt with below.

THE VARNA SYSTEM

The detailed regulations in VIII.v on Marital Relations as well as {3.7.36} show that the *varna* system was an endogamic one. The system was a determining factor in inheritance. Among the sons of a man of higher *varna* by wives of different *varnas*, the lower the varna of the mother, the lower was the share of the son {3.6.17-18}. However, intermarriages did happen giving rise to an elaborate system of subclassifications depending on whether the marriage was *anuloma* (the man being of superior *varna*) or *pratiloma* (the man being of lower *varna*—see Mixed Varnas in VIII.v. The duties of the different *varnas* are prescribed {1.3.5-8}.

The hierarchy was clearly established with the Brahmin at the top and then in the order, Kshatriya, Vaishya and Sudra. The productive role of the three lower varnas was recognized; when settling people in virgin territory, preference was to be given to the three lower *varnas* because of the benefit that farmers, cowherds and traders brought to the economy {7.11.12}.

The system governed all aspects of life and behaviour. In life, different *varnas* inhabited different areas of the fortified city {2.4.9,11,13,15}; in death, the higher and lower *varnas* were cremated in different grounds, not doing so being a punishable offence {2.4.21,22}. Witnesses taking oath in courts of law were cautioned with a different set of words for each *varna* {3.11.34-38}. The punishments for the same crime or transgression were different depending on the *varna* of the offender. In general, the lower the *varna*, the more severe was the punishment. For example: defamation {3.18.5,7 and Note on Translation 5}; assault {3.19.4}; making a person of higher varna eat or drink something prohibited {4.13.1}; selling or keeping as a mortgage an Arya minor {3.13.1}; taking away another man's wife from her village {3.4.18}; having sexual relations with an unprotected Brahmin woman {4.13.32}.

BRAHMINS

Two kinds of Brahmins are distinguished in the text—the *srotriya* (the very learned ones, experts on the Vedas) and the others. The *srotriya* was entitled to even greater respect and privileges than Brahmins in general. The king had to give priority to dealing with their affairs, only those of temples, hermits and heretic ascetics taking precedence over the *srotriya* {1.19.29}. When receiving them, the king had to get up, salute them and take care not to make them angry {1.19.31}. A prince unjustly treated by his father may secretly rob temples, but not those of the *srotriya* {1.18.9}. Their property could not be appropriated by the state in times of emergency {5.2.37}. The king, who took over all intestate property could not do so with that of *srotriyas* {3.5.28}.

When settling virgin territory *srotriyas* were given, free of cost and taxes, land which they could bequeath to their heirs {2.1.7}. A *srotriya* could take salt free {2.12.33} and gather fruits, flowers, rice and barley for ritual purposes from Crown lands {2.24.30}. Wardens of lodging houses were to give them accommodation, probably free of charge {2.36.5}.

Debts owed to a *srotriya* ranked next only to that owed to the king and he was entitled to payment before all other creditors {3.11.20}. They could be called as witnesses only in cases which concerned their own groups {3.11.29}.

As regards the Brahmin in general, the high position of the *varna* is shown by {1.6.5,6} which list kings of yore who perished because they either lusted after Brahmin women or used violence against Brahmins. The *purohita*, the king's chaplain, adviser and preceptor, occupied a position next only to the immediate family and wielded great influence over the king (see IV.iv). Brahmins were also appointed as ambassadors, because they were more immune than other envoys from the wrath of the king to whose court they were sent {1.16.14,15}. On the eve of a battle the king entrusted himself to Brahmins {10.3.37}. Acts of God like fire, floods and pestilence, could be overcome by propitiating Gods and Brahmins. They could not be captured as war booty {3.16.28}.

Brahmins are included in the list of persons whose affairs judges themselves should look into, even if they did not approach the court; no suit of theirs could be dismissed for want of jurisdiction, passage of time or adverse possession {3.20.22}.

Land given as a gift to Brahmins could be sold or mortgaged only to Brahmins similarly placed {3.10.9}. They were not to be compelled to participate or contribute to village festivities if they did not want to {3.10.44}.

If a Brahmin had only one son by a Sudra wife, two-third of the property was to pass on to his kinsmen, teacher or pupils (i.e. other Brahmins) and only a third to the son; this was presumably on the grounds that the son born of a Sudra mother could not perform the rites for his father {3.6.22,23}. A son-less Brahmin could perpetuate his line by getting his wife to bear a son (*kshetraja*—born-on-the-field) with the help of a kinsman or a man of the same *gotra* {3.6.24}.

Torturing a Brahmin, particularly a *srotriya*, was prohibited, whatever the offence; anyone doing so was punished with the Highest Standard Penalty {4.8.19,20,27}. Even for the most serious offence of treason for which the punishment for anyone else was death by burning, the punishment for a Brahmin was reduced to blinding {4.11.11,12}.

Brahmins could travel on the ferries free of charge; making them pay was a punishable offence {2.28.18, 3.20.14}.

Since their special function was celebration of rituals, elaborate rules are given for sharing the fees when a number of them concelebrate. Any priest who had indulged in a sinful activity could be expelled from a ritual {3.14.37,38}.

A Sudra passing himself off as a Brahmin was punished with the blinding of both eyes {4.10.13} and anyone violating the sanctity of a Brahmin's kitchen had his tongue rooted out {4.12.21}. These two verses are considered by J.J. Meyer to be interpolations.[3]

Brahmins could take up arms but were not considered very good soldiers because an enemy could win them over by prostrating himself before them {9.2.23}! The one disadvantage they suffered from was that, unlike others, they could not claim ownership of a building neglected by the owner after living in it for twenty years {3.16.32}.

KSHATRIYAS

To Kautilya, *kshatriyas* were 'protectors of the land' {14.3.35}. He shows a marked preference for the nobility, the protection of *kshatriya* blood and the preservation of the royal line. The preference for noble birth is explained as: 'people will naturally obey a high born king though he be weak....A man of nobility has a natural capacity to rule' {8.2.23}.

Preservation of the royal line through sons is shown by the advice that an only son, even if he revolted against his father, should not be put to death but only be exiled {9.3.14}. If an only son was evil, attempts should be made to get him to father a son {1.17.48}. Or, a daughter was designated to bear a son to carry on the royal line {1.17.49}. A king who could not father any son, might even get one born to his wife using a kinsman or a princely neighbour {1.17.50}. In the detailed discussion on whom to give as a hostage, the advice is that a king might give himself up if there was only one son capable of carrying on the duties because 'all expectations are concentrated on an only son' {7.17.15-31}. It was better to give a daughter as a hostage rather than a son because 'the daughter is not an heir, is useful only to others and costs more to the receiver' {7.17.16}. Kautilya also expresses a preference for a legitimate son over an illegitimate one, even if the illegitimate son was wiser than the legitimate one; the reason given is: 'because the legitimate son is better able to command the loyalty of the people' {7.17.21,22}.

In Kautilya's view, an army composed of *kshatriyas* was the best one, unless the *Vaishya* or *Sudra* forces were much more numerous {9.2.21}.

VAISHYAS

Except where a *varna* distinction has to be made, as in inheritance or differential punishment, *vaishyas*, as a *varna*, are rarely mentioned in the text. However, in their occupation as traders, they formed an important part of the society. Trade, traders and merchants are covered in a subsequent section of this chapter. It may also be noted that, being ubiquitous, the disguise of a trader was often adopted by secret agents (see Part IX).

SUDRAS

As agriculturists, artisans and craftsmen, *sudras* were the backbone of the productive capacity of the country. Entertainers like actors also came from this *varna* {1.3.8}. New settlements were populated mainly by *sudra* agriculturists {2.1.2}. As an *Arya*, a *Sudra* could never be a slave {3.13.4}. Even if he had bonded himself and his family, his children did not lose their *Arya* status {3.13.13}. A more numerous *sudra* (or *vaishya*) army was preferable to a smaller *kshatriya* army {9.2.21-24}.

THE *ASHRAMAS*

An integral part of the varna order was the system of *ashramas* or the four stages of life prescribed for every *Arya* {1.3.9-12}. Since the *dharma* for each *ashrama* is the concern of *Dharmashastras*, the *Arthashastra* deals only with a few aspects relevant to maintenance of social order.

On *brahmacharya*, the student phase, respect for the guru is emphasized throughout. The teacher's wife was like a mother; sexual intercourse with her was punishable by first castration and then death {4.13.30}. Students could have a share in the property of a guru dying without leaving a legitimate Brahmin son {3.7.23}.

The law relating to *grihastas* or householders, will be found in the sections on Marital Life (VIII.v) and Inheritance (VIII.vi). Since the *dharma* of a householder was to sacrifice his own pleasures for the sake of those dependent on him {1.3.9}, abandoning a dependent, without due cause, was a serious offence; examples given are: father abandoning a son, a husband his wife, a brother his sister, a maternal uncle his nephew and a guru his pupil {3.20.18}. In this context, we may note the special role of the maternal uncle, as a protector and almost a second father. Consequently, sexual relations with the wife of the maternal uncle was treated as incest and punished accordingly {4.13.30}.

Vanaprasthas, forest recluses, were allotted parts of forest for their habitation and could take salt free of charge for their own consumption {2.12.33}.

ASCETICS

Ascetics, called by various names in the text (*sannyasin, tapasvin, pravrajita, parivrajaka*, etc.) were a familiar sight on the social scene.

There were men and women ascetics, *Aryas* and those belonging to other sects. Though often equated with Brahmins, they could have originally belonged to any varna. They are often referred to in the text as *munda* (shaven headed) or *jatila* (with matted hair).

They were allotted forest areas for their meditation and contemplation {2.2.2} but they had to live in harmony, make room for newcomers and not annoy each other {3.16.33-36}. Their property could not be claimed as war booty {3.16.28}.

Respect was to be shown to them; reviling, hurting or killing one was equated to similar offences against father, mother or teacher {4.11.13,14}. Torture of ascetics was prohibited {4.8.19}.

They could stay in lodging houses in the city {2.36.5} and take salt free of charge {2.12.38}. As in the case of Brahmins, judges could look *suo moto* into their affairs and not dismiss their suits for want of jurisdiction, etc. {3.20.22}. A wandering monk, *pravrajita*, could travel free on the ferries with a pass from the appropriate authority {2.28.18}.

Since an ascetic had no family, his property passed on to his teacher, pupils, spiritual brother or fellow student {3.16.37}. The theft of their property is mentioned as a separate crime meriting a hefty fine {4.10.6}.

The wife of a man who became a *pravrajita* had the same rights of remarriage as if the man had died or gone on a long journey {3.4.37}.

For secret agents, disguise as an ascetic made an excellent cover, as ascetics were free to wander, their presence anywhere was not unusual and they were held in respect and, perhaps, awe. *Munda* and *jatila* were one class of stationary spies {1.11.4-8} and a wandering nun a class of roving spies {1.12.3,5}. For details of how these were utilized see Part IX. Because spies adopted this disguise, ascetics were also suspect; anyone found wandering at night dressed as a monk was arrested {2.36.39}.

NON-ARYAS

NON-ARYA ASCETICS

Vrishalas and *pashandas* were both ascetics belonging to *Sramana* (non-Brahmanical) sects. It is mentioned in {2.4.23} that *pashandas* should live beyond the cremation grounds; however, from the reference to their quarters being searched periodically for suspicious characters, it seems that they could also live inside the city {2.36.14}. They could stay in lodging houses in the city but their stay had to be reported to the Divisional Officer {2.36.5}. In an emergency their property could be seized {5.2.37}. They were suspected but were also feared; the king was enjoined to listen to their complaints after those of 'gods and temples' but before those of Brahmins {1.19.29}. Those who had no property could do penance instead of paying the fine when convicted of offences less serious than assault, theft, kidnapping or adultery {3.16.39.41}.

Sakyas and *Ajivikas*, mentioned in {3.20.16}, probably refer to Buddhist sects. Anyone feeding them during Brahmanical rites was fined a substantial amount.

OUTCASTS

The general term for all those forced to live outside the perimeter of a city or a village is *antavasayin*, translated here as outcasts, since the *Arthashastra* refers only to *varna* and not to *jati* (caste, in current usage). These could either be those cast out of the *Arya* fold or those who were never admitted to it. On the origins of the system, up to 200 AD., Prabhati Mukherjee's 'Beyond the Four *Varnas*' is highly recommended.[4]

PATITA—THE FALLEN

Those who were cast out of the *Arya* fold for some heinous transgression of the code of conduct became the victims of social ostracism. Anyone cast out was relieved of the responsibility of maintaining his family, except his mother {2.1.28}. Even his wife could abandon him {3.2.48}. Neither an outcast nor his son could inherit family property. They were treated worse than idiots, lunatics and lepers who could at least receive food from their families {3.5.30-32}. Except in cases of defamation and assault, they could be called as witnesses only in cases involving their own group {3.11.28-32}. It is not clear from the text whether they formed an endogamic group of their own or merged with some other group beyond the pale.

CHANDALAS

Among the non-*Aryas*, the most frequently mentioned are the *chandalas*. In view of the heavy fine of 100 panas imposed on a *chandala* for touching an *Arya* woman {3.20.16}, this group was clearly the 'untouchables'. This is further borne out by the reference to '*chandalas* and other impure persons' {3.7.37}, 'the well of the *chandalas* of use only to *chandalas*' {1.14.10} and their being made to live beyond the cremation grounds {2.4.23}. As people who were not permitted to live in settled areas, they were employed by the state as guards for the safety of the land between villages {2.1.6}.

The reference to 'just as a *chandala* stands to benefit when a wild dog fights a wild boar' indicates that they could have eaten meat prohibited to others {9.2.6}. While the fine on *chandalas* for theft of small animals was half that for others {4.10.2}, the punishment for them for defamation or assault was the highest {3.19.10}. They were also classified as a separate group for the purposes of the Law of Evidence {3.11.28}. They seem to have been used to impose punishment thought to be particularly degrading. A woman convicted of misconduct was whipped publicly by a *chandala* {3.3.28}. The body of a suicide was dragged through the streets by a *chandala* {4.7.26}.

SVAPAKAS

Like *chandalas*, *svapakas* (dog breeders) were also a group at the lowest levels of society. For example, an *Arya* man having relations with a *svapaka* woman was branded and exiled while a *svapaka* man having relations with an *Arya* woman was put to death {4.13.34,35}.

SVAGANIN AND LUBDHAKAS

These are translated here, following Kangle, as hunters and fowlers. The hunter's name indicates that he hunted with dogs. For example: 'Just as the cow of a hunter is milked for his hounds and not for Brahmins' {1.14.9}. The two groups are often referred to together as being employed as guards between settlements {2.34.9}; for catching robbers in forests {4.5.15}; for clearing thieves, wild animals and enemies from pastures {2.29.21} and the king's hunting forests {1.21.23} and for guarding the military base camp {10.1.11}. The references in the *Arthashastra* are purely professional and do not indicate their social status as separate endogamic groups. *Sabara* and *Pulinda* are two other communities mentioned as guarding the area between the frontier and the settled regions {2.1.6}.

MLECCHAS

As a group, they could have been of foreign or tribal origin, since they and jungle tribes are often mentioned together, particularly as fighting forces {7.10.16; 7.14.27; 12.4.23}. *Mlecchas* were employed as spies {1.12.21} and, suitably disguised, to poison the enemy {14.1.2}. A *mleccha* could sell or mortgage his children {3.13.3}. After conquering a territory, the king is advised to transfer and disperse *mlecchas* living there {13.5.15}.

JUNGLE TRIBES

Jungle tribes, each with its own chieftain, were feared but were also used as fighting forces. Disagreeing with other unnamed teachers who thought that highway robbers were more dangerous than jungle tribes, Kautilya says: 'Unsubdued jungle tribes live in their own territory, are more numerous, brave, fight in daylight and, with their ability to seize and destroy countries, behave like kings' {8.1.41-43}. Tribal forces are specifically mentioned as one of the six types of troops with the comment that they were unreliable and were interested only in plunder {9.2.18-20}. As troops they were useful in showing the way, putting down a small enemy incursion or when their special skills made them valuable {9.2.8}. Theft by them of small animals was treated more leniently {4.10.2}. On the whole, tribal chieftains seem to have been independent of the king so long as they did not harass the country and came to the king's help when called upon to do so.

SLAVES

All slaves were non-*Aryas*. The regulations regarding slaves and bonded labour, including their rights, may be seen in VIII.x.

FOREIGNERS

Depending on the context, different terms are used for 'foreigners'. The regulations for the city include one which requires that outsiders (*bahirikas*) who may cause harm to the city were not be let in; if at all they were, they had to pay a tax {2.4.32}. The tax called *dvarabahirika* (outsider toll) was important enough to merit a special mention in the revenue for the city. On keeping a watch over strangers in drinking halls, the word used is 'visitor' (*agantuh*) {2.25.12,15}. Foreign artists who had to pay a special tax of 5 panas per show are also called 'visiting artists' (*agantukah*) {2.27.26}. These terms may refer to strangers to the locality rather than true foreigners.

The three references on ports and ferries in chapter {2.28} are to foreigners in the sense of visitors from another country. Foreign merchants could enter the country only if they were frequent visitors or were vouched for by local merchants {2.28.19}. The ferry man at the crossing point was responsible for collecting the import duty, escort charges and road cess {2.28.25}. Foreign sea-going vessels had to pay duty or port dues if they entered territorial waters {2.28.11}.

RELIGION AND SUPERSTITION

The religion of the *Arthashastra* is clearly Brahmanism, with emphasis on the supremacy of the Vedas; for 'the world, when maintained in accordance with Vedas, will ever prosper and not perish' {1.3.17}. The teachings of other religions and sects, like Sakyas or Ajivikas, are not mentioned but their followers were sometimes treated with hostility {3.20.16}. There were holy places, temples and sanctuaries of the various religions and sects but the nature of religious life mentioned below applies mainly to the Brahmanical religion. There was great belief in astrology and similar predictive sciences as well as in the occult sciences such as witchcraft, sorcery and black magic.

TEMPLES AND HOLY PLACES

Temples and shrines were everywhere; in the centre of the city for the guardian deity and for the family deity of the king {2.4.17}; at each of the four gates to the city dedicated to the god of that quarter {2.4.19}; in store houses {2.5.6}; for the tutelary deities of different groups of people in different quarters {2.4.18}. The sanctity of such holy places was emphasized by prescribing a higher scale of punishment for urinating or defecating in them {2.36.28}.

Temples must have owned large properties; the list in {4.10.16} has 'images, crops, cattle, slaves, fields, houses, money, gold and coins' as temple property. The king was to look into temple affairs first {1.19.29} and the judges were instructed to treat them as privileged litigants {3.20.22}. Village elders were charged with the responsibility of looking after temple properties {2.1.27}. Punishments are prescribed for the following crimes relating to temple property: embezzlement by trustees {4.10.13}; riding or killing temple animals {4.13.20}; and theft of temple property {4.10.16}. Two special privileges were accorded to such property: (i) it could not be seized as war booty {3.16.28} and (ii) temple bulls could graze freely in any pasture {3.10.24}. However, temple property, except those of *srotriyas* and *pashandas* could be confiscated in times of emergency {5.2.37,38} and a prince unjustly treated could secretly plunder them {1.18.9}. A strange crime mentioned in the text is the fine of 24 panas levied on anyone caught having sex with images of goddesses! {4.13.41}. A department of the state, headed by the Chief Superintendent of Temples, was responsible for temple affairs {5.2.38}.

A number of gods are mentioned by name; Aparajita, Apratihata, Jayanta, Vijayanta, Shiva, Vaishravana, Ashvins, Sri and Madira {2.4.17}; Brahma, Indra, Yama and Senapati as the gods of the four quarters {2.4.19:00}.[5] In addition, a number of Vedic gods, *asuras* and sages are mentioned in the invocatory mantras for occult purposes in Book 14; many are obscure.

The religious or ritual significance of sanctuaries and holy places, which are often mentioned together, is not clear. Natural objects like trees were also worshipped; e.g. a *caitya* tree {4.3.41}. The reference to thefts in holy places during festivals {4.10.1}, the king organizing spurious ones with the help of secret agents to relieve the public of money {5.2.39,40} and using a festival to kill an enemy {12.5.1} indicate that festivals were frequently orgnized in holy places. During some festivals, liquor could be manufactured and sold {2.25.36}. A king who had newly conquered a territory, was advised to show the same devotion as the local people towards their gods and to participate in their festivals {13.5.8}.

It is obvious that there were rituals in connection with the major events of life: birth, initiation, marriage and death. An interesting aspect of the denial of ritual cremation for a suicide is that any kinsman who performed such rituals was declared an outcast and lost his own right to a ritual cremation {4.7.27}.

SUPERSTITIOUS BELIEFS

Belief in evil spirits {4.3.40, 5.2.41}, magical potions, charms, black magic and sorcery was widely prevalent. Charms and incantations for making someone sleepy or insensible, making oneself invisible, opening locked doors and obtaining wealth are some specifically mentioned {4.5.1-7, 5.2.59}. In addition, the four chapters of Book 14 are wholly devoted to describing 'a number of rites and practices which are supposed to produce occult manifestations and miraculous effects. There are recipes for bringing on blindness or killing people on a mass scale, for mysteriously causing various kinds of diseases, for changing one's appearance, for making objects glow at night, for remaining without food for days together, for walking long distances without getting tired...'[6] Book 14 has not been translated.

The practice of black magic and sorcery {4.4.16, 5.1.33} is condemned but the king was also advised to exploit it for his own purposes. Anyone who brought harm to another using black magic and witchcraft was punished by having the same effects visited on him {4.13.27}. Use of love potions was, however, permitted to be practised without the threat of punishment, by husbands, wives and lovers, towards their loved ones {4.13.28}. Among the methods recommended to the Chancellor for exposing dishonest officials and black money is the use of secret agents exploiting faith in black magic {4.4.14-16}.

Though Kautilya mocks the belief in stars as a means of obtaining wealth {9.4.26}, he recommends that the *Purohita* be also learned in reading omens {1.9.9}. The soothsayer, reader of omens and the astrologer were paid employees of the court {5.3.13}. Astrologers accompanied the king on military expeditions and were used to encourage their own troops and frighten the enemy's on the eve of battle {13.3.44}. The list of such professionals include: *kartantika* (soothsayer), *naimittika* (reader of omens), *mauhurtika* (astrologer) and *ikshanika* (intuitionist) {13.1.7}.

All these beliefs were exploited by artificially producing so-called unnatural manifestations to hoodwink gullible people in order to collect money in emergencies {5.2.39-45} or to draw out the besieged enemy from the protection of his fort {13.2.16, 21-35}. Temples, fairs and festivals could also be used for a variety of nefarious purposes: secret exits could be built into images of gods {1.20.2} and arms could be smuggled in them {13.3.45}. The enemy's visits to worship in temples could be used to poison him {7.17.44} or to kill him by mechanical contrivances {12.5.1-5}. Agents disguised as monks could use temples for their operations {13.2.15}. Festivals of jungle robbers could be used to poison them {13.3.54}. The long list of such tricks may be seen in Part IX.

DAILY LIFE

THE RICH AND THE POOR

There was tremendous disparity in wealth. Apart from the king whose wealth was all the surplus wealth of the state, there were high officials earning 48,000 panas a year, not counting the perquisites of office {5.3.3}. Even if we ignore ascetics and mendicant monks as being poor by choice, the lowest government salary was only 60 panas a year {5.3.17}, making the ratio of the highest to the lowest paid 800 to 1. For the value of a pana, see I.iii.

The lowest monetary fine was one-eighth of a pana, for making a public road impassable with dirt, water or mud {2.36.26} and the highest, 5000 panas levied on a courtesan disobeying an order to attend on someone {2.27.19}, a ratio of 4000 to 1.

Grazing charges in a village for sheep and goats were only one-sixteenth of a pana a day {3.10.22}. At the other extreme, as the detailed regulations in 2.14 show, many private citizens could afford to pay goldsmiths and silversmiths.

The rich were naturally the targets whenever the king needed additional resources in times of emergency. The king could ask them to give gold voluntarily or sell them honours {5.2.35,36}.

CITY LIFE

Though urban life is tackled in the *Arthashastra* only in the form of punishments for violations of rules and regulations, we get from these a picture of how people lived inside the fortified city. The rules on precautions against fire show that fire was a major hazard in a densely packed city {2.36.15-25}. Craftsmen, like smiths, who worked with fire were concentrated in a separate quarter of the city {2.36.20}. Maintenance of cleanliness, sanitation and hygiene was a part of house building regulations {2.36.26-33}; so was privacy {3.8.17}. The people were expected to contribute to building common facilities, not obstruct their use nor destroy them {3.8.26,27}. Causing harm to an entire neighbourhood attracted a fine of 48 panas {3.20.15}.

The sale of houses and tenancy were strictly regulated {3.9.3-8: 3.8.24,25}. The duties and fees of artisans, goldsmiths, silversmiths and even washermen were clearly fixed {4.1.2-42}.

The Governor-General of the City was responsible for the maintenance of law and order which included control of lodgings, curfew and movement control and prevention of crime (see IV.iv). Under him there were four divisional officers, one for each quarter of the city {2.36.4}. Record keepers kept a record of every person in a section of the city, with details including their income and expenditure {2.36.3}.

VILLAGE LIFE

While the Governor General was responsible for administering the more compact City, the Chancellor had to administer the whole of the vast countryside, with its villages, pastures, empty tracts and forests. Though the Chancellor also had under him governors of provinces and record keepers, his control would have been much looser. He relied much more on the secret service {2.35.8-14}.

A lot of responsibility, therefore, fell on the *gramika*, the village headman and the *gramavriddha*, the village elders. The elders were responsible for looking after temple property, holding in trust a minor's property until he came of age {2.1.27; 3.5.20, 00}, arbitrating disputes regarding fields {3.9.15} and overseeing the sale of immovable property {3.9.3}. A debtor could redeem his pledge by depositing the money owed by him with the elders, even if the actual creditor was absent {3.12.12}.

The village headman was responsible for maintenance of the village boundary pillars {3.10.20}, controlling grazing {3.10.25-34} and ejecting undesirables {3.10.18,19}. He could also give asylum to a woman who had run away from home {3.4.9}. Each villager had to take his turn in accompanying the headman whenever he went on official business {3.10.16}.

Usually everyone in the village had to contribute his share of the cost of common projects, festivals and entertainments {3.10.36-38}. However, those belonging to a family, caste, group or locality, were not obliged to take part in festivities, if they did not want to do so {3.10.45}. 'The people of a village shall obey the orders of anyone who proposes any activity beneficial to all' {3.10.39}. 100 panas was the fine for both failing to help a neighbour and, conversely, interfering without reason in the affairs of a neighbour! {3.20.16}.

EATING HABITS

The average food consumption can be deduced from the ration prescribed for an *Arya* male for one meal: one *prastha* (about a kilo) of rice, a quarter of a litre of broth, one sixteenth of a litre of butter or oil and a bit of salt {2.15.43}. Attendants of elephants were given a litre of boiled rice, a cupful of oil, 160 grams of sugar, 800 grams of meat and salt {2.32.17}. An annual salary of 60 panas is said to be equivalent to one *adhaka* (four *prasthas*) of grain a day, enough for four meals. Using the average of the conversion factors suggested by various scholars and assuming that payment was made according to the payment measure (12.5% smaller than the revenue measure), this will, very approximately, be equivalent to four litres or between three to three and a half kilos of grain per person per day. If we assume that the grain was unprocessed, the quantity of dehusked and milled grain would have been between one and a half to two and a half kilos per person per day.

We must note that the ration suggested for an *Arya* male was the highest. The lower classes got the same quantity of rice and salt, but only two-third of the quantity of broth and half the oil given to the *Arya* male {2.15.44}.

Women received three-quarters, and children half, the quantities for the corresponding male of their category {2.15.45,46}.

It is clear, from the punishment prescribed for making someone from a higher *varna* eat or drink a prohibited item, that there were food taboos {4.13.1,2}. Presumably the taboos were as prescribed in the *Dharmashastras*. It is not clear why elephant doctors, unlike other attendants, were not given meat {2.32.17}.

A wide variety of commodities were used for cooking: different kinds of rice, other cereals like wheat, barley and millets, a variety of beans and lentils, butter and ghee, vegetable oils from sesame and mustard, sugar, honey, treacle and molasses, vinegars, fruit juices from tamarind, lemon and pomegranate, milk and yoghurt, spices including pepper, ginger, coriander, cumin seed and anise, root vegetables, other vegetables and fruit, fresh and dried meat and dried fish.

The quantities of other ingredients for cooking fresh meat are given as follows: for every kilo of meat, 50 grams of salt, 50 grams of sugar, 10 grams spices, one and a quarter kilo of yoghurt and a small quantity of oil. For dried meat, the above quantities were doubled and for vegetables, one and a half times the above quantities were used {2.15.47-49}. Kautilya even gives the amount of firewood required for cooking a *prastha* of rice as 25 palas {2.19.26.27}.

We know of the existence of public eating houses where different kinds of cooked food was sold because secret agents often disguised themselves as food vendors; e.g. as the agents of the Chancellor {4.4.3}, for liberating hostages {7.17.45} and for poisoning enemy troops {12.4.8}. In the city such places were periodically searched for undesirables {2.36.14} and the owners were prohibited from giving lodgings to strangers {2.36.8}. There were separate vegetarian and non-vegetarian eating places, bakers selling bread, sweetmeat sellers and broth makers. The Chief Superintendent of Warehouses disposed of broken grains left over from milling grain by selling them to broth makers and cooked food vendors {2.15.61}.

DRESS AND DECORATION

While we do not know what kind of dresses people wore, we have many indications of what the garments were made of. Cotton, wool, bark-fibres, silk-cotton, hemp and flax were used to spin yarn of different qualities, coarse, medium and fine {2.23.2}. Skins and furs were used for garments {2.11.73-96}. Details of the production of various types of fabrics are given later under the textile industry.

People wore a variety of jewellery, made of gold, set with pearls and precious stones, on their heads, hands, feet and waists {2.11.27}. Kautilya goes into great detail in classifying and indicating the sources of diamonds, rubies and other precious stones and naming different types of pearl necklaces {2.11}.

Perfumes, particularly sandal and aloe, were often used; they were considered to be articles of high value, along with gold and precious stones. Kautilya gives a detailed account of the quality of the perfumes and their sources of supply {2.11.43-69}. Garlands of flowers were worn as a decoration. The king had, among his attendants, shampooers, bathpreparers and garland makers {1.21.13,14}. Every courtesan had to be accomplished in shampooing and the preparation of perfumes and garlands {2.27.28}.

LEISURE ACTIVITIES

There is a great deal of material in the *Arthashastra* about how the people spent their leisure and entertained themselves. These leisure activities fall into three broad groups—private entertainment, public entertainment like shows and performances an strictly controlled activities like gambling, drinking and prostitution.

PRIVATE ENTERTAINMENT

It was normal to throw a feat on ceremonial or auspicious occasions like births and marriages. Anyone giving a large feast was asked to make special drainage arrangements for washing {3.8.8}. The king himself, duly protected, attended such feasts {1.21.28}. Such occasions, when people's attention was otherwise engaged, was also used for nefarious purposes such as entrapping a suspected minister {1.10.9}, to obtain money during emergencies {5.2.49} and to storm a fort {13.4.26}.

Hunting was a pastime of the rich, particularly the royal family. However, inordinate addiction to hunting was considered as one of the four serious vices, the others being gambling, drinking and womanizing {8.3.38}. But Kautilya, after extensive analysis, concludes that it is the least serious of the four {8.3.39-64}.

From the reference to betting being allowed in events involving skill or learning, we may deduce that competitions, such as archery, were held {3.20.13}.

Painting and recitation are referred to among the arts.

PUBLIC ENTERTAINMENT

There is a long list of professional entertainers in the *Arthashastra*: actors, dancers, musicians, mimics, reciters, story tellers, acrobats, jugglers and conjurors (see Appendix 6 for a full list of all the professions mentioned in the text). There were shows during the day and at night. From the differential punishments prescribed for a wife attending a show without the consent of her husband, we see that some shows were entirely by female performers and others only by males {3.3.21}.

The cost of putting on shows was shared by the people of a village {3.10.37}. Foreign entertainers paid a special tax {2.27.26}. To prevent the attention of the people in new settlements being diverted from work, no buildings were to be erected for lodging entertainers, who were enjoined not to obstruct the work {2.1.33,34}. Perhaps for the same reason, entertainers were prohibited from moving from village to village during the monsoon {4.1.58}.

Entertainers were permitted to make fun of the customs of the region, castes or families and the practices and love affairs of individuals. However, they were advised not to praise excessively anyone in return for large gifts {4.1.59,61}.

As in other instances when people's attention was diverted, shows could also afford an opportunity to draw out the enemy from the safety of his fort {13.2.4,45} or for storming it {13.4.26}.

GAMBLING AND BETTING

Betting and gambling was strictly controlled by the state. Gambling is described as wagering with inanimate objects such as dice; betting appears to have involved challenges and was concerned with cock fights, animal races and similar contests. Placing bets on literary or artistic challenges was not covered by the regulations.

Since Kautilya considered that all gamblers were cheats by nature, his regulations contained stiff punishments for cheating {3.20.7}. In order to ensure that gambling was conducted under controlled conditions, playing in places other than the authorized gambling halls was prohibited {3.20.1}. The penalty for gambling elsewhere was the most common fine of 12 panas {3.20.2}.

Gambling halls were managed by gambling masters, who were responsible for providing true undoctored gambling equipment, accommodation and water. They could collect an entrance fee, hire charges for the equipment and charges for their expenses {3.20.10}. Since betting beyond their means is common among gamblers, the masters were also permitted to accept articles as pledges and sell them if not redeemed {3.20.11}. The master could be punished for hiring out loaded dice or false equipment, cheating the customer and cheating the government of revenue {3.20.9}.

The state got its revenue from a tax of 5% levied on all winning as well as the fines collected by the Chief Controller of Gambling and Betting {3.20.10}.

There is an interesting contrast between the punishments prescribed, for the same, offence, if it is committed by the gambling master or by the client. For cheating with loaded dice, sleight of hand and other such tricks, the master was fined the Lowest Standard Penalty {3.20.9} and his winnings were confiscated. But the punishment for a gambler was cutting off his hand; he could avoid that only by paying a fine of 400 panas {4.10.9}.

ALCOHOLIC BEVERAGES

The manufacture and sale of alcoholic drinks was a state monopoly, private manufacturing being very limited and strictly controlled {2.25.36}. Alcoholic drinks were widely sold in many places in the city, the countryside and the camps {2.25.1}. These were drunk mainly in drinking halls built for this purpose. The *Arthashastra* prescribes: 'These shall have many rooms, with beds and seats in separate places. The drinking rooms shall be made pleasant in all seasons by providing them with perfumes, flowers and water' {2.25.11}. Only persons of good character could buy and take away small quantities of liquor; others had to drink it on the premises. Moving about while drunk was prohibited {2.25.5}. The liquor seller employed beautiful female servants, who were used to find out information about customers who might have been imposters {2.25.15}.

The duties and responsibilies of the Chief Controller of Alcoholic Beverages may be seen in VII.vi. Details of the types of liquor made are given in Appendix 10.

The prevalence for drinking gave rise to opportunities for poisoning with narcotics or stupefiants during a fight between the chiefs of oligarchies instigated by the king {11.1.24} or for disabling the enemy's troops during a siege {12.4.4}.

COURTESANS, PROSTITUTES AND BROTHELS

Providing sexual entertainment to the public using prostitutes (*ganika*) was an activity not only strictly controlled by the State but also one which was, for the most part, carried on in state-owned establishments {2.27.1}. Women who lived by their beauty (*rupajivas*) could, however, entertain men as independent practitioners {2.27.27}; these could have been allowed to practice in smaller places which could not support a full-fledged state establishment. A third type of women of pleasure, mentioned in a few places, is *pumsachali*, perhaps meaning concubines {3.13.37}.

As befits a treatise on the economy of a state, the emphasis in the *Arthashastra* is on collection of revenue. The state enabled the setting up of establishments with lump sum grants of 1000 panas to the head courtesan and 500 panas to her deputy, presumably to enable them to buy jewellery, furnishings, musical instruments and other tools of their trade {2.27.1}. The madam of the establishment had to render full accounts and it was the duty of the Chief Controller of Entertainers to ensure that the net income was not reduced by her extravagance {2.27.10}. Independent prostitutes, who were neither given a grant nor required to produce detailed accounts, had to pay a tax of one-sixth of their income {2.27.27}. In times of financial distress, both groups had to produce extra revenue with the independents having to pay half their earnings as tax {5.2.21,23,28}.

The establishments were located in the southern part of the fortified city {2.4.11}. Whenever the army marched on an expedition, courtesans also went with them; they were allotted places in the camp, alongside the roads {10.1.10}. During battle, the women were stationed in the rear with cooked food and drinks, encouraging the men to fight {10.3.47}.

It would seem that courtesans not only provided sexual pleasure but also entertained clients with singing and dancing. In specifying their duties, the *Arthashastra* makes a clear distinction between two types of misdemeanours—showing a dislike towards a client visiting her for normal entertainment and refusing to sleep with him, if he stayed overnight {2.27.20,21}. The description of the training given to a couresan, at state expense, indicates how wide her accomplishments had to be—singing, playing on musical instruments, conversing, reciting, dancing, acting, writing, painting, mind-reading, preparing perfumes and garlands, shampooing and, of course, the art of lovemaking {2.27.28}. A courtesan's son, who had to work as the king's minstrel from the age of eight, was also trained as a producer of plays and dances {2.27.29}.

It would appear from the above that some families specialized in the entertainment business. However, the *Arthashastra* specifically states that any beautiful, young and talented girl could be appointed as the head of an establishment, irrespective of whether she came from a family of courtesans or not {2.27.1}.

Once appointed, the madam became a very important person. She could aspire to become the personal attendant of the King or Queen {1.20.20, 2.27.4}. Even otherwise, a very high price - 24,000 panas—had to be paid for obtaining her release from her post {2.27.6}. We must note that the amount was the second highest annual salary paid only to the five top officials (like the Chief of the King's Bodyguards, the Chancellor and the Treasurer). Only such people could afford to buy a madam off as an exclusive concubine.

If a courtesan was promoted to attend on the King, her annual salary was fixed as 1000, 2000 or 3000 panas, depending on her beauty and qualifications {2.27.4}. 1000 panas was the same salary paid to the King's personal advisers and attendants such as the charioteer, physician, astrologer, court poet, etc.

An interesting point is that the courtesan's establishment could not be inherited by her son. On the death, retirement or release of the head of an establishment, her daughter (or sister) could take her place or she could promote her deputy and appoint a new deputy. If neither the daughter nor the deputy succeeded her, the establishment reverted to the state {2.27.2,3}.

The state not only imposed obligations on prostitutes but also protected them. Having been given a grant by the state and having been allowed to spend a part of her earnings on personal adornment, a prostitute could not sell, mortgage or entrust her jewellery and ornaments to anyone except the madam, {2.27.11}. Prostitutes were obliged to attend on any client when ordered to do so, be pleasant to them and not subject them to verbal or physical injury {2.27.12}. In return, stiff punishments were prescribed for anyone cheating or robbing a prostitute, abducting her, confining her against her will or disfiguring her {2.27.14}. Special punishments were also prescribed for depriving a prostitute's daughter of her virginity whether she herself consented or not; the right of the mother was recognized by making the man pay not only a fine but also a compensation to the mother of sixteen times the fee for a visit {4.12.26}.

An imbalance in punishments has to be noted. The penalty for killing the madam of an establishment was three times the release price and that for killing a prostitute in her establishment or her mother or daughter was only the Highest Standard Penalty {2.27.17}. On the other hand, if a prostitute killed a client, she was burnt or drowned alive {2.27.22}.

The expression *bandhakiposhaka* (keeper of prostitutes) occurs thrice in the text, associated always with 'young and beautiful women'. The keepers were obliged to use the women to collect money in times of emergency {5.2.28}, sow dissension among the chiefs of an oligarchy {11.1.34} and subvert the enemy's army chiefs {12.2.11}.

ROLE AND STATUS OF WOMEN

Reading the *Arthashastra*, the question that naturally comes to mind is: Did women of Kautilya's times enjoy more rights than they do today? There can be no clear answer to this question because in some respects, like remarriage or right to property, women had a better position than what they came to have in the subsequent periods of Indian history. However, in terms of subservience and dependence, the principles and traditions were no different. In this summary, the verses relating to women have been collated under the following headings: women as begetters of sons, their right to property, standards of sexual morality as it affected them, their role in the labour force, their legal status in contracts and suits and, lastly, dependency and subservience.

WOMEN AS BEGETTERS OF SONS

The role of women is succinctly stated by Kautilya as: 'The aim of taking a wife is to beget sons' {3.2.42}. From this principle of perpetuating the family line through sons, others follow. 'The frustration of a woman's fertile period is a violation of a sacred duty' {3.4.36}. 'A wife shall not conceal her fertile period and a husband shall not fail in his duty to try to get a son during his wife's fertile period' {3.2.43,44}. If a wife was barren for eight years or if she had borne only daughters over a twelve-year period, the husband could take a second wife without paying compensation to the first or returning her dowry {3.2.38-40}. When a man had more than one wife, the earliest surviving wife or the one who had borne many sons was given priority {3.2.43-44}.

This preoccupation with bearing sons also gave women some rights. A girl, whose father was indifferent about her marriage for three years after her reaching puberty, could find herself a husband, even one from another *varna* {4.12.10}. Likewise, a father lost his rights if he prevented his daughter's husband from approaching her for seven periods {4.12,8,9}. Among the reasons given for a wife's right to refuse to have intercourse with her husband is that she had already borne him sons {3.2.45}.

The principle of perpetuation of the husband's family affected the rights of a widow to remarry; she could retain her husband's property only if she married a man from the husband's own family {3.2.20-30}. Similar restrictions applied to the remarriage of a wife whose husband had gone on a very long journey. The Kautilyan order of preference for *niyoga* (levirate) is: a brother of the husband, any *sapinda* (common ancestor within three generations) male, and lastly, the husband's *kula* (the extended family) {3.4.37-41}. The custom of a wife bearing a *kshetraja* son, referred to earlier, is a further indication of the importance attached to having sons {3.6.24}.

Lastly, though nuns of both Brahmanical and non-Brahmanical orders are often mentioned, it was a crime to induce a woman to renounce her role as a wife {2.1.29}.

WOMEN'S RIGHT TO PROPERTY

The principle is: 'The purpose of giving women the right to own property is to afford protection in case of a calamity' {3.2.34}. This, however, was a right restricted, on the whole, to maintenance. This is made clear in the order of inheritance specified in the text: sons, daughters, the father of the deceased, brothers and nephews; the widow is nowhere mentioned as an inheritor {3.5.10-12}. A widow did not inherit all the property of her husband; if there were no heirs, the king took the property leaving only the amounts needed for her maintenance {3.5.28}.

In general, a woman had control over her dowry and jewellery {3.2.14,15}. She retained this control after the death of her husband, so long as she did not remarry {3.2.19}. If she remarried without the consent of her father-in-law, her new husband was obliged to return all her property to the other family {3.2.23}. A remarrying widow was also obliged to leave her property, at the time of remarriage, to the sons by the first marriage {3.2.28.29}. In short, property passed down the male line, except when there were only daughters.

There are references to rich widows; one example is the case of an unjustly treated prince collecting money by plundering rich widows after gaining their confidence {1.18.9}. Secret agents posing as rich widows were used to sow dissension among the chiefs of an oligarchy {11.1.42} or to draw the enemy from the safety of his sort {13.2.42}.

SEXUAL MORALITY

The *Arthashastra* covers every aspect of sexual morality. Great emphasis is laid on virginity before marriage; there are also references to adultery, rape and abortion.

Not being a virgin at the time of marriage was an offence punishable by a fine of 54 panas; if the bride pretended to be a virgin (by smearing some other blood on the sheets during consummation), the fine was increased to 200 panas. Any man falsely accusing a girl of not being a virgin also had to pay a similar fine and, in addition, lost the right to marry her {4.12.15-19}. As a consequence of the emphasis on virginity for the girl, defloration, including defloration by a woman and auto-defloration, also became punishable offences {4.12.20-22}. Special provisions existed for the defloration of the daughters of slaves and courtesans {4.12.26,27}. It is interesting to note that the *Arthashastra* defines the age of puberty for girls as twelve, while for boys it is sixteen {3.3.1}.

Some types of sexual relations were prohibited. Incest, punishable by the mutilation of sexual organs and then death for the man, and only death for the woman, concerned a parental role: either the man as a father, as in incest with a daughter or daughter-in-law or the woman in a role similar to that of a mother, as in the cases of the teacher's wife, a sister of the father or the mother, and the wife of the maternal uncles {4.13.30-31}. Other prohibited relations attracting punishments were: for men, with the queen, an unprotected Brahmin woman and a woman ascetic; for the woman, slaves and bonded males; and, for both, an *Arya* with a *svapaka* {4.13.32-35}.

Intercourse with a woman, other than through the vagina, was a punishable offence {4.13.40}. The only references to female homosexuality are defloration or rape; male homosexuality, on the other hand, was a punishable offence {4.13.40}. The implication is that male sexual activity was meant only for procreation.

Both husbands and wives were entitled to expect their spouses to fulfil their conjugal duties, the punishment for the husband being double that for the wife {3.3.2}. This may have been due to the fact that prostitution, a state-controlled revenue-enhancing activity, provided an alternative for men. In fact, a husband who falsely accused his wife of refusing to sleep with him was also punished {3.3.14}.

Adultery was treated as a serious crime, the punishment for the wife being the amputation of her nose and an ear {4.12.33}. However, if the adultery was committed when the husband was away on a long journey, the wife was kept under custody by the husband's kinsmen till the husband's return, when he had the option of forgiving both the wife and her lover {4.12.30-32}.

Different punishments are prescribed for the crime of rape, depending on the victim: 12 panas for raping a prostitute, 24 panas for each offender in a gang rape of a prostitute and 100 panas for raping a woman living by herself, the amputation of the middle and index figures for raping a girl who had attained puberty, the amputation of a hand if the girl had not attained puberty and death if the girl died as a result of the rape {3.20.16, 4.13.38, 4.12.1-7}. Among crimes against women, special punishments are prescribed for city guards who misbehave with women; these range from Lowest Standard Penalty if the woman was a slave, to death if the woman was a respectable person {2.36.41}.

Pregnancy carried with it some rights, mainly in the interests of protecting the child. Causing abortion was a serious crime, the punishment varying from the Lowest to the Highest Standard Penalty, depending on the means used {4.11.6}. Procuring the abortion of a female slave also carried a punishment of the Lowest Standard Penalty {3.20.17}. Women were not to be tortured during pregnancy or for a month after childbirth {4.8.17}. For a woman convicted of murder, the sentence of death by drowning was carried out a month after childbirth {4.11.18}. Pregnant women could use the ferries free of charge {2.28.18}.

WOMEN'S EMPLOYMENT

Though the extent to which women were employed in the agricultural sector not clear from the text, it is likely that they also worked in the fields and pastures along with the men. A sector of employment reserved for women, particularly those who had no other means of livelihood, was spinning. The list given under the Chief Textile Commissioner includes: widows, crippled women, unmarried girls, women living independently, women working off fines, mothers of prostitutes, old women, servants of the King and temple dancers whose services to a temple had ceased {2.23.2}.

Special mention is made of women who did not stir out of their houses, for reasons of modesty (or inability?) The list includes: widows, handicapped women, unmarried girls and those whose husbands were away on a journey. Work was sent out to such women by the Chief Textile Commissioner, through his own maid servants. They could also come to the yarn shed, early in the morning, when there was little traffic about {2.23.11.12}. When they came, the official was obliged to do only what was necessary to hand over the raw material, receive the yarn and pay the wages; he was neither to look at a woman's face nor to engage in any conversation unrelated to work {2.23.14}.

Kautilya's concern for protecting the modesty of women was balanced by his concern for ensuring control over the decentralized spinning sector, with the work being done at home unsupervised by an official. The prescribed punishment for cheating (taking the wages but not doing the work, misappropriating the raw material) was drastic—cutting off the thumb and forefinger {2.23.15}.

Women and children were also employed in collecting and preparing the ingredients for making alcoholic liquor {2.25.38}. They worked as attendants of the king and other nobles, their main occupations being shampooing, preparing the bath, making garlands and perfumery and carrying the regalia of office {1.21.13,2.27.4}.

That women were employed by the state for prostitution is obvious from the earlier discussion. There were other types of women entertainers, like actresses. The wives of actors and other entertainers were also to be used, under the cover of profession of their husbands, to detect, delude and murder the wicked {2.27.30}. The use of women to delude or entrap enemies, both internal and external, was quite extensive. Reference was made earlier to the wandering nun belonging to a category of roving spies {1.12.4-5}. 'A woman of bad character' is mentioned as one to be used in trapping a treacherous high official by making her pretend to be the queen {5.1.29}. Women were thus used for a variety of nefarious purposes ranging from tempting a prince unjustly treated to appear before his father, to sowing dissension among the chiefs of an oligarchy. The whole range of such activities of secret agents is given in Part IX of this translation.

The one area where women were protected by law was when they were bonded labour or slaves. A female bonded labourer was not to be beaten, treated violently, made to give a bath to a naked man or deprived of her virginity. If the maltreated woman was a nurse, a cook, a maid or an agricultural tenant, she was freed. A pledged nurse was not to be raped; a master should neither himself rape, nor let some one else rape, a virgin girl under his control. A woman labourer to whom a child of the master was born was entitled to leave the household {3.13.9-12}. A pregnant female slave was not to be sold or mortgaged without making adequate provision for her welfare during her pregnancy. Her pregnancy was not to be terminated by abortion. When a slave gave birth to a child of her master, both she and her child were no longer considered to be slaves {3.13.20,23,24}.

STATUS IN CONTRACTS AND SUITS

A contract made by a woman dependant on her husband or son was not valid; in this, the woman's status was equated with that of other dependant people, such as slaves and bonded labour {3.1.12}. Though contracts had normally to be entered into in public, a contract for inheritance, marriage or deposits was valid, even if made inside a house, provided one of the parties was a woman who did not normally leave her house {3.1.7}.

For the purposes of the law of evidence, a woman was classed with those who could be called upon as witnesses only with respect to cases involving their own group; this did not apply to cases of theft, assault, adultery or secret transactions {3.11.29}. Women were also included in the class of persons whose problems were to be looked into by judges *suo moto* {3.20.22}.

DEPENDENCE AND SUBSERVIENCE

Many aspects of the protection accorded to women were based on the inclusion of women in the list of people who needed the protection of the state because they were helpless and easily exploited. It is a debatable point whether women, as a segment of society, would have needed this protection, if society and the legal system had not placed them from the beginning in an inferior position.

The underlying principle in the *Arthashastra* is that a woman was always dependent on, under the control of and subservient to, her father, her husband or her son. In fact, in the chapter on title to property, women are included in the list of property, along with deposits and pledges {3.16.32}. A wife could not, without the permission of her husband, drink, indulge in unseemly sports or go on pleasure trips. She could not go to see performances, with other men or even with other women, either by day or at night. She could not leave the house when her husband was asleep or drunk; she could not refuse to open the door to him {3.3.20-24}. On the other hand, a wife had certain rights. The physical punishment which a husband could inflict on his wife was limited to three slaps {3.3.8}. She could run away from home if ill-treated {3.4.1}. She could not be prevented from visiting her own family on special occasions like death, illness or childbirth {3.4.13}. Some women, who customarily enjoyed freedom of movement, could travel with a man {3.4.22}. Widows or wives whose husbands had gone on long journeys could remarry, subject to specified conditions. Divorce was possible only in four of the eight forms of marriage {3.3.19}.

The overall picture is thus one of women being placed in a subservient role but given adequate protection to ensure that this did not lead to total exploitation. How well the safeguards operated in practice can only be a matter for conjecture. It is possible that gradual deterioration, over centuries, in the legal protection guaranteed to women in the *Arthashastra*, led to their being given a lower status in later codifications like the *Manusmriti*.

OCCUPATIONS

A classified compilation of the extensive variety of occupations and professions pursued by the population, with references to the appropriate verses, is given in Appendix 6. The lists of artisans and craftsmen as well as that of entertainers each contain fifteen different occupations. There are also detailed lists of attendants, types of jewellers and the specific jobs of those who looked after elephants or horses. The diversity of occupations is also shown by lists of those who practised prediction, sailed in ships or worked in warehouses. The fact that one occupation is mentioned more frequently than another is no indication of the number of people engaged in it. For example, farmers are referred to only about a dozen times in the text; but these must have been very numerous and contributed the most to the wealth of the country.

TRAVEL

Apart from peripatetic people like entertainers, traders and foreign merchants, ordinary people also travelled. They did so for family reasons, to go on pilgrimages or to attend fairs and festivals. We know from the detailed regulations on the absence of husbands from home that some went on long journeys lasting more than a year; some sent no messages and some never returned {3.4.24-37}.

Most journeys must have been on foot; some rode animals or carts. Specifications are laid down for different types of roads {2.4.3-5} and charges for the use of ferries {2.28.21-23}. Traders and caravans of merchants also paid a road cess and escort charges {2.28.25}. Boats and ships could be hired {2.28.3,5}.

Movement within the country was strictly controlled. A passport was needed to enter or leave the countryside {2.34.2}. Immigration into new settlements was prohibited for some categories {2.1.32} and undesirables were not allowed into the fortified city {2.4.32}. Secret agents kept track of arrivals and departures {2.35.10}.

The safety and security of travellers were entrusted to different officials, each one being responsible for a different part of the country. Frontier officers were responsible for the protection of traders and caravans {2.21.25}. Fowlers and hunters kept a watch for thieves and robbers in the forests {2.34.9,10}. The Chief Controller of Pasture Lands and the official responsible for catching thieves guarded the comparatively less densely populated regions between settled villages {2.34.12; 4.13.9-12} and village headmen bore the responsibility for the safety of travellers and traders inside villages {4.13.7-8}. The officials were liable to compensate the victims of any robbery committed within the areas of their responsibility {2.21.25, 4.13.9}.

THE KAUTILYAN ECONOMY

The *Arthashastra* is one of the world's oldest treatises on the economic administration of a state. The aim of the three main types of economic activity—agriculture, cattle rearing and trade—was to generate resources in the form of grains, cattle, gold, forest produce and labour. Using these, the king obtained a treasury and an army, which were then used to bring under his control both his own people and the people of the enemy {1.4.1,2}. Wealth alone enabled the creation of more wealth {9.4.27}. A king with a depleted treasury ate into the very vitality of the country {2.1.16}.

The wealth of the state was the totality of the surplus stored in the king's treasury, the commodity warehouse, the granary, the store for forest produce and the ordnance depots {2.5.1}. Of these, the treasury was the most important; the king is advised to devote his best attention to it, because all the activities of the state depended on it {2.8.1,2}. In the order of importance of the six internal constituents of the state, the treasury is placed immediately below the king and ministers (the state apparatus) and the people, both rural and urban. The treasury is ranked above the army because 'the army is dependent on finance; in the absence of resources, a (disaffected) army goes over to the enemy or even kills the king' {8.1.47,48}. The best treasury was one which had gold, silver, precious stones and gold coins and which was large enough to enable the country to withstand even a long period of calamities when there would have been no income {6.1.10}.

How the state gathered in the surplus by means of revenue from state enterprises, state-controlled activities, taxes, trading, fees and other service charges is explained in 'Sources of Revenue'; see V.ii and Appendix 8.

A king who found himself in financial difficulties could collect additional revenue by special methods {5.2}. The aim of the elaborate structure of punishments was not merely to maintain order but also to collect revenue; even deterrent punishments, like amputation, could be avoided by paying a substantial compensatory fine ranging from 54 panas to 1000 panas, depending on the organ threatened with amputation {4.10.1,2,7-14}.

The accumulation of wealth by the state was made possible by the fact that the king was the principal and residual owner of all property. All land in the country not specifically owned by an individual was state property. All water belonged to the king and users paid a water rate for taking water from irrigation works built by the king {2.24.18}. Irrespective of whether the cost of building a dam or an embankment was borne entirely or only partly by the state, all the fish, ducks and green vegetables produced in or near the reservoirs were the king's property {2.1.24}. When there was a dispute about the ownership of a field or a pasture and neither claimant succeeded in proving his title to it, the property reverted to the king. If the owner of a property disappeared, the king became the owner {3.9.17}. When a man died without heirs, the king inherited his property, except for the amounts needed for the funeral and the maintenance of the widow {3.5.28}. In any auction, either of immovable property by individuals {3.9.3-6} or of goods by foreign traders at city gates {2.21.7-9}, the difference between the price called out by the seller and the price actually realized by the auction, was taken by the state. All lost gems and two-third of lost high value property went to the king. Any treasure trove over 100,000 panas and five-sixth of smaller troves were taken by the king {4.1.52-55}.

PRINCIPLES OF ECONOMIC ADMINISTRATION

The main guiding principles of the administration of the economy were that the state should run a diversified economy actively, efficiently, prudently and profitably.

The king is advised to be 'ever active in the management of the economy because the root of wealth is economic activity; inactivity brings material distress. Without an active policy, both current prosperity and future gains are destroyed' {1.19.35,36}.

All the verses relating to efficient financial administration of the state have been brought together in section V.iii and Part VI of this translation. The topics covered include: the responsibilities of the Chief Comptroller and Auditor, the proper maintenance and timely submission of accounts, inspection and audit, collecting the right amount of revenue (neither more nor less), controlling erring officials and the many ways by which dishonest officials could cheat the government, the public or both. These are mainly in chapters {2.7}, {2.8} and {2.9} of the text.

Apart from the prudence implicit in the verses referred to above, one further example is worth noting. The Chief Superintendent of Warehouses has to keep half the quantity of the commodities in store as reserve stock for use in times of calamities and use only half for current needs. To be even more prudent, he is asked to replace regularly old stock with new {2.15.22,23}.

The king was advised to maintain a diversified economy, within the limits of the technology available at that time, as follows: keep in good repair existing productive forests, elephant forests, reservoirs or mines; start new mines, factories, forests, elephant forests and cattle herds; promote trade and commerce by setting up market towns, ports and trade routes; build storage reservoirs; and organize new settlements {2.1.19,20}. More details on the different sectors of the economy are given later in this chapter.

Efficient management was encouraged. Any official who did not generate adequate profits in a Crown undertaking was punished for 'swallowing the labour of workers'. {2.9.17}

A crucial injunction regarding trade with foreign countries given to the Chief Controller of State Trading is: 'generate profits; avoid losses'. {2.16.25} The regulations for buffer stocks and futures emphasize profitability {2.16.2,3; 4.2.36}. When Crown commodities were sold by private merchants, they had to pay a charge to compensate the state for the profit which it would otherwise have got by selling direct {2.16.9}.

MONEY AND COINAGE

The coin most often mentioned in the text is the *pana*, which is subdivided as follows: sixteen *mashakas* to a pana and four *kakanis* to a *mashaka*. The coinage in circulation was: silver coins of one, half, quarter and one-eighth pana and copper coins of one *mashaka*, half a *mashaka*, one *kakani* and half a *kakani*. An indication of how much a pana was worth is given in I.iii. The value of the coinage was sought to be maintained by stringent punishments for counterfeiting. A special official, the Coin Examiner certified the genuineness of coins {2.5.10}, collected the taxes and charges on coinage and punished those who bought, sold or examined coins {2.12.25}. The punishment for bringing counterfeit money into the storehouse was the Lowest Standard Penalty, for making it or putting it into circulation 1000 panas and for paying it into the government treasury, death {2.5.12, 4.1.48}. The detection of counterfeiting is also dealt with {4.4.20,21}.

THE PUBLIC AND THE PRIVATE SECTOR

Land, the most important natural resource, was primarily in the public sector, with the state holding all virgin land, forests and water resources. Arable land, however, was both in the public and the private sectors. Crown lands were either directly cultivated by the Chief Superintendent of Crown Lands or leased out to tenants {2.24.16}. Land was granted either in perpetuity or for a limited period, on a tax-paying or on a tax-exempt basis. The reference to sale of a field, a park, an embankment, a water tank or a reservoir indicates that such immovable property associated with arable land could also be privately owned with the title transferable by sale {3.9.3}. As with land, animals like cows, sheep and goats, were also in both sectors, in Crown herds and private herds {2.29.1,7}. Deer, birds, wild animals caught in traps or fish were also considered private property since their theft was a punishable offence {4.10.3}.

Mining and fishing were also in both sectors. In these two cases, the concerned official is instructed to reserve for the Crown mines or fishing areas that are easily exploited at lower cost and to lease out the difficult ones {2.12.22, 2.28.6}. While the actual making of salt was done by lessees of salt pans, the Chief Salt Commissioner collected the revenue, before it could be marketed, on both locally produced and imported salt {2.12.28-32}.

The state monopolies on the manufacture and sale of alcoholic liquor and on gambling and betting have been referred to earlier. In addition to prostitution, there were a number of economic activities which were strictly controlled by the state. Sale, purchase and manufacture of gold, silver or precious stones was one. Buying precious metals secretly or from disreputable persons, or receiving stolen metal, were all punishable offences {4.1.26,27}.

The state and private merchants, both local and foreign, were involved in trade. The Chief Controller of State Trading was responsible for the equitable distribution of local and foreign goods, buffer stocking, sale of Crown commodities and public distribution. He could appoint private traders as agents for the sale, at fixed prices, of Crown commodities or sell them direct to the public through stateowned retail outlets {2.16.8,14-16}. The Chief Controller of Private Trading kept a watch over merchants, by inspecting periodically their weights and measures and ensuring that they did not hoard, adulterate or add excessive mark-ups {4.2.2,19,22,28}.

TAX POLICY

Details of the different taxes levied are given under Sources of Revenue (V.ii and Appendix 8). The tax policy distinguished between those who had to pay a tax and those exempt from it. Exemption from tax could be granted in perpetuity to Brahmins with the right to sell or mortgage or as a perquisite of office to specified officials so long as they held that office and without the right to sell or mortgage {2.1.7}. Another kind of exemption, for limited periods ranging between two to five years, was used as an incentive to increase production by granting it to those who brought dry land under cultivation and those who renovated or built irrigation works. The king was, however, advised to treat leniently, like a father would treat his son, those whose exemptions had ceased to be effective {2.1.18}.

The distinction between taxpayers and the tax-exempted affected the rights to residence and sale of property. A taxpayer could not settle in a tax-exempt village and could sell or mortgage his land only to another taxpayer. Tax-exempt land could be sold only by one holding similar land. However, a tax-exempt person could live in a tax-paying village and continue to enjoy his right of ownership of land in a tax-exempt village {3.10.9,11,15}.

RELATIVE MERITS OF DIFFERENT TYPES OF ECONOMIC ACTIVITY

Most of the productive economic activity took place in the *janapada*. 'Power comes from the countryside, which is the source of all activities.' {7.14.19}. An ideal *janapada* was one which was easily defended and which had a lot of productive land with cultivable fields, mines, timber forests, elephant forests and pastures. It should be capable of producing a wide variety of commodities, thus supporting the native population as well as outsiders who might immigrate in times of trouble in their own countries. It should be rich enough to support a high level of taxation and a large army. Its people should be predominantly agriculturists, artisans and craftsmen, devoted to work, honest, loyal and intelligent {6.1.8}.

Agriculture was the most important economic activity. 'Cultivable land is better than mines because mines fill only the treasury while agricultural production fills both the treasury and the storehouses.' {7.11.10-12}. The king had to ensure that agriculture was protected from harassment by not levying onerous taxes or fines and by not making undue demands for free labour {2.1.37}. Other kinds of economic activity were: building forts (i.e. defence preparedness) so as to ensure a haven for the king and the people in times of trouble; water works and reservoirs as the source of crops; trade routes as the means of outmanoeuvring the enemy, because through them the king could send secret agents and bring in weapons and other war material; mines as the source of war material; productive forests for providing material for building forts, carriages and chariots; elephant forests for capturing elephants; and animal herds for providing cattle, horses, donkeys and camels {7.14.21,23-25}.

Availability of water was important. It was better to acquire a smaller tract of land with flowing water than a larger drier one {7.11.3}. Among forests, one watered by a river was better because it was self-sustaining and provided shelter in times of calamities {7.12.7}. It was necessary to build storage reservoirs because the water stored after a good rainfall could be made available continuously for irrigation {7.14.21,22}. A dam built to impound the water of a flowing river was better than a reservoir to which water had to be brought by man-made canals. When damming rivers, preference should be given to one which irrigated a larger area {7.12.4,5}.

Mines should be easily accessible, exploitable at low cost and yield valuable minerals. Kautilya believed that it was better to have a large production of low value minerals than a small production of high value ones {7.12.13,16}.

Productive forests should be large, near the borders of the country, with a river and yield material of high value {7.12.6,7}. Elephant forests should be located on the border near a weak enemy; Kautilya believed that a large number of comparatively dull elephants was preferable to a few brave ones {7.12.8,11} and that elephant forests were more important than other kinds because 'one depends on elephants for the destruction of the enemy's forces' {7.11.13-16}.

It was better to have a large number of trade routes even if they were not all built to high standards. Kautilya's order of preference for establishing trade routes is: land route, preferably to the south; a water route on the coast; an inland waterway. Cart tracks and tracks usable by draught animals were to be preferred to footpaths {7.12.17,20,21,24,27}.

LAND—USE, QUALITY AND SETTLEMENT

The following is the relative importance of the uses to which land was put, in order of decreasing importance: cart shed, storage shed, threshing floor, vegetable garden, irrigated land, dry cultivation, pasture {3.9.25}. Land was classified also according to rainfall: suitable for dry crops if annual rainfall was between 25 to 32 inches; suitable for canal irrigation if annual rainfall is between 21 and 36 inches depending on the region; suitable for wet crops if annual rainfall is about 37 1/2 inches and in areas like the northern foothills and Konkan where rain was plentiful {2.24.5}.

There is an elaborate discussion on the quality of land in the chapters {7.10, 7.11.3-37} in the context of acquiring it by entering into a treaty with another king for a joint attack against a third. Among other things, it is recommended that land which could be defended with its own resources should be acquired {7.10.20}. Incidentally, the order of difficulty of attacking forts of different kinds is also explained as: land forts as the easiest, river forts and mountain forts successively more difficult {7.10.28-32}. See also, from the point of view of the defender, the reverse order {7.12.2,3}.

The quality of cultivable land, starting from the most useful, is given as: irrigated land growing cereals, a large irrigated tract not suitable for cereals but suitable for a variety of other crops and for building forts, and rain-fed land in which both early and late crops could be grown easily with less rain {7.11.3-8}.

All this analysis is subject to the important qualification that human exertion was more important than the actual quality of the land. 'The value of land is what man makes of it.' {7.11.9}. The importance of a united people is further stressed: 'It is the people who constitute a kingdom. Like a barren cow, a kingdom without people yields nothing' {7.11.24,25}.

The Chancellor was expected to keep precise and detailed records of land use and anticipated revenue, helped by magistrates and secret agents {2.36.1-4}.

The organization of new settlements in uninhabited but cultivable areas of the country was an important activity of the state, not only for the increased revenue it would bring but also to make the country more easily defendable. Even in times of great financial stringency, the king was advised to promote new settlements by grants of grain, cattle and money {5.2.4}. The settlements ought to be populated mainly by the three lower *varnas* because of the variety of benefits these provide. 'Farmers are dependable and productive; cowherds make agriculture and other activities possible by opening up pasture lands; and rich traders are a source of goods and money.' {7.11.21}. Though generally officials were paid partly in cash and partly by grant of land, Kautilya recommends that, in new settlements, all salaries should be paid only in cash and no land allotted until the new village had fully stabilized {5.3.32}. All verses on settlements have been collected together under 'land management' in IV.i {2.1.7-18,32-35}.

The pattern of land use can be shown as in Figure 3.

AGRICULTURE, ANIMAL HUSBANDRY, FORESTRY AND FISHERIES

AGRICULTURE

The technical details about agriculture—rainfall, seed and plant preparation, crops and crop protection—are given in IV.v. The list of crops mentioned in the text is in Appendix 2.

Cultivation of land directly by the state was done under the supervision of the Chief Superintendent of Crown Lands (VII.iii). Land not directly cultivated could be leased to share-croppers who got one-fourth or one-fifth of the harvest if they contributed only labour and one-half if they provided all inputs {2.24.16}. If the land was previously uncultivated, the payment to the state was to be agreed beforehand; even this could be waived in times of distress {2.24.17}. The revenue from Crown lands was shown separately in the accounts as *sita* {2.6.3; 2.15.2}.

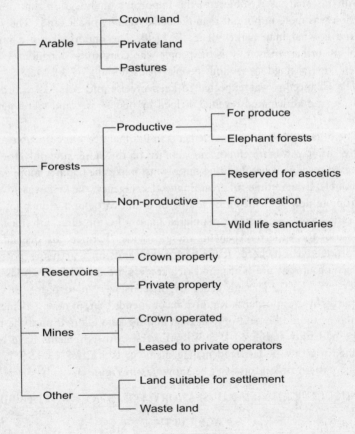

Fig 3. Pattern of Land Use

Private farmers were under an obligation to cultivate their fields. It was a punishable offence for a farmer, or a tenant, to neglect or abandon his field at the time of sowing or for the farmer to take away the land from the tenant; only when circumstances were such that cultivation was impossible was this obligation lifted {3.10.8}. Farmers paid an agricultural tax, in kind, of one-sixth the produce, this being shown separately in the accounts as *bhaga* {2.15.3}. In times of great financial stringency, the tax could be raised to one-quarter or even one-third in case of grains; special levies had to be paid on other commodities and the Chancellor could force farmers to grow a second crop {5.2.2,8,14}.

Labourers in the state sector were given food according to the number of people in their families and a cash wage of one and a quarter panas per month, except for slaves and those working off their fines. Blacksmiths, carpenters, etc. were paid according to their professions {2.24.2,28,29}. In the private sector, the customary rate, unless there was prior agreement to the contrary, was one-tenth of the produce {3.13.28}.

Farmers could not sell crops, fruits, vegetables or flowers at their fields, gardens or orchards but had to bring them to the market; sale elsewhere than at the point of production attracted a heavy penalty {2.22.9,11-13}. The punishment for stealing agricultural produce was 200 panas {4.10.6}. In times of financial stringency, the punishments for a farmer hiding his own produce and for anyone stealing were even more drastic {5.2.12,13}.

The Chancellor is advised to use secret agents disguised as ascetics to find out about dishonest farmers and cowherds {2.35.13}.

ANIMAL HUSBANDRY

Cattle-rearing was the second most important economic activity {1.4.1}. Cows and she-buffaloes were reared for milk and the bulls and he-buffaloes were used as draught animals. Other useful domesticated animals mentioned in the text are: sheep, goats, horses, donkeys, camels and pigs {2.29.41,42}.

Ghee, which had the advantages of being easily stored and transported, was the main end product. Cheese was supplied to the army, buttermilk fed to dogs and pigs and whey mixed with oilcake used as animal feed. Wool was obtained from sheep and goats. Animal byproducts were hides and skins, hooves, horns, etc. {2.29.25-29, 41}; also see Appendix 3.

Crown herds were the responsibility of the Chief Superintendent who either employed cowherds, milkers, etc. on wages or gave some herds to a contractor. Private herds could also be entrusted to the state for protection on payment. Private owners of animals paid a sales tax of a quarter pana for every animal sold. All livestock owners were obliged to pay a special levy in times of financial stringency {5.2.27}. Details about Crown and private herds are in VII.iii. For the specialized nomenclature of male, female and young cattle see Appendix 3 and for rations for animals Appendix 4.

Animal breeding was given special attention; one of the officials of the palace was the king's breeder {5.3.12}. From references to horse doctors and elephant doctors, we know that there were veterinary doctors.

Welfare of animals, a subject given special importance in the *Arthashastra*, is dealt with later in this chapter under 'welfare'.

The Chief Superintendent of Pastures was responsible for organizing pastures in the regions between villages by clearing land and providing watering facilities. He was also responsible for ridding the pasture lands of thieves and wild animals and for ensuring the safety of travellers {2.34.7}. Pasture lands within the village boundary were the responsibility of the village headman; he collected the charges for grazing on common land, ensured that cattle did not stray and damage property and collected the fines payable to the state {3.10.21-29,33}.

Horses and elephants, essential for war, are dealt with in this translation in Part XI.

FORESTRY

Among the different kinds of forests mentioned above under land use, two were important to the economy—those producing useful material like hardwoods, bamboo, creepers and medicinal plants (see Appendix 2 for list) and those maintained exclusively for elephants. Forest produce is classified as a separate commodity group (I.iii) with its own store house under the control of the Chief Superintendent of the Treasury {2.5.1}. Factories were set up in the forests for producing useful articles by the Superintendent of Productive Forests {2.17.17} and the Chief Ordnance Officer {2.18.20}.

The well-protected leisure forest, intended for the king's pleasure, had plantations bearing sweet fruits, thornless trees and pools of water and was stocked with tame deer, wild animals rendered harmless and tame elephants {2.2.3}.

Wildlife sanctuaries and the protection given to wildlife are referred to later in this chapter under 'animal welfare'. A list of wildlife mentioned in the text is in Appendix 3.

FISHERIES

The references to fish and fishing are incidental, as in the one-sixth tax on fishermen, leasing of fishing boats by conch and pearl fishermen {2.28.3,5} or as one of the products from reservoirs {2.1.24}. Kautilya, who provides long lists of agricultural commodities and forest produce, does not give a similar list for fish, indicating that fish did not constitute a significant part of the diet.

MINING AND MANUFACTURING

MINING

Mines, the source of war material, were important because: 'Mines are the source of wealth; from wealth comes the power of government because with the treasury and the army, the earth is acquired.' {2.12.37; 7.14.25}. It appears that mines were usually in remote places, because a discontented, and therefore dangerous, official was posted to a mine, while his family was kept as a hostage {1.13.21}.

The following metals are mentioned in the text: gold, silver, copper, lead, tin, iron and *vaikrantaka* (?). Alloys of copper such as brass, bronze and bell metal are also mentioned. Diamonds and precious stones, quartz and mica, as well as marine products like conches, pearls and coral were also considered as part of the mining industry. All details about metallurgy and the metal industry are in Appendix 5.

A number of officials, under the Chief Controller of Mining and Metallurgy, were responsible for these industries: the Chief Superintendent of Mines for precious stones, quartz and mica, the Chief Superintendent of Metals for workshops making articles from non-precious metals, the Chief Mint Master for minting coins, the Coin Examiner and the Chief Salt Commissioner. The Chief Superintendent of Precious Metals and Jewellery controlled the Crown workshops and his subordinate, the Controller of Gold and Silver Smiths, supervised the jewellers who undertook work for the public. The duties of all these officials are set out in VII.iv.

MANUFACTURING

The four categories of manufacturing industry were: state monopolies such as making weapons or brewing liquor, state-controlled industries such as textiles, salt and jewellery, state-regulated small industries of craftsmen such as goldsmiths, blacksmiths, weavers and dyers and unregulated craftsmen like potters, basket makers, etc. Though not mentioned specifically in the text, there must have been other industries such as the construction industry, ship and boat building and the manufacture of carts and chariots.

TEXTILE INDUSTRY

The spinning of yarn was decentralized, carried out by women, particularly those to whom this was the only means of livelihood. Weaving was both decentralized by contracting work out to weavers on a piece-rate basis and carried out under state supervision in specially built weaving sheds for special types of cloth. The industry also included making of ropes, straps, thongs and similar equipment for animals.

Yarns of different qualities, coarse, medium and fine, were spun from: cotton, wool, silk cotton, hemp, flax, silk and wool from deer. Apart from dress material, bed sheets and coverings and protective wear like quilted armour were also made.

LIQUOR INDUSTRY

The manufacture of alcoholic liquor was predominantly a state monopoly. Specific exemptions were, however provided for: physicians making different kinds of *arishtas*, i.e. alcohol-based medicines, types of liquor like fermented fruit juices not made by the state, home-made alcohol-based medicines, 'white' liquor for own consumption and a special exemption, during fairs and festivals, to make liquor for a maximum of four days.

Liquor was manufactured by the state in a number of places near the points of consumption. It is clearly stated that liquor shall be made in the city, the countryside and the camps, in one place or as many places as required {2.25.1}.

The following kinds of alcoholic drinks were made—*medaka* from rice, *prasanna* from barley flour, *asava* from sugarcane juice, *maireya* from jaggery, *madhu* from grape juice and *arishtas* for medicinal purposes {2.25.16,21}. Many varieties of liquor were made. The basic types were: *sara* and *kinva*. From *kinva*, another liquor made from fermented bean pulp, two kinds of *sura* could be made. These were then flavoured with different spices or fruit juices. A type of liquor was made without using *kinva* by fermenting wood apple or bark, mixed with jaggery or honey. Grape wine was also consumed. The complete list of all types, along with recipes for making, clarifying and flavouring them is given in Appendix 10.

SALT INDUSTRY

Making salt was a state monopoly and unauthorized manufacture or sale was severely punished. Only learned Brahmins, ascetics and labourers could take salt free for their own consumption. Salt pans were leased out either on a share basis or on payment of a fixed quantity as royalty. In order to protect local industry, imported salt had to pay a countervailing duty to compensate the state for breaching the royal monopoly. The punishment for adulterating salt was the Highest Standard Penalty. A distinction was made between edible salt and salt not for human consumption. Details will be found either under the Chief Salt Commissioner (VII.iv) or under the salt industry (IV.v).

TRADE

The *Arthashastra* treats in detail every aspect of trade, the third pillar of economic activity. Apart from promoting trade by improving the infrastructure, the state was required to keep trade routes free of harassment by courtiers, state officials, thieves and frontier guards {2.1.38}.

Traders were mistrusted. 'Merchants...are all thieves, in effect, if not in name; they shall be prevented from oppressing the people.' {4.1.65}. Their propensity to fix prices by forming cartels {4.2.19; 8.4.36}, make excessive profits {4.2.28-29} or deal in stolen property {4.6.3-6} was guarded against by making these offences punishable by heavy fines.

The duties of the Chief Controller of Private Trading are listed in VII.v. Control over prices and trade practices was made easier by prohibiting sale of agricultural products or minerals at their places of production; selling at places other than the designated markets was also punishable {2.22.9-14}. In addition to his supervisory duties, the Chief Controller could also grant the appropriate exemptions if a merchant's goods were damaged due to unforeseen reasons {4.2.32}.

Weights and measures used by merchants were periodically inspected; use of unstamped measures was a punishable offence {2.19.41}. The specifications for making standard weights and measures and their sale prices are laid down (see Appendix 1). An interesting aspect was the use of four different sets of weights and measures—the biggest for payments into the treasury, the second biggest the standard trade measure, the third for payments out of the treasury and the smallest for palace expenditure. By using these, the transaction tax, *vyaji*, was automatically collected. This is fully explained under *vyaji* in V.ii. The interests of the consumer were protected by prescribing even the extra amounts to be given when selling liquids like ghee either because the liquid had expanded by heating it for ease of pouring or because some of it would have stuck to the measure {2.19.43,44}.

The law on dealings between private merchants includes: selling on an agency basis {3.13.28}; revocation of contracts between traders {3.15.1-4,9,10}; and traders travelling together pooling their goods {3.14.19-22}.

The expression 'foreign merchants' in the text has to be understood as meaning traders from outside the state. There are many references to countries and regions within the Indian subcontinent. The truly foreign countries mentioned are: Ceylon, Barbara and Arachosia as the sources of pearls {2.11.2}; Burma (or Sumatra) for aloe {2.11.69}; Nepala for woolen cloth; Gandhara, Vanayu (Arabia or Persia?) and Bahlika (Bactria) for furs and horses {2.11.88, 2.30.29}; Kapisa (Afghanistan) and Harahura (Scythia) for wine {2.25.25}. The importance of foreign trade is indicated by the advice given to the conqueror that he should pause after declaring war, if he could divert to his own country the valuable goods going to the enemy by a trade route {7.4.7}.

Import and sale of foreign goods was encouraged in order to make them freely available all over the country. To promote imports, tax exemptions were given to importers, foreign merchants were given limited immunity from being sued and a higher profit margin allowed for imported goods compared to local products {2.16.4,12,13; 4.2.28}.

The official in charge of exports, the Chief Controller of State Trading, was advised to undertake foreign trade only if there was a profit, except when there were political or strategic advantages in trading with a particular country {2.16.19}. Kautilya's advice on calculating the costs of an export transaction is clear and accurate {2.16.18,24}. Export of weapons and valuable material was prohibited {2.21.22}.

Duty was levied and collected at the city gates where goods were sold by the trader calling out a price; if the actual sale price was higher due to competitive bidding by the buyers, the state took the difference {2.21.7-9}. For import duties and goods exempt from duty see Appendix 9.

LABOUR AND EMPLOYMENT

Apart from the aged, the sick and the handicapped who are all mentioned as requiring the protection of the state, the actual labour force excluded some who voluntarily withdrew from it: ascetics such as monks and nuns, hermits, *vanaprasthas*, brahmins in their *ashrams* and mendicants. Women's employment has been dealt with earlier in this chapter. The references to child labour are: using them to collect the ingredients for the liquor industry {2.25.38}, the bonding or slavery of non-*Arya* children {3.13.3} and the priority of release for a minor of an *Arya* who had pledged himself and his family {3.13.5}.

The total labour force can be classified, in increasing degree of freedom, as follows: slaves, bonded labour, unpaid labour, casual labour working for wages, piece-rate workers, those working for a regular wage and the self-employed. The verses relating to slaves and bonded labour are in VIII.x. Unpaid labourers were those who worked in lieu of paying a tax or a fine: in warehousing processing grains, oilseeds or sugarcane {2.15.8};

in Crown lands {2.24.2}; in mines when caught stealing or mining without permission {2.12.21} and women in spinning yarn {2.23.2}. Piece-rate is mentioned in connection with the Chief of Ordnance awarding work to expert craftsmen {2.18.1} and the assessment of customs duty on jewellery {2.22.5}. The self-employed, such as weavers, washermen, dyers, tailors, goldsmiths, silversmiths and blacksmiths, were paid according to the work done by them {4.1.10-12,22,25,32-35,40,42}.

The wages of agricultural labour have been referred to above under agriculture. Those who looked after Crown herds were paid wholly in cash, for, if paid in milk and ghee, they might be tempted to starve the calves to get a higher yield! {2.29.2,3}.

The law on wages and contract employment is in VIII.x {3.13.26-34}. In some cases, wages were related to productivity; e.g. workers in state retail outlets {4.2.23}. The relationship between wages, productivity and incentives for increasing production is seen clearly in the spinning sector of the textile industry {2.23.3-6}.

A large part of those working for a regular wage or salary were employed by the state, particularly in the civil service, the secret service and the army. The salaries and wages of all state employees is given in {5.3}. It is interesting to note that Kautilya fixes the ceiling on expenditure on salaries of state servants at one-quarter of the revenue {5.3.1}. It is also likely that some employees and craftsmen in a village were paid either a regular wage out of the village revenue or given a share of the village produce {5.2.11}.

Self-employed craftsmen formed guilds, *sreni*, which guaranteed the conduct of its members; the guild was responsible for the return of any material entrusted to a member {4.1.2-3}.

HUMAN AND ANIMAL WELFARE

Just as Kautilya's important qualifications to his advocacy of unethical methods is often ignored, so is the voluminous evidence in the *Arthashastra* of his emphasis on welfare, not only of human beings but also of animals. Welfare in the *Arthashastra* is not just an abstract concept. It covers maintenance of social order, increasing economic activity, protection of livelihood, protection of the weaker sections of the population, prevention of harassment of the subjects, consumer protection and even welfare of slaves and prisoners.

The fact that one of the concerns of the state was the welfare of the subjects should not lead us to confuse it with the concept of a 'welfare state' as we know it today. The two glaring omissions in the Kautilyan concept of welfare are education and health, the promotion of which is now considered to be a state's major duty. Though the duties and responsibilities of thirty-six different Heads of Departments are spelt out, there are no posts of Chief Superintendents of Education or Health. Education is referred to only in the context of the training of a prince to be a king (III.i). Public health is touched upon with reference to public hygiene. The human resource aspect of society was a matter of private, not state, concern.

THE ROLE OF THE KING IN PROTECTING AND PROMOTING WELFARE

Since the king is synonymous with the Kautilyan state, we first note the kind of attitude and behaviour that Kautilya recommends for him. The verse used as the epigraph to this book, 'In the happiness of his subjects lies his own happiness...' summarizes it. A king should be well trained (III.i) and practise self-control (III.ii). An ideal king is one who has the highest qualities of leadership, intellect, energy and personal attributes {6.1.2-6} and behaves like a sage monarch, a *rajarishi*. Among other things, a *rajarishi* is one 'who is ever active in promoting the *yogakshema* of the people and who endears himself to his people by enriching them and doing good to them' {1.7.1}. The word, *yogakshema*, is a compound made up of *yoga*, the successful accomplishment of an objective and *kshema*, its peaceful enjoyment. Thus, peaceful enjoyment of prosperity, i.e. the welfare of the people, is given as much importance as knowledge, self-control and observance of *dharma*.

A king should not only obey his own *rajadharma* but also ensure that his subjects obeyed their respective *dharma*. For, 'when *adharma* overwhelms *dharma*, the king himself will be destroyed' {3.16.42}. Hence, a wicked prince, who hates *dharma* and is full of evil, should not be installed on the throne, even if he is an only son {1.17.51}. In fact, Kautilya prefers an ignorant king who had not been taught *dharma* to a wicked king who, in spite of his learning, deviates from it {8.2.12}.

The king's own *dharma* is to be just, impartial and lenient in protecting his people {8.2.12; 3.10.46; 1.19.33,34; 3.1.41; 3.20.24}. The king's attitude to his people should be like that of a father towards his children, particularly when any danger threatened the population {4.3.43}. He should treat leniently, like a father, those in new settlements whose tax exemptions had ceased to be effective {2.1.18}.

No doubt there was an element of self preservation in this. Discontented and impoverished people might be provoked to revolt; they may then kill their king or go over to the enemy {7.5.27; 1.19.28}. The king should not tax the people unjustly because 'that will make the people angry and spoil the very sources of revenue' {5.2.70}. A weak king who needed to recoup his depleted strength should try to promote the welfare of his people so that he might have the support of countryside {7.14.18}. Nowhere is Kautilya's emphasis on the welfare of the people seen more clearly than in the advice to the king on how to deal with a territory newly acquired by conquest {13.5.4,6,11,21}.

LIFE AND LIVELIHOOD

Protection of life and livelihood constituted, in that order, the elements of securing the welfare of the people. Disagreeing with earlier teachers, Kautilya points out that life was more important than livelihood {8.3.28,35}. Even when a man's property was attached by a decree in a civil suit, he was not to be deprived of the tools of his trade {3.1.31}.

Protection of livelihood extended to protecting the major areas of economic activity. Agriculture was protected from being oppressed by onerous taxes, fines and demands for labour, herds of cattle from the depredations of thieves, wild animals, poisons, crocodiles and diseases and trade routes from harassment by courtiers, state officials, thieves and frontier officers {2.1.37,38}.

The Chief Controller of Shipping was responsible for the welfare of sea-traders and seamen, elimination of piracy, ensuring the seaworthiness of vessels and rescuing vessels in distress. The official had to pay the compensation himself if any vessel was lost due to lack of seamen or equipment or because it was unseaworthy {2.28.8,12,26}.

The principles of fair trading enunciated in the text were designed to promote the welfare of the people. The phrase 'to be sold for the benefit of the public' occurs in the following places: both locally produced and imported goods {2.16.5}; any commodity causing a glut in the market, by centralized sale until the stock was exhausted {4.2.33-35}; and any surplus unaccounted stock in the hands of merchants {4.2.26,27}. When Crown commodities were sold, no artificial scarcity was to be created and even a large profit should be foregone, if it was likely to cause harm to the public {2.16.6,7}. Imported goods were to be sold in as many places as possible in order to make them readily available to people in the towns and the countryside {2.16.4}. Profit margins were fixed at 5% for local goods and 10% for imported ones; making undue profit attracted a heavy fine {4.2.28,29}.

Special favours were shown to those who did things which benefited the people, such as building embankments and road bridges, beautifying villages or protecting them {3.10.46}.

THE WEAKER SECTIONS

The list of the weaker sections of the society, who required special protection, occurs in a number of places: priority of audience before the king {1.19.29}, maintenance at state expense {2.1.26}, free travel on ferries {2.28.18} and the special responsibility of judges on matters concerning them {3.20.22}. The list, with minor variations, always runs: brahmins, ascetics, the minors, the aged, the sick, the handicapped, the helpless and women.

It may seem strange to speak of welfare when discussing torture to elicit a confession. Nevertheless, the list of persons who were not to be tortured is interesting: minors, the aged, the sick, the debilitated, those in a drunken state, the insane, those suffering from hunger, thirst or fatigue after a long journey, those who had eaten too much, those accused of trifling offences and those who had already confessed {4.8.14}. The restrictions on torture of women, particularly pregnant women, have been cited earlier {4.8.17,18}.

Some aspects of the welfare of women, referred to earlier, are: spinning work to be given to handicapped women and taken to those who did not normally leave their houses {2.23.2,11}, protection of women slaves from exploitation {3.13.20,23,24}, punishment for rape (VIII.xv) and protection of prostitutes against exploitation and physical injury {2.27.13-18,23}.

Protection of children is emphasized, especially in the context of slavery and bonded labour {3.13.1,2,4}. When an *Arya* man had bound himself and his family, the minors were the ones to be redeemed first {3.13.5}. A slave less than eight years old was not to be compelled, against his wishes, to do menial jobs or work in a foreign country {3.13.20}. The property of minors was to be held in trust and looked after by the village elders {2.1.27}.

Social security was both a private and a state matter. The primary responsibility for maintaining the family—wife, children, parents, minor brothers and unmarried or widowed sisters—lay with the head of the family; no one could become an ascetic without first providing for his wife and children {2.1.28,29}. Dependents were not to be abandoned, particularly when travelling together {3.20.18}. However, the state had the obligation to provide a safety net and maintain children, the aged, childless women and the helpless {2.1.26}. But, when the state had to maintain the young with no family of their own, these could be recruited into the secret service {1.12.1}.

The extent of Kautilya's concern for the weaker sections is shown by these further examples ranging from chivalry in battle to gleaning on Crown lands. When the enemy fort or camp was attacked, the following were not to be harmed: the non-combatants, the frightened and those who surrender, fall down or turn their backs {13.4.52}. Mendicants and village servants were allowed to glean the grain on Crown lands after the harvest {5.2.11}. Even in times of distress, handfuls of grain could be taken for worship of gods and ancestors, for charity or for cows {5.2.10}.

HARASSMENT OF THE PEOPLE

Using the technique of comparing two different calamities afflicting the people, Kautilya pinpoints the harassment that could be visited on the people by those in positions of power and authority (see introduction to II.iv). A decadent king could oppress the people by seizing what he wanted and taking the wealth of the country for himself and his cronies; quarrels within the royal family could result in harassment; the king's favourite queen or concubine might by her waywardness cause harm to the people; the most powerful officials, like the Treasurer or the Chancellor, might, for their own enrichment, harass the people; the king's own army might exact heavy contributions or go on the rampage {8.4.20,23,26,31-33}. Overzealous tax collectors might collect more than the right amounts and thus impoverish the countryside {2.9.15}. There is a systematic classification of forty ways by which corrupt officials might cheat the government of revenue, cheat the public or both {2.8.21}. Since there was no one in a position of power who could be trusted not to misuse his authority, Kautilya gives clear instructions on how to detect and punish the culprits. For example, people who had suffered at the hands of corrupt officials were compensated after issuing a proclamation asking such victims to come forward {2.8.24,25}.

Other possibilities of harassment of the people were: the nobility seizing common land {8.4.37-40}; profiteering by traders {8.4.34-36}; marauders and robber bands {8.4.41-43}; and, destruction caused by rogue elephants {8.4.45}.

Chapter 4.4 is wholly devoted to detecting the activities of thirteen types of persons who amassed black money by illicit means: village officials, heads of departments, judges, magistrates, perjurers, instigators of perjury, extortioners, practitioners of the occult, black magic or sorcery, poisoners, dealers in narcotics, counterfeiters and adulterators of precious metals.

Kautilya also deals with the welfare of the population when afflicted by natural calamities; the relevant verses have been brought together in this translation under 'Acts of God' in II.iv. Keeping grains and other products as reserve stocks and building forts as places of refuge were part of the system of protecting the people {2.15.22,23}.

MAINTENANCE OF ORDER

The responsibility of maintaining social order was partly individual, to the extent that each person had to follow the *dharma* of his own *varna* and *ashrama*, and partly that of the state. The laws relating to maintenance of order, in the sense of punishing unsocial behaviour, have been grouped together in this translation under criminal investigation (VIII.xii), robbery and theft (VIII.xv), verbal and physical injury (VIII.xiii) and sexual offences (VIII.xv). Punishments for a variety of offences will also be found throughout the text under the appropriate subjects. *Danda*, the coercive power of the state, was exercised through this extensive set of fines and punishments, including amputation and the death sentence.

Order was maintained by controlling movement and activities like drinking and gambling. A curfew was normally imposed in the cities at night. Care was, however, taken to ensure that the city guards did not use it to misbehave with women {2.36.41}. By restricting drinking to authorized drinking halls, not permitting large quantities of alcohol to be bought, taken away or stocked, by not selling on credit and by punishing anyone moving about in a drunken state, the effects of drunkenness on society was contained {2.25.3-5,7}. Both masters of gambling halls and the gamblers themselves were punished for dishonest behaviour {3.20.9; 4.10.9}.

Lodging-house keepers had to report the arrival of undesirable persons {2.36.5}. Doctors had to report treating a wounded person or anyone suffering from food or drink poisoning {2.36.10}. Prostitutes, and owners of drinking halls and restaurants had to report anyone who spent lavishly {2.36.9}.

It is interesting to note that the state was held responsible for any failure to protect the public. If a thief was not apprehended and the stolen property not recovered, the victim was reimbursed from the king's own resources. If anyone's property was unjustly appropriated and not restored, he was paid its value {3.16.25-27}. Judges could modify the rate of interest, if the king was responsible for increasing the risk of loss by not providing adequate protection {3.11.3}.

CIVIC LIFE

Kautilya was aware of the dangers inherent in the confined and densely packed cities, particularly with regard to fire, hygiene and privacy. The welfare of the people could be guaranteed only by having clear regulations fixing the responsibility of the citizen and by providing appropriate penalties for violations. The verses dealing with prevention, house building and hygiene have been collected under 'Civic Responsibility and Municipal

Regulations' (see VII.xi). The rules were not applied indiscriminately. For example, passing urine or faeces in a public place was not punished if it was due to illness, medication or fear {2.3.29}. The rules on sanitation inside houses were relaxed for childbirth and the ten-day lying-in period {3.8.6}. House building regulations could be modified by mutual agreement among neighbours so long as the undesirable was avoided {3.8.18}.

CONSUMER PROTECTION

The rules regarding protection of the welfare of the consumer by control over merchants and weights and measures have been referred to earlier. Other rules take into account the propensity of artisans and craftsmen to cheat the public; these not only refer to goldsmiths and silversmiths palming off precious metals but note that washermen wore their customers' clothes! All verses on consumer protection have been collated in IV.vi.

WELFARE OF GOVERNMENT SERVANTS

While government servants were always under suspicion of wanting to skim off government revenue into their own pockets {2.9.32-34}, they were also rewarded for good work. 'Those officials who do not eat up the king's wealth but increase it in a just manner and are loyally devoted to the king shall be made permanent in service' {2.9.36}. 'An official who accomplishes a task as ordered or better shall be honoured with a promotion and rewards.' {2.9.9} The family of a government servant who died on duty was looked after by the state {5.3.28-30}. An official, whose property was liable to confiscation because he caused loss of revenue, was spared the confiscation if he had many dependents {2.9.24}.

WELFARE OF PRISONERS

The welfare of prisoners (see VIII.xvi) was safeguarded by the following: having separate prisons for men and women, providing halls, water wells, latrines and bathrooms, keeping the prisons free of fire hazards and poisonous insects, protecting the rights of prisoners to their daily activities like eating, sleeping and exercise, putting restrictions on warders from harassing or torturing prisoners, prescribing severe punishments for rape of women prisoners and releasing prisoners periodically as well as by general and special amnesties.

ANIMAL WELFARE

There is extensive evidence in the *Arthashastra* on Kautilya's concern for the welfare of animals. Regulations for the protection of wildlife, a long list of punishment for cruelty to animals, rations for animals, regulations on grazing and the responsibility of veterinary doctors are some of the major topics.

As part of the creation of the infrastructure of a settled and prosperous kingdom, an animal sanctuary, 'where all animals were welcomed as guests', was established {2.2.4}. Live birds and deer received as tax were let loose in them. A list of protected animals and fish is given. Killing or injuring protected species and animals in reserved parks and sanctuarie was prohibited. Even animals which had turned dangerous were not to be killed within the sanctuary but had to be caught, taken outside and then killed {2.26.1,4-6,14}.

Village headmen were responsible for preventing cruelty to animals. If protected animals or those from reserved forests strayed and were found grazing where they should not, they were to be driven away without hurting them; anyone who let such animals stray were to be warned to prevent a recurrence. Stray cattle were to be driven off with a rope or a whip without harming them. Any means could be used to restrain a perrson found to be treating an animal cruelly {3.10.30-34}.

Some animals, like deer, were given special treatment {4.10.5}. Temple bulls, stud bulls and cows for up to ten days after calving were exempt from payment of grazing charges {3.10.24}. Riding or driving a temple animal, a stud bull or a pregnant cow was prohibited {4.13.20}. Animals fights between horned or tusked animals was also prohibited {4.13.19}.

Special regulations applied to animals in Crown herds, horses and elephants, since the latter two were important for war. The possibility of herdsmen starving calves of their mother's milk is foreseen; milking cows twice in seasons when they should be milked only once was punished by cutting off the thumb of the culprit; killing or inducing someone to kill animals in crown herds was punishable by death {2.29.3,16,32}. Special provisions were made for looking after nonproductive cattle {2.29.6}. Rations are laid down for horses and elephants, including special rations for tired horses (see Appendix 4). Attendants who ill-treated elephants or kept them in dirty stalls were punished {2.32.19}. Horses unfit for use in war were used to breed animals for the benefit of the people {2.30.28}.

Veterinary doctors were fined if the condition of a sick animal became worse; they had to repay the cost of the animal if it died {2.30.43,47,48}.

In newly conquered territory, animal slaughter was prohibited for four days around full moon day and during one fortnight in each of the four months of devotion (*chaturmasya*). Slaughter of female and young animals and castration of males was prohibited {13.5.12,13}.

The detailed set of punishments for theft of animals, injuring or killing them will be found in VII.iii.

REALITY AND THE IDEAL

The picture of the ideal Kautilyan state that emerges from the above is one of a well-run state, prosperous and bustling with activity. There were shops with textiles, gold and jewellery and eating houses serving vegetarian and non-vegetarian food. Musicians, dancers, story-tellers and reciters, clowns, acrobats and jugglers entertained the people. Men went to gambling places and drinking halls or visited brothels. Monks and nuns wandered freely.

Some people were given special privileges. The king himself was obliged to grant audiences to deal with matters concerning the weaker sections. Local customs of different regions were preserved {3.7.40}. A good conqueror adopted the dress, language and behaviour of his newly-conquered subjects {13.5.7}.

On the other hand, there were some people automatically suspect, like ascetics and practitioners of the occult {1.21.24; 1.19.31}. There are two long lists of people who were to be arrested on suspicion: in the city {2.36.13} and on ferry crossings {2.28.20}. The outcasts lived both physically on the fringes of the inhabited areas and socially on the fringes of the *Arya* society. Every one was suspected of having designs on the king and the kingdom. Secret agents were everywhere.

But this picture is the ideal. The reality could have been very different. There were kings who impoverished their subjects, whose life could only have been one of unremitting drudgery. Kings imposed extra burdens on the people during calamities or for waging war. Dishonest officials cheated and robbed the people. Robbers and marauding jungle tribes harassed them. An unjust conqueror oppressed his newly conquered subjects.

When reading this translation, it would, therefore, be wise to keep in mind that Kautilya was writing a textbook for kings and not a descriptive history of any particular state.

Part I

INTRODUCTORY SECTIONS

"This *Arthashastra* is a compendium of almost all similar treatises, composed by ancient teachers, on the acquisition and protection of territory. Easy to grasp and understand, free from verbosity, Kautilya has composed this treatise with precise words, doctrines and sense."

{1.1.1, 1.1.19}

"The people of a society, whatever their *varna* or stage of life, will follow their own *dharma* and pursue with devotion their occupations, if they are protected by the king and the just use of *danda* [coercion and punishment]."

{1.4.16}

I.i

ABOUT THIS TREATISE

[This introduction is compiled from the first four chapters of Book 1 and the whole of Book 15 of the manuscript. The detailed contents given in the first chapter of Book 1 have been omitted, since the material is ordered in a different way in this translation. Book 15, on the methodology used by Kautilya, is included here because it provides a glimpse of the flavour of the work; for a treatise written around 2,000 years ago, it is remarkably precise. The logical and stylistic devices used in it are similar to those used in other classical didactic works, such as treatises on medicine. Kautilya's aim in explaining these techniques is to ensure that there is no doubt in the mind of the reader about what the author intends to convey.]

OM

SALUTATIONS TO BRIHASPATI AND SUKRA

[the gurus of the gods and antigods
and the originators of the Science of Politics]

The source of the livelihood of men is *artha* (wealth); that is to say, the territory [and the inhabitants following various professions] is the wealth [of a nation]. The science by which territory is acquired and maintained is *Arthashastra*—the science of wealth and welfare.   {15.1.1,2}

This treatise has been composed by one who, resenting the misrule of the Nanda kings, rescued this neglected science and used it as a weapon to destroy them and save the kingdom. By following [the principles set out in] this treatise one can not only create and preserve *dharma* [spiritual good], *artha* [material well-being] and *kama* [aesthetic pleasures] but also destroy [their opposites, i.e.] unrighteousness, material loss and hatred. It is a guide not only for the acquisition of this world but also the next.

{15.1.73,72,71}

METHODOLOGY

Thirty-two stylistic and logical devices are used in this work: {15.1.3}
A <u>topic</u> is introduced by stating the objective. For example, the subject matter of the whole book is introduced by the sentence above. 'The *Arthashastra* is a compendium....[{1.1.1}]'   {15.1.4,5}
The <u>contents</u> describe briefly the various sections of the book,

{15.1.6,7}

The <u>meaning</u> of a word is [sometimes] <u>implicit</u> in itself. For example, '*mulahara*' is defined [in {2.9.21}] as one 'who squanders his inherited ancestral property in unethical ways'.   {15.1.10-12}
A <u>derivation</u> is so called because of its etymological origin. For instance: 'A *vyasana* (calamity) is derived from "*vyasyati*" [to deprive] a king of his prosperity.'   {15.1.45-46}
<u>Technical terms</u> are words to which special meanings, not used by others, are assigned. For example: [the commonly used words, 'first', 'second' and 'third' are used in verses {6.2.13-15} in the special senses of:] '*vijigishu* or the "first", the potential conqueror; *ariprakriti* or the "second", the hostile king whose kingdom shares a boundary with that of the conqueror; *mitraprakriti* or the "third", the ally, whose territory has no common border with that of the conqueror being separated by the intervening territory of the hostile king.'   {15.1.51,52}
A <u>statement</u> is used to describe a conclusion or a rule. [For example, {1.4.16}:]'The people of the four *varnas* and the four walks of life will follow their own *dharma* and pursue with devotion their occupations if they are protected by the king and the just use of *danda*.'   {15.1.8,9}
A <u>summary</u> is a statement in brief. [For example, {1.6.1}:] 'Discipline and success in learning depend on control over the senses.'   {15.1.15,16}
An <u>explanation</u> is giving details [as in {1.6.2}:] 'Control over the senses means absence of improper indulgence in the [pleasures of] sound, touch, colour, taste and smell by the ear, the skin, the eyes, the tongue and the nose.'   {15.1.17,18}
<u>Application</u> of the same rule to similar situations is shown [in verses such as {3.16.1}:] '[The rules about] non-payment of debts apply also to non-payment of a promised gift.'   {15.1.23,24}
In some cases, an explanation given later is shown by an <u>indication</u>. [For example, {7.14.11}:] 'How conciliation, placating with gifts, sowing dissension and using force are used will be explained in the section on calamities.'   {15.1.25,26}

An <u>implication</u> is a consequence which follows, though not stated explicitly. [For example, in {5.4.1}:] 'One experienced in the ways of the world should win the favour of a worthy sovereign with the help of courtiers and other friends of the king.' It follows that [an aspiring courtier] will not succeed if he fails to make use of those dear to the king.   {15.1.29-31}

A <u>doubt</u> is raised when there are both reasons for and against [a course of action]. [For example: {7.5.12}:] 'Which type of king should be attacked first? One whose subjects are impoverished and greedy or one whose subjects are oppressed and rebellious?'   {15.1.32,33}

<u>Ellipsis</u> is omission of a part of a sentence [as in {8.1.9}:] 'Without competent ministers, a king loses the ability to act, as with clipped wings.' Here the words 'a bird' are omitted.   {15.1.38-40}

An example of <u>emphasis</u> is in [{8.3.64}:] 'And, in particular, in the case of oligarchies and confederacies of kings resembling oligarchies, dissensions are caused by gambling; due to the quarrels, the persons are destroyed. Therefore, gambling is the most evil among vices, because it destroys the ruling class by depriving them of their ability to govern.' {15.1.43,44}

<u>Prior reference</u>, [as in {6.1.7}:] 'The qualifications of a Minister have been described already.'   {15.1.61,62}

<u>Future reference</u> [as in {2.13.28}:] 'Weights and measures will be explained in the section on the [duties of the] Chief Controller of Weights and Measures.'   {5.1.59,60}

<u>Inference</u> is what is not explicitly stated but is to be understood. [For example,: {3.16.5}:] 'Experts shall determine the validity or otherwise of the revocation of gifts in such a manner that neither the giver nor the receiver suffers.'   {15.1.69,70}

<u>Advice</u> is giving guidance [as in {1.7.3}:] 'There is no need for a king to deprive himself of all sensual pleasures so long as he does not infringe his *dharma* or harms his own material well-being.'   {15.1.19,20}

<u>Invariable rules</u> are universally true. [For example, {1.19.5}:] 'A king should himself be always energetic.'   {15.1.57,58}

<u>Restriction, Choice and Combination [of methods]</u>

<u>Restriction</u> is stating 'thus and not otherwise'. [For example, {1.17.33}:] 'Therefore, a prince should be taught what is true *dharma* and *artha*, not what is spiritually unrighteous or materially harmful.'

<u>Either/Or</u> is a choice, [as in {3.5.10}:] '[The sons shall inherit the estate of a man if he had sons,] or the daughters born of pious marriages.'

<u>Combination</u>, [as in {3.7.13}:] '[The son of a woman who has remarried] is the heir to his father as well as his father's kinsmen [if he is born to the husband of the remarriage].'[1]   {15.1.63-68}

<u>Quotations</u> are used to refer to other teachings. [For instance, in {1.15.47-50}, are set out the different views of Manu, Brihaspati, etc. on the question of the number of councillors a king should have.]   {15.1.21,22}

<u>Agreement</u> with the teaching of another writer is indicated when a quotation is not followed by a refutation. [For example, {10.6.1}:] 'Ushanas says that a battle formation shall consist of two wings, a centre and reserves.' [Kautilya agrees.]   {15.1.41,42}

<u>Reasoning</u> is used to prove an assertion. In asserting [in {1.7.7}] that *artha* alone is supreme, the reason is given: 'because *dharma* and *kama* depend on *artha*'.   {15.1.13,14}

<u>Illustration</u> [as in {7.3.3}]: 'A weak king going to war with a stronger king is like a foot soldier fighting an elephant.'   {15.1.47,48}

An <u>analogy</u> is used to establish an unknown with the help of the known. [For example, {2.1.18}:] '(The king) should treat leniently, like a father would treat his son, those settlers whose exemptions from taxes have ceased to be effective.'   {15.1.27,28}

<u>Similarity</u> is used in cases, [such as in {1.11.10},] on the method of recruiting an impoverished farmer as a spy [by reference to the method suggested for a wandering monk].   15.1.34,35}

<u>Exception</u>. [For instance, in {9.2.6}:] 'An army of alien troops should always be stationed in close proximity, except when there is danger of a rebellion.'   {15.1.49,50}

<u>Contrary inference</u> is sometimes used. For example, [after describing the signs which show that a king is pleased with a courtier, it is said, in {1.16.12}, that] 'contrary behaviour will indicate that the king is displeased.'   {15.1.36,37}

<u>Prima facie view</u> is the statement of a view that will be rejected. [For example, [in {8.1.7}:] 'A calamity befalling a minister is more serious than that of the king.'   {15.1.53,54}

<u>Conclusive opinion</u> follows [in {8.1.17,18}:] '[A calamity to the king is worse;] for, all are dependent on him; he is to the state what the head is to the body.'   {15.1.55,56}

I.ii

KNOWLEDGE, *DHARMA* AND *DANDA*

[This section consists of chapters 2, 3, and 4 of Book 1. These are important since they describe the religious and social milieu of Hindu society at the time of Kautilya—a milieu within which the king, his Government and the people had to function. Kautilya does not lay down the laws of *dharma* and social life; these are to be found in the *Dharmashastras*. The *Arthashastra* deals only with different aspects of government. The duties of a state are safeguarding the welfare of the people, promoting their economic well-being and preserving *dharma*. All these are possible only if order and stability are maintained. Hence, the science of government (the *Arthashastra*) is also the science of upholding order by just punishment (*dandaniti*). Stability enables a state not only to share its wealth equitably but also to augment it by enlarging its territory through conquest.]

BRANCHES OF KNOWLEDGE

[Traditionally,] philosophy, the three *Vedas*, economics and the science of government are considered to be the four branches of knowledge. [However,] the followers of [the *Arthashastra* of Prachetasa] Manu say that there are only three branches—the three *Vedas*, economics and the science of government. For, [to them,] philosophy is only a special branch of Vedic studies. The school of Brihaspati considers only economics and politics to be true branches of knowledge; [they argue that] those experienced in the ways of the world use the Vedas only as a cover [in order to avoid the accusation of being materialistic atheists.] The school of Ushanas, maintains that politics is the only science; because, they say, it is in that science all other sciences have their beginning and end. {1.2.1-7}

Kautilya holds that there are, indeed, four branches of knowledge. Because one can know from these four all that is to be learnt about *dharma* [spiritual welfare] and *artha* [material well-being], they are called 'knowledge.'

{1.2.8,9}

Philosophy is the lamp that illuminates all sciences; it provides the techniques for all action; and it is the pillar which supports *dharma*.

{1.2.12}

Samkhya, Yoga and atheistic materialism are [the?] three schools of philosophy. One should study philosophy because it helps one to distinguish between *dharma* and *adharma* [evil] in the study of the Vedas, between material gain and loss in the study of economics and between good and bad policies in the study of politics. [Above all,] it teaches one the distinction between good and bad use of force. When the other three sciences are studied by the light of philosophy, people are benefited because their minds are kept steady in adversity and prosperity and they are made proficient in thought, speech and action.   {1.2.10,11}

The Vedas: The *Sama Veda*, the *Rig Veda* and the *Yajur Veda* are the three Vedas.   {1.3.1}

The *Atharva Veda* and the Itihasas (*Puranas*, epics like the Ramayana and Bharata, history, biographies of gods and men, illustrative stories, works of *Dharmashastra* and the *Arthashastra*) are also part of Vedic studies.

{1.5.14, 1.3.2}

The auxiliary sciences are: phonetics, ritual, grammar, etymology, prosody and astronomy.   {1.3.3}

The three Vedas are most useful because they establish the respective duties of the four *varnas* and the four stages of life [as briefly described below].   {1.3.4}

THE FOUR *VARNAS*

The duties of a Brahmin are: study, teaching, performing the rituals prescribed for him, officiating at other people's rituals, giving and receiving gifts.

{1.3.5}

The duties of a *Kshatriya* are: study, performing the rituals prescribed for him, living by [the profession of] arms and protecting all life.

{1.3.6}

The duties of a *Vaishya* are: study, performing the prescribed rituals, agriculture, cattle-rearing and trade.   {1.3.7}

The duties of a *Sudra* are: service of the twice born [i.e. the three higher *varnas*], [or] an economic activity [such as agriculture, cattle rearing and trade] [or] the profession of an artisan [or] entertainer [such as actor or singer].

{1.3.8}

THE FOUR STAGES OF LIFE

[The order of the *ashramas* below follows the text.]
The duties of a <u>householder</u> are: earning his livelihood by pursuing his
own profession; marrying a woman from the same *varna* but not of the
same *gotra* [deriving from the same primordial paternal ancestor];
procreating children by intercourse with his wife at the appropriate time;
worship of the gods, ancestors and guests; sacrificing his own pleasures
for those dependent on him and being the last to enjoy what is available.
{1.3.9}

The duties of a <u>*Brahmachari*</u> are: study of the prescribed scriptures;
tending the ritual fires; following the ritual ablutions; living on alms only
[i.e. possessing no property]; being devoted, to the end of his life, to his
teacher, the teacher's son and his fellow students.   {1.3.10}

The duties of a <u>*Vanaprastha*</u> (forest recluse) are: observing celibacy;
sleeping on the bare ground, not dressing his hair, wearing deer skins [i.e.
avoiding luxuries]; following the rituals of the fires and ablutions;
worshipping gods, ancestors and guests; and living on things gathered
from the forests [being neither dependent on charity nor on one's own
wealth].   {1.3.11}

The duties of a <u>*Parivrajaka*</u> [a wandering ascetic] are: complete control
over his senses [i.e. renouncing the temptation of all sensual pleasures];
refraining from all active life; renouncing all possessions; giving up
all attachment to worldly ties; living on the charity of the many, never
staying in one place for long; living in forests; maintaining inner and
outward purity.   {1.3.12}

Duties common to all: *Ahimsa* [abstaining from injury to all living
creatures]; *Satyam* [truthfulness]; cleanliness; freedom from malice;
compassion and tolerance.   {1.3.13}

ON FOLLOWING ONE'S OWN *DHARMA*

[The observance of] one's own *dharma* leads to heaven and eternal bliss.
When *dharma* is transgressed, the resulting chaos leads to the extermination
of this world. Whoever upholds his own *dharma*, adheres to the customs
of the Aryas and follows the rules of the *varnas* and the stages of life, will
find joy here and in the hereafter. For the world, when maintained in
accordance with the Vedas, will ever prosper and not perish. Therefore,
the king shall never allow the people to swerve from their *dharma*.
{1.3.14-17}

ECONOMICS

Agriculture, cattle rearing and trade constitute economic activity. They are the main sources of wealth—i.e. grains, cattle, gold, forest produce and labour. The king obtains through them the treasury and the army, which [are then used to] bring under control both his own people and the enemy's people.   {1.4.1,2}

MAINTENANCE OF ORDER

The pursuit of [the people's] welfare as well as the maintenance of the philosophic tradition, the Vedas and the economic well-being [of the society] are dependent on the sceptre wielded by the king. The maintenance of law and order by the use of punishment is the science of government. By maintaining order, the king can preserve what he already has, acquire new possessions, augment his wealth and power, and share the benefits of improvement with those worthy of such gifts.   {1.4.3}

The progress of this world depends on the maintenance of order and the [proper functioning of] government.   {1.4.4}

Some teachers say: 'Those who seek to maintain order shall always hold ready the threat of punishment. For, there is no better instrument of control than coercion.' Kautilya disagrees for the [following reasons]. A severe king [meting out unjust punishment] is hated by the people he terrorises while one who is too lenient is held in contempt by his own people. Whoever imposes just and deserved punishment is respected and honoured. A well-considered and just punishment makes the people devoted to *dharma*, *artha* and *kama* [righteousness, wealth and enjoyment]. Unjust punishment, whether awarded in greed, anger or ignorance, excites the fury of even [those who have renounced all worldly attachments like] forest recluses and ascetics, not to speak of householders. When, [conversely,] no punishment is awarded [through misplaced leniency and no law prevails], then there is only the law of fish [i.e. the law of the jungle]. Unprotected, the small fish will be swallowed up by the big fish. In the presence of a king maintaining just law, the weak can resist the powerful.   {1.4.5-15}

I.iii

SOME GENERAL TOPICS

[This section is a compilation of a number of miscellaneous topics which are necessary for a clearer appreciation of the text. For instance, some knowledge of the approximate value of the '*pana*', the currency used, is necessary for understanding the complexity of the Kautilyan economy. In view of the difficulty of finding exact modern equivalents of the weights and measures used at that time, one has to guess the approximate values to get an idea of things like rations for men and animals. Special terms used by Kautilya for classifying commodities and prescribing standard penalties are also explained herein. Lastly, the set of four traditional Indian methods of conflict avoidance and conflict resolution, used with great acumen by Kautilya, is explained.]

VALUE OF MONEY

[Throughout the text the currency almost always used is a *pana*, a silver coin; in {5.2.17-22}, there is mention of '*kara*' which, from the context, seems also to mean a pana. Half, quarter and one-eighth pana silver coins were also in circulation. There were sixteen *mashakas* to a pana and four *kakanis* to a mashaka. There were one mashaka, half a mashaka, one kakani and half-kakani copper coins. The smallest coin was, therefore, one hundred and twenty-eighth the value of the highest. More details about coinage, testing coins, charges payable to the Treasury and punishments for counterfeiting will be found in VII.iv under the Chief Master of the Mint and the Examiner of Coins.

What was the pana worth? According to the salary list in 5.3, the highest salary paid in cash, excluding perquisites, was 48,000 panas a year and the lowest 60 panas a year. The ratio of the highest salary to the lowest, was eight hundred to one. While we find that, in {3.2.15}, 2000 panas is prescribed as the maximum for a wife's endowment on marriage, we also see that {2.27.6} the amount payable for redeeming a courtesan in the King's service was 24,000 panas!

Fixed monetary fines ranged between one-eighth pana to 5000 panas, with 12 or 24 panas being the fine for a large number of offences. However, the three levels of standard fines (explained below) were 48 to 96 panas (lowest SP), 200 to 500 panas (middle SP) and 500 to 1000 panas (highest SP).

The charges for washing clothes {4.1.22} ranged from one or two mashakas for rough white fabrics to one pana for delicate garments needing special care. For normal work, silversmiths were paid one-sixteenth of the metal worked, goldsmiths one eighth and base metal workers five per cent {4.1.32-35}

Four and a quarter panas was the reward for bringing in a pair of tusks of an elephant dying naturally {2.2.9}. The reward for saving someone from a wild animal was 12 panas {4.3.32}.

A more direct indication of the value of a pana in relation to the cost of living is in {5.3.34}; an annual salary of 60 panas could be substituted by an *adhaka* of grain per day, enough for four meals for one Arya male {2.15.43}. However, in {2.24.28}, the wages of cowherds, labourers and watchmen is prescribed as food in accordance with the number of persons dependant on the workman and, in addition, a monthly wage of one and a quarter panas (i.e. 15 panas per annum). Thus, a cash wage of 60 panas a year may be considered as adequate for a family of normal size of the lowest paid. The other criteria, such as the endowment for a wife or a courtesan's ransom, must have applied to the relatively better off and the richest in the land.

Given the fact of a cash wage of 5 panas a month for the lowest paid, the pana was, indeed, a valuable coin; the kakani and the mashaka were, perhaps, the coins which most people ever saw or used.]

CLASSIFICATION OF COMMODITIES

[Reference is often made in the text to three types of commodities—*sara, phalgu* and *kupya*; these are rendered in this translation, following Kangle, as articles of high value, articles of low value and forest produce. We also find references to 'precious objects' which were even more valuable than the other three. These included *ratna* (precious and semi-precious stones), gold, silver and articles made of precious metals. A broad guide to the classification is given below. These are commodities stored in state warehouses under the control of the Chief Superintendent of the Treasury. This is not a comprehensive classification of all commodities and products in the Kautilyan economy. Agricultural products like grains, edible and non-edible oils, livestock products like ghee and meat, fruit and vegetables, sugar and honey and forestry products are listed under the appropriate Head of Department. Lists of all commodities mentioned by Kautilya are given in Appendix 2].

Ratna   Pearls, diamonds, coral, precious stones (like ruby, beryl, sapphire and pure crystal) and semi-precious stones.

{from 2.11.2-42}

Sara   Articles of high value—perfumery such as sandal wood, aloe, incense and camphor.   {from 2.11.43-72}

Phalgu   Articles of low value—woollen articles, skins and furs, silk and silk-type fabrics, cotton cloth.   {from 2.11.73-115}

Kupya   Forest produce—[i.e. raw material, gathered not cultivated:] timber, bamboo and reeds, creepers, leaves for writing, medicinal herbs, poisonous plants, animal products such as skins, metals, products and by products made from any of these.

{from 2.17.4-16}

WEIGHTS AND MEASURES

[Complete details of weights and balances, linear and capacity measures and measurement of time are given in Appendix 1. The weights and capacity measures frequently used in the text are:

Measures:	4 *prasthas*	= 1 *adhaka*
	4 *adhakas*	= 1 *drona*
Weights:	10 *dharanas*	= 1 *pala*

It is difficult to give modern equivalents for these since the scale of weights is based on the weights of beans and berries {2.19.2,5} and the volume measure is based on the volume occupied by a certain weight of beans {2.19.29}. A good guess is:

    1 *pala*   = approximately 40 grams or 1 1/2 ounces.

    1 *drona*   = between 8 and 9 litres or between 1 3/4 to 2 British gallons.

It must also be noted that four different kinds of measures and weights were in use depending on the use to which they were put—payments into the Treasury, normal trade, payments out of the Treasury and payments to the palace. These are explained in the section on Sources of Revenue (see *vyaji*) and in Appendix 8.]

STANDARD PENALTIES

[References to three levels of standard fines are scattered throughout the text; the actual penalties are explained in {3.17} on 'Robbery with violence'. Kautilya appears to have used the terms 'lowest fine for robbery with violence', 'middle fine' and 'highest fine' as shorthand expressions to avoid repetition. In this translation these penalties are referred to as Lowest SP (LSP), Middle SP (MSP) and Highest SP (HSP) and mean:

Lowest SP	48 to 96 panas
Middle SP	200 to 500 panas
Highest SP	500 to 1000 panas

There are two other levels of penalties for robbery with violence of articles less valuable than those itemised for the Lowest SP. These are for stealing flowers, fruits and similar low value articles (12 to 24 panas) and for stealing articles made of iron, wood or ropes (24 to 48 panas). In fact, in {3.17.6-10}, five different grades of fines are prescribed—12 to 24 panas, 24 to 48, 48 to 96, 200 to 500 and 500 to 1000, according to the value of the article robbed. Kautilya prescribes the highest level for crimes involving the use of force in order to effect a change in the state of liberty of human beings—either putting them under bondage unjustly or releasing them without cause.]

Lowest level standard penalty:
For depriving a person forcibly of articles made of materials such as copper, *vritta*, bronze, glass or ivory the fine shall be not less than 48 panas and not more than 96 panas and shall be called the lowest penalty for robbery with violence.   {3.17.8}

Middle level standard penalty:
For robbery with violence of large animals, human beings, land, house, money, gold or fine cloth the fine shall be 200 to 500 panas and shall be called the middle penalty for robbery with violence.   {3.17.9}

Highest level standard penalty:
For forcibly depriving a man or a woman of liberty [abduction, confinement, bondage or slavery] or causing another to deprive a person of liberty or forcibly releasing a man or a woman from bondage or slavery the fine shall be between 500 to 1000 panas and this shall be called the highest penalty for robbery with violence.   {3.17.10}

Magistrates shall determine whether to levy the highest, the middle or the lower Standard Penalty, taking into account the person sentenced, the nature of the offence, the motive and its gravity, the circumstances prevailing [at the time of the offence] including the time and the place as well as the consequences, while maintaining a balance between the interests of the king [i.e. the State] and the offender. {4.10.17,18}

METHODS OF DEALING WITH CONFLICTS

[A well-known concept in Indian tradition is the set of four methods used in dealing with situations of potential or actual conflict: *sama*, *dana*, *bheda* and *danda* (i.e. adopting a conciliatory attitude, placating with rewards and gifts, sowing dissension among enemies and using force). These are referred to in many different places in the text. A detailed consideration of the use of the appropriate method is found mainly in Book 9 which deals with the planning and preparation needed before undertaking a military campaign. {9.5.3-29] in III.v and {9.6.21-73} in X.vi on tackling revolts and rebellions are particularly important. Other references are: against confederacies {7.14.11} in X.ix; a strong king controlling his circle of kings {7.16.3-8} in X.iv; a recaptured hostage {7.17.59} in X.iii; sowing dissension or using force among the Chiefs of an Oligarchy {11.1.6-8} in X.ix and a weak king threatened by an aggressor {12.1.18} in X.x.

In the case of conciliation, the first five methods are mentioned in the chapter on edicts and the last in connection with revolts within the country. Placating with gifts is elaborated in {9.6.24}. Many of the techniques for sowing dissension involve the use of clandestine agents and methods, details of which will be found in this translation in Part IX.

The methods can be used singly or in combination; Kautilya correctly calculates in {9.7.77-78} that there are fifteen possible ways of choosing one, two, three or all four from a set of four objects. The order of employing the methods could be an easier one first or a harder one first. There are thus thirty possible combinations from which to choose.]

The four [standard] methods [for dealing with conflict situations] are: conciliation, placating with gifts, sowing dissension and use of force.

It is easier to employ a method earlier in the order than a later one. Placating with gifts is twice as hard as conciliation, sowing dissension three times as hard and use of force four times. {2.10.47,9.6.56-61}

1. CONCILIATION

There are six kinds.

(i) <u>Praising the merits</u> [of someone who is, or likely to be, inimical]: Appreciating the merits of the person's pedigree, personal qualities, occupation, good nature, learning or wealth, either personally or to third parties.

(ii) <u>Mutual connections:</u> Extolling common relationships (such as blood relationship, relationship by marriage, a common teacher, a common ritual system, common friends or family connections).

(iii) <u>Mutual benefits:</u> Explaining the advantages that will accrue to each of the two parties (one's own side as well as the side addressed).

(iv) <u>Inducement:</u> Raising the hopes [of the other] by pointing out the beneficial results that will accrue to both, if a particular course of action is adopted.

(v) <u>Identity of interest:</u> Shown by placing oneself at the other's disposal (saying: 'What I am art thou, the wealth that is mine is thine, use it as it pleases thee.')   {2.10.48-53}

(vi) <u>Awards and honours:</u> Giving a high rank or awarding an honour is also a method of conciliating a potential [internal] enemy.   {9.5.10}

2. PLACATING WITH GIFTS

Rewarding with money, granting favours, exempting from taxes and giving employment.   {2.10.54,9.5.11}

Gifts are of five kinds: relinquishing what is owed; continuing a payment already being made; return of something received; giving something new out of one's own wealth; permission to take something from the enemy.
{9.6.24}

3. SOWING DISSENSION

[Between two enemies] is done by creating mutual suspicion between them or by threatening one of them.   {2.10.55}

4. USE OF FORCE

Force can be used to deprive a person of his property, liberty or life—(plunder, harassment and death).   {2.10.56}

[War, particularly the use of force for capturing the enemy by open, deceptive or secret war and the methods for capturing a fort are mentioned in {7.16.3-8} in X.iv and elaborated in appropriate places.]

COMBINATION OF METHODS

The methods can be used singly or in combination depending on the seriousness of the situation. There are four ways of using any one method, six ways of using two at a time, four ways of using three at a time and one way of using all four simultaneously. Thus, there are fifteen ways of using the methods singly or in any of the possible combinations in the *anuloma* [natural] order. Likewise, there are fifteen ways of using them in the *pratiloma* [unnatural] order.

If only one method is recommended, it is defined as 'placing a restriction', if a choice is suggested, it is an 'option' and if two or more are to be used together, it is a 'combination'.   {9.7.73-79}

RECOMMENDED METHODS

In the case of a son, a brother or a kinsman, the appropriate methods are conciliation and placating with gifts. In the case of citizens of the city, the people of the countryside or the army, placating with gifts or sowing dissension among them are the right methods. In the case of neighbouring princes or forest chiefs, one should show dissension or use force. This order is *anuloma* [natural and, therefore, recommended]; if the methods are used in reverse order [*dana* before *sama* or *danda* before *bheda*] it is *pratiloma*.   {9.7.68,69}

In the case of allies and enemies, a combination of methods ensures success because the different methods mutually reinforce each other.
{9.7.70,71}

Some methods are ideal in some cases and render the use of others unnecessary. For example, conciliation is adequate for dealing with the enemy's ministers whose loyalty is uncertain, placating with gifts for traitorous ministers of the enemy, dissension in case of confederacies and force against the powerful.   {9.7.72}

Part II

THE STATE, ITS CONSTITUENT ELEMENTS AND THREATS TO THEM

"Kautilya says: 'There cannot be a country without people and there is no kingdom without a country.'"

{13.4.5}

"The value of land is what man makes of it."

{7.11.9}

"It is the people who constitute a kingdom; like a barren cow, a kingdom without people yields nothing."

{7.11.24,25}

"In the interests of the prosperity of the country, a king should be diligent in foreseeing the possibility of calamities, try to avert them before they arise, overcome those which happen, remove all obstructions to economic activity and prevent loss of revenue to the state."

{8.4.50, 8.5.21}

II.i

INTRODUCTION TO PART II

The two chapters of Book 6 contain the foundations of Kautilya's theory of the State. {6.1} describes the seven constituent elements of any state and {6.2} is an exposition of the theory of the Circle of States (the *mandala* theory) as the basis for a foreign policy of expansion by conquest. Of the seven elements, six (the King, the ministers, the people, the fortified city, the Treasury and the army) are internal elements; only the ally is an element outside the borders.

The structure and organization of the six internal elements of a well-ordered state are fully developed and explained by Kautilya in Books 1 to 5. Nevertheless, he has placed the theoretical chapter, {6.1}, at the end so as to act as a prelude to the further development of the theory of conquest. Indeed, the aim of creating a well-run state is to provide the base for expansion. Continuing this logic, Kautilya deals in Book 7 with all theoretical possibilities of conducting an expansionist foreign policy. Before a King actually sets out on an expedition of conquest (treated from Book 9 onwards) he has to take steps to guard himself against the dangers which might weaken any of the constituent elements of his own state. Kautilya uses the word 'calamity' (*vyasana*) in the precise sense of any event which weakens any constituent element of a state, thereby preventing it from being used to its full potential in the conduct of foreign policy or war. The five chapters of Book 8 deal with the topic of calamities and adversities.

Kautilya's ordering of topics is logical. However, it is also logical to describe first the theory of the internal structure of a state before elaborating on the details. Likewise, one can place {6.2} at the beginning of the part dealing with foreign policy. In the rearrangement adopted in this translation, chapters {4.3}, {8.1}, {8.3} and {8.4} dealing with calamities are grouped together after the theory of the state; {8.3}, dealing with vices of men is, in fact, a general chapter, not specifically related to any one constituent element but to man in general. {8.2} is dealt with in III.vii, {8.4.49} in V.i and {8.5} in XI.ii.

A reason for including the section on calamities of the population in this part is that it brings out clearly the obligations of a ruler towards his subjects. Governed as he was by his own *dharma*, the King was not an unfettered, absolute monarch. His first duty towards his people was to protect them in times of natural calamities and from enemies, both internal and external. He also had the duty to provide a clean, efficient administration, though this was also in his own interest, since a contented and prosperous citizenry was essential for augmenting revenues. But the aim of increasing state revenues was not an unqualified objective, to be achieved at the cost of the welfare of the people. Hence, in describing the adversities to which the population might be subjected, Kautilya includes harassment by queens, King's mistresses, princes, ministers, customs officials and traders. The threefold obligation of a King towards his people were thus *rakshana* (protection), *palana* (administration) and *yogakshema* (welfare).[1] The welfare aspect is most clearly brought out in 4.3 on Acts of God, particularly the verses relating to famine.

Each one of the constituent elements briefly mentioned in II.ii is fully developed in later parts of this translation—the King in III, the *janapada* and the city in IV.i, the Treasury in V, the Army in XI.ii, and the ally in X.iv. The *janapada*, in particular, is covered in numerous places such as settlement of virgin land and the duties of the Chancellor.

One of the elements referred to is *amatya*, translated as 'councillors, ministers and high officials'. There is some confusion in the text in the use of the terms *amatya*, *mantri* and *mantriparishad*, probably because the text 'has preserved the terminology of the sources,...representing different stages in the process of development'.[2] In this translation, *mantri* is generally translated as councillor (one of the few close advisers of the King), *amatya* as minister or Head of Department depending on the context and *mantriparishad* as council of ministers. A detailed explanation is given in Notes on Translation No. 3.

Kautilya does not simply list the various calamities that can affect each constituent element but also indicates the relative seriousness by considering them in pairs. Examples are: a decadent King is worse than a decadent people; a favourite queen or mistress is worse than a wayward prince.]

II.ii

THE CONSTITUENT ELEMENTS OF A STATE

The elements which constitute a state are:

(i) the king;

(ii) [the group of] councillors, ministers and other high officials (the *amatya*);[1]

(iii) the territory of the state along with the population inhabiting it (the *janapada*);[2]

(iv) the fortified towns and cities (the *durga*);

(v) the treasury (*kosa*, the wealth of the State);

(vi) the forces (of defence and law and order) and

(vii) the allies.   {6.1.1}

THE KING

> [An ideal king is one who has the highest qualities of leadership,
> intellect, energy and personal attributes.]

The <u>qualities of leadership</u> (which attract followers) are: birth in a noble family, good fortune, intellect and prowess, association with elders, being righteous, truthful, resolute, enthusiastic and disciplined, not breaking his promises, showing gratitude [to those who help him], having lofty aims, not being dilatory, being stronger than neighbouring kings and having ministers of high quality.

The <u>qualities of intellect</u> are: desire to learn, listening [to others], grasping, retaining, understanding thoroughly and reflecting on knowledge, rejecting false views and adhering to the true ones.

<u>An energetic king</u> is one who is valorous, determined, quick and dexterous.

As regards <u>personal attributes</u>, an ideal king should be eloquent, bold and endowed with a sharp intellect, a strong memory and a keen mind. He should be amenable to guidance. He should be well trained in all the arts and be able to lead the army. He should be just in rewarding and punishing. He should have the foresight to avail himself of the opportunities (by choosing) the right time, place and type of action. He should know how to govern in normal times and in times of crisis. He should know when to fight and when to make peace, when to lie in wait, when to observe treaties and when to strike at an enemy's weakness. He should preserve his dignity at all times and not laugh in an undignified manner. He should be sweet in speech, look straight at people and avoid frowning. He should eschew passion, anger, greed, obstinacy, fickleness and backbiting. He should conduct himself in accordance with the advice of elders.   {6.1.2-6}

COUNCILLORS AND MINISTERS

<u>A councillor or minister</u> of the highest rank should be a native of the state, born in a high family and controllable [by the king]. He should have been trained in all the arts and have logical ability to foresee things. He should be intelligent, persevering, dexterous, eloquent, energetic, bold, brave, able to endure adversities and firm in loyalty. He should neither be haughty nor fickle. He should be amicable and not excite hatred or enmity in others.[3]

{1.9.1}

[The king should appoint advisers in different grades of the hierarchy, depending on how many of the qualities described above they possess].

Those who have all the qualities are to be appointed to the highest grade (as Councillors), those who lack a quarter to the middle grades and those who lack a half to the lowest grades.   {1.9.2}

THE TERRITORY AND THE POPULATION

All economic activities (relating to the fortified cities, the Treasury, the Army, waterworks and trade) have their source in the countryside.

{8.1.29}

The kingdom shall be protected by fortifying the capital and the towns at the frontiers. The land should not only be capable of sustaining the [native] population but also outsiders [when they come into the kingdom] in times of calamities. It should be easy to defend from [attacks by] enemies and strong enough to control neighbouring kingdoms. It should have productive land (free from swamps, rocky ground, saline land, uneven terrain and deserts as well as wild and [unruly] groups of people). It should be beautiful, being endowed with arable land, mines, timber forests, elephant forests, and good pastures rich in cattle. It should not depend [only on] rain for water. It should have good roads and waterways. It should have a productive economy, with a wide variety of commodities and the capacity to sustain a high level of taxation as well as a [large] army. The people shall be predominantly agriculturists [artisans and craftsmen], devoted to work, honest, loyal and with intelligent masters and servants. {6.1.8}

THE FORT

[For the planning and construction of forts and fortified towns, which are the fourth constituent element, see IV.i]

THE TREASURY

The wealth of the state shall be one acquired lawfully either by inheritance or by the king's own efforts. It shall consist of gold, silver, precious gems and gold coins. It should be large enough to enable the country to withstand a calamity, even of long duration during which there is no income.

{6.1.10}

THE FORCES

The army shall consist mostly of men of tested loyalty, *kshatriyas*, having come down from the king's father and grandfather. The soldiers should be strong, obedient, not averse to a long expeditions, with powers of endurance, skill in handling all weapons and experience of many battles. They should keep their wives and sons contented. They should have no interest other than that of the king and should share his prosperity and adversity.

{6.1.11}

THE ALLY

The ideal ally is one who has the following qualities: a friend of the family for a long time, constant, amenable to control, powerful in his support, sharing a common interest, able to mobilise (his forces) quickly and not a man who double-crosses [his friends].[4] {7.9.38, 6.1.12}

THE KING IN RELATION TO THE OTHER CONSTITUENTS

However ideal the other constituent elements of the state may be, they are all subordinate to the qualities of the king. A king endowed with the ideal personal qualities enriches the other elements when they are less than perfect. [On the other hand,] a weak or wicked king without doubt destroys the most prosperous and loyal elements of the kingdom. An unrighteous and vicious king, however mighty an emperor, is sure either to be killed by his infuriated subjects or subjugated by his enemies. A wise king, though only ruling over a small territory, will surely conquer the world if he gathers round him the best as the other constituent elements. {6.1.15-18}

II.iii

ON ADVERSITIES

CALAMITIES AND ADVERSITIES

That which deprives (*vyasyati*) a person of his strength and goodness is a *vyasana* (a vice, adversity or calamity).   {8.1.4}

[We need to consider the adversities that can affect the constituent elements of a state because,] when more than one element is affected, or when the (would be) conqueror and the enemy are both affected, the king has to decide whether to attack or to adopt a defensive posture. Calamities can be due to Acts of God or men and may arise from misfortune or bad policies. The following are to be considered as calamities—(i) when any of the constituent elements has characteristics opposite to those described as ideal [in the previous section]; (ii) when one of the elements is absent [such as not having an adequate treasury or a good ally]; (iii) a great defect [such as a disaffected population]; (iv) personal vices [such as addiction to women and gambling] and (v) natural calamities [like fire and flood].

{8.1.1-3}

Some teachers have said that: 'Of the calamities befalling the king, the ministers, the populated territory, the fort, the treasury, the army and the ally, that which affects the one mentioned earlier in the order is more serious than that affecting one later.'   {8.1.5}

[Other teachers, however, hold that a calamity of a constituent lower in the order could sometimes be more serious than that of the one immediately preceding.]

ORDER OF PRIORITY

KING AND MINISTERS

[For example], Bharadvaja is of the view that a calamity befalling a minister is more serious than that of the king. [His reasoning is that] a great deal of state activity depends on ministers—deliberation in council, acting on such deliberation, implementing the decisions made, collecting revenue and meeting expenditure, enforcing order, defending the kingdom from enemies and jungle tribes, taking remedial measures against calamities, protecting princes and ensuring the succession of the heir-apparent. In the absence of ministers, all the above activities are not done [properly] and the king, [like a bird] with clipped wings, loses the ability to act. The enemy then finds it easy to intrigue against the king. An unreliable minister, close to the king, threatens his very life.   {8.1.6-11}

Kautilya disagrees. It is the king alone who appoints the councillors, the *purohita* and other high officials. He directs the activities of heads of departments, takes counter-measures against calamities affecting the life or the prosperity of his people and promotes [the state's] development. If some ministers are afflicted by calamities, he can appoint others who are not affected. A good king is ever diligent in rewarding those who are worthy and in punishing the traitors. When the king is endowed with all that is good, he enriches all other constituents by his own prosperity. Whatever character the king has, the other elements also come to have the same, for they are all dependent on him for their progress or downfall. For the king is to the state like a head (to a body).   {8.1.12-18}

THE MINISTER AND THE *JANAPADA*

According to Vishalaksha, a calamity affecting the populated territory (the *janapada*) is more serious than the one affecting the minister; because, out of the territory and the people one obtains the treasury, the army, forest produce, labourers, means of transport and commodities. One cannot secure any of these if a calamity affects the territory and the people and [as a result] soon there will be neither minister nor king.   {8.1.19-21}

Kautilya disagrees. All state activities have their origin in the minister, whether these be the successful execution of works for [the benefit of] the territory and the population, maintenance of law and order, protection from enemies, tackling [natural] calamities, settlement of virgin lands, recruiting the army, revenue collection or rewarding the worthy.[1]   {8.1.22-23}

THE JANAPADA AND THE FORTS

The followers of Parasara consider a calamity to the fortified towns to be more serious than one to the territory and the people outside the towns. For, the treasury and the army are both situated inside the fortifications, where the people can take refuge in times of trouble. The people of the towns are more powerful and, being more loyal, are of greater help to a king in trouble. The people outside the fortified towns are common to the king and the enemy. [When they are conquered by the enemy, they transfer their allegiance.]   {8.1.24-27}

Kautilya disagrees. For the fort, the treasury and the army all depend on the people; so do the water reservoirs. All economic activity has its source in the countryside. Bravery, stability and cleverness are also found among the country people. They are also more numerous. If there is no populated territory, remote forts in mountains and islands would remain unoccupied [and unguarded.]   {8.1.28-31}

However, [Kautilya adds] if a country consists predominantly of agriculturists, the calamity [to the few fortifications] would be more serious. Conversely, in a country inhabited mostly by martial people, calamities to the [comparatively more limited] country territory would be more serious.

{8.1.32}

THE FORT AND THE TREASURY

Pisuna thinks that a calamity to the treasury is more serious than that of the fort, arguing that the building, maintenance and repair of forts depend on finance. With wealth, one's own people, allies and the people of the enemy can be kept under control; the people inside an enemy's fort can be tempted to defect; those in the enemy's countryside can be incited to vacate the land; and the army can be managed better. It is possible to remove the treasury in times of danger but not the fort.

Kautilya disagrees. [A fort has many uses.] The treasury is kept safe there and the army is well protected in it. It is from the fort that secret war is waged, one's own people controlled, allies received and enemy troops and jungle tribes kept at bay. In the absence of a fort, the treasury will fall into the hands of enemies. It is well-known that those with forts are not destroyed.   {8.1.33-40}

THE TREASURY AND THE ARMY

Kaunapadanta considers a calamity to the army to be worse than a calamity to the treasury. One is dependent on the army for controlling allies and enemies, winning over an enemy's army and reinforcing one's own. In the absence of an army, the treasury is sure to be lost, whereas, even without finance, an army can be used not only to collect raw material and agricultural produce but also to seize enemy land. [Eventually,] the treasury can be replenished by the army. Being close to the king, the army is like the minister [and a calamity to it has to be ranked as high as that of a minister.]

Kautilya disagrees. It is the army which is dependent on finance. If not paid, [the soldiers] either go over to the enemy or kill the king. Finance is necessary to undertake any state endeavour and is the chief means for both *dharma* [righteous duty] and *kama* [enjoyment].

[However,] Kautilya adds that the relative importance of the army and the treasury may depend on the circumstances. The time, the place and the nature of the task determine which is more important. For, the army is [sometimes] the means of acquiring and protecting the treasury. But the treasury is [always] the means of acquiring wealth as well as the army. [On the whole,] the calamity to the treasury is more serious since it affects all others. {8.1.41-52}

THE ARMY AND THE ALLY

Between these two, Vatavyadhi says that a calamity to the latter is more serious. An ally, though far away, helps even without being paid. He repels the enemy in the rear, the allies of the enemy, the enemies in the front and the unsubdued tribes. He also helps the king with money, troops and land in times of trouble.

Kautilya disagrees. When one has an army, the ally continues to be friendly and [even] the enemy becomes a friend. However, when there is work that can be done equally well by [his own] army and [that of] the ally, the king should choose the appropriate instrument depending on the circumstances [the time, the place and the nature of the action] and on whichever is more profitable. [But the king must remember that] no ally can be relied upon in cases of speedy expedition, internal rebellion or subduing jungle tribes. In case both the king and the enemy suffer from calamities or when the enemy grows stronger, an ally [only] looks to his own interests [and maintains the alliance only if it is profitable to him.] {8.1.53-59}

[To summarise, Kautilya generally agrees with the accepted teaching that a calamity of a constituent higher in the order is more serious than that affecting one lower. There are, however, some important qualifications. The relative importance of the countryside and the forts depends on whether there is a population balance between the two; a calamity to a weaker constituent is a more serious one. Though the treasury is almost always more important, there may be circumstances when a threat to the army should be considered more serious. Kings must also remember that five of the other six constituents, excepting the ally, are domestic and hence more under his control; allies are not to be considered reliable in all circumstances.]

PARTIAL CALAMITY

[A constituent element does not become totally useless just because it is affected.] Depending on the particular nature of the calamity, the extent, loyalty and strength of the other [serviceable] parts of the same element may be enough to accomplish a task.   {8.1.61}

Even if the King cannot save the whole of a constituent element, he shall try to save a part.   {9.7.48}

SIMULTANEITY

When two elements are affected equally, they should be judged according to whether the damage is increasing or decreasing, so long as neither of them affects any other element.   {8.1.62}

[When two elements are equally and simultaneously affected, that which is likely to suffer increasing damage should be considered more serious. However, if the calamity to one element is likely to affect other elements, then that should be considered more serious.]

ORDER OF PRIORITY

[The following verses in the chapter on the priorities of a king about to go on a military expedition but faced with a wrong acquisition on one side and uncertainty on the other (see X.vi) are relevant.]

The conqueror shall save from misfortune, one by one, the constituents of his state, in order of their importance; for, it is better that the ally remains in danger but not the army; likewise the army but not the treasury. If the constituent as a whole cannot be saved, at least parts shall be rescued; i.e. in the case of the army, the more numerous or the more loyal troops shall be saved leaving out the sharp and the greedy; in the case of the treasury the most valuable or the most useful shall be saved. The least important [constituents or parts of constituents] shall be saved by peace, inactivity or a dual policy and the most important by other means [seeking help, preparing for or actually waging war.]   {9.7.46-50}

[Lastly,] a calamity which threatens to destroy all other elements shall be considered as [the most] serious, irrespective of what position the element affected occupies in the list of priorities.   {8.1.63}

II.iv

CALAMITIES OF THE POPULATION

[A variety of calamities can afflict the population of a state, most of them living in the countryside, outside the fortified towns. The sufferings of the people could be due to Acts of God or men. Acts of God are mentioned in the text in a variety of chapters {4.3, 8.4 and 9.7}; of these, {4.3} has the most extensive treatment. Calamities brought about by men are more numerous. The army (either one's own or the enemy's), or those near the king (such as his favourite wife or a mistress or a prince), can harass the population; there may be civil strife among the people or among the members of the royal family; the king and the people may become lax, giving themselves over to pleasure. There may be marauding fighting units or oppression by chiefs, high-ranking ministers and customs officials. Traders may make exorbitant profits at the cost of the people. Common lands may be seized by nobles. Highway robbers and jungle tribes may harass the population. Any of these affects the welfare and contentment of the people and thereby weakens the nation. In line with his habit of exhausting all possibilities of a subject, Kautilya also adds his advice on two topics: the effect of calamities on common people and on chiefs; and the target population for relief works.]

ACTS OF GOD

GENERAL

Calamities due to acts of God are: fire, floods, diseases and epidemics, and famine.   {8.4.1}

Other calamities of divine origin[1] are: rats, wild animals, snakes and evil spirits. It is the duty of the king to protect the people from all these calamities.   {4.3.1-2; 9.7.82}

Whenever danger threatens, the King shall protect all those afflicted like a father [protects his children] and shall organize continuous [day and night] prayers with oblations.   {4.3.42,43}

All such calamities can be overcome by propitiating Gods and Brahmins. When there is drought or excessive rain or visitations of evil, the rites prescribed in the *Atharva Veda* and those recommended by ascetics shall be performed. Therefore, experts in occult practices and holy ascetics shall be honoured and thus encouraged to stay in the country so that they can counteract the calamities of divine origin.   {9.7.83,84; 4.3.44}

Worship with offerings, oblations and recitals of benediction shall be organized on full moon and new moon days [against different calamities as follows]:

Calamity	Worship offered to
fire	Agni [God of fire]
flood	rivers
rats	rats
wild animals	mountains
snakes	Naga [the cobra divinity]
evil spirits	Chaityas

Offerings made to Chaityas may include umbrellas, food, small flags and goatmeat.   {4.3.5,10,26,33,38,41}

FIRE

Villagers shall do their cooking during the summer months outside their houses. They shall always have the [ten] firefighting implements.[2]

{4.3.3,4}

[The responsibilities of the municipal administration and the citizens for preventing outbreaks of fire in the more crowded cities are given in detail in {2.36.15-25} (see VII.xi, Civic Responsibility and Municipal Regulations); the verses also include a set of punishments. Verses {1.20.4-8}, also on Acts of God, deal with occult remedies for warding off dangers to the Royal Palace from fire, snakes and poison.]

FLOODS AND DROUGHT

A drought is worse than too much rain, because drought destroys livelihood.

{8.2.25}

During the rainy season, villagers living near river banks shall move to higher ground; they shall keep a collection of wooden planks, bamboo and boats.

Persons carried away by floods shall be rescued using gourds, skin bags, tree trunks, canoes, boats and thick ropes. Owners of canoes shall be punished if they do not try to save someone in danger.

Persons learned in the Vedas and experts in occult practices shall use prayers and incantations against [excessive] rain. [Conversely,] Indra, the Ganges, the mountains and the God of the Sea shall be worshipped in times of drought. {4.3.6-12}

HUMAN AND ANIMAL DISEASES AND EPIDEMICS

The following shall be called upon to counteract diseases and epidemics affecting human beings: physicians by using medicines, ascetics by purificatory or expiatory rites and experts by occult means. Making oblations to or organising night festivals in honour of Gods, worship of the God of the Sea, milking cows in cremation grounds and burning effigies are other methods of averting the danger of epidemics. {4.3.13-15}

In case of diseases or epidemics affecting cattle, purificatory rites of their sheds and special worship of the appropriate Gods shall be performed. {4.3.16}

FAMINE

The methods of counteracting the effects of famine are:
- distribute to the public, on concessional terms, seeds and food from the royal stores;
- undertake food-for-work programmes such as building forts or irrigation works;
- share out the royal food stocks;
- commandeer for public distribution private stocks of food;
- seek the help of friendly kings;
- shift the affected population to a different region;
- encourage [temporary] migration to another country;
- move the entire population [with the King and Court] to a region or country with abundant harvest or near the sea, lakes or rivers;
- supplement the harvest with additional cultivation of grain, vegetables, roots and fruits, by fishing and by hunting deer, cattle, birds and wild animals. {4.3.17-20}

RATS, LOCUSTS, ETC.

In case of danger from rats, locusts, birds or insects, the appropriate animals [e.g. cats, mongoose] shall be let loose and [these predators] protected from being killed or harassed by dogs. Poisoned grain may be strewn around and purificatory rites may be performed by experts. Or, the rat tax [a quota of dead rats to be brought in by each one] may be fixed. {4.3.21,23-25,27}

WILD ANIMALS

In case of danger from marauding wild animals (such as tigers, crocodiles, herds of animals, or flocks of birds) the following methods may be adopted:
- leave poisoned carcasses of adult or young animals;
- get hunters and fowlers, hidden in pits or cages, to trap or kill them;
- send men, suitably armed and armoured, to kill them.

Failure to try to save someone threatened by a wild animal is a punishable offence. The reward for saving someone is the same, i.e. 12 panas.

{4.3,28-32,34}

SNAKES AND AQUATIC DANGERS

In case of snake bite, an expert in poisons shall be called to apply his medicines and incantations. The people shall join together in [finding and] killing poisonous snakes and dangerous things living in water. Experts in *Atharvaveda* shall perform the necessary rites [to ward off the dangers].

{4.3.35-37,39}

EVIL SPIRITS

Experts in *Atharvaveda* and in occult sciences shall perform rites of exorcism.

{4.3.40}

RELATIVE SERIOUSNESS

[Which of the divine calamities are more serious than others?] Some teachers say that fire is more serious than floods because destruction by fire is irremediable, consuming all; one can escape from floods and its damage can be alleviated. Kautilya, however, considers floods to be more dangerous because it destroys hundreds of villages while fire destroys [only] one village, or a part of it.

Some teachers say that disease and epidemics are worse than famine, because pestilence brings all state activities to a stop with men falling ill and dying but during famine all work does not stop and it is still possible to collect revenue in gold or commodities or cattle.

Kautilya disagrees. Pestilence [usually] devastates only a region [of the country] and remedies can be found for the disease. Famine, on the other hand, affects the whole country and deprives the people of their livelihood

{8.4.2-8}

[The reasoning is: floods and famine, which affect agricultural production, the livelihood of people and state revenue are more serious than fire and disease, the effects of which tend to be more local. The other adversities, like rats, etc. have consequences even more limited.]

CALAMITIES DUE TO ACTS OF MEN

DEPRADATIONS OF ARMIES

Some teachers consider harassment by one's own army to be more serious than that by an enemy's army; for, one's own army harasses people by excessive violence or exactions and cannot be remedied. When an enemy's army goes on the rampage, one can fight, escape by flight or neutralise it by a treaty.

Kautilya disagrees, saying: harassment by one's own army can be countered by winning over or destroying the leaders; [in any case] such harassment affects [only] a part of the country. Harassment by the enemy's army [not only] affects the whole country but also ruins it by plunder, slaughter, burning and destruction. {8.4.13-15}

INTERNAL STRIFE

Some teachers say that civil strife among the people is worse than quarrels among members of the royal family. Civil strife, creating a split among the people, invites attacks by enemies. When there is a quarrel within the royal family, the people benefit by double food and wages as well as exemption from taxes [by each side wooing them].

Kautilya disagrees. Quarrels among the people can be resolved by winning over the leaders or by removing the cause of the quarrel; people fighting among themselves help the king by their mutual rivalry. Conflicts [for power] within the royal family, on the other hand, bring about harassment and destruction to the people and double the exertion is required to end such conflicts. {8.4.16-20}

DECADENCE

[Which is worse—decadence of the people or decadence of the king?] Some teachers say that it is worse having a people given over to pleasures because they bring three-fold (past, present and future) ruin to production. [They do not care for crops sown in the past; they do not sow crops at the right time; and they do not prepare the land for future sowing.] A decadent king, [at least] fosters artisans, actors, reciters, courtesans and traders.

Kautilya disagrees. People taking to pleasures consume little; they do so to relax from the fatigue of work and they get back to work again after relaxation. A decadent king, on the other hand, oppresses the people by demanding gifts, seizing what he wants and grabbing for himself and his favourites the produce of the country [i.e. the king and his coterie consume more than their due share thus considerably impoverishing the treasury and the people].   {8.4.21-23}

HARASSMENT BY QUEENS, MISTRESSES AND PRINCES

Some teachers say that a prince harasses more by demanding gifts and seizing for himself and his friends the production of the country; a favourite queen or mistress is [only] interested in her own pleasures.

Kautilya disagrees. A [wayward] prince can be kept in check with the help of ministers and the *purohita*. The king's favourite cannot be controlled because she is [stubbornly] childish and [usually] associates with harmful persons.   {8.4.24-26}

REBELLIOUS GUILDS OR CHIEFS

Some teachers say that, between a rebellious [fighting] guild and a rebellious chief, the guild is worse. A guild harasses the people by robbery and looting and is more difficult to suppress because of larger numbers; a rebellious chief [only reduces revenue] by favouring some and obstructing production by others.

Kautilya disagrees. A guild, which behaves as a unit, can be subdued by capturing its leader or a part of the unit. A rebellious chief is [usually] haughty and oppresses people by destroying lives and property.

{8.4.27-30}

HARASSMENT BY IMPORTANT MINISTERS

[The two highest ranking ministers are the *Samahartr* or Chancellor and the *Samnidhatr* or the Treasurer.] Some teachers say that oppression by the Treasurer is worse because he harasses by finding fault with whatever is done and levies fines [which he pockets?]. The Chancellor, on the other hand, cannot do much harm since he is supervised by an [audit] bureau and can only enjoy what is legitimately assigned to him.

Kautilya disagrees [by pointing out that the avenues open to the Chancellor for harassing the people are more.] The Treasurer can only appropriate what is brought into the treasury by others. But the Chancellor collects his own revenue first and then he may collect the king's revenue or even let it go to ruin; he can do as he pleases with other people's property.

{8.4.31-33}

DISHONEST CUSTOMS OFFICIALS AND TRADERS

Some teachers say that frontier [customs] officers harass the people by levying excessive duties or permit robbers [by colluding with them] to attack trade routes; traders, on the other hand, bring prosperity to the people through trade.

Kautilya disagrees. It is the frontier officer who promotes trade, whereas traders form cartels in order to raise prices [for the goods they sell] or lower them [for the goods they buy]; they are profiteers making one hundred panas on one pana or one hundred measures on one measure [of grain].

{8.4.34-36}

SEIZURE OF COMMON LAND

[Should the king allow common land to be seized by a nobleman or let it be used as pasture? In either case it is not available to the people for cultivation.] Some teachers say that it is better to use it as pasture. A person of noble birth occupying land makes it productive; he [also] supplies men for the army. It is [therefore] difficult to retrieve, for fear that the owner might create trouble. Pasture land, being suited for agriculture, is fit to be reclaimed.

Kautilya disagrees. Though highly productive, land seized by a noble should be liberated because he might [become too powerful and] cause difficulties. It is not necessary to convert pasture land held for grazing cattle, since it enriches the treasury and produces animals for transport. The [only] exception is when such pasture impedes sowing of crops [in other cultivable lands.] {8.4.37-40}

MARAUDERS

[Which are more dangerous—highway robbers or jungle tribes?] Some teachers hold highway robbers to be more dangerous because they ambush and attack people at night, steal hundreds of thousands of panas and make chiefs angry [by creating problems for them.] Tribes, on the other hand, operate in [uninhabited] jungles or remote frontier regions, move about openly and harm only a part of the country.

Kautilya disagrees. Robbers rob only the negligent, are few in numbers, and are [relatively] weak; it is also easy to know [their whereabouts] and capture them. Unsubdued jungle tribes live in their own territory, are more numerous, brave, fight in daylight and, with their ability to seize and destroy countries, behave like kings. {8.4.41-43}

DANGERS FROM FORESTS

Forests with many animals [such as deer], produce abundant meat and skins; the animals [which eat naturally growing grass] do not need to be fed specially with fodder; they are easy to control. Elephant forests are the reverse; the elephants are difficult to capture and tame, and rogue elephants can cause havoc.   {8.4.44,45}

> [Kautilya then examines two special aspects of calamities which can affect the population—the relative harm when such calamities afflict the people or their chiefs and then the choice of helping only natives or both natives and aliens during calamitous times.]

EFFECT ON COMMON PEOPLE AND ON CHIEFS

[Some teachers consider a calamity to the common people to be more serious than one affecting chiefs because:] When common people are affected, [all] state undertakings come to a standstill; when chiefs are affected, they can only obstruct the work of the state [but not totally stop them].

Kautilya disagrees. The loss of common men can be made good, because there are so many of them. Not so the loss of chiefs, for they are few; one in a thousand, maybe not even one, has leadership qualities. Common men look up to such men because of their courage and wisdom.

{8.4.9-12}

RELIEF MEASURES

In times of calamities it is better to direct the relief activities towards one's own people, by giving them grains, cattle, money and forest produce. This will sustain them through the calamity. The help given to aliens or the people of the enemy can bring harm [later].   {8.4.46,47}

> [To summarize Kautilya's views on oppression and harassment of people: power conflicts among members of the royal family is worse than civil strife among the people; a decadent king is worse than a decadent people; a favourite queen or mistress of the king causes more damage than a wayward prince; a haughty and rebellious chief destroys life and property more than a rebellious guild. The harassment of an administrator is worse than that of a revenue collector and profiteering traders are worse than corrupt customs officials. It is better to let fallow land be used as pasture than let it be seized by noblemen. Protecting people from robbers is less important

than subduing remote forest tribes because the tribes can challenge
the authority of the king. A harassing army, even one's own, should
be subdued by destroying its leaders. The first preference in relief
works is to one's own people. At all times, courageous and wise
chiefs should be cherished.]

PUNISHMENTS

Failure to save someone carried away by floods, though having a canoe.	12 panas	{4.3.9}
Catching or killing predatory animals; not restraining dogs from harassing them.[3]	12 panas	{4.3.22}
Not trying to save someone threatened by a wild animal.	12 panas	{4.3.31}

II.v

ON VICES

We shall now consider [people's] vices because they are [the cause of] personal adversities. Vices are due to ignorance and indiscipline; an unlearned man does not perceive the injurious consequences of his vices.

{8.3.1-3}

ANGER AND DESIRE

Three kinds of vices are due to anger and four due to uncontrolled desire. Of the two, anger is worse because it knows no boundaries. It is well known that angry kings have often been killed by popular fury, whereas greedy and lustful kings have perished by disease, poverty or enemy action.

{8.3.4-7}

Bharadvaja disagrees [and is of the view that anger and desire are good things. He says:] Anger provides the proper motivation for a righteous man enabling him to put down enemies, avenge insults and cause fear in people. And, resort to anger is always needed to put down sin. Likewise, desire [is the motivating force] for attainment of success, reconciliation, generosity and endearing oneself to all. Desire is always necessary for one who wants to enjoy the fruits of his labour. {8.3.8-12}

Kautilya disagrees. Anger makes one the object of hatred, creates enemies and brings suffering on oneself. Excessive greed and lust bring about humiliation, loss of wealth and association with undesirable persons like thieves, gamblers, hunters, singers and musicians. [While both have bad consequences,] being hated is worse than humiliation; whereas one humiliated is held in thrall by his own people and by enemies, a hated one is destroyed. [Likewise,] making enemies is worse than losing one's wealth; the latter [only] causes financial distress while the former endangers life [itself]. Suffering on account of vices is worse than associating with undesirable persons; the latter can be got rid of in a moment while vices cause suffering for a long time. Hence, [on every count] anger is a more serious evil. {8.3.13-22}

ANGER

The three kinds of vices arising from anger are: inflicting verbal injury, causing injury to another's property and inflicting physical injury. Injuring another's property includes: not giving what is due, taking away unjustly, destroying it and neglecting entrusted property.

[Which is worse—abuse and insult, violation of property or physical violence?] Vishalaksha says that verbal injury is worse than destruction of property for 'a brave man retaliates when spoken to harshly; the arrows of abuse [and insult] which lie embedded in the heart inflame the spirit and affect the senses'.

Kautilya disagrees [on the grounds that] while gifts of money can assuage the pain of the darts of speech, destroying property means depriving another of his livelihood. {8.3.23-29}

The followers of Parasara say that violation of property is a worse evil than physical injury. [In their view,] *dharma* and *kama* are both dependent on *artha*, which binds the world together.

Kautilya disagrees, saying: 'no one would want to lose his own life even for a large sum of money.' [In any case,] one who inflicts physical injury is likely to suffer the same fate from others. {8.3.30-36}

[Therefore, causing physical injury is worse than injury to property which, in turn, is worse than verbal injury.]

EXCESSIVE DESIRE

The four vices springing from excessive desire are addiction to hunting, gambling, women and drink. {8.3.38}

[We now consider the relative seriousness of these vices.]

Pisuna says that, of hunting and gambling, hunting is a worse vice; for, many are the dangers of hunting. One may fall into [the hands of] robbers or enemies, [be trampled by] wild elephants, [be engulfed by] forest fire, or lose one's way. One may suffer from hunger and thirst and even lose one's life. In gambling, however, an expert like Jayatsena or Duryodhana always wins. {8.3.39-41}

Kautilya disagrees. Of the two parties [in gambling] one has to lose, as we know from the stories of Nala and Yudhishtira. The same wager won by one is, to the loser, a fish-hook which becomes a source of enmity. A gambler never knows how much wealth he has got, tries to enjoy wealth which he has not got and loses it before he can enjoy it. Being irregular in his habits, he contracts stomach, urinary and bowel disorders. [On the other hand, there are some good points about hunting.] The physical exercise helps to gets rid of [not only] phlegm and bile, [but also] fat by sweating it out. Skill in hitting moving and stationary targets is acquired. Knowledge of animals, when they are angry, afraid or at rest, is gained. There is only occasional need for walking [long distances]. {8.3.42-46}

Kaunapadanta considers gambling to be worse than lusting after women. [A gambler's addiction is total.] He plays continuously, [during the day and] at night by lamplight, and even when his mother is dying. He gets angry when somebody talks to him when he is in trouble. [On the other hand,] conversation on *dharma* and *kama* is possible with one infatuated with women, when he is bathing, dressing or eating. Women could also be useful in influencing the king towards good things. A bad woman can be got rid of by clandestine methods or by accusing her of being diseased.   {8.3.47-51}

Kautilya disagrees. A gambler can be reformed but not so a man who lusts after women; [the evils of lust are:] failure to see reality, neglect of work, the loss of *dharma* and material wealth due to not doing things at the right time, loss of political acumen and addiction to drink.

{8.3.52-54}

Vatavyadhi considers lust worse than addiction to drink. 'For, many are the dangers arising from the foolishness of women, as has been explained in the section on the women of the palace.[1] Drink, on the other hand, gives pleasure to the senses, helps to show affection to others and is a way of honouring followers [by drinking with them]. It helps to relieve the fatigue caused by work.'   {8.3.55-57}

Kautilya disagrees. In having relations with women of the house, [there are] two advantages—begetting children and self-protection. If one lusts after outside women, or those with whom relationship is forbidden, then one loses these advantages. It is the same with drink. There are also [other adverse] effects of drink: loss of one's senses, acting like a madman, loss of health to the extent of looking like a corpse even when alive, shamelessness in exposing oneself, separation from good people, association with harmful ones, [excessive] indulgence in music and singing, throwing away one's wealth as well as loss of learning, intellect, strength and good friends.   {8.3.58-61}

[Kautilya continues:] Of gambling and addiction to drink, gambling is worse. Gambling with one's property and betting on animal races leads to a win for one and a loss to the other. The consequence is that factions are formed and strife ensues. Particularly in the case of oligarchies and confederacies of kings resembling oligarchies,[2] gambling promotes factionalism and the [ruling] groups are thus destroyed. Gambling is the most evil among vices, because it destroys the ruling class by depriving them of their ability to govern. {8.3.62-64}

[To summarize: subject to the qualification that gambling is most dangerous in cases where there is more than one entity sharing power, the vice with the most serious consequences is addiction to drink, followed by, lusting after women, gambling and, lastly, hunting.]

Excessive desire leads to the cultivation of evil things while anger causes the abandonment of good things. Since both result in a multitude of evils, both are classified as calamities [affecting men]. A king should hence learn to control his senses by associating himself with [wise] elders. By exercising self-control, he can free himself of excessive desire and anger, the starting points of all calamities which [eventually] destroy the inherited kingdom. {8.3.65-66}

Part III

THE KING

"The king and his rule encapsulate [all] the constituents of the state."

{8.2.1}

"A king who observes his duty of protecting his people justly, according to law, goes to heaven, unlike one who does not protect his people, or inflicts unjust punishment."

{3.1.41}

"A king who flouts the teachings of the *Dharmashastras* and the *Arthashastra*, ruins the kingdom by his own injustice."

{8.2.12}

[In the *Arthashastra*, 'King' is often used to signify the state, since he embodies all the constituents. In this translation, the two are used interchangeably, depending on the context. The seven sections of this Part deal only with the personal aspects of kingship.]

III.i

THE TRAINING OF A FUTURE KING

THE IMPORTANCE OF SELF DISCIPLINE

The three sciences [philosophy, the three Vedas and economics] are dependent [for their development] on the science of government. [For, without a just administration, no pursuit of learning or avocation would be possible.] [Government by] Rule of Law, which alone can guarantee security of life and the welfare of the people, is, in turn, dependent on [the] self-discipline [of the king].   {1.5.1-2}

Discipline is of two kinds—inborn and acquired. [There must be an innate capacity for self-discipline for the reasons given below.] Instruction and training can promote discipline only in a person capable of benefiting from them; people incapable of [natural] self-discipline do not benefit. Learning imparts discipline only to those who have the following mental faculties—obedience to a teacher, desire and ability to learn, capacity to retain what is learnt, understanding what is learnt, reflecting on it, and [finally] ability to make inferences by deliberating on the knowledge acquired. Those who are devoid of such mental faculties are not benefited [by any amount of training.] One who will be a king should acquire discipline and follow it strictly in life by learning the sciences from authoritative teachers.   {1.5.3-6}

THE TRAINING OF A PRINCE

A prince [who is likely to become a king] should learn the alphabet and arithmetic as soon as the tonsure ceremony is performed [in the third year after birth]. [After a few years] when the ceremony of the sacred thread is performed [and the Prince enters the *ashrama* of a *Brahmachari*], he should learn philosophy and the three Vedas from authoritative teachers, economics from the heads of [various government] departments, and the science of government from [not only] theoretical exponents of political science [but also] from practising politicians. He should remain a *brahmachari* [a celibate student] till he is sixteen. He should then have the second tonsure ceremony and get married.   {1.5.7-10}

[A prince's education does not stop with his reaching manhood and getting married.] With a view to improving his self-discipline, he should always associate with learned elders, for in them alone has discipline its firm roots. [His training programme shall be as follows.] During the first part of the day, he shall be trained in the martial arts—with elephants, horses, chariots and weapons [as an infantryman]. In the latter part of the day, he shall listen to *Itihasas*.[1] In the remaining part of the day and at night, he shall prepare new lessons [for the next day], revise old lessons and listen repeatedly to things which he had not understood clearly.

For, a [trained] intellect is the result of learning [by hearing]; from intellect ensues *yoga* [successful application]; from *yoga* comes self-possession. This is what is meant by efficiency in acquiring knowledge.

{1.5.11-13,15,16}

Only a king who is wise, disciplined, devoted to a just governing of the subjects and [ever] conscious of the welfare of all beings will enjoy the earth unopposed.   {1.5.17}

III.ii

SELF-CONTROL

RENOUNCING THE SIX ENEMIES

The sole aim of all branches of knowledge is to inculcate restraint over the senses.   {1.6.3}

Self-control, which is the basis of knowledge and discipline, is acquired by giving up lust, anger, greed, conceit, arrogance and foolhardiness. Living in accordance with the *shastras* means avoiding over-indulgence in all pleasures of [the senses, i.e.] hearing, touch, sight, taste and smell.

{1.6.1,2}

A king who has no self-control and gives himself up to excessive indulgence in pleasures will soon perish, even if he is the ruler of all four corners of the earth.   {1.6.4}

[Verses {1.6.5-10} contain examples of kings who were destroyed for falling prey to one or the other of the vices mentioned above:[1] - Dandakya, a Bhoja king and Karala, a Videha king, for having lusted after Brahmin girls; Janamejaya and Talajangha for showing anger against Brahmins; the son of Ila and Ajabindu of the Suviras, out of greed; Ravana and Duryodhana for refusing to restore another's wife or a portion of the kingdom, out of conceit about their own invulnerability; Dambodhbhava and Arjuna of the Haihayas because of their arrogance; and Vatapi and Vrishni (against Agastya and Dvaipayana respectively) because of their foolhardiness.]

All these, and many others, lacking self-control and falling prey to the six enemies [lust, anger, greed, conceit, arrogance and foolhardiness] perished with their kinsmen and kingdoms. On the other hand, kings like Jamadagnya and Ambarisha, who had conquered their senses, long enjoyed their kingship on earth.   {from 1.6.4-12}

RAJARISHI—A WISE KING

A *rajarishi* [a king, wise like a sage] is one who:
- has self-control, having conquered the [inimical temptations] of the senses,

- cultivates the intellect by association with elders,
- keeps his eyes open through spies,
- is ever active in promoting the security and welfare of the people,
- ensures the observance [by the people] of their *dharma* by authority and example,
- improves his own discipline by [continuing his] learning in all branches of knowledge and
- endears himself to his people by enriching them and doing good to them.

Such a disciplined king should:
- keep away from another's wife,
- not covet another's property,
- practise *ahimsa* [non-violence towards all living things],
- avoid daydreaming, capriciousness, falsehood and extravagance, and
- avoid association with harmful persons and indulging in [harmful] activities.

There is no need for such a king to deprive himself of all sensual pleasures [and lead a life of total austerity] so long as he does not infringe his *dharma* or harm his own material well-being.

[Some teachers say that] the three objectives of human endeavour [*dharma, artha* and *kama*] are interdependent and should be pursued equally. Excessive importance given to any one brings harm not only to that objective but to others as well.

Kautilya, however, says: *artha* (sound economics) is the most important; for, *dharma* and *kama* are both dependent on it.

A *rajarishi* shall always respect those councillors and *purohitas* who warn him of the dangers of transgressing the limits of good conduct, reminding him sharply (as with a goad) of the times prescribed for various duties and caution him even when he errs in private.   {1.7.1-8}

> [Only a just king commands the loyalty of the people. The subjects of
> a just king attacked by another will follow him until death, even if he
> is weak. On the other hand, when a strong but unjust king is attacked,
> his people will either topple him or go over to the enemy {7.5.9,10} in
> X.i); see also {7.13.12} in X.viii. The *rajadharma* also includes just
> behaviour towards conquered kings {7.16.24-28} in X.iv and peoples
> {13.5.3-21} in XI.xi. A disloyal vassal may be got rid of but the
> conqueror shall not covet the slain king's wealth, sons or wives and,
> instead, give them appropriate positions.]

III.iii

DUTIES OF A KING

If the king is energetic, his subjects will be equally energetic. If he is slack [and lazy in performing his duties] the subjects will also be lax and, thereby, eat into his wealth. Besides, a lazy king will easily fall into the hands of his enemies. Hence, the king should himself always be energetic.

{1.19.1-5}

He shall divide the day and the night, each, into eight periods of one and a half hours[1] and perform his duties as follows:

Day:

First 1 1/2 hours after sunrise	Receive reports on defence, revenue, and expenditure.
Second 1 1/2 hours after sunrise	Public audiences, to hear petitions of city and country people.
Third 1 1/2 hours after sunrise	(Personal—bath, meals, study).
1 1/2 hours before noon	Receive revenue and tributes; appoint ministers and other high officials and allot tasks to them.
First 1 1/2 hours after noon	Write letters and dispatches; confer with councillors; receive secret information from spies.
Second 1 1/2 hours after noon	(Personal—recreation, time for contemplation).
Third 1 1/2 hours after noon	Inspect and review forces.
1 1/2 hours before sunset	Consult with Chief of Defence.

The day shall end with evening prayers.

Night:

First 1 1/2 hours after sunset	Interview with secret agents.
Second 1 1/2 hours after sunset	(Personal—bath, meals, study).

3 hours before and first 1 1/2 hours after midnight	(Retire to the bed chamber to the sound of music; sleep.)
Second 1 1/2 hours after midnight	(After waking to the sound of music, meditate on political matters and on the work to be done.)
Third 1 1/2 hours after midnight	Consult with councillors; send out spies.
1 1/2 hours before sunrise	(Religious, household and personal duties; meetings with his teacher, adviser on rituals, *purohita*, personal physician, chief cook and astrologer.)

At daybreak, he shall circumambulate a cow, its calf and a bull, and then proceed to his court.　　　　　　　　　　　　　　　　{1.19.6,9-24}

[A king is, therefore, allowed 10 1/2 hours out of twenty four as his personal time—three hours for bath and meals, one and a half hours for recreation and six hours at night, during which he can sleep for four and a half hours. The hour and a half before sunrise is to be spent on palace affairs and personal needs. Out of the twelve hours each day to be spent on state duties, one and a half hours are to be devoted to public audiences, three hours to defence, three hours to secret consultations and intelligence and the balance four and a half hours on the administration of the state.]

The [above is only a suggestion and the] king may, in accordance with his capacity, alter the timetable and carry out his duties.　　{1.19.25}

When in court, he shall not make petitioners wait at the door [but attend to them promptly himself]. When a king makes himself inaccessible to his people, and he is seen [only] by those near him, wrong decisions are bound to be made; the people will become angry and may go over to the enemy.
{1.19.26-28}

A king shall, therefore, attend to the people in the order given below, except in cases where a matter [concerning one lower in the order] is more urgent or more important: gods and deities, hermits, heretics, Brahmins learned in the Vedas, cows, sacred places, minors, the aged, the sick, the handicapped, the helpless and women.　　　　　　　　　{1.19.29}

He should hear at once all urgent matters and not postpone them; for, postponement makes them more difficult and [sometimes] even impossible to settle.　　　　　　　　　　　　　　　　　　　　　　{1.19.30}

He should decide on the affairs of persons learned in the Vedas and of ascetics with due respect to them. Such hearings shall be conducted in the room with the sacred fire, and in the presence of his teacher and the high priest. He should be particularly careful with ascetics and those expert in magic, for such people are easy to anger. Their affairs should never be heard alone but in the presence of those learned in the three Vedas.

{1.19.31-32}

[Brahmins take religious vows, perform sacrificial rituals, offer a fee to those who perform them and undergo initiation ceremonies.] Likewise, for a king, the vow is readiness to action, the ritual is the satisfactory performance of his duties, impartiality towards all the reward that he can offer and his coronation the initiation into a [lifelong] vocation. {1.19.33}

In the happiness of his subjects lies his happiness; in their welfare his welfare. He shall not consider as good only that which pleases him but treat as beneficial to him whatever pleases his subjects. {1.19.34}

Hence the king shall be ever active in the management of the economy. The root of wealth is [economic] activity and lack of it [brings] material distress. In the absence of [fruitful economic] activity, both current prosperity and future growth will be destroyed. A king can achieve the desired objectives and abundance of riches by undertaking [productive] economic activity. {1.19.35-36}

III.iv

THE KING'S SECURITY

[In addition to advice on the personal security of the king and the means of protecting the royal residence, this section also contains the precautions to be taken against danger of assassination by close family members such as queens or princes.]

THE ROYAL RESIDENCE

The king shall have his royal residence built on a site recommended by experts in the science of buildings. The complex shall be surrounded by ramparts and a moat and be provided with [guarded] gates. There shall be many halls [for different purposes, as described below].

The king's own chambers shall be built in the centre of the complex, with emergency exits for use in cases of sudden danger. Any of the following models can be adopted:

– a protected treasury [in three underground floors];[1]
– the middle of a labyrinth with concealed passages in walls;
– an underground chamber (connected by a stairway hidden in the wall to the living quarters above) having a concealed underground passage leading to a nearby shrine, the exit from which is hidden by a wooden image of a god;
– with an emergency exit built in an upper storey with a stairway hidden in a wall, a hollow pillar or behind a concealed trap door.

The type of construction can be varied [depending on actual conditions] so long as the need to safeguard oneself against attack by palace intimates is kept in mind.   {1.20.1-3}

[Kautilya describes a number of methods, mostly of an occult nature, for averting dangers like fire, snakes and poisons in the grounds outside the palace. Verses {1.20.4-8} have not been translated in full.]

The residential quarters shall be protected against snakes and other poisons; plants which deter snakes shall be planted; snake-killers like peacocks and mongooses and birds which give warning of the presence of poison (like the parrot, shrike, heron and partridge) shall be reared.

{from 1.20.4-9}

OTHER BUILDINGS IN THE PALACE COMPLEX

Behind the king's own chambers, there shall be built the following: the residences of the royal ladies, the maternity ward, the infirmary, water tanks and groves. The residences of the princes and princesses shall be beyond [this group of structures].   {1.20.10-11}

The following shall be built in front of the king's chamber: the king's dressing room, the council chamber, the audience hall and the hall for the education of princes. Palace guards shall be stationed in the spaces between the buildings.   {1.20.12-13,1.21.3}

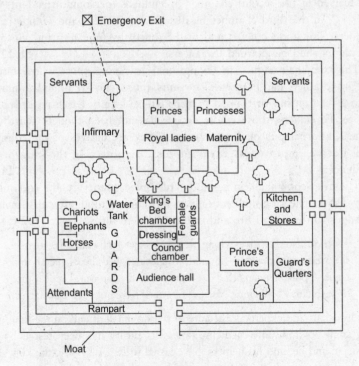

Fig 4. The Palace Complex
{1.20.1, 2, 10-13}

MOVEMENT CONTROL

Everyone [in the residential complex] shall live in the quarters assigned him and shall not move to the quarters of another. No one staying inside shall establish contact with any outsider.

Every object which comes into the palace complex or goes out of it shall be examined, its arrival and departure recorded and sent to its destination [only] after affixing the [appropriate] seal.   {1.20.22-23}

THE KING'S PERSONAL SECURITY

Just as a king watches over the security of others through secret agents, so shall a wise king guard himself against dangers from others. {1.21.29}

The king's personal guard of female archers shall guard him from an adjacent chamber while he is asleep in his own. On waking up, he shall be received in the second chamber by eunuchs (personal attendants and dressers), in the third chamber by dwarfs, hunchbacks and *kiratas* [cave-dwellers?, for good omen?] and in the fourth by ministers and kinsmen. The doors shall be guarded by lancers.   {1.21.1}

The king shall employ as his personal attendants those whose fathers and grandfathers had been royal servants, those who are bound to him by a close relationship or trained persons whose loyalty has been proved in service. Foreigners, those whose service has not been thought worthy of reward, and persons of ill will (even if they are natives of the country) shall not be employed as royal guards for protecting the king or his residence.   {1.21.2}

The head-cook shall, in a well-guarded place, supervise the cooking of tasty dishes. The king shall eat only freshly cooked food, after first making oblations to the sacred fire and offering food to birds.   {1.21.4,5}

> [Kautilya then gives a long list of signs by which one can recognize the presence of poisons—in food, wine, water, bed sheets, metals and gems. A poisoner can also be recognized by his unnatural appearance or suspicious behaviour. Verses {1.21.6-8} have not been translated.]

Physicians and experts in the cure of poisons shall attend on the king. The king shall not take any medicine unless its purity has been tested by the physician and he, and his helpers, have tasted it first. Likewise, the king shall not drink water or wine without it first having been tasted by others.
                                                           {1.21.9-11}

Barbers and valets shall wait on the king only after they have had a bath and put on clean clothes. They shall receive, with clean hands, implements [of their trade], toilet articles and dresses, in a sealed condition from the concerned officer.

The king's female servants, of proven integrity, shall either supervise the work of bath-attendants, shampooers, bed-makers, launderers and garland-makers or do the work themselves. They shall offer garments and flowers [to the king] after [testing them by first] putting them to their eyes and bath oils, fragrant powders, perfumes and all other substances used for the king's toilette by applying them to their own arms and breasts. Anything received from persons outside shall be similarly tested.

{1.21.12-15}

Entertainers [actor and acrobats] shall not use weapons, fire or poison in their performances. The instruments of musicians shall always remain inside the palace complex. Likewise, all accoutrements of elephants and horses and all chariots shall remain inside. {1.21.16-17}

The king shall mount a carriage or an animal [only] when attended by trustworthy servants and get into a boat only when there is a trustworthy boatman and never if it is towed by another or when there is a high wind. His troops shall be on guard at the water's edge. {1.21.18-20}

He shall not go for a swim unless the water has been cleared of crocodiles and dangerous fish. Similarly, he shall not go into a park unless cleared of snakes. He shall practise game hunting only in jungles cleared by hunters of robbers, wild animals and enemies. {1.21.21.23}

[There are some people whom a king should not receive alone.] A holy ascetic shall be received only when there are trusted armed guards [because it may be a disguise]. Envoys from foreign states shall be received only in the presence of ministers. {1.21.23}

He shall inspect fully armed troops only when fully armed himself and riding a horse, an elephant or a chariot [and not on foot]. {1.21.25}

When the king leaves or enters the fortified area, the royal road shall be lined on both sides by armed men and truncheon-bearers. The roads should be cleared of men carrying arms, ascetics and cripples [since the latter two are likely to be enemy agents]. He shall not plunge into crowds. He should go to [crowded functions such as] fairs and festivals only when protected by units of ten soldiers. {1.21.26-28}

PROTECTION FROM QUEENS AND PRINCES

A king can protect his kingdom only when he himself is protected from persons near him, particularly his wives and children. {1.17.1}

QUEENS

[There are many cases of kings being murdered by queens or in the queen's apartments.] Bhadrasena was killed by his own brother, concealed in the queen's chamber; similarly, Karusha was killed by his own son, hiding under his mother's bed. Other queens have killed their husbands by putting poison in their food, with a poisoned ornament or jewel, or by a concealed weapon. Therefore, a king shall always be careful and avoid such dangers.
{1.20.15-17}

The king shall visit the queen in her own apartment only after an old [trusted] maidservant assures him that there is no danger from the queen. He shall forbid the queen from having contacts with ascetics with shaven heads or matted hair, jugglers and magicians or female servants from outside. Nor should the members of the queen's family visit her except in the maternity ward or in the infirmary [i.e. when she is giving birth or is ill]. Courtesans, who attend on the queen, shall first cleanse themselves with baths and change into fresh garments. The integrity or otherwise of the queen's [personal] attendants shall be ascertained by old men over eighty years of age or old women over fifty (pretending to be a parent of some other servant), retired servants or eunuchs. These supervisors shall do their duties in the interests of the king.
{1.20.14,18-21}

PRINCES

As regards princes, [there are a variety of opinions. For example,] Bharadvaja says: 'Princes, like crabs, eat their begetters. A king should, therefore, guard himself against them, right from their birth. It is better to kill them quietly if they are found wanting in affection.'
{1.17.3-6}

'Killing is cruel', says Visalaksha. 'An innocent one may be killed [by mistake]. It is better to keep them under guard in one place, rather than destroy a *kshatriya*.'
{1.17.7,8}

'This is like nurturing a viper', say the followers of Parasara. 'A [confined] prince would think that his father had done so out of fear and try to bring his father under his influence. Better send him off to a frontier fort.'
{1.17.9-11}

'This is like dragging away a fighting ram which will only rush back', says Pisuna. 'Knowing why he had been sent off, a prince might make an alliance with a frontier chief against his father. Better to let him spend his time in the fort of another king, far from [the king's] own territory.'
{1.17.12-14}

'This is like giving a calf as a hostage', says Kaunapadanta. 'The king to whom the prince is entrusted will surely start milking the father. Better send the prince to live with his mother's kinsmen.'

{1.17.15-17}

'That, surely, raises the rallying flag!' says Vatavyadhi. 'His relations are certain to go on importuning [on behalf of the prince]. Better let him be free to dissipate himself, because a son engrossed in pleasures does not hate his father.'

{1.17.18-21}

Kautilya [totally] disagrees. This [to treat a prince with suspicion from the moment of his birth] is living death. A royal family, with undisciplined princes, will collapse under attack like a worm-eaten piece of wood. [One should take every possible precaution against a prince turning against his father.] Therefore, when the queen is ready to conceive, priests should make the necessary oblations to Indra and Brihaspati. When she is pregnant, her health shall be protected by specialist physicians so that she delivers safely. After the birth, the priests shall perform the necessary purificatory rituals. When the prince is of the right age, he should be trained by experts.[2]

{1.17.22-27}

[Some teachers say that, even after all these safeguards, the loyalty of a prince should be tested.] For example, the school of Ambhi recommend that secret agents should tempt the prince with hunting, gambling, wine and women and then suggest to him that he seize the kingdom. Other secret agents should try to dissuade him.

{1.17.28-29}

'There can be no greater crime or sin', says Kautilya, 'than making wicked impressions on an innocent mind. Just as a clean object is stained with whatever is smeared on it, so a prince, with a fresh mind, understands as the truth whatever is taught to him. Therefore, a prince should be taught what is true *dharma* and *artha*, not what is unrighteous and materially harmful.'

{1.17.30-33}

[Instead of tempting the prince with harmful suggestions] secret agents should guard him while declaring their loyalty to him. If, in the exuberance of youth, he were to cast his eyes towards the wives of others, the [friendly] agents should make him terrified by arranging for unclean women, posing as high-born, to meet him in lonely houses at night. If he were to be tempted by wine, they should turn him off by giving him drugged liquor. If tempted by gambling, fraudulent gamblers should create an aversion. If tempted by hunting, he should be frightened by agents disguised as highway robbers. If he seems to turn his mind against his father, secret agents should first win his confidence by seeming to agree with him and then dissuade him from attacking the king. They should tell him that, if he fails in the attempt, he would be killed but [even] if he succeeds, he would be condemned to hell [for the sin of patricide]; there will also be great anger among the people who will break him like a clod of earth.   {1.17.34-39}

PUNISHMENTS

<u>For offences against the king and royal property:</u>

Riding a royal chariot, horse or elephant	Cutting off of a hand and a foot or a fine of 700 panas	{4.10.12}
Reviling the king; spreading false rumours about the king	Tongue pulled out	{4.11.21}
Stealing or killing a royal elephant or horse; stealing a royal chariot	Death by impaling	{4.11.7}
Having sexual intercourse with the Queen	Boiled alive	{4.13.33}

III.v

REVOLTS, REBELLIONS, CONSPIRACIES AND TREASON

[Treason, treachery, revolt and rebellion were ever-present dangers for the King. Because he was the embodiment of the state, eliminating him was the best means of capturing the state. Every one posed a threat. People near the king—queens, princes who wanted to usurp the throne, the *purohita*, councillors and ministers, the Chief of Defence—could turn treacherous. The people of the countryside might rebel. A commander of a frontier region might want to carve out a kingdom for himself; tribal chiefs and vassal kings might seek to escape the authority of the king. All these potential traitors may act on their own, collude with each other or be instigated by the enemy king. The possibility of a revolt or a rebellion was particularly acute when the king was away on a military campaign; his absence for a long period from the state and his capital city provided opportunities for the traitors. The question of tackling treachery is, therefore, given importance in Book 9, dealing with preparations for a military campaign.

A particular cause of rebellion was discontent in the population. The king is advised to anticipate discontent and take steps to prevent them from becoming worse. Kautilya attaches great importance to the well-being of the people; if they become impoverished, they become greedy and rebellious. A list of sixteen different types of policies which lead to the impoverishment and disaffection among the people is given in {7.5.19-26} and analysed in {7.5.27-37}.

Palace coups are dealt with as a special case in {9.3.9-34}. A rebellion entirely within the constituents of the state could arise in the heartland of the kingdom or in the outer regions, remote from the capital. This could be abetted in the heartland or in the outer regions, giving rise to four possibilities; these are analysed logically in {9.5.4-32}. The instigation and abetting by the enemy king of internal treachery is dealt with in this translation in Part X on war. While the king had to be on guard against the treachery induced by the enemy, he is also advised, in {9.3.35}, to practise similar subversion of the enemy's people!]

The pursuit of wrong policies [i.e. those which are not in accordance with the principles and methods described in this treatise] gives rise to the danger of a revolt. {9.5.1-2}

Immoderation [excessive drinking, womanising, etc.] is a devilish practice which rouses one's own people to revolt. {9.7.1-2}

A king shall employ, without hesitation, the methods of secret punishment[1] against traitors in his own camp and against enemies; but he should do so with forbearance keeping in mind the future consequences as well as immediate results. {5.1.57}

ANTICIPATING AND AVOIDING DISCONTENT

Spies in the guise of ascetics [*mundajatila*, those with shaven heads or matted locks] shall find out who among the following are happy and who discontented:
- those dependent on the King for grains, cattle or money;
- those who help the King in prosperity and adversity;
- those who [help to] restrain an angry relative or region and
- those who repel enemies and forest chiefs. {1.13.15}

The contented shall be appreciated by giving them additional honours and wealth. {1.13.16}

In order to make the discontented happy, conciliation shall be the method used. If [conciliation fails and] they continue to be unhappy, they shall be used to collect taxes and fines so that they may incur the wrath of the public. When the people come to hate them, they shall be eliminated either by inciting a popular revolt against them or by secret punishment. Alternatively, they may be sent to work in mines and factories while keeping their wives and sons under close security in order to prevent them from being used by enemies.

The [different] discontented persons shall not be allowed to come together or join hands with neighbouring princes, jungle chiefs, kinsmen who covet the throne and disgruntled princes; [in case there is a danger of this happening] sowing dissension is the method to be used.

{1.13.17-21}

DISAFFECTION AMONG SUBJECTS

When a people are impoverished, they become greedy; when they are greedy, they become disaffected; when disaffected, they either go over to the enemy or kill their ruler themselves. {7.5.27}

Impoverishment, greed and disaffection are engendered among the subjects when the king:

(i) ignores the good [people] and favours the wicked;

(ii) causes harm by new unrighteous practices;

(iii) neglects the observation of the proper and righteous practices;

(iv) suppresses *dharma* and propagates *adharma*;

(v) does what ought not to be done and fails to do what ought to be done;

(vi) fails to give what ought to be given and exacts what he cannot rightly take;

(vii) does not punish those who ought to be punished but punishes those who do not deserve to be;

(viii) arrests those who should not be arrested but fails to arrest those who should be seized;

(ix) indulges in wasteful expenditure and destroys profitable undertakings;

(x) fails to protect the people from thieves and robs them himself;

(xi) does not do what he ought to do and reviles the work done by others;

(xii) causes harm to the leaders of the people and insults those worthy of honour;

(xiii) antagonizes the [wise] elders by lying and mischief;

(xiv) does not recompense service done to him;

(xv) does not carry out his part of what had been agreed upon; and

(xvi) by his indolence and negligence destroys the welfare of his people.
{7.5.19-26}

[A king who is profligate with ancestral wealth, spendthrift with his own wealth or miserly also practises wrong policies; see {7.13.13} in X.viii.]

Therefore, the king shall not act in such a manner as would cause impoverishment, greed or disaffection among the people; if, however, they do appear, he shall immediately take remedial measures. {7.5.28}

What are the consequences [and types] of disaffection among the subjects? {7.5.29}

An impoverished people dread extortion and destruction of their property. They prefer an immediate peace, war or emigration: [i.e. reducing the expenditure on war, hoping for riches after victory or escaping from misery]. [As regards different types,] impoverishment due to depletion of money or grains [is more serious because it] poses a danger to everything in the state and is difficult to remedy. Depletion of useful animals and men can be made good with money and grains. {7.5.30,33}

Greedy people are always discontented and easily fall prey to the instigations of the enemy. [The problem is easier to remedy]. If the greedy are only a few chiefs, [they] can be satisfied by [promising them a share of] the enemy's wealth or by getting rid of them.   {7.5.31,34}

The disaffected rise in revolt when there is an enemy attack on the king. Disaffection can be countered by suppressing the leaders. Without the leaders, people are more easily governed, less susceptible to enemy instigations, and less capable of enduring the sufferings [of revolt]. When the leaders are seized, the people become fragmented, restrained and more able to withstand calamities.   {7.5.32,35-37}

REVOLTS AND REBELLIONS

The king may be threatened by dangers in the interior or in the remote regions, particularly when he is about to start on an expedition.[2] An internal rebellion is one led by a Crown Prince, the *purohita*, the Chief of Defence or a minister. A rebellion in the outer regions is one led by a chief of a region, the commander of a frontier post, a chief of a jungle tribe or a [previously subdued] vassal king.   {8.2.2, 9.3.12,22}

An internal rebellion is more dangerous than one in the outer regions because it is like nurturing a viper in one's bosom.

{9.3.11, 8.2.3, 9.5.31}

A revolt among the councillors and ministers is a greater evil than any other type of internal revolt. Therefore, the king shall keep the treasury and the army under his [own] control.   {8.2.3,4}

Protection against rebellion: A king who is about to go on an expedition [of conquest], should take with him [as hostages]: (i) in case of a suspicion of internal revolt, the persons suspected and (ii) in case of suspicion of a frontier revolt, the wives and sons of those suspected.   {9.3.9}

Overcoming internal rebellions: A king should not go on an expedition until he had suppressed the rebellion, appointed a Viceroy and placed the capital under different types of troops and under many different chiefs. If the rebellion is due to the king's own faults, he shall correct them. If the rebellion is due to no fault of his, it should be dealt with according to the power [or importance] of the rebel and the gravity of the offence. For example, a rebel Crown Prince shall be put to death, if the king has another virtuous son; if [however, the rebellious] Crown Prince is an only son, he shall be imprisoned. A *purohita*, however great his offence, [shall not be executed but] shall be punished by exile or imprisonment.

{9.3.10,13,14}

Revolt by close kinsmen: A king shall energetically suppress a revolt by a son, a brother or a close kinsman. If he lacks the means to do so, the king may allow the rebel [to keep] what he had seized and enter into a treaty with him, in order to prevent him from joining the enemy. It is better to send a harassing force, the forces of a neighbouring king or those of a jungle chieftain against him and while the rebel is busy fighting these, attack him from a different direction. Alternatively, the means recommended for use against a disgruntled prince should be employed.[3] [Lastly,] the means suggested for instigating sedition inside an enemy's fort can also be used to create a revolt in the rebel's camp.[4]   {9.3.15-18}

Revolt by Ministers, etc.: Internal revolts by a minister or Chief of Defence and a rebellion in the outer regions by a chief shall be dealt with by methods similar [to those described above.] Conciliation shall be tried first in the case of ministers suspected of treason; if it succeeds, the use of the other (three) methods becomes unnecessary. [Likewise,] placating traitorous ministers with gifts shall be tried first making it unnecessary to use any of the other methods.   {9.3.19-21,9.7.72}

Revolts in the outer regions by jungle chiefs, etc.: [Revolts by a commander of a frontier region, a jungle chief or a vassal king are different in character because they are more likely to seek independence from the King.] The following methods shall be used to suppress these successfully. A revolt by one can be tackled by setting another against him. If the rebel is strongly entrenched in a fort, he shall be subdued by using a neighbouring king, a jungle chieftain, a kinsman or a prince out of favour. [If this is not possible,] the rebel should be made an ally, so as to prevent him from going over to the enemy. [If necessary,] secret agents shall be used to sow discord between the rebel and the enemy. The agents shall warn the rebel that (i) the enemy king was only making use of him temporarily and would discard him once his aim was achieved (by sending him on expeditions, posting him to a difficult place or sending him far away from his family) or (ii) if the rebellion should fail, the enemy king would either sell him or make his own peace with the king, abandoning the rebel to his own fate. If the rebel agrees [not to join the enemy], he should be rewarded with honours. If he refuses, the secret agent shall reveal himself and get the rebel killed by his own warriors instigating them with promises of reward, or by using other agents.   {9.3.23-34}

A king shall instigate rebellion against an enemy but suppress those against himself. He should understand how an enemy can instigate revolt in his territory, adopting the same kind of techniques which he himself would use against the enemy.   {9.3.35}

[The various methods of instigating rebellion in enemy territory, depending on the type of target, are given in IX.iv.]

TYPES OF REVOLT

[Since a revolt can arise either in the interior or in the outer regions, there are four logical possibilities, depending on where it arises and where it is abetted. The four types, their relative seriousness and the methods of dealing with them are shown in the table below.

Type	Instigator in	Abettor in	Seriousness	Tackle	Method
1.	Interior	Outer	Least serious	Abettor	Conciliation Gifts
2.	Outer	Interior	2nd least	Abettor	Dissension Force
3.	Outer	Outer	2nd most	Instigator	Dissension Force
4.	Interior	Interior	Most	Instigator	All four

It is seen, from the above, that a cross revolt between two regions is less serious than one instigated and abetted within the same region; a wholly internal revolt is the most serious.]

Understanding clearly the nature of various types of rebellion, a wise king shall always be on guard against the following: (i) rebels in the outer regions joining up with other rebels in the outer regions, (ii) those in the interior joining up with others in the interior and (iii) potential rebels in the two regions conspiring together. He shall always protect himself from both those near him and those in the remote regions [of the kingdom].
{9.3.42, 9.5.3}

Of the four types of rebellion, the one [wholly] in the interior shall be tackled first.
{9.5.30}

The above order is subject to the qualification that a revolt instigated by a strong personality is [always] more serious than one started by a weaker man, wherever he may be.
{9.5.32}

Types 1 and 2—Cross-regional: The way of successfully overcoming these two types is by tackling the one who responds. More than the instigators, the abettors make the success [of the conspiracy] possible; for, if the abettors are subdued, the instigators will find it difficult to tempt others. To instigate a conspiracy in a different region requires enormous effort and this [itself] is an advantage to the King.
{9.5.4-8}

<u>Type 1</u>: In this case, [of the responders living within the country,] the king should make use of either conciliation or placating with gifts.

{9.5.9}

<u>Type 2</u>: In this case, the king should either [try to] sow dissension or use force. [There are two ways of sowing dissension.] (i) Secret agents, posing as friends of those (in the outer regions) likely to succumb to instigation, should cast doubts on the motives of the internal instigators by implying that the king was, in fact, using the latter as agents to subdue those in the outer regions. (ii) Agents may act as if they themselves were traitors in league with the instigators and then sow dissension between the two groups. [The two ways of using force are:] (i) assassins may be sent to befriend the abettors and kill them with weapons or poison and (ii) the abettors may be invited [to the capital] and then killed.   {9.5.12-16}

<u>Types 3 and 4</u>: The way of successfully overcoming these two types of conspiracies is to tackle the instigator. For, when the cause of treason is removed, there will be no traitors. If one removes only abettors, others may become so [by falling prey to the instigator.]   {9.5.17-19}

<u>Type 3</u>: Sowing dissension and force are the methods to be used in cases where the instigators and the abettors are both in the outer region. [Dissension:] Secret agents may cast doubts on the abettors, implying that they really were the agents of the king, who intends to subdue them all. [Force:] Assassins should infiltrate the troops of the responder and attack them [stealthily] with weapons, poisons and other means; then, other secret agents should accuse the responder of the crimes.   {9.5.20-23}

<u>Type 4</u>: In the case of a conspiracy wholly in the interior, the king should use any of the [four] means, as appropriate. He may use conciliation if the instigator acts as if contented even if he is not (or acts discontented without really being so). Gifts may be given to him, on happy and sad occasions, on the pretext of appreciating his loyalty or in ostensible consideration of his welfare [thus placating him]. A spy, posing as a friend could warn him that the king was about to test his loyalty, and that he should tell the truth. Attempts may be made to divide the conspirators by telling each one that the other was carrying tales to the king. (Lastly,) the different methods of secret punishment could be used.   {9.5.24-29}

VILLAINS AND UPRIGHT CONSPIRATORS

[In order to counteract revolts and rebellions, particularly conspiracies between the interior and outer regions, it is necessary to understand the motivations of the instigator, who may be an upright man or a villain. Kautilya argues that the intention of an instigator is only to use for a time the one who responds in order to get rid of the king and then eliminate the responder himself later. An upright conspirator shall be tackled by making an agreement with him, satisfying his legitimate demands; a villain shall be dealt with by force.]

A king shall try to win over secretly any one who can start a revolt or can put one down. He shall approach one who is true to his word, capable of helping the king in achieving his objectives or of saving him from difficulties. He shall first form a judgment about whether the man is upright or a villain. Upright men conspire for the sake of others similarly placed [while villains do so only for their own benefit?]

The king shall make a treaty with an upright man [and keep it.] With a villain, a treaty shall be made with a view to outmanoeuvring him.

{9.3.36,37,40,41}

The villain from the outer regions instigates one in the interior to revolt with the following intentions. He expects that, if the revolt succeeds, the one in the interior will accept the villain as king, thereby making the villain a double gainer—death of the king and obtaining the kingdom. If, however, the revolt fails, the king will kill the interior rebel, with the result that the rebel's family and supporters will come over to the villain. Others in a situation similar to that of the dead conspirator will also become a large conspiratorial faction, for fear of being punished by the king. Even if they do not become rebels, the king will be suspicious of them and they can be eliminated one by one through [false] letters, carried by condemned men, implicating them.   {9.3.38}

The villain in the interior instigates one in the outer regions to revolt with the following intentions. While the villain appropriates the king's treasury and destroys the king's troops, he induces the other conspirator to kill the king. Or, the villain will embroil the one in the outer regions in a war with enemies or jungle tribes, in order to entangle his army, deepen his enmities and thus bring him under the control of the villain; then, the villain will either please the king by betraying the fellow-conspirator or seize the kingdom himself. Once brought under control, the villain could also imprison his fellow-conspirator and thus gain his land as well as the king's land; or, he may invite the fellow-conspirator to pay a visit and when he trustingly responds, get him killed; or, when he is away from his base, may absorb his territory.   {9.3.39}

TREACHERY

[There are three possibilities:
(i) treason wholly within the constituents of a state;
(ii) treachery instigated by the enemy; and
(iii) enemy-instigated treachery compounded by internal treason.
The first two are called 'simple' types and the third, 'compounded'.]

There are two [distinct] types of (simple) treachery [not complicated by collusion between the two]: internal treachery and treachery by the enemy. {9.6.1}

The king shall use all the means except force [i.e. conciliation, placating with gifts and sowing dissension] to prevent the people of the city and the *janapada* from being corrupted into treason by traitors. For, force cannot be used against a large number of people. Even if used, it might not produce the desired result and might even become counterproductive. However, the king shall [be free to] use any method of secret punishment against the ring-leaders. {9.6.2-5}

A bigger conspiracy is born if the traitors and those still loyal join hands. [To avoid this danger] success [should be sought] through those [still] loyal. For, in the absence of support [from the people], treachery which needs support cannot exist. {9.6.8-10}

[For unmixed enemy treachery and enemy treachery compounded by internal treason see X.v.]

Of the four means of dealing with dangers, [conciliation, placating with gifts, sowing dissension and use of force], it is easier to employ a method earlier in the order. In the case of a son, a brother or a kinsman, the appropriate methods are conciliation and placating with gifts. In the case of city people, people of the countryside or the army, placating the leaders with gifts or sowing dissension among them are the right methods. In the case of neighbouring princes or jungle chiefs, the right methods are sowing dissension and using force. This order is *anuloma* [natural and, therefore, recommended]; if the methods are used in the reverse order [*dana* before *sama* or *danda* before *bheda*] it is *pratiloma* [unnatural]. {9.6.56-61; 9.7.68-69}

SECRET METHODS

[High officials, who benefit from service under the king, may become inimical to the king of their own accord or in league with the enemy.

They should be dealt with using clandestine agents {1.12} or by winning over those in danger of being seduced by them {1.13}. the methods suggested for (taking over) an enemy town could also be adopted {13.1,13.3}.]

Sometimes, traitorous high officials, who cause harm to the kingdom, cannot be dealt with openly either because they are powerful or because they are united. It is the duty of the king to suppress such people using secret methods. Three kinds of secret methods can be used—using kinsmen, entrapment and playing one against the other.   {5.1.4,20,37}

[All the secret methods recommended in the *Arthashastra* have been consolidated in Part IX on clandestine operations.]

The traitor may surrender with his troops to the Crown Prince or the Chief of Defence. They should immediately show the traitor some favours but later proceed against him. The king shall then send the traitor to his death with a weak army and [chosen] assassins [as described under secret methods].   {5.1.53-54}

Among the sons of the traitors who had been eliminated, the one who is not disloyal shall get the patrimony.   {5.1.55}

Thus the kingdom will continue to be enjoyed by the king's sons and grandsons, free from the dangers caused by [seditious] men.   {5.1.56}

[Traitors are also fair game for collecting revenue by a variety of fraudulent means, though Kautilya recommends these only in extreme cases of financial difficulty and after exhausting all other means of supplementing revenue. See {5.2.52-68} in V.ii.]

PUNISHMENTS

Propagating treason	Blinding of both eyes a fine of 800 panas	{4.10.13}

III.vi

SUCCESSION

[Kautilya lays considerable emphasis on the importance of the royal line. In {7.11.28}, it is said that the people will desert even a strong king, if he is not of royal blood. Nobility of birth is also referred to in verses {8.2.20,23} translated in the next section. The importance of sons for continuing the royal line is dealt with extensively in {7.17} on the giving of hostages (see X.iii). {7.17.20}, in particular, stresses the importance of legitimate sons over illegitimate ones.

While the eldest son is normally the successor to the throne, he can be by-passed if he is unfit to hold the office. Any other successor must, however, be one who can assure the continuity of the lineage of the monarchy. Chapters {1.7} and {1.8} also deal with disgruntled princes as well as worthy ones unjustly treated by the King.

An important chapter, {5.6}, deals with orderly succession in the event of the death of the king due to natural causes or in the battlefield. Since the integrity of the kingdom is likely to be threatened in such times of transition, the chief councillor has the responsibility of averting dangers from princes, other relatives, ministers, rebellious chiefs and neighbouring kings. {5.6} also deals with the interesting topic of regency, when the chief councillor has to act not only as the regent but also as the guardian of a young prince. The designation of chief councillor, as such, does not exist in the *Arthashastra*; we have to presume that the seniormost or the most respected among the councillors managed the succession.]

PRINCES

Sons are of three kinds. A wise son is one who understands *dharma* and *artha* when taught and also practises these. A lazy son is one who understands what he is taught but does not practise them. A wicked son is he who hates *dharma* and *artha* and [therefore] is full of evil.

{1.17.44-47}

If the only son of a king turns out to be evil, efforts shall be made to get a son born to him. Alternatively, grandsons shall be begotten through daughters.   {1.17.48-49}

SUCCESSION

<u>Rules for succession</u>: Unless there are dangers in it, succession of the eldest son is praiseworthy.

An only son, if he is wicked, shall not [under any circumstances] be installed on the throne.

An old or sick king shall get a child begotten on his wife by one of the following: his mother's kinsman, a close relation [of the same *gotra*[1]] or a virtuous neighbouring prince.

A king with many sons acts in the best interests [of the kingdom] only if he removes a wicked one from the succession.

Sovereignty can [sometimes] be devolved on the royal family [collectively]. An [oligarchic] family is difficult to conquer and, being free of the dangers of anarchy, can survive forever on this earth.   {1.17.50-53}

DISGRUNTLED SONS

Secret agents shall inform a king if a son is disgruntled [and likely to become a rebel]. If the prince is an only son and is loved, he shall be imprisoned. If a king has many sons, the disgruntled prince shall be sent off to the frontier or somewhere else [where there is no danger of his becoming powerful] avoiding regions where he can cause a disturbance or where the people may adopt him as a native son, or use him as a bargaining counter in order to increase their power. If the disgruntled son has good personal qualities, he shall be made the Chief of Defence or heir-apparent [to assure him of his succession without having to rebel against his father].   {1.17.40-43}

   <u>A son unjustly treated</u>: [It may so happen, sometimes, that a prince of good qualities and worthy of succeeding the king is unjustly treated by his father. In such a case:] a disciplined prince, who is harassed and given unworthy tasks, shall [nevertheless] obey his father, unless the work is such that (i) his life is threatened (ii) it arouses the people against him or (iii) involves committing a heinous sin. If, however, he is given a worthwhile job to do, he shall take the help of efficient officers and perform the task with zeal, duly supervised by the officers. He shall send to his father the normal profit from the work as well as the additional profit gained through his efforts. If the king is still not pleased with him and shows partiality to another son or another wife [other than his mother], the prince shall ask to withdraw to the forest.

If the prince is afraid that the king may imprison him or put him to death, he shall seek refuge with a worthy neighbouring king, one who is known to be just, righteous and truthful, who keeps his promises and welcomes and respects those who have sought asylum. Under the protection of such a king, the prince shall collect together an army and resources, marry into influential families, make alliances with jungle tribes and win over people [in his father's kingdom, with a view to taking over the throne by force].

If he [cannot find a suitable refuge and] acts alone, he shall maintain himself by working in gold, precious stones or articles of gold and silver. After entering into their confidence and giving them stupefying drugs, he shall secretly rob the wealth of: heretical groups, rich widows, traders in caravans and sailing ships or temples (which are not used by Brahmins learned in the Vedas). He shall then use the methods suggested for instigating sedition inside an enemy's fort[2] to incite a rebellion in his father's fort. Or, he shall attack the king with the help of people from his mother's family.

[The prince could also act in a covert manner.] He may disguise himself as an artisan, an artist, a minstrel, a physician, a story-teller or a heretic and, accompanied by assassins similarly disguised, enter the king's palace [clandestinely] and kill him with weapons or poison. He shall then announce to the king's supporters that, as the Crown Prince, the kingdom should have been enjoyed jointly and not by one person alone. He shall then offer to reward with double food and double wages all those who agree to serve him.
{1.18.1-12}

The king's countermeasures: [Faced with a disgruntled prince who is likely to become a traitor] the king shall use the sons of high officials or the prince's mother (if he has confidence in her) to persuade the prince to come to the king's court. [If he refuses to come] he shall be abandoned to be killed by assassins with weapons or poison. If the king does not want the prince killed, secret agents shall capture him by making him drunk, or while hunting or at night using women of bad character; he shall then be brought before the king.

When he is brought before the king, an only son shall be pacified by promising him the kingdom after the father's death but kept under confinement. If there are other sons, the disgruntled prince shall be killed.
{1.18.13-16}

ORGANIZING SUCCESSION ON THE DEATH OF A KING

The following shall be done by councillors when the king is seriously ill or about to die, in the interests of continuity and peaceful transfer of sovereignty without loss to the corpus of the kingdom.   {5.6.1,23}

Well before the anticipated death of the king, the councillor shall, with the help of his friends and followers, allow visitors [to see the king] once in a month or two; [in order to conceal the seriousness of the king's illness, more frequent visits shall be avoided] on the plea that the king was very busy in performing special rites for the prevention of national calamities, the destruction of enemies, long life or getting a son. When [unavoidably] necessary, a double of the king may be shown to the people and envoys (of allies and enemies), at such times when the deception would not be obvious; the double shall hold discussions with envoys [only] through the councillor. With the connivance of the Commandant of the Palace Guards and the King's Chamberlain, the councillor shall give the impression that the king performs all his daily duties. He shall keep the people happy by punishing those who do harm and rewarding those who have been helpful.

{5.6.2-6}

The councillor shall collect both the treasury and the army together in one place, either within the fort or at the frontier, and place them under the charge of two trustworthy men. Princes, close relatives of the king and important officials shall also be brought together under some pretext.

{5.6.7}

If a commander of a fort or of a jungle region shows hostility, he shall be won over or sent off on a dangerous expedition or to visit an ally of the king.

{5.6.8,9}

A neighbouring king, from whom an attack is feared, shall be captured by inveigling him to visit the kingdom for a festival, wedding, elephant hunt, horse sale or land grant; or, he shall be captured by an ally. Then, an agreement, which is not treasonable [i.e. not against the interests of the dying king], can be concluded with him. [If this is not possible] trouble shall be caused to the threatening king by [inciting] jungle chiefs or other enemies against him. [Alternatively,] a kinsman of his family who covets the throne or an unjustly treated prince of his house shall be won over with promises of territory and set against the suspected king. If, however, a commander or a neighbouring king [actually] rises in revolt, the councillor shall invite him with promises of crowning him as king and [then] have him killed. Or, he shall use [against the rebel] the methods suggested for dealing with conspiracies.[3]

{5.6.10-13,16,17}

[After having made sure of the conditions for a peaceful transfer of sovereignty,] the councillor shall:
– first get the support of the other members of the royal family, princes and important officials to declare a prince as having already been crowned [even before the death of the king],

– announce the serious illness of the king after gradually transferring the burden of the kingdom to the Crown Prince,
– or continue the administration, taking due care against internal and external conspiracies.[4]   {5.6.14,18,15}

<u>Death of a king during war</u> In case a king dies in enemy territory [during a war], the councillor shall:
– retreat, after making a treaty with the enemy with the help of a friend posing as an enemy [in order to get the best terms],
– install a neighbouring king in the capital and then retreat [from the war],
– crown the heir-apparent [at once] and fight back; or
– if attacked by the enemy, take the measures described elsewhere.[5]
                                                                {5.6.19-22}

REGENCY

[There may be cases where there is either no Crown Prince or one too young.] Bharadvaja argues that, in such a case, the councillor himself shall take possession of the kingdom. [His argument is:] If, for the sake of a kingdom, fathers can fight sons, and sons fathers, why not a councillor, one of the principal constituents of the state? He shall not disdain what has, of its own accord, fallen into his hands. As the popular saying goes: 'If you scorn a woman who comes to you voluntarily, she will only heap curses on you.' [So it is with a kingdom—*rajyasri*[6]] Therefore, [says Bharadvaja,] when the king is dying, the councillor shall make the members of the royal family, the princes and important officers fight with each other or with other officers. Those who oppose shall be eliminated by [engineering] a popular uprising. Or, he shall secretly get rid of the contenders to the throne. 'The right time comes but once to one who is waiting for an opportunity; it will not come again when he next wants to achieve the same thing.'   {5.6.24-31}

Kautilya considers the above advice immoral and one likely to provoke the people to revolt. In any case, the councillor cannot be certain that he will be accepted as king. It is better that he installs on the throne a worthy royal prince [such as the brother of the dead king?] If there is none such, he shall choose a prince (who may not be fully worthy) or a princess or a pregnant queen. He shall then call a meeting of all the high officials and tell them: 'This is our fate. Think of the father and of your own duty as persons of virtue and nobility. This person [prince, princess or unborn child] is only a symbol and you are the masters. Advise me on what I shall do.' As he is talking, clandestine agents, having been briefed beforehand, shall say: 'Who else but this one can protect the people of the four *varnas*, [so long as] as you

guide him?' [The other ministers are then certain to agree to the proposal.]
The councillor shall then install the prince, princess or pregnant queen on
the throne and proclaim the fact to kinsmen and to envoys of allies and
enemies. He shall increase the rations and salaries of ministers and armed
forces. He shall also promise that, when the [young] prince grows up, there
will be further increases. Similar raises and promises shall also be given to
the commanders of forts and senior officers in the countryside. [As a regent,]
he shall deal with allies and enemies as appropriate and strive to educate
and train the prince.   {5.6.32-39}

[If there is neither a young prince nor a pregnant queen,] he shall cause
an offspring to be born to a princess by a man of the same caste. The
prince thus born shall be crowned. [While the prince is growing up,] a
poor but handsome man of the same family shall be kept near the mother,
lest her mind wavers [and she takes on a lover who may become a danger
to the state and the young prince]. He shall ensure that the mother does
not become pregnant again. The prince shall be provided with a young
playmate. The regent shall not enjoy any luxuries himself but shall provide
the young king with chariots, riding animals, ornaments, dresses, women
and palaces.

When the prince grows up, the councillor shall seek to retire, to find
out the young king's mind. If the king is unhappy with him, he shall give
up his duties. If the king is pleased, he shall continue to protect him. If he
is tired of his responsibilities, he shall retire to a forest or perform lengthy
sacrifices, but [only] after instructing a specially selected secret group to
continue to protect the king. If the king falls under the influence of some
high officials, the councillor shall, with the help of those dear to the king,
teach him the principles of politics and government by illustrative stories
from the Itihasas and Puranas. [If this does not succeed,] he shall put on
the appearance of an ascetic, bring the king under his influence and punish
the traitors by appropriate secret practices.   {5.6.40-48}

III.vii

ABNORMALITY OF KINGSHIP

[Just as calamities can affect any of the other six constituent elements of a state, kingship too may be affected by adversity. Most of chapter 8.2 is, therefore, devoted to an examination of different types of kings, seen from the point of view of the kingdom as a whole. The technique used is that of comparison by pairs.]

Dyarchy and Foreign Rule: Some teachers say that rule by a single [king, even if he is a] foreigner is better than a joint rule by two kings. The kingdom is destroyed [if there are two kings] by each one showing partiality to his own group, or by mutual rivalry and hatred. But a foreign king leaves things alone, being anxious to win the affection of the people and enjoy the kingdom as it is.

Kautilya disagrees. Rule by a father and a son, or by two brothers, has been known to have happened; with equal concern for the welfare [of the people] they keep the ministers in check. A foreign king, on the other hand, is one who has seized the kingdom from a [legitimate] king still alive; because it does not belong to him, he impoverishes it [by extravagance], carries off its wealth or sells it. If the country becomes too difficult for him to handle, he abandons it and goes away. {8.2.5-8}

An uneducated king and a deviant one: The teachers say that, between a king who is blind [to the light of knowledge] and a king who deliberately deviates from the teachings, the former is a greater evil. For, an uneducated king does not discriminate between good and bad, is obstinate or is [easily] led by others; such a king ruins the kingdom by his [acts of] injustice. A king who deviates from the right teachings can be persuaded to return [to the right path] whenever his mind goes astray.

Kautilya disagrees. An unlearned king can be made to follow the [right] courses of action, if advised by good helpers. A deviant king, on the other hand, is always bent on acting contrary to the [right] teachings and, by his injustice, ruins the kingdom himself. {8.2.9-12}

A sick king and a new [usurping] king: The teachers say that a sick king is worse; either he loses the kingdom (due to the intrigue of his ministers) or he loses his life by trying to carry on [as if he was healthy]. A new king, on the other hand, pleases the people by actions designed for their benefit such as performing his duties properly, bestowing favours, remitting taxes, distributing gifts and conferring honours.

Kautilya disagrees. A sick king can carry out his duties as he had done before. A new king who has acquired the kingdom by his own might [usually] does as he pleases, as if it was his personal property. If he has been helped by others in the takeover, he has to tolerate them [even] if they oppress the country. [There is also the danger of instability because] a usurper, with no firm roots among the people, is easily overthrown.

{8.2.13-18}

[The advice given above has to be qualified by taking into account the nature of the illness of the sick king and the nobility of birth [or otherwise] of the usurper.] In the case of a sick king, a distinction has to be made between one suffering from a foul disease [due to immoral behaviour] and one who is sick due to normal causes. In the case of a new king, a distinction has to be made between one of noble birth and a low-born one.

{8.2.19-20}

A weak but noble king and a strong but low-born one: The teachers say that the people prefer a strong king, though low-born, [precisely] because he is strong. Though nobly-born, the people can be induced to follow a weak king only with difficulty.

Kautilya disagrees. People will naturally obey a high-born king though he is weak, because a man of nobility has a natural capacity to rule. Furthermore, people frustrate the intrigues of the low-born, however strong he may be, because, as the saying goes: 'When there is love, one sees all the virtues in the beloved.'

{8.2.21-24}

Part IV

THE WELL-ORGANIZED STATE

"A king can reign only with the help of others; one wheel alone does not move (a chariot). Therefore, a king should appoint advisers (as councillors and ministers) and listen to their advice."

{1.7.9}

"Ever victorious and never conquered shall be that *kshatriya*, who is nurtured by Brahmins, made prosperous by the counsels of able ministers and has, as his weapons, the precepts of the *shastras*."

{1.9.11}

"No enemy shall know his secrets. He shall, however, know all his enemy's weaknesses. Like a tortoise, he shall draw in any limb of his that is exposed."

{1.15.60}

"The root of wealth is economic activity and lack of it brings material distress. In the absence of fruitful economic activity, both current prosperity and future growth are in danger of destruction."

{from 1.19.35,36}

IV.i

ESTABLISHING THE BASIC STRUCTURES OF THE COUNTRY

[The creation of a settled, well-protected and prosperous kingdom is a prerequisite for expansion by conquest. Part IV of this translation is concerned with three of the constituent elements of the state—the *janapada*, the fortified city and the group of high officials. IV.i is only a preliminary development of the characteristics of a well-ordered *janapada* and city with their different aspects being elaborated later. For example, chapters {7.10}, {7.11} and {7.12} of the text contain a precise analysis of the good and bad points of different kinds of land, forts, irrigation works, forests, mines, trade routes and roads. This analysis is placed in the chapters of Book 7 dealing with treaties because a king has to weigh the relative merits and disadvantages of entering into a treaty to acquire land or build forts and other undertakings. But the king has to take his own country as he finds it and then develop it into a secure base for further expansion. He has to start with populating empty regions of his country and building forts, roads etc. While some aspects of planning the capital are mentioned in this part, municipal regulations on fire prevention and planning houses are elaborated elsewhere.

Organising the kingdom with arable land, pasture land, elephant and timber forests, forts, frontier posts, roads and trade routes was a complex exercise. A map of a Kautilyan State has been included in the introductory chapter on 'The Kautilyan State and Society'.

Some of the details given here may appear trivial but are not really so. The reason for prescribing the precise details of boundaries between villages becomes clear when the law relating to boundary disputes is spelt out in VIII; the distinction between tax-paying and tax-exempt villages or the actual location of cremation grounds outside the city are necessary because these topics are also picked up later.]

SETTLEMENT OF VIRGIN LAND

The king shall populate the countryside by creating [new] villages on virgin land or by reviving abandoned village sites. Settlement can be effected either by shifting some of the population of his own country or by immigration of foreigners [by inducement or force]. The settlers in the villages shall mainly be *Sudra* agriculturists, with a minimum of one hundred families and a maximum of five hundred. The villages shall be sited so as to provide mutual protection. Each boundary of a village shall be one or two *krosas*[1] and be [clearly identifiable using] a river, a mountain, a forest, a dry river-bed, a cave, an embankment, or trees like the silk cotton, acacia and milktree. {2.1.1-3}

The king shall avoid [settling] any part of the country which is liable to attack by enemies or jungle tribes and which is likely to be afflicted by disease and famine. He shall avoid excessive expenditure.[2] {2.1.36}

He shall establish a *sangrahana* (the headquarters of a sub-district) for each group of ten villages, a *karvatika* (a district headquarters) in the middle of two hundred villages, a *dronamukha* (a divisional headquarters) in the middle of four hundred and a *sthaniya* (provincial headquarters) for every eight hundred.

On the frontiers, he shall construct fortresses under the command of frontier chiefs to guard the entrances to the kingdom.

The area between the frontier forts and the settled villages shall be guarded by trappers, archers, hunters, *Candalas* and forest tribes.

{2.1.4-6}

He shall grant land to Brahmins [of different categories]: —teachers, *purohitas*, experts in the Vedas and those who officiate at ritual sacrifices. Such land shall be exempt from fines and taxes and be transferable to heirs.

He shall [also] grant land [after the village is fully established[3] to heads of departments, accountants, record keepers (*gopas*), divisional officers (*sthanikas*), doctors, couriers and horse trainers. Such land shall not be sold or mortgaged by the possessor [being a perquisite associated with the job].

Arable land shall be allotted to tax-payers for their lifetime [only].[4] Unarable land, prepared for cultivation by any one [by their own efforts] shall not be taken away from them. Land allotted to those who do not cultivate it shall be confiscated and given to others. Alternatively, employees of the village, whether salaried or not, or [village] merchants may cultivate them. The loss suffered by the state due to non-cultivation shall be made good by the offending holder.

[On new settlements] the cultivators shall be granted grains, cattle and money which they can repay at their convenience.[5] Favours and exemptions shall be granted either at the time a settlement is organised or as and when people move in. Grants can also be made later [to people in existing settlements] provided that such grants result in increased revenue and/or avoid losses to the Treasury; for, a king with a depleted Treasury eats into the very vitality of the country. He shall, however, treat leniently, like a father [would treat his son], those whose exemptions have ceased to be effective.   {2.1.7-18}

The following shall not enter the country for purposes of settlement: ascetics belonging to heretical sects (i.e. other than Brahmin *vanaprasthas*); groups of people who were not born in the country; and [cooperative] societies other than those specifically formed for [developing] the settlement.
{2.1.32}

Ascetics who live in *ashramas* and *Pashandas* [who live in reserved areas] shall do so without annoying each other; they shall put up with minor irritations. Those who are already living in an area shall make room for newcomers; any one who objects to giving room shall be expelled.
{3.16.33-36}

The king shall, under threat of punishment, prevent misconduct among mendicant orders. For, when *adharma* overwhelms *dharma*, the king himself will be destroyed.   {3.16.42}

There shall be no grounds or buildings intended for recreation [in the new settlements]. Actors, dancers, singers, musicians, professional story-tellers and minstrels shall not obstruct the work [of the people], because in villages which provide no shelter [to outsiders], the people will be [fully] involved in the work of the fields. [Consequently] there will be an increase in the supply of labour, money, commodities, grains and liquid products.
{2.1.33-35}

[Also see {7.11.3-25} in X.v. in which Kautilya advises that, when making a settlement, land with the following qualities should be preferred—with water, capable of sowing two crops, specially grains, with elephant forests and trade routes on land. If a tract is difficult to settle because of heavy expenditure or losses, the king is advised, in {7.11.26-40}, to sell it first to some one who is likely to fail in the attempt to settle it and then reacquire it; a list of kings who are likely to fail is also given in X.v.]

PROMOTION OF ECONOMIC ACTIVITY

[The importance of economic activity is explained by Kautilya in the context of a king who lacks power to withstand an attack from a confederacy of kings {7.14.18-25} in X.ix. A king shall augment his power by promoting the welfare of his people; for power comes from the countryside which is the source of all economic activity. He shall build forts, because they provide a haven to the people and the king himself; waterworks since reservoirs make water continuously available for agriculture; trade routes since they are useful for sending and receiving clandestine agents and war material; and mines for they are a source of war material; productive forests, elephant forests and animal herds provide various useful products and animals. For a comparison of the relative methods of different kinds of forts, waterworks, roads, mines, productive forests, elephant forests, trade routes, pastures and herds see {7.12.2-28} in X.v 'Joint activities'.]

He shall protect agriculture from being harassed by [onerous] fines, taxes and demands for labour. {2.1.37}

Not only shall the king keep in good repair productive forests, elephant forests, reservoirs and mines created in the past, but also set up new mines, factories, forests [for timber and other forest produce], elephant forests and cattle herds and [shall promote trade and commerce by setting up] market towns, ports and trade routes, both by land and by water.
{2.1.19,39}

He shall build storage reservoirs, [filling them] either from natural springs or with water brought from elsewhere; or, he may provide help to those who build reservoirs by giving them land, building roads and channels or giving grants of timber and implements. Similar help shall be given to those who build shrines and sanctuaries.

If anyone refuses to participate in a cooperative effort [of all the people in a settlement] to build a reservoir, his labourers and bullocks shall [be made to] do [his share of] the work. He shall pay his share of the cost but shall not receive any share of the benefits.

The ownership of the fish, ducks and green vegetables obtained from the reservoirs shall rest with the king. {2.1.20-24}

He shall allot land for cattle pastures on uncultivable land and shall protect the herds from harassment by thieves, wild animals, poisonous creatures and cattle disease. {2.2.1, 2.1.37}

He shall also allot land in forests to ascetics for *soma* plantations and for Vedic learning. These shall be at least one *goruta*[6] in extent and the safety of all movable and immovable things therein shall be assured.
{2.2.2}

He shall set up a forest area of similar size as a recreational forest for the king.

Near the frontier or in any other suitable area, he shall set up an animal sanctuary where all animals are [welcomed as] guests.

He shall further demarcate forest areas, one for each kind of forest produce and set up factories for goods made from such produce and create settlements of foresters near these productive forests.

On the border of the kingdom he shall establish a forest for elephants, protected by other forests and under the supervision of the Chief Elephant Forester.   {2.2.3-6}

He shall protect trade routes from harassment by courtiers, state officials, thieves and frontier guards and from being damaged by herds of cattle.
{2.1.38}

He shall show special favours to those in the countryside who do things which benefit the people, such as building embankments or road bridges, beautifying villages, or helping to protect them.   {3.10.46}

RULES OF SOCIETY

[The detailed rules regulating the stable order of the society are found mainly in the chapters on civil and criminal law. However, verses {2.1.25-31} in the chapter on the organization of the kingdom mention five principles, presumably on the grounds that these are fundamental to good order.]

The king shall enforce the laws regarding discipline among members of a family, slaves and persons mortgaged.[7]

He shall maintain, at state expense, children, the old, the destitute, those suffering from adversity, childless women and the children of destitute women. The village elders shall act as trustees of temple property and the inheritance of minors (till they come of age).

Every man has an obligation to maintain his wife, children, parents, minor brothers and dependent (unmarried or widowed) sisters. This does not apply to those excommunicated from their *varna*, except that even an outcast shall continue to have the duty of supporting his mother.

No one shall renounce the life of a householder in order to become an ascetic without providing for the maintenance of his wife and children. No one shall induce a woman [still capable of bearing children?] into becoming an ascetic.

A man, who has passed the age of sexual activity can renounce family life, with the approval of the judges [who shall ensure that the family is well provided for] but if the judges do not approve, he shall be prevented from doing so.   {2.1.25-31}

CONSTRUCTION OF FORTS

On the frontiers of the country [four] forts shall be built, one for each quarter, equipped for defence against enemies. These shall be built in places best suited by nature for defence. The eight kinds of forts with natural defences are shown in Figure 5.

> [A land fort is the easiest to capture, a river fort more difficult and the mountain fort most difficult. From the point of view of a besieged king, a mountain fort is preferable to a river fort which is better than a land fort, as explained in {7.12.2} in X.v.]

ROADS IN THE KINGDOM[8]

The following roads shall be fifty four feet wide: Royal Highways, roads leading to a divisional or a provincial headquarters, roads in the countryside and pasture lands, roads in port towns and cantonments and roads leading a village or to a cremation ground.

Forest roads, roads on reservoir embankments and roads within the city shall be twenty-seven feet wide.

Roads in elephant forests shall be thirteen and a half feet wide.

The width of chariot roads shall be seven and a half feet, that of cattle paths three and three quarter and that of footpaths and paths for small animals half of that. {2.4.3-5}

CONSTRUCTION OF THE CAPITAL—FORTIFICATION

He shall build his capital (as the seat of the Treasury) in the centre of the country. The site [or the capital] shall be chosen by experts in the science of building and be naturally best fitted for the purpose—[for example:] at the confluence of rivers or near a perennial lake; near an artificial tank (round, rectangular or square in shape, depending on the nature of the land) with canals to fill it. The place shall be well served by both land and water trade routes and [be capable of being] a market town. {2.3.3}

The fort shall be surrounded by three moats, either filled by natural springs or by water brought in from elsewhere; they shall have adequate drainage and be filled with lotuses and crocodiles. {2.3.4}

There shall be a rampart all round the fort, built up by earth obtained in digging the moats. The rampart shall be planted, [on the outward side,] with thorny bushes and poisonous creepers. Surplus earth shall be used to level up low-lying areas [inside the fort] or the palace grounds. The top of the rampart shall be covered with rounded stones with chariot tracks made of trunks of palm trees. {2.3.5,6}

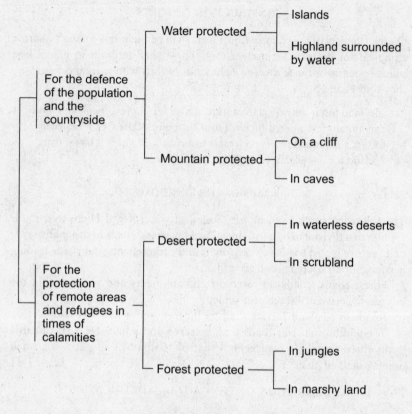

Fig. 5 Types of Forts
{2.3.1-2}

A parapet, of height between 18 and 36 feet and breadth half its height, shall be built on top of the rampart with stones or bricks; on no account shall it be made of wood, for in it fire finds a happy home. Along the ramparts there shall be turrets and, between every two turrets, a square tower. Between each tower and turret, a high wooden board with holes and covers shall be erected, big enough for three archers [to defend the ramparts using the board as protection]. In between these structures, there shall be strong wooden planks projecting outwards [to make boarding difficult]. Paths [for soldiers to go out on attacks], an escape door and an exit door shall also be built in an unassailable part of the ramparts.   {2.3.7-14}

Various defensive structures (such as speed-breakers and concealed traps) shall be made outside the ramparts [in order to obstruct the movement

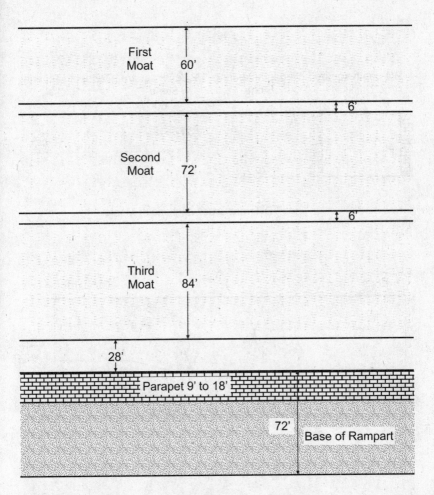

Fig. 6 Plan-Moats, Ramparts and Parapet
{2.3.4-9}

of an attacking force]. A gateway shall also be built with a tower consisting
of a hall, a well and a border post [in the ground floor], an upper chamber
and a turret. The gateway shall have a main door and a side door, and
defences against [ramming by] elephants. The bridge [over the moat] in
front of the gateway shall be removable. Arms and equipment for the defence
of the fort[9] shall be stored in pits [dug inside along the rampart.] [In places
where all these fortifications are not possible] different types of gateways
can be built, depending on the [availability of] space and materials.

{from 2.3.15,19,22,30,33-35}

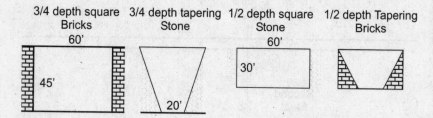

Fig. 7 Different Cross-sections of Moats

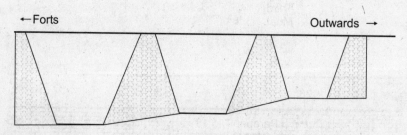

Fig. 8 Arrangements of Moats

Door specifications: Of size three-fifth of the width of the gateway with two bars to each door, 1 1/2' stake (bolt) into the ground inside. Four elephant bars on the outside.   {2.3.24-28}

<u>Other types of gates</u>   {2.3.31-32}

Gopura—same width as the parapet, shaped like a lizard's mouth;

Pushkarini—a well dug in the parapet;

Kumaripura—Four rooms surrounding a courtyard, 9' from each other, with holes for archers;

Mundaka—a two-storeyed hall

Similar forts shall be built at the frontiers.   {2.4.31}

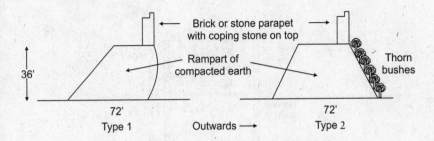

Fig. 9 Cross-sections of Ramparts and Parapets

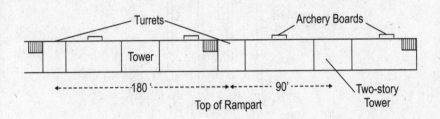

Fig. 10 Location of Towers, Turrets and Archery Boards

THE CAPITAL CITY—LAYOUT

The land inside the fort shall be demarcated by six royal roads, three running from east to west and three, from north to south, with twelve gates. The city shall be provided with water, drainage and covered passages.
{**2.4.1,2**}

The royal buildings shall be erected, facing north or east, on a good building site, in the middle of the residential areas of the four *varnas*, to the north of the centre of the fortified city, occupying one-ninth of the residential area. {**2.4.6,7**}

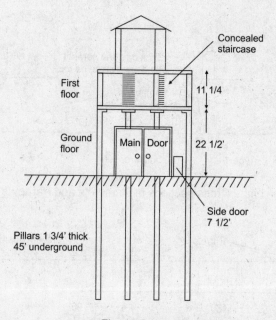

First
floor

Ground
floor

Main Door

Concealed
staircase

11 1/4

22 1/2'

Side door
7 1/2'

Pillars 1 3/4' thick
45' underground

Fig. 11 Gateway

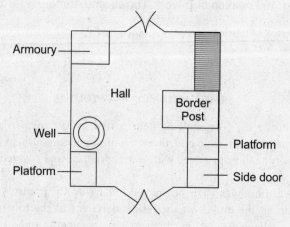

Armoury

Hall

Well

Platform

Border
Post

Platform

Side door

Fig. 12 Gateway Tower-Ground Floor Plan

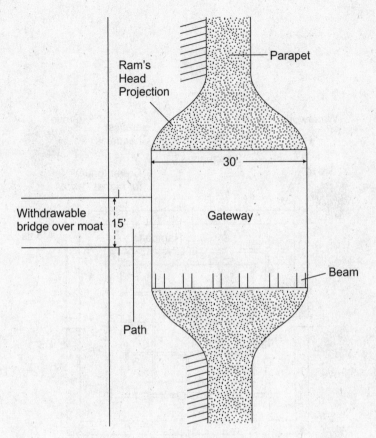

Fig. 13 Gateway-Cross-section

The Governor-General of the City shall make all those who work with fire [e.g. blacksmiths] live in one locality. {2.36.20}

Shrines to the gods of victory as well as temples of Siva, Lakshmi, Vaishravana, Ashvins and Kali shall be built in the centre of the city. Tutelary deities [of the people] shall be installed in different parts of the city and guardian deities at [each of the four principal] gates.

{2.4.17-19}

Outside the city, at a distance of six hundred feet from the moats, sanctuaries, holy places, groves and waterworks shall be made. Cremation grounds shall be designated for the higher *varnas* in the northern or eastern part and for the lower *varnas* in the southern part. {2.4.20,21}

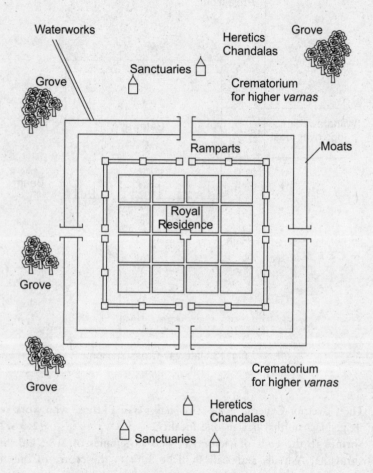

Fig. 14 The City and Environs

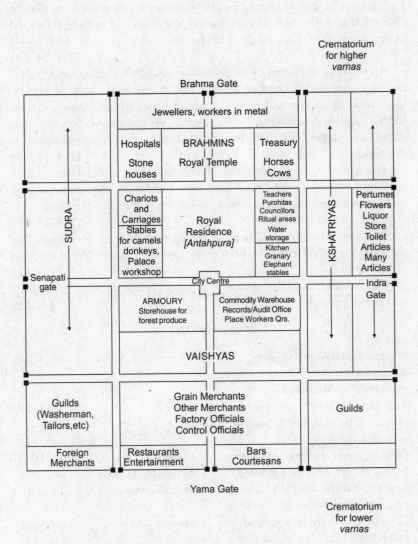

Crematorium
for higher
varnas

Brahma Gate

Jewellers, workers in metal

| Hospitals | BRAHMINS | Treasury |
| Stone houses | Royal Temple | Horses Cows |

SUDRA

| Chariots and Carriages Stables for camels donkeys, Palace workshop | Royal Residence [Antahpura] | Teachers Purohitas Councillors Ritual areas / Water storage / Kitchen Granary Elephant stables | KSHATRIYAS | Pertumes Flowers Liquor Store Toilet Articles Many Articles |

Senapati gate

City Centre

Indra Gate

| ARMOURY Storehouse for forest produce | Commodity Warehouse Records/Audit Office Place Workers Qrs. |

VAISHYAS

| Guilds (Washerman, Tailors,etc) | Grain Merchants Other Merchants Factory Officials Control Officials | Guilds |
| Foreign Merchants | Restaurants Entertainment | Bars Courtesans | |

Yama Gate

Crematorium
for lower
varnas

Fig. 15 Schematic Plan of Fortified City

THE CAPITAL CITY—SECURITY AND WELFARE

Each household shall be allotted the land necessary for its work. They shall be allowed, if so authorised, to grow flowers and fruits and to store grains and other commodities. Each group of ten houses shall be provided with a well.
{2.4.24-26}

Appropriate quantities of the following, enough for a number of years' consumption, shall be kept in storage: oils, grains, sugar, salt, perfumery, medicines, dried vegetables, fodder, dried meat, hay, firewood, metals, hides, charcoal, gut, poisons, horns, bamboo, yarn, strong timber, weapons, shields and stones. Old items in storage should be constantly replaced by new ones.
{2.4.27,28}

The armed forces—elephants, chariots, cavalry and infantry—shall each be under more than one chief. For, with many chiefs, mutual fear will prevent them from succumbing to the temptations of the enemy.
{2.4.29,30}

Outsiders who can cause harm to the country shall not be allowed into the city. They shall either be driven out into the countryside or made to pay all the taxes.
{2.4.32}

Heretics and Candalas shall stay in land allotted to them beyond the cremation grounds.
{2.4.23}

PUNISHMENTS

For not maintaining children, wife, parents, minor brothers and unmarried or widowed sisters	12 panas	{2.1.28}
Becoming an ascetic without providing for the maintenance of wife and children	Lowest SP	{2.1.29}
Entering a fort without permission; leaving a fort with an entrusted object[10] through a [secret] passage or a hole in the wall	Cutting off the sinews of the foot or 200 panas	{4.10.7}
Cremating a body in a ground not reserved for that *varna*	Lowest SP	{2.4.22}

IV.ii

THE ROYAL COUNCILLORS AND MINISTERS

ON THEIR APPOINTMENT, INVESTIGATION OF THEIR LOYALTY AND SEEKING THEIR ADVICE

[The qualities essential for high officials, such as the different grades of councillors and ministers, have been summarised in {1.9.2,1} in II.ii above. The first part of this section deals with the type of men who could be appointed as the king's councillors, as distinct from ministers, a councillor's main function being an adviser to the king. The close advisers to the king accompanied him on military campaigns and were housed near him in the Base Camp {10.1.6} in XI.iv. One of their responsibilities was to boost the morale of the troops before the battle {10.3.32} in XI.iv.

The second part of this section is concerned with the king's deliberations, in secret, with his advisers, before undertaking any task. *Mantra*, or counsel is an important and comprehensive concept in the *Arthashastra*. It does not mean just advice; it implies the whole sequence of deciding on a good policy—collecting the right information, inferring correctly what is not available, analysing all the relevant factors, evaluating them giving each one its due weight and then arriving at the right judgment on the course of action to be followed. According to Kautilya, the power of good counsel, is superior to military strength; with good judgment a king can overwhelm even kings who are mighty and energetic {9.1.14,15}. Kautilya considers weakness in intellectual judgment as much a disadvantage as weakness in morale or resources {7.14.14-27} in X.ix.

The last part of this section deals with ministers—their number and role, ascertaining their qualifications and how to investigate their honesty and integrity.]

THE NEED FOR COUNCILLORS AND MINISTERS

The work of government is threefold—that which the king sees with his own eyes, that which he knows of indirectly through reports made to him and that which he infers about work not done by knowing about work that has been done.

> [While his personal knowledge and the reports coming to him give the king an idea of the accomplishments of his government, he has to infer for himself what his officials have failed to do.]

Because the work of the government is diversified and is carried on simultaneously in many different places, the king cannot do it all himself; he, therefore, has to appoint ministers who will implement it at the right time and place. {1.9.4-8}

APPOINTING COUNCILLORS

Bharadvaja says that the king shall appoint his classmates as royal councillors; for, [having known them since childhood,] the king knows their capability and integrity and can have confidence in them.

Vishalaksha disagrees [and advises against appointing such people] because, having been his childhood friends, they would treat the king with contempt [born of familiarity]. [Instead,] the king shall appoint, as councillors, his associates in secret activities. Such associates are [likely to be] of the same character and temperament; being afraid of the king's knowledge of their secrets, they will not offend the king.

The followers of Parasara disagree with the above, contending that the defect applies to both; [i.e. if the king knows their secrets, so do they know the king's.] The king, too, may be afraid of their knowledge and forgive them their [acts of] omission and commission. [As the old saying goes:] 'Any leader of men becomes subservient to all those to whom he has divulged a secret, by the very act of doing so.' It is better to appoint as a councillor one whose loyalty has been proved by his having helped the king in times of danger to his life.

'No', says Pisuna, 'Such a councillor shows only devotion and this has little to do with intellectual qualities. The king shall appoint as a councillor one who has proved his worth in governmental activities—[for example,] one who, when he had been entrusted with a productive task, had produced as much or more revenue than anticipated in the budget'.

Kaunapadanta disagrees [with the above suggestion] on the grounds that ability to earn more revenue alone is not enough; there are other essential qualities. The King shall appoint as councillors those who belong to hereditary ministerial families. Men whose families have been councillors [or ministers] for generations will have long experience [of administration] and close knowledge [of the royal family]. Such ministers never abandon the king, even if he does not behave well with them. Such faithfulness is seen even among dumb animals; cows, for example, pass by a strange herd and stay with their own.

Vatavyadhi disagrees, pointing out the danger of a hereditary minister bringing everything under his control and becoming, in effect, the ruler. It is better to bring in new blood, from those well-versed in the art of politics. Such new holders of power know that the king can take away what he had bestowed and, therefore, do not offend him.

Bahudantiputra warns against appointing theoreticians without practical experience of politics; they will commit blunders when given a task. The qualities of an individual are of supreme importance [in assessing fitness to be a councillor]. Only those persons who are born of a noble family, wise and possessed of integrity, bravery and loyalty shall be appointed as councillors.

Kautilya considers that everything [referred to in the analysis] above is relevant [depending on the circumstances].   {1.8.1-27}

> [The king may appoint a childhood friend, so long as lie is not allowed to overreach himself; or an associate in secret activities so long as he is not allowed to blackmail the king; or one of proven loyalty, provided he has also proved himself efficient in government; or one from a hereditary family so long as he does not become all-powerful; or bring in new blood, if he has both theoretical ability and practical experience. In any case, anyone who is appointed as a councillor must have the highest personal qualities.]

DELIBERATIONS

A king shall deliberate on undertaking tasks after he has secured the allegiance of his own people as well as of [some] people in the enemy territory.
                                                                {1.15.1}

Just as the ritual offerings of one unlearned in the Vedas is unfit to be eaten by good men, likewise one should not listen to the advice given by those ignorant of the science [of politics].   {1.15.61}

SECRECY

No work shall be undertaken unless it has been carefully examined. Such a scrutiny shall take place in a secret [secluded and well guarded] place from where the discussion cannot be overheard and into which even birds cannot peep; for it is said that the secrecy of deliberations have been breached by parrots and starlings and even by dogs and other animals. Therefore, no unauthorised person shall approach the place of the meeting.

{1.15.2-5}

Secrecy shall be maintained and vigilance exercised over officers who take part in the deliberations till the time of starting the work. Carelessness, intoxication, talking in one's sleep, indulgence in amorous pursuits and similar bad habits are the causes of betrayal of secrets. Persons of an inherently secretive nature or those despised [by the king earlier] will also betray; one should be on one's guard in protecting secrets from falling into the hands of such people.

{1.15.10-12}

Observations of the attitudes and expressions of envoys, ministers and chiefs can reveal that a secret had been divulged [by someone]. [One should be on the lookout for] abnormal behaviour and expressions.

{1.15.7-9}

Anyone who betrays a secret shall be torn to pieces.   {1.15.6}

THE NUMBER OF ADVISERS

Bharadvaja says: 'A secret [prematurely] divulged is fatal to the well-being of the king and the officials entrusted with the task. Every adviser has his own adviser, and the latter, in turn, his adviser [and so on]. Thus, [the series becomes too long and] the secret is divulged [somewhere along the line]. Therefore, a king shall deliberate by himself [without advisers]. (As the saying goes:) 'None shall know what a king sets out to do. Only those who have to implement it should know when the work is begun or when it has been completed.'   {1.15.13-17}

Vishalaksha says: 'Never can a single person arrive at the right decision. The work of government is dependent on [complete] knowledge—that which the king personally knows, that which is reported to him and that which he has to infer. To find out what is not known, to clarify doubts when there are alternatives, to obtain more information when only a part is known—all these can be done only with the help of advisers. Hence, a king shall conduct his deliberations with advisers of mature intelligence. (As the saying goes:) 'Despise no one, [but] listen to all views; for, a wise man pays heed to all sensible advice, even those of a child.'

{1.15.18-22}

The followers of Parasara, however, say: 'This advice tells one how to get different opinions but has nothing to do with maintaining secrecy. [A king should ascertain the views of his advisers indirectly.] He should pose to them a problem similar to the one in mind and then ask for their advice with questions like: "Supposing this or that were to happen, how should we proceed?" He can then follow their advice [in the hypothetical case]. By this method, one obtains advice while maintaining secrecy.'

{1.15.23-26}

Pisuna disagrees. 'Advisers, when asked questions about hypothetical situations, either do not take it seriously [thus giving ill-considered advice] or talk about it openly [thus breaking secrecy]. In neither case is the purpose served. Therefore, the king should consult [only] those who will be involved in the task to be accomplished. Both objectives—getting sound advice and maintaining secrecy—will be achieved.'   {1.15.27-31}

Kautilya disagrees. This method is inherently unstable. [To involve everyone concerned with the work would impose no limit on the numbers. To change advisers for every task would mean a different set for each one.] A king shall confine his deliberations to [at the most] three or four advisers. If he consults only one, he may find it difficult to reach a decision on complicated questions; for a single adviser can behave as he pleases without restraint. If there are only two advisers, they may either combine together and overwhelm him or fight and neutralise each other. If there are more than two, they [may either form a clique or split into factions and] become difficult [to control]. If ever three or four councillors all combine against the king or become involved in a fight among themselves, it spells great danger [for by then it will be too late to regain control].

[There should be no more than four advisers] because, with more than four, secrecy is rarely maintained.   {1.15.32-40}

[While, normally, the king should consult three or four advisers,] he may, depending on the nature of the work and the special circumstances of each case, take a decision by himself, consult just one adviser, or even two.

{1.15.41}

The opinions of the advisers shall be sought individually as well as together [as a group]. The reason why each one holds a particular opinion shall also be ascertained.   {1.15.43,44}

ASPECTS OF DELIBERATION

The five aspects of deliberating on any question are:
  (i)   the objectives to be achieved;
  (ii) the means of carrying out the task;
  (iii) the availability of men and materials;
  (iv) deciding on the time and place [of action]; and
  (v)   contingency plans against failure.   {1.15.42}

Deliberations shall not be unduly delayed once an opportunity for action arises.   {1.15.45}

No one who belongs to the side likely to be adversely affected by the project shall be consulted.   {1.15.46}

THE ROLE OF THE MINISTERS

[The few councillors, who may themselves be ministers, are advisers at the highest levels of policy making. The ministers, who are not councillors, are, primarily, the body of officials who execute these policies. It is worth mentioning here Dr. Kangle's comment that this body was, by no means, 'a Cabinet armed with powers to enforce its decision on the King.'[1]]

Every man shall be judged according to his ability to perform [a given task]. The king shall appoint as ministers, but not as councillors, all those judged to be fit [to hold ministerial office] and divide the work of the government among them, taking into account each one's ability and the nature of the work assigned to him.   {1.8.28-29}

The followers of Manu say that a king should appoint a council of twelve ministers. The students of Brihaspati suggest sixteen and those who follow Ushanas, twenty.

Kautilya says: "The number shall be according to need. Indra, indeed, had a council of one thousand ministers; they were his eyes. That is why he is called the 'thousand-eyed one', though he had only two eyes."
                                        {1.15.47-50,55-57}

The ministers shall [constantly] think of all that concerns the king as well as those of the enemy. They shall start doing all that has not [yet] been done, continue implementing that which has been started, improve on works completed and, in general, ensure strict compliance with orders.
                                                  {1.15.51-52}

The king shall personally supervise the work of those ministers near him. With those farther away, he shall communicate by sending letters.
                                                  {1.15.53-54}

In an emergency, the king shall call together both the group of councillors and the council of ministers and seek their advice. He shall follow whatever the majority advise or whatever is conducive to the success of the task in hand.   {1.15.58-59}

INVESTIGATION BEFORE APPOINTMENT

[The king shall thoroughly investigate all the qualities of anyone whom he is considering for appointment as a minister.] Of these qualities, nationality, family background and amenability to discipline shall be verified from reliable people [who know the candidate well]. The candidate's knowledge of the various arts shall be tested by experts in their respective fields. Intelligence, perseverance and dexterity shall be evaluated by examining his past performance, while eloquence, boldness and presence of mind shall be ascertained by interviewing him personally. Watching how he deals with others will show his energy, endurance, ability to suffer adversities, integrity, loyalty and friendliness. From his intimate friends, the king shall find out about his strength, health, and character (whether lazy or energetic, fickle or steady). The candidate's amiability and love of mankind [absence of a tendency to hate] shall be ascertained by personal observation. {1.9.3}

TESTING THE INTEGRITY OF MINISTERS

The king, after appointing someone as a minister in consultation with his councillors and the *purohita*, shall test his integrity by a [variety] of secret tests. {1.10.1}

[He shall make use of the appropriate person to conduct each of the four kinds of tests based on *dharma*, *artha*, *kama* and fear. These tests are designed to entice someone to defect by appeals to their religious sentiments or piety, by promise of financial reward, by temptation of the flesh or by playing on fear. Details of the four tests, as given by earlier teachers, are in IX.iii. Kautilya, however, warns of the dangers of attempting to corrupt innocent minds.]

The ancient teachers have laid down that the king shall allot duties to the ministers appropriate to their integrity as determined by the four tests. For example, he shall appoint those proved pure by the test of *dharma* to judicial and law and order posts. Those proved pure by the *artha* test shall be appointed as the Chancellor or the Treasurer, those proved pure by the test of *kama* as controllers of recreation inside and outside the palace and those proved by the test of fear to duties near the [person of the] king. Those who succeed in every test shall be appointed to the highest office of councillor. Those who fail every test shall be sent off to [difficult] posts such as mines, forests, elephant forests or factories. {1.10.13-16}

[However, Kautilya cautions that these ancient teachings shall not be accepted completely.] Kautilya says: 'Under no circumstances shall the king make himself or his [principal] Queen the target for ascertaining the probity of a minister. Furthermore, he shall not corrupt the uncorrupted; that would be like adding poison to water: for, it may well happen that a cure may not be found for one so corrupted. Even the mind of the steadfast and the valiant may not return to its original purity if it is perverted by the fourfold secret tests. Hence, the king shall make an outsider the object of reference for the tests and then investigate through secret agents the integrity of his ministers.   {1.10.17-20}

[After verifying the integrity of his high officials, the next duty of the king was to create the secret service {1.11.1} see IX.ii]

PUNISHMENT

Divulging a state secret   Tongue pulled out   {4.11.21}

IV.iii

SERVICE WITH A KING

[The previous section dealt with how a king should choose his councillors and ministers. Kautilya also examines the question from the point of view of one aspiring to high office under a monarch.]

SEEKING SERVICE

Whoever is experienced in the ways of the world shall seek service with a king possessing the highest personal qualities [of leadership, intellect, energy and other personal attributes as described in [{6.1.2-6} in II.ii] and the [best] attributes of a state with the help of courtiers and other friends of the king. He may even seek service with a monarch who lacks the best of the other attributes, so long as the ruler has qualities of leadership and is accessible. Under no circumstances shall he seek a position with a king whose character is not good. Such a ruler, however mighty he may be, will cease to exist due to his contempt for political science or due to association with harmful persons.   {5.4.1-3}

After obtaining an audience with a good king, the aspirant shall discuss [political] science with him. [The reason being:] His position will be secure only when the ruler holds opinions which are not contrary to [the teachings of] political science. If the king asks questions which require intelligent consideration, the aspirant shall reply briefly, [strictly] in accordance with the eternal principles of *dharma* and *artha*, without being afraid of those present.   {5.4.4-6}

If the king wants to appoint him [to a post], the aspirant shall stipulate that the monarch shall not seek the advice of those who have not distinguished themselves in [the sciences of] *dharma* and *artha* or punish those who have powerful support; the ruler shall also agree to show consideration to the appointee by agreeing that his livelihood will not be harmed or his secrets divulged, and those associated with him not harmed or punished summarily.   {5.4.7}

BEHAVIOUR AFTER APPOINTMENT

If the king agrees to the stipulations and the aspirant is appointed, the official may take up the duties assigned to him.

He shall always be at the side of the king, neither too close nor too far away, and

– not talk slyly against other advisers;
– not say things which are not carefully thought out and which are untrue, uncultured, or outside his knowledge;
– not laugh loudly when there is nothing to laugh about; when there is cause, he may laugh but not too loudly;
– avoid [uncouth behaviour like] spitting and breaking wind;
– neither talk in secret with another [adviser] nor become quarrelsome in public debate;
– not dress [above his station] like royalty nor in a gaudy or clownish fashion;
– not openly ask for gems or special favours;
– not indulge in [unseemly gestures like] winking, biting the lips and frowning;
– not interrupt while another is speaking;
– not antagonise the powerful;
– not associate with [disreputable] women, pimps, envoys of neighbouring kings, those supporting the enemy, dismissed officers, wicked people, those who form a group for a single objective nor with specialised lobbies.

{5.4.8-10,14}

He shall [try to] turn the king away from saying evil things about others and shall not himself use evil words against anyone. He shall tolerate evil spoken to him and show as much forbearance as Mother Earth.

{5.4.15}

GIVING ADVICE

He shall give his advice always in accordance with *dharma* and *artha*. If it is a matter in the king's interest, he shall speak without procrastination; if it is a matter in his own interest, he shall speak when in the company of persons friendly to him and if in the interest of someone else, he shall choose an appropriate time and place.   {5.4.11}

[In some situations, the courtier may be faced with a dilemma; the course of action which is in the best interests of the king and the Kingdom ('good' advice) may not be the one which the king wants to hear ('pleasing' advice).]

When asked, he shall say those things which are both good and pleasing [to the king]. He shall never give advice that is harmful [just] because it pleases the monarch; but he may, provided the king is prepared to listen and gives permission, give, in private, good advice which may not please the monarch. {5.4.12}

He may even remain silent when asked for his opinion but shall never say anything that is unwelcome to or likely to provoke the king. Even competent people may be cast out if they say unwelcome things and undesirable people who know the mind and inclinations of the monarch may become favourites. {5.4.13,14}

SURVIVAL

Service under a king has been compared to living in a fire [but is, in fact, worse]. A fire may burn a part of one's body and, at its worst, all of it; but a king [goes from one extreme to another. He] may either confer prosperity or may have the whole family, including wives and children, killed. [Therefore,] a wise man makes self-protection his first and constant concern. {5.4.16,17}

When assigned to a [particular] task, he shall report to the king the net income after meeting all expenditure. {5.5.1}

He shall advise the monarch on the work to be done, giving details about whether it pertains to the city or to the countryside, whether open or covert and whether urgent or postponable. {5.5.2}

He shall keep a watch over the king's [harmful] activities such as hunting, gambling, drinking or women. He shall endeavour, by flattery, to wean the king away from [such] evil habits. He shall guard the monarch from intrigues, plots and machinations of enemies. {5.5.3,4}

He shall watch carefully the king's gestures and expressions; a wise man will know the mind of another who is trying to reach a decision by looking out for the following: liking and hatred, joy and distress, resoluteness and fear. {5.5.5,6}

That the king is satisfied with a courtier is shown by the following: looking pleased at the sight of the courtier, returning his greeting, giving him a seat, giving him a private audience, not suspecting him when suspicion is possible, taking pleasure in conversing with him, attending to [his] matters without being reminded, tolerating what he says reasonably, giving orders with a smile, touching him, not ridiculing him when praise is due, praising him in his absence, remembering [to invite] him during meal times, going with him on pleasure trips, telling him secrets, honouring his followers, according him greater honours, granting him favours, preventing any harm that may come to him and helping him when in trouble. {5.5.7}

That the king is dissatisfied with a courtier is shown by the following opposite indications: looking angry at the sight of the courtier, ignoring or not returning his greeting, neither giving him a seat nor looking at him, changing his expression or speech when talking to him, looking at him with expressions of disapproval (with eyes, eyebrows or lips), perspiring in his presence, smiling or sighing without cause, talking with another [while ignoring the courtier], going away suddenly, showing favours to others, showing signs of impatience like scratching his body or the ground, instigating others [against the courtier], showing contempt for the courtier's knowledge, *varna* or region, censuring some one for doing something similar [to that done by the courtier in disfavour], finding fault with everything the courtier does, praising his enemies, not acknowledging his good work, talking about his bad work, looking somewhere else [like the far end of the room] when the courtier is speaking, showing extreme indifference and telling him lies. Such displeasure can also be seen when there is a change in the behaviour towards the courtier of those who frequently see the king.   {5.5.8,9}

The courtier shall also watch out for signs [of the king's displeasure] by observing changes in animate beings and inanimate things.

> [Kautilya then gives examples from history of courtiers who managed to leave a King's service in time. One minister took took the hint when a servant carelessly poured water on him from above. Another did so on seeing an evil omen—a heron flying from right to left. Other courtiers left when a negligible gift was bestowed in place of a better one which was deserved, when given a cold instead of a warm garment, when made to look ridiculous by being drenched by an elephant, when their chariots or horses were praised by the King but not their ability in riding them and when a King's dog barked at them.]
>   {from 5.5.10,11}

When a king deprives a courtier of wealth and honour, it is better to resign. Alternatively, he may recognise his own defects and, in the light of his understanding of the king, reform himself.

[When he leaves the king's service,] the courtier may seek the intervention of a close friend of the monarch. He shall stay with the friend and, through him and other friends, try to remove the [king's] misunderstanding about him. If he succeeds, he can return to his position.

Otherwise, he may return [only] after the death of the king.

{5.5.12-15}

IV.iv

HIGHEST LEVEL OFFICIALS

[In the Kautilyan state, there were eighteen categories of *mahamatras* (high officials), there being more than one official in some of the categories. However, not all of them can be considered to have occupied posts in the highest echelon. When describing the duties of senior officials, such as Heads of Departments, Kautilya does not separately list those considered to be of the highest rank. It is also not clear which of these were deemed to be ministers or, the even more exalted councillors. However, we can deduce the rank of an official from his salary and the reason Kautilya gives for fixing his salary at a particular level. The nature and extent of the duties of the official provide another indication; for example, the *Samahartr* (Chancellor) was obviously a very high official, since he had under his charge both revenue collection and maintenance of law and order of the whole of the countryside, including the secret service. Another clue is the fact that some of the Heads of Departments were clearly subordinates, as in the cases of the Chief Superintendents of the Treasury, the granaries and warehouses who worked under the *Samnidhatr* (Treasurer).

The highest salary, 48,000 panas a year, ('enough to prevent them from succumbing to the temptations of the enemy or rising up in revolt'), was a princely sum; those entitled to it were no doubt also recipients of other perquisites and special gifts, favours and tax exemptions from the king. Apart from the king's councillors (who numbered not more than four and one of whom also functioned as the Royal Scribe), seven others are named ex officio. Three are obvious—the king's mother, the principal Queen and the Crown Prince, these being the closest relatives entitled to Privy Purses. While, as shown in III.iv, there is a great deal in the text about princes who may try to usurp the throne, there is very little about the actual duties of the Crown Prince. An heir-apparent, who was content to wait his turn to succeed, appears to have performed whatever duties were assigned to him; in two cases he was an alternative to the Chief of Defence. A treacherous high official may surrender to either {5.1.53} in III.v. The Crown Prince or the Chief of Defence could also be designated to lead a military campaign when the king himself was obliged to stay in the capital to deal with the threat of a revolt in the rear {9.3.7} in X.vi.

Three among the seven were Brahmins who occupied special positions. The priest officiating at sacrifices was paid the highest salary for his special knowledge of rituals. The second, the king's guru, was owed respect and reverence. The duties of the third, the *Purohita*, are described later in this section. The seventh officer, paid the highest salary, was the Chief of Defence whose duties are described in this translation in XI.ii on military organization.

It is in the next grade—annual salary of 24,000 panas ('enough to make them efficient in their work')—that we find a list of those civilian officials placed highest in the hierarchy. Very little is known about three of the five in the list. The offices of *Dauvarika* and *Antarvamsika* appear in the salary list (see section VI.ii); they 'are also mentioned as people of importance who had to be watched over by spies and whose cooperation was essential in the event of the imminence of the king's death. The duties of the *Dauvarika* (literally 'doorkeeper'), were those of a Chamberlain—arranging the king's programme, looking after his comforts, ensuring that the king's valet and barber were issued clothes and implements in sealed packages, etc. The *antarvamsika* (inner palace official) was an important official controlling the king's appointments. We find a mention of the *antarvamsikasainya* (the King's Own Guards) as guarding the king, not only in the palace {1.20.13 and 1.21.3} but also in the camp when on a military expedition {10.1.3}. Both the *dauvarika* and the *antarvamsika* played an important role in organizing the succession to a king seriously ill, by making it appear that the king was as active as ever {5.6.5} in III.vi. Even less is known about the official called *Prasastr*. Since his office is named immediately after the *Dauvarika* and the *Antarvamsika*, he may also have been a high official of the palace. On the other hand, since his name precedes those of the Treasurer and the Chancellor, he could have been an official with responsibilities outside the Palace, such as the judiciary or the administration of the capital city. Apart from the salary list and the list of *mahamatras*, the *Prasastr* is mentioned only in one other place in the text {10.1.17}.

The two remaining officials on a salary of 24,000 panas a year are the Treasurer and the Chancellor. Their duties are explained in detail in this section. While both the Treasurer and the Chancellor had to be persons of the highest integrity, Kautilya considers that a dishonest Chancellor does more harm to the State than a dishonest Treasurer {8.4.31-33} in II.iv.

One level below—at 12,000 panas per annum ('enough to ensure that they remain loyal and powerful servants of the King')—we find provincial and frontier governors. These had to be kept happy with a high salary in order to prevent them from succumbing to the temptation of becoming independent.

It is necessary to add to the above list the office of the Chief Comptroller and Auditor. It is clear from his responsibilities and the fact that he reported directly to the king that the Chief Comptroller performed a very important function. His role is described immediately after that of the Chancellor and before that of the Royal Scribe. Three chapters {2.7}, {2.8} and {2.9} are devoted to book-keeping and accounts, fraud and misappropriation by government servants and to inspection. Though a specific scale has not been laid down by Kautilya for this official it is difficult to believe that he would have been treated on par with other Heads of Departments and paid a salary of only 1000 panas, particularly as the office could not have had many perquisites associated with it.

Kautilya's description of the duties of the Royal Scribe, one of the councillors, is primarily a short treatise on how to write good Royal Edicts. This is included in full in this section.

Only the duties and responsibilities of high civilian officials are described in this section. Those of military officials, including those in charge of elephants, elephant forests and ordnance, are given under 'military organization' in XI.i.

One other official mentioned in the text is 'Sunyapala'. This was not a regular post but a designation temporarily given when a mahamatra was put in charge of the state by the king, especially when the king was away on a military expedition. The Viceroy is mentioned in {13.2.25-31} and {9.3.10} as well as in {12.3,5,7,9} as a target for subversion.

Three of the officials mentioned here—nayaka, prasastr and antapala—are also referred to in Book 10 on war. It is clear that they were not the same as the civilian officials but were military officers who performed similar functions in a military camp. For example, the nayaka might have been the Camp Administrator, the prasastr the Camp disciplinary officer and the antapala, the perimeter commander; see {10.1.1}, {10.2.4}, {10.6.45} and {10.1.8,16,17} in XI.iv.

We also note that there was no separate diplomatic service. Envoys of three different grades were chosen from among the high officials. The duties of envoys are described in X.i.

According to {1.12.6}, there were eighteen mahamatras. There is no agreement among different translators even on who the eighteen were; translations of the nomenclature also differ widely. The terminology used by Kangle, Shamasastry and R.K. Mookerji is shown in a comparative

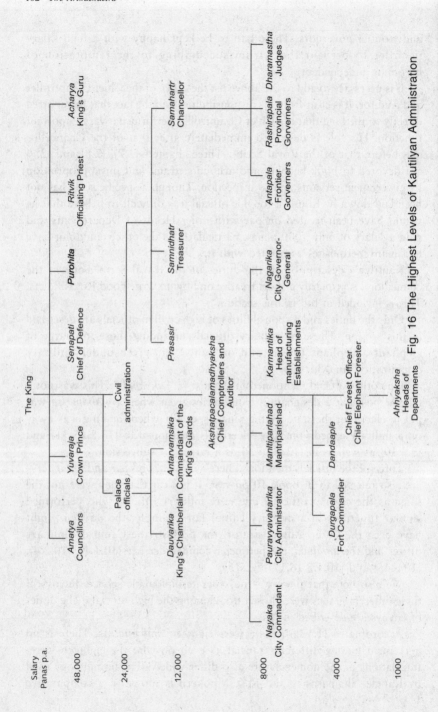

Fig. 16 The Highest Levels of Kautilyan Administration

Table, along with that used in this translation, in Appendix 7. An explanatory note is given in Notes on Translation No.4.]

PUROHITA

(Salary—48,000 panas a year)

The king shall appoint as the *purohita* (the Royal Chaplain) one from the very highest family, of the most exemplary character, learned in all the Vedas and their branches, expert in reaching omens, well-versed in the science of politics and capable of performing the correct expiatory rites against acts of God and human calamities. The king shall follow him as a pupil does his teacher, a son his father and a servant his master.

{1.9.9,10}

[The *purohita*, though highly respected and very well paid, had no direct role in the administration of the state. He had considerable personal influence over the ruler because of his knowledge of religion, ritual and politics and because he was presumed to give disinterested advice. He was consulted on the appointment of ministers {1.10.1} in IV.ii. Kautilya emphasises the special position of the *purohita* by enjoining that, even if he commits a grave offence like treason, he shall not be killed but only imprisoned or exiled {9.3.14} in III.v. His presence in court was required whenever the king received Brahmins and ascetics in audience {1.19.31} in III.iii. He could also be used to test the integrity of ministers {1.10.24} in X.iii. He accompanied the king on expeditions of conquest and was accommodated near the king in the base camp {10.1.6} in XI.iv. His duty was to give encouraging talks to the troops before the battle.]

THE ROYAL SCRIBE

(Salary—48,000 panas a year)

QUALIFICATIONS:

A person fit to be appointed as the Royal Scribe shall have the same qualifications as those for a Royal Councillor. He shall have a [thorough] knowledge of all conventions, be quick in composition and have good handwriting. He shall also be able to read [clearly] documents and edicts.

{2.10.3}

RESPONSIBILITIES

The scribe shall listen attentively to the king's instructions and write them down precisely.   {2.10.4}

ROYAL EDICTS

It is the [accepted] teaching that a Royal Edict (a *sasana*) is so called because it is used to issue a command [order or directive] or for purposes of administration.[1]

The rule of kings depends primarily on [written] orders; even peace and war have their roots in them.

GENERAL PRINCIPLES

Tone: Every document shall be composed keeping in mind the circumstances for which it is written and in a manner befitting the recipient. The latter shall take into account the recipient's caste, family background, social position, age learning, profession, property, character and relationship by blood or marriage [with the king].   {2.10.5}

CHARACTERISTICS OF A GOOD EDICT[2]

(a) Topical Order: is stating the principal subject first and arranging the rest logically.

(b) Non-contradiction: is ensuring that a statement made later is not incompatible with one made earlier, throughout the edict.

(c) Completeness: is avoiding redundancy or deficiency of letters, words and subject matter; citing reasons, quotations and illustrative examples; avoiding tired words (i.e. cliches); and using [appropriately] expressive words.

(d) Sweetness: is using words which are pleasant and precise in their meaning.

(e) Dignity: is [achieved by] avoiding vulgarisms.

(f) Lucidity: is [achieved by] using words which are well-known.

{2.10.6-12}

DEFECTS

The defects [to be avoided] are:

(a) Absence of Charm: Using bad paper (black palm leaf) and writing unattractively, unevenly and illegibly result in clumsiness.

(b) Contradiction: is making part of the edict incompatible with another part.

(c) <u>Repetition</u>.

(d) <u>Bad grammar:</u> is using wrong gender, number, tense or case.

(e) <u>Confusion:</u> arises when mistakes of arrangement are made; examples are: dividing into paragraphs where inappropriate or not marking new paragraphs where they should be.   {2.10.57-62}

TYPES OF DOCUMENTS

There are nine types of Royal Edicts:

(a) <u>Informatory:</u> documents are of various kinds, such as:
  – report of information received [e.g. from an envoy];
  – report of an oral communication;
  – a conditional order [e.g. 'If there is any truth in this report, then the following shall be done.'];
  – 'The good work done by you has come to our notice'.

(b) <u>Commands:</u> deal with the king's favours and punishments, particularly when they are addressed to servants of the Crown.

(c) <u>Awards:</u> Honours bestowed according to merit, help given to some one in distress and gifts in general.

(d) <u>Exemptions:</u> Grant of favours [such as remission of taxes], by the order of the king, to a caste, village or a region.

(e) <u>Authorizations:</u> to do a work, to issue orders or a general authorization to do whatever is necessary.

(f) <u>Guidance:</u> about remedial action to be taken in case of calamities due to Acts of God or actions of evil men.

(g) <u>Response:</u> a reply, prepared strictly according to the words of the king, after he has read and discussed a communication received.

(h) <u>Proclamations:</u> [Orders] applicable everywhere and publicised widely within the country. [An example is a proclamation] calling on all Governors and other officials to give protection to and provide adequate comforts for travellers.   {2.10.38-46}

COMPOSITION

(a) <u>Salutation:</u> Every document shall begin with an [appropriate] salutation, in polite terms, of the following:

–in the case of kings and nobles: country, riches [territory, treasury and army], pedigree and name [with full titles];

–in the case of others: country and his name.   {2.10.4}

(b) <u>Subject matter:</u> The theme of a Royal Edict can be any one of the following [thirteen]:

- <u>Derogatory remarks</u>: i.e. mentioning defects of birth, body or actions;
- <u>Praise</u>: i.e. mentioning the good points of the above;
- <u>Query</u>;
- <u>Statement</u>: [of a position or circumstance];
- <u>Request</u>;
- <u>Refusal</u>;
- <u>Reproof</u>: e.g. 'This is unworthy of you';
- <u>Prohibition</u>: e.g. 'Do not do so';
- <u>Command</u>: e.g. 'Do this';
- <u>Conciliation</u>: e.g. 'What I am, thou art that; whatever is mine is yours';
- <u>Offer of help</u>;
- <u>Menace</u>: i.e. pointing out the dangerous consequences which will follow [an action];
- <u>Propitiation</u>: which is of three kinds: propitiating someone for the sake of money, to right a wrong done to someone or to assist someone in trouble. {2.10.23-37}

(c) <u>Conclusion</u>: Every document shall end with 'Thus in the words of'[3] followed by the name and title of the king. {2.10.22}

PUNISHMENTS

Royal Scribe deliberately writing down wrongly a Royal Edict, by omission or commission	Cutting off both feet and a hand or a fine 900 panas	{4.10.14}

THE TREASURER

(Salary—24,000 panas a year)

QUALIFICATIONS:

[Kautilya has laid down the qualities necessary for appointment to one of the two highest paid Grade II administrative offices of the Crown, in {1.10.13} in IV.ii where it is noted that he shall be incorruptible.]

RESPONSIBILITIES:

(i) Construction of Storehouses:
The Treasurer shall be responsible for the construction of all buildings concerned with storing Government property, namely, the Treasury, the

commodity warehouse, the granary, the store for forest produce and the ordnance depots. He shall also be responsible for the construction of jails. {2.5.1}

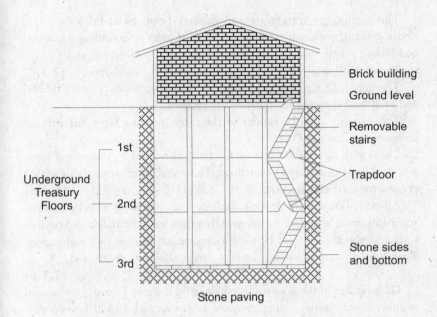

Fig. 17 Treasury-Cross-section

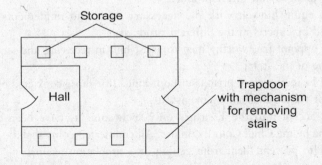

Fig. 18 Ground Floor Plan of Brick Building

Underground floors [shall have] different sized rooms [to store different types of commodities?].

Alternatively, the whole treasury could be built above ground.

{2.5.2-3}

The <u>commodity warehouse and granary</u> [shall be a] brick building, above ground, with many rooms on all four sides surrounding a covered quadrangle on two rows of pillars and with only one entrance.

There shall be a rain-gauge in the commodity warehouse.   {2.5.7}

The <u>store for forest produce</u> shall have many long sheds [to store timber] and with walled rooms for other forest produce.

The <u>armoury</u> shall be similar to the forest produce store but with an underground room.

There shall be separate prisons for those convicted by judges and those punished by Ministers and Councillors. There shall be separate well-guarded prisons for men and women.   {2.3.5}

All store-houses and prisons shall be provided with a well, latrines, and bathrooms, and shall be adequately protected against fire and poison. Cats and mongooses shall be used as protection against rats and snakes. Shrines for the [appropriate] tutelary deities shall be constructed.

{2.5.6}

On a border of the country, he shall build a secret Treasury to be used in times of calamities, using convicts as labour, who shall be executed after the work is done.   {2.5.4}

(ii) <u>Receipt and Storage of Government Property</u>:

The Treasurer shall:

(a) be responsible for the receipt on government account of gems (old and new), precious metals, articles of high value (*sara*), articles of lesser value (*phalgu*) and forest produce;[4]

(b) equip himself with the necessary tools and implements and be assisted by experts in the different products;

(c) appoint trustworthy men to assist him in receiving and storing the revenue of the state;

(d) be in charge of prisons of both kinds [for those convicted by judges and for those punished by magistrates];

(e) accept into the Treasury only such coins as have been certified genuine by the Chief Coin Examiner. All counterfeit coins shall be cut into pieces [to prevent them from getting into circulation again].

(f) accept into the granary new grain, clean and in full measure.

{2.5.8,10,11,13,21}

(iii) <u>Reporting</u>:

He shall have so thorough a knowledge of the receipts and disbursements from the city and from the countryside that, when questioned, he shall not falter in giving details of the income, expenditure and net balance for [accounts relating to] a period of even a hundred years.   {2.5.22}

(iv) <u>Discipline</u>:

If the Treasurer causes loss to the Treasury due to ignorance he shall be censured and if it is deliberate he shall be whipped; those abetting him shall receive half the punishment.   {2.5.16-19}

[For punishments relating to offences against the Treasury, see end of this section.]

THE CHANCELLOR

(Salary—24,000 panas a year)

[The Chancellor was one of the most important high officials under the Crown. He was responsible for collecting revenue from the whole of the country. The administration of the countryside (i.e. all settled parts of the country excepting the fortified towns), particularly law and order and the secret service, were also his responsibility. His counterpart in the cities for these specific duties was the Governor General of the City. The qualifications necessary for appointment to this post were the same as those required for appointment as Treasurer.]

RESPONSIBILITIES:

(i) Revenue collection:

The Chancellor shall be responsible for:

(a) the collection of revenue from the fortified towns, the countryside, the mines, the irrigation works, forests and trade routes; and   {2.6.1}

(b) the preparation of the budget and maintenance of detailed accounts of revenue and expenditure as prescribed.[5]   {from 2.6.10-27}

A wise Chancellor is one who collects revenue so as to increase income and reduce expenditure. He shall take remedial measures if income diminishes and expenditure increases.   {2.6.28}

(ii) <u>Administration of the Countryside</u>:

(a) The Chancellor shall divide the countryside into four provinces and [clearly] demarcate the boundaries of each village. He shall appoint a Governor (*sthanika*) for each province and a Record Keeper (*gopa*) for every group of five to ten villages.

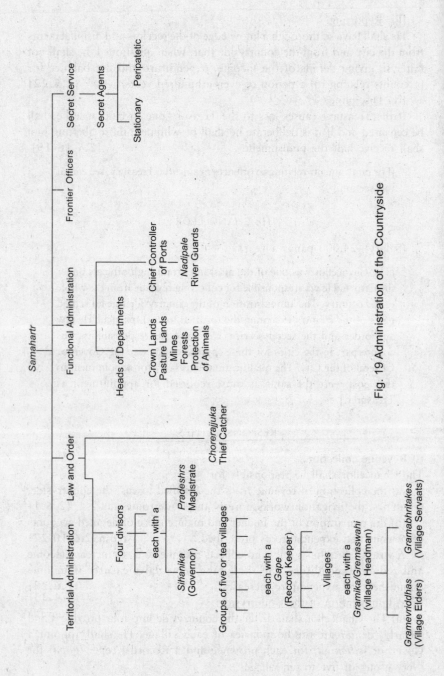

Fig. 19 Administration of the Countryside

(b) [The Record Keepers (for the villages under their charge) and the Governors (for their provinces) shall maintain records as follows.] The villages shall be classified as best, average or lowest. They shall also be classified according to whether they are [tax paying or] tax-exempt, whether they supply soldiers [in lieu of tax], and whether they supply [fixed amounts of] grain, cattle, gold, forest produce, labour or other commodities. [Within each village,] every plot of land shall be numbered and its use recorded according to the classification: cultivated or fallow, dry or wet cultivation, park, vegetable garden [and orchard], enclosed area, forest, sanctuary, temple, water works, cremation ground, rest-house, public drinking-water facility, holy place, pasture and road. These records shall be used for determining the location of fields, forests and roads [in case of boundary disputes] and to record transactions such as gifts, sales, charitable endowments and tax exemptions. [Likewise,] each house shall be numbered and classified as whether tax-paying or tax-exempt. Records of the inhabitants shall also be kept under the following headings: (i) the *varna*, (ii) occupation (such as farmer, cowherd, trader, craftsman, labourer or slave); (iii) the number of males and females as well as the number of children and old people, their [family] history, occupation, income and expenditure; (iv) livestock and poultry owned; (v) the amount of tax payable in cash or in free labour; and (vi) tolls and fines that may be due.

In each place where there is a Record Keeper or Governor [responsible for collection of revenue] magistrates shall [also] be posted to inspect their work and to ensure proper collection of taxes, particularly the Special Emergency Dues. {2.35.1-7}

(iii) <u>Control</u>:

The Chancellor shall be always diligent in administering the *Janapada* and shall employ the [appropriate] secret agents to ensure that servants of the State perform their duties.[6] {2.35.15}

(iv) <u>Eliminating anti-social persons</u>:

There are thirteen types of undesirable persons who amass wealth secretly by causing injury to the population. [These are: corrupt judges and magistrates, heads of villages or departments who extort money from the public, perjurers and procurers of perjury, those who practise witchcraft, black magic or sorcery, poisoners, narcotic dealers, counterfeiters and adulterators of precious metals.] When they are exposed by secret agents, they shall either be exiled or made to pay adequate compensation proportionate to the gravity of the offence.[7]

{4.4.23}

When thieves and robbers are arrested, the Chancellor shall parade them before the people of the city or the countryside [as the case may be] and proclaim that the criminals were caught under the instructions of the King, an expert in detecting thieves. The people shall be warned to keep under control any relative with criminal tendencies, because all thieves were bound to be caught [like the ones paraded before them].   {4.5.13}

If the Chancellor comes to know through spies that someone has stolen [a trifling object like] a yoke pin or a goad, the culprit shall be paraded before the people as proof of the [omniscient] power of the king.

{4.5.14}

Likewise, the Chancellor shall parade before the people forest bandits and [criminal] tribes caught with stolen goods as proof of the king's omniscience.

{4.5.18}

(v) Control over Government Servants:

The Chancellor, working through the magistrates, shall be responsible for inspecting Heads of Departments, judicial officers and their subordinates.

{4.9.1}

> [For punishments prescribed for crimes committed by civil servants, such as stealing or falsifying documents, see {4.9.2-12}, under Civil Servants. For punishments for improper behaviour by judges, their assistants and jailers, see {4.9.13-27} in VIII.iii.
>
> The Chancellor is also responsible, in times of urgent need to augment the resources of the state, for making farmers cultivate summer crops {5.2.8-13} and for seeking voluntary contributions from the public {5.2.31-34} in V.ii.]

THE GOVERNOR GENERAL OF THE CITY

(Salary—12,000 panas a year)

> [The qualifications required for appointment as *nagarika*, the officer in charge of administering a fortified city, would be similar to those of the Chancellor, except that, with a salary probably half of that of the Chancellor, the Governor General would be a more junior official with half the standard expected of the former.]

RESPONSIBILITIES:

(i) Record Keeping:

The City Governor General shall be responsible for the administration of the city just as the Chancellor is responsible for the administration of the countryside. He shall divide the city into four parts and appoint a Governor for each one. (Under the Governors, he shall appoint Record Keepers (*gopas*) in charge of ten, twenty or forty families. The Record Keepers and the Governors shall keep records of the number of people (in each family), their sex, caste, family name, occupation, income and expenditure. {2.36.1-4}

(ii) Other duties:

> [The other duties of the City Governor General have to be gleaned from {2.36} which prescribes the duties of the citizens and the punishments for breach of civic discipline. Translations of these verses concerning citizens will be found in Vii.xi. The duties of the Governor General, briefly described below, are consequential to the characteristics of urban living—higher density of population, greater dependence on trade, need for efficient distribution of essential commodities to the public, urban crime, fire hazards, sanitation, internal security and maintenance of prisons.]

The City Governor General shall be responsible for:

(a) control over charitable lodging houses and ensuring that visitors to the city stay at the places specified for them;

(b) control over trade, particularly sale at fair prices and prevention of sale of stolen goods;

(c) maintenance of law and order, particularly observance of curfew regulations;

(d) ensuring observance of fire precautions and providing fire fighting equipment;

(e) ensuring cleanliness and sanitation, including control over cremation grounds;

(f) prisons; and

(g) custody of lost property.   {Summary of 2.36.5-39,43-47}

Fire prevention:

The Governor General shall make all those who work with fire [e.g. blacksmiths] live in one locality and shall remove any thatch found in that locality.

He shall arrange to have thousands of water jars kept in the following places: main roads, cross roads, city gates and all royal buildings [including the Treasury and the commodity warehouses.]   {2.36.19,20,22}

(iii) Control:

The Governor General shall make a daily inspection of water reservoirs, roads, drains, underground passages, ramparts and other fortifications.
{2.36.43}

He shall maintain control over the City Guards and punish them for any transgressions.   {2.30.42}

[Punishments for misbehaving guards given at end of section.]

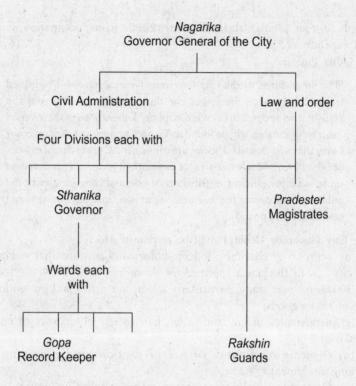

Fig. 20 City Administration

CHIEF COMPTROLLER AND AUDITOR

(Salary—Not given)

RESPONSIBILITIES

(i) <u>Construction</u>:

The Chief Comptroller and Auditor is responsible for the construction and maintenance of the Records Office which shall be built facing north or east, with separate seats for accountants and well-ordered shelves for account books. {2.7.1}

(ii) <u>Maintenance of Records</u>:

The following shall be maintained:

(a) [a consolidated] Account Book showing, for each Department, the nature of its activity and the total income received from it;

(b) in the case of manufacturing establishments, the following:

[a stock register showing] the [raw] materials [bought or received], the quantities consumed in manufacturing, stock changes due to transaction tax or use of different weights and measures and changes due to mixing of materials;[8]

–[a manufacturing costs register showing] expenditure on the labour employed and wages paid;

(c) in the case of stores of all kinds (jewellery, articles of high and low value and forest produce): the price, the quality, the quantity (by weight or by volume) and description of the containers in which they are stored;

(d) for each region, village, caste, family and guild [or corporation]: a rule book of customary laws regarding social customs and economic transactions;

(e) for servants of the Crown: all grants, titles to land, gifts, land allotted for use (as part of the conditions of service), exemptions and remissions, salary and perquisites;

(f) for the Royal Household [Queens and Princes]: gifts of jewellery and land, special allowances and provisions made against sudden calamities [emergency funds];

(g) for Foreign Affairs: payments and receipts, both for making peace and waging war, with allies as well as enemies.[9]   {2.7.2}

The Closing Day for the Accounting Year shall be the full moon day of the month of *Asadha* [June/July], the year consisting of 354 days (according to the lunar calendar) with a separate book for the intercalary month.[10]

{2.7.6-8,16}

[The form for maintaining Account Books is given in V.iii]

(iii) <u>Rule Compilation:</u>

The Comptroller shall be responsible for the compilation of all fixed rules as well as the conventions used [in administering the State].

{2.7.3}

(iv) <u>Inspection:</u>

The Comptroller shall appoint inspectors, [of different grades] high, middle and low, as appropriate to the revenue-earning capacity of each undertaking.

The inspectors shall be [selected from among] those whom the king will have no hesitation in punishing [if they cause loss of revenue].[11]

The Comptroller shall have the activity of the [various] departments watched by spies.   {2.7.4,9}

(v) Audit:

On the Closing Day for Accounts, all Accounts Officers [of the regions, undertakings, etc.] shall present themselves with sealed account books and with the [net] balance [of revenue over expenditure] in sealed containers. The officers shall be kept separate and shall not be allowed to talk [to each other].   {2.7.17}

The Chief Comptroller and Auditor shall have the accounts [thoroughly] audited [by Audit Officers] checking daily entries as well as weekly, fortnightly, monthly, four-monthly and annual totals.

For each of the above periods, the details shall be audited [according to the check list below]:

For income	For expenditure	For the net balance
1. Place of receipt	1. Place	1. Place
2. Time of receipt	2. Time	2. Time
3. Head of Income	3. Head of Expenditure	3. Head of Account
4. Current Income or outstanding dues	4. Gain (counter value received)	4. Dues left outstanding
5. Quantity received	5. Occasion	5. Form in which balance is received into the Treasury
6. Name of payer	6. What was paid	6. Quality
7. By whose order	7. Amount	7. Amount
8. Person receiving payment	8. For what use	8. Details of storage
9. Person recording payment	9. Authority ordering payment	9. Treasury official responsible
	10. Person withdrawing it from store	
	11. Person delivering it	
	12. Person receiving it	

{2.7.30-33}

After the [net] balances are physically verified, they shall be taken into the Treasury [or appropriate warehouse].   {2.7.18}

High officials shall [also] render accounts in full for their respective activities, without contradicting themselves.   {2.7.24}

(vi) <u>Reporting to the King:</u>

The Chief Comptroller and Auditor shall compile, for every department, the estimated revenue, the actual revenue, the outstanding revenue, income, expenditure and balance. He shall also compile reports on the presentation of accounts [by other officials] and a description of the activities [of the Government for the period under review]. {2.7.3}

[For punishments for causing loss of revenue, discrepancy between book balance and physical balance, delays in presenting accounts or delivering the net income, failure to follow rules, improper maintenance of account books and delays on the part of Audit Officers see V.iii.]

FRONTIER OFFICERS

(Salary—12,000 panas a year)

RESPONSIBILITIES

(i) <u>Defence:</u>

Frontier Officers shall be in charge of forts built at each of the points of entry into the country. {2.1.5}

(ii) <u>Revenue:</u>

Frontier officers shall levy [and collect] the road cess (*vartani*) as follows:

Head loads	1/16 pana
Small animals	1/4 pana
Cattle	1/2 pana
One-hoofed animals	1 panas
Cart loads	1 1/4 panas

{2.21.24}

(iii) <u>Control of caravans:</u>

Frontier Officers shall be responsible for examining the goods of foreign caravans, classifying them as goods of high or low value, sealing the packages with the official stamp and issuing the passes for the merchants. Frontier officers shall then send [all the relevant] information about these caravans to the Chief Collector of Customs.

They [shall be responsible for the safety of the merchandise travelling on the roads] and shall make good whatever is lost or stolen [on the way].[12] {2.21.25,26}

RASHTRAPALA

(Salary—12,000 a year)

[Though mentioned in the salary list as an official administering the 'country', this official's duties are not specified anywhere. The nomenclature must have been taken from an earlier source and probably refers to the *sthanika* (provincial governor) who was a subordinate of the Chancellor in charge of one of the four regions of the *janapada*.]

PUNISHMENTS

TREASURY OFFENCES

Fraud (both culprit and abettor to be punished)		{2.5.9}
gems	Highest SP	
articles of high value	Middle SP	
articles of low value and forest produce	payment of compensation and equal amount as fine	
Bringing in		{2.5.12-15}
counterfeit coins	Lowest SP	
unclean or old grain or short measure	Double the value[13]	
Goods not according to specified quality	Double the value[14]	
Theft		
Thieves breaking into Treasury	Death by torture	
		{2.5.20;4.9.7}

OFFENCES OF CITY GUARDS

Stopping authorised movement and failing to stop unauthorised movement	Double that for movement during curfew[15]	{2.36.40}
Not reporting to the Governor General any unusual happening (by the animate or inanimate)	According to the nature of the offence	{2.36.42}
Negligence	According to the gravity of the offence or the adverse consequences of their negligence	{2.36.42}

{2.36.41}

Misbehaving with a woman:

a slave	Lowest SP
free courtesan	Middle SP
exclusive mistress	Highest SP
respectable woman	Death

IV.v

ASPECTS OF THE ECONOMY

[Kautilya gives details of agriculture or different industries under the appropriate Head of Department. For reasons explained in the Introduction, only the duties and responsibilities of different Heads of Department are given in Part VII of this translation. Aspects of different types of economic activity are in this section.]

AGRICULTURE

RAINFALL

In regions where cultivation is dependant solely on the rain, land is classified as suitable for dry crops if the rainfall is about sixteen *dronas* [about 25 inches] a year and for wet crops if the rain fall is one and a half times that [about 37 1/2 inches a year].

Among regions where canal irrigation is practised, *Asmaka* [Deccan?] has a rainfall of 13 1/2 *dronas* [about 21 in.] and *Avanti*-twenty three *dronas* [about 36 in.]; in *Konkan* and snowy regions rain is plentiful in all seasons.

A good rainy season is one when one-third of the annual rainfall occurs at the beginning (*Sravana*—July/August) and at the end of the season (*Kartika*—October/November) and two-third in the middle (*Praushtapada*—August/September and *Asvayuja*—September/October).

A forecast of the rainfall can be made by observing the position, movement and cloudiness(?) of Jupiter, from the rise, setting and movement of Venus, and from changes in the appearance of the Sun.

Inferences can also be made about the [likely] rainfall from Venus, the [successful] sprouting of seeds by observing the Sun and the [healthy] growth of stalks by observations of Jupiter.

Even and beneficial rainfall is three clouds raining [almost] continuously for seven days, eight clouds raining intermittently and sixty clouds alternating with sunshine.

A good harvest is certain when, rain, wind and sunshine are distributed properly and there are three dry periods.   {2.24.5-10}

SEED AND PLANT PREPARATION

Cereals	to be soaked in dew by night and dried in the sun by day for seven days and nights
Beans and pulses	as above but for three or five days and nights
Grown from the stalk (crops such as sugarcane)	to be smeared at the cut with a mixture of honey, ghee and lard and covered with cowdung
Root crops	to be smeared with ghee and honey
Cotton seed	to be smeared with cowdung
Trees	to be planted in a pit in which grass, leaves, etc. are burnt and then manured with bones and cowdung at the right time. {2.24.24}

CROPS

To be sown at the beginning of the season: *Sali* rice, *Vrihi* rice, *Kodrava*, sesame, *Priyangu*, *Udaraka* and *Varaka*.

To be sown in the middle of the season: *Mudga*, *Masha* and *Saibya* beans.

To be sown later in the season: safflower, lentils, *Kulutha*, barley, wheat, linseed and mustard.

[Of these,] *Sali* and the other crops listed with it are the best, vegetables are next best and sugarcane, the worst. For, sugarcane is very difficult to grow being susceptible to diseases and requiring much more expenditure.

Banks of rivers are best suited for creeper plants [e.g. pumpkins], regions prone to flooding for pepper, grapes and sugarcane, the vicinity of wells for vegetables and edible roots, lakes, tanks and canal beds for green crops and furrows between rows of other crops for perfumery plants, medicinal herbs, *hribera*, *pindaluka*, etc. {2.24.12-14,20-22}

[For a complete list of crops mentioned in the *Arthashastra* see Appendix 2.]

CROP PROTECTION

Manuring:	Freshly caught fish and juice of *sunhi* plant are recommended.
Snakes:	The smoke from burning cotton seed and snake skin drives away snakes. {2.24.25,26}

[For agricultural taxation, *bhaga, kara,* and *bali* and the special tax, *amsa* see V.ii]

Anyone who brings new land under cultivation shall be granted exemption from payment of agricultural taxes [on the newly cultivated land] for a period of two years.   {3.9.33}

CALAMITY

A loss of [ripe] crops is worse than a loss of seedlings, because, with grown crops, the labour put in is also lost.   {8.2.25}

IRRIGATION

For building or improving irrigation facilities the following exemptions from payment of water rates shall be granted:

New tanks and embankments	five years
Renovating ruined or abandoned water works	four years
Clearing water works overgrown with weeds	three years {3.9.33}

Waterworks such as reservoirs, embankments and tanks can be privately owned and the owner shall be free to sell or mortgage them.   {3.9.34}

The ownership of tanks shall lapse, if they had not been in use for a period of five years, except in cases of distress.   {3.9.32}

Anyone leasing, hiring, sharing or accepting a waterwork as a pledge, with the right to use them, shall keep them in good condition. {3.9.36}

Owners may give water to others (by dredging channels or building suitable structures), in return for a share of the produce grown in the fields, parks or gardens.   {3.9.35}

In the absence of the owner, either charitable individuals or the people of a village acting together, shall maintain waterworks.   {3.10.3}

The following are the taxes to be paid for use of water for cultivation:

From water works built by the King:

manually transported	one-fifth of the produce
carried by bullocks	one-fourth
lifted by mechanism into channels	one-third

From natural reservoirs:

irrigated from rivers, lakes, tanks and springs	one-fourth of produce	{2.24.18}

OBSTRUCTION

No one irrigating his field from a reservoir or tank shall cause danger to the ploughed or sown field of another. {3.9.27}

The water from a lower tank shall not submerge a field fed from a higher tank built earlier. A higher tank shall not prevent the filling up of a lower tank, except when the latter has not been in use for three years. {3.9.29,30}

No one shall:

(a) let water out of dams out of turn;

(b) obstruct, through negligence, the [rightful] use of water by others;

(c) obstruct a customary water course in use;

(d) make a customary water course unusable [by diverting the water];

(e) build a dam or a well on land belonging to someone else; or

(f) sell or mortgage, directly or indirectly, a bund or embankment built and long used as a charitable public undertaking except when it is in ruins or has been abandoned. {from 3.9.38;3.10.1,2}

PUNISHMENTS

Causing damage to another's ploughed or sown field by letting water overflow from a reservoir, channel or field	Compensation according to damage	{3.9.27}
Causing damage to gardens, parks and embankments	Double the damage	{3.9.28}
A higher tank preventing the filling up of a lower one, in use for at least three years.	Lowest SP and emptying of higher tank	{3.9.31}
Failure to maintain an irrigation facility	Double the loss caused by the failure	{3.9.37}
Letting water from a dam out of turn; obstructing the flow of water to a user with a right to it	6 panas	{3.9.38}
Obstructing a customary water course or diverting it	Lowest SP	{3.10.1}
Building a well or a dam on someone else's land	Lowest SP	
Selling or mortgaging a charitable waterworks still in use:		{3.10.2}

the person selling or inducing someone to sell	Middle SP
witnesses to the transaction (for not preventing it)	Highest SP
Breaking a dam	{4.11.17}
if the reservoir had water	Drowing in the same place
if without water	Highest SP
if abandoned or in ruins	Middle SP

INDUSTRY

TEXTILE INDUSTRY

INCENTIVES

For better work [or greater productivity] women who spin shall be given oil and myrobalan cakes as a special favour. They shall be induced to work on festive days [and holidays] by giving them gifts.   {2.23.4,5}

Weavers, specialising in weaving fabrics of flax, *dukula*, silk yarn, deer wool and [fine] cotton shall be given gifts of perfumes, flowers and similar presents of encouragement.   {2.23.8}

WEAVING CHARGES

cotton	value of yarn
line or silk	1 1/2 times the value of yarn
woollen garments, blankets, etc.	twice the value of yarn

{4.1.10}

TOLERANCES

Cotton fabrics shall weigh 10% more than the yarn supplied, to take into account the sizing used.   {4.1.8}

An allowance of 5% is to be allowed for loss of wool in carding.

{4.1.13}

SALT INDUSTRY

SALE

Of locally produced salt:
Sale price = cost prise + 5% transaction tax + inspection fee.

Of imported edible salt:

Duty and tax payable: customs duty, one-sixth (quantity taken into government stores) + countervailing duty (= 5% transaction tax + manufacturing charge + inspection fee)

The buyer [of the imported salt] shall be responsible for payment of the duty and the countervailing duty equal to the loss sustained on the king's goods. Imported salt shall not be sold unless the customs duty and the countervailing duty have been paid on it.   {2.12.30,31}

Salt not for human consumption:

Duty payable: basic duty (one-sixth) but no countervailing duty.
                                                                {2.12.34,2.15.15}

PUNISHMENTS

Adulteration of salt	Highest SP	{2.12.32}
Evading taxes on imported salt	600 panas	{2.12.31}
Buying salt at a place other than the designed customs post	600 panas	
Unauthorized manufacturer of salt	Highest SP	{2.12.32}

METAL INDUSTRY

Base metals:
Charges:

Copper, steel, bronze, *vaikrantaka*, brass	5% of value of metal	
Lead or tin	1 kakani per pala	
Iron	2 kakanis per pala	{4.1.35,40,42}

Tolerances—loss in working allowed:

Copper, steel, bronze, *vaikrantaka*, brass	10%
Lead or tin	5%
Iron	20%
	{4.1.36,39,41,43}

PUNISHMENTS

For losses exceeding permissible allowances in base metal work	Double the [excess] loss	{4.1.37}

TRADE ·

The king shall promote trade and commerce by setting up trade routes by land and by water and market towns/ports.   {2.1.19}

Trade routes shall be kept free of harassment by courtiers, state of officials, thieves and frontier guards and from being damaged by herds of cattle.   {2.1.38}

PROTECTION OF TRADE

Frontier officers shall be responsible for the safety of the merchandise passing on the roads and shall make good what is lost.   {2.21.25}

Traders may stay inside villages after letting the village officers know of the value of their merchandise. If any of these is lost or driven away,[1] the village headman shall recompense the trader, provided that these had not been [deliberately] sent out at night.   {4.13.7,8}

If any property of a trader is lost or driven away in an area between villages, the Chief Superintendent of Pastures shall be held responsible. In the regions which are not under the control of the Chief Superintendent of Pastures, the responsibility shall be that of the *Chorarajju*, the official in charge of catching thieves. If no official can be held responsible, the people of the village (within whose boundary the loss occurred) shall contribute to the reimbursement. If the place of loss cannot be fixed within the boundary of any village, the *gopa* (the record keeper of five or ten villages, as the case may be) shall be held responsible.   {4.13.9-12}

TRADERS AND MERCHANTS

Merchants...are all thieves, in effect, if not in name; they shall be prevented from oppressing the people.   {4.1.65}

MARKETING SYSTEM

TRADE CONTROL SYSTEM

Commodities and products [of the countryside] shall not be sold in the places of their production [but sold only at the designated markets or brought into the city and sold after payment of duty].   {2.22.9}

GOODS PRODUCED LOCALLY

Crown commodities: The sale of all commodities belonging to the Crown [either produced on Crown property or received into the Treasury] shall be centralised.   {2.16.4}

<u>Direct sale:</u> Officers in charge of sale of Crown commodities shall deposit the proceeds in a wooden box with a lid with only one hole on top. At the close of the day, they shall render complete accounts and hand over the money [box], the balance stocks and their weighing and measuring instruments. {2.16.14-16}

<u>Sale through merchants:</u> Merchants in different places may be authorised to sell Crown commodities at prices fixed by the Chief Controller of State Trading. They shall compensate the Government for the loss sustained [i.e. the extra profit that would have been made on direct sale].

{2.16.8,9}

IMPORTED GOODS

These shall be sold in as many places as possible [in order to make them readily available to people in the towns and the countryside]. {2.16.4}

The following incentives shall be provided [to encourage the imports of foreign goods needed in the country]:

(i) [local] merchants who bring in foreign goods by caravans or by water routes shall enjoy exemption from taxes, so that they can make a profit;

(ii) foreign merchants shall not be sued in money disputes unless they are legal persons in the country; their local partners can, however, be sued.

{2.16.12,13}

ALL COMMODITIES—PROFIT MARGINS

The profit margins allowed to merchants shall be:

(i) 5% for locally produced goods and

(ii) 10% for imported goods. {4.2.28}

PRICE SUPPORT

When there is an excess supply of a commodity, the Chief Controller of State Trading shall build up a buffer stock by paying a price higher than the market price. When the market price reaches the support level, he shall change the price, according to the situation. {2.16.2,3}

FUTURES

Prices shall be fixed taking into account the investment, the quantity to be delivered, duty, interest, rent and other expenses. {4.2.36}

EXPORTS—SALES ABROAD OF CROWN COMMODITIES

General principles:

The Chief Controller of State Trading shall ascertain the profitability of a trading operation with a foreign country using the following method. The price of the goods to be sold in the foreign country and the price likely to be realised on the goods imported in exchange shall be estimated. From the gross margin, all expenses, as described below, shall be deducted:

for caravans: customs duty, road cess, escort charges, tax payable at military stations, ferry charges, daily allowances paid to merchants and their assistants and the share payable to the foreign king.

for trade using ships: all the above plus the following additional charges: i.e. the cost of hiring ships and boats, provisions for the journey.

He shall, in general, trade with such foreign countries as will generate a profit; he shall avoid unprofitable areas.

If no profit is likely to be made, he shall keep in mind the economic, political or strategic advantages in exporting to or importing from a particular country.   {2.16.18,19,24,25}

Precautions:

If the Chief Controller of State Trading sends a caravan by a land route, he shall choose a safe route. One quarter of the goods shall be of high value. Jungle chieftains, frontier officers and governors in the City and the countryside shall be contacted beforehand for assuring security. Steps shall be taken to ensure the protection of the members of the caravan and the goods of high value. If the caravan is unable to reach its destination, the goods may be sold in the country itself after payment of all dues.

If exports are to be made by water route [by sea or river], the Chief Controller shall ascertain the seasons best suited for the journey, port regulations and the dangers likely to be encountered.   {2.16.20-23}

IMPORTS

CLASSIFICATION

Goods traded are classified into three kinds:
    those produced in the countryside
    those produced in the city and
    those imported from other countries.   {2.22.1}

All three types of goods are liable to payment of customs duty whenever they are imported [into the city] and or exported [from it].   {2.22.2}

CUSTOMS REGULATIONS

Duty Free goods:
- goods intended for [celebrating] a wedding;
- gifts taken by a bride [going to her husband's home];
- gifts for presentation;
- goods intended to be used in rituals or worship of the gods;
- goods intended for rituals connected with birth, tonsure, sacred thread investiture, consecration [into *sanyasa*] etc.; and
- any items that, at his discretion, the Chief Controller of Customs may consider to be highly beneficial to the country (such as rare seeds).

{2.21.18,31}

Prohibited exports:
- weapons and armour of all kinds including coats of mail;
- metals;
- chariots;
- jewels and precious stones;
- grains; and
- cattle. {2.21.22}

Prohibited imports:
- those harmful to the country and
- those that are useless. {2.21.31}

IMPORT AND SALE OF FOREIGN GOODS

The frontier officer shall inspect the caravans carrying foreign goods and classify the goods as those of high value or of low value. The packages shall be sealed with the official seal and identity papers issued to the merchants. He shall also collect the appropriate road cess. All details about the caravans shall then be communicated to the Chief Collector of Customs. {2.21.24,26}

On arrival at the city gates, the Chief Collector of Customs shall inspect the caravan and make his appraisal on the basis of information received from frontier officers, spies or the king. Goods enjoying exemption from payment of duty shall be allowed in. All dutiable goods shall be weighed, measured or counted and the duty payable on goods of low value shall be determined carefully [not ignoring them as insignificant]. Customs collectors shall record the details: name of merchant, place of origin, quantity, place of issue of merchant's identity pass and place where goods were sealed. [The merchant shall then pay the duty as assessed and any penalty levied for violations.] {2.21.2,15,16}

[The Schedule of Import and Export Duties is given in Appendix 9.
Punishments for trading offences are in VII.v.]

After the duty is paid, the merchant shall place himself near the customs house and declare the type, quantity and price of his goods. He shall call out for bids three times and sell to anyone who is willing to buy at the price demanded. If there is competition among buyers and a higher price is realised, the difference between the call price and the sale price along with the duty thereon shall go to the Treasury.   {2.21.7-9}

Sale of prohibited goods:

Goods whose export is prohibited shall not be brought into the city for sale. They shall be sold outside the city gates [to the state?] without payment of duty.   {2.21.23}

LAW REGARDING SALES

SALE THROUGH AGENTS/RETAILERS

[Verses {3.12.25-30} seem to apply, at least for the most part, to the sale of royal goods through private merchants; they may also apply to transactions between wholesalers and retailers in the private sector.]

An agent selling goods on behalf of someone else, at the right time and place [i.e. realising the best price], shall hand over to the owner of the merchandise the price as received (the cost price plus the profit made) [less their commission]. If the price realised is lower because of missing the best opportunity for sale, the agent shall pay the owner the cost of the goods at the time he received them and the normal profit.

If it is so agreed upon beforehand between the two, the retail seller may pay to the wholesaler, whenever no profit is made, only the price of the goods.

If the price falls [between the time of entrusting the goods and the time of sale], only the lower price [actually realised] shall be payable.

Reputed dealers who have not been convicted of any offence [in trading in royal goods] shall not be held responsible for paying even the cost price in case the goods are destroyed due to deterioration or lost due to unforeseen accidents.

In the case of goods sold abroad and those sold after a lapse of time, the amount payable (the cost price and the profit) shall be reduced by the expenses and losses, if any.

A separate account shall be rendered for each type of goods.
          {3.12.25-30}

PUNISHMENTS

Merchants for adding a profit margin higher than those prescribed or for making undue profit	200 panas	{4.2.28,29}

Security of caravans

Leader of caravan abandoning a companion:		{3.20.18}
in an inhabited place	Lowest SP	
in a forest	Middle SP	
if the companion comes to harm	Highest SP	

Other merchants who were present when a companion was abandoned

if the companion comes to harm	Highest SP	
in an inhabited place	Half Lowest SP	
in a forest	Half Middle SP	
if the companion comes to harm	Half Highest SP	
Selling something which has already been sold to someone else	48 panas	{3.20.15}

IV.vi

CONSUMER PROTECTION

[An essential aspect of the welfare of the population was the protection of the interests of the consumer. All verses relating to control over artisans, craftsmen, entertainers, etc. are brought together in this section. The tendency to pilfer precious metal from articles entrusted to them by customers must have been widely prevalent among goldsmiths and silversmiths for Kautilya to give an exhaustive description of the methods of pilferage.]

Merchants, artisans, craftsmen, nomadic mendicants, entertainers and similar persons are all thieves, in effect, if not in name; they shall be prevented from harassing the people.   {4.1.65}

GOLDSMITHS AND SILVERSMITHS

<u>CHARGES</u> (In terms of value of metal worked)   {4.1.32-34}
<u>Precious metals</u>

Silver	one-sixteenth
	one-eighth for work requiring skill
Gold	one-eighth
	one-fourth for work requiring skill

<u>Doing work on time:</u>
The smiths shall complete the work agreed upon within the stipulated time. No time limit need be stipulated, if the work to be done is of a special nature.   {2.14.2,3}
<u>Returning the work entrusted:</u>
The smiths shall return to the customer the same quantity of [precious] metal, of identical quality, as was entrusted to him, even if the customer claims it after a lapse of time. Allowance is to be made for loss in manufacture and normal wear and tear.   {2.14.5,6}
<u>Allowances:</u>

Gold and silver articles	- 1/64th
Enamelling	-1/6th of the colouring material used

(Amount of colouring matter to be used is: 1/64th for colouring gold and 1/32nd for colouring silver.)   {2.14.8,9}

<u>Weights and Balances:</u>

All balances and weights shall be bought from the Chief Superintendent of Weights and Measures.   {2.14.15}

Making solid objects or hollow ware, covering with thick or thin plates, fixing [precious stones, etc.] and gilding are the [types of] work done by the craftsmen [employed by goldsmiths and silver smiths.]   {2.14.17}

METHODS OF STEALING {2.14.18}

<u>(i) Fraud in weighing</u>: The following are the types of false balances used by goldsmiths to steal gold—balances with an arm that bends too easily; with an arm hollowed out and weighted inside; with a split head that allows one arm to tilt more; with a wrong pivot; with unequal strings; with defective pans; with a magnet to attract a pan downwards and balances which are unstable. [In all cases one pan goes down more easily; the object to be weighed is placed in this pan in the case of sale or return to the customer and the standard weight is placed in this pan in the case of purchase or taking over an article from a customer.]   {2.14.19}

<u>(ii) Substitution</u>: Gold may be removed and substituted by: an alloy of two-third silver and one-third copper; wholly by copper; or a mixture of half gold and half copper. The gold may be removed by: using a crucible with a false bottom; mixing with dross in the course of manufacturing the article; using hollow pincers, the blowpipe, or a pair of tongs; concealing in the water vessel or using borax. Or, the stolen gold may be mixed with sand placed in the crucible and recovered later by breaking the crucible.
{2.14.20-24}

<u>(iii) Interchanging</u>: When putting together pieces with decorative gold leaf on them, or when testing the plating, the gold inside may be interchanged with silver; or bits of gold interchanged with iron pieces.   {2.14.25}

<u>(iv) Substitution in apparently solid objects:</u> A piece of lead may be covered by gold leaf and bound with lac, thus firmly fixing the gold. Or, the lead may be loosely covered with gold leaf [with the intention of removing the lead later and making the object hollow instead of solid]. A thick gold plate may be fixed on to a copper or silver base, the plating being well-polished on the outside or both inside and outside.

These methods can be detected by heating and testing on the touchstone, or by sound or by scratching. Loose covering can be detected by immersing in salt water or a suitable chemical.   {2.14.26-33}

(v) Embedding: Foreign objects may be embedded in a gold article:

(a) by heating bits of vermilion with the gold;

(b) by heating together lac or a paste of red lead when making solid objects;

(c) by heating together salt and sand when making gold leaf;

(d) by fixing, using lac, a layer of mica to substitute for the thickness of gold leaf; and

(e) setting inferior gems instead of precious stones.

For (a), (b) and (e), the test is to break up the articles after heating. To detect (c), the article should be boiled. For (d), the test is checking the density or piercing [with a sharp instrument].   {2.14.34-42}

(vi) Knocking off: Under the pretext of discovering substitution the goldsmith may hammer out a piece [of genuine gold] or cut out a part of a string of gold beads.   {2.14.45}

(vii) Cutting out: is replacing a part of the interior of hollowware by a piece of lead covered with gold.   {2.14.46}

(viii) Scratching out: is scraping away gold with a sharp tool.

{2.14.47}

(ix) Rubbing out: A piece of cloth impregnated with the appropriate chemical (e.g. red arsenic) is rubbed on the article removing gold.

{2.14.48}

BASE METAL WORKERS

CHARGES

Base metals:		{4.1.35,40,42}
Copper, steel, bronze, *vaikrantaka*, brass	5% of value of metal	
Lead or tin	1 kakani per pala	
Iron	2 kakanis per pala	

TOLERANCES FOR LOSS IN WORKING		{4.1.36,39,41}
Copper, steel, bronze, *vaikrantaka*, brass	10%	
Lead or tin	5%	
Iron	0%	

CONTROL OVER SERVICES

[Includes repairers, weavers, washermen, tailors, doctors and entertainers.]

ARTISANS AND CRAFTSMEN

All goods entrusted to repairers of articles, employers of [groups of] artisans, middlemen who undertake to get work done as well as self-employed artisans and craftsmen shall be covered by a guarantee from the appropriate guild. The guild shall be responsible for compensating [the owner] in case of death of the person to whom the article was entrusted. {4.1.2-3}

The artisans shall complete the work agreed upon] within the stipulated time. No time limit need be stipulated, if the work to be done is of a special nature. {4.1.4}

Every artisan or craftsman shall be responsible [for compensating the owner] if the entrusted article is lost or destroyed, unless it is due to sudden calamity; normal wear and tear is excepted. {4.1.6}

WEAVERS

For every ten palas of yarn supplied weavers shall return eleven palas of cloth [the excess being accounted for by the sizing material or starch used]. The cloth shall be woven with the right yarn and be of the correct length and weight.

Charges:

Cotton fabrics	Value of yarn
Linen or silk	One and a half times the value
Woollen garments, blankets and similar articles	Twice the value

{4.1.8,10}

WASHERMEN AND TAILORS

Washermen and tailors shall not wear,[1] sell, hire out, mortgage, lose or change a customer's garment. They shall return the garments within the time prescribed. {4.1.16,25}

Disputes about dyeing shall be adjudicated by experts.
{from 4.1.21}

Loss due to washing [shrinkage, loss of colour, etc.] shall be allowed at the rates of one-fourth of the value for the first wash and one-fifth for the second and subsequent washes. {4.1.23,24}

Washermen shall wash the garments only on wooden boards or smooth stone slabs [so as not to damage them]. If they damage the clothes by washing them on rough surfaces, they shall pay compensation and a fine.
{4.1.14,15}

Time allowed for washing/dyeing:

Whites	Unbleached	1 day
	Stone washed	2 days
	Semi-bleached	3 days
	Fully bleached	4 days
Coloureds	Light red	5 days
	Blue	6 days
	Saffron, lac or blood red	7 days
Fine cloth which requires care and skill		7 days

{4.1.18,19}

If the garments are returned after the prescribed period the customer need not pay the charge for washing and dyeing.   {4.1.20}

Charges for washing:

Plain	Rough garments	1 or 2 mashakas
	Lower quality	1/4 pana
	Medium quality	1/2 pana
	Fine quality	1 pana
Coloured		Double above scale

{4.1.22}

DOCTORS

Physicians shall inform the authorities before undertaking any treatment which may involve danger to the life of the patient. If, as a result of the treatment, the patient dies or is physically deformed, the doctor shall be punished.   {from 4.1.56,57}

ENTERTAINERS

Entertainers shall not move from place to place during the rainy season [so as not to hamper agricultural activities].   {4.1.58}

In their performances, they may, if they so wish, make fun of the customs of regions, castes or families and the practices or love affairs [of individuals]. [However,] they shall neither praise anyone excessively nor receive excessive presents.   {4.1.59,61}

Payment for work done by artists and artisans not specifically mentioned in this text shall be determined in accordance with the work done.   {4.1.64}

BEGGARS AND NOMADIC MENDICANTS

Like entertainers, these shall also not move about during the rainy season. The punishment for transgression shall be whipping with an iron rod.

{4.1.62,63}

PUNISHMENTS

GOLDSMITHS AND SILVERSMITHS

Anyone who makes a smith work in an unauthorized place without the knowledge of the Controller of Goldsmiths.	12 panas	{2.14.11}
Goldsmiths and Silversmiths, if caught working in an unauthorized place without the knowledge of the Controller	24 panas	{2.14.12}
If there was a valid reason	24 panas	{2.14.12}
No valid reason	Taken before a magistrate	{2.14.13}
Gold and Silversmiths, proved after a magisterial enquiry to have worked clandestinely	200 panas or cutting off the fingers	{2.14.14}
Goldsmiths and Silversmiths buying precious metal from suspicious persons without informing the Controller		{4.1.26}
if article was intact	12 panas	
if article was altered or melted down	24 panas	
if bought from a thief, in secret, modified articles, at a lower price	48 panas or punishment for theft	{2.14.27}
If the work is not done as specified	loss of wages for the period agreed upon + a fine of double the amount	{2.14.3}
If the work is not done within the stipulated time	the wages to be reduced by one-quarter and a fine	{2.14.4}

	of double the amount	
Loss of quality		{2.14.10}
up to 4 carats	Lowest SP	
Loss of quantity		
up to 1/16th	Middle SP	{2.14.10}
by using fraudulent scales or weights	Highest SP	
Fraud	Highest SP	
Deception of the article made:	Punishment for theft	{4.1.27}
Use of non-certified scales and weights	12 panas	{2.14.16}
Stealing Precious Metal		
In making new objects		
(i) Fraud in weighing	For every 1/16th part stolen from a customer a fine of 200 panas for gold and 12 panas for silver	{4.1.28,29}
(ii) Substitution by cheaper metal or alloy	500 panas	{4.1.30,31}
(iv) Interchanging gold by cheaper metal in plated articles		
(v) Substitution of base metal in apparently solid gold objects		
(vi) Embedding various things		
In testing or repairing old articles	Same as above	{2.14.44,49}
(gold stolen from articles without any apparent damage)		
(i) Knocking off		
(ii) Cutting out		
(iii) Scratching out		
(iv) Rubbing off		
BASE METAL WORKERS		
For losses exceeding tolerances	Double the loss	{4.1.37,38}

ARTISANS AND CRAFTSMEN

If the work is not done as specified	loss of wages for the period agreed upon + a fine of double the amount	{4.1.7}
If work is not done within stipulated time	the wages to be reduced by one-quarter and a fine of double the amount	{4.1.5}

MERCHANTS

Fraud in weights and measures

The permitted tolerance is 1/400th. {4.2.3-12}
For every deviation of 1/200th part:
Quantities weighed or measured:

Up to 50 palas	3 panas	
Between 50 and 100 palas	6 panas	
Above 100 palas	12 panas	
If the trader deliberately uses short weights for selling and excess weights for buying	Double the above fines	{4.2.13}

Fraud in articles sold by counting

Miscounting:		{4.2.14}
for every one-eighth part	96 panas	

False description in selling or pledging for credit

Describing an article of lower quality as one of higher quality	8 times the actual value	{4.2.15}
(i) Misrepresenting an article as one of high value; or	Punishment for all five types of offences, depending on the value of article:	{4.2.16}
(ii) Misrepresenting the source of origin; or	Below 1 pana—54 panas	
(iii) Deceit as to quality; or	Between 1 and 2 panas—108 panas	
(iv) Giving a false shine; or	Above 2 panas in value: —200 panas	
(v) Showing one product and selling another		

<u>Charging a higher price</u>

than the authorized price | Same scale as for false description {4.2.17}

<u>Higher profit margins</u>

than the ones authorized for local products (5%) or imports (10%) | For every additional 5%—200 panas {4.2.28-30}

<u>Adulteration</u>

of grains, fats, sugars, salts, perfumes and medicines with similar articles of no quality | 12 panas {4.2.22}

<u>Cartelisation</u>

By artisans and craftsmen with the aim of lowering the quality, increasing the profits or obstructing the sale or purchase | 1000 panas {4.2.18}

By merchants conspiring to hoard with the aim of selling at a higher price | 1000 panas {4.2.19}

<u>Brokers and middlemen</u>

Accumulation of stocks (in excess of the quantities authorized by the Chief Controller) | Confiscation of excess {4.2.26}

<u>Employees of merchants</u>

Servants who weigh or measure and who, by sleight of hand, give short weight or short measure: | For every loss of 1/8th pana—200 panas {4.2.20,21}

<u>Visiting merchants</u> | {2.36.7}

Host merchants shall report if a visitor sells goods at an unauthorized time or place or sells articles of which they are not full owners.

WEAVERS | {4.1.9,11,12}

Single and double woven cloth:

Not having correct sizing | Double the shortfall

Measuring less | Value of shortage deducted from payment and a fine of double the shortfall

Weighing less | Four times the shortfall

Substituting another cloth	Twice the difference in value	
WASHERMEN		
Not washing clothes on wooden boards or smooth stone slabs	Compensation for damage + fine 12 panas	{4.1.15}
Wearing customer's clothes	3 panas	{4.1.16}
Selling, hiring out or pledging customers clothes	12 panas	{4.1.17}
Losing or substituting customer's garment	Compensation of value of garment + twice the value as fine	
DOCTORS		{4.1.56,57}
Doctor not giving prior information about treatment involving danger to life with the consequence of		
Physical deformity or damage to vital organ	Same punishment as for causing similar physical injury[2]	
Death of patient	Lowest SP	
Death due to wrong treatment	Middle SP	
ENTERTAINERS		
Praising someone excessively in return for large gifts	12 panas	{4.1.60}
BEGGARS AND NOMADIC MENDICANTS		
Moving about during the rainy season	Whipping with an iron rod; as many strokes as the fine imposed	{4.1.63}

Part V

TREASURY, SOURCES OF REVENUE, BUDGET, ACCOUNTS AND AUDIT

"All [state] activities depend first on the Treasury. Therefore, a King shall devote his best attention to it."

{2.8.1,2}

"A King with a depleted Treasury eats into the very vitality of the citizens and the country."

{2.1.16}

"Just as one plucks fruits from a garden as they ripen, so shall a King have the revenue collected as it becomes due. Just as one does not collect unripe fruits, he shall avoid taking wealth that is not due because that will make the people angry and spoil the very sources of revenue."

{5.2.70}

"Wealth will slip away from that childish man who constantly consults the stars. The only [guiding] star of wealth is itself; what can the stars of the sky do?"

{9.4.26}

"Just as elephants are needed to catch elephants, so does one need wealth to capture more wealth."

{9.4.27}

V.i

THE TREASURY

[The word Treasury (*kosa*) is used by Kautilya in a broad as well as a narrow sense. The word is often used to denote the wealth of the state. For example, when Kautilya says that 'all [State] activities depend on the Treasury', we have to understand it as 'without wealth, there is no production or acquisition'.

The Kautilyan dictum, in {2.12.37}, is: 'From wealth (*kosa*) comes the power of the Government (*danda*). With the treasury and the army (together—*kosadanda*) the earth is acquired with the treasury as the ornament.' The word, *kosadanda*, the Treasury and the army together, occurs repeatedly in the books on foreign policy and war as the objectives of acquisition by conquest or other means. The interrelationship between the Treasury and the army and the primacy of the Treasury as between the two are explained fully in verses {8.1.41-52} in II.iii.

Because of the importance of the Treasury, Kautilya cautions the king that he should always keep the army and Treasury under his own control {8.2.4}. Likewise, one of the precautions which the Councillor had to take when an old king was dying was to collect together the Treasury and the army in one place under the charge of trusted people {5.6.7}.

The importance of accumulation of wealth is emphasized throughout the text. For example, whenever the State suffered a loss, the punishment levied on the one responsible for it was reimbursement of the loss suffered or a multiple of it, in addition to a monetary fine. A clear distinction is maintained between tax payers and tax-exempt persons as well tax-paying and tax-exempt villages; a tax payer was not allowed to settle in a tax-exempt village {3.10.11}. Actors and other entertainers were prohibited from entering new settlements so that the people might devote themselves wholly to productive work without being distracted {2.1.33-35}.

The Chief Superintendent of the Treasury was not only in charge of gold and precious objects but also of all types of produce. However, when the *Arthashastra* describes how a Treasury building (*koshagriha*) is to be constructed {2.5.2,3}, it refers only to the building where precious objects were stored. Other types of storehouses, such as granaries and warehouses, are described for other commodities. The location of the treasury and warehouses within the fortified city is given in the town plan diagram in IV.i.]

The following are the means of increasing the wealth of the State:
- ensuring the prosperity of state activities [and enterprises];
- continuing well tried [and successful] policies;
- eliminating theft;
- keeping strict control over government employees;
- increasing agricultural production;
- promoting trade;
- avoiding troubles and calamities;
- reducing [tax] exemptions and remissions; and
- increasing cash income.   {2.8.3}

Obstruction, misuse of government property and false accounting by government servants lead to a reduction of wealth.   {2.8.4}

With no distraction, the people will be fully involved in the work in the fields and there will be an increase in the supply of labour, money, commodities, grain and liquids to the Treasury.   {2.1.33-35}

[See also financial misbehaviour of government servants, VI.iii.]

CALAMITY TO THE TREASURY

[The relative adverse consequences of a calamity to the Treasury as compared to a fortified city or the army (which come just before and just after the Treasury in the list of the constituents of a state), have been described earlier in verses {8.1.33-52} in II.iii. In Kautilya's opinion, a calamity to the fort was more serious than one to the Treasury, because the fort protected the Treasury. But a calamity to the Treasury was more serious than one affecting the army because, with wealth, all other things including the army could be acquired.]

Calamities to the treasury can be any internal or external action which has the effect of reducing the revenue. Financial health can be affected by misappropriation by chiefs, remission of taxes, scattered collection, false accounting and looting by enemies and tribes before the revenue reaches the Treasury.   {8.4.49}

As a provision against calamities, a substantial Treasury shall be built on a border of the country using persons condemned to death who shall be executed after the work is done [so that none save the king may know its location.]   {2.5.4}

Each household . . . can store grains and other commodities only if authorized to do so; these can be requisitioned in times of calamities.

{2.4.25}

If receipts and expenditure are properly looked after the king will not find himself in financial difficulties. {5.3.45}

V.ii

SOURCES OF REVENUE

[How did the Kautilyan state get its wealth in order to have adequate resources to acquire new territories and conquer other kingdoms? This is not an easy question to answer since the references to sources of revenue are scattered throughout the text, though most of them are found in Book 2.

{2.6.2-9} purport to give a classified list of income sources, but this is a rather confusing mixture of many things—revenue from Crown enterprises, taxes and tolls, service charges and fines. Sometimes only the title of the Head of a Department is specified, perhaps to indicate revenue resulting from his activities. Sometimes it is just a list: of different kinds of forests, flowers or fruit or the list under mines (gold, silver, diamonds, etc.). How revenue is obtained from these is not clearly spelt out. Of the different lists in the eight verses, {2.6.2} enumerating the types of revenue collected from within the fortified towns, and {2.6.3} those collected from the countryside are the most extensive.

Another detailed list is found in {2.15.1-11}, describing the duties of the Chief Superintendent of Warehouses. Apart from the Treasury proper, where precious metals and jewellery were stored and coins minted, the wealth of the state was kept in the commodity warehouses granaries, storehouses for liquids, salt and sugar and warehouses for forest produce. The list in {2.15.1-11} indicates how the goods received into these warehouses were to be classified in the stock registers. Not all the items in this list can be considered to be independent sources of revenue; for example, commodities borrowed or received in a barter transaction did not add to the net wealth of the state though they had to be entered as such in the registers. Nevertheless, there are a few items which can be thought of as revenue receipts.

In {2.15.3}, which is itself a part of the above, we find yet another list of sources of revenue from the country-side. The items are not the same as those sources of revenue given in {2.6.3}, though both are called 'rashtram'.

One more list is found in {2.6.10}, a verse which describes how revenue receipts are to be classified in the accounts books. This is more analytical, giving details of taxes, fees and service charges. An important tax, *vyaji* or transaction tax, is mentioned here as a separate item. A similar analytical list is also found in {2.12.35.36} dealing with the classification of revenue accruing from mines, minerals, metal-working, coinage and salt.

As one would expect, a list of taxes and dues is found in {2.35}, which describes the duties of the Chancellor, the official responsible for collection of revenue from the countryside. This list is noteworthy for the use of a special term, *pratikara*, to denote payment of taxes in kind—grains, cattle, gold, or forest produce. *Pratikara* also includes *vishti* (labour), i.e. doing work for the state in lieu of paying taxes. Two terms in this chapter are *parihara* and *aakarada* used to describe authorized exemptions from payment of tax. *Ayudhiya* (supply of soldiers in lieu of tax payable by villages as a whole, a tax not elsewhere mentioned in the text), is also found here. We also note from this chapter that, while the responsibility for collection of revenue rested with the local record keepers and provincial governors, in each place a magistrate was also entrusted with the tasks of inspection and ensuring proper collection, particularly that of the Special Emergency Dues (*bali*).

A number of miscellaneous sources of income, such as lost property, intestate property or treasure trove, are listed in {2.6.20}. Two identical verses {2.6.21 and 2.15.10} describe three kinds of savings from expenditure, which are to be counted as revenue.

Lastly, payment of fines by the citizens for failure to obey rules or codes of conduct and for misdemeanours, crimes and other infractions of the law constituted a separate source. Such fines are prescribed under almost every Head of Department for breaches of administrative laws and regulations as well as under civil and criminal law. As mentioned earlier, the punishment was often related to the loss suffered by the state. Even when deterrent punishment (such as amputation of different parts of the body) is prescribed, chapter 4.10 provides for payment of monetary fines in lieu of the physical penalty.

All the lists referred to above are given in Appendix 8, with the terminology used by Kautilya, the translation and the appropriate verse reference.

From {3.11.20}, we note that, in case anyone became bankrupt, debts owed to the state had priority over other creditors.

The various lists are, in fact, intended for mnemonic purposes, to be used by different officials in the performance of their duties. There is no analytical classification, showing whether a particular source was a tax, a service charge or from a productive enterprise. They give no indication about the relative importance of the sources in the accumulation of wealth by the state. This has to be inferred from the type of income and the importance given to it in the text.

For the purposes of state budgeting, it would clearly have been impossible to predict accurately the collection from some sources. For example, there could have been no assurance of a given quantum of revenue from people dying intestate or by the discovery of a treasure trove The amount of revenue collected from fines, as a proportion of total revenue, would also have been difficult to estimate. The main aims of levying fines were to ensure the observance of the laws and regulations of the state and to protect the corpus of revenue. We can, therefore, assume that the regime of fines was used to prevent loss of revenue and not specifically to augment it. This is borne out by {3.17.15,16}, in which the practice of levying a surcharge of 8% on fines below 100 panas and 5% on those above is condemned as unjust. Such surcharges were obviously fairly common and were imposed, according to Kautilya, either due to increase in lawlessness or due to kings being misguided.

The state also levied a number of fees or charges for services rendered to the public—issuing passports, providing ferry services or escorts for caravans, making standard weights and measures and so on. In these cases, the aim was to recover the cost of providing the service and not to augment revenue.

This leaves four major areas of state economic activity as the main sources of raising revenue—income from state property, state-controlled manufacturing and leisure activities, taxes paid in cash or in kind and trading. The full range of revenue-raising measures is explained below, starting with the most important. In this note, only an indication of the ways in which revenue was raised is given; translations of relevant verses will be found in the various subject sections.

Kautilya devotes a chapter to methods of increasing the resources of a state when they are depleted after an expensive operation, such as a war. He suggests different sets of methods for collecting additional revenue. Firstly: levying special taxes on all groups within the population; secondly: cultivating an extra summer crop; thirdly: seeking voluntary contributions and selling honours; fourthly: expropriating temple property; and fifthly: using a variety of methods to extract money from the gullible. The last was to be used only against traitors and the wicked and consisted of methods which, to us, appear to be of dubious morality. Presumably, these were to be used in the order prescribed and the last to be used only when all other methods had failed to raise adequate resources.

The sources of revenue described in this section are those of the state; i.e. the central government. Villages had their own independent sources of income, mainly from charges for grazing and the fines levied on owners of cattle which strayed and caused damage. For details see VII.xi—Village Village Headmen {3.10.21,25-34}.

As explained in the Introduction, a large part of this section is a compilation by the translator; only the verses relating to 'Special levies. taxes and collections' are translations of verses in the text.]

1. INCOME FROM CROWN PROPERTY

REVENUE FROM CROWN AGRICULTURAL LANDS (SITA):
{2.15.1,2.24.16,18}

Most of chapter {2.4} is devoted to this subject. The state raised revenue both by direct cultivation and by leasing out land to tenants. The crops grown on these lands (grains, beans and lentils, oilseeds, sugarcane, textile fibres, etc.) constituted a major part of the revenue and were accounted for separately {see 2.15.1}.

Direct cultivation:

Crops grown on Crown land:

Net revenue to state was equal to value of production less expenditure on seeds, labour, etc.

Leased cultivation:

Leased land

State's share 3/4 or 4/5 if lessee provided only labour; 1/2 if lessee provided seeds and implements as well as labour.

Water rate for taking water from water works built by the king: one-fifth if lifted manually; one-fourth if lifted by bullocks; one-third if lifted mechanically; one-fourth for taking water from natural reservoirs, or irrigated from rivers lakes, and tanks.

REVENUE FROM MINING AND METALLURGY:
{2.12.18,19,22-24,26,27}

[The importance of mining and metals in the economy is indicated by the following verse.]

The wealth of the state has its source in the mining and [metallurgical] industry; the power of the state comes out of these resources. With [increased] wealth and a [powerful] army more territory can be acquired, thereby further increasing the wealth of the state.   {2.12.37}

[The importance of metals lay not only in their sale to the public but also as the raw material for the manufacture of goods for the king, particularly weapons for the army. Mines which were neither too expensive nor too difficult to exploit were worked directly by the Crown and the rest were leased out. Smelting was state owned and trade in metals centralized {2.12.18}. The following officials were all concerned with raising revenue from metals and precious stones—The Chief Controller of Mining and Metallurgy, the Chief Superintendent of Mines, the Chief Superintendent of Metals, the Chief Master of the Mint, the Coin Examiner and the Chief Salt Commissioner.]

Mines worked directly by the Crown:

Proceeds from: sale of precious stones, less cost of mining.sale of metals, less cost of mining and smelting; sale of alloys less cost of alloy manufacture.

Leased mines:

Revenue: lease payment, either a share of the ore recovered or payment of a fixed royalty.   {2.12.22}

REVENUE FROM ANIMAL HUSBANDRY:
{2.29.5-7,25,30,35-37,41}

Crown herds:

Directly looked after by wage labour	Ghee and all animal by-products
Looked after by contractor	I pana per annum per animal; 8 varakas of ghee p.a. per 100 animals; skins of all dead animals
Non-productive herds	According to capacity
Private cattle: Tax on sale	Quarter pana per animal

Miscellaneous revenue:

Animal by-products:	Hair, skins, bladder, bile, tendons, teeth, hooves and horns; Wool from sheep and goats

REVENUE FROM IRRIGATION WORKS: {2.1.24}

Fish, ducks and green vegetables, produced in or near reservoirs, was the property of the state, on the grounds that land on which the water storage stood was state property.

REVENUE FROM FORESTS: {2.17.3,4}

Dues levied for right to collect forest produce; sale of forest produce and by-products; sale of output of factories based on forest products.

2. INCOME FROM STATE-CONTROLLED ACTIVITIES

MANUFACTURING INDUSTRY—TEXTILES: {2.23}

Net revenue: realization from sale of textiles and products less cost of raw materials and wages.

MANUFACTURING INDUSTRY—SALT: {2.12.28-31,34}

Revenue:
Lease rent on salt pans, (paid either as a share of the salt produced or as a fixed quantity) received in kind and sold to public.

Duty on imported salt (1/6th) and countervailing duty (equal to the sum of manufacturing charge, transaction tax and inspection fee, all levied on locally produced salt); no countervailing duty on non-edible salt.

MANUFACTURING/LEISURE INDUSTRY—ALCOHOLIC LIQUOR: {2.25.39,40}

Made in state undertakings:
Revenue from sale of alcoholic beverages made in state undertakings and sold in drinking places under the control of the Chief Controller of Alcoholic Beverages, calculated by taking into account the transaction tax, the countervailing duty and the sticking allowance.

Made privately:
5% of the quantity manufactured as 'monopoly tax'.

LEISURE ACTIVITY—COURTESANS, PROSTITUTES AND ENTERTAINERS: {2.27.6-8,10,24-27}

Courtesans and Prostitutes: Revenue collected by the Chief Controller of Entertainers:

Regular income:
Net income from courtesans' establishments, for which the courtesans had to provide detailed accounts of payments received, person making payment and net gain (payment less expenses).

Private prostitutes	1/6th of income
Foreign entertainers	5 panas per show

Occasional income:

Release money for courtesans.	24,000 panas
Release money for courtesan's sons	12,000 panas
Retired prostitutes not working in the kitchens, etc.	1 1/4 panas p.m.

LEISURE ACTIVITY—BETTING AND GAMBLING: {3.20.10}

Revenue from Chief Controller of Gambling—5% tax on winnings

3. TAXES—IN CASH AND IN KIND

The complete list of taxes mentioned in the text are:

1. Customs duty (*sulka*) which consists of:
   import duty (*pravesya*)
   export duty (*nishkramya*) and
   octroi and other gate tolls (*dwarabahirikadeya*)
2. Transaction tax (*vyaji*) including
   manavyaji (transaction tax for Crown goods)
3. Share of production (*bhaga*) including
   1/6th share (*shadbhaga*)
4. Tax (*kara*), in cash
5. Taxes in kind (*pratikara*) including
   Labour (*vishti*)
   Supply of soldiers (*ayudhiya*)
6. Countervailing duties or taxes (*vaidharana*)
7. Road cess (*vartani*)
8. Monopoly tax (*parigha*)
9. Royalty (*prakriya*)
10. Taxes paid in kind by villages (*pindakara*)
11. Army maintenance tax (*senabhaktham*)
12. Surcharges (*parsvam*)

While *kara* is generally assumed to be a tax paid in cash, and *pratikara* that paid in kind, the text does not usually make a distinction between the two. For example, customs duty, expressed as a fraction, could be paid either way; only in the case of manufactured jewellery, a cash payment of 20% of the value added was to be paid as export duty. The taxes paid by butchers, or the production share paid by farmers, lessees of mines or fishermen must almost always have been paid in kind. Only brief indications of the different taxes are given below; full details will be found in the appropriate places elsewhere in this translation.

CUSTOMS DUTIES (*SULKA*): {2.24.4-7}

Collected at the city gates on both goods coming in and going out:

import duty   - 20% ad valorem

export duty   - 1/25th, 1/20th, 1/15th, 1/10th or 1/6th

(For dutiable goods and goods exempt from duty, see {**2.22.22,23,31**})

OCTROI AND OTHER GATE TOLLS (*DWARABAHIRIKADEYA*)

Normally, 1/5th of the customs duty levied; this could, however, be reduced
if it was in the interest of the country.   {**2.22.8**}

Foreigners had to pay all taxes at the city gate.   {**2.4.32**}

Gulma was a tax payable at military stations and pickets.

{**2.16.18; 2.35.12; 3.20.14**}

TRANSACTION TAX (*VYAJI*)

This was a very important tax, affecting every transaction in goods. It
was, at the same time, a sales tax, a revenue surcharge and a discount on
payments made by the government. It is mentioned often as a separate
item in recording revenues {2.7.2; 2.6.22; 2.12.35; and 2.15.11}. It is also
mentioned in {2.12.30} (as a charge payable on salt produced in the country
and countervailing duty on imported salt), {2.25.40} (in relation to sale of
alcoholic beverages), {2.12.26} (for coins received into the Treasury) and
{4.1.45} (on the legal circulation of coins).

The transaction tax was automatically collected in most transactions
by the use of different weights and capacity measures. There were four
categories:

- the biggest weight or largest measure when anything was paid into the
government treasury;
- the second biggest ones for normal trade;
- the third biggest for payments out of the treasury;
- the smallest for payments to the palace.

Each of the different sets of weights had to be used with its own balance.
Details of these weights, measures and balances are given in the table on
page 264.   {**2.19.21-23,29**}

The transaction tax is also referred to as '*manavyaji*' in relation to
sale of Crown goods. In addition to the 6.25% for sales by volume and
5% for sales by weight, the rate of tax for goods sold by counting is given
as 1/11th (about 9%).   {**2.16.10**}

For commodities weighed in large quantities (in panless balances of
the steelyard type) an additional 5% was to be given in trade transactions

and in payments to the treasury to compensate for inaccuracy. This addition did not apply to meat, metals, salt or gems.   {2.19.24}

Two other items are referred to in the chapter on Weights and Measures; neither is a tax but an additional outgo meant to compensate the receiver of liquids for incidental losses.

Taptavyaji: - an extra quantity given as 'heating allowance' for loss of volume on heating - 1/32 for ghee and 1/64 for oil.

Manasrava: - an 'sticking allowance' given in the case of all liquids, in lieu of the quantity which sticks to the measure; 1/50th.   {2.19.43,44}

Different weight and capacity measure system for automatic collection of transaction tax
{2.19.12-17}

Type of Transaction	Weights		Weighing Machines				Capacity Measures
	Objects weighed in		Samavritta		Parimani		
	Tulas	Palas	Length of beam in inches	Weight of beam in palas	Length of beam in inches	Weight of beam in palas	
Revenue - Ayamani for receiving payments into the Treasury	100 palas	10 dha-ranas	54	35	82	70	100%
Trade	95 palas	91/2 dharanas	491/2	33	66	66	93.75%
Payments (out of the Treasury)	90 palas	9 dharanas	45	31	60	62	87.5%
Palace Expenditure	85 palas	81/2 dharanas	40 1/2	29	54	58	81.25%

SHARE OF PRODUCTION (*BHAGA*): {2.15.3; 2.28.3,6; 2.12.22}

This, sometimes referred to as '*shadbhaga*', is usually 1/6th and applies to tax on agricultural production in private lands and fishermen. Private animals under Crown protection paid 1/10th.

The royalty paid by lessees of mines, pearl and conch fishermen leasing boats and lessees of salt pans is not specified in the text.

TAX ON BUTCHERS: {2.26.3}

<u>*Sale of meat*</u>: revenue collected by Chief Protector of Animals and Controller of Animal Slaughter:
Animals, not in sanctuaries, whose slaughter is permitted   1/6th
Fish and birds   11/60th
Deer and cattle   1/60th + (4 or 5%)

TAX PAID IN CASH: (*KARA*)

General term applicable to all taxes paid cash.

TAX PAID IN KIND (*PRATIKARA*): {2.15.8; 2.35.1}

Free Labour (*Samhanika*): work, such as processing grain, oilseeds or sugarcane in warehouses, done in lieu of payment of tax.

SUPPLY OF SOLDIERS: (*AYUDHIYA*)

Supplying soldiers in lieu of taxes payable by villages as a whole.

COUNTERVAILING DUTY OR TAX: (*VAIDHARANA*)

as in: countervailing duty on imported salt   {2.12.31,35}
compensatory payments by merchants   {2.16.9}
alcoholic beverages   {2.25.40}

ROAD CESS (*VARTANI*): {2.21.24; 2.28.25}

Collected at frontiers by ferry-men:
Head loads   1/16 pana
Small animals   1/4 pana
Cattle   1/2 pana
Animals without cloven hooves   1 1/4 panas
Cartloads   1 1/4 panas

MONOPOLY TAX (*PARIGHA*)

Collected whenever private manufacture or trade of a state monopoly item was permitted; a licence fee.

ROYALTY (*PRAKRIYA*): {2.12,22; 2.28.6}

A fixed amount paid in the case of leased mines, salt pans and boats for conch or pearl fishing in lieu of payment of share of production.

TAXES IN KIND PAID BY VILLAGES (*PINDAKARA*)

For example, for the provision by government of a ferry service.

ARMY MAINTENANCE TAX (*SENABHAKTHAM*)

Appears to have been an occasional tax levied when the army was sent to a location specifically to protect it or rid it of danger.

SURCHARGES (*PARSVAM*)

No details given in the text.

4.TRADE

STATE TRADING: {FROM 2.15 AND 2.16}

The profit margins on the sale of monopoly goods was a significant source of revenue. This was under the control of the Chief Controller of State Trading who was responsible for orderly marketing, maintaining buffer stocks, avoiding excessive profits and collecting the transaction tax. He was also responsible for the export of Crown commodities, keeping in mind the advantages to the country and the people of importing goods in exchange. (See the responsibilities of the Chief Controller, principles of fair trading, incentives for import trade and rules for exports.)

COMPENSATION PAYMENTS: {2.16.9}

Merchants who were authorized to sell Crown commodities, at prices fixed by the Chief Controller, had to compensate the government for the loss sustained in foregoing the profit that would have been made had the goods been sold through Crown outlets.

EXCESS VALUE REALISATION: {2.21.7-9; 3.9.5}

Merchants selling foreign goods were to call out the price three times, after paying the duty. Likewise, owners of property were to call out the price of whatever property they were selling three times. If, due to competition among buyers, the goods or the property was sold at a higher price, the difference between the sale price and the call price had to be paid into the treasury.

5. FEES AND SERVICE CHARGES

WEIGHTS AND MEASURES (*PAUTAVAM*): {2.19.36-39}

Sale of standard weights and measures (for prices see Appendix 1 on Weights, Measures and Time.)

STAMPING FEE FOR WEIGHTS AND MEASURES: {2.19.40-42}

1 kakani per weight or measure per day since the date of last stamping

PASSPORT FEES (*MUDRA*): {2.34.1}

Service charge—1 masha per pass.

FERRY CHARGES (*TARA*): {2.28.21-24}

Cost of ferry services borne by nearby villages which (i) paid a licence fee and (ii) bore the expenses on food and wages of ferry-men. For ferry charges see table.

PORT DUES (*PATTHANAM*): {2.28.7}

Rates not specified.

LAND SURVEY CHARGES (*RAJJU*): {2.6.3}

Rates not specified.

COINING FEE (*RUPIKAM*): {2.12.26}

For new coins issued—a coining fee of 8% of value.

TESTING FEE (*PARIKSHIKAM OR RUPAM*): {2.12.26}

For coins received into the Treasury or certified as genuine 1/8 the of one percent of value.

ESCORT CHARGES (*ATVAHIKAM*): {2.28.25}

Collected by ferry-man at the frontier.

FIXED CHARGES/TAXES (*KLIPTHAM*): {2.28.2}

Not elsewhere specified.

Ferry charges

Ferry charges	on small rivers	on big rivers
Small animals; man with hand luggage	1 masha	2 mashas
Man with head load or back load	2 mashas	4 mashas
Camel; buffalo	4 mashas	8 mashas
Small cart	5 mashas	10 mashas

Bullock cart	6 mashas	12 mashas
Large cart	7 mashas	14 mashas
Bhara of 20 tulas of merchandise	1/4 pana	1/2 pana

Chartering:

| Passengers chartering a boat for a voyage (*yatravetanam*) | Hire charges and cost of crew (subsistence and wages) |

Freight charges:

| *sulkabhagam* | Freight charges paid in kind |

6. MISCELLANEOUS

LOST PROPERTY: {3.16.23,24}

Share of the State:

| Gems | all (no share to finder) |
| Articles of high value | two-third (one-third to finder) |

Charges for claiming lost property:

Living:

Slaves	5 panas
One-hoofed animals	4 panas
Cows and buffaloes	2 panas
Small animals	1/4 pana

Objects:

| All types | 5% of value |

REVENUE FROM CONTROLLER OF TEMPLES AND HOLY PLACES: {5.2.38}

Special levy (*bali*)

RECOVERY FROM THIEVES (*CHORARAJJU*): {4.13.10}

(in unpoliced lands)

INTEREST ON COMMODITIES LOANED (*PRAYOGAPRATYADANAM*):{2.15.4}

Interest paid to be accounted for as revenue

RECEIVED AS AID (*YACHANAM*): {2.15.6}

From 'begging' from a foreign king

PRESENTS (*UTSANGA*): {2.15.3}

Presents from the people on festive occasions

COMPENSATORY PAYMENTS (*PARIHINIKAM*): {2.15.3}

For example, for damage done by cattle

REDEMPTION OF PRISONERS: {2.36.45,46}

Paid by prisoners themselves or by others

REVERSION OF PROPERTY TO STATE: {3.9.17,23; 3.16.22}

Disputed property when the claims of all disputants fail. Lost property not claimed within six weeks of deposit at the lost property office

COURT CASES: {3.1.20,21}

Penalty for loss of suit:
if admitted voluntarily	one-tenth of disputed amount
if court decrees against	one fifth

DEBTS: {3.11.40,42}

If no judgement is possible on available evidence and if the claim cannot be split down the middle, the king shall take over the disputed property. If the evidence proves a higher amount than that claimed by the plaintiff, the defendant shall pay the full amount the king shall take the difference.

FOREIGN AFFAIRS

Tributes received
Treaty payments received

UNFORESEEN RECEIPTS (*ANYAJATHA*): {2.15.11,2.6.20}

Receipts of outstanding arrears already written off
Gifts to the king (*aupayanikam*)
Recovery of lost or forgotten items (*nashtaprasmrtam*)

CONFISCATED PROPERTY (*DAMARAGATAKASVAM*): {2.1.12}

For example, non-cultivation of land

INTESTATE PROPERTY (*APUTRAKAM*): {3.5.28}

Ownerless property (*adayadakam*), less amounts needed for funeral rites and maintenance of widow, shall go to the king. This does not apply to the property of Brahmins learned in the Vedas.

TREASURE TROVE (*NIDHI*): {4.1.52-54}

Share of the State (except when the finder can prove that it is ancestral property):

any trove over 100,000 panas	100% (nothing to finder)
less than 100,000 panas	5/6th (1/6th to finder)

SAVINGS FROM EXPENDITURE (*VYAYAPRATHYAYA*): {2.15.10, 2.6.21}

Savings from demobilisation, works abandoned and economies made in budgeted expenditure.

7. FINES

Monetary fines were of three kinds: *danda* (fines levied by Heads of Departments), *athyaya* (those levied by judges and magistrates) and *ayuktadanda* (those paid by government servants). Details will be found in appropriate places.

SPECIAL LEVIES, TAXES AND COLLECTIONS

A king, who finds himself in great financial difficulty, may collect [additional] revenue [using the methods described below].   {5.2.1}

SPECIAL LEVIES:

All demands [under this heading] are to be made only once and not twice.
<u>(i) On farmers:</u>

(a) From land not dependent on rain and yielding abundant crops, irrespective of whether the holding is big or small, a tax of one-third or one quarter of the stocks of grain shall be demanded.

(b) If the [quality of the land or] yield is middling or poor, the additional levy shall be proportional to the yield.

(c) No demand shall be made on a region which is useful [for defence or a productive enterprise, e.g.] forts, reservoirs, trade routes, new settlements, mines, forests of both kinds (commodity producing or elephant rearing) or small regions near the frontier [to avoid the additional burden driving the people into the hands of the enemy].

(d) Assistance, in the form of grain, cattle, money, etc. shall, however, be provided to new settlements [notwithstanding the depleted resources].

{5.2.16,2-4}

(ii) Compulsory Purchase:

(a) [After the harvest,] a quarter of the surplus, after deducting the grain needed for subsistence and seeds, shall be [compulsorily] acquired for cash.

Forest produce and grain held by Brahmins learned in the Vedas shall be exempt from compulsory purchase, unless the holders agree to sell.

{5.2.5-7}

(iii) Other commodities:

The proportion for [special levy or compulsory purchase] for other commodities shall be as follows:

One sixth	Silk cotton, lac, linen, barks, cotton, wool, silk, medicinal plants, perfumery plants, flowers, fruits and vegetables, firewood, bamboo, meat and dried meat.
One half	Ivory and skins.

Any one selling any of these commodities without permission shall be fined the lowest level standard fine.　　　{5.2.14,15}

(iv) Levies on Merchants, Craftsmen and Professionals:

The rates for special levies on traders in different commodities and professionals shall be:

Item	Levy
Gold, silver, diamonds, gems, pearls, coral, horses and elephants	50 panas
Yarn, cloth, copper, brass, bronze, perfumes, medicines and alcoholic liquor	40 panas
Grain, liquids, metals not specified above, carts	30 panas
Workers in glass and highly skilled craftsmen	20 panas
Other craftsmen; brothel keepers	10 panas
Wood, bamboo, stoneware and earthenware craftsmen and sellers of cooked food and vegetables	5 panas
Actors and prostitutes	Half the earnings

The tax shall be recovered, in cash, from all those skilled in their work. Their offences shall not be forgiven, for they are apt to [evade the tax and] pretend that the sales made by them were on behalf of someone else.

{5.2.17-26}

(v) Levies on Livestock Owners

Item	Levy
Cocks and pigeons	Half
Small animals	One-sixth
Cows, buffalos, mules, donkeys and camels	One-tenth

{5.2.27}

(vi) Miscellaneous

Brothel keepers shall make use of young and beautiful women sent by the king to collect [more] revenue.   {5.2.28}

DIRECT CULTIVATION

If these [special levies and purchases] do not produce enough grain, the officers working under the Chancellor [i.e. *sthanikas* and *gopas*] shall make farmers prepare the ground, in summer, for a summer crop [in addition to the normal rainy season crop]. Seeds shall be distributed [free] to the farmers on condition that anyone who neglects to take proper care shall pay a penalty of double the estimated loss.

When the crops ripen, the officials shall prevent the farmers from taking green or ripe grain; however, handfuls of vegetables or grain plucked by hand may be taken, if they are intended for worship of gods and ancestors, for charity or for feeding cows.

[After the harvest], the grain on the ground shall be left behind to be gleaned by mendicants and village employees.

Anyone taking away grain cultivated by himself shall pay a fine of eight times the amount taken. Anyone taking grain cultivated by someone else shall pay a fine of fifty times the quantity, if he belongs to the same village. If the thief is an outsider, he shall be put to death.   {5.2.8-13}

VOLUNTARY CONTRIBUTIONS AND SALE OF HONOURS

If adequate resources have not been raised by the above means, the Chancellor shall ask the people of the city and the countryside to make voluntary contributions, giving as a reason some state activity which needs to be executed. Secret agents shall then be the first to give large amounts. They shall be pointed out as examples and the people asked for [similar large] contributions. Other secret agents shall be used to reproach those who give little.   {5.2.31-34}

The king may also ask the rich to give as much gold as they can, either voluntarily or in expectation of favours. Honours and status symbols (umbrella, headgear, decorations) may be bestowed on them in return for gold.   {5.2.35,36}

EXPROPRIATING TEMPLE PROPERTY

Agents appointed by the state shall first take away the property of temples (so long as they are not the property of Brahmins learned in the Vedas) and groups of *Pashandas*. They shall then pretend that the property was lost because the person with whom it was deposited had died or his house had burned down.

The Chief Superintendent of Temples shall collect together the wealth of temples in the city and in the countryside. Then, [using a similar pretext] the property shall be taken away to the Treasury. {5.2.37,38}

EXPLOITING THE GULLIBILITY OF THE PEOPLE

[Kautilya then describes, in {5.2.39-45}, a number of ways by which the gullibility of the public can be exploited to collect money. These include:
 - building overnight, as if it happened by a miracle, a temple or a sanctuary and promote the holding of fairs and festivals in honour of the miraculous deity;
 - exploiting an unnatural happening, such as an unseasonal flower or fruit, by making it into a divine phenomenon;
 - using secret agents to frighten people into making offerings to drive away an evil spirit;
 - playing tricks on people by showing a cobra apparently with many heads, or a stone cobra coming alive;
 - selling remedies against evil occult manifestations.
If people are not taken in so easily, they should be frightened into doing so. Secret agents should give unbelievers an anaesthetic in water and blame their condition on a curse of the gods; or, a condemned man shall be killed by poison and his death blamed on divine retribution.]

OTHER METHODS OF CHEATING TO COLLECT REVENUE

[{5.2.46-51} describe methods of collecting revenue while making it appear that the King was not responsible. For example, it is suggested that a secret agent, posing as a trader, coin examiner or goldsmith, should collect money on deposit and as loans. These should then be 'stolen' by other agents, for the benefit of the Treasury.]

The following are the methods to be used against traitors and wicked people. They shall not be used against others. {5.2.69}

When a person stands accused of a crime, after being trapped by any of the methods described below, his property shall be confiscated.

(a) use women to entrap and then blackmail him;

(b) in a family quarrel, arrange for one member of the family to be killed by a poisoner and blame it on another.

(c) induce a person condemned to death, by offering him clemency, to falsely accuse a traitor of having cheated him out of a deposit or an inheritance.

(d) make a condemned person abuse the traitor, kill the condemned man and accuse the traitor of the murder.

(e) use an agent to pose as an ascetic and trap a traitor into doing some occult rituals for gaining great wealth and then accuse him of indulging in black magic.

(vi) accuse the traitor falsely of child sacrifice, counterfeiting, theft, poisoning or of being in the pay of the enemy.

{Summary of 5.2.52-68}

PUNISHMENTS

Selling commodities without permission in times of declared emergency	Lowest SP	{5.2.15}
Taking away grain from special crops in times of declared emergency:		{5.2.12,13}
from own field	Eight times the quantity stolen	
from another's field	Fifty times if from the same village	
a stranger caught stealing	Death	

V. iii

BUDGET, ACCOUNTS AND AUDIT

BUDGET

REVENUE BUDGETING

The Chancellor shall first estimate the revenue [for the year] by determining the likely revenue from each place and each sphere of activity under the different Heads of Account, total them up by place or activity, and then arrive at a grand total.

Actual revenue shall then be estimated by adding receipts into the Treasury for the current year and receipts on account of [delayed] payments due from the previous year and deducting from this the following: expenditure on the king, standard rations for others, exemptions granted [by the king] by decree or orally, and authorised postponements of payments into the Treasury.

Outstanding revenue shall be estimated by taking into account the following: works under construction from which revenue will accrue only on completion, unpaid fines and penalties, dues not yet recovered, dues defiantly withheld and advances to be repaid by officials; outstandings of little or no value shall be ignored.   {2.6.13-16}

> [The net resources available to the State was thus calculated be estimating revenue during the year, adding outstanding dues of the previous year collected during the current year and subtracting from this total committed Crown expenditure, remissions, uncollectables and loans and advances.]

INCOME, EXPENDITURE AND BALANCE

Actual income is to be calculated under the headings—(i) current income; (ii) transferred income and (iii) miscellaneous revenue.

Current income consists of receipts due and paid in the same year.

Transferred income is income from outstandings of earlier year as well as income earned [by one department] transferred to another.

<u>Miscellaneous income</u> is [of three kinds]:

(i) Recovery of debts and dues which were earlier written off, fines paid by government servants, additional income (from surcharges and unanticipated revenue), compensation collected for loss or damage, gifts, confiscated property, intestate property and treasure trove.

(ii) The following deductions from [anticipated] expenditure [are to be treated as income]: savings due to demobilisation of [a part of] the army, works abandoned before completion and economies made in [actual] investment as against original [planned] budget.

(iii) Income due to profit, on sales: increase in the price of a commodity at the time of sale, profit from the use of differential weights and measures and increased income due to competition from buyers.

Actual expenditure shall be shown under the headings:

(i) budgeted day-to-day expenditure

(ii) unbudgeted day-to-day expenditure

(iii) foreseen periodic (fortnightly, monthly or annual) expenditure.

The [net] revenue is to be calculated after deducting expenditure from income, taking into account the actuals as well as deferred amounts.

{2.6.17-27}

ACCOUNTS

[In the account books,] every entry shall have the date of the transaction.[1]

{2.6.12}

On the receipt side, the revenue shall be classified according to the major Heads of Account: cost price, share *(bhaga)*, transaction tax *[vyaji]*, monopoly taxes, fixed taxes, manufacturing charges, fines and penalties.

On the debit side, expenditure shall be classified according to the major Heads, as given below:

1. Worship (of gods and ancestors) and charitable expenses.

2. The Place [expenditure of the King, Queens, Princes etc.]

3. Administration.

4. Foreign Affairs.

5. Maintenance of granary, ordnance depots and warehouses for commodities and forest produce (under separate subheads).

6. Manufacturing expenses.

7. Labour charges.

8. Defence (with separate subheads for each of the four wings).

9. Cattle [and pastures].

10. Forests and game sanctuaries.

11. [Consumables like] firewood and fodder.   {2.6.11}

FORM OF ACCOUNTS

Income Side

{2.7.31}

Place	Period of accounting	Date and time of receipt	Head of account	Classification current year or outstanding dues	Quantity received	Name of payer	By whose order	Received by	Recorded by
1	2	3	4	5	6	7	8	9	10

Expenditure Side

{2.7.32}

Place	Period of accounting	Date and time of payment	Head of Expenditure	Counter value received	Occasion	What was paid	Amount paid	For what use	Authority ordering payment	Withdrawn from store	Delivered by	Received by
1	2	3	4	5	6	7	8	9	10	11	12	13

Balance Columns

{2.7.33}

Place	Date and time	Head of account	Dues left outstanding	Form in which balance received into the treasury	Quality	Amount received	Details of container	Delivered to (name of treasury official)
1	2	3	4	5	6	7	8	9

DEPARTMENTAL OR REGIONAL ACCOUNTS OFFICERS

Proper Maintenance of Account Books

All accounts shall be maintained in the proper form and legibly written without corrections. Failure to do so shall be a punishable offence.

{from 2.7.35}

Timely Submission of Accounts:

Monthly accounts: Day-to-day accounts[2] [to be submitted once a month] shall be presented before the end of the following month and late submission shall be penalised.   {from 2.7.26.27}

Accounts of specific transactions: If the net balance to be remitted to the Treasury is small, a grace of five days shall be allowed for making the remittance. If the accounts are delayed [beyond five days], the net balance shall first be remitted to the Treasury and then a thorough audit done taking into account the rules of business, [relevant] precedents, the circumstances and the calculations; a physical verification of the work shall be carried out. Whether the smallness of the remittance was justified or not shall then be judged by inference [supplemented] by information from secret agents.   {2.7.28,29}

AUDIT

RESPONSIBILITY OF ACCOUNT OFFICERS

Accounts officers shall:

- present themselves for audit at the appointed time bringing with them their account books and the income to be remitted to the Treasury;
- be ready for audit when the audit officer calls him;
- not lie about the accounts [when questioned during audit; and
- not try to interpolate an [omitted] entry as if it was forgotten [inadvertently].

Failure to conform to any of the above regulations is a punishable offence.

{from 2.7.21-23, 39, 40}

In case a discrepancy is discovered during audit:

- the official concerned shall pay a penalty if the discrepancy has the effect of either showing a higher actual income of a lower actual expenditure [in both the state being the loser].
- the official shall keep the difference for himself in the converse case [where a lesser amount than the one shown by the official is actually due to the state].   {2.7.19,20}

RESPONSIBILITY OF AUDITORS

An auditor shall be ready when an accounts officer presents himself for audit; otherwise, he shall be punished.   {from 2.7.22}

RESPONSIBILITY OF HIGH OFFICIALS

High officials that shall be responsible for rendering the accounts in full for their sphere of activity without any contradiction in them. Those who tell lies or make contradictory statements shall pay the highest level standard penalty.   {2.7.25}

PUNISHMENTS

<u>Departmental or regional accounts officers:</u>

Writing in a disorderly manner, not following the prescribed from, writing illegibly or rewriting <u>over a previous entry:</u>		{2.7.35,36}
any column of the account book	12 panas	
in the column for net revenue	24 panas	
If the account books are destroyed [accidentally]	restitution of loss to state + one-fifth of the amount as fine	{2.7.38}
Losing account books [deliberately]	96 panas	{2.7.37}
Failure to submit day-to-day accounts for a given month by the end of the following month	200 panas for each month's delay	{2.7.27}
Not coming on time for audit; coming without account books or without the net balance	One-tenth of amount due	{2.7.21}
Not having accounts ready for audit; not maintaining accounts in accordance with written orders; disobeying accounting instructions	Lowest SP	{2.7.34}
Discrepancy involving loss to state	Eight times the amount of discrepancy	{2.7.19}
Lying about accounts	As for theft	{2.7.39}
Lie discovered after audit is completed	Twice the penalty for theft	{2.7.40}

| Interpolating entries | Twice the penalty for theft | {2.7.40} |
| Not being ready for audit | Twice lowest SP | {2.7.22} |

Audit Officers:

| Not being ready for audit | Twice Lowest SP | {2.7.23} |

High Officials:

| For telling lies or making contradictory statements | Highest SP | {2.7. 25} |

PART VI

CIVIL SERVICE REGULATIONS

"Just as it is impossible not to taste honey or poison that one may find at the tip of one's tongue, so it is impossible for one dealing with government funds not to taste, a little bit, of the King's wealth."

{2.9.32}

"Just as it is impossible to know when a fish moving in water is drinking it, so it is impossible to find out when government servants in charge of undertakings misappropriate money."

{2.9.33}

"Those officials who do not eat up the king's wealth but increase it in just ways and are loyally devoted to him shall be made a permanent in service."

{2.9.36}

"He who causes loss of revenue eats the king's wealth, [but] he who produces double the [anticipated] revenue eats up the country and he who spends all the revenue [without bringing any profit] eats up the labour of workmen.}

{2.9.13, 15, 17}

VI.i

ESTABLISHMENT AND FINANCIAL RULES

[There general principles for running an efficient and disciplined civil service are given in the verses in the title page to this part of the translation. The first is that, unless controlled, civil servants will make money in unauthorized or fraudulent ways. The second is that good civil servants shall be suitably rewarded. The third is the very important principle enjoining civil servants to collect the right amount of revenue, neither more nor less and to reduce expenditure in order to leave a net balance to the state.

This section brings together the verses relating to general principles of establishment, financial discipline, embezzlement, etc. The actual duties of the Heads of different Departments are dealt with in detail in Part VII. The topics in this section are spread over a number of books, particularly 2 and 5. There is a lot of repetition, partly because similar things are said about collectors of revenue, officials involved in running undertakings such as mines, accounts officers, audit officers, etc. In the text, the same ideas are put in different places by Kautilya because each Head of Department had to memorise all his duties described in that particular chapter.

Some aspects of the Code of Conduct of government servants have been translated in earlier sections. For example, misbehaviour or negligence of duty by guards at night during curfew hours has been dealt with under the responsibilities of the Governor-General of the City. Financial misbehaviour by government servants is dealt with in section VI. iii and punishments for crimes committed by them in VI. iv.

Attention was paid to recruitment of proper personnel for the civil service. In {1.11. 19, 20}, spies, masquerading as ascetics, were required to be on the lookout for men of spirit, intelligence and eloquence and to predict for them prosperity and close association with a minister. Their names were then to be secretly recommended to a minister for appointing them to suitable positions.

The first three verses below continue the general principles enunciated in the title page.]

GENERAL

It is possible to know even the path of birds flying in the sky but not the ways of government servants who hide their [dishonest] income.

{2.9.34}

The King shall forgive a trifling offence and be content even if the [net] revenue is small. He shall honour with rewards [those] officials who bring great benefit [to the State.]

{2.7.41}

Those officials who have amassed money [wrongfully] shall be made to pay it back; they shall [then] be transferred to other jobs where they will not be tempted to misappropriate and be made to disgorge again what they had eaten. {2.9.35}

ESTABLISHMENT OF THE CIVIL SERVICE

Heads of Departments shall not remain permanently in one job and shall be rotated frequently.[1] {2.9.31}

Officials, who have the [necessary] qualifications for being appointed as ministers[2] shall be appointed as Heads [of Departments] according to their ability. {2.9.1}

Heads of Departments shall carry out their duties with the assistance of accounts, clerks, coin examiners, store keepers and [military] supervisors. Clever and loyal assistants of military supervisors shall watch over [the activities of] subordinate officials such as accountants and clerks.

{2.9.28-30}

Inspection: The King shall have the work of Heads of Departments inspected daily, for men are, by nature, fickle and, like horses, change after being put to work. Therefore, the King shall acquaint himself with all the details [of each Department or undertaking, such as]—the officer responsible, the nature of the work, the place of work, the time taken to do it, the exact work to be done, the outlay and the profit. {2.9.2-4}

GENERAL INSTRUCTION ON WORKS

No work shall be started without authorization, except in cases of emergencies.

{2.9.7}

Officers shall carry out the work as ordered without either colluding with each other or quarrelling among themselves. For, when they collude they swallow revenue and when they quarrel they ruin the work.

{2.9.5,6}

An officer negligent or remiss in his work shall be fined double his wages and the expenses incurred.   {2.9.8}

An officer who accomplishes a task as ordered or better shall be honoured with promotion and rewards.   {2.9.9}

Every official who is authorized to execute a task or is appointed as a Head of Department shall communicate [to the King] the true facts about the nature of the work, the income and the expenditure, both in detail and the total.   {2.9.19}

ON COLLECTING THE CORRECT REVENUE

[There are three kinds of faults in revenue collection—causing loss through negligence, collecting more than the just dues due to overzealousness and being careless about keeping expenditure well within income.]

He who causes loss of revenue swallows the King's wealth. If he causes loss through ignorance [and the seven other causes mentioned in {2.7.10}— see below] he shall be made to pay an amount equal to the loss multiplied by an appropriate number [depending on the circumstance of each case].
                                                              {2.9.13,14}

He who produces double the [anticipated] revenue eats up the *janapada* [the countryside and its people, by leaving them inadequate resources for survival and further production]. If the official brings in [to the Treasury] the whole of the excess revenue, he shall be given a small punishment. If the offence is grave, [i.e. using part or whole of the excess collection for his own benefit] he shall be punished according to the amount involved.
                                                              {2.9.15,16}

He who spends all the revenue [without bringing in any profit] swallows the labour of workers. He shall be punished according to the nature of the offence—depending on whether the profit was misappropriated or not. The amount lost shall be calculated by taking into account the work done, the number of days spent in doing it, the amount spent, the price received for goods produced, the number of workmen employed and the wages paid.   {2.9.17,18}

[Some] teachers say: 'An official who brings in little revenue and spends too much [must be a corrupt one who] eats it up. Conversely, one who manages the expenditure [under his control] according to the income does not misappropriate.'

Kautilya [does not think that the conclusions automatically follow and] says that the reasons for loss of revenue can be found out only through spies.
                                                              {2.9.10-12}

ERRANT OFFICIALS

The King shall watch out for those [errant] officials who are <u>prodigal</u> (one who squanders his inherited ancestral property in unethical ways), <u>spendthrift</u> (one who spends whatever he earns as soon as he earns it) or <u>miserly</u> (one who amasses wealth while making his dependents suffer).

In all cases, an official [who has caused loss of revenue to the State] shall not be deprived of his property if he has many dependents [but shall be dismissed from service]. Otherwise, his property shall be confiscated.

In the case of a miserly official, who hoards the King's property and uses it for his own benefit (by storing it in his own house, by depositing it with others or by trading with it with foreigners), the facts shall be ascertained by a secret agent. The agent shall find out the details of the receipt and despatch of the goods as well as who are the official's advisers, friends, dependents, kinsmen and supporters. In the case of trading with foreigners, the agent shall penetrate the [establishments of] foreign buyers in order to ascertain concealed information. When all facts have been ascertained, the errant official shall be [falsely] accused [of being in the pay of the enemy] using, as a pretext, a [forged] letter; he shall then be killed.   {2.9.2027}

FINANCIAL DISCIPLINE

OF INSPECTORS

The loss caused [due to inadequate supervision] by an inspector failing in his duty shall be made good by the following: his fellow officials, sureties, subordinates, sons, brothers, wife, daughters and servants [the one later in the list becoming liable if an earlier one fails to compensate].

{2.7.5}

OF OFFICIALS RESPONSIBLE FOR DEPARTMENTS

The following are the causes of loss to the Treasury due to officials failing to collect the revenue required from them:

- <u>ignorance</u> of the work to be done or of the rules, regulations and customs;
- <u>laziness</u> and disinclination to work hard;
- <u>neglect</u> of duty due to indulgence in sensual pleasures;
- <u>timidity</u> due to feat of public discontent or uproar, [reactions from] evil persons or of untoward results;
- <u>corruption</u> [particularly] showing favours to selfish persons with whom the official has had dealings;

- short temper and tendency to violence [alienating those from whom he has to collect the revenue];
- arrogance about his learning, his wealth or the support he gets from highly placed persons; or
- greed which prompts him to use false balances, weights or measures, or to make false assessments and calculations.   {2.7.10}

According to the school of Manu, the punishment shall be a fine equal to the loss suffered multiplied by the number of the reason for loss [given above—i.e. 1 for ignorance, 2 for laziness, etc]. The penalty recommended by the school of Parasara is, in all cases, eight times the loss, by the school of Brihaspati ten times and by Ushanas twenty times.

Kautilya disagrees and recommends that the penalty shall be commensurate with the [gravity of the] offence. [i.e. not follow a rigid pattern but to take into account the circumstances of each case.]

{2.7.11-15}

PUNISHMENTS

For not being present at the right place or time (day or night) on government duty	12 panas	{3.20.14}
Negligence in work	Double the wages and expenses incurred.	{2.9.8}
Loss of revenue through ignorance, or any of the seven other causes in {2.7.10}	A multiple of the loss	{2.9.13-15}
Bringing in excess revenue		{2.9.15,16}
all remitted to Treasury	Small punishment	
excess embezzled in whole or in part	of offence	
All income spent and no net revenue	According to the offence	{2.9.17,18}
Prodigal, spendthrift and miserly officials		
with many dependants	dismissal from service	{2.19.24}
few or no dependants	dismissal and confiscation of property	
Miserly official using government money for own benefit	Death after false accusation	{2.19.27}

VI. ii

SALARIES OF GOVERNMENT SERVANTS

[The section deals with the principles of determining salaries and wages, actual scales of pay, special payments for rituals, travelling allowances and death benefits. Salaries were fixed on a cash basis but could be paid in kind or as a mixture of the two; a formula is given for converting a part of the salary into a mixture of mostly grains and a little cash. An official could, in lieu of a part of his salary, be allotted land to be farmed by him for his own benefit—see {3.1.7}; but such land could neither be sold nor mortgaged and could be used only as long as he held the office.]

PRINCIPLES OF SALARY FIXATION

The [total] salary [bill] of the State shall be determined in accordance with the capacity [to pay] of the city and the countryside and shall be [about] one quarter of the revenue of the State. The salary scales shall be such as to enable the accomplishment of state activities [by attracting the right type of people], shall be adequate for meeting the bodily needs of state servants and shall not be in contradiction to the principles of *dharma* and *artha*.   {5.3.1,2}

If the [amount of actual cash in the] Treasury is inadequate, salaries may be paid [partly] in forest produce, cattle or land, supplemented by a little money. However, in the case of settlement of virgin lands, all salaries shall be paid in cash; no land shall be allotted [as a part of the salary] until the affairs of the [new] village are fully stabilised.   {5.3.31,32}

Grain may be substituted for cash wages according to the following formula: an annual salary of 60 panas is equal to one *adhaka* of grain per day.[1]

Salaries and wages of any individual employee, permanent or temporary, shall be fixed in accordance with the above principles, taking into account each one's level of knowledge and expertise in the work allotted.

{5.4.33}

SALARIES

Grade	Annual Salary (in panas)	Position	Remarks
A. The Higher Grades			
1.	48,000	Palace Officiating Priest King's guru *Purohita* Crown Prince King's mother The Queen Civil Service Councillors Armed forces Chief of Defence	This is enough to prevent them from succumbing to the temptations [of the enemy] or rising up in revolt.
2.	24,000	Palace *Prasastr* (?) The Chancellor The Treasurer	Enough to make them efficient in their work.
3.	12,000	Palace Princes, (other than the Crown Prince) Queens (other than the seniormost) Civil Service Ministers Governor General of the City Head of manufacturing establishment Provincial Governors	Enough to ensure that they remain loyal and powerful supporters of the king.

Grade	Annual Salary (in panas)	Position	Remarks
		Governors of frontier regions	
		Armed forces City Commandant	
4.	8,000	Civil Service Magistrates	Enough to enable them to carry their men with them.
		Armed forces Chief Commanders of: Infantry Horses Elephants Chariots	
5.	4,000	Civil Service Chief Elephant Forester Chief Superintendent of Productive Forests Armed forces Divisional Commanders of: Infantry Horses Elephants Chariots	

{5.3.3-11}

Grade	Annual Salary (in panas)	Position	Remarks

B. The Middle Grades

6.	3,000	**Palace** Grade I courtesan	
7.	2,000	**Palace** Grade II courtesan King's charioteer King's physician Elephant trainer Horse trainer Chief Engineer Animal breeders **Armed forces** Camp superintendent	
8.	1,000	**Palace** Grade III courtesan Soothsayer Reader of omens Astrologer Narrator of *Puranas* Story tellers Court poet Bard/Praise Singers Deputy *purohitas* **Civil Service** HEADS OF DEPARTMENTS **Secret Service:** Intelligence officer; Agents under the cover of monks, householders, merchants and ascetics.	

Grade	Annual Salary (in panas)	Position	Remarks
9.	500	<u>Palace</u> Instrumental musicians and instrument makers <u>Civil Service</u> Accountants, clerks and similar subordinates <u>Secret Service:</u> Village-level secret agents, assassins, poisoners and female agents disguised as wandering nuns. <u>Armed forces</u> Commandos and other specialist soldiers	
10.	250	<u>Palace</u> Minstrels, actors, etc. <u>Civil Service</u> Occasional secret agents (minimum)	Secret agents pay to be increased according to work done.

{5.3.12-15,21-24}

C. The Lower Grades

{5.3.16,17}

Grade	Annual Salary (in panas)	Position	Remarks
11.	120	<u>Palace</u> Artisans, sculptors	
12.	60	<u>Palace</u> Servants in charge of animals and birds Labour foremen Valets [of the King] Bodyguards of the King Mahout of the King's elephant *Manavaka* Miners (?) King's servants not elsewhere specified.	

SPECIAL PROVISIONS FOR RITUALS

The honorarium for teachers and learned men shall be a minimum of 500 panas and a maximum of 1000 panas [for each occasion?]

He who represents the King in sacrificial rites, such as the *Rajasuya*, shall be paid three times the amount paid to those similar in learning. The charioteer of the King's chariot for the ritual shall be paid 1000 panas.

{5.3.18,20,21}

TRAVELLING ALLOWANCE

Middle grade envoy:
- 10 panas per *yojana*,[2] up to 10 *yojanas*
- 20 panas per *yojana*, between 10 to 100 *yojanas*   {5.3.19}

DEATH OF GOVERNMENT SERVANT IN SERVICE

If a Government servant dies while on duty, his sons and wives shall be entitled to his salary and food allowance. Minor children and old or sick relatives shall be [suitably] assisted. On occasions such as funerals, births or illnesses, the families [of the deceased government servant] shall be given presents of money and shown honour [as a mark of gratitude to one who died in the King's service].   {5.3.28-30}

VI.iii

FINANCIAL MISBEHAVIOUR OF GOVERNMENT SERVANTS

[Government servants could enrich themselves improperly in two ways—either by cheating the government or by exploiting the public. In {2.8.4-19}, Kautilya describes succinctly the ways in which misbehaviour by government servants leads to a reduction in revenue and prescribes the appropriate punishment for each type of misbehaviour. The translation has been set out in a tabular form for better understanding.

The single verse—{2.8.21}—listing forty ways of 'stealing' is very difficult to translate. Since a later verse deals with making restitution, after due investigation, to the victims of the mischief of dishonest officials, it must be assumed that the forty ways are concerned with enrichment at the cost of the public. In any case, the ways in which officials could cheat the State have been separately dealt with by Kautilya. The forty ways become more understandable if they are viewed as opportunities for corruption and exploitation of the public and the symmetrical pattern of this verse reinforces this judgment. Of the forty ways, the last ten simply list the areas in which fraud is possible; two more deal with cheating about the time of transactions (months in annual accounts and days in monthly accounts). The other twenty-eight show two types of symmetry: (i) each statement is paired with another and (ii) there are three groups of transactions, often with very similar expressions. These 28 ways are, therefore, set out in this translation in the form of a table, bringing out this symmetry. The public is affected in all cases while in some, the state coffers also suffer.

It should be noted that civil servants were encouraged to confess while, at the same time, were also protected against false accusation. The interest of the public was protected by providing for compensation to the victims of malpractices.]

CHEATING THE GOVERNMENT

Type	Details	Punishment
Obstruction	Failure to carry out [orders or] a task [or to collect due taxes]	A fine of one-tenth of the amount involved
	Failure to realise the profit from an undertaking Failure to deliver the profit to the Treasury	
Using government property for personal profit	Lending government property at interest	Double the [personal] profit made
	Trading in government goods	
Falsification of the date	Showing a later date than the one on which income was received	One-fifth of the amount involved
	Showing expenditure as having been incurred on an earlier date [in both cases, using the money for personal benefit for a period]	
Causing loss to Government	Collecting less than the fixed amount of revenue or exceeding the sanctioned amount of expenditure	Four times the amount lost
Misuse of Government property		Death
(i) by the official himself,	if gems and jewellry	Middle SP
(ii) by allowing others, or	if high valued articles	Restitution plus equal amount as fine
(iii) by substituting one article [of higher value] by another [of lower value]	all others	
Misappropriation	Not delivering revenue to the Treasury	
	Not paying authorised expenditure [such as not handing over the gifts, as ordered by the king]	
	Misrepresenting income received	

STEALING IN TRANSACTIONS WITH THE PUBLIC

TWENTY-EIGHT OF THE FORTY WAYS OF STEALING

	Revenue collection	Making Payments	Sale and Purchase
Favour shown for a bribe	1. Revenue due on a given date is allowed to be paid later [for a consideration]	11. Making payments [to a favourite] earlier than due	19. Goods bought [wholesale but shown as bought retail and a higher price paid]
Public exploited	2. Revenue not due till later is collected earlier [by force, to compensate for above]	12. Delaying a payment due on a given date	20. Goods sold at retail prices but shown as sold wholesale [at a lower price]
Favour shown	3. Revenue due [from a bribe-giver] is suppressed	13. Making payment not due to someone [for a bribe]	21. Suppressing a sale by giving away the goods
Public exploited and revenue embezzled	4. Revenue not due is made to be paid [and is misappropriated]	14. Not paying the due amount to someone [and pocketing it]	22. Suppressing a purchase
Corruption	5. Revenue not paid is shown as paid [for a bribe]		23. [In a supposed purchase] goods not received but payment made
Public exploited	6. Revenue paid is shown as not paid [but misappropriated]		24. [In a supposed sale] price received but goods not delivered

	Revenue collection	Making Payments	Sale and Purchase
Corruption	7. Small amount of revenue paid is made out as paid in full	15. Large payment misrepresented as a small one	25. Selling a high-priced item but charging a lower price
Public exploited	8. Though paid in full, only small amount shown as received	16. Small payment made, shown as large amount	26. Buying a high-priced item but paying a lower price
Corruption	9. Revenue paid in by one shown as paid by another [a bribe giver]	17. Payment due to one person paid to another [for a cut]	27. Lowering the price [for a favourite]
Public exploited	10. Revenue paid in one kind [of higher value] shown as another [of lower value]	18. Payment made in one kind [of lower value] shown as another [of higher value]	28. Raising the price [to someone who does not give a bribe]

The remaining twelve are:

29,30. Fraud in periods of payment:

(i) discrepancy in months in a year

(ii) discrepancy in days in a month.

[In both cases, not recording receipts or payments to the advantage of the fraudulent official and the disadvantage of the public.]

31-40. Discrepancies in the following:

– personally supervised work

– Heads of Account

– labour accounts

– measurement of work

– totalling

– quality

– price

– weighing

– measuring

– containers for goods

{2.8.20,21}

INVESTIGATION AND COMPENSATION

In all these cases, the subordinate officers, the storekeeper, the ledger-keeper, the receiver, the payer, the official who authorised the payment, the adviser, and the assistant shall be interrogated individually. If any one of these tells a lie, he shall receive the same punishment as the officer concerned.

{2.8.22,23}

A proclamation shall then be issued calling on all those who had suffered at the hands of the [dishonest] official to inform [the investigating officer]. All those who respond to the proclamation shall be compensated according to their loss.

{2.8.24,25}

TRIAL AND PUNISHMENT

When an official, accused of many [instances of fraud], denies them all, he shall be held liable for all of them, if he is found guilty [even] in a single instance. If he admits to some of them, each [charge] shall be tried separately.

Likewise, if an official is accused of defrauding a large amount and if the accusation is proved even for a small part of it, he shall be held liable for the whole.

{2.8.26-28}

INFORMERS—REWARDS AND PUNISHMENTS

REWARDS

Any informant, to whom an assurance against punishment has been given [even if he had participated in the fraud], shall, if the case is proved, receive [as reward] one-sixth of the amount involved; if the informant is a state servant, one-twelfth.

If, in a case involving a large amount, only a small part is proved, the reward shall be a proportion of [only] that part which is proved.

{2.8.29,30}

PROTECTION

If the case is proved, the informant [shall be permitted to escape the wrath of the guilty and] may either remain in hiding or attribute the information to someone else.

{2.8.32}

PUNISHMENTS

If the case [against the accused official] is not proved, the informant shall be given corporal punishment or fined and no mercy shall be shown to him.

If an informant withdraws the charge at the instigation of the accused, he shall be condemned to death.

{2.8.31,32}

VI.iv

PUNISHMENT OF GOVERNMENT SERVANTS

[The crimes and punishments described in this section are criminal offences; i.e. those in Book 4 on 'The Removal of Thorns'. A summary of the punishments prescribed for administrative lapses has been added.]

The scale of punishments for crimes committed by civil servants shall be as given below.

A. STEALING THE KING'S PROPERTY

A.1 - Stealing from the Treasury

Crime	Punishment
Gems or articles of high value	Death
Articles of low value or implements	Lowest SP

A.2 - Stealing from other places

[See Table on page 300]

For abetting thieves to break into the King's Treasury, warehouses, etc. the punishment shall be death by torture. {2.5.16,20; 4.9.4-8}

B. THEFT OF PROPERTY OTHER THAN THAT OF THE KING

From a field, a threshing floor, a house, a shop and stores of forest produce, commodities, tools or implements. See Table on pages 302 and 303.

C. FALSE DOCUMENTATION

Making counterfeit documents or copying the seals of:

The public	Lowest SP
Heads of Departments	Middle SP
Ministers	Counsellors
The King	Death

[The above are normal penalties. However,] the punishment shall be commensurate with the gravity of the offence. {4.9.12}

Stealing from other places

Value of goods stolen (in panas)			Punishment
From place of production	From granaries, armoury, warehouses for commodities and forest products	From Treasury goldsmithy or storehouses for valuable articles	(in panas)
1/16 to 14	1/32 to 1/8		12
1/4 to 1/2	1/8 to 1/4	1/64 to 1/16	24
1/2 to 3/4	1/4 to 3/8	1/16 to 1/1/8	36
3/4 to 1	3/8 to 1/2	1/8 to 3/16	48
1 to 2	1/2 to 1	3/16 to 1/4	Lowest SP
2 to 4	1 to 2	1/4 to 1/2	Middle SP
4 to 8	2 to 4	1/2 to 1	Highest SP
above 8	above 4	above 1	Death

D. WRONGFUL CONFINEMENT

Keeping anyone confined after acquittal   Lowest SP   {4.8.8}

E. PUNISHMENTS FOR ADMINISTRATIVE LAPSES

[Punishments for lapses and misdemeanours of specific officials are given under the appropriate official. Some examples are:

Misbehaviour of judges, judges' clerks and jailors—{4.9.13-27};

Corrupt Coin Examiner—{4.1.44,46,47};

Chief Controller of Customs concealing offences of merchants-{2.21.14}

Chief Controller of Shipping failing to maintain boats or have them manned properly-{2.28.26};[

Chief Textile Commissioner misbehaving with women workers—{2.23.14}

Chief Superintendent of Pasture Lands failing to ensure safety of travellers on roads between settlements—{4.13.9};

Frontier Officers personally responsible for loss of theft of merchandise on the way—{2.21.25};

Gate keepers who allow corpses to be taken out by an unauthorized gate—{2.36.32};

Cheating by masters of gambling houses—{3.20.9,12};

Game keepers/game sanctuary attendants who permit protected species to be trapped, injured or killed—{2.26.6.}

Attendants of horses not doing their duties, or riding a ceremonial or sick horse—{2.30.45,46}.

Veterinary doctors not treating a sick horse properly—{2.30.47,48}.]

THEFT OF PROPERTY OTHER THAN THAT OF THE KING

Value of goods stolen (in panas)			Punishment
Stealing secretly	Seizure by force during day or at night during curfew	Seizure by force with weapons during day or at night	Fine in panas plus as specified
Below 1/16	Below 1/32	Below 1/64	Nil
1/16 to 1/4	1/32 to 1/8		3 panas or public humiliation 1
1/4 to 1/2	1/8 to 1/4	1/64 to 1/16	6 panas or pub. hum. 2
1/2 to 3/4	1/4 to 3/8		9 panas or pub. hum. 2 or 3
3/4 to 1	3/8 to 1/2	1/16 to 1/8	12 panas or pub. hum. 3 and exile
		1/8 to 3/16	18 panas or pub. hum. 2 or 3
1 to 2	1/2 to 1	3/16 to 1/4	24 panas or pub. hum. 4 and exile
2 to 4	1 to 2		36 panas
4 to 5	2 to 2 1/2	1/4 to 1/2	48 panas
		1/2 to 1	72 panas
		1 to 1 1/4	96 panas
5 to 10	2 1/2 to 5		Lowest SP

Value of goods stolen (in panas)			Punishment
Stealing secretly	Seizure by force during day or at night during curfew	Seizure by force with weapons during day or at night	Fine in panas <u>plus</u> as specified
		1 1/4 to 2 1/2	Middle SP
10 to 20	5 to 10		200 panas
		2 1/2 to 5	400 panas
20 to 30	10 to 15		500 panas
30 to 40	15 to 20	5 to 7 1/2	1000 panas
		7 1/2 to 10	2000 panas
Above 40	Above 20	Above 10	Death

<u>Public humiliation</u>
1. Smearing with cowdung in public.
2. Smearing with cowdung and ashes in public.
3. As in 2 above <u>or</u> a parading with a belt of broken pots.
4. Shaving off the head.   {4.9.9-11}

Part VII

THE DEPARTMENTS OF THE GOVERNMENT

"The source of the financial strength of the State is the mining [and metallurgical] industry; the State exercises power because of its Treasury. With [increased] wealth and a [powerful] army more territory can be acquired, thereby further increasing the wealth of the State."

{2.12.37}

"Trade shall be [directed towards markets which are] profitable; losses must be avoided."

{2.16.25}

"Any official who incurs the displeasure of the people shall either be removed from his post or transferred to a dangerous regions."

{13.5.21}

VII.i

HEADS OF DEPARTMENTS

[Dr. Kangle notes that 'the kind of state control over the economy *Arthashastra* presupposes is not possible without an efficient administration. We, therefore, find in it a description of an elaborate administrative machinery.'¹The structure of the administration of an ideal state is primarily given by Kautilya in Book 2. As one would expect from a text book on the practical aspects of government, Book 2 is the longest book containing 36 chapters and as many as 1285 verses (nearly a quarter of the entire work). It is titled *adhyakshaprachara*—'Duties of Heads of Departments'. Since the *adhyaksha* or Head of Department was in overall charge of all the activities of his Department, the thirty-six chapters, in effect, describe the work of the different departments of the state.

The word *adhyaksha* is used by Kautilya primarily in the specialised sense of someone responsible for a clearly delimited field of government activity. In order to preserve this special usage, the word 'Chief' is used in this translation, whether the official is called a 'Controller' or a 'Superintendent' or by any other name such as 'Chief Mint Master' or 'Chief Elephant Forester'.

There are thirty *adhyakshas* listed in Book 2. Four more are mentioned elsewhere—the Chief Controller of Gambling {3.20}, the Chief Controller of Private Trade {4.2}, the Chief Superintendent of Jails {4.9.23} and the Chief Superintendent of Temples {5.2}, making a total of thirty-four. Of these, the office of the Chief Comptroller of Accounts has been dealt with in IV.iv under 'Highest Level Officials', for reasons explained therein.

The complete list of the remaining thirty-three Heads of Departments is given below.

LIST OF *ADHYAKSHAS*
(in textual order)

1.	{2.2}	*Nagavanadhyaksha*	Chief Elephant Forester
2.	{2.11}	*Kosashadhyaksha*	Chief Superintendent of the Treasury
3.	{2.12}	*Akaradhyaksha*	Chief Controller of Mining and Metallurgy

4.	{2.12.23}	Lohadhyaksha	Chief Superintendent of Metals
5.	{2.12.24}	Lakshanadhyaksha	Chief Master of the Mint
6.	{2.12.27}	Khanyadhyaksha	Chief Superintendent of Mines
7.	{2.12.28}	Lavanadhyaksha	Chief Salt Commissioner
8.	{2.13}	Suvarnadhyaksha	Chief Superintendent of Precious Metals and Jewellery
9.	{2.15}	Koshtagaradhyaksha	Chief Superintendent of Warehouses
10.	{2.16}	Panyadhyaksha	Chief Controller of State Trading
11.	{2.17}	Kupyadhyaksha	Chief Superintendent of Forest Produce
12.	{2.18}	Ayudhagaradhyaksha	Chief of Ordnance
13.	{2.19}	Pauthavadhyaksha	Chief Controller of Weights and Measures
14.	{2.20}	Manadhyaksha	Chief Surveyor and Timekeeper
15.	{2.21}	Sulkadhyaksha	Chief Controller of Customs and Octroi
16.	{2.23}	Sutradhyaksha	Chief Textile Commissioner
17.	{2.24}	Sitadhyaksha	Chief Superintendent of Crown Lands
18.	{2.25}	Suradhyaksha	Chief Controller of Alcoholic Beverages
19.	{2.26}	Sunadhyaksha	Chief Protector of Animals and Controller of Animal Slaughter
20.	{2.27}	Ganikadhyaksha	Chief Controller of Entertainers (Courtesans, Brothels, Prostitutes and other Entertainers)
21.	{2.28}	Navadhyaksha	Chief Controller of Shipping
22.	{2.28.7}	Pattanadhyaksha	Chief Controller of Ports and Harbours
23.	{2.29}	Go-adhyaksha	Chief Superintendent of Crown Herds
24.	{2.30}	Asvadhyaksha	Chief Commander of Cavalry
25.	{2.31}	Hastyadhyaksha	Chief Commander of Elephant Corps
26.	{2.33}	Rathadhyaksha	Chief Commander of Chariot Corps
27.	{2.33}	Pattyadhyaksha	Chief Commander of Infantry
28.	{2.34}	Mudradhyaksha	Chief Passport Officer
29.	{2.34}	Vivitadhyaksha	Chief Controller of Pasture Lands
30.	{3.20}	Dhyutadhyksha	Chief Controller of Gambling
31.	{4.2}	Samsthadhyaksha	Chief Controller of Private Trade
32.	{4.9.23}	Bandanagradhyaksha	Chief Superintendent of Jails
33.	{5.2.38}	Devatadhyaksha	Chief Superintendent of Temples

Of these thirty-three, five (the Chief Corps Commanders of Infantry, Cavalry, Chariots and Elephants and the Chief of Ordnance) properly belong to the Defence establishment. The Chief Elephant Forester, being a subordinate of the Chief Commander of the Elephant Corps was also probably a part of this. The duties of these officials are described in section XI.ii on Defence.

The responsibilities of the remaining twenty-seven have been collected together in this section, grouped under different subheadings, according to the nature of their duties:

Treasury officials (2):

The Chief Superintendent of the Treasury;
The Chief Superintendent of the Warehouses.

Agriculture, Forestry and Livestock officials (4):

The Chief Superintendents   of Crown Lands;
                                    of Productive Forests;
                                    of Crown Herds;
The Chief Protector of Animals (and Controller of Animal Slaughter).

Industry officials (7):

The Chief Textile Commissioner;
The Chief Controller of Mining and Metallurgy with his subordinates;
The Chief Superintendents of Mines and Metals, the Chief Master of the Mint and the Chief Salt Commissioner.

Though not an *adhyaksha*, the work of another subordinate, the Coin Examiner, is also included. The sixth *adhyaksha* described in this subsection is the Chief Superintendent of Precious Metals and Jewellery; the work of his important subordinate, the Controller of Goldsmiths and Silversmiths, is also covered.

Trade and Transport officials (7):

The Chief Controllers of State Trading, Private Trade, Weights and Measures, Shipping including Ferries and Ports; the Chief Collector of Customs and Octroi and the Chief Surveyor and Time Keeper.

Leisure Control officials (3):

The Chief Controllers of Alcoholic Beverages, of Entertainers, Prostitutes and Courtesans and of Gambling and Betting.

Movement Control officials (2):

The Chief Superintendent of Pasture Lands; the Chief Passport Officer.

Miscellaneous (2):

The Chief Superintendent of Jails and the Chief Superintendent of Temples and Holy Places.

Book 2 is long because it is not confined only to a description of the duties of Heads of Departments but also contains a mass of material relevant to their duties. For example, everything about precious metals and jewellery, including a description of how goldsmiths and silversmiths cheat, is found under one or the other of the two officials responsible for this subject. Much information about agriculture, forest produce, elephants, recipes for making liquor and other similar topics is given under the appropriate Head of Department. In addition, of course, the revenue to be collected by each one and the fines and penalties for contravention of rules and regulations are given in detail for each Head. All this, presumably, made it easier for each one to memorise all that was relevant to him. Since this translation is organized differently, information about agriculture or industry has been collated separately. Many of Kautilya's lists have been put together in Appendices. This section, therefore, only contains translations of those verses which describe the duties and responsibilities of each Head of Department. Where available, the qualifications which an official ought to have for being appointed to a post has also been given.

Though the thirty-three officials are all called *adhyakshas* they were clearly not all of the same grade. Chapter {5.3} of the text gives a salary scale for 'all *adhyakshas*' as 1000 panas per annum. But, in the same chapter, the salary of Heads of Manufacturing Establishments is specified as 12,000 panas per annum and that of the officials in charge of forests (both productive and elephant) as 4000 panas. That one *adhyaksha* could be paid differently from another is also borne out by the fact that the Chief Controller of Mining and Metallurgy, himself and *adhyaksha* had four other *adhyakshas* working under him, the implication being that the superior officer was of a higher grade. It is also likely that some Heads of Departments (e.g. of Crown Lands, Crown Herds, etc.) could have had a lower cash salary but perquisites in the form of land for private cultivation etc. It is also worth recalling that 'officials, who have the qualifications of a minister...shall be appointed as Heads [of Departments and] Undertakings, each according to his capacity' {2.9.1} and that those who have all the qualities necessary to be a minister shall be appointed as Councillors and those with three quarter or half to other jobs {1.9.2}. Thus, there were at least two grades of ministers and Heads of Departments, apart from the Councillors who need not have had direct administrative responsibilities. In verse {1.10.15}, Kautilya says that one who fails all four tests (*dharma, artha, kama* and fear) shall be sent to difficult posts such as forests, mines or factories. Hence, the salary of a Head of Department could have been anywhere between 1000 to 12,000 panas per annum, with or without perquisites. This lack of precision, in one who is almost always very precise, is not surprising: for Kautilya describes in his work an ideal state. In a real state, the grade of a Head of Department would have been decided, within the above range, by the contribution his Department made to the state, for instance, to revenue, law and order or welfare.

Book 2 also contains information about the administrative hierarchy in the countryside and fortified city as well as the organization of administrative offices and productive enterprises. These have been brought together in a separate subsection.

Likewise, the organization of a village, the duties of the village headman and the responsibilities of the villagers towards the community have been collated in VII.x. Lastly, municipal regulations, which include also the obligations of the citizens, will be found in VII.xi.]

VII.ii

TREASURY OFFICIALS

[Under the *Samnidhatr* (the Treasurer), there were two officials in charge of all stores—the Chief Superintendent of the Treasury and the Chief Superintendent of the Warehouses. The latter could have been a subordinate of the former, who had the overall responsibility for 'precious articles, high and low valued commodities as well as forest products'. The Treasury proper, situated in the capital, was used to store precious metals, coins, jewellery and very high valued articles. There were also, as pointed out in {2.4.10} and {2.5.5}, granaries and warehouses for various types of commodities. Though they are not mentioned in the text, there must have been supervisors (*ayuktah*) in charge of individual warehouses in the city and the countryside. Treasury and commodity warehouses similar to the permanent ones were also set up in the base camp during military expeditions {10.1.4,6}.]

CHIEF SUPERINTENDENT OF THE TREASURY

QUALIFICATIONS

The Chief Superintendent shall be the officer in charge of the Treasury for gems, jewellery and precious metals, the storehouses for products of high value (*sara*), the warehouses of products of low value (*phalgu*) and the warehouse for forest produce. He shall be conversant with the qualities of all the items described in detail {in 2.11} as well as other precious articles not specifically listed therein. He shall be knowledgeable about the quality differences in each of the products and where they come from and shall also be conversant with identification of adulterated goods. He shall know how to store each item, any losses that may occur during storage and the means of preventing deterioration during storage.

{from 2.11.116,117}

RESPONSIBILITIES

The Chief Superintendent shall:

(i) receive into the Treasury [or appropriate storehouse] precious articles, commodities of high value, commodities of low value and forest produce;

(ii) form panels of experts in each field [to assist him in evaluating the articles received];

(iii) keep a record of each item indicating class of item, form,[1] description, quality, amount, price and place of storage;

(iv) be responsible for the repair and refurbishment of stored articles.

{2.11.1,116,117}

[Chapter {2.1} contains a detailed description of the qualities and sources of the following:

(a) precious stones (diamonds, pearls, gems like ruby, beryl and sapphire), semi-precious stones and coral;

(b) perfumery articles (sandalwood, aloe, incense, camphor and *kaleyaka*);

(c) manufactured jewellery;

(d) woollen cloth and blankets;

(e) silk and silk-type fabrics; and

(f) cotton fabrics.

[See Appendix 2 for lists of commodities in the text.]

THE CHIEF SUPERINTENDENT OF WAREHOUSES

QUALIFICATIONS

[None laid down]

RESPONSIBILITIES

The Chief Superintendent of Warehouses shall:

(i) be in charge of granaries and warehouses for fats and oils, sugar and honey, salt, vinegars, fruit juices, sour liquids, spices, dried fish, dried meat and vegetables; and cotton and flax.

(ii) keep an account of all commodities received into the warehouses, duly classified as follows:

(a) brought in by the Chief Superintendent of Crown Lands (*sita*);

(b) received revenue from the countryside—i.e. taxes paid in kind by villages as a whole (*pindakara*), the 1/6th share from leased lands, animal slaughter, etc. (*shadbhaga*), contributions from the people for the maintenance of the army[2] (*senabhaktham*), special agricultural tax (*bali*), taxes paid in cash (*kara*), presents from the people on festive occasions [e.g. the birth of a prince] (*utsangha*), surcharges (*parsva*), compensatory payments[3] (*parihinikam*), gifts to the king (*aupayanikam*) and income from water reservoirs and parks (*kaushteyakam*);

(c) received in lieu of cash taxes, bought for cash, or repayment of borrowings including interest therefrom;

(d) received in exchange on a barter basis;

(e) received as aid;

(f) borrowed [from a foreign king];

(g) free labour (processing grain, oilseeds or sugar-cane) contributed in lieu of tax;

(h) miscellaneous receipts;

(i) savings from budgeted expenditure—i.e. demobilisation of [part of] the army, works abandoned before completion and economies made in the investment originally budgeted;

(j) changes in stock: on account of the transaction tax [use of differential weights and measures for receiving and paying out] or due to gain or loss in weight or volume in storage or leftovers; and

(k) receipts of outstanding arrears already written off.

{2.15.1-11}

(iii) personally inspect the conversion of grains and pulses (e.g. husking, pounding, grinding, frying or cooking), the extraction of oil, the making of sugar and spinning of cotton and flax and be conversant with the conversion ratios[4] for each of these operations;

{from 2.15.24-41}

(iv) be knowledgeable about the rations for armed forces, civil personnel and animals [and issue commodities strictly in accordance with the prescribed rations];[5]

{from 2.15.42-59}

(v) be responsible for the profitable use of by-products such as oilcake and bran (for feeding bullocks), charcoal and husk (in metal workshops and for plastering walls) and broken grains (given to labourers or sold to brothmakers and cooked food vendors);

{2.15.52,60,61}

(vi) be in charge of all implements—standard weights and measures, grinding stones, mortars and pestles, wooden mortars for dehusking and hulling, [oil] expellers, winnowing fans, sieves, baskets, boxes and brooms;

{2.15.62}

(vii) be in charge of all labour employed—sweepers, watchmen, weighingmen, measurers, supervisors of receipts and deliveries, accountants and miscellaneous slaves and labourers;

{2.15.63}

(viii) ensure the proper storage of all commodities by storing grain on elevated platforms, sugar in close-knit grass bags, oils in earthen or wooden vessels and salt on the ground.

{2.15.64}

The Chief Superintendent shall, at all times, keep half of the commodities in store as reserve stock for use in times of calamities and use [only] the other half [for current needs]; he shall [constantly] replace old stock with new.

{2.15.22,23}

VII.iii

AGRICULTURE, FORESTRY AND
LIVESTOCK OFFICIALS

[The responsibilities of the following officials are described in this section:
the Chief Superintendent of Crown Lands;
the Chief Superintendent of Productive Forests;
the Chief Superintendent of Crown Herds; and
the Chief Protector of Animals and Controller of Animal Slaughter.

The Chief Superintendent of Crown Lands was concerned only with
land owned by the State, whether cultivated directly or leased out.
Agricultural taxation on production from privately owned land was the
responsibility of the *Samahartr* (the Chancellor). The importance of revenue
from Crown lands, whether directly cultivated or leased, is shown by the
separate classification given to it in the accounts as *sita*.

In the Kautilyan state forests were either reserved strictly for wild elephant
herds from which elephants were caught almost always as mature animals
or for collecting a variety of forest products. A different Superintendent was
in charge of each type of forest. A list of useful forest products is given in the
Appendix 2 on Commodities.

Apart from a limited responsibility for collecting the tax on privately
owned cattle and restoring recovered stolen cattle, the Chief Superintendent
of Crown Herds was primarily responsible for the State's herds of domesticated
animals. Though {2.29} deals almost wholly with cattle (cows, bulls and
buffaloes), other herds (of goats, sheep, horses, donkeys, camels and pigs)
also come under the same regulations.

The text refers to the Chief Protector of Animals and Controller of
Animal Slaughter simply as the Head of the Department of Meat. However,
his main responsibility was the protection of animals, thereby making
him responsible also for control over butchers and the sale of meat.]

CHIEF SUPERINTENDENT OF CROWN LANDS

QUALIFICATIONS

The Chief Superintendent of Crown Lands shall be conversant with the science of cultivation, water management and the proper care of plants.
{2.24.1}

RESPONSIBILITIES

The Chief Superintendent shall employ such experts as are necessary in order [to cultivate profitably Crown lands and] supervise the following farming operations:

(i) <u>Seed collection:</u> Seeds of all kinds of cereals, flowers, fruits, vegetables, bulbous roots, other edible roots, creeper products, flax and cotton shall be collected at the appropriate time. {2.24.1}

(ii) <u>Land preparation:</u> The work force shall be made to plough many times the land appropriate to each kind of crop. The Chief Superintendent shall ensure that ploughing is not delayed due to lack of ploughs, implements and bullocks or due to failures of artisans such as blacksmiths, carpenters, basket makers, rope-makers, snake-catchers, etc. {2.24.2,3}

(iii) <u>Seed preparation and sowing:</u> The Chief Superintendent shall decide on the sowing of wet crops, dry crops or summer crops according to the water available, the nature of the land and the season.

He shall have the seeds prepared as prescribed.[1]

Whenever a crop is sown for the first time [in a season], he shall take a handful of seed soaked in a pot of water containing gold, and sow it after reciting the *mantra:*

'Salutations to Lord Prajapati Kashyapa!
Let the crops flourish always!
Let the goddess reside in the seeds and the grains!'
{2.24.11,15,19,23,27}

(iv) <u>Manuring and protection:</u> When the seeds sprout, manure - freshly caught small fish and the juice of the *sunhi* plant—shall be applied.

Since snakes do not remain in smoky places, he shall have cotton seed and snake skins burnt [round the fields]. {2.24.25,26}

(v) <u>Harvesting and threshing:</u> Crops shall be harvested at the right time. All products of the harvest shall be [carefully] collected together. For, a wise man leaves nothing in the fields, not even chaff.

The harvested sheaves shall be piled high, with roofs of the same material. The tops of the heaps shall be neither too tight nor too loose.

The sheaves shall be threshed on a threshing floor and the grain collected in heaps in a circle around the floor. Workmen engaged in threshing shall be provided with water but shall be forbidden from carrying any fire on to the floor.   {2.24.31-33}

Ascetics and those learned in the Vedas may take rice and barley for ritual purposes, and flowers and fruits that have fallen on the ground for the worship of the gods.

Those who live by gleaning can take what is left [in the fields and the threshing floors] after the crops have been removed to storage.
                                                          {2.24.30}

The responsibilities of the Chief Superintendent also include the following:
(vi) Workforce:

On Crown lands, he shall employ slaves, labourers and persons working off their fines.

Slaves, labourers, watchmen in flower gardens and orchards and those who look after bullocks shall be supplied food according to the number of members in their families. They shall also be given a cash wage of one and a quarter panas per month.

Artisans shall be paid in accordance with the nature of their work.
                                                      {2.24.2,28,29}

(vii) Leased cultivation:

The Chief Superintendent may lease out land that cannot be cultivated [directly].

Those lessees who provide only labour [the seeds and implements being provided by the Crown] shall get one-fourth or one-fifth of the harvest.

Those lessees who provide all the inputs shall get one-half of the harvest.

Those who prepare new [Crown] land and bring it into cultivation for the first time shall pay an agreed amount. In times of distress, the payment may be foregone.   {2.24.16,17}

(viii) Water rate:

The Chief Superintendent shall also be responsible for collecting the water rate from farmers for the areas under his charge.[2]   {2.24.18}

PUNISHMENTS

Artisans and workers not being ready in time with their implements at the time of sowing or reaping	Amount equal to the loss incurred	{2.24.4}

CHIEF SUPERINTENDENT OF PRODUCTIVE FORESTS

QUALIFICATIONS

The Chief Superintendent shall know:

(i) how to identify the different kinds of useful trees and plants;

(ii) the uses, including those of by-products, to which these can be put;

(iii) the useful products (including poisons) that can be obtained from the animals in the forests; and

(iv) the metals that can be extracted from the forests.   {from 2.17}

RESPONSIBILITIES

The Chief Superintendent shall be responsible for:

Collection and manufacture:

(i) organizing the collection of forest products by forest rangers;

{2.17.1}

(ii) establishing separate factories, both inside and outside the forests, for making different kinds of [end] products (i.e. those necessary for everyday life as well as those necessary for defence);   {2.17.2,17}

(iii) fixing the scale of dues for the right to collect forest produce;

(iv) fixing the scale of penalties for collecting forest produce without payment of dues. Such fines may be waived when produce is collected in times of acute distress;   {2.17.3}

Storage:

(v) creating enclosures for deer, other tame animals, birds and wild animals;

Sale:

(vi) selling the end-products and by-products;

Control:

(viii) keeping precise accounts of the demand for various products, the supply available, the places where these are available, income, expenditure, net profit, normal losses and losses due to fraud.   {2.18.20}

THE CHIEF SUPERINTENDENT OF CROWN HERDS

RESPONSIBILITIES

(i) General:

The Chief Superintendent shall be responsible for cattle (cows, bulls and buffaloes),[3] goats, sheep, horses, donkeys, camels and pigs.

{from 2.29.8,41,42}

He shall keep a record of every animal in the different types of herds (as detailed below), the total of all such animals, the number that die or are lost and the total collection of milk and ghee [and other products].

{2.29.1}

(ii) Breeding:

For breeding purposes, the following proportion of male animals shall be kept for every herd of 100 animals:

Donkeys and horses	5 stallions
Goats and sheep	10 rams
Cows, buffaloes and camels	4 bulls.

{2.29.48}

(iii) Types of Herds:

(a) Looked after by attendants on cash wages:

The Chief Superintendent shall employ, for each herd of 100 animals, one cowherd or buffalo herdsman, a milker, a churner and a hunter-guard [to protect the herd from wild animals].

They shall be paid only in cash, because if they are paid in milk or ghee, they will starve the calves to death [by milking the cows dry, leaving nothing for the calves].   {2.29.2,3}

(b) Looked after under contract:

A balanced herd[4] of 100 animals may be given to someone on contract. [See below for payment to be made by contractor]   {2.29.4,5}

(c) Unproductive animals:

A balanced herd of 100 animals, (made up of sick or crippled cows, those that allow only an accustomed person to milk them, those that are difficult to milk and those which give birth only to dead calves) may be given to someone for an annual payment, related to what the herd can produce.   {2.29.6}

(d) Private cattle looked after for a share:

Private cattle owners can place their animals under the protection of the King on payment of a protection share.   {2.29.7}

(iv) Accounting for animals:

The Chief Superintendent shall keep an account of the animals as follows:

All calves shall be identified [by branding or by nicking the ear] within a month or two of birth; all stray cattle shall also be marked if they remain unclaimed for more than two months.

Every animal shall be identified in the records with the details of the branding mark, any natural identification marks, the colour and peculiarity of horns.

An account shall be maintained of cattle lost (by theft, straying into another herd or disappearance) and of cattle totally lost [by death].[5]

Those in charge of herds shall report to the Chief Superintendent the total loss of any animals and the reason for it. In case of death due to natural causes, proof of death shall be furnished.[6]

{2.29.15,9-13,24,25}

(v) By-products:

Churned buttermilk [from which butter for making ghee had been removed] shall be fed to dogs and pigs.

Cheese shall be delivered to the armed forces.

Whey shall be mixed with oilcake [from the expeller] for [use as] animal feed.

Hair, skin, bladder, bile, tendon, teeth, hooves and horns of all animals dying naturally shall be delivered to the Chief Superintendent. The flesh may be sold by the herdsman, either as fresh meat or dried.

{2.29.26-29}

(vi) Responsibilities of herdsmen

Herdsmen shall graze their herds in forests from which thieves, tigers and other predators had been eliminated. The pasture shall be chosen keeping in mind the movement of the cattle, their strength and their safety and shall be appropriate for the season. The animals shall be grazed, under suitable guards, in groups of ten according to their type. Bells shall be hung around the necks of timid animals in order to frighten snakes and to locate them easily when grazing. The animals shall be taken to safe watering places which shall be free of crocodiles, approachable by broad and even paths and not be muddy. They shall be guarded from dangers while drinking.

In the rainy season, autumn and early winter, cows and she-buffaloes shall be milked twice a day and in late winter, spring and summer only once a day.

Herdsmen shall pay [particular] attention to the young, the old and the sick animals. {2.29.20-23,31,39,40}

(vii) Revenue:

Cattle looked after for wages	Ghee according to the norms laid down.[7] All animal by-products.
Cattle looked after by contractor	1 pana per animal per annum and 8 *varakas* of ghee per 100 animals. Skins of dead animals.
Non-productive animals	According to capacity of herd.
Private animals given state protection	1/10th of production.

| Tax on sale of private cattle | 1/4 pana |
| Sheep and goats | Wool |

{2.29.5-7,30,35-37,41}

(viii) Control:

Those who look after state animals shall not be negligent and allow animals to stray, be stolen or lost.

Stealing, inciting to steal, killing and inciting to kill state animals shall be punishable offences.

Replacing an animal with the royal mark by another [inferior] animal is a punishable offence.   {from 2.29.14,16,17}

(viii) Animals in private herds:

Anyone recovering stolen cattle from within the country shall receive the appropriate reward.

Anyone recovering stolen cattle from a foreign country shall receive half the value [as reward].

On the sale of private animals, a tax of one quarter of a pana per head shall be paid by the seller.   {2.29.18,19,30}

PUNISHMENTS

Animal husbandry

For not milking cows in time	Value of milk lost	{2.29.33}
For negligence in not training bulls at the right time[8]	Value of work lost due to delay	{2.29.34}
Negligence of herdsmen	Restitution equal to loss	{2.29.14}
Not reporting loss of cattle by natural causes, theft, wild animals, snakes or crocodiles	Restitution of the value of the animal lost	{2.29.24}
Replacing an animal in the state herd by a private one	Lowest SP	{2.29.17}
For letting two bulls fight	Lowest SP	{2.29.38}
For letting a bull die in a fight with another	Highest SP	{2.29.38}
For milking cows twice in seasons [spring, summer, late winter] when they should be milked only once a day	Cutting off of the thumb	{2.29.32}
Killing, inciting to kill, stealing or inciting to steal an animal	Death	{2.29.16}

Punishments for veterinary doctors {2.30.47-49}

When a sick animal's condition
becomes worse due to wrong
treatment or carelessness

If the animal is cured	Twice the cost of treatment
If the animal dies	The value of the animal

THE CHIEF PROTECTOR OF ANIMALS
(AND CONTROLLER OF ANIMAL SLAUGHTER)

RESPONSIBILITIES

Protection of animals:
   (i) The following shall be declared as protected species:
      (a) sea fish which have strange or unusual forms;
      (b) fresh water fish from lakes, rivers, tanks or canals;
      (c) game birds or birds for pleasure such as curlew, osprey, *datyuha*, swan, *chakravaka*, pheasant, *bhringaraja*, partridge, mattakokila, a cock, parrot and mynah; and
      (d) all auspicious birds and animals. {2.26.5}

The Chief Protector shall ensure their protection from all dangers of injury.

He shall not allow the catching of fish, or the trapping, hurting or killing of animals whose slaughter is not customary.

He shall not allow the slaughter of animals in reserved parks [and sanctuaries].

Among animals customarily slaughtered for meat, the killing of the calf, the bull and the milch cow shall be prohibited.

Live birds and deer received by him as tax shall be let loose in the sanctuaries.

If any of the animals (wild or tame) in the sanctuaries turn out to be dangerous, they shall be taken out of the sanctuary and then killed.

{from 2.26.1,2,4,10,14}

Revenue:
   (ii) Butchers shall pay tax at the rates given below:

Animals, not in sanctuaries, whose slaughter is permitted	1/6th
Fish and birds	11/60th
Deer and cattle	1/6 th + *sulka* of 4% or 5%

{2.26.3}

Control of butchers:

(iii) Only meat from freshly killed animals shall be sold. The sale of swollen meat, rotten meat and meat from [naturally] dead animals is prohibited. Fish without head or bones shall not be sold.

Meat may be sold with or without bones. If sold with bones, equivalent compensation [for the weight of the bone] shall be given.{2.26.7,8,12}

ANIMAL WELFARE

Village headmen shall be responsible for preventing cruelty to animals. If stray protected animals and those from reserved forests are found grazing where they should not, they shall be driven away without hurting them; those responsible for such shall be informed [to prevent recurrence].

Stray cattle shall be driven off with a rope or a whip. They shall not be otherwise harmed. Anyone who attacks such cattle or seen to be hurting them shall be prevented from doing so, by any means available.

{3.10.30-34}

PUNISHMENTS

For trapping, injuring or killing of

Protected species	Highest SP	{2.26.1}
Animals in sanctuaries	Highest SP	{2.26.1}
For the above offences		
committed by householders	Middle SP	{2.26.1}
[for their personal use]		
gamekeepers and sanctuary	Lowest SP	{2.26.6}
guards who let the above happen		
For trapping, injuring or killing		
Fish and birds whose slaughter is not customary	26 3/4 panas	{2.26.2}
Deer and animals whose slaughter is not customary	53 1/12 panas	{2.26.2}
Violations by butchers:		
giving short weight	Eight times the shortage	{2.26.9}
selling bad meat	12 panas	{2.26.13}
(from Book 4 on 'Control of Anti-social elements)	Cutting off both feet and a hand or a fine of 900 panas	{4.26.14}

killing or torturing to death a calf, bull or milch cow	50 panas	{2.26.11}
Castrating the male of a small animal used for breeding	Lowest SP	{3.26.17}
<u>Injuring animals with a stick, etc.</u>		
for small animals	1 to 2 panas	{3.19.26,27}
for big animals	2 to 4 pana + cost of treatment	
<u>Causing bleeding wounds to animals</u>		
small animals	2 to 4 panas	{3.19.26,27}
big animals	4 to 8 panas + cost of treatment	
Letting horned or tusked animals fight and kill one another	Compensation to owner and equal amount as fine	{4.13.19}
<u>A temple animal, a stud bull or a cow not yet calved</u>		{4.13.20}
Riding	500 panas	
Driving away	Highest SP	
<u>Theft of animals</u>		
Theft or killing of small animals (e.g. cocks, cats, dogs, pigs etc.) of value less than 25 panas	Cutting off the tip of the nose or 54 panas (fine for *Candalas* and forest dwellers - 27 panas)	{4.10.2}
Theft or killing of a small animal useful for its milk or hair, for riding or for stud	Compensation to owner + equal amount as fine (killing for ritual purposes permitted)	{4.13.21}
Theft of deer, cattle, birds, fish, wild animals caught in some body else's trap or net	Value of animal + equal amount as fine	{4.10.3}
Theft of deer from protected forests or objects from productive forests	100 panas	{4.10.4}
Theft of deer or birds held in captivity for pleasure	200 panas	{4.10.5}

Theft of adult cattle	Cutting off both feet or a fine of 600 panas	{4.10.11}
Theft of a temple animal	Highest SP or death (depending on the gravity of the offence)	{4.10.16}
Theft of a herd (more than ten heads) of cattle	Death without torture	{4.11.15,16}

VII.iv

INDUSTRY OFFICIALS

[The officials covered in this section are those concerned with mines and metals, precious metals and jewellery and textiles. Of these, the Chief Controller of Mining and Metallurgy had under him a number of Departments, such as mines, metals, the mint and salt. Though each one was headed by a Head of Department (*adhyaksha*) it would seem that they were of a rank lower than the Chief Controller, who probably had to have the qualifications of a minister to hold this important post.

The Chief Superintendent of Precious Metals and Jewellery was not only in charge of the Crown workshops but also of goldsmiths and silversmiths who handled precious metal work for private citizens. The smiths doing work for the public were employees of the State and worked under the supervision of the Controller of Goldsmiths, who himself was subordinate to the Chief Superintendent of Precious Metals. All precious metal work was thus a state monopoly. Though employees of the State, the smiths doing work for the public had greater freedom than their counterparts in the Crown workshops. For example, the former could keep in their custody the work entrusted to them, while the latter had to deposit all the work and the implements with the supervisor at the end of each shift.

Instead of the normal practice in this translation of giving the fines and penalties pertaining to a particular Head of Department at the end of the concerned subsection, the penalties for which the Controller of Goldsmiths and Silversmiths was responsible have been grouped together under Consumer Protection in IV.vi as being a more logical place for them. This is in accordance with Kautilya's scheme of putting them in Book 4 under 'Removal of Thorns'.

The officials described in this section can be classified as follows:

<u>Chief Controller of Mining & Metallurgy</u>

    Chief Superintendent of Mines;
    Chief Superintendent of Metals;
    Chief Master of the Mint;

Examiner of Coins;

Chief Salt Commissioner.

<u>Chief Superintendent of Precious Metals and Jewellery</u>

Controller of Goldsmiths and Silversmiths

<u>Chief Textile Commissioner</u>

THE CHIEF CONTROLLER OF MINING AND METALLURGY

QUALIFICATIONS

The Chief Controller in charge of mining operations shall be conversant with the geology of metal-bearing ores, the techniques of smelting [different metals] and with the identification of gems.[1]   {2.12.1}

RESPONSIBILITIES

Supervision:

(i) He shall [be responsible for supervising the work of the Chief Superintendent of Mines, the Chief Superintendent of Metals, the Chief Master of the Mint, the Examiner of Coins and the Chief Salt Commissioner.]

<u>Opening up mines:</u>

(ii) He shall take the help of experts in those fields of mining and metallurgy [in which he himself is not an expert];

(iii) be responsible for equipping fully [the units under his charge] with the necessary implements and labour;

(iv) identify locations for mining by looking either for signs (such as tailings of an earlier working, old crucibles, coal or ashes) of an old [abandoned] mine or geological evidence of mineral-bearing ores. In the case of new mines, the quality of the ore, including whether it is liquid or solid, shall be ascertained by weight, depth of colour, strength of smell and taste.   {2.12.1}

<u>Crown working and leasing:</u>

(v) He shall lease out mines which are too expensive or too difficult to exploit, on payment of either a share of the ore recovered or a fixed royalty and develop as Crown mines those easily exploited with reasonable expenditure.

{2.12.22}

<u>Recovery of metals:</u>

(vi) He shall send metal ores to the smelters for recovering the metals and gem ores to the recovery plants for gems.   {2.12.18}

<u>Trade:</u>

(vii) He shall centralize the sale of metals and fix penalties for manufacture, sale or purchase at any places other than the designated ones.   {2.12.19}

<u>Control:</u>

(viii) He shall ensure that there is no unauthorized mining.

(ix) He shall ensure that metal ores, and particularly gem ores, are not stolen. {from 2.12.20.21}

PUNISHMENTS

<u>Miners stealing ores:</u>

gem ores	Death	{4.9.2}
other ores	Eight times the	{2.12.20}
	amount stolen (Instead	
	of paying the fine, the	
	culprit can opt to do	
	labour without	
	payment.)	
Unauthorized mining or stealing from mines	Forced labour	{2.12.21}

OFFICIALS SUBORDINATE TO THE CHIEF CONTROLLER OF MINING AND METALLURGY

[The qualifications necessary for appointment to the posts mentioned below have not been specified in the text.]

THE CHIEF SUPERINTENDENT OF MINES

RESPONSIBILITIES

The Chief Superintendent of Mines shall

(i) establish [and run] factories for recovery of mother-of-pearl, diamonds, gems, pearls, coral, quartz and mica.

(ii) organize [and supervise] trade in the above products. {2.12.27}

CHIEF SUPERINTENDENT OF METALS

RESPONSIBILITIES

The Chief Superintendent of Metals shall

(i) establish [and run] factories for recovery of metals such as copper, lead, tin, iron and *vaikrantaka*.

(ii) manufacture alloys of copper with tin or zinc such as brass, *vritta*, bronze and bell metal as well as alloys of iron.

(iii) organize [and supervise] trade in metals. {2.12.23}

CHIEF MASTER OF THE MINT

RESPONSIBILITIES

The Chief Master of the Mint shall be responsible for the

(i) minting of silver coins, made up of [an alloy consisting of] 11/16th part silver, 1/4th part copper and 1/16th part hardening metal (such as iron, tin, lead or antimony) in the following denominations—one pana, 1/2 pana, 1/4 pana and 1/8 pana [the weight of each coin being proportional to its value.]

(ii) minting of copper coins, made up of [an alloy consisting of] three-quarters copper and one-quarter hardener, in the denominations

1 mashaka [= 1/16th pana],

1/2 mashaka,

1 kakani [= 1/4 mashaka] and

1/2 kakani.

[The weight of the coins, in copper alloy, being the same as those of silver coins of 1 pana, 1/2 pana, 1/4 pana and 1/8 pana respectively].

{2.12.24}

EXAMINER OF COINS

RESPONSIBILITIES

The Examiner of Coins shall

(i) be responsible for certifying that the coins used in trade and commerce as well as those used for making payments into the Treasury

(ii) levy the charges for his services as follows:

(a) [for new coins issued] a coining fee	8% of value
(b) for coins paid out from or received into the Treasury	the transaction tax of 5% of value
(c) [for coins received into the Treasury only]	an additional testing fee of 1/8%
(d) for certifying the genuineness	testing fee of 1/8%

{2.12.25,26}

(iii) ensure that no new coin is put into circulation unless all charges and taxes have been paid;   {4.1.45}

(iv) levy and collect the fines for illegal minting of coins, buying or selling them or certifying their genuineness;   {4.1.48}

(v) Discipline:

The Examiner of Coins shall not reject genuine coins or certify spurious ones as genuine; if he does so, he shall be fined 12 panas.   {4.1.44}

He shall not put a new coin into circulation on payment of [only] a one masha per pana [i.e. paying only 1/16th or 6 1/4%; the correct fee is 13 1/8%, adding up *vyaji*, testing fee and coining fee]. If he does so, he shall be fined on a *pro rata* basis of 12 panas for every pana.   {4.1.46,47}

PUNISHMENT

For minting coins illegally, for buying, selling or certifying them in places other than the official mint	25 panas	{2.12.24}
Minting, putting into circulation or receiving counterfeit coins	1000 panas	
Paying counterfeit coins into the Treasury	Death	{4.1.48}

CHIEF SALT COMMISSIONER

RESPONSIBILITIES

The Chief Salt Commissioner shall
    (i) lease out salt pans and salt mines on a share basis or on payment of a fixed quantity;
    (ii) collect the State's share at the right time;
    (iii) be responsible for the sale of salt at the right price, including the manufacturing charge and the transaction tax;
    (iv) levy and collect the duty on imported salt, and at the time of its sale, collect the countervailing duty [equal to the total of the manufacturing charge, transaction tax and inspection fee levied on locally produced salt];
    (v) collect the penalties for infringements.   {from 2.12.28-34}

Revenue:
[For lease rent, rates of duty and countervailing duty—see Sources of Revenue, V.ii.]
    The duty payable on imported salt not used for human consumption[2] shall be the duty [1/6th] only and not the countervailing duty.

{2.12.29,34}

Exemptions:
    (a) Vanaprasthas can produce [or mine] salt for their own requirements.
    (b) Brahmins learned in the Vedas, ascetics and labourers [in the salt industry] can take salt without payment.   {2.12.32,33}

PUNISHMENTS

Buying imported salt without paying duty and countervailing duty	600 panas	{2.12.31}
Selling adulterated salt	Highest LSP	{2.12.32}
Unauthorized manufacture of salt	Highest LSP	{2.12.32}

CHIEF SUPERINTENDENT OF PRECIOUS METALS AND JEWELLERY

QUALIFICATIONS

The official shall have expertise in:

(a) the qualities of different types of gold, silver and touchstones;

(b) the methods of purification, hardening and softening of precious metals;

(c) testing gold of different carats;

(d) the different ways of making jewellery such as setting or stringing precious stones, making solid or hollow articles and making beads;

(e) gold plating and enamelling in different colours;

(f) making white silver;

(g) the treatment of iron and copper for manufacturing;

(h) use of precious stones; and

(i) the quantities of precious metals required to make different articles.

{from 2.13}

RESPONSIBILITIES

Control over goldsmiths and silversmiths:

(i) The Chief Superintendent of Precious Metals and Jewellery shall establish [the office and workshops of] the Controller of Goldsmiths and Silversmiths in the middle of the market street [in fortified towns and major townships in the countryside]. {2.13.2}

The Crown Workshop:

(ii) For the manufacture of jewellery and articles of gold and silver, the Chief Superintendent shall cause to be built a workshop which shall have only one entry. There shall be four rooms, not interconnecting, around an inner courtyard.[3] {2.13.1}

Testing:

(iii) The Chief Superintendent shall be responsible for testing the quality of gold. Pure gold, (*suvarna*), is the standard. Copper can be added to pure gold in proportions 1/64, 2/64 . . . up to 16/64, in order to produce sixteen other standards.[4] {2.13.15,16}

He shall ensure that the testing is done correctly by examining the touchstone the gold is to be tested and on which the standard gold had been rubbed. The rubbing shall be on a level part of the stone and not on any part which has elevations or depressions. Over-rubbing, rubbing heavily, colouring the stone with red powder concealed under fingernails are all attempts at deception, and appropriate chemicals shall be smeared on the streaks to verify that no attempt is made.

As for touchstones, that which shows the exact colour is best for both sale and purchase. A greenish-grey stone shows a higher carat and is better for sale, whereas a stone of uneven colour shows a lower carat and is better for buying gold.   {2.13.17-19,22-24}

Control over workshops:

(iv) No unauthorised person shall approach the workshop under pain of death.

No one, even an official, shall carry gold or silver into the workshop.

All workers—gem setters, bead makers, platers, gilders, blowers, servants and sweepers—shall be thoroughly searched in both dress and body, on entering and leaving the workshop. They shall leave their tools and equipment where they have been at work. They shall [fully account for the gold received by them and] shall hand over to the Superintendent the work completed and the balance of the gold. At the end of each shift, the gold and the articles made shall be sealed with the seals of the worker and overseer.   {2.13.30-36}

In setting gems in gold, he shall guard against the use of one-quarter copper with silver or one-quarter silver with gold [in parts which are not visible].   {2.13.42}

PUNISHMENTS

Unauthorized person approaching Crown workshop	Death by beheading	{2.13.31}
One carrying gold or silver into the workshop	confiscation of the metal carried.	{2.13.32}

CONTROLLER OF GOLDSMITHS AND SILVERSMITHS

QUALIFICATIONS

The Controller of Goldsmiths and Silversmiths shall be a person of high birth, skilled in his profession and of reliable character.   {2.13.2}

He shall be conversant with every detail of the characteristics of gold [and silver] and the method of manufacture of various articles.

He shall be aware of all the methods used by goldsmiths to cheat the public by stealing the precious metal entrusted to them.

He shall be knowledgeable about all aspects of the work of goldsmiths and silversmiths—making solid objects, hollow ware, plating, gilding, enamelling and setting stones as well as the characteristics of diamonds, gems, pearls and coral.   {from 2.14}

RESPONSIBILITIES

The Controller of Goldsmiths and Silversmiths shall be responsible for:
Supervision:

(i) supervising the work of the smiths who undertake work for the citizens of the towns and the countryside;
Control over illegal trafficking:

(ii) ensuring that goldsmiths and silversmiths do not buy precious metal from suspicious persons or from thieves, either as metal or as melted down articles;
Control over unauthorized working:

(iii) ensuring that work in precious metals and jewellery is carried out only in authorized places and with the knowledge of the Controller; (if the Controller suspects a smith of having worked clandestinely, he shall order a magisterial enquiry and, if the suspicion is proved true, the smith shall be punished severely.)
Inspection:

(iv) inspecting the finished new articles or repaired old articles [before delivery to the customer] for the following characteristics: type of article, appearance, quality and quantity of metal used;

(In the case of old articles from which metal has been stolen by cutting, scratching or rubbing, he shall infer the quantity stolen by comparing them with similar pieces. In the case of plated articles, the quantity stolen shall be estimated by cutting out an identical area. Where the appearance of an article gives rise to suspicion, it shall be tested by heating, washing or treatment with chemicals. In the case of silver articles, fraud can be detected by smell, bad colour, roughness, hardness due to alloying and changes in shape. Penalties, as prescribed, shall be imposed on the smiths if the inspection reveals pilferage.)

(v) watching over the smiths as they work with a view to detecting pilferage of precious metals. (He shall, in particular, be on the lookout for precious metal hidden, by sleight of hand, by fiddling with the balance, in the fire, the anvil, the firepan, the tool box, the waste, the metal and water vessels, the bellows and the rubbish as well as the body of the smith (especially his head, lap, the folds of his dress and his loincloth). He shall also listen to their conversation for indications of pilferage.

{from 2.14}

[For details of the methods used by goldsmiths and silversmiths to steal metal and the relevant punishments see Consumer Protection in IV.vi.]

CHIEF TEXTILE COMMISSIONER

RESPONSIBILITIES

Manufacture:

(i) The Chief Textile Commissioner shall be responsible for the [manufacture of and] trade in yarn, clothing, bed sheets and covers, protective wear, ropes, thongs, straps, bindings and similar requirements. He shall employ persons expert in each type of work. {2.23.1,9,19}

Workforce:

(ii) Spinning shall be carried out by women [particularly those who are dependent on it for a living] such as widows, cripples, [unmarried] girls, [unattached] women living independently, women working off their fines, mothers of prostitutes, old women servants of the King and temple dancers whose services to a temple have ceased. {2.23.2}

Employment may be given to women who do not move out of their houses [e.g. women whose husbands are away, widows, handicapped women or unmarried girls] by the Chief Commissioner sending his women servants out to them with the raw materials for spinning. Or, such women may come to the yarn shed at dawn to collect raw materials, return the yarn spun and receive their wages. {2.23.11,12}

(iii) Weaving shall be carried out by men; ropes, protective wear, straps and similar articles shall be made by specialists in their manufacture.

{2.23.7,10,17,18}

Wages:

(iv) Spinning: Wages shall be fixed according to the quality (fine, medium or coarse) of the yarn and the quantity spun. Wages shall be reduced if the quantity of the yarn produced is not commensurate with the quantity of the raw material supplied. Special incentives shall be given for better work [or productivity] and for working on festive days.

Weaving: The Chief Commissioner shall come to an agreement [beforehand] with artisans regarding the amount of weaving to be done in a given period and corresponding wages to be paid. Incentives shall be given to weavers of special types of fabrics such as those made from silk yarn, [fine] wool from deer, etc. {from 2.23.3-8}

<u>Control:</u>

(v) The Chief Commissioner shall maintain a strict watch over weavers [to prevent theft of yarn or cloth].   {2.23.7}

<u>Discipline:</u>

(viii) [The Chief Commissioner shall not misbehave with women with whom he has to deal officially.]

When women who do not move out of their houses come to the yarn shed early in the morning, there shall only be a lamp for the inspection of the yarn.

For looking at the face of a woman or talking to her about anything other than work, he shall be punished with the lowest level standard fine.

For delaying the payment of wages and for paying wages for work not done, he shall be punished with the middle level standard fine.

{2.23.12-14}

PUNISHMENTS

Weavers not doing their work properly	In accordance with the gravity of the offence.	{2.23.16}
Women who do not carry out the work after having been paid, misappropriate the raw material or run away with it	Amputation of thumb and finger.	{2.23.16}

VII.v

TRADE AND TRANSPORT OFFICIALS

[The duties and responsibilities of the following officials are covered in this section:
the Chief Controller of State Trading;
the Chief Controller of Private Trading;
the Chief Controller of Weights and Measures;
the Chief Collector of Customs and Octroi;
the Chief Controller of Shipping and Ferries;
the Chief Controller of Ports; and
the Chief Surveyor and Time Keeper.

As mentioned in {1.4.1}, trade was the third most important constituent of the economy of the Kautilyan State, after agriculture and cattle-rearing. It is therefore not surprising that a large part of trading was done directly by the State and that private trade was also strictly controlled. Augmenting the revenues of the state through trade was, no doubt, an essential objective. However, the welfare of the public was also an important objective. From the chapters dealing with state and private trading {2.16} and {4.2} one can deduce the 'Principles of Fair Trade'. These include the welfare of the public, orderly marketing and reasonable profit margins. These principles have been collected together at the beginning of the section.

The main responsibilities of the Chief Controller of State Trading were sale of goods over which the state exercised monopoly, collecting the transaction tax (*vyaji*) and export of Crown commodities. Ensuring orderly marketing and preventing the making of excessive profits by private merchants were the responsibilities of the Chief Controller of Private Trading. The Chief Controller of Weights and Measures safeguarded the public interest by checking the accuracy of the weights, balances and capacity measures used by the traders and merchants. Details about the trading system have been collected together in section IV.v on Aspects of the Economy. The penalties relating to private merchants, under the control of the Chief Controller of Private Trading have been grouped under the subsection on Consumer Protection in IV.vi.

There is an interesting point to note about the Chief Collector of Customs and Octroi. Though *sulka* was clearly a customs duty levied on imports and exports, it was not collected at the frontier posts but at the gates of fortified cities, particularly the capital. Thus, not only foreign goods but also goods entering the city from the countryside had to pay duty; likewise, goods produced in the city and taken out of it were dutiable. This would, normally, lead to the anomalous situation of goods produced in the countryside and sold therein being outside government control. However, such control was, in fact, exercised by prohibiting the sale of goods at the places of production (e.g. mines, fields and gardens). Sales could take place only at the designated markets where the private merchants came under the control of the Chief Controller of Private Trading. Stiff penalties are prescribed for violation of the prohibition of sale at places of production.

The Chief Controller of Shipping and Ferries had a wide range of responsibilities—supervising maritime safety and rescue, running shipping services, hiring ships and boats with or without crew, organizing ferries, controlling the movement of foreign merchants, collecting revenue such as road cess, customs duty and ferry charges and ensuring security by keeping a watch over undesirable persons using the ferries.

Not much information is available about the Chief Controller of Ports or the Chief Surveyor and Time Keeper.]

PRINCIPLES OF FAIR TRADING

1. Both locally produced and imported goods shall be sold for the benefit of the public. {2.16.5}
2. When there is an excess supply of a commodity, a buffer stock shall be built up by paying a price higher than the prevailing market price. When the market price reaches the support level, the buying price shall be changed according to the situation. {2.16.2,3}
3. When there is a glut in a commodity, its sale shall be canalised [through state-controlled outlets] and merchants shall sell only from the accumulated stock, until it is exhausted, on a daily wage basis [with no profit margin for them]. {4.2.33-35}
4. Surplus stocks unaccounted for in the hands of merchants shall be sold for the benefit of the public. {4.2.26,27}
5. Even a large profit shall be foregone if it is likely to cause harm to the public. {2.16.6}
6. No artificial scarcity shall be created by accumulation of commodities constantly in demand; these shall [be made available at all times and] not be subjected to restrictions on when they may be sold. {2.16.7}

THE CHIEF CONTROLLER OF STATE TRADING

QUALIFICATIONS

The Chief Controller State Trading shall be conversant with the details given below for all state monopoly commodities, whether locally produced (on land or in water) or imported (by land or water):
- the state of public demand
- price fluctuations
- relative prices of high and low value goods, and
- optimum time for buying, selling, [buffer] stocking and disposal [from stocks]. {2.16.1}

RESPONSIBILITIES

The Chief Controller of State Trading shall be responsible for the marketing (internally or by export) of state monopoly goods and of all commodities belonging to the Crown [either produced on Crown property or received into the Treasury].

[In detail] he shall

(i) either canalise the sale of these goods or appoint merchants as agents for sale at prices fixed by him;

(ii) encourage the import of foreign goods by providing [suitable] incentives;

(iii) be responsible for the prompt collection of sale proceeds and accounting of balance stock by sales officers;

(iv) be responsible for the export of Crown commodities, keeping in mind the profit that can be made; if no profit is likely, he shall keep in mind the advantages of importing goods from a country [to satisfy local demand or for political and strategic reasons];

(v) be responsible for the collection of the transaction tax;

(vi) fix prices for trade in futures (i.e. for goods to be received at a future date or at a different place) after taking into account the investment, the quantity to be delivered, duty, interest, rent and other expenses; and

(vii) fix the wages of the sales agents taking into account the sales made by them during the day. {2.16.8-11,14-16,18,19; 4.2.23,36}

[Details of the trading system for Crown commodities are in IV.v. 'Aspects of the Economy'.]

THE CHIEF CONTROLLER OF PRIVATE TRADING

RESPONSIBILITIES

The Chief Controller shall
General responsibilities:

(i) be responsible for fair trading in new and old articles;

(ii) allow the sale or pledging of old articles only if the seller or mortgagor can provide proof of ownership;

(iii) inspect the weights and measures used by merchants in order to prevent the use of fraudulent weights and measures;   {4.2.1,2;4.6.6}
Control over merchants:

(iv) ensure that the profit margins (5% for locally produced goods and 10% for imported goods) are adhered to;

(v) ensure that the goods are sold at the prices fixed for them;
{4.2.28}

(vi) ensure that they do not deal in stolen goods.[1]   {4.6.4,5}
Orderly marketing:

(vii) prevent the collective purchase by merchants of a commodity as long as the goods of an earlier joint purchase remain unsold; {4.2.31}
Assistance to merchants:

(viii) provide appropriate exemptions, if the goods held by a merchant are damaged [for unforeseen reasons];   {4.2.32}
Brokers and middlemen:

(ix) ensure that merchants do not count the brokerage paid to middlemen as part of their costs [in calculating their profit margins];

(x) allow brokers to hold stocks of grain and other commodities [only] to the extent authorized;

(xi) confiscate any stocks held by brokers in excess of authorised limits and deliver them to the Chief Controller of State Trading for sale to the public
{4.2.24-27}

THE CHIEF CONTROLLER OF WEIGHTS AND MEASURES

RESPONSIBILITIES

Manufacture of Standard Weights and Measures:

(i) The Chief Controller shall be responsible for setting up the workshops for making standard weights, balances, and measures of capacity.
{2.19.1}

Weights shall be made of iron or stones from Magadha and Makala, or of such materials that will neither increase in weight when wet [i.e. not porous] nor decrease in weight when heated.   {2.19.10}

Measures of capacity shall be made of dry, hard wood. They shall be of different types as follows: (1) [For dry goods] the measure shall be so made as to include the conical heaped-up portion on top, the proportion being three-quarters of the volume in the flat top measure and one quarter in the heap and (2) [For liquids] the measure shall show the correct quantity when full to the brim, except that in the case of wine, the measure shall be one and a quarter times the size for other liquids. (3) In the case of flowers, fruits, bran, charcoal and slaked lime, the full measure shall be flat top and, in addition, a heaped-up quantity equal to one-fourth shall be given.
{2.19.34,35}

Sale:

(ii) Standard measuring instruments shall be made for different types of articles in different sizes and sold [to merchants] at the prices prescribed.
{2.19.36-38}

Control:

(iii) All measuring instruments shall be inspected and stamped once every four months, on payment of stamping fee. {2.19.40}

[All details about measuring instruments are given in Appendix 1.]

PUNISHMENTS

Use of unstamped weights, balances or measures of capacity	27 1/4 panas	{2.19.41}

THE CHIEF COLLECTOR OF CUSTOMS AND OCTROI

RESPONSIBILITIES

General:

(i) The Chief Collector shall prevent the import of whatever is harmful or useless to the country. He shall grant exemption from duty to [and thus promote the import of] goods that are highly beneficial [to the country]; such as rare seeds. {2.21.31}

Customs Posts:

(ii) The Custom House shall be set up near the main gate [of the fortified city] facing east or north; the King's flag shall be flown at the post.
{2.21.1}

Appraisal:

(iii) [All goods entering the city shall be appraised and] goods enjoying exemption from duty allowed in after verification. The duty payable on goods of low value shall be determined after careful consideration. Dutiable goods shall be allowed to be sold only after they had been weighed, measured or counted [and duty paid accordingly]. {2.21.15}

Staff:

(iv) There shall be four or five customs collectors in each post.

{2.21.2}

Records:

(v) The collectors shall record the following details about merchants: their names, places of origin, the quantity of merchandise, place of issue of identity pass and place where the goods were sealed.   {2.21.2}

Collection of revenue:

(vi) [The Chief Collector shall be responsible for the collection of the prescribed customs duties, octroi (gate toll) and fines.]

The Chief Collector shall determine the rates of duty for new and old commodities, taking into account the traditions of the region and its communities.

Fines shall be fixed according to the [nature of the] offence.

The octroi shall [normally] be one-fifth of the customs duty but can be fixed at a lower rate if it is beneficial to the country.   {2.22.8,15}

Information gathering:

(vii) Frontier officers shall send information about caravans from foreign countries to the Chief Collector of Customs after examining the goods, classifying them as high or low value, stamping the sealed packages and issuing the passes for the merchants.   {2.21.26}

Clandestine agents [disguised as traders, woodcutters or shepherds] operating on roads and roadless places shall gather information [about merchants and caravans].   {2.21.17}

Or, secret agents, acting as merchants, shall communicate information about a caravan to the King who shall then pass it on to the Chief Collector. Armed with this knowledge, the official shall caution the merchants not to conceal the goods or evade the duty.   {2.21.27-29}

Import of articles whose export is prohibited:

(viii) All goods, the export of which is prohibited [such as weapons, etc.] shall be sold outside the city gates without payment of duty.

{2.21.23}

Discipline:

(ix) A Chief Collector who is guilty of concealing a merchant's offences shall pay a fine of eight times the fine levied on the merchant for the same offence.   {2.21.14}

PUNISHMENTS

Documentary violations:

Goods not stamped	Double the duty payable	{2.21.3}

Forged stamps	Eight times the duty	{2.21.4}
Broken stamps	Goods to be kept in the warehouse [until the genuiness of the broken stamp is established]	{2.21.5}
Changing the royal stamp on sealed packages or wrong description of goods	1 1/4 panas per load	{2.21.6}

Sale price violations:

Declaring a lower quantity	Excess quantity to be confiscated	{2.21.10}
Declaring a lower price in order to pay less duty	Eight times the difference between actual and declared price	{2.21.11}
Showing a sample of lower value in a package of goods of higher value or concealing goods of higher value under a few pieces of lower value on top	Same as above	{2.21.12}
Calling out too high a price at the gate [anticipating competitive bidding]	Difference between actual sale and the price originally called or double the duty	{2.21.13}

Evasion

Non-payment of duty	Eight times the duty	{2.21.16}
False declaration of a dutiable commodity as exempt from duty	As punishment for thef	{2.21.19}

Caravans from foreign countries

Evasion on goods of low value	8 times the duty	{2.21.16,30}
Evasion on goods of high value	Confiscation	{2.21.30}

Exports

Attempting to export goods while paying duty only on a part or adding more goods to a sealed package by breaking the seal	Confiscation and equal amount as fine	{2.21.20}

Attempting to export high value goods after declaring and paying duty on them as low value goods (e.g. straw)	Highest SP	{2.21.21}
Attempting to export prohibited articles	Confiscation and Highest SP	{2.21.22}
Sale at places of origin or production and not at the authorized markets		
Metals from smelters and minerals from mines	600 panas	{2.22.10}
Flowers and fruits from gardens and orchards	54 panas	{2.22.11}
Vegetables and root vegetables from vegetable gardens	51 3/4 panas	{2.22.12}
Crops from fields	53 panas	{2.22.13}
Resale of Crown land produce	1 pana on vendor and 1/2 pana on buyer	{2.22.14}

THE CHIEF CONTROLLER OF SHIPPING AND FERRIES

RESPONSIBILITIES

General:

(i) The Chief Controller of Shipping and Ferries shall be responsible for sea voyages, ferries at mouths of rivers, ferries over natural and artificial lakes, ferries across rivers and water transport in provincial headquarters and towns.

He shall ensure the observance of the regulations laid down by Port and Harbour Commissioners regarding goods and navigation.

{2.28.1,7}

State-owned vessels:

(ii) Big vessels shall be used as ferries on large [perennial] rivers which are crossable throughout the year only by boats. These shall have a captain, a steersman, a rope and hook handler and a bailer.

Small boats shall be used as ferries on small [seasonal] rivers which need them [only] in the rainy season.

(iii) The King's vessels may be used for transporting freight and passengers on payment of charges as laid down. Boats may be hired out to fishermen, pearl and conch fishers. In the case of pearl and conch fishers, the principles laid down for the Chief Controller of Mining and Metallurgy shall apply. [If the fishing is either too expensive or too hazardous, boats shall be hired out on payment of a share of the catch or a fixed royalty. Fishing grounds easy to fish in at reasonable cost shall be exploited directly by the State.]   {from 2.28.13,3-2.12.22}

Safety and Rescue:

(iv) If a boat is lost through of lack of seamen or equipment or because it was unseaworthy, the Chief Controller shall pay compensation [to the victims] for the loss or damage.

(v) Pirate ships, vessels which are bound for enemy countries and those which violate port regulations shall be destroyed.

(vi) The Chief Controller shall, like a father, rescue vessels that have strayed from their course or are buffeted by storms. He shall show concessions by exempting goods that have been damaged by water from payment of duty or by reducing the duty to half. The rescued vessels may be allowed to proceed to their original destinations when it is safe for them to do so.   {2.28.26,12,8-10}

Ferries:

(vii) Ferries shall cross waterways only at fixed points, in order to prevent traitors to the King crossing [into the country].

Ferry-men shall provide a surety and shall deposit earnings daily. Villages near the crossings shall pay the ferry-man his salary in food and in cash. The following shall be allowed to cross ferries free by issuing them a pass, stamped with the seal of the Chief Controller: Brahmins, wandering ascetics, children, old people, the sick, royal messengers and pregnant women.

When the ferry service is seasonal, it shall be available from the eighth day after full moon in Asadha till the corresponding day in Kartika.

{from 2.28.14,18,24,27}

(viii) Revenue:

Boat hire charges:

Fishermen	1/6th of catch
Pearl and conch fishers	As fixed
Passengers chartering for a voyage	Hire charges and cost of crew subsistence and wages
Merchants:	
Freight charges	(paid in kind)
Port dues	As fixed by the Port Commissioner

Customs duty	On all goods when sea-going vessels come within territorial waters
Customs duty on goods damaged by water	Half the duty prescribed or total exemption from duty

Ferries:

Maintenance	Villages on the banks served by a ferry shall pay a fixed tax (*klptam*) and subsistence and wages for the ferry-man

Ferry charges on small rivers:

Small animals; man with hand luggage only	1 mashaka
Man with head load or load carried on the back; a cow or a horse	2 mashakas
Camel; buffalo	4 mashakas
Small cart	5 mashakas
Bullock cart	6 mashakas
Big cart	7 mashakas
1 Bhara (20 tulas) merchandise	1/4 pana

Ferry charges on big rivers shall be double the rates given above.

{2.28.2-5,9,11,21-24}

Frontier:

(ix) Ferry-men at the frontier shall collect the customs duty, escort charges and road cess.   {2.28.25}

Law and order:

(x) Foreign merchants may be allowed to cross into the country if they are frequent visitors or if local merchants vouch for them.   {2.28.19}

(xi) The following shall be arrested if they try to cross by ferry:
- one who has stolen the wife, daughter or wealth of another;
- one who acts suspiciously or appears agitated;
- one who carries too heavy a load;
- one who disguises himself as an ascetic;
- an ascetic who has erased the signs of asceticism;
- one who pretends to be ill [to avoid paying the fare];
- one who is panic-stricken;

- one who carries secretly valuable objects, letters, weapons, fire-making equipment or poison;
- one who has travelled a long way without a pass.

{2.28.20}

PUNISHMENTS

Merchants entering the country without a pass, or coming with a heavy load at short notice or trying to cross at a place other than the authorized ferry	Confiscation of goods brought over	{2.28.25}
Passengers crossing at unauthorized hours or unauthorized places	Lowest SP	{2.28.15}
Passengers crossing without authority even if they do so at the right time and place	26 1/4 panas	{2.28.16}
For making a Brahmin pay ferry charges	12 panas	{3.20.14}

(xi) Exemptions from punishment:

There shall be no penalty for the following for offences of unauthorized crossing: fishermen, carriers of wood and grass, attendants at flower gardens, vegetable gardens and orchards, cowherds, those who supply villages along the river or lake with seeds, foodstuffs and other necessities of life, those who use their own boats, those following an envoy and those who supply the army.   {2.28.17}

THE CHIEF CONTROLLER OF PORTS

[This official is mentioned only once, in {2.28.7} and is the one who makes the regulations for the Chief Controller of Shipping. There must have been Port or Harbour Controllers, working under this Head of Department, for each port, harbour or ferry point.]

CHIEF SURVEYOR AND TIME KEEPER

[The whole of chapter 20 of Book 2, apart from the first verse which refers to this official, is a description of linear measures and time. No specific qualifications or duties are laid down for this official. Unlike the Chief Controller of Weights and Measures, he was not even concerned with the manufacture and certification of standard measuring implements; presumably, linear measures were so well known that standards were not needed. One responsibility of the

Surveyor could have been to settle boundary disputes; another, to demarcate plans on the ground for forts, camps, etc. He could also have issued standard calendars for regulating government accounts, payments to defence forces and indicating intercalary months. For details about time see Appendix 1.]

The Chief Surveyor and Time Keeper shall be conversant with the measurement of space and time.   {2.20.1}

VII.vi

OFFICIALS CONTROLLING LEISURE ACTIVITIES

[This section describes the duties and responsibilities of the Chief Controller of Alcoholic Beverages, the Chief Controller of Entertainers (Courtesans, Brothels, Prostitutes and Other Entertainers) and the Chief Controller of Gambling and Betting.

The manufacture and sale of alcoholic liquor was a state monopoly, private manufacture being very limited and strictly controlled. Liquor sellers and drinking places were closely supervised and used to obtain information for maintaining law and order. The responsibilities of the Chief Controller were diverse; his department was, no doubt, a major revenue earner. However, no special qualifications for this post have been laid down. Details of the types of liquor manufactured and recipes for making them are given in the Appendix 10 on Alcoholic Beverages.

Verse {2.27.25} shows that the Chief Controller of Entertainers, though called by Kautilya the Head of the Department of Courtesans/Prostitutes, not only supervised prostitutes but also other entertainers such as actors, dancers, singers and musicians. The text also shows that the places of entertainment were strictly controlled by the State though individual prostitutes could ply their trade on payment to the State of a tax on their earnings. The official was also responsible for the training of courtesans and for protecting the interests of prostitutes as well as their clients. No special qualifications have been laid down.

Almost the entire chapter {2.27} deals with prostitutes and courtesans. It would seem that these not only provided sexual services but also entertained clients with singing and dancing. A piece of evidence for this is that a distinction is made between a courtesan showing dislike to a client visiting her and she refusing to sleep with him. The establishments of the courtesans were to be located in the south-east part of the city {2.4.11}, see town plan in IV.i; their establishments also accompanied the army on an expedition {10.1.10} in XI.iv. They were obliged to pay additional amounts in times of financial stringency {5.2.23,28} in V.ii.

The text distinguishes between gambling (as with dice) and betting (on cock fights and animal racing) though the same rules applied to both and the same official was put in charge of ensuring that these were conducted fairly. No special qualifications have been laid down for the Chief Controller in charge of these leisure activities.]

CHIEF CONTROLLER OF ALCOHOLIC BEVERAGES

RESPONSIBILITIES

State Manufacture:

(i) The Chief Controller shall make arrangements for the manufacture of alcoholic beverages in the city, the countryside and the camps, with the help of experts in brewing and fermenting.   {2.25.1}

Women and children shall be employed in searching for special ingredients (such as herbs and spices) used in the industry and in preparing them [by roasting, grinding, etc.].   {2.25.38}

Private Manufacture:

(ii) Physicians can make *arishtas* [medicines based on alcohol] for different illnesses.   {2.25.21}

Types of liquor, including fermented fruit juices, not made in the state units, can be made by [private] manufacturers, on condition that they pay 5% of the quantity as royalty.   {2.25.39}

Householders shall be permitted to make white liquor for special occasions, *arishtas* for medicinal purposes and other liquor [for similar needs].

Permission to make and sell liquor shall be given on special occasions such as festivals, fairs and pilgrimages, for a period of four days [only]. Those who make liquor without permission shall pay a daily fine, till the end of the festive period.   {2.25.35-37}

Trade:

(iii) The Chief Controller shall organize, through appropriate persons, the sale of liquor (in the city, the countryside and the camps) in as many places as are necessary.   {2.25.1}

(iv) Drinking places: The Chief Controller shall be responsible for the construction of drinking places. These shall have many rooms, with beds and seats in separate places. The drinking rooms shall be made pleasant in all seasons by providing them with perfumes, flowers and water.

{2.25.11}

(v) Liquor sellers: Vintners shall sell liquor only for cash at the price fixed[1] and shall not sell for credit.

Spoilt liquor may be sold at a different price [i.e. less than the fixed price,] but only at a different place [and not at the drinking house itself]. Alternatively, spoilt liquor may be given to slaves and labourers, or used to feed draught animals and pigs.   {2.25.7-10}

Revenue:

(vi) At the end of each day the Chief Controller shall ascertain the quantity sold, the transaction tax collected, the out-go on *manasrava* (sticking allowance), the cash received and the countervailing tax collected; he shall strike the balance accordingly [i.e. the net profit for remitting to the Treasury].[2]   {2.25.40}

> [Since the trade measure for liquids was 6.25% smaller than the revenue measure (in which liquor manufactured or bought in from private manufacturers was measured), for every litre of liquor sold 62.5 millilitres of liquor should have been in stock. On the other hand, the customer was entitled to 1/50th or 2% for all liquids sold by measure as sticking allowance; hence, the surplus stock would actually been only 42.5 millilitres.
>
> Thus, the stock verification of each kind of liquor was to be calculated according to this formula:
>
> Closing stock = Opening stock - quantity sold + transaction tax - sticking allowance.
>
> The money to be accounted for by the vintner was the sale price multiplied by the quantity sold at the trade measure for each kind of liquor.
>
> The net profit was:
>
> Net profit = Sale realisation - cost of production of liquor manufactured by the Crown—95 % of the sale realisation on private liquor paid to private manufacturers—wages and other expenses.
>
> Since the retail outlets had to maintain daily accounts, the Chief Controller was obliged to submit the accounts for a given month before the end of the following month; if he failed to do so, he was fined 200 panas for each month's delay {2.7.26,27} in V.iii.]

Control over movements and stock:

(vii) Liquor shall only be drunk in the drinking house, and no one shall move about while drunk.

Liquor shall not be stored [in large quantities] nor taken out of a village. The dangers in allowing large stocks or unrestricted movement are that workers may spoil the work allotted to them, the Arya may behave immodestly and assassins may be encouraged to behave rashly.

However, persons known to be of good character may be allowed to take away small quantities in certified containers of 1/2 kuduba, 1 kuduba, 1/2 prastha and 1 prastha.   {2.25.3-5}

Law and order:

(viii) Some people may try to buy liquor by misappropriating articles entrusted to them [for manufacture or repair] or by selling a pledged or stolen article. If anyone is found in a drinking place with an article or money that is not his, he shall be arrested elsewhere [i.e. not in the drinking house itself].

A watch shall be kept over those who spend lavishly and those who spend without having a known source of income.

Secret agents shall be posted in drinking houses to note whether the spending by customers is normal or abnormal and they shall gather information about visitors [to the village or city].

Secret agents shall also make a note of the ornaments, clothes or cash of customers who are drunk or asleep. Any loss suffered by these customers shall be the responsibility of the liquor seller who shall repay the loss and pay a fine.

Liquor sellers shall be responsible for finding out correct information about strangers and natives who may pretend to be Aryas. Beautiful female servants shall find out the information when the client is drunk or asleep in a secluded place.   {2.25.6,12-15}

PUNISHMENTS

Making, selling or buying liquor other than in the authorized places	600 panas*	{2.25.2}
Loss suffered by customers	Vintner to pay compensation to client and fine equal to loss	{2.25.14}

* - [For a more lenient, but unspecified, punishment for the same offence during exempted festive periods see above {2.25.35-37}.]

THE CHIEF CONTROLLER OF ENTERTAINERS (COURTESANS, BROTHELS, PROSTITUTES AND OTHER ENTERTAINERS)

RESPONSIBILITES

Professions to be supervised:

(i) The regulations regarding courtesans and prostitutes also apply to actors, dancers, singers, musicians, story-tellers, bards, rope dancers [acrobats?], jugglers, wandering minstrels, people who deal in women and women who follow a secret profession.[3]   {2.27.25}

The wives of actors and similar entertainers shall be taught languages and the science of signs and signals. They shall be employed, using the profession of their relatives [as a cover], to detect, delude or murder the wicked.   {2.27.30}

Training of prostitutes and courtesans:

(ii) The state shall bear the expenditure on training courtesans, prostitutes and actresses in the following accomplishments: singing, playing musical instruments (including the *vina*, the flute and the *mridangam*), conversing, reciting, dancing, acting, writing, painting, mind-reading, preparing perfumes and garlands, shampooing and making love.

Their sons shall also be trained [at state expense] to be producers of plays and dances.   {2.27.28,29}

Management of brothels:

(iii) A beautiful, young and talented woman, whether a member of a courtesan's family or not, shall be appointed as the 'madam' of a brothel; she shall be given, on appointment, a grant of 1000 panas [for setting up the establishment].

A deputy shall be appointed, with a grant of 500 panas.

If the madam of a brothel dies or goes away, her daughter or sister shall take over the establishment. Or, the madam can [before her departure] appoint a deputy [promoting her own deputy to be the head].

If no such arrangements are possible, the establishment shall revert to the King [and the Chief Controller shall place it under the charge of someone else].   {2.27.1-3}

Court attendants:

(iv) Courtesans shall be appointed to attend on the King in one of three grades, according to their beauty and the splendour of their make-up and ornaments. The lowest grade, on a salary of 1000 panas per month, shall hold the umbrella over the King, the middle grade, on a salary of 2000 panas per month, shall carry his water jug and the highest, on a salary of 3000 panas per month, shall be his fan bearer. In order to add distinction, courtesans of the lower grade shall attend on the King when he is carried in his palanquin, the middle grade when he is seated on his throne and the highest shall accompany him in his chariot.

Courtesans who are no longer beautiful shall be put in charge of supervising court attendants.

Sons of courtesans shall work as the King's minstrels from the age of eight.   {2.27.4,5,7}

[Reference has been made in III.iv to preventing dangers to the King from Queens by ensuring that only trusted courtesans attended on them.]

Courtesans shall cleanse themselves with baths and change into fresh garments before attending on the Queen.   {1.20.20}

Release and retirement:

(v) The payment for obtaining the release of a courtesan [the head of an establishment] shall be 24,000 panas and for her son, 12,000 panas.

When they can no longer work prostitutes under a madam in an establishment shall be given work in the pantry or kitchen. Any one who does not work but is kept by someone shall pay 1 1/4 panas [per month?] as compensation. {2.27.6,8,9}

Obligations of a prostitute:

(vi) A prostitute shall not hand over her jewellery and ornaments to anyone except the madam and shall not sell or mortgage them.

(vii) A prostitute shall not show dislike [and refuse service] to a client after receiving payment from him.

She shall not abuse a client, disfigure him or cause him physical injury.

She shall not refuse to sleep with a client staying overnight, unless the client has physical defects or is ill.

(viii) She shall not disobey the King's command to attend on a particular person. {from 2.27.11,12,19-22}

Protection of prostitutes:

(ix) The proper procedure shall be used to take a virgin daughter of a prostitute, whether she is willing or not; coercive methods shall not be used.

(x) No one shall abduct a prostitute, keep her confined against her will or spoil her beauty by wounding her.

(xi) A client shall not rob a prostitute of her jewellery, ornaments or belongings nor cheat her of the payment due to her. {2.27.13,14,23}

Revenue:

(xii) In establishments:

Every prostitute shall report the persons entertained, the payments received and the net income to the Chief Controller.

The Chief Controller shall keep an account of the payments and gifts received by each prostitute, her total income, expenditure and net income.

He shall ensure that prostitutes do not incur excessive expenditure.

{2.27.24,10}

(xiii) Independent prostitutes:

Women who live by their beauty (*rupajiva*) [not in state-controlled establishments] shall pay a tax of one-sixth of their earnings.[4]

{2.27.27}

[The special taxes levied in times of financial distress on prostitutes and brothel keepers are described in {5.2.21, 28} in V.iii.]

<u>Foreign entertainers:</u>

(xiv) Foreign entertainers shall pay a licence fee of 5 panas per show.
{2.27.26}

PUNISHMENTS

In all cases, the punishment prescribed shall be imposed for the first offence; it shall be doubled for the second and trebled for the third. If the offence is committed a fourth time, any punishment may be awarded, as the king pleases.
{2.27.18}

<u>Violations by a prostitute:</u>

Handing over ornaments and jewellery to an unauthorized person	4 1/4 panas	{2.27.11}
Selling or mortgaging her belongings	50 1/4 panas	{2.27.12}
Abusing a client	24 panas	{2.27.12}
Causing physical injury to a client	48 panas	{2.27.12}
Disfigurement (e.g. cutting off a client's ear)	51 3/4 panas	{2.27.12}
Showing dislike to a client after receiving payment	Double the fee	{2.27.20}
Refusing to sleep with an overnight client	8 times the fee	{2.27.21}
Disobeying a command of the King to attend on someone	1000 strokes of the whip or 5000 panas	{2.27.19}
Killing a client	Death by burning alive or by drowning	{2.27.22}

<u>Offences against a prostitute:</u>

For making a courtesan's daughter lose her virginity without her mother's consent	54 panas fine + compensation to the mother of 16 times the fee for a visit	{4.12.26}
Cheating a prostitute or robbing her of her ornaments, or belongings	8 times the amount	{2.27.23}
Using coercion to take a consenting virgin from a prostitute's family	Lowest SP	{2.27.13}

Using coercion to take an unwilling virgin from a prostitute's family	Highest SP	{2.27.13}
Raping a prostitute	12 panas	{4.13.38}
Gang rape of a prostitute	24 panas for each offender	{4.12.39}
Abducting, confining or disfiguring depending on the status of the victim	1000 to 2000 panas	{2.27.14,15}
Killing a courtesan who has been appointed head of establishment	3 times the release price	{2.27.16}
Killing a mother, daughter or a prostitute in an establishment	Highest SP	{2.27.17}

Miscellaneous

For having sexual relations with the exclusive mistress of another	48 panas	{3.20.15}

CHIEF CONTROLLER OF GAMBLING AND BETTING

GENERAL

The regulations regarding gambling also apply to betting, except when the bets pertain to challenges concerning learning or skill.　{3.20.13}

　　Gamblers, by nature, cheat.　　　　　　　　　　　　　{3.20.7}

RESPONSIBILITIES OF CHIEF CONTROLLER

Gambling establishments:

　(i) The Chief Controller shall be responsible for ensuring that gambling is carried out [only] in designated places under the supervision of honest gambling masters, in order to detect men who follow secret activities [like spying].

　Gambling masters shall hire out to the players gambling equipment (such as dice, cowries, ivory rollers and leather cups) and provide water and other necessities.

　They can levy an entrance fee, hire charges for the equipment and charges for water and accommodation and can accept articles as pledges from the players which may be sold [if not redeemed].

{3.20.1,2,8,10-11}

Revenue:

(ii) Gambling masters shall recover five per cent of the winnings [as tax]. {3.20.10}

Disputes:

(iii) Some teachers say that, in a dispute between gamblers, [the judge shall impose] the lowest level standard penalty on the winner and the middle level standard penalty on the loser. [They argue that the loser should be punished more because,] being anxious to win, he could not bear to be the loser and had filed the suit, though the loss was due to his own lack of skill.

Kautilya disagrees. If the loser is always to be fined double, no one will come to the courts for justice [even if he has a valid case]. All gamblers, winners as well as losers, cheat as a matter of course. {3.20.3-7}

PUNISHMENTS

General:		
Gambling in an unauthorized place	12 panas	{3.20.2}
Gambling masters:		
Hiring out loaded dice and similar offences	12 panas	{3.20.9}
Cheating as a player himself[5]	Lowest SP and confiscation of winnings	{3.20.9}
Allowing players to cheat with loaded dice or sleight of hand	Double the above	{3.20.12}
Cheating the State of revenue and repayment of amount stolen	Fine for theft	{3.20.9}
Players:		
Cheating with loaded dice, false equipment, or sleight of hand	Cutting off of one hand or 400 panas fine	{4.10.9}

VII.vii

MOVEMENT CONTROL OFFICIALS

[The movement of the people in the Kautilyan state was strictly controlled, both in the countryside and within the fortified city. As mentioned in IV. iv, the Governor-General of the City was responsible for controlling entry into the city and for enforcing the night curfew. For travel within the countryside, the Chief Passport Officer issued passes, set with an official seal. This was checked by frontier officers, river guards at ferry crossings and by the Chief Controller of Pasture Lands. Notwithstanding the designation, this official was primarily responsible for the security of the realm and of travellers. He was responsible for clearing the land between settlements and, incidentally, converting it into pastures as well as keeping these free of all dangers, particularly threats to safety from thieves and enemies. It is, therefore, more appropriate to consider him as a movement control officer rather than an officer involved in production or servicing of the livestock industry.

The responsibility for ensuring security within the kingdom was thus clearly demarcated. The Governor-General or his equivalent was responsible within the fortified cities. In the settled areas of the countryside the overall responsibility rested with the Chancellor and his officials though individual villages were also responsible, within the village boundaries, for the safety of travellers and traders. For the regions between the villages, the Chief Controller of Pasture Lands was responsible. For remote, uninhabited or sparsely populated areas, there was a special officer called the thief-catcher. The frontier areas were, of course, controlled by frontier governors and commanders of frontier forts.

In protecting the safety of the realm, extensive use was made of the secret service and clandestine agents, both within the city and in the countryside. Some aspects of curfew, movement control and detection of undesirables are included in this section; others will be found in Part IX on Clandestine Activity.]

CHIEF CONTROLLER OF PASTURE LANDS

RESPONSIBILITIES

Clearing land for pasture:

(i) The Chief Controller shall clear the land in the regions between villages and establish pastures thereon. In waterless lands, he shall construct wells, tanks and embankments and create orchards and flower gardens.

{2.34.6,8}

Providing security:

(ii) Valleys and forests shall be cleared of all dangers, such as thieves and wild animals. Hunters, with their hounds,[1] shall [be employed to] roam forests. At the approach of thieves or enemies, they shall not let themselves be caught but hide themselves in trees or mountains or escape from the place quickly; they shall then sound the alarm by blowing conches or beating drums.

The Chief Controller shall promptly report to the King the movements of enemies or jungle tribes by sending sealed letters through carrier pigeons or by using smoke or fire signals.

It shall be his duty to protect timber and elephant forests, keep roads in good repair, provide protection against robbers and ensure the security of caravans, cattle and trade within the region.

If any one is robbed or killed in the regions between settlements, he shall be [personally held] responsible for paying the compensation.

{2.34.7,9-12; 4.13.9}

Control:

(iii) The Chief Controller shall check [the movement of people by asking them to show] the sealed passes [issued by the Chief Passport Officer].

{2.34.5}

CHIEF PASSPORT OFFICER

RESPONSIBILITIES

Regulations:

(i) No one shall enter or leave the countryside (*janapada*) [or the fortified city] without a valid pass. {2.34.2; 2.36.38}

Issue of passports:

(ii) The charge for issuing passports shall be one mashaka per pass.

{2.34.1}

PUNISHMENTS

A citizen entering or leaving without a pass	12 panas	{2.34.3}
A citizen using a forged pass	Lowest SP	{2.34.4}
A non-citizen using a forged pass	Highest SP	{2.34.4}

MOVEMENT CONTROL

WITHIN THE CITY

LODGING

Every houseowner shall report the arrival and departure of his guests.

If a houseowner fails to report the arrival or departure of a guest and a crime is committed during the night, the householder shall be held responsible for the crime. If no crime was committed, he shall [still] pay a fine.

{2.36.10-12}

Persons in charge of lodging places run by charities [providing free accommodation and food to travellers] shall permit ascetics and Brahmins learned in the Vedas to stay, after satisfying themselves about their bonafides. They shall allow *pashandas* (ascetics of heretical sects) to stay only after informing the Divisional Officer.

Artisans and artists shall provide accommodation in their own places of work to visitors following similar professions. [Likewise] merchants shall stay with other merchants, on the basis of reciprocity. Merchants providing accommodation shall be responsible for informing the authorities if the visitor sells goods of which they are not full owners or at an unauthorised time or place.

Those in charge of drinking places, vegetarian and non-vegetarian eating houses and brothels shall allow only those well known to them to stay with them. They shall report to the authorities anyone spending extravagantly or behaving rashly.   {2.36.5-9}

CURFEW

The curfew period shall start 6 *nalikas* (2 hours and 24 minutes) after sunset and last till 6 *nalikas* before sunrise [i.e. a period of curfew of approximately seven and a half hours]. A bugle shall be sounded to mark the beginning and the end of the curfew period.

The following shall be permitted to move during the curfew period: midwives attending a delivery, doctors attending to illness, those who are obliged to do so due to a death in the family, those who go with a lamp in their hand [i.e. move about openly], visitors to the city officials for official purposes, those summoned by a trumpet-call, firefighters and those having a valid pass.

All those found moving about in a suspicious manner, in unauthorised places or with a previous conviction [for curfew violation] shall be interrogated.

On special occasions when no restrictions on movement are imposed, persons in disguise, those masquerading as the opposite sex or as wandering monks, those armed with sticks or weapons shall be punished according to the gravity of the offence.

{2.36.34,36,38,39}

CRIMES

Any doctor who is called to a house to treat a severely wounded person or one suffering from unwholesome food or drink shall report the fact to the *gopa* and the *sthanika*. If he makes a report, he shall not be accused of any crime; if he does not, he shall be charged with the same offence [which he helped to conceal].

{2.36.10}

SAFETY OF THE REALM

Frontier officers and the Chief Controller of Pasture Lands shall be responsible for the safety of the persons and merchandise travelling on the roads.

{2.21.25,4.13.9}

No one shall move about carrying arms, unless they have a special permit, with the proper seal.

{5.3.38}

Frontier officers shall take away weapons carried by caravans or [where necessary,] issue them a special permit with the proper seal affixed to it.

{5.3.41}

[Clandestine agents shall be posted in drinking houses to watch if any customer spends lavishly, gather information about visitors and make sure that the ornaments and property of visitors is not stolen {2.25.12,13}.]

PUNISHMENTS

<u>Moving about near the king's palace</u>

in the first third and last third of the curfew period	1/4 panas	{2.36.35}
in the middle third	2 1/2 panas	
Moving about in the palace grounds	5 panas	
Approaching the royal buildings	Middle SP	{2.36.37}
Climbing the city's fortifications	Middle SP	
Householder failing to report arrival or departure of guests	3 panas	{2.36.12}

VII.viii

MISCELLANEOUS OFFICIALS

CHIEF SUPERINTENDENT OF TEMPLES AND HOLY PLACES

[This official is mentioned only twice in the entire text. In {2.6.2}, he appears as a source of revenue and in {5.2.37,38} he is given special responsibility for collecting revenue in times of financial distress. It is not clear whether, in normal periods, he contributed any revenue to the State.]

A King who finds himself in great financial difficulty may collect [additional] revenue. If adequate resources have not been raised [by special levies, direct cultivation of an additional summer crop or by voluntary contributions and sale of honours], the Chief Superintendent of Temples shall collect together the wealth of temples in the city and the countryside. He shall then pretend that the property was lost because the person with whom it was deposited had died or that his house had burned down. The property shall be taken to the Treasury.   {5.2.37,38}

CHIEF SUPERINTENDENT OF JAILS

[This official is mentioned only once in the text, in {4.9.23}. He appears to have responsible for both judicial lock-ups and prisons. Since imprisonment by itself is unknown in the *Arthashastra*, the persons in lock-ups must have been mostly debtors, accused awaiting trial, etc. The Chief Superintendent alone seems to have had the power to decide whether to allow free movement of a prisoner without actually releasing him, transfer a prisoner from one prison to another, change his status, deprive him of food or drink or torture him. See VIII.xvi.]

PROTECTOR OF DEPOSITS

[The *Adhipala*, Protector of Deposits, is mentioned only once in the text, in {3.12.14}. He was not a Head of Department and may have been an officer of the court, charged with looking after unclaimed pledges and deposits.]

VII.ix

SUBORDINATE OFFICIALS

[The duties and responsibilities of the heads of some subordinate offices, such as the Controller of Goldsmiths and Silversmiths or the Examiner of Coins, have been given in detail by Kautilya. In addition, the text mentions a number of other subordinates, by designation, without any significant details about their actual duties. All these have been collected together in this subsection. Charts of the structure of civil offices and productive enterprises have been added at the end.

Officials under the Treasurer:

Tajjata	Experts in valuation (valuers)	{2.5.8}
Rupadarshaka	Examiner of coins	{2.5.10}

Official under the Chancellor:

Chorarajju	Catcher of thieves	{4.13.10}

Official under the Chief Controller of Ports:

Nadipala	River guards	{2.6.3}

Officials under the Comptroller of Accounts and Audit:

Karmic	Works officer	
Karanika	Accounts officer	{2.7.22}

Officials in 2.8.22:

Upayukta	Subordinate officer	
Nidhayaka	Store keeper	
Nibandhaka	Ledger keeper	

Under the Chief Superintendent of Warehouses:

Workers in his establishment:

Sweepers, watchmen, weighingmen, measurers, supervisors of receipts and deliveries; accountants and miscellaneous slaves and labourers. [For the designations, see Appendix 6 'Professions'.]   {2.15.63}

Officials under Chief Controller of State Trading:

Panyadhishtatharah   Retail outlet managers in state service {2.16.14-16}

Officials under the Chief Superintendent of Productive Forests:

Vanapala   Forest guard (Ranger?)   {2.17.1}

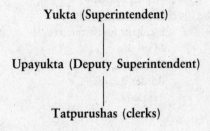

Fig. 21 Organization of an Office
{2.5.16}

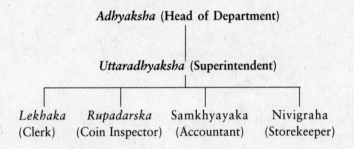

Fig. 22 Organization of Productive Enterprises
{2.9.28-30}

<u>Working under the Chief Controller of Entertainers:</u>

Ganika	Heads of Establishment of Prostitutes	
Pratiganika	Deputy Heads	{2.27.1}

<u>Team under the Chief Elephant Forester:</u>

Nagavanapala	Elephant forest rangers	
Hastipaka	Mahouts	
Padapasika	Tetherers	
Saimika	Border guards	
Vanacharika	Trackers	
Parikarmika	Attendants	{2.2.10}

<u>Miscellaneous</u>

<u>Under the Chief Superintendent of Jails</u>

Warders in lockups and jailors in prisons.   {4.9.21-27}

VII.x

VILLAGE/VILLAGE HEADMAN

[The organization of administration at the level of the individual village is not very clear from the text. The lowest level in the official hierarchy was the *gopa* (record keeper), who was in charge of five or ten villages. {2.35.2} in IV.iv. In the text, four different words are used to denote village officials. *Gramakutam* appears only once {4.4.9} in connection with a secret agent tempting the integrity of a headman; the word may have crept in inadvertently since the verse mainly deals with Heads of Departments. *Gramaswami*, the master (?) of a village, appears in {4.13.8} as the person responsible for making good losses if a trader is attacked in daytime and killed or his goods stolen. The other two words are *gramika* and *gramabhritaka* though the latter, usually translated as 'village servant', does not seem to be used in the same sense throughout the text.

The salary of the *gramabhritaka* is given as 500 panas a year in the salary list {5.3.23}; such servants are to cultivate land left uncultivated by someone to whom it had been given as a grant {2.1.11}; and these servants are not to be called as witnesses in civil cases, except when the case concerns one of their own group {3.11.29}. On the other hand, in {5.2.11}, the village servants are grouped together with *bhikshukas* (mendicants) as people who can gather left over grain from fields and threshing floors in times of serious financial difficulty. Since an official with a salary of 500 panas a year cannot be equated to a mendicant, the word is usually translated in this verse as a 'village servant' in the sense of a village craftsman such as a barber, washerman or blacksmith.

Gramika is mentioned twice {3.10.16 and 18} in Book 3 on civil law and justice in the chapter on damage to pastures, fields and roads. Some translators have assumed that only verses {3.10.16-20} deal with the office of the *gramika*.[1] However, it seems more logical to attribute subsequent verses also to the duties of the village headman and the obligations of villagers; otherwise one has to strain to find a different subject for each verse.

Gramavriddah (village elders) occupied an important position of trust in a village. They were trustees of temple property as well as the property of a minor until he came of age {2.1.27,3.5.20}. Boundary disputes between villages were decided on the basis of evidence given by elders who were farmers or cowherds; within villages, they acted as judges in disputes about fields {3.9.11,15}. The sale of any immovable property had to be conducted in public in their presence {3.9.3}. In the absence of a creditor from the village, a mortgagor could deposit the redemption money with the elders and reclaim his property {3.12.12}.]

VILLAGE HEADMAN (*GRAMIKA*)

RESPONSIBILITIES

Erecting boundaries:
(i) The village headman shall have a fence with pillars erected all the way around the village at a distance of 600 feet from it.   {3.10.20}
Cattle grazing:
(ii) He shall ensure that cattle do not graze or stray into cultivated private fields or gardens or eat the grains in storage sheds and threshing fields and shall be responsible for protecting them from injuries or harsh treatment.[2] He shall have the right to cut the grass in pasture lands for his living.   {from 3.10.21,25-34}
Revenue:
(iii) The headman shall collect the revenue for the village from the charges levied on grazing in common land, from the prescribed fines and the fines levied by the State.   {3.10.22-24}
Village population:
(iv) The headman shall not eject any settler from a village except for reasons of theft or adultery. For unjust eviction, the headman and the village as a whole are liable to punishment. An ejected person who re-enters the village is to be held guilty of trespass.[3]   {3.10.18,19}

[See also {3.4.9} in VIII.v on headman as one who can give asylum to women who run away from home.]

RESPONSIBILITIES OF VILLAGERS

Village Organization:
(i) The village shall organize a hierarchy of its society, from the Brahmin downwards.
Brahmins,[4] the people of a locality, a caste, a family or group shall not be obliged to take part in any festivities [if they do not want to].
                                        {3.10.43-45}

Participation in village life:

(ii) All the people in a village shall contribute their share of the [community] work and the costs of festivals and entertainments.

Anyone who does not contribute his share of the cost of production of a performance shall not be allowed to see it; his family shall also be banned. Watching or listening to it secretly is a punishable offence.

The fines collected from anyone for not doing his share of the work or for not contributing his share of the costs of festivities shall go to the village [and not to the State].

The people of a village shall obey the orders of anyone who proposes any activity beneficial to all. They shall not conspire against such a person to [attack or] harm him.   {from 3.10.35,37-41}

Miscellaneous:

(iii) When the headman has to travel on village business, he shall be accompanied by some of the residents of the village, [who shall take the duty] in turns.   {3.10.16}

VILLAGE REVENUE

Grazing charges:

Bulls belonging to village temples, stud bulls and cows up to ten days after calving are exempt from payment of grazing charges.   {3.10.24}

	Grazing only	Grazing and resting	Grazing and staying overnight
Small animals [goats, sheep]	1/16 pana	1/8 pana	1/4 pana
Cattle, horses, donkeys	1/8 pana	1/4 pana	1/2 pana
Buffaloes and camels	1/4 pana	1/2 pana	1 pana

{3.10.22,23}

PUNISHMENTS

Compensation:

Animals eating crops: owner of offending animal to pay the specified amount to one who has suffered	Double the damage calculated according to [expected] harvest	{3.10.25}

Fines payable to State: {3.10.26,27}

Domesticated and protected animals	Owner of cattle	Herdsman

Animals grazing on village pastures

without prior permission [from the headman]	12 panas	6 panas
due to owner's negligence	24 panas	12 panas

Animals straying: {3.10.28,29}

into gardens	24 panas
and breaking down fences	48 panas
eating grain in stores and threshing floors	48 panas

Causing injury to animals and, in particular to protected species in reserved forests	Same fines as for causing physical injury to people	{3.10.33}

Other punishments:

A resident not accompanying the village headman going on a journey on official duty (when it is his turn to do so)	1 1/2 panas per yojana	{3.10.17}

Ejecting a legitimate settler: {3.10.18}

Fine on village headman	24 panas
Collective fine on village	Highest SP

Fines paid into village revenues:

A resident who does not: {3.10.36}

do his share of community work	Double the wages of work not done
contribute his share of the cost	Double the contribution of each member [of his family]
contribute his share of food and drink for festive occasions	Double the contribution
contribute his share of a performance but listens to or watches it secretly	Double his contribution to be made for some other common purpose {3.10.38}
carry out the orders beneficial to all	12 panas {3.10.40}

Villagers conspiring to attack or beat one who gives orders for the good of the village	Each one in the conspiracy to pay double the penalty for the offence	{3.10.41}
causing serious injury to such a person as a result of the conspiracy	The highest level of punishment for causing physical injury	{3.10.42}

VII.xi

CIVIC RESPONSIBILITY AND MUNICIPAL REGULATIONS

[Collected together in this section are verses relating to fire prevention, hygiene, house-building and tenancy in urban areas and damage to public and private property.]

CIVIC RESPONSIBILITY

RESPONSIBILITIES APPLICABLE TO ALL

No one shall cause injury to others by:
- [the collapse of] a rickety dwelling or
- an unsupported pillar [or beam];
- an unsheathed weapon;
- an uncovered or concealed pit or well; or
- allowing his horned or tusked animal to hurt someone, particularly by failing to come to the rescue when entreated to do so.

A person shall not be held guilty of assault by causing injury, if he gives suitable warning (such as 'get out of the way!') when:
- felling a tree;
- leading by the rope an animal being trained;
- driving or riding an untrained animal;
- throwing sticks, clods of earth, stones, weapons or arrows when on the move [riding a horse, elephant or chariot]; or
- [riding or leading] an elephant.   {from 4.13.13,14,18}

TRAFFIC CODE

A cart shall not [be allowed to] move with no driver in it; only an adult can be in charge of a cart; a minor driver shall be accompanied by an adult.
                                          {from 4.13.25,26}
One who injures another by driving his cart [recklessly] shall be punished except [in cases of unforeseen accident as] when:
- the nose string of a bullock or the yoke of the cart breaks [accidentally];
- the draught animals move [suddenly] backwards or sideways; or
- there is a large throng of animals and men.   {4.13.22}

PRIVACY AND MUTUAL HELP

No one shall interfere in the affairs of a neighbour, without due cause. However, every one has the duty to run to the help of a neighbour in distress.

{from 3.20.16}

COMMON FACILITIES

Every one shall contribute his share to the building of common facilities. No one shall obstruct or prevent the lawful use of such facilities by others in the neighbourhood. Such facilities shall not be destroyed.

{from 3.8.26,27}

No one shall damage plants and trees in city parks, sanctuaries, holy places and cremation grounds, particularly those which bear fruits or flowers or provide shade.   {from 3.19.28-30}

GOOD NEIGHBOURLINESS

No one shall behave in a manner likely to cause harm to the immediate neighbourhood.[1]   {from 3.20.15}

RESPONSIBILITIES OF TOWNSMEN

Fire Prevention:
  In the summer, citizens shall take appropriate precautions against fire. They shall not light fires during the [two] middle quarters of the day; if food has to be cooked during this period, it shall be done outside the house.

  Every householder shall provide five water pots, a big jar, a trough, a ladder, an axe [for chopping down pillars and beams], a winnowing basket [for fanning away the fire], a hook [to pull away burning parts], a hooked rake [for pulling away thatch] and a skin bag.

  During the night, householders shall stay near the front doors of their houses and shall not collect together.

  If a house catches fire, every occupant, owner or tenant, shall take immediate steps [to put it out].   {from 2.36.15-18,21,23}
Hygiene:
  No one shall throw dirt on the streets or let mud and water collect there. This applies, particularly, to royal highways.

  No one shall pass urine or faeces in [or near] a holy place, a water reservoir, a temple or a royal property, unless it is for unavoidable reasons like illness, medication or fear.

  No one shall throw out dead bodies of animals or human beings inside the city.

Corpses shall be taken out of the city only by the prescribed route and the gate for corpses and cremation or burial done only at the designated places.

{from 2.36.26-33}

COMMON FACILITIES

It is preferable that sheds, courtyards, latrines, fire places, places for pounding grain and all open spaces are used as common property.

{3.8.28}

HOUSE-BUILDING REGULATIONS

The boundaries of every residential property shall be clearly demarcated by pillars at the corners with wires strung between them. Houses shall be built in conformity with the [nature and] extent of the land. There shall be adequate rain water drainage.   {3.8.3,4,23}

The house and its various facilities shall be built at a suitable distance from a neighbour's property so as not to cause inconvenience to the neighbour. The roof of a house may either be three inches away from the roof of a neighbour's house or may [even] overlap it. There shall be a lane between two houses with a side door for access to repair damage and to avoid overcrowding. Rain water falling from the roof of a house should not damage a verandah [of the neighbouring house]; if it is likely to do so, it shall be protected either by a wall or by matting. The doors and windows shall be so made as not to cause annoyance by facing directly a door or a window of a neighbouring house, except when the two houses are separated by a wide road such as the royal highway. Any window made for lighting shall be high up [so that it does not overlook a room of another house]. No part of the house (ditch, step, water channel, ladder or dung hill) shall be built in a manner which will cause obstruction and prevent the enjoyment of others. When the house is occupied, the doors and windows shall be suitably covered [with curtains].   {3.8.14-17,19-21}

Every house shall be so built so that the following facilities are at the specified distances from a neighbouring house in order to avoid causing nuisance to the neighbour.

Facility	Distance from neighbouring property
Boundary	2 aratnis/3 padas [about one yard]
Between the house or any projecting part of it and the neighbour's house or any	1 kishku/3 padas [about 2 to 3 feet]

projecting part of it

Dung hill, sewage channel, well	Appropriate distance
Temporary facilities (such as water closets, pits and wash water outlets) built for festive occasions	Appropriate distance
Fresh water course—a channel of sufficient slope or a cascade, so that the water may flow easily	3 padas/1 1/2 aratnis [a yard or more]
Places for: carts, domestic animals, fire, water jar, grinding mill, pounding mortar	1 aratni/1 pada [about a foot and a half]

The regulation about sewage channels does not apply to temporary facilities provided for childbirth and lying-in for ten days after delivery.

Neighbours may, by mutual agreement, modify the above so long as they avoid the undesirable. {3.8.5,6,8,9,11,13,18}

PUNISHMENTS

<u>General Responsibilities</u>

Causing injury by the collapse of a rickety dwelling or cart; an unsupported pillar or beam; an unsheathed weapon; an uncovered or concealed pit or well.	As for causing corresponding physical injury	{4.13.13}
Not coming to the rescue of someone being hurt by his horned or tusked animal		{4.13.18}
normally	Lowest SP	
if failing to respond to cries for help	Middle SP	

<u>Traffic Code</u>

Reckless driving of a cart except when it was due to an unforeseeable accident

causing injury to human beings or animals	Same as for causing corresponding physical injury	{4.13.23}
Death of animal	Above + payment of compensation	{4.13.24}

Person to be punished, if there is no adult driver:

driver is a minor	Owner of cart or accompanying adult	{4.13.25}
unaccompanied minor or driverless	Confiscation of cart	{4.13.26}

Fire Prevention:

Lighting a fire inside the house during the two middle quarters of the day	1/8 pana	{2.36.16}
Not providing fire fighting equipment	1/4 pana	{2.36.18}
Not hastening to save his own house on fire		{2.36.23}
if he is the owner	12 panas	
if he is the tenant	6 panas	
Letting a house catch fire through negligence	54 panas	{2.36.24}
Arson [deliberately setting fire]	Death by fire	{2.36.25}

Hygiene:

Throwing dirt on the road	1/8 pana	{2.36.26}
blocking it with mud or water	1/4 pana	
Throwing dirt on the royal highway	1/4 pana	{2.36.27}
blocking it with mud or water	1/2 pana	

For using as a urinal/latrine:	As urinal	As latrine	{2.36.28}
a holy place	1/2 pana	1 pana	
a water reservoir	1 pana	2 panas	
a temple	1 1/2 panas	3 panas	
a royal building	2 panas	4 panas	

For throwing dead bodies inside the city:		{2.36.30}
cat, dog, mongoose or snake	3 panas	

donkey, mule, camel horse or cattle	6 panas	
human corpse	50 panas	
For taking out a dead body by an unauthorized route or through an unauthorized gate	Lowest SP	{2.36.31}
A gate keeper who lets the above happen	200 panas	{2.36.32}
Burial/cremation in a place other than the designated grounds	12 panas	{2.36.33}

<u>Damage to public property:</u>   {3.19.28-30}

Damaging plants and trees in city parks, sanctuaries, holy places and cremation grounds, particularly those which bear fruits or flowers or provide shade:

Plants and creepers	Trees	Important trees*	Others
A sprout	3	6	12
Small branches	6	12	24
Big branches	12	24	48
Cutting off trunks	Half Lowest SP	Lowest SP	Double Lowest SP
Uprooting	Half Middle SP	Middle SP	Double Middle SP

* (Including those which mark boundaries, are objects of worship or those in Royal enclosures)

<u>Damage to Private Property:</u>   {3.19.24-27}

Immovable property:

Damaging the wall of someone else's house by hitting it	3 panas	{3.19.24}
Breaking or demolishing a wall	6 panas + compensation for repair or rebuilding	{3.19.24}
Throwing damaging things inside another's house	12 panas	{3.19.25}
Throwing things which may endanger life into another's house	Lowest SP	{3.19.25}
Breaking open the sealed door of a house	48 panas	{3.20.15}

House-building:

Not having adequate rainwater drainage	12 panas	{3.8.23}
Causing damage to the wall of another house by letting water collect	12 panas	{3.8.22}
Causing damage to another house by letting urine or dung collect	24 panas	{3.8.22}
Having a cart shed, animal shed, fireplace, water jar, grinding mill or pounding mortar too near	24 panas	{3.8.12}
Having a fresh water course too near a neighbour's house	54 panas	{3.8.10}
Having a dung hill, a sewage channel or a well too near a neighbour's house as to cause nuisance	Lowest SP	{3.8.7}
Neighbour's verandah needing protection from rain not protected; house built with door or window directly facing a door or window of a neighbour's house	Lowest SP	{3.8.20}
Causing obstruction and preventing the enjoyment of others	Lowest SP	{3.8.21}

Tenancy:

Tenant who refuses to leave after being asked to	12 panas	{3.8.24}
Landlord who evicts, without due cause, a tenant who has paid his rent	12 panas	{3.8.24}

Common facilities:

For not helping to build common facilities, for	12 panas	{3.8.26}

obstructing their use, or for
preventing their rightful use

Destroying a common facility	24 panas	{3.8.27}
Causing harm to entire neighbourhood	48 panas	{3.20.15}
Causing injury by [collapse of] unstable house	According to scale for physical injury	{4.13.13}

Privacy

Interfering in a neighbour's affairs without reason	100 panas	{3.20.16}

Mutual help

Not running to help a neighbour in distress	100 panas	{3.20.16}

Part VIII

LAW AND JUSTICE

"A king who observes his duty of protecting his people justly and according to law will go to heaven, whereas one who does not protect them or inflicts unjust punishment will not."

{3.1.41}

"It is the power of punishment alone, when exercised impartially in proportion to the guilt, and irrespective of whether the person punished is the King's son or an enemy, that protects this world and the next."

{3.1.42}

"Because the King is the guardian of the right conduct of this world with its four *varnas* and four *ashramas*, he [alone] can enact and promulgate laws [to uphold them] when all traditional codes of conduct perish [through disuse or disobedience]."

{3.1.38}

"Judges shall discharge their duties objectively and impartially so that they may earn the trust and affection of the people."

{3.20.24}

VIII.i

THE KAUTILYAN LEGAL SYSTEM

[An essential duty of government is maintaining order; Kautilya defines this broadly to include both maintenance of social order as well as order in the sense of preventing and punishing criminal activity. Thus the subject covers civil law (including family law, law of contracts and law of labour) and criminal law (including the Penal Code). A broad distinction is maintained between the two in the *Arthashastra* by placing most aspects of civil law in Book 3 and criminal law in Book 4. The titles indicate this: Book 3 is called 'Concerning upholders of *dharma*' and Book 4, 'The removal of thorns', i.e. elimination of anti-social activities. A description of the legal system has also to mention procedures, the law of evidence in civil cases and, for criminal activities, investigation and forensic science.

The fact that a judge is called a '*dharmastha*'—upholder of *dharma*—indicates that the ultimate source of all law is *dharma*. So long as every Arya follows his *svadharma* having due regard to his *varna* and *ashrama* and the king follows his *rajadharma*, social order will be maintained. Kautilya, however, recognizes that the customary law of the people of a region or a group is also relevant. In addition, there is law as promulgated by the king. 'When all traditional codes of conduct cease to operate due to disuse or disobedience, the king can promulgate written laws through his edicts, because he alone is the guardian of the right conduct of this world' {3.1.38}.

Pradeshtr, usually translated as magistrates, were another class of judicial officers. The distinction between judges and magistrates seems to be that, while the former dealt with all cases concerning transactions between two parties, the latter were concerned with crimes against society in general. This distinction is not strictly kept; for example, deception in arranging marriages is dealt with as a criminal activity in Book 4. The magistrates also combined executive and judicial functions. They were in charge of criminal investigation and assisted revenue officials in collecting taxes and dues {2.35.7}.

Both judges and magistrates were subordinates of the *Samahartr*, the Chancellor. The opening verses of the two books indicate that, in each place, there were benches of three judges or three magistrates. Both categories of judicial officers were expected to have the qualifications prescribed for a minister. It is not clear whether there were different grades, depending on the size of their charge (large towns or groups of ten, 400 or 800 villages), or whether there was one bench in each provincial headquarter, moving around as needed within the province. There is no reference in the text to a hierarchy of courts or to appeals from the decisions of a lower court to a higher one. An appeal could always be made to the king.

In this translation, the material in Books 3 and 4 and other relevant verses from other books has been reorganized. The sources of law, the duties of judges, magistrates and judges' clerks, civil procedure and the law of evidence are in Sections ii to iv. All aspects of family law are covered in Sections v (marital life) and vi (inheritance). Civil transactions are in Sections vii (loans and similar transactions), viii (law of property), ix (law of contracts), x (law of labour and slavery) and xi (partnership). Sections xii to xv are concerned with criminal law (investigation, causing injury, theft and sexual offences). Section xvi deals with prisons and welfare of prisoners. The last section is on the penal system and includes the general principles regarding punishment, the monetary fines payable in lieu of mutilation and amputation, capital punishment and some miscellaneous punishments from {3.20} and {4.13}.

The prevention of crime is an aspect of maintenance of law and order which is not separately spelt out but is referred to in a number of places in the text. Clandestine agents working under the Chancellor were responsible for collecting information about various crimes. They kept a look-out for treacherous activities, cheating on taxes, fraud by merchants, dishonesty of officials and movement of thieves {2.35.8-13} in IX.iii. Verse {2.23.14} gives a list of places where anti-social persons might gather. Similar lists of suspicious places in the city and the duties of agents operating there are given in {2.36.14} in IX.iii. A list of thirteen types of undesirable persons is in {4.4.4-22} in IV.iv; another list of people to be arrested on suspicion is in {2.28.20} in VII.v. The Chief Controllers of Alcoholic Beverages and of Gambling and Betting were also responsible for collecting information about enemy agents and thieves (VII.vi). Entertainers and their wives were also used as agents. Doctors were obliged to report cases of secretly treating wounded persons; dead bodies could be taken out of the city only through designated gates. All this points to an elaborate system of crime prevention.

VIII.ii

SOURCES OF LAW

SOURCES OF LAW

Any matter in dispute shall be judged according to the four bases[1] of justice. These, in order of increasing importance, are:
- *Dharma*, which is based on truth;
- Evidence, which is based on witnesses;
- Custom, i.e. the tradition accepted by the people; and
- Royal Edicts, i.e. law as promulgated. {3.1.39,40}

A King who administers justice in accordance with *dharma*, evidence, custom and written law will be able to conquer the whole world.

Whenever there is disagreement between custom and the *dharmashastras* or between the evidence and the *shastras*, the matter shall be decided in accordance with *dharma*.

Whenever there is a conflict between the *shastras* and the written law based on *dharma*, then the written law shall prevail; for, the reasoning explaining the derivation of a [particular] *shastra* from *dharma* is no longer available to us. {3.1.43-45}

VIII.iii

JUDGES AND MAGISTRATES

JUDGES

There shall be established a bench of three judges who shall hold court at frontier posts, sub-district headquarters, and provincial headquarters[1] [as necessary]. The judges shall be learned in *dharma* and have the qualifications of a minister. They shall judge [civil] cases arising from disputes between two parties.   {3.1.1}

Judges shall discharge their duties objectively and impartially so that they may earn the trust and affection of the people.   {3.20.24}

A judge shall not:
- threaten, intimidate, drive away or unjustly silence any litigant;
- abuse any person coming before the court;
- fail to put relevant and necessary questions or ask unnecessary or irrelevant ones;
- leave out [of consideration] answers relevant to his own questions;
- give instructions [on how to answer a question];
- remind [one of a fact];
- draw attention to an earlier statement;
- fail to call for relevant evidence;
- call for irrelevant evidence;
- decide on a case without calling any evidence;
- dismiss a case under some pretext;
- make someone abandon a case by making them tired of undue delays;
- misrepresent a statement made in a particular context;
- coach witnesses; or
- rehear a case which had been completed and judgment pronounced.

All these are punishable offences; in case the offence is repeated, the judge shall be fined double and removed from office. {from 4.9.13-16}

JUDGES' CLERKS

The clerks [who record statements made before the court] shall:
- record the evidence correctly;

- not add to the record statements not made;
- hide the ambiguity or confusion in evidence badly given;
- make unambiguous statements appear confused; or
- change, in any way, the sense of the evidence as presented.

All these are punishable offences.   {from 4.9.17}

MAGISTRATES

A bench of three magistrates (*pradeshtr*), each of the rank of minister, shall be responsible for the suppression of anti-social activities. {4.1.1}

Wherever there is a Record keeper or a Provincial Governor [responsible for revenue collection], magistrates shall be posted to inspect their work and to ensure proper collection of taxes, particularly the Special Emergency Dues.
{2.35.7}

SENTENCING BY JUDGES AND MAGISTRATES

[Judges and] magistrates shall determine whether to levy the Highest, the Middle or Lowest penalty [in the prescribed scale] taking into account the person sentenced, the nature and gravity of the offence, the motive and the circumstances prevailing [at the time of the offence], as well as the consequences while maintaining a balance between the interest of the king [i.e. the State] and the individual.   {4.10.17,18}

Judges and magistrates shall not:
- impose a fine when it is not prescribed;
- impose a fine higher or lower than the prescribed one;
- award physical punishment when it is not prescribed;
- disallow a just claim; or
- allow an unjust claim.   {from 4.9.18-20}

IMPERSONATION

No one shall pretend to be a magistrate and examine a suspect under oath.
{3.20.17}

PUNISHMENTS

<u>Judges:</u>

Threatening, intimidating, driving away or unjustly silencing a litigant	Lowest SP	{4.9.13}
Abusing a litigant	Double Lowest SP	{4.9.13}
Not asking right questions or	Middle SP	{4.9.14}

asking irrelevant ones; ignoring
answers; instrucing, reminding or
prompting witnesses

Failing to call relevant evidence or calling irrelevant evidence; deciding a case without calling evidence; dismissing a case on a pretext; tiring out a litigant with undue delays; misrepresenting a statement; coaching witnesses; rehearing a case already decided	Highest SP	{4.9.15}
A repetition of any of the above offences	Double the fine and removal from office.	{4.9.16}

Judges' clerks:

Not recording correctly evidence given; recording statements not made; hiding the ambiguity in statements; making clear statements ambiguous; misrepresenting the sense of the evidence	Lowest SP or according to the offence	{4.9.17}

Sentencing by Judges and Magistrates:

Imposing a wrong fine	Eight times the [shortfall or excess]	{4.9.18}
Imposing a fine when none is to be levied	Twice the fine levied	{4.9.18}
Imposing unjustly physical punishment	Same punishment or twice the redemption money	{4.9.19}
Wrong decree whereby one litigant is obliged to pay the fine for loss of suit	Eight times the claim	{4.9.20}

Inpersonating a judge

For pretending to be a magistrate and examing someone under oath	Lowest SP	{3.20.17}

VIII.iv

DETERMINATION OF CIVIL SUITS
AND THE LAW OF EVIDENCE

PROCEDURES IN CIVIL CASES

COGNIZANCE

The judges themselves shall take charge of the affairs of gods, Brahmins, ascetics, women, minors, old people, the sick and those that are helpless [e.g. orphans], [even] when they do not approach the court. No suit of theirs shall be dismissed for want of jurisdiction, passage of time or adverse possession.   {3.20.22}

The plaintiff and the defendant shall both be persons fit to sue and be sued; they shall provide adequate sureties [to cover fines and payments for loss of suits as explained below in {3.1.21}].

The court clerk shall, [after the sureties have been provided,] record the statements of both the plaintiff and the defendant. These shall include the substance of the dispute and the questions raised.

The record shall show the date and time the case was filed,[1] the place, the amount in dispute and personal details of the plaintiff and the defendant.[2]

The statements shall be recorded in due order of subject matter. They shall be scrutinised [by the judge for accuracy].   {3.1.17,18}

The same case shall not be filed against a defendant twice.
                                                        {3.1.26}

COUNTERSUITS

Except in cases of riots, forcible seizure or trade disputes among merchants, the defendant shall not have the right to file a countersuit against the plaintiff.
                                                        {3.1.25}

REJOINDERS

Plaintiffs must file a reply on the same day to a statement or counter-statement filed by the defendant, for it is the plaintiff and not the defendant who has been determined to bring the action.

Defendants may be allowed time, between three to seven days [depending on the complexity of the case], to prepare their defence. If the rejoinder is not filed in time, the judge shall impose a fine.

The maximum time allowed for a defendant to file his defence shall be three fortnights. After that, the suit shall be decreed against him with costs, as specified below.   {3.1.27-31}

If a person accused of assault does not file his defence within the permitted period, the case shall be heard on the day the period expires.

{3.19.22}

PRODUCTION OF WITNESSES

The parties themselves shall be responsible for producing those witnesses [called by them] who do not live too far away [from the court] or who have no valid reason for postponing their appearance.[3] Unwilling witnesses and those who live far away may be summoned by royal writ.

{3.11.50}

The servant of the court [who summons witnesses] shall be paid his actual travelling expenses and a fee of one-eighth pana. These costs shall be borne by the loser.   {3.1.22-24}

LAW OF EVIDENCE

GENERAL

[In any case before the judges] admission [by the defendant of the claim against him] is the best. If the claim is not admitted, then the judgment shall be based on the evidence of trustworthy witnesses, who shall be persons known for their honesty or those approved by the Court.

[Normally,] there shall be at least three witnesses. If, however, the parties so agree, two shall suffice. Judgments in cases involving debt shall never be based on the testimony of only one witness.   {3.11.25-27}

WITNESSES

The following shall not be cited as witnesses: the brother of the wife of the claimant, his [business] partner, a dependent, a creditor, a debtor, an enemy of his, a cripple or anyone with an earlier conviction.[4]

{3.11.28}

The following shall be called as witnesses only in cases concerning their own groups: the king, Brahmins learned in the Vedas, village officials, lepers, people with open wounds or sores, an outcast, a *Candala*, anyone following a despicable profession, blind, deaf or dumb persons, women, government officials and those who volunteer to be a witnesses. However, in cases involving assault, theft or adultery, any one may be called as a witness, except the following: any brother of the wife of the accused, a business partner or an enemy. In the case of secret transactions, the testimony of a single witness, man or woman, may be accepted if he or she had seen or heard the transaction. The King or an ascetic shall not be called to testify to secret transactions.

Masters may appear as witnesses on behalf of their servants, priests and teachers for their students and parents for their sons but they shall not be forced to do so. If masters and servants sue each other, the punishment to the servant for loss of suit shall be double that levied on the master.

{3.11.29-33}

TAKING THE OATH

Witnesses shall take the oath in the presence of a Brahmin, a water jar or fire.

The judge shall caution the witness to tell the truth and point out the consequences of not doing so.

A Brahmin shall be exhorted to tell the truth.

A *kshatriya* or a *vaishya* shall be warned that if he gives false testimony, he shall lose all the merit he had accumulated [for the hereafter] by his performance of rites or acts of charity and be reduced to begging from his enemies.

A *sudra* shall be warned that, if he gives false testimony, all his merits shall go to the King and all the King's sins shall fall upon him. He shall be threatened with punishment for perjury and told that the true facts will always be revealed, even after some time, by aural or visual witnesses.

{3.11.34-38}

PERJURY

[There is considerable difference of opinion among earlier teachers on the punishment to be awarded for witnesses giving false or contradictory evidence.]

The school of Ushanas recommends the following punishments for witnesses who give contradictory evidence due to stupidity:

testimony about place	Lowest SP
testimony about time	Middle SP
testimony about subject matter of dispute	Highest SP.

The school of Manu recommends a fine of ten times the amount involved for testifying falsely. The followers of Brihaspati recommend that a witness who, by his testimony is responsible for miscarriage of justice, shall be put to death.

Kautilya disagrees. Witnesses are obliged to tell the truth. For not doing so, the fine shall be 24 panas and half that for refusal to testify.
{3.11.44-49}

GUIDELINES TO JUDGES

The testimony of witnesses alone shall be the basis for judgment if the case arises out of:
- folly of the plaintiff;
- a misunderstanding [of the terms of the deal] between the plaintiff and the defendant;
- a badly written document; or
- a document written by someone who had died in the meantime [and cannot, therefore, vouch for its accuracy].   {3.11.43}

Disputes about wages shall be settled only on the basis of the evidence of witnesses. If there are no witnesses, an on-the-spot investigation shall be made.   {3.13.32}

In determining a suit in favour of one or the other party, the following shall be taken as strengthening a party's case: statements of eye witnesses, voluntary admissions, straightforwardness in answering questions and evidence tendered on oath. The following shall go against a party: contradiction between earlier or later statements, unreliable witnesses or being brought to court by secret agents after absconding.   {3.1.46,47}

The following shall [also] be adequate grounds for finding a suit against one of the parties, if:
-he abandons the suit as set out in the records and changes it to another;
-his later statement does not corroborate an earlier one;
-he is unable to refute an assertion of the other party;
-he is unable to substantiate with evidence an assertion he had made, particularly when asked to do so;
-his witnesses are weak, or unfit to be witnesses;
-his evidence is quite different from what he had offered to produce;
-his own witnesses depose something contrary to what he himself had asserted;
-he denies the truth of evidence given by others; or
-he conspires with witnesses by talking to them in secret when such conversation is prohibited.   {3.1.19}

The evidence of a witness who dies [after the suit was instituted and cannot be examined by the Court] and that of a witness who suffers from a misfortune [and hence unreliable] shall be disregarded.   {3.1.34}

[See also 'Scuffles and Affrays' in VIII xiii for Kautilya's view that there should be no limitation on bringing an action and that judgement should be based on evidence and not on who brought it before the Court.]

EXECUTION OF DEGREES

If there is a conflict in the evidence given by different witnesses, the judgment shall take into action the number of witnesses, their reliability and [opinion of the court on their] disinterestedness. [If no decision can be reached on these grounds] the judgment shall be half-way between the two claims. [If even this is not possible, both parties shall lose their suits and] the King shall take over the disputed property. If the testimony of witnesses justifies a degree less than the amount claimed [by the plaintiff] he shall pay one-fifth of the excess claim as a fine. If, however, the testimony justifies a degree for a higher amount [than claimed, the plaintiff shall get only the amount claimed and] the King shall take the difference.

{3.11.39-42}

The [successful] plaintiff may, after paying the fine [on behalf of the losing defendant] make the defendant work for him. Or, the defendant may hypothecate his property to the plaintiff [until the degree amount is paid], or may get Brahmins to perform, at his cost, special rituals to ward off evil on behalf of the [successful] plaintiff[6]   {3.1.35-37}

PUNISHMENTS

Refusal to testify:

Up to a period of seven days	Nil	{3.11.38,39}
From seven days to three weeks	12 panas	
Beyond three weeks	Amount of the suit	

Perjury:

Perjury	24 panas	{3.11.49}

Filing rejoinders:

Defendant who does not file his rejoinder within the time allowed (3 to 7 days)	3 to 12 panas, depending on the case	{3.1.30}
Defendant against whom decree is entered for not filing his defence within six weeks	Fine for loss of suit and payment of amount	{3.1.31}

	defendant's property, excepting the tools his trade	
Loss of suit:		
By defendant who admits his liability [before witnesses are heard]	one-tenth of amount in dispute	{3.1.21}
Plaintiff or defendant against whom suit is decreed	one-fifth of the amount of decree	{3.1.20}
In a suit and countersuit between master and servant, priests or teachers and their students, parent and son:		{3.11.33}
for the superior	one-tenth of amount	
for the inferior	one-fifth of amount	
Decree less than amount claimed:		
Plaintiff who claims more	one-fifth of the difference between claim and decree	{3.11.41}
Absconding:		
Defendant	Same as for not filing rejoinder	{3.1.32}
Plaintiff	Same as for loss of suit	{3.1.33}

VIII.v

MARITAL LIFE

[The role of the *grihasta*—householder—is an important stage in every Arya's life because it is during this period that a man contributes to economic activity and maintenance of social order, particularly the perpetuation of his family line. All the verses in the text dealing with marriage and married life, whether in Book 3 on civil transactions or in Book 4 on criminal offences, have been brought together in this section. The bulk of the material is found in chapters {3.2}, {3.3} and {3.4}; the parts falling under criminal law are in {4.12}.

Prof. Kangle mentions a mnemonic verse according to which Manu begins the discussion on the topic of civil transactions and disputes with the law on debts, Ushanas with property, Brihaspati with deposits and Kautilya with marriage. Kautilya's arrangement is said to be the most rational.[1]

The general rule in Hindu society of marriages being permitted only between a man and woman of the same *varna* had, by Kautilya's time, been broken often enough to give rise to mixed *varnas* and sub-*varnas*. The names given in the *Arthashastra* to these sub-classifications are tabulated below. It must be noted that these need not correspond to the names given in other classical texts.[2]

		Varna of WIFE			
		Brahmin	Kshatriya	Vaishya	Sudra
		Anuloma marriages—Husband of superior *varna*			
H	Brahmin		Brahmin	Ambastha	Nishada Parasava
U					
S	Kshatriya	Suta		Kshatriya	Ugra
B					
A	Vaishya	Vaidehaka	Magadha		Sudra
N					
D	Sudra	Chandala	Kshatta	Ayogava	
		Pratiloma marriages—wife of superior *varna*			

{3.7.20-23,25-28,30}

Note 1. *Vratya*: One who does not undergo the twice-born ceremony, even if he is the son of a couple of the same *varna* [among the three higher *vanas*].   {3.7.24}

Further sub-*varnas*

WIFE--	Ugra	Nishada	Ambastha	Vaidehaka	Kshatta
H Ugra		Kukkuta			Svapaka
U					
S Nishada	Pulkasa				
B					
A Ambastha				Vainya	
N					
D Vaidehaka		Kusilava			

{3.7.31-34}

Note 2. *The Suta and Magadha* mentioned in the *Puranas* are special types of Brahmins and Kshatriyas and are not to be confused with the mixed *varnas* of the same names above.   {3.7.29}

Note 3. A *Rathakara* is a [*Vaishya*?] [*Vainya*?] because of his profession.
{3.7.29,35}

[In this section, general information on types of marriages, dowries and gifts is given first, followed by marriage agreements, including revocation and deception in concluding these agreements. A daughter's right to find herself a husband, if a father is indifferent for three years after her puberty, is also included in this subsection. Consummation of marriage and restrictions on conjugal rights are then dealt with. Two points are worth noting; the aim of marriage is to beget sons, and the girl has to be a virgin at the time of consummation. Indeed, the thread that runs throughout this section is that producing a son to perpetuate the male family line (and, perhaps, to save the couple from falling into the hell reserved for the sonless) is a sacred obligation imposed on both.

The subsection on women's property rights is also important as it is a clear exposition of the right of women, as wives or widows, to hold property for their survival and maintenance. Limitations on a man marrying more than one wife are covered in the next subsection.

Marriages could break down for a variety of reasons: cruelty, misconduct or incompatibility; the wife abandoning her husband without cause or committing adultery; the husband going away on short or long journeys or renouncing family life for the life of a *sannyasin* (ascetic). Kautilya enumerates, in considerable detail, the rules for dealing with the different situations.

All the punishments relating to the laws of marriage have been brought together in the last sub-section. The list given therein applies only to punishments where the state is involved, in levying a fine or other punishment (e.g. mutilation for women and death for men for adultery). Cases where compensation to the injured party is the only kind of punishment are dealt with in the appropriate places in the relevant sub-sections.]

GENERAL

[An examination of] civil transactions begins with marriage.   {3.2.1}

The aim of taking a wife is to beget sons.   {3.2.42}

TYPES OF MARRIAGE

There are eight types of marriage:[3]

Brahma	- a father giving away in marriage a well-adorned daughter;
Prajapatya	- the joint performance of sacred duties [by a man and a woman] without the prior consent of the woman's father;
Aarsha	- a marriage subsequently regularised by the husband presenting two cows to the father of the wife;
Daiva	- the giving away of a girl to the officiating priest inside a sacrificial altar;
Gandharva	- lovers marrying secretly;
Aasura	- the giving away of a girl in exchange for bride price;
Rakshasa	- Abduction of a woman [for marriage by force];
Paisacha	- Abduction of a woman while she is sleeping or intoxicated.

With the approval of the woman's father, the first four become *dharmya* [lawful and sacred]. The latter four become lawful [only] with the approval of the father and the mother [of the woman].   {3.2.2-10}

Members of mixed *varnas* shall marry among themselves.

{3.7.36}

DOWRY AND GIFTS

Any dowry paid [on giving consent] shall go to the father and mother or either one in the absence of the other.

[They shall be entitled to only one dowry, and] if a second dowry is paid [on remarriage] the woman shall receive it.

In all forms of marriage, giving gifts [voluntarily] to please the bride is not forbidden. {3.2.11-13}

MARRIAGE CONTRACTS

REVOCATION OF MARRIAGE CONTRACTS

In the case of the three higher *varnas*, a marriage agreement can be revoked up to the stage of *panigrahana* [bride and groom joining hands]. It can be revoked even after this if a sexual defect [loss of virginity, impotency] is discovered after it. In the case of Sudras, a marriage agreement can be revoked until consummation.

Under no circumstances can an agreement be revoked if the girl has conceived a child by the man. {3.15.11-13}

DECEPTION IN MARRIAGE AGREEMENTS

Giving away a girl in marriage by hiding the fact of her having a sexual defect is a punishable offence. [Likewise,] arranging the marriage of a man married without mentioning a sexual defect is also an offence punishable with a fine double that for a girl. {3.15.14,15}

It shall be an offence for anyone who, while pretending to arrange a marriage to a particular groom, has the girl married to another. The marriage so made shall be invalid, if the girl rejects it.

It shall be an offence to show one girl and substitute another at the time of marriage. {from 4.12.12-14}

DAUGHTER'S RIGHT TO MARRY

[It shall be the duty of a father to get his daughter married within three years after her reaching puberty.]

It shall not be an offence for a daughter, remaining unmarried for three years after her first menstruation, to marry a man of the same *varna*, and she shall be free to marry a man of [even] another *varna* provided that she does not take with her the ornaments [given to her by her father]. {4.12.10}

MARRIED LIFE

CONSUMMATION OF MARRIAGE

A woman attains majority when twelve years of age and a man, sixteen. [Their obligation to carry out marital duties begins at these ages.] Failure to carry out marital duties is punishable. {3.3.1,2}

[A father shall not keep postponing the marriage for too long after the betrothal.]

A bridegroom shall have the right to have marital relations with the betrothed girl, if seven menstrual periods have passed since the date of betrothal. The bridegroom shall not then be obliged to pay the dues owed to the father, since the latter loses his rights by wasting his daughter's fertile periods. {4.12.8,9}

The bride shall be a virgin at the time of consummation of marriage; if she is not, she shall pay the dowry and marriage expenses and a fine. Pretending to be a virgin and deceiving by substituting some other blood [to indicate falsely the rupture of the hymen] shall be a punishable offence.

No man shall falsely accuse a girl of not being a virgin. If anyone does so, he shall lose the right to marry her if she does not want to and he cannot claim back the dowry and marriage expenses. {from 4.12.15-19}

CONJUGAL DUTIES

A husband shall not have intercourse with a wife against her will if she:
- has already borne him sons
- wants to lead a pious life
- is barren
- has given birth to a still-born
- is beyond her menopause.

A husband is not obliged to have intercourse with a wife who is either insane or a leper. However, a wife can have intercourse with a leprous or mad husband, in order to beget a son [to carry on the family name]. {3.2.45-47}

[See also below: obligations to many wives {3.2.43,44}; incompatibility {3.3.12-14}.]

PROPERTY RIGHTS OF WIVES AND WIDOWS

A woman shall lose all her property (i.e. her *stridhana*, gifts from her family and her dowry) if she is guilty of treason, [persistent] misconduct or becoming a vagrant. {3.3.32}

WIFE'S PROPERTY RIGHTS

A wife's property (*stridhana*) consists of an amount for her support and her jewellery.[4] The former shall be in the form of an endowment of more than 2000 panas; there is no limit to the amount of jewellery. {3.2.14,15}

USE OF WIFE'S PROPERTY

It shall not be an offence:

(i) for the wife to use her property for maintaining herself or her sons and daughters-in-law, if a husband makes no provision for the maintenance of the family before going away on a long journey;

(ii) for the husband to use his wife's property for the performance of religious acts or to meet emergencies such as disease, famine and [unanticipated] dangers;

(iii) for the couple to use, by mutual consent, if they beget [twins] [a son and a daughter].[5]

> [If the wife had not objected to her husband using her property over a period of three years, the wife's rights vary depending on the type of marriage.]

If the husband has had the use of his wife's property for three years:

First four types of marriage	Wife loses any claim to compensation
Gandharva and *Aasura* marriages	Husband shall repay both [support and jewellery] with interest
Rakshasa and *Paisacha* marriages	Husband to pay the penalty for theft.

{3.2.16-18}

WIFE PREDECEASING HUSBAND

If the wife dies before her husband, her property shall be divided as follows:
 - sons and daughters in equal shares;
 - daughters in equal shares if there are no sons;
 - the husband, if there are no children.

The dowry, the marriage gifts and any other gifts given by relatives shall revert back to the donors. {3.2.36,37}

WIDOW'S PROPERTY RIGHTS

WIDOWS WHO DO NOT REMARRY

Women who do not expect to remarry shall receive, on the death of the husband, the support endowment, her jewellery, the balance of dowry (if any) and whatever had been given to her by her husband [in his lifetime].

[This property shall pass, on her death, to her sons.] A widow without sons, who remains faithful to her [deceased] husband's bed, shall enjoy, to the end of her life, her property, under the protection of the elders [of the husband's family]. For, the purpose of giving her right to property is to afford her protection in case of calamities. After her death, the property shall pass to kinsmen [in accordance with the laws on inheritance].

{3.2.19,27,33-35}

WIDOWS WHO REMARRY

If a widow remarries after receiving all the above, she shall forfeit what was left to her by her [previous] husband and shall also be obliged to return the rest with interest. {3.2.20,26}

If, however, a widow marries [someone from the late husband's family] with a view to begetting a son, she shall retain whatever was given to her by her late husband and father-in-law. If the remarriage is without the consent of the father-in-law, she shall forfeit whatever was given to her by him and her late husband.

If a widow remarries outside her late husband's family, her new family shall be obliged to return all her property [by the previous marriage] to the previous husband's family, except that, when the later marriage is agreed to in a proper manner, the new husband shall safeguard her property [by the earlier marriage].

If a widow with sons remarries, she shall forfeit the rights to her property [by the previous marriage] and this shall pass on to her sons [by that marriage]. If, [however,] she continues to look after these sons, she shall endow the property in their names.

Even if the remarrying widow has full rights of enjoyment and disposal, she shall settle the property on her sons, and if there are many sons, born of different fathers, the property shall be divided among them according to [the share in it of] the respective fathers. {3.2.21,23-25,28-32}

POLYGAMY AND PAYMENT OF COMPENSATION

A man may marry any number of wives [subject to the conditions spelt out below] provided that he pays [each of] the wives their dowry, their property and adequate maintenance. In the case of wives without a dowry or property of their own, appropriate compensation for supersession shall be paid, in addition to the maintenance payment. {3.2.41}

DELAY BEFORE REMARRIAGE

Before taking another wife a husband shall wait:

-eight years if the wife is barren, always miscarries or conceives only daughters;

- <u>ten years</u> if all the children are still-born;
- <u>twelve years</u> if the [surviving] children are all daughters.

After the prescribed period, a husband may marry another wife [only] for the purpose of begetting a son.

If a husband marries before the prescribed period, he shall:
- pay the superseded wife her dowry and her property (*stridhana*) and a compensation equal to half the total of the above
- and pay a fine not exceeding 24 panas.   {3.2.38-40}

OBLIGATIONS OF A HUSBAND WITH MORE THAN ONE WIFE TOWARDS HIS WIVES

If more than one wife has her fertile period at the same time, the husband shall lie with that wife to whom he had been married longer or with one who has living sons.

A wife shall not conceal her fertile period and a husband shall not fail in his duty to try to get a son with a wife in this period.

{from 3.2.43,44}

[See, under punishments later in this section, for penalties for transgressions of the above two rules.]

BREAKDOWN OF MARRIAGES

WIFE'S RIGHTS

A wife may abandon her husband if he:
- has a bad character;
- is away from home a long time in a foreign country;
- is a traitor to the king;
- threatens the life of his wife;
- is declared an outcast; or
- becomes impotent.   {3.2.48}

CRUELTY

A wife shall be taught proper behaviour but the husband shall not use [abusive] expressions such as: 'You are lost [beyond redemption]'; 'You are thoroughly ruined'; 'You are a cripple'; 'You do not know who your father was'; 'Your mother abandoned you'. Breach of this rule is a punishable offence.

Physical punishment shall be [limited to] slapping her on her behind three times with the hand, a rope or a bamboo cane. Any beating exceeding this shall be punishable offence.

A woman who is known to abuse or beat her husband shall be subject to the same punishments as a cruel husband. If a wife, out of jealousy, goes outside her marital home for her pleasures, she shall be punished.

{from 3.3.7-11}

INCOMPATIBILITY

A wife who, out of dislike for her husband, refuses to adorn herself and does not let her husband sleep with her for seven menstrual periods shall:

- return to her husband the endowment and jewellery [given to her by him]; and
- let him sleep with another woman.

A husband who dislikes his wife shall permit her to live apart, under the protection of a guardian, kinsman or mendicant woman.

A husband who falsely accuses his wife of refusing to sleep with him or of informing him through another woman of the same *varna* [of her intention to do so] shall be punished.

{3.3.12-14}

MISCONDUCT

A man and a woman [not married to each other] shall refrain from gestures or secret conversations with a view to sexual intercourse.

Neither a man nor a woman shall touch the hair or the knot of the lower garment of another of the opposite sex; marking another with teeth or nails is forbidden.

Neither a man nor a woman shall give presents to anyone to whom the giving of presents is prohibited.

A woman shall not have dealings [such as buying, borrowing, etc.] with anyone with whom having such transactions is forbidden.

A wife shall not indulge in drinking or unseemly sports, if so prohibited [by her husband]. She shall not go [without her husband] on pleasure trips or to see performances, with other men or even with other women, either by day or by night. She shall not leave the house when the husband is asleep or intoxicated or refuse to open the door to her husband.

{from 3.3.20-31}

[All the above are punishable offences; see below for punishments.]

WIFE RUNNING AWAY

A woman shall not run away from the marital home, except when [she has been] ill-treated [by her husband]. {from 3.4.1}

A husband shall not prohibit his wife from going to the house of a kinsman on occasions such as death, illness, calamity or childbirth and if she still goes, it shall not be considered as running away from the marital home. [However, she shall not use the opportunity to hide herself in her kinsman's house.] If the wife does so, she shall forfeit her property and the kinsman the balance of any dowry due to him.   {3.4.13-15}

A graded set of punishments shall be prescribed for the wife who runs away and the one who gives her asylum.   {from 3.4.1-7}

No man shall give asylum to another man's wife except to save her from danger. He shall not be punished if he had forbidden the woman to enter or if she does so without his knowledge.   {3.4.8}

Some teachers say: 'It shall not be considered an offence for a wife, ill-treated by her husband, to seek shelter in the house of any of the following, provided that there are no [other] males in it: a kinsman of the husband, a trustee, the village headman, a guardian, a female mendicant or her own kinsman.'

Kautilya disagrees. 'There is no harm in seeking shelter with a kinsman, even if there are other males in the household. For how can a chaste woman be tempted to deceive, when it is [so] easily found out?'

{3.4.9-12}

GOING ON A JOURNEY WITH A MAN

Accompanying a man on a journey shall not be an offence (i) for women who [customarily] enjoy greater freedom of movement and (ii) the wives of dancers, minstrels, fishermen, hunters, cowherds and vintners except if this is prohibited [by the customs of that community].   {3.4.22,23}

A wife shall not go on a journey to another village without her husband, particularly if she is with a man with whom she could have sexual intercourse [i.e. a man not included in the list of prohibited relationships]. Doing so shall be a punishable offence for both the woman and the man accompanying her, except when the man is a kinsman.

Adultery shall be presumed if the wife:
- meets a man [by prearrangement] during the journey;
- goes to an out of the way place with a man;
- accompanies a man who is suspected of having carnal intentions; or
- accompanies a man with whom contact is forbidden.   {3.4.16-23}

ABSENCE OF HUSBAND
CONDITIONS FOR WIFE'S REMARRIAGE

BEFORE CONSUMMATION

Kautilya says: 'The frustration of a woman's fertile period is a violation of a sacred duty.'   {3.4.36}

Therefore, a wife who is still a virgin shall be free to remarry as she wishes after she has waited for the prescribed period and with the approval of the judges.

[The waiting period shall depend on whether the husband informed his wife before his departure, whether the wife received news of her husband during his absence, and whether he had paid the full dowry.]

The prescribed periods shall apply [only] to the first four kinds of marriage.

Period of waiting before wife can remarry
(in menstrual periods)

	No news about husband - (period counted from date of departure)	News received (period counted from date of receipt of last news)
Prior information of departure given to wife	5	10
Departure without informing wife	7	12
Only part dowry paid	3	7
Dowry paid in full	5	10

{3.4.31-36}

AFTER CONSUMMATION/HUSBAND GOING AWAY ON A SHORT JOURNEY

Period of waiting before wife can remarry
(in years)

	No maintenance		Maintenance provided by husband	
	No children	With children	No children	With children
Sudra	1	2	2	4
Vaishya	2	3	4	6
Kshatriya	3	4	6	8
Brahmin	4	5	8	10

In cases where the husband has not made provision for the maintenance of his wife [and/or children], the family shall be looked after by trustees during the prescribed waiting period. After that, they shall be looked after, for a period of four to eight years, by the wife's kinsmen. The wife shall then be free to remarry, after returning the presents given to her at the time of her marriage to the [husband's] kinsmen.

If the kinsmen's family is in straitened circumstances or if the trustees abandon her, the wife shall be free to remarry (as she pleases) anyone who will relieve her of distress and look after her without waiting for the full prescribed period.

Special provisions:

The wife of a Brahmin, who has gone away to study, shall wait ten years [before remarrying] if she has no children and twelve if there are children.

The wife of a servant of the King shall not remarry [at all].

[In both cases?] [In the latter case?] she shall be blameless if she bears a child from a man of the same *varna* [in order to avoid extinction of the family]. {3.4.24-30}

AFTER CONSUMMATION/HUSBAND AWAY ON A LONG JOURNEY

The following conditions shall apply in the case of remarriage of a wife whose husband has left on a long journey or who has become an ascetic [renouncing the life of a householder].

The same conditions shall also apply to the remarriage of widows provided that the rules regarding widows' property rights are observed. {3.4.37}

In all three cases [long absence, becoming an ascetic and death of the husband] the period of waiting shall be:

without children	seven menstrual periods
with children	one year

After the waiting period, the wife shall seek to marry someone from the family of her husband, in the following order of priority:

- the only brother of the husband;
- one of the following brothers of the husband, when there are many:
- immediate elder or younger brother;
- one who is virtuous;
- one who can maintain her;
- the youngest unmarried one;
- if there are no such brothers, a male member of the husband's extended (*sapinda*) family;
- if there are none such, any male member of the husband's family (*kula*).

The above order shall be strictly observed. If the wife violates it and marries someone while spurning her husband's family, she, the man whom she marries, the man who gives her away in marriage and those who consent to it shall be given the punishment for adultery. {3.4.38-42}

ADULTERY

A kinsman or a servant of a husband who is away on a long journey shall keep an adulterous wife under guard till the husband returns. If, on return, the husband does not raise any objections, neither the woman nor her lover shall be prosecuted; otherwise the wife shall suffer mutilation and the lover, death.

No one shall conceal adultery. Anyone who catches an adulterer but declares him to be a thief [so that the culprit may escape with a lower punishment] shall himself be punished. No one shall take a bribe to let an adulterer escape.

The proofs of adultery are: finding the hair of one person on another, marks of carnal enjoyment, opinion of experts or the woman's admission.

{from 4.12.30-35}

[See {4.6.18,19} under 'Criminal Investigation', VIII.xii for a list of possible suspects in cases of theft and adultery.]

RENUNCIATION

No man shall renounce his marital life [to become an ascetic] without providing for his wife and sons.

No one shall induce a woman [still capable of bearing children?] into becoming an ascetic.

A man, who has passed the age of sexual activity can renounce family life, with the approval of the judges [who shall ensure that the family is well provided for] but if the judges do not approve, he shall be prevented from doing so. {2.1.29-31}

DIVORCE

There is no divorce in cases of marriages of the first four kinds.

{3.3.19}

[In the case of the latter four kinds] a marriage can be dissolved only when there is mutual hatred. Neither a husband nor a wife may seek a divorce on the grounds of unilateral hatred, if the other is unwilling to end the marriage. {3.3.15,16}

If a husband seeks a divorce on the grounds of his wife's misconduct, he shall return to her all he has received from her. However, if a wife seeks a divorce on the grounds of her husband's misconduct, he need not return to her whatever he has received from her. [i.e. one who seeks a divorce shall not benefit by it.] {3.3.17,18}

MAINTENANCE OF WIFE AFTER SEPARATION/SUPERSESSION

If the maintenance payments to a wife are to be made periodically, the husband shall calculate and pay the required amounts in [suitable] instalments.

If no regularity of payment has been decided upon, the husband shall provide the necessary food and clothing, or more than necessary, according to the income of the husband.

Such maintenance shall also be paid in cases where the wife had not received the dowry, her property and her compensation for supersession.

The husband shall not be sued for maintenance if the wife is supported by the family of her father-in-law or if she is [financially] independent.

{3.3.3-6}

PUNISHMENTS

(Fines in panas)

	Punishment by State	Rights of injured party	
Deception in marriage agreements:			
Hiding a girl's sexual defect	96	Man to get back dowry and *stridhana*	{3.15.14}
Hiding a groom's sexual defect	192	Girl to keep dowry and *stridhana*	{3.15.15}
Misrepresentation:			
Substitution of:			
a different groom	200	Girl can reject the substitute	{4.12.12,13}
a girl of same *varna*	100		{4.12.14}
a girl of different *varna*	200		
Daughter's right to marry:			
Marrying a man of a different *varna* but taking her ornaments with her	Punishment for theft		{4.12.11}

<u>Conjugal duties:</u>

Failure to carry out marital duties:			{3.3.2}
woman	12		
man	24		
Polygamous marriages:			{3.2.44}
Concealing or wasting fertile period (wife or husband)	96		
<u>Virginity:</u>			
Bride not a virgin at the time of consummation expenses	54	Husband to get back dowry and marriage	{4.12.15}
Bride claiming to be a virgin but found not to be so	108	"	{4.12.16}
Deception by substituting some other blood	200	"	{4.12.17}
Man accusing bride falsely of not being a virgin	200	Girl can reject him and keep dowry and not reimburse marriage expenses	{4.12.17-19}
<u>Incompatibility:</u>			
Husband falsely accusing wife of refusing to sleep with him	12		{3.3.14}
<u>Woman's right to property:</u>			
Husband using wife's property in *Rakshasa* and *Paisacha* marriages	Punishment for theft		{3.2.18}
<u>Polygamy:</u>			
Husband marrying another wife without waiting for the prescribed period	Maximum fine 24 panas.	Pay superseded wife her dowry, property and compensation	{3.2.40}

	of half the total of first two	
Cruelty:		
Husband abusing wife/ wife abusing husband	Half the fine prescribed in {3.18} for verbal injury	{3.3.9,10}
Husband beating wife beyond prescribed limits/ wife beating husband	Half the fine prescribed in {3.19} for causing physical injury	
Misconduct:		
Wife enjoying herself:		
drinking	3	{3.3.20}
going to see a show or on a pleasure trip		{3.3.21,22}
with women		
by day	6	
by night	12	
with men		
by day	12	
by night	24	
Leaving home when husband is asleep or intoxicated	12	{3.3.23}
Not opening the door to husband		{3.3.23}
by day	12	
at night	24	
Going out at night	24	{3.3.24} {3.3.25}
Sexual gestures or conversation		
woman	24	
man	48	
Conversation in a suspicious place	5 strokes of the whip on the back in public or 5 panas fine	3.3.26-29}
Touching hair, knot of lower garment, making marks with nails or teeth		{3.3.26}

of a member of the
opposite sex

woman	Lowest SP
man	Double above

<u>Prohibited gifts and transactions:</u> Gifts to a person {3.3.30,31}
of the opposite sex when it is forbidden; a woman's
forbidden business transactions with men.

	Man	Woman
Recipient is one with whom sexual intercourse is forbidden		
Small articles	12	6
Big articles	24	12
Money or gold	54	27
Recipient is one with whom sexual intercourse is not forbidden		
Small articles	24	12
Big articles	48	24
Money or gold	108	54

<u>Wife leaving home:</u> (except in cases of ill treatment by {3.4.1-7}
husband and going to the house of a kinsman with
good reason - {3.2.13} above)

	Not forbidden	Forbidden
Punishment to wife:		
Leaving home and going to		
the house of a neighbour	6	12
stranger	24	
Punishment to giver of asylum:		
A neighbour who gives the wife shelter; a mendicant who gives her food or a merchant who gives her goods	12	Lowest SP
Stranger who gives asylum, except in times of danger	100	B
Punishment to husband:		{3.4.14}
Preventing wife from going to the house of a kinsman for death, illness, calamity or childbirth	12	

Wife going to another village leaving her husband's house:

	Women who customarily enjoy freedom of movement and intercourse between the man and woman is:		All other women and intercourse between man and woman is:	
	Permitted	Prohibited	Permitted	Prohibited
Woman	12	6	24	12
Man (except blood relation):				
of same or superior *varna*	1/2 LSP	1/4 LSP	LSP	1/2 LSP
of inferior *varna*	1/2 MSP	1/4 MSP	MSP	1/2 MSP

[Furthermore,] in the case of a woman going to another village in the company of one with whom intercourse is permissible, she shall lose all her rights except support from her husband, who shall continue to have his conjugal rights. In case the man is one with whom intercourse is prohibited, the wife shall lose her support endowment and ornaments.   {3.4.16-20,23}

Adultery: {4.12.33,34;4.10.10}

Wife caught in adultery	Mutilation by cutting off the nose and an ear or 500 panas
Her lover	Mutilation by cutting off the nose and both ears or 1000 panas; [Death in 4.12.33] {4.10.10}
Helping an adulteress	Cutting off the nose and an ear or 500 panas {4.10.10}
Letting an adulterer escape with a smaller punishment:	
by making him out to be a thief	500 panas
by taking money from him in {4.10.14}	Eight times the bribe taken Mutilation by

| | cutting off both feet and a hand or 900 panas | {4.10.14} |

[Adultery was also a sufficient reason for banishing the guilty from the village.][6]

Maintenance:

| Man failing to maintain his wife and children, excluding those who had become outcasts | 12 panas | {2.1.28} |

Renunciation:

| Renouncing family life without providing for wife and sons | Lowest SP | |
| Inducing a woman to become an ascetic | Lowest SP | {2.1.29} |

Miscellaneous: Crimes against members of the family

For dragging by the hand a brother's wife	48 panas	{3.20.15}
Attacks against mother, father, son or brother		{4.11.13,14}
Reviling/vilifying	Cutting off the tongue	
Wounding a limb	Cutting off same limb	
Killing	Death by setting fire to the shaved head	

Family life

| Abandoning a dependant, i.e. father abandoning son; husband, his wife; a brother, his sister; a maternal uncle, his nephew; a teacher, his pupil. | Lowest SP | {3.20.18} |

VIII.vi

INHERITANCE AND
PARTITION OF ANCESTRAL PROPERTY

[Kautilya's description of the law relating to division of ancestral property is a succinct summary of the traditional Hindu practice, as given in the *Dharmashastras*. In this translation, the verses have been rearranged, starting with the general principles of partition, followed by the order of inheritance among successors.

The basic principle is that sons inherit, because a son has the responsibility for performing the ritual funereal and annual *pinda* ceremonies for his father. This responsibility extends to three prior generations—father, grandfather and great-grandfather. Among the sons, the eldest bears the primary responsibility and hence is entitled to a special share of the ancestral property. The eldest son also takes on the role of father towards his younger brothers, unmarried sisters, mother and his father's other wives. Inheritance bears a direct relationship with the obligations for the performance of rituals; a man adopting a son or fostering an abandoned one has the obligation to perform the initiation and other ceremonies. A consequence of this direct relationship is that the only son of a Brahmin born of a Sudra wife cannot inherit the whole of his father's property (but only a third) since he, not being a twice-born, is not authorized to perform the ceremonies for his dead father. Two-third go to those competent to do so, however remote the relationship.

Kautilya describes twelve types of sons, including sons conceived clandestinely, sons of unmarried girls, sons of girls who were pregnant at the time of marriage and sons from wives of different *varnas*. Of the different types, the most important, and the one taking precedence over all others, was the *aurasa* son—one born between a couple of the same *varna* married according to one of the four lawful forms of marriage.

In cases where there were no sons and the family line was likely to become extinct, it was permissible to have a son born to the wife by a close relative. It is likely that, for the purpose of begetting a son, the order of priority for choosing the man would have been the same as that for remarriage of widows and wives whose husbands had left them. See {3.4.38-41} in VIII.v above. The verses translated under this heading also answer the question of which property such a son should inherit—that of the mother's husband or that of the natural father.

The special shares and entitlements in dividing ancestral property are described in the last subsection. Special cases such as the property of a man with wives of different *varnas*, and of craftsmen, non-householders, prostitutes, mistresses, slaves and bonded labourers are included at the end.]

GENERAL

Partition of inherited property shall be made in accordance with the customs prevalent in the region, caste, guild or village [of the family]. {3.7.40} Sons, whose fathers are alive, cannot be [independent] masters of the [ancestral] property. {3.5.1}

[A father may divide his ancestral property among his sons during his lifetime.] In the case of such partition, the father shall neither show a special favour to anyone nor exclude any rightful heir from the inheritance without good reason. {3.5.16,17}

[If there had been no division of ancestral property during a father's lifetime,] a partition can be made after the death of the father. {3.5.2}

The laws of inheritance do not apply to self-acquired property (*swayamarjitham*) [but only to ancestral property], and that part of the property earned by using ancestral property. {3.5.3}

When there is no ancestral property, after his father's death the eldest son shall support his younger brothers, except those of bad character.

{3.5.18}

Some teachers say: 'If there is nothing to inherit, even mud pots can be divided.' Kautilya says: 'This is a contradiction in terms and is only a play on words. One can only divide what exists; there can be no division of the non-existent'. {3.5.23-25}

Liabilities shall be divided just like assets. {3.5.22}

Only those who have attained the age of majority shall receive their share of the partitioned inheritance. The share of minors, net of debts, shall be placed in trust with a kinsman of the mother or with village elders till they attain majority as shall the net share of any one who is away on a journey. Unmarried brothers shall be given, in addition to their share, an amount equal to that spent on the marriages of the other brothers. Provision shall also be made for the expenses of marriage of unmarried daughters.

{3.5.19-21}

Partition shall be made in the presence of witnesses and the property about to be divided and the specific share of each one shall be publicly announced. {3.5.26}

REPARTITION

A repartition shall be made if
(i) the original partition was wrongly made;
(ii) one inheritor had unjustly deprived another of his share; or
(iii) if hidden or previously unknown property comes to light.
{3.5.27}

If the inheritors live together [in a Hindu undivided joint family], repartition can be made irrespective of an earlier partition or there having been nothing to divide. {3.5.7}

Anyone who brings the ancestral property to a prosperous condition [so that there is something to divide] shall receive a double share.
{3.5.8}

PROPERTY WITH NO CLAIMANTS

If there are no heirs, the property shall go to the King, except for the amounts needed for the maintenance of the widow and for the funeral rites.

The King shall not take the property of a Brahmin learned in the Vedas without heirs; this shall be handed over to those well-versed in the three Vedas. {3.5.28,29}

The disinherited:
The following shall not inherit their due share:
- outcasts;
- the progeny of outcasts;
- eunuchs/impotent persons;
- idiots;
- the insane;
- the blind; and
- lepers.

However, the wives and children, if any, of the above (except of the outcasts) shall receive a share, provided they are not also impotent, idiot, mad, blind or leprous. If they also fall under any of these categories, they shall receive only [enough for their] maintenance. The children of outcasts, but never the outcast, shall also receive maintenance. {3.5.30-32}

ORDER OF INHERITANCE

Because a man's descendants in the male line up to the fourth generation [the man himself, his son, grandson and great-grandson] have the unbroken responsibility for the *pinda*[1] of the man, these shall have the right to the [prescribed] share in the property of the man, including that which was acquired using that property. Beyond the fourth generation, the property shall be shared equally [without preferential shares].   {3.5.4-6}

FIRST FOUR TYPES OF MARRIAGE

The order of inheritance of the estate of a man who was married according any one of the first four types of marriage shall be:

- sons, if there are [living] sons;
- daughters, if there are no sons;
- the father, if alive, of the deceased;
- if the father has died earlier, then equally between brothers and nephews [sons of brothers only] [subject to the condition below].

If any of the brothers has died earlier, his sons, however many they may be, shall receive only the single share of their father.

As between the father, brothers and sons of the deceased, the older among them shall not be made to be dependent on one younger. So long as the eldest son is alive, the youngest shall await his share.

                {3.5.10-13,15}

SECOND FOUR TYPES OF MARRIAGE

The order of inheritance in case the marriage was one of the latter four kinds shall be:

- sons, if there are living sons;
- brothers, or persons who had been living with the deceased;
- daughters.   {3.5.9}

Of uterine brothers born to more than one father, the inheritance shall be according to the corresponding father.[2]   {3.5.14}

NIYOGA (LEVIRATE)

If a person is disinherited [for reasons of being made an outcast, madness, etc. as described in {3.5.31}] the rule shall be: if the person concerned had been married before the event [of banishment, etc.] and if his line was likely to become extinct, his wife may bear a son for him by one of his kinsmen. A son so born shall get his share of the property [of the disinherited person].

                {3.5.33}

In the case of the property of a Brahmin dying without legitimate heirs, the wife may bear a son [*kshetraja*—born in the field] by a person of the same *gotra* or her kinsman; such a son shall inherit the property [of the wife's husband]. {3.6.24}

Some teachers say that the seed sown in the field of another shall belong to the owner of the field while others say that the mother is only the receptacle for the seed and so the son must belong to him from whose seed he is born. Kautilya [disagrees and] says that the son belongs to both [the fathers]. {3.7.1-3}

CLASSIFICATION OF SONS

The following are types of sons:

1. *Aurasa*	The son born by a wife he had married in accordance with all the rituals.
2. *Putrikaputra*	The son of a nominated daughter; he shall be equal in rank to an *aurasa* son.
3. *Kshetraja*	The son born to a wife by an authorized person [other than the legal husband], irrespective of whether he is of the same *gotra* or not. Clarification: If, when the authorized person dies, he had no other son, the *kshetraja* son shall be the son for both the fathers, have both *gotras*, perform the death ceremonies for both and inherit both properties. [If the blood father had other sons, the *kshetraja* son shall belong only to the family of the husband of the mother.]
4. *Gudaja*	The son secretly begotten in the house of a kinsman [of the husband]; he shall rank *pari passu* with a *kshetraja* son.
5. *Apaviddha*	A son, abandoned by his own family but brought up by another; he shall be considered the son of the man [i.e. the foster father] who performs the [initiation and other] religious ceremonies for him.
6. *Kanina*	The son of an unmarried girl. [Whether he belongs to the husband's family or that of the mother is not clear.]
7. *Sahoda*	The son of a girl who was pregnant at the of marriage.
8. *Paunarbhava*	The son of a woman who has remarried. Clarification: If the son is born of the husband [of the remarriage], he shall be a full heir of the father and of the father's family. If he had been born of someone else, he shall be the son of only the step-father (who performs the religious rites for him) but not have a share in the property of the father's family.

9. *Datta*	An adopted son, given away by formal ceremony;[3] such a son shall be the heir of only the father adopting him but shall not have a share in the property of the family of the adopted father.
10. *Upagata*	One who offers himself or is offered by his kinsman as a son [to another].
11. *Kritaka*	A son appointed in that capacity.
12. *Krita*	A son bought.

An *aurasa* son has priority over all others, even if born later. [See, 'Entitlements' below, for the share of other sons when an *aurasa* son is born.]   {3.7.4-19}

AMONG CHILDREN FROM DIFFERENT WIVES

The order of seniority among sons born of different wives shall be determined according to the following criteria:

- the son of a wife married according to the rites [i.e. any one of the first four forms] shall rank higher than a son by any other wife.

- the son of a wife who was a virgin at the time of her marriage shall rank higher than a son by a wife who was not [irrespective of when the sons were born].

- among sons of the same wife or among twins, the one born earlier shall rank higher.   {3.6.13}

PARTITION ENTITLEMENTS

AMONG CHILDREN FROM THE SAME WIFE

Daughters do not have a share in the father's property; they can, however, share bronze household utensils and their mother's jewellery, after the mother's death.

All articles, including unique ones, shall be equally divided among all the sons from the same wife, except for special shares as given below.

Kautilya agrees that the special shares shall be as suggested by Ushanas (reproduced below):

Division of animals in the property of the deceased:

Animals	Eldest
Brahmins	Best goats
Kshatriyas	Best horses
Vaishyas	Best cattle
Sudras	Best sheep

Middle sons shall receive the same kinds of animals but those which are blind in one eye or lame, and youngest sons, those which are not pure-bred.

When there are no animals: the eldest [of whatever *varna*] shall have an additional share of one-tenth of the property, excepting precious stones; the eldest has this special share because he has the primary obligation to perform the rites for his ancestors.

Personal belongings:

Eldest	Middle	Youngest
Carriage and ornaments	Bed, seat and father's bronze eating plates	Black grains, personal iron articles and bullock cart

The allotment of the special share of any son, particularly the eldest, shall be dependent on his having manly qualities, such as ability to manage the property.

Any son who does not have the necessary qualities shall receive only one-third of the special share due to him. If he behaves in an unjust manner, or if he lapses in the performance of his religious duties, he shall receive only one-fourth of the special share. If he is wanton [avaricious, lustful, etc.] he shall not receive it at all.

When the eldest son is disqualified, half the special share due to him shall be given to another who has the necessary qualifications.

{3.6.1-12}

SPECIAL CASES

[Among the different kinds of sons described in the provisions below] sons of the same *varna* shall have [only] a one-third share when an *aurasa* son is born. Sons of different *varnas* shall receive only maintenance.

{3.7.19}

If a man from any of the three higher *varnas* had wives from different *varnas*, the shares of the sons shall be according to the *varna* of the mother, as given below:

			(Shares)
Varna of wife	*Varna* of husband		
	Brahmin	Kshatriya	Vaishya
Brahmin	4	-	-
Kshatriya	3	3	-
Vaishya	2	2	2
Sudra	1	1	1

{3.6.17,18}

An alternative arrangement operates in case a man had only two wives, one of the same *varna* and another from a *varna* next below.

			(Shares)
Varna of wife	*Varna* of husband		
	Brahmin	Kshatriya	Vaishya
Brahmin	1	-	-
Kshatriya	1	1	-
Vaishya	-	1/2 or 1*	1
Sudra	-	-	1/2 or 1*

(*one share if the son is as well endowed with manly qualities as the son of the wife of the higher *varna*)　　　　　　　　　　　　{3.6.19.20}

If a man had two wives of different *varnas* but only one son, that son shall inherit everything but shall have the obligation of maintaining all the family.　　　　　　　　　　　　{3.6.21}

In case a Brahmin has only one son by a Sudra wife, that son shall have only one-third of the property. The other two-thirds shall go to a *sapinda* [proximate agnate] member of the family or to a *kula* [wider cognate] member, depending upon whom the obligation of performing the rites of the dead man devolves. If there are none of these, the two-thirds shall go to the man's teacher or student.　　　　　　　{3.6.22,23}

In the case of castes of craftsmen, (*Suta, Magadha, Vratya* and *Rathakara*), the sons who are proficient in the craft shall inherit everything and maintain the others. If no son is a skilled craftsman, all sons shall share equally.　　　　　　　　　　　　{3.6.14-16}

Mixed *varnas*: Children born of parents of mixed <u>*varna*</u> shall have equal shares.　　　　　　　　　　　　{3.7.39}

Bonded labour: A self-mortgaged Arya shall have the right to inherit his father's property.　　　　　　　　　　{3.13.14}

Slaves: The property of a slave shall be inherited by his kinsmen; if there are none, his master shall inherit it.　　　　{3.13.22}

PUNISHMENTS

Misappropriating family wealth	100 panas	{3.20.16}

VIII.vii

LOANS, DEPOSITS, PLEDGES, MORTGAGES, ETC.

[Chapters {3.11} and {3.12} of the text are closely related to each other. {3.11} deals with loans (literally, *rina*, debt) and <u>inter alia</u> with the law of evidence since, as Dr. Kangle says: 'The law of evidence was indeed formulated primarily in connection with debts'.[1] This branch of law has been dealt with earlier in section VIII.iv.

{3.12} deals with the following:

upanidhi	- deposits
aadhi	- pledges
aadhana	- mortgages
aadesa	- delivery orders
anvadhi	- courier deliveries
yachithakam	- borrowings
avakritakam	- hiring
vaiyavritya vikraya	- sale through agents
nikshepa	- entrusting articles to artisans and
mithas-samavaya	- secret agreements.

All these have this in common—they involve entrusting one's goods to another, the latter being in temporary charge of the goods. They are also related to debts in the sense that goods pledged or mortgaged for a loan, which may be interest-bearing. Thus, {3.12.1} states that the law on loans also applies to deposits. Similarly, the law about deposits also applies to pledges and mortgages {3.12.8,17}, delivery orders {3.12.21}, borrowings {3.12.24}, sale through agents {3.12.31}, articles entrusted to artisans and craftsmen {3.12.33} and secret agreements {3.12.52}. Hence, the general law on all such transactions was covered under loans and the general law on the nine types of transactions starting from pledges were covered by the law on deposits. The most important guiding principle on all such transactions is given in {3.12.53}. In this translation all these general principles are brought together at the beginning of the section.

Though all these transactions were similar in nature, each one had its own peculiarity. For example, a pledged article (inanimate or animate) could be used by the creditor for his own benefit (e.g. a house could be rented, a field cultivated, a cow milked, or a slave worked); special rules were needed to cover this possibility. Articles entrusted by one to another for delivery to a third party could be lost on the way through no fault of the carrier and rules are needed for this eventuality. Since Kautilya considered that all artisans were, by nature, dishonest, an elaborate set of rules and methods of investigation for establishing the guilt or innocence of the artisan had to be laid down. All such special provisions are included in this section with the exception of investigatory methods which are dealt with in VIII.xii.]

GENERAL PRINCIPLES

APPLICABLE TO ALL TRANSACTIONS

[For the reasons that will be clear from the law on loans and similar transactions], all agreements, with one's own people or with strangers, shall be arrived at openly, in the presence of witnesses and with all details such as time, place, quantity and quality [unambiguously expressed].

{3.12.53}

PRINCIPLES APPLICABLE TO LOANS AND ALL SIMILAR TRANSACTIONS

1. Suing for recovery:
    Debts mutually contracted between the following are not recoverable in law:
    - a husband and a wife;
    - a father and a son;
    - brothers in a joint family.
    A wife shall not be sued for a debt incurred by her husband if she had not agreed to the borrowing, though this rule does not apply to herdsmen's families or to farmers leasing land jointly.
    A husband shall be responsible for the debts incurred by his wife if he has gone away without providing for her.
    Farmers and servants of the Crown shall not be arrested for nonpayment when they are at work.   {3.11.21-24}
    2. Obligations of debtors and creditors:
    The obligation of a debtor [e.g. interest on loan] shall not increase if he is:
    - engaged in performing rites which take a long time;
    - ill;
    - under tutelage in a teacher's house;

- a minor; or
- insolvent.   {3.11.10}

A creditor shall not refuse [to accept the] repayment of a loan. [Nor shall a person refuse to return the goods pledged or mortgaged with him if the conditions of the pledge are fully met.] If there is good reason for such a refusal, the payment involved shall be held in trust by another with no increase in the obligations of the debtor.   {3.11.11-12}

3. Sureties:

Any surety given shall only apply to that particular transaction [and shall not be extended to matters extraneous to it].[2] Minors cannot legally be sureties.   {3.11.15,16}

4. Limitation:

A debt ignored [by the creditor] for ten years shall not be recoverable; this does not apply to minors, the ill, the aged, those involved in [unforeseen] calamities, those away on long journeys and those gone abroad as well as in times of disorder in the kingdom; [i.e. all cases where proceedings for recovery could not be started for valid reasons.]   {3.11.13}

5. Obligations of heirs and successors:

In case a debtor dies, the responsibility for repayment, with accrued interest, shall devolve upon:
- sons;
- heirs inheriting the property of the deceased;
- co-signatories;
- sureties.

When there is no limitation as to time or place, the obligation to repay shall devolve upon sons, grandsons and kinsmen who inherit the debtor's property, and any surety given in respect of guarantee of life, the performance of a marriage or land shall be fulfilled by sons and grandsons.
                                                               {3.11.14,17,18}

6. Many creditors:

Unless a debtor was about to go abroad, two creditors shall not simultaneously sue the [same] debtor. Even in the case of a debtor going abroad [and thus being sued simultaneously], the debts shall be recoverable in the order in which they were contracted; the debts owed to the King or Brahmins learned in the Vedas shall have priority.   {3.11.19,20}

PROVISIONS APPLICABLE TO DEPOSITS,
PLEDGES AND SIMILAR TRANSACTIONS

7. Exemptions for unforeseen circumstances:

A person entrusted with some property [e.g immovable property, an animal or a slave] shall not be obliged to return it if he himself was involved in [any the following circumstances of civil strife, Acts of God or of Princes]:

- pillaging of the fortified city or countryside by enemies or jungle tribes;
- plundering of villages, caravans or herds;
- breakdown of law and order;[3]
- extensive destruction of a village by fire or floods;
- loss of a ship by sinking or plundering [by pirates].   {3.12.2}

8. Use of deposits:

Anyone who uses a deposit for his own benefit shall pay compensation to the depositor according to the circumstances and also be liable to a fine. If the deposit is lost or disappears completely through use, the person entrusted with it shall compensate the depositor and pay a [heavier] fine. The same rule applies to a live deposit [animal or slave] which runs away [due to negligence or ill-treatment], except when the live deposit dies or is involved in a calamity.

A person to whom a property is entrusted shall not misappropriate, substitute, sell, mortgage or lose it nor allow live property to escape.

{from 3.12.3-7}

LOANS

[In addition to general principles 1 to 6, the following special rules apply to 'rina'—'debt'.]

Rules on charging interest:

No one shall recover interest without agreeing on the rate with the debtor at the time of making the loan.

Once agreed upon an interest rate shall not be changed during the course of the loan.

No one shall claim as principal the original loan with the accumulated interest added to it. [Interest cannot be charged on unpaid interest and claims for repayment of principal and interest shall be kept separate.]

No one shall claim repayment of a loan never made. Those who make such a claim and those who provide false witnesses who support such a claim shall all be punished.   {from 3.11.7-9}

Interest rates:[4]

The lawful rates of interest [on money lent] for different purposes shall be:

Normal transactions	11/4% per month [15% p.a.]
Commercial transactions:	
Normal	5% per month [60% p.a.]

Risky travel:

Through forests	10% per month [120% p.a.]
By sea	20% per month [240% p.a.]

No one shall charge or cause to be charged a rate higher than the above, _except_ in regions where the King is unable to guarantee security; in such a case, the judges shall take into account the customary practices among debtors and creditors.

Grains lent shall be repaid at the time of harvest one and a half times over [i.e. the grain lent plus half as interest—a rate of 50% for the crop season]. If not repaid [at that time], the value of the grain returnable shall be treated as a money loan and interest charged accordingly.

Commodity stocks: Interest on money lent on stocks of commodities, [actual or future,⁵] shall be paid yearly and shall be 50% per annum [until the loan is repaid]. Anyone who misses an interest payment deliberately or through being away on a journey shall pay an interest of 100%.   {3.11.1-6}

DEPOSITS

[See special rules 7 and 8.]

PLEDGES

SPECIAL PROVISIONS

Usufructory and non-usufructory pledges:

A pledge shall not be used by the person entrusted with it for his own benefit without the prior agreement of the owner. If he does so, he shall pay to the owner the profit earned less any interest due; he shall also pay a fine.   {3.12.16}

If an item pledged is useful [e.g. a cow whose milk can be used by the creditor,] no interest shall be payable on the money lent against it and the debtor shall never lose his right to redeem it; interest may be charged with prior agreement [in cases where the profit realised by use is inadequate to cover the normal interest payable].

If an item pledged yields no benefit, interest may be charged on the amount lent and the pledge may be forfeited [if not redeemed within the stipulated period].   {3.12.9-10}

Pledges of immovable property can be of two kinds—those which can be of benefit with labour [e.g. a cultivable field] or without [e.g. a rentable house]. In either case, if the net earnings are more than the interest due, the creditor can keep all the earnings and need not use the excess towards reduction of the principal.   {3.12.15}

Redemption:

A creditor shall not decline to return a pledge to a debtor who had come to redeem it. When a debtor is unable to redeem a pledge because of the absence of the creditor, he may deposit the amount due with village elders and take away his pledge. The debtor may also leave the pledge where it was after fixing its exact value; no further interest shall be payable and the responsibility for preventing loss or damage to the pledge shall rest with the creditor. If, however, the debtor apprehends that the pledge may suffer damage, he may sell it for the highest price obtainable either with the approval of the judges or to the satisfaction of the Protector of Deposits.

{3.12.11-14}

TRANSPORT AND DELIVERY ORDERS

SPECIAL PROVISIONS

There are two kinds of transactions in which a property is entrusted to another for [transport and] delivery to a third person. *Aadesa* is giving an order [to, say, a servant] and *anvadhi* is giving it to a courier or an agency [for a fee?].

The person in charge of the property to be delivered shall not be held responsible if:

- the caravan in which he was travelling does not reach its destination or
- he and the caravan are robbed and abandoned on the way.

If the person loses his life, not even his heirs and successors shall be held responsible. {3.12.18-20}

BORROWING AND HIRING

SPECIAL PROVISIONS

Anything borrowed or hired shall be returned in the same condition in which it was received. The borrower or hirer shall not be held responsible [for damage] or loss if the lender had placed restrictions as to time or place on its use, or if the damage was due to an unforeseen calamity.

{3.12.22,23}

WORK ENTRUSTED TO ARTISANS AND CRAFTSMEN

SPECIAL PROVISIONS

Artisans are [by nature] dishonest. It is not a custom among them to have a witness when things are entrusted to them. {3.12.36,37}

An artisan who hands over an object to anyone other than the person who had entrusted it to him shall be deemed to have lost it.   {3.12.34}

If an artisan is accused of misappropriation, the judges shall make a decision after enquiring into the character, antecedents and previous convictions, if any, of both the artisan and the accuser.   {3.12.35}

In all suits involving property entrusted to artisans, the judges shall enquire into how the property came to be in their hands, the various transactions to do with the property and whether the accuser had the wealth to be its owner.   {3.12.51}

When, after investigation, it is proved that the artisan had misappropriated property entrusted to him, he shall not only be made to return it but also be punished as a thief.   {from 3.12.41,44,48,50}

[Also see {4.1.2-3} under Consumer Protection in IV.vi for the responsibility of the appropriate guild for compensating a depositor in case of death of the artisan to whom the article was entrusted].

SECRET AGREEMENTS

[The same investigatory methods as in the case of artisans {3.12.38-50} are to be used.]   {3.12.52}

PUNISHMENTS

General principles:

Depositor not returning at the right time or place an item borrowed, hired, pledged or deposited	12 panas	{3.20.14}
Creditor refusing repayment of a loan or depositor refusing return of pledged goods	12 panas	{3.11.11} {3.12.11}
Person using something deposited with him for his own benefit (fine in addition to compensation to depositor)	12 panas	{3.12.3}
If the item deposited is lost or disappears completely through use; if a live deposit runs away (but not if it dies or is in distress)	24 panas	{3.12.4,5}

Loans:

Anyone charging a rate of interest higher than permitted	Lowest SP	{3.11.2}

Witness to a transaction in which a higher than permitted rate of interest is claimed	Half Lowest SP	{3.11.2}
Recovering interest without prior agreement; increasing rate of interest during the course of a loan; claiming principal and interest together as principal	Four-fifths of the amount as fine	{3.11.7}
Claiming repayment of a loan never made		{3.11.8,9}
claimant	Two and two-third of the amount falsely claimed	
anyone giving false evidence to support above claim	One and one-third of the amount falsely claimed	
Creditor refusing to accept repayment of a loan without valid reason	12 panas	{3.11.11}

Deposits, Pledges:

Mortgaging, selling or losing a deposit	Four-fifths of value	{3.12.6}
Substituting a deposit or allowing it to escape	Value of deposit	{3.12.7}

Pledges:

Person entrusted with a pledge using it without prior agreement of owner	one-tenth or one-fifteenth of value	{3.12.16}
For not returning borrowed, hired, pledged or entrusted objects at the due time or place	12 panas	{3.20.14}
		{3.12.11}

Delivery orders:

Not delivering the object entrusted	48 panas	{3.20.15}

Artisans:

One proved after investigation to have misappropriated an object entrusted to him	Punishment for theft	{3.12.41,44,48,50}

VIII.viii

PROPERTY LAWS

[Chapters {3.8, 3.9, 3.10} and parts of {3.14, 3.16} and {4.1} all deal
with property, both immovable and movable. Three verses of {3.16}
contain the laws about title to property.

The only common thread in the three chapters, {3.8, 3.9} and {3.10},
is that they all relate to immovable property. However, some verses
deal with civic responsibility in urban areas, others with use of irrigation
facilities, others with sale of immovable property, obstruction,
boundary disputes, etc. The rules governing building houses so as not
to annoy neighbours have been described earlier in VII.xi under
Municipal Regulations and those relating to irrigation in Aspects of
the Economy. Only verses concerning boundary disputes, tenancy,
sale of immovable property, and obstruction and damage to immovable
property are translated in this section.

{3.16.10-28} of are called, in the text, 'sale without ownership', i.e. an
attempt to sell something without having the legal title to it; these rules
pertain to lost property, recovered stolen property and enemy property.
Finally, the verses {4.1.49-55} dealing with treasure trove and found
objects are also included in this section.]

OWNERSHIP AND TITLE

In the case of owners who cannot produce proof of ownership of goods,
proof of continuity of possession shall be enough to establish title.

Owners who have neglected their property and let it be enjoyed by
others for a period of ten years shall lose their title to it. This rule does not
apply to [cases with a valid reason for the owners not taking care of their
property, i.e.]: minors, the aged, the ill, those afflicted by a calamity and
those away in another country as well as during times of national disturbance.

Owners shall lose the title to buildings which they have neglected and
in which they have not lived for twenty years. However, the mere
occupation of a building by a kinsman, a Brahmin, a heretic or a nominee
of the King shall not give the occupier the title to it. The same rule also

applies to deposits, pledges, treasure trove, women, boundaries, state property or property belonging to Brahmins learned in the Vedas.

{3.16.29-32}

IMMOVABLE PROPERTY

GENERAL

Houses, fields, embankments, tanks and reservoirs are types of immovable property. {3.8.2}

Disputes about immovable property are to be decided on the basis of the evidence of people living in the neighbourhood. {3.8.1}

A tax-payer shall sell or mortgage only to another tax-payer. Brahmins shall sell or mortgage gift land only to similar Brahmin owners of gift lands. A tax-payer shall not settle in a village exempt from tax. [Doing so is a punishable offence.] [However,] a tax-payer may settle in any tax-paying village and have the right to buy and hold property with the exception of [existing] houses, which can only be bought with prior permission.

{3.10.9.13}

A non-tax-payer, [even] if not living in the tax-exempt village, shall continue to enjoy the right of ownership [of properties in that village].

{3.10.15}

The owner of a field shall not neglect it at the time of sowing or abandon it for a neighbour to do so except in cases of some irremediable defect, an unforeseen calamity or intolerable conditions. {3.10.8}

If the owner of inalienable land does not cultivate it, another may do so for five years; when the land is returned, the cultivator is entitled to compensation for his efforts. {3.10.14}

BOUNDARY DISPUTES

BETWEEN VILLAGES

Boundary disputes between two villages shall be decided by a group from the neighbouring five or ten villages, using natural or man-made boundary marks. The marks shall first be described to the group by one or more of the following who do not belong to the side making the claim: elders among farmers or cowherds, or any outsider who has owned property there. The witnesses shall then lead the group to the marks described. If the marks are not there as described, the witnesses shall be punished severely. If the marks have been removed or destroyed, the culprit shall be punished. In case of absence of any marks, the land shall be distributed among the claimants in a fair manner. {3.9.10-14}

FIELDS, PASTURE LANDS, ETC.

The following shall apply to all disputes regarding fields, hermitages, pasture lands, highways, cremation grounds, temples, land for performing sacrificial rites and holy places: {3.9.23}

No one shall occupy the property of another except with good reason.[1] The occupier shall pay due compensation to the owner after deducting the cost of his labour and the profit due to him.   {from 3.9.19,20}

Disputes [about the above mentioned types of immovable property] shall be decided by the elders of the neighbourhood. If there is no unanimity, the decision shall be made either by majority or by adopting the opinion of those honest people who are acceptable to both parties. Otherwise, a fair division [down the middle] shall be made.

Where the claims of all the disputants fail, the property shall revert to the Crown.

All ownerless property shall also revert to the Crown; the King can divide it in any way he considers fair.   {3.9.15-18}

SALE

RESTRICTIONS ON SALE

Tax payers shall sell [or mortgage] immovable property only to other tax payers.

Land given as a gift to Brahmins and exempt from taxes and fines shall be sold or mortgaged only to Brahmins holding similar property.
{3.10.9}

RIGHT TO PURCHASE

The following shall be the order of priority of the right to purchase: kinsmen, neighbours, creditors, others.   {3.9.1,2}

PLACE OF SALE

The owner selling a house shall proclaim its sale in front of the property and in the presence of representatives from among the (forty)[2] neighbouring families.

An owner selling a field, garden, an embankment, a tank or a reservoir shall proclaim the sale at the boundary of the property and in the presence of the elders of the neighbouring village.   {3.9.3}

METHOD OF SALE

The owner shall name his price and ask three times: 'Who is willing to buy at this price?' If, during this time, no one has challenged [the owner's right to sell,] prospective buyers may make their bids.

Bids by proxy are not allowed.

If there is a competition among buyers and a higher price is realised, the difference between the call price and the sale price along with any tax payable shall go to the Treasury.   {3.9.3-5,7}

TAXATION

The tax [due on the transaction] shall be paid by the successful bidder.

{3.9.6}

RESALE

If the successful bidder fails to [pay and] take possession within seven days, the owner shall be free to offer it for sale again.   {3.9.8}

OBSTRUCTION/DAMAGE

DAMAGE TO FIELDS, ETC.

[The seriousness of an obstruction depends on the use to which the land encroached upon is put.]

The obstruction of an item earlier in the following list by one mentioned later shall be permitted [i.e. the later an item, the more important its use]:
    pasture;
    dry land;
    [irrigated] land;
    vegetable garden;
    threshing floor;
    building [for storing agricultural products];
    cart shed.

This rule does not apply to *ashrams* of Brahmins, *soma* plantations, temples and holy places in dry lands; [access to none of these shall be obstructed].   {3.9.25,26}

Anyone irrigating his fields from a reservoir or a tank shall avoid damage to the ploughed or sown field of another. If there is damage, adequate compensation shall be paid according to the extent of damage. In case the damage is extensive and affects fields, gardens and embankments, there shall also be a fine of double the damage.   {3.9.27,28}

All disputes regarding obstruction and damage shall be decided on the testimony of neighbours.   {3.9.24}

DAMAGE TO ROADS

A public path or road, including forest paths and roads to cremation grounds shall neither be obstructed nor destroyed by ploughing over. The prescribed width of each type of road[3] shall be respected. Breaking any of these rules is a punishable offence.   {from 3.10.5-7}

TRESPASS

The following shall not be considered to have committed trespass: beggars, tradesmen, drunks or madmen. Entry of close neighbours, when driven by force [of circumstances] or by a calamity shall not also be considered trespass, unless they have been [expressly] prohibited from doing so.

{4.13.5}

RESIDENTIAL PROPERTY

A tenant shall not continue to occupy forcibly a house from which he has been asked to leave; nor can a landlord evict a tenant who has paid his rent, except when the tenant is involved in a case of verbal or physical injury, theft, robbery, abduction or wrongful possession. A tenant who leaves of his own accord shall pay the balance of the annual rent.   {3.8.24,25}

LOST OR STOLEN PROPERTY

LOST PROPERTY

If anyone thinks that someone else has his lost property, he shall approach a judge for having the object seized. If this is not possible, due to [lack of] time or [the judge being in a different] place, the claimant may seize the object himself and produce it before a judge.

The judge shall then interrogate the person who had the [alleged] lost object how he came by it. If the possessor had bought it legitimately but cannot produce [before the judge] the one who had sold it to him, he shall be let off on his surrendering the object [to the original owner]. If the seller is produced, he shall in turn be interrogated and the same procedure repeated. The last person who is incapable of establishing how he came to have the object shall be held to be culpable. He shall pay back the price to the person who had bought it from him and shall also be fined for theft.

{3.16.10-16}

The claimant [of the lost property] can take possession [only] after providing the necessary proof. If proof of ownership is not produced, the claimant shall be fined one-fifth of the object's value [for making a false claim] and the property shall revert to the King. A claimant shall not take possession of an [alleged] lost property without the approval of the judges.

{3.16.17-20}

If a person is found with something of which he is not the owner, he can plead that it had strayed, been abandoned or discarded. If he can prove his assertion he shall be declared innocent, otherwise he shall be punished.

{4.6.13-15}

LOST PROPERTY OFFICE

The Governor-General of the City shall be responsible for the custody of lost property and strays [e.g. runaway slaves or animals]. {2.36.43}

A lost property office shall be set up in the customs house/toll booth.[4]

Lost property may be reclaimed by its owner on providing proof of ownership within six weeks [of its being deposited in the Lost Property Office].

The following charges shall be paid:

slaves	5 panas
one-hoofed animals	4 panas
cows and buffaloes	2 panas
small animals	1/4 pana
articles of high or low value and forest produce	5% of value

If a property is not claimed within six weeks, it shall revert to the King.

{3.16.21-24}

RECOVERED PROPERTY

A King who recovers the property of his own citizens from jungle tribes or enemies shall return them to their owners.

STOLEN PROPERTY

If a King is unable to apprehend a thief or recover stolen property, the victim of the theft shall be reimbursed from the Treasury (i.e. the King's own resources).

Property [unjustly] appropriated[5] shall be recovered [and returned to the owner]; otherwise, the victim shall be paid its value.

A King may, at his pleasure, allow any of his subordinates to enjoy specified spoils of war. This, however, shall not include keeping an *Arya* in slavery or keeping the properties of temples, Brahmins and ascetics.

{3.16.25-28}

[See Criminal Investigation VIII.xii for the procedure for investigation of lost or stolen property.]

TREASURE TROVE AND FOUND OBJECTS

All finds such as mines, gems and treasure trove shall be reported to the authorities; failure to do so is a punishable offence.

The reward to sweepers and cleaners for finding objects of high value, except gems, shall be one-third of the value. There is no reward for gems. The object found shall be taken to the Treasury.

The reward for reporting a find of a mine, a gem or a treasure trove shall be one-twelfth [of the value of the find] if the finder is an official and one-sixth otherwise.

Any treasure trove worth over 100,000 panas shall go [wholly] to the King. The reward for the finder of a treasure trove of value less than 100,000 panas shall be one-sixth of the value.

An honest citizen may keep the whole of a treasure trove if he can prove that it was ancestral property of which he was the rightful heir.

{4.1.49-55}

PUNISHMENTS

Immovable property:

Tax-payer buying property in a tax exempt village, selling or mortgaging to a non-tax-payer, Brahmin selling gift land to one not owning similar land	Lowest SP	{3.10.10,11}
Owner of a field neglecting it at the time of sowing	12 panas	{3.10.8}
Witnesses giving misleading information about boundary marks between villages	1000 panas	{3.9.12}
Anyone removing or destroying a boundary mark between villages to hide encroachment	1000 panas	{3.9.13}
Occupation by force of an immovable property like a field (list in {3.9.23})	Punishment for theft	{3.9.19}

Destruction of boundary marks between fields, etc.	24 panas	{3.9.22}
Encroachment into fields, etc. by removal of boundary marks	Lowest SP	{3.9.21}
Bidding on behalf of someone else	24 panas	{3.9.7}
Owner failing to hand over property after a sale	200 panas	{3.9.9}

Obstruction:

For causing extensive damage to another while irrigating his own field	Twice the value of the damage	{3.9.28}

Obstruction to roads   {4.11.13,14}

Nature	For obstructing or ploughing over	Reducing the width (1/4 of fine for obstruction)
Footpaths or paths for small animals (width—13 1/2 ft.)	12 panas	3 panas
Paths for large animals (27 feet)	24 panas	6 panas
Elephant paths and paths leading to [cultivated] fields (13 1/2 feet)	54 panas	13 1/2 panas
Paths to waterworks and forests (27 ft.)	106 panas	26 1/2 panas
Roads to cremation grounds and villages (54 ft.)	200 panas	50 panas
Roads leading to Divisional or Provincial Headquarters (54 feet)	1000 panas	250 panas
[Main] roads in the country-side and in pasture land [connecting villages]	1000 panas	250 panas

Tenancy: {3.8.24}

Tenant who refuses to leave when asked to do so	12 panas
Landlord who evicts a tenant who	12 panas

has paid his rent without due cause

Trespass

Trespass into another's house		{4.13.3,4}
by day	Lowest SP	
by night	Middle SP	
with weapons, by day or night	Highest SP	
Entry into a house, after midnight by climbing over		{4.13.6}
one's own house	Lowest SP	
another's house	Middle SP	
Into public parks		{4.13.6}
by breaking the hedge	Middle SP	

Movable Property

Seller failing to hand over movable property along with immovable property	24 panas	{3.9.10}

Lost Property:

Anyone who cannot produce a legitimate reason for possessing property claimed as lost	Punishment for theft	{3.16.16}
Making a false claim of ownership to lost property	One-fifth of value	{3.16.18}
Owner of alleged lost property keeping it without getting the approval of a judge.	Lowest SP	{3.16.20}
Anyone found with something of which he is not the owner:		
if he pleads, but cannot prove, that it had strayed, been abandoned or discarded	Return of object + equal value as fine	{4.6.14}
if he has no excuse	Punishment for theft	{4.6.15}

Treasure trove and found objects:

Sweepers and cleaners who keep gems found by them	Highest SP	{4.1.50}
Keeping a treasure trove of ancestral property without producing proof	500 panas	{4.1.55}
Not reporting a treasure trove	1000 panas	{4.1.55}

VIII.ix

LAW OF CONTRACT; REVOCATION

VALIDITY OF CONTRACTS

Any contract entered into, in person, by anyone with others of his own class, community or group shall be valid, provided that the contract is concluded in a suitable place and at a suitable time, observing all the due formalities, including presence of witnesses, and further provided that all the details [of the object of the contract] such as the appearance, distinguishing marks, quality and quantity are properly noted down.

{3.1.15}

Judges shall declare as invalid any contract that is concluded:

(i) in the absence [of any party to the transaction or of the object involved in it];

(ii) [concealed] inside a house;

(iii) at night;

(iv) in a forest;

(v) with fraudulent intention; or,

(vi) in secret;

provided that the following contracts shall be considered valid [in spite of falling under one of the above deficiencies]:

(i) absence:

(a) in a transaction concerning a loan, the absence of the object pledged; and

(b) in one where one party was absent at the time of the transaction provided that it is agreed by all others as a valid one;

(ii) inside a house:

(a) in transactions concerning inheritance, marriage, deposits, or articles entrusted [to an artisan], [even] if concluded inside a house, if the reason for so doing was that one of the parties was sick but of sound mind or was a lady who did not [normally] leave the house;

(iii) at night:

(a) those concerning robbery, trespass with criminal intent and provoking unrest;

(b) those relating to marriage or implementation of the King's order;

(c) those concluded by persons who [usually] carry on their business during the first part of the night [such as prostitutes, drinking house keepers and inn keepers];

(iv) <u>in a forest:</u>

(a) those concluded by persons who habitually live in [or travel through] forests [such as hermits, cowherds, hunters, spies, and merchants in caravans], if they happen to be inside a forest at the time of the transaction;

(v) <u>fraud:</u>

(a) those made by clandestine agents;

(vi) <u>secret agreements:</u>

(a) those entered into by members of any secret association.

{3.1.2,6-11}

Contracts entered into by dependants or unauthorized persons are invalid, unless the person was specifically authorized to do so. Examples are: a son dependant on his father, an aged father dependant on his son, a brother cast out of the family, the younger sons in an undivided family, a woman dependant on her husband or son, a slave, a bonded labourer, anyone who is either too young or too old to enter into contracts, a person accused of a crime, a wandering monk, a cripple or a person in distress.

{3.1.12}

Contracts entered into when one of the parties was angry, intoxicated, mad or under duress shall be invalid.   {3.1.13}

In the case of several agreements in series [on the same subject], the last one shall be considered the authoritative one. This does not apply to contracts involving hypothecation or entrusting a property to another for delivery to a third person.   {3.1.16}

REVOCATION OF SALE, PURCHASE AND GIFTS

GENERAL

Those called upon to judge the validity of the revocation of a sale contract or a gift, shall give their judgement in such a manner that neither of the two parties involved in the transaction suffer.   {3.15.10,19; 3.16.5}

SALE AND PURCHASE CONTRACTS

The seller shall deliver, and the buyer shall receive, an article sold under a valid sale and purchase contract unless:

- the contract is revoked within the time limit set out below;
- the article was defective;

- it was likely to be seized by the King,[1] stolen by thieves or destroyed by fire or floods;
- it was not up to specifications in many respects; or
- the sale or purchase was done in distress or under duress.

{3.15.1-4,9,10}

The period within which a sale or purchase contract can be revoked by either party shall be:

Traders	1 day
Agriculturists	3 days
Cattle owners	5 days
A collection of different types of articles	7 days
Precious objects	7 days
A going concern or business	7 days
Four-legged animals	3 fortnights*
Human beings	One year*

* - [In the case of living things the longer period is necessary because] it will take that long to ascertain their worth.

As regards perishable goods, a buyer may agree to revocation of a contract on condition that the seller does not sell the goods to anyone else.

{3.15.5-7,17,18}

GIFTS

The rules regarding non-repayment of loans also apply to gifts promised but not made.   {3.16.1}

[The following are the general principles applicable to loans and similar transactions {3.11.11-13,17,18,21,24} which are also applicable to gifts. Gifts promised but not made between a husband and wife or father and son and between brothers are not recoverable in law. Though a wife is not to be held responsible for gifts made by her husband without her knowledge, a husband is responsible for all gifts promised by his wife. Anyone to whom a gift is made cannot refuse it without good reason. A gift ignored for ten years cannot be claimed, except in those cases where proceedings cannot be started for valid reasons. Sons and heirs shall be responsible for the gifts promised by someone who dies before he himself had transferred them. Unconditional gifts, particularly gifts of land or wedding gifts, shall be honoured until the third generation.]

Invalid gifts:

Gifts invalid in law shall continue to be the property of the donor. Those called upon to judge the validity of gifts [judges or experts] shall disallow the following:

- a promise [made in extreme distress] by a man to hand over his entire property, his sons, his wife and himself;
   - a charitable [*dharma*] gift made to a wicked person or for an evil purpose;
   - a gift of wealth [*artha*] made to an unhelpful or inimical person;
   - a love [*kama*] gift made to an unworthy recipient.   {3.16.1-4}
A gift shall neither be made nor accepted if it is:
-, demanded with threats or intimidation;
- made in anger to force the recipient to harm another;
- made out of arrogance surpassing that of kings;
- accepted in fear of punishment, abuse or retaliation.   {3.16.6-8}

PROMISES NOT BINDING ON OTHERS

Any one inheriting property need not pay, if he does not want to, the following kinds of debts incurred by the deceased: sureties given, balance of fines or dowry due, a gambling debt, promises made when intoxicated or out of love.

PROMISES MADE WHEN IN DISTRESS

A person in extreme distress (such as when swept away by a current, engulfed in flame or attacked by a wild animal) may promise his rescuer everything—not only all his property but also himself, his wife and children as slaves. In such cases, [the promise shall not be binding and] the amount of reward shall be determined by experts. The same rule [of determination of reward by experts] shall also apply in all cases of assistance given to one in distress.   {3.13.35,36}

PUNISHMENTS

<u>Contracts:</u>
    For entering into contracts invalid *ab initio* for any of the six reasons listed above or those entered into by dependents and unauthorized persons:

for the proposer and the accessory	Lowest SP
for each witness	Half lowest SP

There shall be no [state] punishment for those who enter into such contracts in good faith but they shall bear any loss that they may have suffered.
    {3.1.3-5,14}

<u>Revocation of sale or purchase:</u>

Seller not delivering, without due cause, an article sold	12 panas	{3.15.1}

Seller not delivering movable property sold along with immovable property	24 panas	{3.9.9}
Selling perishable goods when, under a revoked contract, it could not be resold	24 panas or one-tenth of value of goods	{3.15.8}
Sale of bipeds and quadrupeds wrongly certifying them as strong, healthy or clean	12 panas	{3.15.16}
Buyer not accepting, without due cause, an article bought	12 panas	{3.15.9}

Gifts:

Donor of a gift under threat or intimidation; receiver who takes it out of fear	Punishment for theft	{3.16.6}
Donor of a gift made in anger or haughtiness; receiver who accepts it.	Highest punishment [for theft?]	{3.16.7,8}

VIII.x

LABOUR, BONDED LABOUR AND SLAVERY

[Chapter {3.13} and a part of {3.14} which deal with the law on labour and employment have given rise to a variety of different interpretations by different translators and commentators. The cause of the controversy is the question: 'Did slavery exist in ancient India?' Depending on the answer to this question, a number of theories on the nature of Indian society in Kautilya's time have been postulated—that it was prefeudal slave-owning, feudal or a society in transition.[1] The accepted view is that slavery, in the form it was practised in contemporary Greece, did not exist in Kautilyan India. This view is based on Arrian (derived from the first-hand observation of Megasthenes) that 'all Indians are free and not one of them is a slave.'[2] From this Kangle concludes that 'the *dasa* in India is not the same as the Greek *doulos* and was certainly no *helot*.' R.K. Mookerjee's view is: 'the supposed slavery in India was of such mild character and limited extent as compared with the slavery known to the Hellenic world that Megasthenes could not notice its existence.'

Nevertheless, the word *dasa* is always translated as 'slave'. This was a condition of 'unfree' labour, i.e. a worker, male or female, who enjoyed fewer rights than other categories of employees. Kautilya, in fact, uses a variety of expressions to denote different aspects of this phenomenon—*dasa* (a slave), *dasatva* (the concept of slavery), *dasabhava* (the state of being a slave) and *dasakalpa* (the rules regarding slavery). That even an *Arya* could be a slave is clear from {3.13.21}. Whether this kind of slavery was milder than ancient Greek slavery or the modern slavery of the African by the Occident can be debated; but the fact remains that *dasabhava* represented, in Kautilyan society, the most unfree state of labour.

Though any man, woman or child could be bonded and enslaved, the main aim of the laws of Kautilya was the protection of the rights of those most easily exploited, particularly women and children. The special position of *Aryas* (belonging to any one of the four Hindu *varnas*), particularly that of minors, is recognized throughout.

Dasabhava was the most unfree form of labour because Kautilya uses special terminology to distinguish two other forms of labour with limited rights. *Udaradasatva* is a concept of working in lieu of maintenance—a person in distress placing himself, with or without his family, under the protection of someone who looks after them in return for work. An aspect of the restriction of freedom of slaves and bonded labour was that they could not enter into valid contracts {3.1.12}.

A more important category was *ahitaka*—persons who were pledged or mortgaged against a debt. This form of bonding, almost always due to an inability to repay a debt, took many forms. One could mortgage oneself or one's slave in repayment of a loan or to work off a fine or a ransom demanded after being captured in war. In all these cases, there was a contractual obligation based on the amount owed and the time that had to be spent working it off. In this translation, the term 'bonded labour' is used to identify this type of unfree labour.[3] Even in the case of individual free workmen, Kautilya distinguishes two categories. Chapter {3.13} deals with *karmakara* and {3.14} discusses *brithaka*. Conceptually they are different. Judging from the context, the karmakara seems to have been casual labour engaged for a specific task while brithaka was labour employed under some kind of a contract.

The term *brithaka* has also been noticed in the context of *gramabrithaka* or village servants—i.e. blacksmiths and carpenters who did specialised work for the village in return for a contractual annual payment or a retainer, most probably in the form of grain. The conceptual difference between the two forms is maintained in this translation.

Kautilya also recognizes a kind of collective labour—a guild or a cooperative—which offered its services on a group basis.

The last three verses of chapter {3.13 35-37} have little to do with the law on labour and employment and appear to have crept into the text. They are translated elsewhere.]

GENERAL

The King shall enforce the laws regarding slaves and bonded labour.[4]

{2.1.25}

Changing by force the free or unfree status of a person is a serious offence punishable with a fine of 1000 panas. {3.20.19}

MINORS

An *Arya* minor [i.e. a Hindu child of any of the four *varnas*] shall never be sold or mortgaged into slavery. {3.13.4}

It is, [however,] not a crime for a *mleccha* [a non-Hindu or foreigner] to sell or mortgage his child. {3.13.3}

Selling or mortgaging an *Arya* minor of the same *varna* is a punishable offence; the higher the *varna* the higher shall be the punishment. A set of [more severe] graded punishments shall be prescribed for selling or mortgaging an *Arya* minor of a different *vana*. The seller, the buyer and the witnesses to the transaction shall all be punished.

Handing over a minor, when in distress, to work for another in return for maintenance shall not be considered selling or mortgaging the child.
{from 3.13.1,2}

If, in times of distress, an *Arya* family had bound itself as a whole [including minor children], a minor child or any one who can help the family shall be the first ones to be redeemed when the family has collected enough money to do so. {3.13.5}

BONDED LABOUR

APPLICABILITY

The regulations about bonded labour apply to anyone (i) who mortgages himself; (ii) is mortgaged by someone else; (iii) is sent, in times of distress, to work for someone in return for maintenance (*udaradasa*); (iv) works off a fine or (v) is captured in war. {3.13.16,18,19}

REDEMPTION

A bonded labourer who mortgages himself or has been mortgaged by someone else [against a debt] shall be redeemed by paying the amount owed.
{3.13.15,17}

An *Arya* captured in war shall be freed if he pays the ransom in cash or if he works for a period on the basis that the amount of bonding shall be equal to twice the ransom. {3.13.19}

RIGHTS OF BONDED LABOUR

The children of an *Arya* who has mortgaged himself shall be *Aryas* [i.e. they are not also to be considered bonded].

A self-mortgaged *Arya* shall have the right to keep what he earns on his own without prejudice to his master's work. He shall also have the right to inherit his father's property. {3.13.13,14}

Cheating a bonded labourer of the due wages or depriving him or her of the rights due as an *Arya* shall be punishable offences.[5] {3.13.7}

A bonded labourer [man or woman] shall not be made to carry dung, urine, dirty food plates[6] or corpses.

A female bonded labourer shall not be beaten, treated violently, made to give a bath to a naked man or deprived of her virginity.

For the offences against bonded men or women described above, the master shall forfeit the amount owed by them. If the woman against whom such an offence is committed is a nurse, a cook, a maid or an agricultural tenant,[7] she shall be freed. A woman labourer to whom a child of the master is born shall be entitled to leave the household.

Raping a pledged nurse is a punishable offence.

If a master himself rapes or lets someone else rape a virgin girl under his control, he shall not only forfeit the amount owed but shall also pay the dowry for her marriage and a fine of double the dowry.

{from 3.13.9-12}

OBLIGATIONS OF BONDED LABOUR

A bonded labourer shall not run away [from the household of the master]. A labourer who has pledged himself shall forfeit the right to redemption if he or she runs away. A labourer pledged by another shall forfeit if he or she attempts to run away twice. Both categories shall forfeit it if they run away with the intention of going to another country.   {3.13.6}

OBLIGATIONS OF MORTGAGER

The mortgager shall continue to be liable for repayment of the amount owed if the bonded labourer runs away, dies or cannot work. {3.13.8}

SLAVERY

Slaves are of four kinds—born in the house, inherited, bought or obtained in some other way [captured, received as a present, etc.]

{from 3.13.20}

The period within which a contract for sale or purchase of a slave can be revoked is one year, since it will take the long to ascertain the worth of the slave.   {3.15.17,18}

MINORS AND WOMEN

A minor, below eight years of age and with no relatives, shall not be made to work, against his will, in menial jobs or in a foreign country.

A pregnant female slave shall not be sold or mortgaged without making adequate provision for her welfare during her pregnancy. Procuring the abortion of a pregnant slave is a punishable offence.

All those involved in crimes against minors and women—buyers, sellers and witnesses—shall be punished. {3.13.20; 3.20.17}

Children born to a slave and her master: When a slave gives birth to a child of her master, both the mother and the child shall be recognised as free. If the mother continues to stay with the master and look after the house, her brothers and sisters shall also be considered free.

{3.13.23,24}

REDEMPTION

Anyone who fails to set free a slave on receipt of redemption money shall not only be fined but the culprit shall be kept in detention until the slave is freed. {3.13.21}

Resale of redeemed slaves: No one shall resell or remortgage a redeemed (male or female) slave without his or her consent. {3.13.25}

PROPERTY OF SLAVES

A slave's property shall pass on to his kinsmen; if there are none, the master shall inherit it. {3.13.22}

CASUAL LABOUR

WAGES

The agreement between a labourer and the one hiring him shall be made in public.[8]

Labourers shall be paid wages as agreed upon. If there is no prior agreement, the labourer shall be paid in accordance with the nature of the work and the time spent on it [at customary rates].

The customary rate for the following categories are one-tenth of what they had produced:

cultivators   crops;
cowherds   ghee;
merchants   goods traded.

The customary rate can be modified by prior agreement.

Special case of self-employed professionals: Those providing a service (such as artisans, craftsmen, minstrels, doctors, story-tellers, cooks, etc.) shall be paid a remuneration similar to others of the same profession or [in exceptional cases] as decided by experts in their profession.

Disputes about wages shall be settled only on the basis of the evidence of witnesses. If there are no witnesses, an on-the-spot enquiry shall be held. Denying that any wages whatsoever are due and not paying the wages for work done are both punishable offences.   {3.13.26-34}

CONTRACTUAL WORK

OBLIGATIONS OF EMPLOYEES

An employee shall not refuse to do the work allotted to him, if he has already received his salary. He shall be detained till he does the work and also fined.

If there is an agreement that no one other than a particular employee may do a specified job, that employee shall do the work accordingly; otherwise, he shall be fined.

An employee shall perform his duties at the right place and time and in the correct manner.   {from 3.14.1,4,10}

RIGHTS OF EMPLOYEES

An employee shall have the right, if he is ill, in distress, incapable of doing the work or if the work is vile:
- to have his contract annulled or
- to have it done by someone else.

Some teachers say that, if an employer does not allot work to an employee who has presented himself for duty, the work shall be deemed to have been done [and the employee paid accordingly]. Kautilya disagrees. Wages are paid only for work done and not for not doing it. An employee shall have the right to full wages only if the employer prevents an employee from finishing a job of which he had already done a part. An employee shall not be obliged, against his will, to continue working for his previous employer if he had completed the task allotted to him and already accepted employment under another.

An employee shall have the right to additional compensation if he does more work than agreed upon.   3.14.2,5-9,11}

OBLIGATIONS OF EMPLOYERS

If there is an agreement that only a particular employee may do a specified task, the employer shall allot the work accordingly; otherwise, he shall be fined.

If an employee does more work than agreed upon, his employer shall compensate him [app ropriately] for the extra work done.   {3.14.4,11}

RIGHTS OF EMPLOYERS

The employer has the right to:

get the work done at the cost of an employee, if the contract of employment has been annulled [for the reasons given above];

disqualify [for the purposes of calculating the wages due] work not done at the right time or place or in the right way.   {3.14.3,10}

COLLECTIVE LABOUR

The rules about rights and obligations of [individual] labour also apply to groups of workmen who contract collectively to do a specified task.

{3.14.12}

ADDITIONAL PROVISIONS

A workman sent by the collective labour group shall stay on a job for seven days; another shall be sent [for the next seven days and so on] until the work is completed.

The group shall neither remove nor send a workman without the approval of the employer. For abandoning the work without informing the employer, both the group and the workman shall be fined.

Workmen belonging to collective groups shall divide the earnings among themselves either equally or according to shares agreed upon earlier.

{3.14.13-18}

PUNISHMENTS

<u>General</u>

Depriving a person of his/her liberty; making someone deprive the liberty of another; forcibly releasing a person from bondage, slavery, or confinement; putting a minor under bondage or confinement, making someone else put a minor under bondage or confinement	1000 panas	{3.20.19}

<u>Offences against *Arya* Minors:</u>   {3.13.1,2}

Selling or mortgaging a minor—punishment for seller, buyer and each witness:

Offender	Minor of the same *varna*	Minor of different *varna*
Sudra	12 panas	Lowest SP
Vaishya	24 panas	Middle SP
Kshatriya	36 panas	Highest SP
Brahmin	48 panas	Death

Bonded Labour

Cheating a bonded labourer or depriving him or her of the rights as an *Arya*:		{3.13.7}
Sudra	6 panas	
Vaishya	12 panas	
Kshatriya	18 panas	
Brahmin	24 panas	
Rape of a bonded nurse:		{3.13.11}
one under his own control	Lowest SP	
one under control of another	Middle SP	
Rape of a bonded virgin:	Payment of dowry + twice the dowry as fine	{3.13.12}

Slavery {3.13.20}

Making an unwilling minor work in a menial job or a foreign country;	Lowest SP	
Selling or mortgaging a pregnant slave without making arrangements for her and her child: buyers, sellers and witnesses, all to be punished		
Not freeing slave after receiving redemption money	12 panas and detention till slave is freed	{3.13.21}
Rape by a man of a female slave due for redemption	12 panas and a present of clothes and ornaments	{4.12.28}
Reselling or remortgaging an unwilling or redeemed slave	12 panas	{3.13.25}

Deflowering the daughter of a male or female slave (when the daughter herself was not a slave)	24 panas + payment of dowry and ornaments	{4.12.27}
Procuring the abortion of a pregnant slave	Lowest SP	{3.20.17}
Stealing a male or female slave	Cutting off both feet or 600 panas	{4.10.11}
Kidnapping a slave along with money	Cutting off both feet and a hand or 900 panas	{4.10.14}
Woman having sexual relations with slave, servant or pledged man	Death	{4.13.31}

Casual Labour

Non-payment of wages	One-tenth of wages due or 6 panas whichever is higher	{3.13.33}
Denying an obligation to pay wages	One-fifth of wages due or 12 panas whichever is higher	{3.13.34}

Contract Labour

Employee not doing his work after receiving his wages	12 panas	{3.14.1}
Employee refusing to do a job when there was prior agreement that no one else should do it	12 panas	{3.14.4}
Employer not allotting a specified task to an employee in spite of prior agreement that no one else should do it	12 panas	{3.14.4}

Collective Labour

Sending a workman without prior approval of the employer—fine on the collective	24 panas	{3.14.16}
Removing a workman without prior approval of the employer on the collective	24 panas	{3.14.16}
on the workman	12 panas	{3.14.17}

VIII.xi

PARTNERSHIP

PARTNERSHIP/COOPERATIVES

Partners in an enterprise shall divide the profits among themselves either equally or by prior agreement [over unequal shares].   {3.14.18}

Once the work collectively undertaken has been started, no partner shall refuse to do his share of the work, except on the grounds of illness. Abandoning the partnership halfway shall be a punishable of fence.

{3.14.23,24}

ILLNESS

[The general rule in the case of a partner ceasing to be active due to illness is as follows:] when a partner ceases to take an active interest in the work [e.g. cultivation or trading] after it has begun but before it is completed, he shall be paid his share commensurate with the work done by him. He shall, however, be entitled to his full share if he provides a substitute to do his share of the work.

[There is a special rule for merchants travelling together and pooling their goods.] Because success or failure is equally possible on the road, a trader shall be entitled to his share of the profits as and when they are earned.   {3.14.19-22}

MISAPPROPRIATION

A partner suspected of embezzling partnership money shall be caught [i.e. made to confess] by promising him forgiveness and a continuing share in the partnership. If it is the first such offence, the promises shall be honoured. For the second such offence, he shall be thrown out of the partnership.

OTHER OFFENCES

A partner who leaves the place of work shall be thrown out.

If a partner commits a very serious offence, he shall be treated like a traitor [and ostracized].   {3.14.25-27}

CONCELEBRATION BY PRIESTS

All priests who participate in a ritual shall divide the fees equally or by prior agreement [over unequal shares]; each one can keep for himself gifts made to him for special duties.   {3.14.28}

Whether a ritual lasts one day or many days, priests who participate in only a part of the ritual shall be paid one-fifth, one-fourth, one-third, one-half, three-quarters or a full share of the fees due to them depending on the stage up to which they had participated.[1]   {from 3.14.29-33}

If a concelebrant falls ill or dies during a ritual, the others shall continue performing it; in case of death, the funeral rites of the dead priest shall be performed for ten days and nights, either by his relatives or by the other priests.

If the *yajamana* ['master' of ceremonies][2] dies during the performance, the priests shall complete it and be entitled to receive the full fees.

No celebrant shall abandon the ritual or the *yajamana* once it has started; doing so is a punishable offence.   {3.14.34-36}

It is not an offence to expel a priest from a ritual who is found to have [made it impure by having] been guilty of any of the following: not performing his daily rituals, not performing his special rituals,[3] being drunk, marrying a heretic, killing a Brahmin, having immoral relations with the wife of his guru, taking gifts from evil persons, stealing and performing rituals for a degraded person.   {3.14.37,38}

PUNISHMENTS

Partnership:

A partner in good health who abandons the work halfway through it	12 panas	{3.14.23}

Concelebrating priests:

A priest abandoning a ritual or its principal organizer halfway	Lowest SP	{3.14.36}

VIII.xii

CRIMINAL INVESTIGATION

[The topics covered in this section are: arrest, investigation of burglary and theft, dishonesty of artisans and craftsmen, unnatural death, and torture of suspects. There are three kinds of arrest—on suspicion, for possession and for a crime such as murder. Investigation of unnatural death also includes suicide and investigation on the discovery of bodies of strangers. Suicide was considered a heinous sin and no funeral rites could be performed for the dead; relatives were required to treat the person as a posthumous outcast.

Torture appears to have been common practice in the Kautilyan state to elicit confessions. There are detailed regulations regarding prohibitions of torture of some types of suspects and on prevention of excessive torture.

An investigating officer was liable to be punished if he held under restraint any one who was clearly not guilty {4.8.8} in VI.iv.]

ARREST ON SUSPICION

GENERAL

Because of the difficulties of [conducting a proper] investigation, no one shall be arrested for a crime committed more than three nights earlier, unless he is caught with the tools of the crime.

No one shall falsely accuse another of being a thief; doing so is a punishable offence.

Protecting a thief [by hiding him] is also a punishable offence.

{4.8.5,6}

ARREST ON SUSPICION

If there are adequate grounds [as detailed below], a person can be arrested on suspicion of having committed any of the following crimes:
- murder;
- theft [including robbery, dacoity and burglary]; or

- having a secret income from misappropriation of treasure trove, fraud concerning an entrusted article or spying for the enemy.

A person is to be arrested on suspicion if he is one:

- whose family lives [well] on a meagre inheritance, income or salary;
- who identifies himself fraudulently, i.e. misrepresents his place of origin, caste, *gotra*, name or occupation;
- who conceals his profession or calling;
- who spends lavishly on meat, liquor, dinner parties, perfumes, garlands, clothes and ornaments;
- who is prodigal;
- who spends his time in drinking or gambling halls or with loose women
- who travels frequently;
- who keeps his stay or travel secret from others;
- who moves about at odd hours in isolated places like forests and mountains;
- who has many meetings in secret or suspicious places;
- who has his recent wounds secretly treated;
- who always stays inside his house;
- who avoids meeting people;
- who is infatuated;
- who is inordinately curious about other people's women, wealth or houses;
- who has the tools of an evil trade;
- who moves stealthily in the shadows at night;
- who sells objects either at abnormal times and places or by changing their appearance [in order to conceal their original identity];- who is known to be an enemy;
- who conceals his low caste or occupation;
- who pretends to be a monk;
- who, though a monk, pretends not to be one;
- with a previous conviction;
- whose actions give rise to suspicion;
- who shows fear at the sight of soldiers; and
- who, at the sight of the Governor-General of the City or [similar] high official, does any of the following: attempts to hide, runs away, becomes immobile or agitated, or displays [symptoms of panic such as] a dry or changed face or voice. {4.6.2}

Peripatetic agents [who are to patrol regularly various areas inside and outside the city] shall arrest for suspicious behaviour any stranger, or anyone wounded, with implements which can cause injury, hiding behind a heavy load, appearing agitated, sleeping unnaturally long hours or looking tired after a long journey.   {2.36.13}

The Chief Controller of Shipping and Ferries shall be responsible for arresting the following if they try to cross by ferry:

- anyone who has stolen the wife, daughter or wealth of another;
- anyone who acts suspiciously or appears agitated;
- anyone who carries too heavy a load;
anyone who disguises himself as an ascetic;
- an ascetic who has erased the signs of asceticism;
anyone who pretends to be ill [to avoid paying the fare];
- anyone who is panic-stricken;
- anyone who carries secretly valuable objects, letters, weapons, fire-making equipment or poison or anyone who has travelled a long way without a pass.   {2.28.20}

BURGLARY AND THEFT

STOLEN PROPERTY

A trader shall not handle any article unless he is sure that the person who offers it has the right to sell or pledge it.

Information about objects stolen or lost, but not yet recovered, shall be communicated to all those who deal in similar goods. If any trader (who comes to know of an article about the loss or theft of which he has been informed,) were to conceal it, he shall be punished as an accessory [after the crime]. If he has no prior knowledge of its loss or theft, he shall be acquitted provided he hands it over [to a magistrate]. A trader shall not buy or receive as a pledge a used article without informing the Chief Controller of Private Trade.   {4.6.3-6}

If an article reported lost or stolen is found, the person who had it shall be [arrested, brought before a magistrate[1] and] interrogated about how he came to have it. He can plead that he inherited it, received it as a gift, bought it, had it made to his order or received it as a secret pledge; he can also adduce evidence about the time and place of its acquisition, the price paid, the quantity of material [used for making it], distinguishing marks or countervalue given [in case of a secret pledge]. If the evidence supports the plea, he shall be acquitted. If the person who claims to have lost the article also produces [satisfactory] evidence of his ownership, the case shall be decided on the basis of (i) who had it earlier, (ii) who had it longer or (iii) whose title is clearer. [Kautilya comments that it is not easy to judge questions of ownership.] Even among quadrupeds and bipeds there are similarities in appearance and form; how much more difficult it is [to distinguish between two similar articles] in the case of forest produce, jewellery and vessels which are [often] made from identical materials by the same maker?

The person arrested with the lost or stolen article may also plead that he had borrowed it, hired it, had it mortgaged to him or had it entrusted to him [all these cases involving an identifiable third party] and name the person concerned. If the person so named corroborates the pleas, the arrested person shall be acquitted. If the person named does not so corroborate, the accused can produce evidence about the reasons of the donor [denying his involvement] and his own reasons for accepting it; these shall be substantiated by evidence relating to the donor, his associates, anyone recording the transaction, the receiver, as well as by witnesses who had seen or heard of the transaction.   {4.6.7-12}

If a living being [animal or slave] strays, disappears or runs away and is later found, the person finding it shall not be held guilty if he can prove where, when and how he found it. If he cannot substantiate these facts, he shall be punished [for theft].   {4.6.13-15}

INVESTIGATION OF BURGLARY

Robbery from a house can be external by breaking into it, from within or both.

The entry or exit of the thief: [shall be investigated by looking for] passage other than through doors, uprooting of doors, holes made in them, broken lattice windows, entry into an upper chamber through the roof, tunnelling and marks on a wall in climbing or descending. Evidence of attempts to bury or transport secretly the stolen objects [shall also be looked for].

If the evidence such as the rubbish and tools left behind points to the cutting or breaking as having been done from the inside and if the knowledge of the things stolen could only have been gathered only from inside, the burglary shall be deduced as an internal one; conversely [if there is no such evidence,] it shall be deduced as external. If the evidence supports both, it shall be held to be a joint burglary [by someone inside abetting one outside.]   {4.6.16,17}

If an insider is suspected of having committed the burglary, the following shall be interrogated:

- a close relative who is addicted to vice, known to associate with ruthless people or is found to have the tools for burglary;
- a servant with similar characteristics;

- a woman from a poor family or one with a lover outside [the family];
- anyone who shows signs of: sleeping too much or too little; agitation; a dry and pale face; an indistinct or changed voice; restlessness; overtalkativeness; stiffness of body due to climbing; body or clothes cut, scratched or torn; hands and feet scratched or bruised; torn hair, broken nails or both full of dust; having just bathed and anointed one-self; having freshly washed hands and feet; having footprints similar to those found in the dust or mud [near the scene of the crime]; having garlands, wine, perfumery, clothing, unguents, or perspiration similar to those found at the entrance or exit.   {4.6.18}

Any one who displays the signs mentioned above can be either a thief or an adulterer.   {4.6.19}

If the burglary has been committed by breaking into the house from outside, the Divisional Officers and Record Keepers shall search for thieves in the countryside and the Governor-General of the City inside the fortified city, using the evidence gathered.   {4.6.20}

ARREST AND INTERROGATION OF SUSPECTS

Because interrogation after some days is inadmissible [unreliable?], no one shall be arrested on suspicion of having committed theft or burglary if three nights have elapsed since the crime, unless he is caught with the tools of the crime.   {4.8.5}

Anyone who is accused of being a thief out of enmity or hatred shall be acquitted.   {4.8.7}

Anyone arrested [on suspicion of having committed a theft or burglary] shall be interrogated in the presence of the accuser as well as witnesses from inside and outside [the house of the accuser]. The accused shall [first] be asked to state his place of origin, caste, family name, personal name, occupation, economic situation, friends [and associates] and residence. These shall be verified from others.

The accused shall then be interrogated about his movements on the day of the crime and where he stayed till the time he was arrested.

If the statements proving his innocence are corroborated, he shall be acquitted; otherwise he shall be tortured [to elicit a confession].

In case the suspicion is confirmed, corroborative proof of the following shall be sought: implements of the theft or burglary, advisers, accomplices, the stolen articles or agents [selling the stolen goods]. The modus operandi shall also be sought to be established with reference to entry [into the house], possession [of the stolen articles] and division [between accomplices].

If there is no such corroborative proof and the accused protests his innocence,[2] he shall be declared to be not a thief. It is likely that a person may be arrested on suspicion of being a thief [though not actually one] because of being accidentally present at the scene of the crime, of similarity in dress, weapons or articles with those of the thieves or [accidental] proximity to the stolen goods. A suspect may admit to being a thief, as Ani-Mandavya[3] did, for fear of the pain of torture. Therefore, conclusive proof is essential before a person is sentenced.   {4.8.1-4,9-13}

DISHONESTY OF ARTISANS AND CRAFTSMEN

If an artisan denies having been entrusted with an object and if there are no witnesses to the transaction, [the following investigatory methods may be adopted to discover the truth]:

- the artisan may be made to admit his being given the article by the investigator gaining his confidence and engaging him in a conversation in a garden, a park or at a dinner party, the admission being attested to by hidden witnesses;

- a valuable object or one with a [secret identification] mark may be used to trap the artisan. An old or sick merchant shall entrust the marked object with him and go away; [after a while] the merchants's brother or son shall ask for its return on behalf of the depositor. Or, a reliable person shall give the artisan a marked object, go away for some time and ask for it back on return. A third alternative is for a person pretending to be simple-minded and in fear of arrest for violation of curfew, to hand over at night a [marked] valuable object to the artisan and ask for its return, allegedly from the prison. In all these cases, if the artisan returns the object he is honest; otherwise, he shall not only be obliged to return it but also punished as a thief.

- [a secret agent may leave with two objects the artisan, one marked and the other unmarked.] He shall then ask for the return of both. If only one is returned, the artisan shall be punished for theft.   {3.12.38-50}

SECRET AGREEMENTS

The methods described for uncovering the dishonesty of artisans are also to be used to establish the truth in the case of secret agreements claimed to exist by one but denied by the other.   {3.12.52}

UNNATURAL DEATH

Anger is the motive for murder.   {4.7.18}

POST-MORTEM EXAMINATION

The magistrate shall conduct a post-mortem on any case of sudden [unnatural] death after smearing the body with oil [to bring out bruises, swellings and other injuries].   {4.7.1}

The examination on the cause of death shall be conducted [even in cases where it appears that the person had committed suicide by hanging] because, sometimes for fear of punishment, marks are produced on the throat of the body after the murder.   {4.7.11}

[Death can be caused by four ways of stopping the breathing (strangling, hanging, asphyxiation or drowning); two ways of physical injury (by beating or by throwing from a height); or poisoning (by poisons, snake or insect bite or narcotic drugs). The forensic evidence for establishing the cause of death is as follows.]

Symptoms:

strangling: urine and faeces thrown out, skin of the abdomen inflated with wind, swollen hands and feet, eyes open, marks on the throat;

hanging: in addition to indications above [for strangling], contraction of arms and thighs;

asphyxiation: swollen hands, feet or abdomen, sunken eyes, inflated navel;

drowning: protruding eyes or anus, bitten tongue, swollen abdomen;

beaten to death with sticks or stones: broken or dislocated limbs, body covered in blood;

hurled down [from a height]: limbs shattered and burst;

poisoning: dark hands, feet, teeth or nails; loose flesh, hair or skin; foamy mouth;

snake or insect bite: as above, with bloody bite marks;

narcotic drugs: clothes strewn about, body spread-eagled, excessive vomiting and purging.   {4.7.2-10}

FURTHER INVESTIGATION

In case death [is suspected to be] due to poisoning, the undigested parts of the meal shall be tested by [feeding it to] birds. If these parts, when thrown in fire, produce a crackling sound and become multicoloured, poisoning is proved. If the heart [or stomach] does not burn when the body is cremated, then poisoning is also proved.   {4.7.12,13}

MOTIVES FOR MURDER

In all cases of sudden death, one of the following can be the cause for anger, which becomes the motive for murder: an offence against one's wife or kinsman; professional jealousy; hatred of a rival; a trade dispute; a partnership quarrel or a litigation before a court of law.

In cases of death by poisoning or [suspicion of] hanging after a murder, the following are likely suspects: a servant who may have been excessively abused, verbally or physically, by the deceased; a wife who has a lover but [hides it by] showing excessive signs of grief; a kinsman coveting inheritance, wealth or a woman.   {4.7.14,15,17,18}

EXAMINATION OF WITNESSES

Those closely associated with the victim of the murder shall be questioned about whether the crime could have been committed by agents of the deceased, by thieves for the sake of money or by enemies of someone else due to mistaken identity. They shall also be questioned about who summoned the deceased, who went with him, with whom he stayed and who took him to the scene of the crime. Those who were near the scene of the crime shall be questioned individually about who brought the deceased to that place and whether they had seen anyone behaving suspiciously, i.e. armed, in hiding or agitated. Further investigation shall proceed on the basis of the information gathered from the above examination of witnesses.   {4.7.19-22}

UNIDENTIFIED BODIES

On finding the murdered body of a stranger, his personal belongings such as clothes, dress and ornaments shall be examined. Dealers in these articles shall be questioned about their meeting with the dead man, his stay in that place, the reason for his stay, his occupation and his [business] dealings. Further investigation shall be made on the basis of these enquiries.
{4.7.23,24}

SUICIDE

Cases of suicide by hanging shall be investigated to ascertain whether any injustice had been done to the deceased.

If any person under the influence of passion or anger, or any woman captivated by sin, were to commit suicide (by hanging, a weapon or poison), the body shall neither be cremated with rites nor shall the relatives perform the subsequent ceremonies. The body shall be dragged by a *Candala* on a royal highway.

Any kinsman performing the funeral rites shall meet the same fate [i.e. no rites, body dragged through the streets] on his death or be declared an outcaste by his relatives.

Anyone associating with those who perform forbidden rites shall lose the right to perform rites, to teach and to give or receive [ceremonial] gifts for a year. This shall extend to the associates of associates.

{4.7.16,25-28}

TORTURE OF SUSPECTS

GENERAL RULES

Only those about whom there is a strong presumption of guilt shall be tortured [to elicit a confession].

The following shall not be tortured:
- those suspected of minor offences;
- minors;
- the aged;
- the sick;
- the debilitated;
- those in a drunken state;
- the insane;
- those suffering from hunger, thirst or fatigue after a long journey;
- those who have eaten too much; and
- those who have already confessed.

A pregnant woman shall not be tortured; nor any woman within a month of childbirth.

Women shall [preferably] be [only] interrogated; if tortured, they shall be subjected to half the prescribed scale.

Brahmins learned in the Vedas and ascetics shall not be tortured, whatever the offence. Their guilt shall be established only by using secret agents. Torturing or ordering the torture of Brahmins and ascetics is an offence punishable by highest SP.

A person can be tortured only on alternate days and only once on the permitted days.

Torture shall not result in death; if it does so, the person responsible shall be punished.

The following types of criminals may be tortured repeatedly, either individually or together:
- recidivists;
- [those who confess and then retract] or [those who steal after vowing not to do so];[4]
- anyone caught in the act of burglary or theft;
- anyone caught with stolen goods;

- anyone who tries to rob the Treasury; or
- anyone who is sentenced by the King to death by torture.

{4.8.14,17-20,25-27}

METHODS OF TORTURE

There are eighteen—four for ordinary offences and fourteen for serious ones.
The four ordinary ones are:
- six strokes with a stick;
- seven lashes with a whip;
- suspending twice by the arms [tied together?] from above;
- the water tube [pouring salt water through the nose].
The fourteen kinds of torture for serious offences are:
- nine strokes with a cane;
- twelve lashes with a whip;
- tying the right leg to the head;
- tying the left leg to the head;
- twenty strokes with a *naktamala*[?] stick;
- thirty-two slaps;
- tying the right hand and foot at the back;
- tying the left hand and foot at the back;
- hanging from above by the arms;
- hanging from above by the feet;
- pricking with a needle under the finger nails;
- burning one of the joints of a finger after being made to drink gruel;
- making one stand in the sun for a day after being made to drink oil; and
- making one lie on a [bed of] *balbaja* points.[5]

The instruments to be used, the conditions, the methods of infliction, the duration and the termination of torture shall be ascertained from the appropriate Manual.   {4.8.21-24}

INVESTIGATION OF SUSPECTS NOT TORTURED

In case of suspects for whom torture is prohibited, the truth shall be ascertained by having them watched secretly by people of similar occupations, concubines, attendants in drinking halls, story tellers, hotel keepers and cooked food sellers. Otherwise, the methods of investigation suggested for trapping artisans who appropriate articles entrusted to them may be used.[6]   {4.8.15,16}

PUNISHMENTS

<u>Theft—false accusation:</u>

Falsely accusing another of being a thief	As for theft	{4.8.6}

<u>Lost or strayed living beings:</u>

Person who finds a stray animal or slave and cannot prove where, when and how he found it:		{4.6.14,15}
if not held culpable of theft	Compensation of value to owner + equal amount as fine	
if stolen	Punishment for theft	

<u>Suicide:</u>

Deceased	No funeral rites; body dragged through the streets	{4.7.25,26}
Relative who performs rites declared an outcast	Same as above; or	{4.7.27}
[Priests] who perform rites	Suspension from right to perform religious duties for a year	{4.7.28}

<u>Torture</u>

Causing death by torture	Highest SP	{4.8.20}
Torturing a Brahmin learned in the Vedas	Highest SP	{4.8.20}

<u>Murder:</u>

[For punishments for murder with cruelty see VIII.xvii.]

<u>Miscellaneous:</u>

Stealing from a corpse	Cutting off both feet or fine of 600 panas	{4.10.11}

VIII.xiii

DEFAMATION AND ASSAULT

[Kautilya says that the vice of causing injury verbally, or physically to another's person or property arises from anger. Injury to property is defined as not giving another what is due, taking away something from someone unjustly, destroying another's property or neglecting trust property. In Kautilya's view, causing physical injury is the most serious offence, causing damage to property less serious and verbal injury the least serious {8.3.23-36} in II.v. The punishments for crimes of this nature are found in a number of booms, particularly {3.18, 3.19 and 4.11}. Verses {3.19.8-10} have been omitted, on the grounds that these are clearly interpolations.[1] Verses {3.18.7,8} are ambiguous and different interpretations are possible; see Note on Translation 5.]

GENERAL

[In general, the fines prescribed for causing verbal or physical injury are for offences, without extenuating circumstances, against an equal in social status.]

The fines shall be increased or decreased proportionately as follows:

towards superiors in status	double the fine
towards inferiors in status	half the fine
towards wives of others	double the fine
if there is a case for diminished responsibility (mistake, intoxication, or temporary loss of sense)	half the fine.

{3.18.5; 3.19.4}

DEFAMATION

A verbal attack is of three kinds—simple defamation, aggravated defamation and intimidation. {3.18.1}

Simple Defamation:

The offense is categorized as simple defamation when a person is disparaged about any of his qualities such as his body, his nature or character, learning and attainments, profession or place of origin.

{3.18.2}

Defamation of physical characteristics: can be of three kinds, depending on the truth of the statement:

(i) true ['You are one-eyed', when the person was, in fact, blind in one eye];

(ii) false ['You are lame', when the person was not];

(iii) sarcastic ['What lovely eyes!', when the person was actually blind].

The punishment shall be highest for a sarcastic defamation and lowest for a true one.   {3.18.2,3}

Defamation of character, learning, profession or place of origin:

[The punishment shall depend on whether the person defamed belongs
to a superior or inferior *varna*.]

If one lower in the *varna* order (Brahmin, Kshatriya, Vaishya, Sudra or outcast) defames one higher, the fine shall be three panas and above. If one higher defames one lower in the order, the fine shall be two panas, decreasing successively.

The above shall also apply to defamation of the learning of professional story tellers, the profession of artisans, actors and musicians or the country of origin or persons from Prajjuna, Gandhara, etc.   {3.18.7.8}

Aggravated Defamation

Taunting a person with being leprous, mad or impotent or of low birth (e.g. a low Brahmin) is aggravated defamation.

The fines in the case of defaming an equal of having a serious malady shall be 12 panas if the taunt is true and more than 12 panas if false or used sarcastically.

The truth or otherwise of leprosy and madness shall be established on the evidence of doctors and neighbours. For impotence, the evidence shall be that of women or based on urine and faecal tests. The punishment for taunting a person as being of low birth shall be the same as the scale prescribed for defamation of character etc.   {3.18.4,6,7}

Verbal Intimidation

If a person threatens another with injury but is either incapable of carrying it out or pleads diminished responsibility (anger, intoxication or loss of sense) the fine shall be 12 panas.

For threatening someone with injury but not actually carrying it out shall be half that prescribed for causing that type of physical injury.

One who threatens another out of enmity and is capable of carrying it out shall provide a surety of lifelong good behaviour.   {3.18.9-11}

[Punishments for calumny, reviling elders and blasphemy are given at the end of this section.]

ASSAULT

Physical assault is of three kinds:
touching, [including pushing, kicking, throwing things and bodily restraint];
hurting; and
wounding.
If a person accused of assault does not file his defence within the permitted period, he shall be convicted of the offense on the same day [the period expires].
Attack by a group: If a number of persons are responsible for assault, each one shall be punished with double the relevant fine.

{3.19.1,16,22}

SCUFFLES AND AFFRAYS

Limitation: Some teachers say that judges shall not take cognizance of quarrels or assault which had happened some time earlier. Kautilya disagrees: an offender shall not go scot-free [just because of passage of time].

{3.19.17,18}

Judgment: Some teachers say that in a suit involving a scuffle, the case shall be decided in favour of one who approaches the court first, because he has run to the court unable to bear the pain. Kautilya disagrees: who approaches the court first is irrelevant; only the evidence of witnesses is relevant to the judgment of such a case. If there are no witnesses, the nature of the injuries shall be the basis for judgment.   {3.19.19-21}

Destroying property during an affray is a punishable offence.

{from 3.19.23}

[For punishments for stealing or destroying property during an affray, see Punishments later in this section].

DAMAGE TO PROPERTY

[Penalties for damaging public or private property, including animals, are tabulated below under Punishments.]

PUNISHMENTS

<u>Defamation:</u>

<u>Simple defamation of physical attribute</u>		{3.18.2,3}
if true	3 panas	
if false	6 panas	
sarcastic	12 panas	
Simple defamation of character, learning, etc. see Notes on Translation No.5		{3.18.7,8}
<u>Aggravated defamation against equal</u>		{3.18.4}
if true	12 panas	
false or sarcastic	More than 12 panas	
taunting about low birth	Same as for defamation of character; see Notes on Translation No.5	
<u>Verbal intimidation</u> but incapable of carrying it out or pleading diminished responsibility	12 panas	{3.18.9-11}
Threatening physical injury but not actually causing it	Half the punishment for causing that type of injury	
<u>Calumny and Blasphemy</u>		{3.18.12}
Reviling one's own village or country	Lowest SP	
Vilifying one's own caste or group	Middle SP	
Blasphemy of gods and holy places	Highest SP	
Insulting one's mother, father, brother, teacher or an ascetic	Cutting off of the tongue	{4.11.14}
<u>Special Cases</u>		
Insulting the king; divulging state secrets; spreading false rumours [about the king]	Cutting off of the tongue	{4.11.21}[2]

| Prostitute abusing a client | 24 panas | {2.27.12} |

Assault

Pushing, kicking or throwing
things:

Offences against an equal in status (Fines in Panas)
{3.19.2,3}

[Fines doubled or halved in accordance with {3.19.4} above for offences against
persons of superior or inferior varnas.]

	Below the navel	Above the navel	On the head
Pushing with the hand or throwing mud, ashes or dust	3	6	12
Spitting, kicking with the foot or throwing impure things	6	12	24
Throwing vomit, urine, faeces, etc.	12	24	48

{3.19.5}

Holding:

| Holding another by the feet dress, hand or hair | 6 panas and above | |

Restraining: {3.19.6}

| Trying to crush, bear-hug, twist with force, drag or sit on another | Lowest SP |

Throwing someone down: {3.19.6,7}

| without attacking further | Half lowest SP |

Hurting: {3.19.11}

Hurting with the hand	3 to 12 panas
Kicking with the foot	6 to 24 panas
Hitting with an object	Lowest SP
Hitting with a lethal object	Middle SP

<u>Wounding:</u>   {3.19.12-15}

Causing a bloodless wound with a stick, earth, stone, metal rod or rope	24 panas
Causing a bleeding wound with any of the above (except when bleeding happens due to an existing wound)	48 panas
Beating a person to the point of death without causing bleeding; dislocating or fracturing a hand or foot; breaking teeth; cutting off an ear or nose; causing an open wound, except when an existing wound reopens	Lowest SP
Injuring the thigh, neck or eye; any injury affecting speech, movement or eating	Middle SP + cost of treatment

<u>Striking another with a weapon:</u>   {4.11.3-5}

all cases except those below	Highest SP
in a crime of passion	200 panas
when intoxicated	Cutting of a hand
resulting in death	Death

Injuring the tongue or nose	Cutting off thumb and a finger	{4.11.25}
For injuring the penis or testicles of another	The same organ to be cut off	{4.11.24}
Making someone blind in both eyes	Both eyes to be blinded or 800 panas fine	{4.10.13}
Causing wounds which result in death	To be tried by magistrates; see {4.11.1,5} in VIII.xii	

<u>Special cases:</u>

A person of high *varna* beating or kicking a guru	Cutting of a hand and a foot, or 700 panas fine.	{4.10.12}

Wounding a limb of one's mother, father, son, brother, teacher or an ascetic	Cutting of the same limb	{4.11.14}
Prostitute causing physical injury to a client	48 panas	{2.27.12}
Disfigurement (cutting off an ear) of a client	51 3/4 panas	{2.27.12}
Anyone abducting, confining or disfiguring a courtesan/prostitute	1000–2000 panas depending on the status	{2.27.14,15}

Affray: {3.19.23}

Stealing someone's property during an affray	10 panas	
Destroying property		
of small value	Compensation to owner + equal value as fine	
of higher value	Compensation to owner + twice the value as fine	
clothes, ornaments, money or gold articles	Compensation to owner + Lowest SP	
Death as a result of a scuffle or affray		{4.11.1,2}
on the spot	Death with torture	
within seven days	Death without torture[*]	
within a fortnight	Highest SP[*]	
within a month	500 panas[*]	

[*]In these three cases, the cost of treatment of the injured shall be borne by the aggressor.

Abortion: {4.11.6}

Causing abortion

by harassing the woman	Lowest SP
by medicine	Middle SP
by a [physical] blow	Highest SP
Procuring abortion of a female slave	Lowest SP

Arson: {4.11.20}

Setting fire to a pasture, a field, a threshing ground, a house, a productive forest or an elephant forest	Death by burning

VIII.xiv

THEFT AND VIOLENT ROBBERY

[Robbery is dealt with in Book 3, but punishment for theft is in Book 4. Theft, which must have been a fairly common crime, is not dealt with under its own heading anywhere in the text. Two important aspects of theft (investigation of reported theft and a graded set of punishments for theft) are covered in {4.6} on arresting suspects and {4.10} on payment of redemption money in lieu of mutilation. In addition, the term 'same as for theft' is given as the punishment for a variety of offences throughout the text to indicate that the actual penalty should be varied according to the scale prescribed. Theft of precious metals by goldsmiths and silversmiths has been covered in IV.vi.

The chapter on payment of redemption money in order to escape mutilation also includes some purely monetary fines; strictly speaking, these entries should not be in chapter {4.10}. It would seem that the prescribed punishment in many cases was, in principle, cutting off different parts of the body according to the nature of the theft. Perhaps, as in the case of capital punishment accompanied by torture {4.11.26}, the cruel punishments were traditional, i.e. 'laid down in the Shastras by great sages'. A monetary fine was always available as an alternative to succumbing to mutilation. Since any one convicted could work off a fine in a state establishment {2.24.2 and 2.23.2}, or pledge himself and/or his family to someone in return for paying the fine, cases of actual mutilation may not have been many. It is also not clear whether theft and robbery were dealt with by judges or by magistrates, since these subjects are dealt with in Books 3 and 4.]

Robbery with violence is seizing forcibly a person or property in the presence of the owner. If the owner is absent, or if the seizure is indirect [e.g. by fraud] it shall be considered theft.   {3.17.1,2}

The school of Manu holds that the fine, in the case of precious objects, articles of high or low value and forest produce, shall be equal to the value of the goods seized. The school of Ushanas advocates a fine of twice the value. Kautilya is of the view that the punishment must be commensurate with the offence and agrees with the scale recommended by other teachers, as described below.   {3.17.3-5}

The school of Brihaspati advocates increasing the fines for one who instigates another to commit robbery with violence. Kautilya agrees, subject to the condition that only the basic fine [and not the multiple thereof] shall be levied if the instigation was done in a moment of diminished responsibility such as anger, intoxication or passion.   {3.17.11-14}

When a territory is newly acquired by conquest, thieves shall be removed from their usual places of residence and dispersed.   {13.5.15}

PUNISHMENTS

PURELY MONETARY FINES FOR THEFT

Stealing deer, cattle, birds, wild animals or fish caught in snares, nets or traps set by someone else	Value of animal + equal amount as fine	{4.10.3}
Theft of a small animal useful for its milk or hair, for riding or for stud	compensation to owner + equal amount as fine	{4.13.21}
Theft of deer or objects from protected or productive forests	100 panas	{4.10.4}
Theft of deer or birds held in held in captivity for pleasure	200 panas	{4.10.5}
Killing deer or birds in protected forests	200 panas	{4.10.5}
Theft of property of artisans, craftsmen, actors and ascetics:		{4.10.6}
of small value	100 panas	
large articles	200 panas	
Theft of agricultural produce	200 panas	{4.10.6}
Robbing a prostitute of her belongings or ornaments	Eight times the amount stolen	{2.27.23}
A soldier stealing weapons or armour	Highest SP	{4.11.23}

MUTILATION AND ALTERNATIVE FINES

Crime	Mutilation	Monetary Equivalent (in panas)	
Theft at holy places on festive occasions; pickpocketing or stealing money tied up in a garment			{4.10.1}
First offence	Thumb and forefinger (of right hand)	54	
Second offence	All four fingers (of right hand)	100	
Third offence	Right hand	400	
Fourth offence	Death, simple or with torture		
Stealing or killing [small animals such as] cocks, mongooses, cats, dogs or pigs of value less than 25 panas	Tip of the nose (Half for *Chandalas* and jungle dwellers)	54	{4.10.2}
Stealing a cart, a boat or a calf	A foot	300	{4.10.8}
Stealing adult cattle; a male or a female slave; stealing from a corpse	Both feet	600	{4.10.11}
Concealment or embezzlement of temple property	Blinding of both eyes	800	{4.10.13}
Theft of temple property such as images, cattle, persons, fields houses, money gold, gems or crops	Death	Highest SP	{4.10.16}

DEATH PENALTY FOR THEFT

Theft of a herd (of more than ten heads)	Death	{4.11.15}
Stealing or inciting to steal an animal in the Crown herd	Death	{2.29.16}
Theft of weapons or armour by one not a soldier	Death by firing squad of archers	{4.11.22}
Theft by breaking into the Treasury, government warehouses or the workshop of the Controller of Goldsmiths	Death by torture	{4.9.7}
Highway robbers	Impaling	{4.11.7}

ACCESSORIES AND ABETTORS

Helping a thief (or adulterer)	Cutting off the nose and an ear or a fine of 500 panas	{4.10.10}
Hiding a thief	Same as for theft	{4.8.6}
Giving food, shelter, tools or fire to murderers and thieves;	Highest SP	{4.11.9}
Advising them or helping them	Highest SP	
if done unknowingly	Reprimand	
Wife or son of murderer or thief		{4.11.10}
if not an accessory	Acquit	
If an accessory	Arrested and tried	

ROBBERY WITH VIOLENCE
{3.17.6-10}

Flowers, fruits, vegetables, root vegetables, cooked food, leather, bamboo and earthenware.	12 to 24 panas
Articles made of iron, wood or ropes; small animals; cloth.	24 to 48 panas
Articles made of copper, *vrtta*, bronze, glass or ivory.	48 to 96 panas

Large animals, human beings, land, house, money, gold or fine cloth.	200 to 500 panas	
Depriving a man or woman of liberty; making someone deprive another's liberty; forcibly releasing a person from bondage or slavery.	500 to 1000 panas; also given as 1000 panas in -->	{3.20.19}

INSTIGATION
{3.17.11-14}

With assurance of accepting responsibility	Twice the above scale
With promise of reimbursing the costs incurred	Four times the above scale
With promise of a specified amount as reward	Four times the above scale + amount of reward promised

VIII.xv

SEXUAL OFFENCES

[This section consists mainly of the punishments for:
—defloration of a virgin by a man, a woman or by herself;
—rape
—prohibited relationships such as incest, unnatural intercourse and bestiality.
Reference is also made to the right of a man to have sexual intercourse with a woman whom he rescues from danger. The punishment for guards who misbehave with a woman detained during curfew hours is dealt with in {2.26.41} in IV.iv.]

DEFLORATION

[Given the fact that the preservation of virginity of a girl until her marriage was an important preoccupation of Kautilyan society, defloration of a virgin was a serious offence; that of a minor was considered more heinous. This applied also to daughters of courtesans. The full set of punishments is given at the end of this section.]

{from   4.12.1-7,20-29}

RAPE

[Even] a prostitute shall not be enjoyed against her will; each member of a gang raping a prostitute shall be punished.   {from   4.13.38,39}

RESCUED WOMEN[1]

A man may, with her consent, enjoy a woman [previously] unknown to him, if she has been rescued by him: from robbers, enemy troops or jungle tribes; from being carried away in a current; if found abandoned in a forest, during a famine or due to civil disturbance; if lost or left for dead.

If she is unwilling, of higher *varna* or caste, already a mother, saved by the King's forces or by her own kinsmen, he shall not enjoy her but restore her on payment of a ransom.   {4.12.36-40}

PROHIBITED RELATIONSHIPS

TEACHERS

Sexual relations with the wife of a teacher is prohibited.

{from 4.13.30}

ASCETICS

Both the man and the woman who have taken the vow [of an ascetic] if found to have had sexual relations, shall be punished. {4.13.36}

INCEST

For a man, sexual relations with the following are prohibited, under pain of punishment of cutting off the penis and both testicles and death thereafter: aunt (sister of mother or father); wife of maternal uncle; daughter-in-law; daughter or sister.

Any woman who permits such a relationship shall also be sentenced to death. {4.13.30,31}

BETWEEN *VARNAS*

A person of inferior *varna* shall not have sexual relations with an unprotected Brahmin woman; the lower the *varna* of the man, the higher shall be the punishment. {from 4.13.32}

ROYALTY

Any man [caught] having sexual relations with the Queen shall be boiled alive. {4.13.33}

SLAVES, ETC.

A woman shall not have sexual relations with a slave, a servant or a pledged man. {4.13.31}

OUTCASTS

No *Arya* [male] shall have sexual relations with a *Svapaka* woman. Those of the three higher *varnas* shall be branded [with the brand of a headless torso] and exiled; a *Sudra* shall [cease to be an *Arya*] and become a *Svapaka* himself.

A *Svapaka* man [caught] having sexual relations with an *Arya* woman shall be condemned to death.

A *Svapaka* woman [caught] having relations with an *Arya* male shall be mutilated by having her ears and nose cut off. {4.13.34,35}

UNNATURAL INTERCOURSE

Having sex with a man or with a woman other than vaginally are punishable offences.   {4.13.40}

BESTIALITY

He who forgets himself so much that he has sex with beasts shall be fined 12 panas; for doing so with images of goddesses, 24 panas.[2] {4.13.41}

PUNISHMENTS

DEFLORATION

Deflowering by a man of a minor girl (not yet attained puberty)

of the same *varna*	Cutting off a hand or fine of 400 panas	{4.12.1,2}
if the girl dies	Death	

Deflowering by a man of a virgin (after puberty):

Girl not willing to marry violator (who will have no right to marry the girl)	Cutting off middle and index fingers or fine of 200 panas + payment of compensation to the father of the girl	{4.12.3-5}
Girl willing to marry violator		{4.12.6}
man	54 panas	
girl	27 panas	
Girl betrothed to someone else (and dowry received)	Cutting off of hand or fine of 400 panas + repayment of the dowry	{4.12.7}

Defloration by a woman:

Girl of the same *varna* and willing		{4.12.20,21}
girl	12 panas	
violator	24 panas	
Girl unwilling (heavier punishment for violator satisfying her passion)	100 panas + dowry	

Auto-defloration: {4.12.22}

Any girl who deflowers herself shall become the King's slave.

Defloration outside the girl's own village:	Twice the prescribed punishment	{4.12.23}

Defloration of virgin daughters of prostitutes, slaves, etc.:

Of a courtesan	54 panas + dowry at sixteen times the rate for a visit	{4.12.26-28}
Using coercive methods to deflower a virgin from a prostitute's family		{2.27.13}
girl consenting	Lowest SP	
girl unwilling	Highest SP	
Daughter of a male or female slave, but one who is herself not a slave	24 panas + payment of dowry and ornaments	
Of a slave held for ransom	12 panas + payment for clothes and ornaments	
False accusation of loss of virginity	Twice the prescribed punishment	{4.12.23}

ABDUCTION

Abduction of a virgin:		{4.12.24,25}
without her jewellery	200 panas	
with her jewellery	Highest SP	

(If many persons are involved in the abduction of a virgin, each one shall pay the prescribed fine.)

Abettors/Accessories:

For giving help or shelter	Same as for the offender	{4.12.29}

RAPE

Rape of minor girls and unmarried girls	See above under defloration	
Rape of a bonded nurse:		{3.13.11}
one under his own control	Lowest SP	
one under control of another	Middle SP	

Rape of a bonded virgin:	Payment of dowry + twice the dowry as fine	{3.13.12}
an Arya minor	Death	
Jailor raping		
a married slave or a mortgagee wife of a prisoner	Lowest SP Middle SP	
an Arya woman	Highest SP	
Rape by a man of a female slave due for redemption	12 panas and a present of clothes and ornaments	{4.12.28}
Raping a widow living by herself	100 panas	{3.20.16}
Raping a prostitute	12 panas	{4.13.38}
Gang rape of a prostitute	24 panas for each offender	

PROHIBITED RELATIONSHIPS

<u>Teacher's wife:</u>		
Man	Cutting off of penis and testicles and then death	{4.13.30,31}
<u>Woman ascetic:</u>		{4.13.36,37}
the man	24 panas	
consenting woman ascetic	24 panas	
<u>Royalty</u>		
Man having relations with the Queen	Boiled alive	{4.13.33}
<u>Slaves, etc.:</u>		
Woman having relations with a slave, a servant or a pledged man	Death	{4.13.31}
<u>Outcasts:</u>		{4.13.34,35}
Arya having relations with a *Svapaka* woman		
the three higher *varnas*	Branded and exiled	
Sudra	Demoted to a *Svapaka*	

Svapaka man having relations with an *Arya* woman:

man	Death
woman	cutting off of nose and both ears

Incest:

Sexual relations between a man and his maternal or paternal aunt, maternal uncle's wife, daughter-in-law, daughter or sister	{4.13.30,31}
man	Cutting off of penis and testicles and then death
consenting woman	Death

Unprotected Brahmin woman: {4.13.32}

Kshatriya man	Highest SP
Vaishya man	Confiscation of his entire property
Sudra	Burnt alive

UNNATURAL INTERCOURSE

Between man and woman (unnaturally)	Lowest SP	{4.13.40}
Homosexuality between men	Lowest SP	

BESTIALITY AND BLASPHEMY

Bestiality	12 panas	{4.13.41}
Sex with images of goddesses	24 panas	{4.13.41}

VIII.xvi

PRISONS, LOCK-UPS AND WELFARE OF PRISONERS

[Imprisonment, as such, is not prescribed as a punishment anywhere in the *Arthashastra*. People were locked because they were under investigation for a serious offence or unable to pay a fine imposed on them. There were two types of jails—prisons for those convicted by judges and lock-ups for those punished by high officials for non-payment of fines. Only the Chief Superintendent of Jails, *Bandhanagaradhyaksha*, who is mentioned in only one verse, {4.9.22}, had the authority to order the harassment or torture of prisoners. A large part of the regulations are conceived with protection of the welfare of the prisoners in mind.]

PRISONS AND LOCK-UPS

The lock-ups for [those remanded in custody by] judges shall be separate from the prisons for [those sentenced by] high officials. Both these shall have well guarded rooms and with separate accommodation for men and women. They shall have halls [for common use?], a water well, latrines and bath rooms. Adequate precautions shall be taken against fire and poisonous insects.   {from 2.5.5,6}

RESPONSIBILITIES OF PRISON OFFICERS

CUSTODY

A warder of a remand lock-up shall not set free or allow the escape of a person remanded into judicial custody.

A jailer who sets free or allows the escape of a prisoner shall [not only] be condemned to death [but also] have his entire property confiscated.
{from 4.9.22,27}

Without the approval of the Chief Superintendent of Jails a jailer shall not:
- allow a prisoner free movement;
- torture any prisoner;

- change the place [or status] of confinement;
- withhold food and drink;
- torment, maim or kill a prisoner. {from 4.9.23}

WELFARE OF THOSE IN CUSTODY

An officer in charge of a prison or a judicial lock-up shall not harass those in custody by:
- hindering [their daily essential activities such as] sleeping, sitting down, eating, exercise or going to the lavatory; or
- tying any of them down in one place. {from 4.9.21}

WELFARE OF WOMEN PRISONERS

It is a serious offence for a jailer or a prisoner to rape a married woman in custody who is:
- either a slave or has been pledged;
- the wife of someone in custody [such as] a thief or someone locked up for causing civil disturbance; or
- an Arya woman. {from 4.9.24,25}

RELEASE OF PRISONERS

Continuing to confine anyone acquitted is a punishable offence.
{from 4.8.8}

The Governor-General of the City may release some prisoners every day or [at least] once in five days for the following reasons:
- if they had paid off, by their work, the amount owed by them;
- after receiving a payment for redemption; or
- if they agree to corporal punishment in lieu of imprisonment.
{2.36.46}

Charitable persons can secure the freedom of a prisoner by paying redemption money in accordance with the crime.

A prisoner can also be redeemed by anyone coming to an agreement with him or her [undertaking to work in return for the redemption money paid]. {2.36.45}

GENERAL AMNESTY

Children, old people, the sick and the helpless shall be released every month on full moon days and on the day of the King's birth star.
{2.36.44}

SPECIAL AMNESTY

Prisoners are usually set free when:
- a new country has been conquered;
- the Crown Prince is installed;
- a son is born to the King.   {2.36.47; 13.5.11}

PUNISHMENTS

Duties of jailers

Holding anyone acquitted in custody	Lowest SP	{4.8.8}

Setting free, allowing the escape, or assisting the escape: {4.9.22,23,27}

Warder of judicial lock-up (without damaging the lock-up)	Middle SP + payment of amount involved in the suit
If by breaking the lock-up	Death
Jailer of prison	Confiscation of property and death

Jailer who, without the approval of the Chief   {4.9.23}

Superintendent of Prisons:

allows a prisoner free movement	24 panas
tortures a prisoner	48 panas
changes the place or status of a prisoner	96 panas
withholds food or drink	96 panas
torments or maims a prisoner	Middle SP
kills a prisoner	1000 panas

Welfare of persons in custody: {4.9.21}

Hindering daily activities like eating, sleeping, etc.—the jailer who does so and the one who gives him the order	3 panas and above

<u>Women prisoners:</u>

Warder of judicial lock-up raping a
woman locked up for curfew
violations:[1]

a slave	Lowest SP
an Arya woman	Death

Jailer raping:

a married slave or a mortgagee	Lowest SP
wife of a prisoner	Middle SP
an Arya woman	Highest SP
Prisoner raping a woman prisoner	Death (immediate execution)

VIII.xvii

THE PENAL SYSTEM

[The highly centralized Kautilyan state was regulated by an elaborate system of penalties. That is why the *Arthashastra* (economics) is also called *dandaniti* (the science of punishment). The aims of punishment were to maintain social order; to prevent misbehaviour by civil servants, including exploitation of the public and causing loss to state revenue; and to avoid the danger of disaffection, revolts and rebellions. The punishment ranged from as little as one-eighth of a pana to death with torture or impaling on a stake.

Kautilya repeatedly admonishes that the punishment awarded must always be just, neither too lenient nor too harsh. This does not mean that no leniency or clemency was to be shown. The prescribed penalties could be modified to take into account both the prevailing local conditions as well as the particular circumstances of the case under trial. Leniency was to be shown to anyone in distress. Often lesser punishments are prescribed if a crime was committed through ignorance or inadvertence. For example, an official who caused loss to the treasury through ignorance suffered only censure {2.5.19}. Diminished responsibility (inadvertence, intoxication or temporary insanity) could be pleaded and, if accepted, a lower penalty was imposed {3.18.5, 3.19.4}.

There were rewards as well as punishments. A civil servant who performed his task well was made permanent {2.9.36}. People who accomplished things beneficial to the community were honoured.

Chapter 10 of Book 4 contains a list of crimes for which the punishment is mutilation or amputation, which could be avoided by paying a monetary compensation appropriate to the organ. Some of the crimes listed have been reclassified according to subject in previous sections.

Chapter 11 of Book 4 is titled 'Capital punishment, with or without torture', but is in fact a miscellany of punishments, some of which have little to do with the death sentence.

In the course of making this translation, a comprehensive list of all penalties classified by type was made; this could not be included for want of space.]

PRINCIPLES OF THE PENAL CODE

Only the Rule of Law can guarantee security of life and the welfare of the people. {1.5.2}

The maintenance of law and order by the use of punishment is the science of government (*dandaniti*). {from 1.4.3}

It is the power of punishment alone which, when exercised impartially in proportion to guilt and irrespective of whether the person punished is the king's son or the enemy, that protects this world and the next. {3.1.42}

A severe king [meting out unjust punishment] is hated by the people he terrorises, while one who is too lenient is held in contempt by his own people. Whoever imposes just and deserved punishment is respected and honoured. {1.4.8-10}

An innocent man who does not deserve to be penalised shall not be punished, for the sin of inflicting unjust punishment is visited on the king. He shall be freed of the sin only if he offers thirty times the unjust fine to *Varuna* (the god who chastises unjust behaviour of kings) and then distributes it to Brahmins. {4.13.42,43}

The special circumstances of the person convicted and of the particular offence shall be taken into account in determining the actual penalty to be imposed. {3.20.20}

Fines shall be fixed taking into account the customs (of the region and the community) and the nature of the offence. {2.22.15}

In all cases, the punishment prescribed shall be imposed for the first offence; it shall be doubled for the second and trebled for the third. If the offence is repeated a fourth time, any punishment, as the king pleases, may be awarded.[1] {2.27.18}

Leniency shall be shown in imposing punishments on the following: a pilgrim, an ascetic, anyone suffering from illness, hunger, thirst, poverty, fatigue from a journey, suffering from an earlier punishment, a foreigner or one from the countryside. {3.20.21}

Those who are known for their learning, intellect, valour, nobility of birth or achievements shall be honoured. {3.20.23}

Whenever *brahmacharis*, *vanaprasthas* or *sanyasins*[2] have to pay fines, they may instead perform rituals and penances for the benefit of the King, for as many days as the amount of the fine (in panas). Likewise, heretics without money shall observe a fast for the number of days equivalent to the fine. This rule does not apply to [serious crimes such as] defamation, theft, assault and abduction; in such cases, the prescribed punishment shall be implemented. {3.16.38-41}

Thus, the king shall first reform [the administration], by punishing appropriately those officers who deal in wealth; they, duly corrected, shall use the right punishments to ensure the good conduct of the people of the towns and the countryside. {4.9.28}

Either due to the increase in criminality of the population or due to the misguided [greedy?] nature of kings, it has become customary to levy a surcharge of eight per cent on fines below one hundred panas and five per cent on fines above that; this is illegal. Only the basic fine [as prescribed in this text] is legal. {3.17.15,16}

DEATH PENALTY

The cruel punishments listed below are prescribed by great sages in the *shastras*. [However,] for crimes which are not cruel, the simple death penalty [without torture] is equally just. {4.11.26}

Theft

Of cattle herds (more than 10 heads)	Death without torture	{4.11.15,16}
Stealing or killing a royal elephant or royal horse; stealing a royal chariot	Impalement	{4.11.7}
Theft of weapons or armour by anyone who is not a soldier[3]	Death by a firing squad of archers	{4.11.22}

Damage to water works

Breaking the dam of a reservoir	Death by drowning in the same place	{4.11.17}

Death as a result of scuffle or affray

(No capital punishment if death occurs after seven days)

On the spot	Death with torture	{4.11.1}
Within seven days	Death without torture	{4.11.2}

Manslaughter

With a weapon	Death without torture	{4.11.5}

<u>Murder</u>

With cruelty[4]	Impalement[5]	{4.11.7}
Murder during highway robbery		
Murder during housebreaking		

<u>Poisoning</u>

Poisoner—man or woman not pregnant	Death by drowning[6]	{4.11.18}
(special provision of delayed implementation of punishment for pregnant women)		
<u>Sale of human flesh</u>	Death	{4.10.15}

<u>Treason</u>

Anyone who tries to usurp the throne, attacks the royal residence, encourages enemies or jungle tribes to rebel, incites a revolt in the city, countryside or army.	Death by burning from head to foot. (Does not apply to Brahmins, who shall be blinded)[7]	{4.11.11,12}

<u>Parricide, fratricide, etc.</u>

Killing mother, father, son, brother, teacher or ascetic	Death by burning the shaved head	{4.11.13}
<u>Accidental death</u>	Death without torture	{4.11.15}

<u>Crimes by women</u>

Murdering husband, guru, child or children, by a weapon, poisoning or setting fire to the house	Death by being torn apart by bullocks	{4.11.19}
Prostitute murdering a client	Death by being burnt alive or by drowning	{2.27.22}

<u>Arson</u>

Setting fire to a pasture, a field, a threshing ground, a house, a productive forest or an elephant forest	Death by burning	{4.11.20}

MUTILATION

MONETARY FINES IN LIEU

Mutilation	Equivalent Fine (in panas)
Thumb and forefinger	54
Tip of nose	54
All fingers of the [right] hand	100
Sinews of the feet	200
Middle and index fingers	200
A foot	300
A hand [usually right hand?][8]	400
An ear and the nose	500
Both feet	600
A hand and a foot	700
Blinding both eyes	800
Left hand and both feet	900
Both ears and nose	1000

{from 4.10.1,2,7-14; 4.12.1,3,7}

[For those who remove or cremate criminals executed by impaling them on a stake, the prescribed punishment is also death by impaling; the monetary equivalent in this case is the Highest SP {4.11.8}. There is no monetary equivalent to the cutting off of penis and testicles {4.13.30}]

MISCELLANEOUS PUNISHMENTS

BRAHMINS

[The punishment for a Brahmin guilty of a serious offence is branding and exile.]

The guilt of a Brahmin shall be displayed publicly and permanently so that he may be excluded from all activities of Brahmins. The brand shall indicate the nature of the offence as follows:

theft	dog
drinking alcoholic liquor	the vintner's flag
murder	a headless torso

rape of teacher's wife   the female sexual organ.

After publicly proclaiming a Brahmin's guilt and branding him, he shall be exiled or sent to [work in] the mines.   {4.8.28,29}

FOOD AND DRINK TABOOS

Eating or drinking prohibited things

If done voluntarily	Exile	{4.13.2}

Making someone eat or drink a prohibited item.   {4.13.1}

depending on the *varna* of the person made to do so

Brahmin	Highest SP
Kshatriya	Middle SP
Vaishya	Lowest SP
Sudra	54 panas

DEATH BY BEING GORED BY AN ELEPHANT

Being gored to death by an elephant is as meritorious as having the sacred bath at the end of the *Asvamedha* [horse] sacrifice. Hence, anyone who seeks such a death [voluntarily] shall make oblatory gifts of the following: a *drona* of rice, a jar of wine, garlands and a piece of cloth to clean the tusks.   {4.13.15,16}

WITCHCRAFT AND BLACK MAGIC

Performing magic or witchcraft is a punishable offence except when it is done in order to arouse love in a wife towards her husband, in a husband towards his wife or in a suitor towards his beloved.   {4.13.28}

PUNISHMENTS

Mahout of an elephant which gores to death someone who did not volunteer	Highest SP	{4.13.17}
Anyone who practises witchraft	Same results to be meted out	{4.13.27}
Causing injury by black magic	Middle SP	{4.13.29}

Part IX

COVERT OPERATIONS

"A king shall have his agents in the courts of the enemy, the ally, the Middle and the Neutral kings to spy on the kings as well as their eighteen types of high officials."

{1.12.20}

"Miraculous results can be achieved by practising the methods of subversion."

{13.1.21}

"A single assassin can achieve, with weapons, fire or poison, more than a fully mobilized army."

{9.6.54,55}

IX.i

COVERT ACTIVITIES

[The creation of a secret service, with spies, secret agents and specialists such as assassins, was a task of high priority for the king. After the Royal Councillors and Ministers had been appointed, their integrity had to be tested using one of the four tests as appropriate to the work allotted to them {1.9} and {1.10}. The creation of an entire network of secret agents was the next task, because they were necessary for ensuring the security of the kingdom and for furthering the objective of expansion by conquest. How these clandestine agents were to be used is described in a number of places in the text in the appropriate context.

The general term used in the text for all clandestine agents, both men and women, is *guda* (concealed). There were two basic groups of agents— those who stayed in one place and those sent wherever they were required. The word *samstha* (established) is used to denote agents settled in one place; these established agents were used to collect, collate and transmit in code the information received from other agents. Both the agents in one place and the roving agents could pursue 'cover' occupations. Both groups were permanent state employees on fixed salaries.

From the list of salaries of state employees in {5.3}, it appears that some agents were employed on a temporary basis for a specific task and paid accordingly.

In addition to these agents who worked directly under the king, the Chancellor, who was in charge of revenue collection and security of the countryside, had his own network of spies. (See Notes on Translation No. 6). These were primarily concerned with ensuring that government revenue did not suffer by people hiding income and keeping a watch over strangers and anti-social elements.

Among the agents permanently in one place, two types are distinguished. The Intelligence Officer, operating under the cover of a monk, a householder or a merchant, was in charge of the intelligence station. Other established agents adopted the disguise of ascetics, both of Brahminical and non-Brahminical sects.

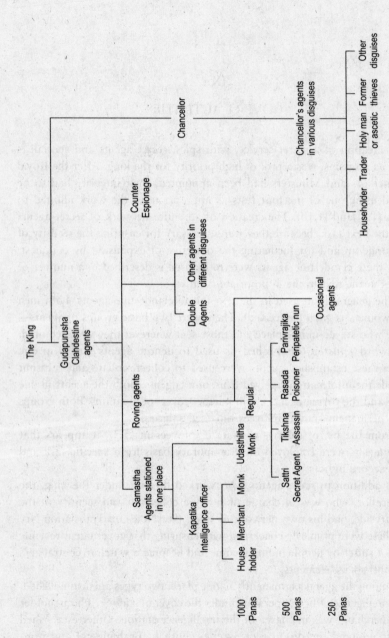

Fig. 23 Organization of the Secret Services.

Of the different types of roving agents, the most ubiquitous was the *sattri* (here translated as secret agent), a word derived from 'ambush'. Forty-nine different instances of the use of this general purpose agent are mentioned in the text. Next in importance (mentioned in over twenty tricks) were assassins, called *tikshna* (agents using sharp practice), who were used mainly to kill secretly enemy chieftains and kings. Poisoners, wandering nuns and ascetics were the other categories.

A special category of agents was the double agent who was in the employment of the enemy but who also worked for the conqueror. To ensure the double agent's good behaviour, the conqueror is advised to hold the agent's wife and children as hostages.

The secret agents were everywhere, both inside the country and in foreign countries. They worked inside houses; they stationed themselves inside cities, near cities, in the countryside, in the forests and along the frontier, adopting a cover profession which was appropriate to the location or the particular trick to be played on the victim. The list of occupational cover (called the ....*vyanjana*, the word before indicating the nature of the cover) is almost as long as the list of legitimate professions mentioned in the text. There are twenty-nine distinct categories of cover with fifty subtypes. The agents could disguise themselves as: ordinary citizens; holy men (including ascetics, *pashandas*, and their assistants); merchants; doctors; teachers; entertainers (such as brothel keepers, actors, singers, story tellers, acrobats and conjurers); household attendants (cooks, bath attendants, shampooers, bed makers, barbers and water-bearers); caterers (vintners, bakers and sellers of vegetarian and nonvegetarian food); astrologers, soothsayers, readers of omens, intuitionists, reciters of *puranas* and their attendants; artisans and craftsmen; cowherds and elephant handlers; foresters, hunters, snake catchers and tribals; and even as thieves and robbers. Women agents could adopt the disguises of a nun, a rich widow, an actress, a musician or an expert in love affairs. An agent could pretend to be a deserter, a friend or an envoy. They could even act out the parts of gods and evil spirits such as snake gods, fire gods or *rakshasas*. The fact that the exact cover to be used is specified in over a hundred places in the text is indicative not only of the extensive use of clandestine agents but also the thought that Kautilya has given to their precise use in different situations. There are many other references to clandestine agents in the text where the exact trick to be employed is not specified.

Some covers are very strange. In {12.4.7}, an agent of the weak king is described as the 'chief in the aggressor's army'; it is not clear how such a treacherous person could rise to be an important officer of the attacking army. Another is the use of a female agent of the weak king, 'wife of a high official' of the aggressor, being used to subvert the official {12.2.21}; this does not seem very plausible. All other cover jobs, including two references to 'pretending to be a wife' {4.5.6 and 7.17.38} are logically relevant to the trick being played.

Clandestine agents had extra legal protection. Though, according to the Law of Contract, any contract made with fraudulent intent was invalid, all contracts entered into by clandestine agents were valid, irrespective of intent.

Clandestine agents were employed for the following purposes within the country: testing the integrity of ministers, surveillance over the population in general and high officials in particular, secretly eliminating treacherous high officials, preventing subversion by enemy kings, trapping criminals and forest bandits and detecting anti-social elements, especially the thirteen types mentioned in {4.4.3-22}. The compilation of these internal duties is in the third section of this Part.

As one would expect, the use of clandestine agents is extensive with regard to relations with other kingdoms, both in the context of foreign policy and in war. In IX.iv, following a general theory of the people who can be subverted and the specific type of approach to be made to them, the special cases of oligarchies and confederacies (both characterised by there being a number of chiefs or kings acting collectively) are dealt with. The obvious method of weakening such groups is to sow dissension among them. The latter part of this section has two cases which are mirror images of each other. In one the conqueror is the weaker party facing an aggressor who might, eventually, pin him down in a fort. In the other, the conqueror is stronger and is bent upon eliminating an enemy king at least cost to himself. The treatment of the two subjects, therefore, is elaborate, taking into account the different tactics using clandestine agents, depending on the stage of the attack. Section iv of this Part is, in effect, a text book on the use of clandestine agents abroad in all possible situations.

Some of the methods suggested are very convoluted and involve the use of as many as three different types of agents; for example, {5.1.9-11}, {9.6.34-41} and {13.3.11-14}. Some methods are also common to two different target situations; e.g. an agent in the guise of a wine seller distributing liberally poisoned wine {11.1.24} and {12.4.11}. In general, the methods play on the weaknesses of men, such as ambition or lust. The use of false rumours to create mistrust is quite frequent. Often associated with this is the sending of a man, already condemned to death, with a forged letter confirming the false rumour. The condemned man gets a temporary reprieve and if he is unmasked and killed, it is no loss to the conqueror!

Section v of this Part is a very brief summary of the use of magical and occult practices, omitting most of Book 14 of the text due to the difficulties of translating with any degree of clarity the proper names of plants and other material used in the preparation of chemicals and spells.

In addition to clandestine agents, others could also be used to play tricks. For example, the conqueror about to eliminate the enemy may also use allies, loyal tribal chiefs and so-called friends and supporters of the enemy to into a false sense of security {13.4.27-38} in XI.x.]

IX.ii

CREATING THE SECRET SERVICE

After verifying the integrity of high officials by means of seven tests,[1] the king shall create a secret service consisting of the following types:

(i) <u>agents based in one place</u>: the intelligence officer, spies under the cover of monks, householders, merchants or ascetics;

(ii) <u>roving agents</u>: the secret agent, the assassin, the poisoner and the woman mendicant.   {1.11.1}

Any information corroborated by three [different] spies shall be taken to be true.   {1.12.15}

Any agent who is consistently unreliable shall be eliminated.

{1.12.16}

AGENTS BASED IN ONE PLACE

[The salary of this group was fixed at 1000 panas p.a. {5.3.22}]

Agents stationed in one place shall be [suitably] honoured and rewarded by the king so that they may [be trusted to] ascertain the integrity of government servants. Any government servant angry with the king for a good reason shall be pacified with honours and rewards. Those who act against the king and those angry without reason shall be quietly eliminated.

{1.11.21,22}

INTELLIGENCE OFFICER: (*KAPATIKA*)

A courageous and sharp student shall be trained to be an intelligence officer. [After training] he shall swear to be loyal to the king and the Chancellor. He shall be well rewarded with honours and money and sent out with instructions to report back any activity against the king.

{1.11.2-3}

USING DIFFERENT ROLES AS COVER

Honest and intelligent persons shall be recruited to act as spies according to the cover specified below:

    <u>monk</u> (*udasthita*) —a monk who has relinquished his vocation but pretends to be one after recruitment;

    <u>householder</u> —an impoverished farmer;

    <u>trader</u> —an impoverished merchant.   {1.11.4,9,11}

These agents, having been provided with plenty of money and assistants, shall pursue a [profitable] occupation at the places assigned to them. Out of the profits, they shall give others [monks, farmers, or traders as applicable] food, clothing and shelter. Among those thus helped, the ones who want to earn money shall be recruited to act as spies using the appropriate cover. They shall swear loyalty to the king and be promised payment of salaries and expenses. With the new recruits also recruiting others, a network of spies shall be set up.   {from 1.11.5-8,10,12}

ASCETICS AS SPIES

An authentic ascetic (*mundajatila*—with shaven head or matted locks)[2] who wants to earn money shall be established, as an agent, near a city along with many disciples with shaven heads and matted hair like him. He shall pretend to practise austerities by eating very sparingly in public, just a handful of barley every month or two; he may eat secretly as much as he likes.

    [He shall then establish his reputation with the help of other secret agents]. Agents, acting under the cover of merchants, shall come to worship him seeking their prosperity with the help of his occult powers. His own disciples shall proclaim his accomplishments. [His agents shall also find out beforehand information about visitors]. When the people come to him, praying for wealth, he should make predictions with the help of palmistry and similar techniques as well as the [secret] signs made by his disciples. He may predict any of the following: an unexpected gain, a loss by fine or theft, death of a traitor, a reward from someone pleased with the recipient, news from abroad, an event which will occur in the next day or two or a royal decision.

    Secret agents and other clandestine operators shall make the predictions come true.

    [Such an agent shall also be on the lookout for suitable recruits for Government service]. If he finds, among the visitors, someone with spirit, intelligence, and eloquence, he shall predict for him good fortune from the king and association with a minister, who shall then appoint the recommended person in a Government post.   {1.11.13-20}

ROVING AGENTS

SECRET AGENT: (*SATTRI*)

Secret agents shall be recruited from orphans who have to be looked after by the state. They shall be trained in the following techniques: interpretation of signs and marks, palmistry and similar techniques of interpreting body marks, magic and illusions, the duties of the *ashramas* [stages of life], and the science of omens and augury. Alternatively, they can be trained in [physiology and sociology,] the art of men and society.   {1.12.1}

ASSASSIN: (*TIKSHNA*)

These shall be recruited from the bravest in the land, particularly those who, for the sake of money, are willing to fight wild elephants and tigers, in total disregard for their own personal safety.   {1.12.2}

POISONER: (*RASADA*)

Those who are cruel, lazy and devoid of any affection for their relatives shall be recruited as poisoners.   {1.12.3}

WANDERING NUNS: (*PARIVRAJIKA, MUNDA-VRISHALA*)

A wandering nun may be a Brahmin (*parivrajika*) or from another sect (*vrshala* with their heads shaven). Such agents shall be recruited from poor but intrepid widows, who need to work for their living. They shall be treated with honour in the palace so that they may go into the houses of high officials freely.   {1.12.4,5}

> [In addition to the above categories employed on a permanent basis, occasional agents could also be used. Their salary was fixed at 250 panas p.a. which could be increased according to the work done {5.3.24}.]

TRANSMISSION OF INTELLIGENCE

The intelligence gathered from roving spies shall be collected together in the establishments of spies based in one place and shall be transmitted by code. The transmitters shall not know who the gatherers were. [Sometimes transmission of intelligence gathered by agents within the house may become difficult if nuns are prevented from entering it.]. In such a case, the intelligence gathered shall be transmitted by means of songs, speech, signs or messages in code hidden inside musical instruments or vessels, to other agents appearing at the door in disguise (as the parent of a servant, an artist, a singer or a slave). Alternatively, the agent inside the house may attempt to get out either secretly or by pretending to be ill, mad, or feigning escape from fire or poison. {1.12.11-14}

DOUBLE AGENTS

Double agents are those clandestine operatives who, while employed by a king, spy for another king. They can adopt as cover any of the guises mentioned as cover for clandestine operatives under the Chancellor.[3]

The king who employs the servant of another as a double agent shall hold the agent's wife and children [as hostages]. Every king shall be aware of [the possibilities of] his own servants being double agents. Therefore, the loyalty of government servants shall be ascertained using other agents, adopting the same type of cover as the one under investigation.

{1.12.17-19}

AGENTS ABROAD

A king shall have his own set of spies, all quick in their work, in the courts of the enemy, the ally, the Middle, and the Neutral kings to spy on the kings as well as their eighteen types of high officials. {1.12.20}

The different kinds of spies are as follows:

inside their houses—hunchbacks, dwarfs, eunuchs, women skilled in various arts, dumb persons, *mlecchas*;

inside their cities—traders, espionage establishments;

near the cities—ascetics;

in the countryside—farmers, monks;

frontiers—herdsmen;

forests—forest dwellers, such as *shramanas* and foresters.

{1.12.20-23}

COUNTER ESPIONAGE

In order to uncover enemy agents [operating in his own territory] the king shall: (i) employ his own roving and non-roving spies, who shall adopt disguises or covers similar to those of enemy agents and act with great secrecy; (ii) post at the frontiers high officials of unquestioned loyalty but acting as if they had a reason for acting disloyally [in order to attract approaches from enemy agents]. {1.12.24-25}

AGENTS EMPLOYED BY THE CHANCELLOR

The Chancellor shall employ in the *janapada* clandestine agents taking any of the following disguises: ascetic, wandering monk, [long distance] cart driver, wandering minstrel, juggler, fortune teller, soothsayer, astrologer, physician, lunatic, blind, dumb or deaf person, idiot, merchant, artist, craftsman, actor, brothel-keeper, vintner, baker, vegetarian or non-vegetarian restaurant-keeper.

These agents shall report on the honesty or otherwise of village officials and heads of departments. Anyone suspected of leading a secret life [and secretly amassing wealth] shall be spied upon by an agent conversant with the [suspected] officials job.   {4.4.3-5}

[The methods of exposing the thirteen types of criminals who make money by causing injury to the people (*janapada*) are given in IX.iii.]

WORK OF CLANDESTINE AGENTS[4]

The [different types of] agents described above shall be employed to:
  (i) neutralize the principal officers who, though living by service under the king, work for the enemy;
  (ii) keep under surveillance people of the country who are likely to fall prey to the incitement of the enemy;
  (iii) wage psychological warfare against the enemy; and
  (iv) weaken the enemy.   {5.1.3}

IX.iii

INTERNAL SECURITY

TESTING THE INTEGRITY OF MINISTERS

[The king, after appointing someone as a minister, has to test his integrity, using one of the four tests described below, depending on the nature of the work assigned to him. See above, IV.iv 'Royal Councillors and Ministers.]

For the *Dharma* test, the king shall [ostensibly] dismiss the *purohita* on some [alleged] grounds such as refusal to teach someone or officiate at the rites of a person not entitled to perform them. The seemingly disgruntled *purohita* shall then use secret agents to persuade each minister, under oath of secrecy, to join a conspiracy to overthrow the king for his impiety. If any minister refuses to join, he is clean [i.e. loyal].

Likewise, for the *Artha* test, the Chief of Defence should [ostensibly] be dismissed for some crime, such as showing favours to evil men. He shall then use secret agents to offer bribes to various ministers to destroy the king. Any minister who refuses is to be considered clean [i.e. honest].

For the *Kama* test, a wandering nun shall be used to gain the confidence of a minister in order to convey the suggestion that the Queen is in love with him. Much wealth and a meeting with her shall be promised. If any minister refuses to be tempted he is clean [i.e. upright].

For the test by fear, a minister shall invite all other ministers for a party. Seemingly apprehending a conspiracy, the king shall throw them all in jail. An Intelligence Officer, previously placed in the same jail, shall try to induce them to kill the king who had deprived them of their honour and prosperity. Anyone who refuses is clean [i.e. steadfast].

{Summary of 1.10.2-12}

[However, Kautilya cautions that these ancient teachings shall not be accepted completely.] Kautilya says: 'Under no circumstances shall the king make himself or his [principal] Queen the target for ascertaining the probity of a minister. Furthermore, he shall not corrupt the uncorrupted; that would be like adding poison to water: for, it may well happen that a cure may not be found for one so corrupted. Even the mind of the steadfast and the valiant may not return to its original purity if it is perverted by the fourfold secret tests. Hence, the King shall make an outsider the object of reference for the tests and then keep the ministers under surveillance using clandestine agents.' {1.10.17-20}

SURVEILLANCE

OF HIGH OFFICIALS

The king shall select, from among the roving spies, those who are diligent, can disguise themselves credibly conforming to different regions, and who know various languages and professions to spy on the activities of the [eighteen ranks of] high officials within the country. They shall serve the king with devotion and to the best of their ability. {1.12.6}

Assassins shall obtain employment under the officials as attendants (e.g. bearers of the umbrella, water-vessel, fan or shoes and attendants when the king is seated on the throne, riding on animals or by chariot).[1] They shall report to the king, by a secret agent, the outdoor activities of the official concerned. {1.12.7,8}

Poisoners shall spy on the indoor activities of the official. They shall either get themselves employed (as a cook, waiter, bath attendant, hair washer, bed-maker, barber, valet or water bearer), or adopt a disguise (as a woman, dwarf, *kirata*, or as deaf, dumb, blind, or idiotic), or work as an entertainer (as an actor, dancer, singer, instrumentalist, story teller, or minstrel). They shall report through wander ing nuns. {1.12.9,10}

OF THE PEOPLE

After organizing the system of surveillance over high officials, the king shall set up the system of keeping a watch over the population in the cities and countryside, [in order to ascertain who are the dissatisfied among them]. {1.13.1}

Secret agents shall [ostensibly] enter into arguments with each other, whenever people gather together in places of pilgrimage, assemblies, communal gatherings, shows or festivals. One of them shall [start the argument] and say that, in spite of the king's reputation for virtue and nobility, he is totally without good qualities because he oppresses the people with taxes and fines. Other agents shall disagree with him and say that a king uses the taxes take on themselves the jungle. Subjects who do not pay fines and taxes take on themselves the people take on themselves the sins of the subjects. Kings shall never be insulted because divine punishment will be visited on whoever slights them.[2] Thus, the people shall be discouraged from having seditious thoughts.

Spies shall also find out [and report] the rumours circulating among the people.   {from 1.13.2-14}

Spies in the guise of ascetics [*mundajatila*—those with shaven heads or matted locks] shall find out who, among the population, is discontented. They shall, in particular, keep a watch over those who receive grants of grain, cattle or money from the king, who contribute these in good times and in bad, who provide assistance in putting down revolts and rebellions and who repel an attack by an enemy or a jungle chief.[3]   {1.13.15}

The Chancellor shall appoint spies in the guise of householders to ascertain [independently] in the villages they are stationed, the facts about fields (size and production), households (taxes and exemptions) and families (*varna* and occupation). They shall also keep track of those who leave the village and those who come in as well as the reasons for such movement. They shall also watch out for men and women of bad character and enemy spies.

Likewise, spies in the guise of merchants shall keep a watch over the quantity and price of the goods produced on Crown property (such as mines, water works, forests, they shall ascertain the amount stations, ferry charges, share and subsistence expenses as well as the quantities stored in the warehouses.

Spies in the guise of ascetics shall be [directly] responsible to the Chancellor for reporting on the honesty or dishonesty of farmers, cowherds, merchants and Heads of Departments.

Spies disguised as old thieves shall keep track of the entry, sojourn or departure of thieves and desperadoes of the enemy, particularly in [vulnerable places such as] sanctuaries, cross-roads, ancient ruins, bathing places in tanks and rivers, river crossings, places of pilgrimage, hermitages, jungles, mountains and desert tracks.   {2.35.8-14}

Secret agents shall patrol along the roads and roadless places, both inside and outside the city. They shall patrol [especially] temples, holy places, forests and cremation grounds. They shall arrest for suspicious behaviour any stranger and anyone who is wounded, having implements which can cause injury, hiding behind a heavy load, appearing agitated, sleeping unnaturally long hours, or looking tired after a long journey.

Inside the city, they shall search deserted houses, workshops, drinking places, vegetarian and non-vegetarian eating houses, gambling places and the quarters of heretics.   {2.36.13-14}

[Secret agents shall be posted in drinking houses to watch spending {2.25.12}, to gather information about visitors {2.25.12} and to look after the ornaments and property of visitors {2.25.13}.]

Watch shall be kept over those who spend lavishly and those doing so in drinking houses without having a known source of income.   {2.25.6}

TREACHEROUS HIGH OFFICIALS

Sometimes treacherous high officials, who cause harm to the kingdom, cannot be dealt with openly either because they are powerful or because they are united. It is the duty of the king to suppress such people by secret methods.   {5.1.4}

Using relatives

(i) Against a traitorous minister, or the son of a Brahmin by a Sudra wife, or the son of a maid servant, a brother should be used. A secret agent shall tempt the brother of the traitor to kill him with the promise of being given his brother's property; when the deed is done, by weapon or by poison, he himself should be killed for the crime of fratricide.

(ii) The brother of a seditious minister may be instigated by a secret agent to demand his inheritance; other secret agents, pretending to be close to the minister, shall threaten the claimant with death. When the claimant is either lying at the minister's doorstep [till his demand is met] or asleep elsewhere he shall be killed by an assassin. The minister shall be blamed for the murder and the king shall have him [also] killed, as if avenging the murdered man.

(iii) A secret agent may mislead the seditious minister's son (who has a high opinion of himself) into thinking that he is really the son of the king and is being kept in ignorance of his 'true' origin for fear of the enemy. When the son believes the story, he shall be showered with honours in private and then told that, though he is fit to be installed as the Crown Prince, the king was not doing so for fear of his father [the minister]. The son shall thus be instigated to murder his father. When the deed is done, the king shall have him [also] executed on the very ground that he was a parricide.

(iv) A mendicant woman agent, having won the confidence of the wife of a seditious minister by providing her with love potions, may, with the help of the wife, contrive to poison the minister.   {5.1.5-13,15-19}

Entrapment

(i) The seditious official shall be sent with a weak army, and with chosen assassins, on a [dangerous] expedition (such as subduing a jungle tribe or an enemy village, to set up a district or frontier zone in a [remote] region near a wilderness, to suppress a rebellion in a fort, or to escort a caravan from an area threatened by an enemy king). In any fight that ensues, at night or by day, the assassins, posing as highway robbers, shall kill the traitor and proclaim that he was killed in battle.

(ii) The seditious officials shall be invited to meet the king, when he is out on a visit or an expedition. They shall be accompanied by [chosen] assassins, who, just before entering the king's chamber, let themselves be searched for weapons. When their weapons are discovered by the doorkeepers, they shall [falsely] declare that they were the agents of the traitors, who should thereupon be killed. Instead of the actual agents, some others should be killed [to give credibility to the story].

(iii) When on a pleasure trip outside the city, the king shall honour the traitors with accommodation near his own. A woman of bad character, dressed like the queen, shall be caught in their apartment. For this [alleged] attempt to molest the queen, they shall be killed.

(iv) The king, during a long voyage, may praise the traitor's cook or wine-maker and get himself invited for food or drink. The food or drink shall be [secretly] poisoned [by a secret agent] and the traitor shall be asked to taste it first. The discovery of poisoned food or drink shall be denounced publicly and the traitors put to death as poisoners.

(v) If the traitor is addicted to witchcraft, a spy in the guise of a holy man should inveigle him into a secret rite, during which he shall be killed by poison or with an iron bar. The death shall be attributed to some mishap during the secret rites.

(vi) A spy in the guise of a doctor may make the traitor believe that he is suffering from a malignant or incurable disease and kill him by poisoning his medicine or diet.

(vii) The traitor may be poisoned by secret agents in the guise of sweet makers or cook's assistants.   {5.1.21-36}

Playing one against the other

The following methods may be used when there is more than one seditious official.

(i) If there is an adulterous relationship between members of the two families (an official with the daughter-in-law of another, a son of one official with the wife of the other, or a son with the daughter-in-law of another) a mischief maker shall cause a quarrel among them. An assassin shall kill one; the other shall be blamed for it and killed.

(ii) A quarrel shall be engineered between the two by sending one of them on an expedition into the other's territory, with a weak army and [chosen] assassins. The assassins shall create trouble by raising an army, extracting money, kidnapping the other's daughter, or undertaking government works [without the other's consent] (such as building forts or reservoirs, opening a trade route, settling virgin land, starting a mine, organizing a timber or elephant forest, setting up a district, or marking a boundary). The officer who has been sent shall be instructed to arrest anyone who does not help him or actively hinders him; at the same time, the other official shall be instructed not to let the first one to do the work. When the two start quarrelling, assassins shall kill one and blame the other who shall, in turn, be killed.

(iii) A quarrel can also be engineered by a mendicant woman agent, [falsely] suggesting to one of them that the wife, daughter or daughter-in-law of the other was in love with him. When the deluded traitor gives the agent jewellery [to be given to the supposed lover], she shall show them to the other as proof of designs on his wife, daughter or daughter-in-law. When they quarrel, assassins shall kill one of them and blame it on the other, who shall then be punished.

(iv) In case the regions of the two traitors have a common border, a quarrel can be engineered between the two by damaging the property, implements, crops or transport, using as an excuse a boundary dispute between villages, fields, threshing floors or houses. On a [crowded] occasion like a show, ceremony or festival, assassins shall kill one of the traitors and declare that he deserved it because he was quarrelling with the other. For this [alleged] offence, the other shall also be punished.

(v) If there is already a deep-rooted quarrel between the two traitors, this shall be exacerbated by secret agents who shall either set fire to fields, houses or threshing floors or attack the kinsmen, relatives or draught animals of one or the other. Then, as in the previous cases, assassins shall kill one and so on.

(vi) One of the traitors may be persuaded by secret agents to be the guest of the other and be poisoned during the visit. The blame shall be cast on the host, who shall then be punished.   {5.1.14,38-52}

[For other provisions relating to treacherous officials, see III.v]

SUBVERSION/INTRIGUE

A wise king shall protect his people (his important chiefs and the ordinary population) against the intrigues of the enemy, irrespective of whether the persons are likely to be subverted or not.   {1.13.26}

The kinds of people easily subverted by the enemy are: the angry, the greedy, the frightened and the haughty.

In his own country, spies in the guise of soothsayers, readers of omens and astrologers shall keep a watch over those likely to be subverted and find out whether these have contacts among themselves or with enemies or jungle chiefs. Appreciation shall be shown, by awarding honours and gifts, to those who are happy with the king [and, therefore, loyal]. The discontented shall be tackled by the four methods (conciliation, placating with gifts, sowing dissension, and use of force). {1.13.22-25}

In the enemy's country, those who are easily subverted shall be won over by conciliation and gifts. Those who are not easily subverted shall be tackled by sowing dissension, use of force or by pointing out to them the defects of their king. {1.14.12}

ENTRAPMENT OF CRIMINALS

[A variety of methods shall be used to trap criminals (such as thieves, adulterers and bands of robbers) using agents adopting suitable disguises. Different methods are to be used for thieves operating in settled areas like villages and bandits who operate in forests and wildernesses.]

THIEVES IN THE SETTLED AREAS

Secret agents shall try to gain the confidence of thieves by pretending that they know the secrets of their favourite tricks, such as charms for inducing sleep, making oneself invisible or opening locked doors. The agents shall arrange to give proof of these powers by preparing the people of a village beforehand. A band of thieves shall be promised a demonstration in a village [of their choice] but instead be taken to the prepared village on some excuse such as difficulty in getting to the other village. [On reaching the prepared village], the gates shall be opened by [ostensibly] using a gate-opening charm. The robbers shall then enter, passing guards who shall pretend not to see them because they had been made invisible by a *mantra*. The sleep-inducing charm shall be demonstrated by making the guards [pretend to be asleep] and the robbers shall move the guards with their beds. The robbers shall then enjoy themselves with [paid] women who pretend to be [chaste] wives who had succumbed to a love-potion.

After thus convincing them, the robbers may be taught the use of the [so-called] charms, *mantras* and potions.

Alternatively, secret agents may pose as old [retired] thieves in order to gain the confidence of the robbers. [The trap shall then be set].

The thieves shall be asked to rob a particular house and be apprehended while actually burgling it. Or, secret identification marks may be put [in advance] on the goods in the house and the thieves arrested when trying to sell, exchange or pledge the marked articles. Or, [after the burglary] they may be made to drink drugged liquor and arrested [with the marked articles] while intoxicated.

After the arrest, the robbers shall be interrogated about other of fences and accomplices.   {4.5.1-12}

The Chancellor shall then parade the criminals before the people of the city or the countryside [as the case may be] and proclaim that the criminals were caught under the instructions of the king, an expert in detecting thieves. The people shall be warned to keep under control any relative of theirs with criminal intentions, because all thieves were bound to be caught [like the ones before them].   {4.5.13}

FOREST BANDITS

Old thieves, cowherds, fowlers and hunters shall, after gaining the confidence of forest bandits and [criminal] tribes, persuade them to attack caravans, which had earlier been loaded with a large amount of spurious gold, commodities and forest produce. The bandits may be killed by concealed soldiers when the caravan is attacked. Or, they may be rendered insensible, by giving them food mixed with narcotic drugs. Or, they may be arrested with the stolen goods when they are asleep after a tiring journey. Or, they may be given stupefying drinks when celebrating their robbery and then arrested.   {4.5.15-17}

AGAINST ANTI-SOCIAL ELEMENTS

The agents of the Chancellor shall report on the honesty or otherwise of village officials and heads of departments. Anyone suspected of leading a secret life [and secretly amassing wealth] shall be spied upon by an agent conversant with the [suspected] official's job.   {4.4.3-5}

The methods of exposing the thirteen types of criminals who make money by causing injury to the people (*janapada*) are given below. In all cases, the recommended punishment is exile, or payment of the appropriate redemption, depending on the gravity of the offence.   {4.4.23}

Testing the honesty of judges and magistrates:

After making friends with a [suspected] judicial officer the agent should try to bribe him to treat leniently an [alleged] relative [accused of a crime]. If the judge or magistrate accepts the bribe, he should be exiled.

{4.4.6-8}

Village/Department Heads:

A secret agent shall point out to an official a wealthy but unscrupulous man who had got into difficulties, and suggest that money could be extorted from him. If the official agrees, he shall be exiled for the crime of extortion.
{4.4.9-10}

Perjurers and procurers of perjury:

An agent, pretending to be the accused in a case, shall tempt perjurers and those who procure perjurers with large amounts of money. Whoever succumbs shall be exiled. {4.4.11-13}

Witchcraft, Black Magic, and Sorcery:

One who is reputed to procure the love of a woman by means of charms, love potions or ceremonies in cremation grounds shall be sought by an agent, pretending to be in love with someone else's wife, daughter, or daughter-in-law. The punishment is exile for these practitioners and for those who practise black magic and sorcery. {4.4.14,16}

Poisoners and dealers in narcotics:

Anyone who makes, sells or buys poison and sellers of cooked food suspected of being poisoners shall be approached by an agent offering money [ostensibly] for procuring the death of an enemy. The punishment is exile for the poisoners and also for dealers in narcotics. {4.4.17-19}

Counterfeiters and adulterators of precious metals:

A counterfeiter can be identified by (i) his frequent purchase of metals, chemicals, bellows, pincers, vices, anvils, dies, chisels and crucibles; (ii) having blacksmith's tools [necessary for making coins] and (iii) clothes and body blackened with smoke, soot and ashes. A secret agent shall join him as an apprentice, gain his confidence and then expose him. A similar technique shall be adopted for exposing those who adulterate precious metals. The punishment is exile for both types. {4.4.20-22}

[See also: cheating the public or exploiting their gullibility—
{5.2.39-45,52-68} in V.ii.]

MARAUDING JUNGLE TRIBES AND ROBBER BANDS

[Clandestine agents were used to tackle tribes and robber bands who, from the shelter of the jungle, raided villages or ambushed caravans. Some special tricks to be used against them are given in {13.3}, which is a chapter mainly concerned with weakening or killing an enemy who had taken refuge in a fort.]

The agents employed in deceiving an enemy who had taken shelter in a fort, and those used in removing anti-social elements, can also be used against marauding jungle tribes and robber bands.   {from 13.3.50}

Clandestine agents shall [gain the confidence of the raiders] and make them attack a herd of cattle or ambush a caravan near the jungle. Arrangements shall be made beforehand for the cowherds or the caravan escorts to carry food and drink laced with a narcotic. On being attacked by the raiders, the cowherds or the caravan shall run away leaving everything behind. When the raiders become insensible after consuming the poisoned victuals, the cowherds or caravan merchants shall attack them.

An ascetic (with shaven head or matted locks and posing as a devotee of *Samkarshana*[4]) shall trick the raiders by offering, during a festival, wine laced with a narcotic. An agent in the guise of a vintner may, likewise, sell or offer poisoned wine using the occasion of a celebration in honour of a god, a funeral rite or a festival. When insensible, the raiders shall be attacked.

When the raiders come to plunder villages, they may be dispersed into many groups and then destroyed one-by-one.   {13.3.51-58}

IX.iv

AGAINST OLIGARCHIES AND ENEMY KINGS

Miraculous results can be achieved by practising the methods of subversion.
{13.1.21}

In the enemy's country, those who are easily subverted shall be won over by conciliation and gifts. Those who are not easily subverted shall be tackled by sowing dissension, use of force or by pointing out to them the defects of their own king. {1.14.12}

SUBVERSION IN ENEMY TERRITORY

TARGETS

The types of persons who are likely to be <u>angry</u> with the king are:
- someone to whom a promised reward has not been given;
- of two people equally skilled or efficient, the one who is humiliated;
- someone out of favour due to a favourite of the king;
- someone defeated in a challenge;
- someone unhappy due to banishment;
- someone who has not gained anything after incurring expenditure [on behalf of the king];
- someone who is thwarted from doing his duty or obtaining his inheritance;
- a government servant dismissed or reduced in rank;
- someone suppressed by his own kinsman;
- a male relative of a raped woman;
- someone imprisoned;
- someone fined for losing his court case;[1]
- someone disciplined for misconduct;
- someone whose entire property has been confiscated;
- someone suffering from bondage; and
- the relative of someone exiled. {1.14.2}

The <u>greedy</u> are:
- the impoverished;
- someone who has lost his property to another;

- a miser;
- someone suffering from adversity;
- someone involved in a risky transaction.   {1.14.4}

The <u>frightened</u> are:
- someone who has offended or wronged [an important person];
- someone whose sins have been found out;
- someone who fears the same punishment, as given to another for the same offence;
- someone who has occupied someone else's land;
- a rebel subdued by force;
- a government servant who has enriched himself [by fraudulent means];
- someone supporting a pretender to the throne; and
- someone who hates or is hated by the king.   {1.14.3}

The <u>haughty</u> are those who:
- are conceited, rash or violent;
- are fond of honours or resentful of honours given to their rivals; and
- are unhappy because they think they are placed in too low a position or paid too little.   {1.14.5}

METHODS OF SUBVERSION

Those susceptible shall be subverted by an agent in the guise of an ascetic, choosing as a target one who had become his devotee. [Each type of potential traitor shall be approached according to the method best suited to his character, as described below].

When the targeted person agrees to work for the [foreign] king, a contract with agreed terms shall be entered into with him. He shall then be used, according to his capacity, in association with [or, under the supervision of] the king's own spies.   {1.14.6,11}

APPROACH TO THE ANGRY

These shall be instigated by comparing their [actual] king to a mad elephant. 'Just as a mad elephant ridden by a drunk tramples under foot whatever comes in its way, so does [your] king, blind due to ignorance of *Shastras*, has started destroying the city and the country people. The way to control him is to set him against a rival elephant. Show your anger [by joining our king]'.   {1.14.7}

APPROACH TO THE GREEDY

These shall be instigated by comparing their [actual] king to the cows kept by hunters. 'Just as a hunter's cows are milked to feed dogs and not

Brahmins, your king rewards those without valour, intelligence or eloquence and not those of noble character. Our king knows how to distinguish between [good and bad] men. Let us go to him.'   {1.14.9}

APPROACH TO THE FRIGHTENED

The king shall be compared to a snake. 'Just as a hidden snake spits poison at whatever it sees as a danger, so with your king, seeing you as some danger, will soon spit anger at you. Let us go elsewhere'.{1.14.8}

APPROACH TO THE HAUGHTY

The king shall be compared to a *chandala* [outcast]. 'Just as the well of *chandalas* is of use only to *chandalas*, so does this low-born king patronize only low persons and not *Aryas* like you. Our king knows how to distinguish between men. Let us go to him.'   {1.14.10}

When someone agrees [to change sides] he shall be rewarded with money. Any money or food needed by them shall be given as a gift. If someone refuses the gifts, ornaments may be presented to his wife or sons.

{13.1.17-19}

APPROACH TO OTHER TYPES

Each type shall be compared to an exemplar as below:

– the diligent: to an ordinary donkey [that toils for little reward];

– the officers of the army: to a stick used to strike the branches of a fruit tree [it is the wielder who gets the fruit, not the stick itself];

– those alarmed: to a goat that has strayed [and is easily caught and killed];

– those insulted: to one struck by lightning.

In the following cases their king is to be compared to the exemplar as below:

– those disappointed in their expectations: to (i) a cane which bears no fruit or (ii) someone who throws meagre balls of rice to the crows or (iii) a mirage of a cloud [which brings no rain];

– those denied their rewards for meritorious service: to a husband who denies a hated wife her ornaments;

– those whose loyalty had been secretly tested: to a tiger whose claws are hidden or to a death trap.

–those who give constant help: to a bark or a bitter fruit which gives no nourishment or the milk of she-asses, the churning of which gives no butter.

{13.14-16}

AGAINST OLIGARCHIES

[As explained in {Book 11} in X.ix, oligarchies were characterised by collective leadership of a council of chiefs. Because of their unassailable cohesiveness, winning over an oligarchy to one's own side was, for the conqueror, even better than winning over an army or gaining a king as an ally. If an oligarchy could not be won over by using the methods of conciliation or gifts, it was better to sow dissension among the chiefs. After dividing them, the weaker party should be removed and settled away from their territory. Given below are the secret methods (*upamsudanda*—stealthy or underhand use of force) recommended for use against oligarchies. These are so classified because they involve killing secretly one chief of an oligarchy and blaming it on another. In most cases the plausible cause of murder is by provoking lust; in one case it is stoking a chief's ambition. See also {5.1.15-18} in IX.iii.]

In all cases of strife among the members of an oligarchy, whether they arise by themselves or incited by assassins, the conqueror shall assist the weaker party with money and arms, make them fight the hostile group and urge them to kill their rivals.   {from 11.1.15,53}

1. BY ENCOURAGING AMBITION

A secret agent shall get hold of an ambitious son of a chief of the oligarchy and make him believe that he was really the son of a king but kept hidden for fear of enemies. When he comes to believe this, he shall be helped with money and arms to fight the oligarchy. When the oligarchy is destroyed, the [deluded] son shall also be killed.[2]   {11.1.31-33}

2. BY EXPLOITING LUST

(i) Brothel keepers, acrobats, actors/actresses, dancers and conjurors shall make the chiefs of the oligarchy infatuated with young women of great beauty. When they are duly smitten with passion, the agents shall provoke quarrels among them by making one of them believe that [he had lost her to another chief, either because] she had gone voluntarily or had been abducted. In the ensuing fight, assassins shall do their duty [of killing one of them and blaming it on the other] giving lust as the motive. If the disappointed chief is not roused to anger, the woman shall complain that though she loved only him, another chief was harassing her. She shall then incite him to murder the other. If the ruse was the pretence that she was abducted, the [alleged] abductor shall be murdered, an assassin luring the victim to a pleasure house or the outskirts of a park; or, the woman herself may poison him. Then she shall blame it on another chief. {11.1.34-39}

(ii) An agent in the guise of a holy man shall gain the confidence of an enamoured chief of the oligarchy addicted to love potions, poison him and escape. Then, other agents shall blame the murder on another chief.[3] {11.1.40,41}

(iii) Women secret agents may pose as a rich widow, one with a secret income, a dancer, a singer or an expert in abetting love affairs. One posing as a rich widow may use an inheritance dispute, one with a secret income a dispute about a deposit and the others may use their particular abilities to approach a chief of the oligarchy and then make him infatuated with her. He shall then be lured to a secret house for an assignation at night, where an assassin shall kill him or carry him away to prison. {11.1.42,43}

(iv) A secret agent shall inform a chief of the oligarchy, known to run after women, of a beautiful woman fit for a king, allegedly impoverished and persuade the chief to get hold of her. A fortnight after she has been seized, a condemned man, dressed as an ascetic, shall be made to accuse the chief, in front of the other chiefs, of having raped a woman of his family (wife, daughter-in-law, daughter or sister).[4] If the group punishes the accused chief, the conqueror shall take his side and make him fight the others. If the group does not punish the chief, assassins shall kill the so-called ascetic and brand the chief of not only having committed adultery with a Brahmin woman but also as a killer of Brahmins. {11.1.44-48}

(v) An agent in the guise of a soothsayer shall incite a chief to seize, by money or by force, a girl who was betrothed to another [chief] on the grounds that she was fit to be the wife of a king and mother of kings. If he does get her, a quarrel is certain. If he does not succeed, the other party shall be instigated to fight. {11.1.49-51}

(vi) A mendicant woman [agent] shall provoke a chief who is fond of his wife by saying that another chief, conceited because he was younger, had sent her with a letter and ornaments to the [first] chief's wife. She shall claim that she agreed to do so out of fear and that the wife was guiltless. She shall then incite the chief to attack the other chief secretly and promise to convey the alleged agreement of the wife [to prevent the other from becoming suspicious]. {11.1.52}

SOWING DISSENSION WITHIN A CONFEDERACY

[Verses {9.6.28-48} are found in Book 9 dealing with the precautionary steps that a conqueror should take before setting out on a campaign of conquest. One of them is to avoid the danger of external treachery, particularly from a confederacy of kings, who join together to attack the conqueror. The best method of tackling this danger is to sow dissension among them, mainly by making one of them out to be a villain, in league with the conqueror, against the interests of the confederacy. Clandestine agents shall be used to implement the methods of deception and trickery described below. The same methods can also be used against the Chief of Defence, Princes or army commanders in the confederacy {9.6.50}.]

(i) When one of the members of the confederacy gets presents from his own land or from outside, the [conqueror's] secret agents shall spread the rumour that these had been received [as a bribe] from the conqueror against whom the confederacy was to start a military campaign. Once the rumours had become widely current, a condemned man shall carry a [fictitious] letter, as if confirming that the conqueror had sent the presents as part payment for fighting or deserting his fellow confederates, with the promise of more payments later. Then secret agents shall make this letter widely known among other members of the confederacy.

(ii) The conqueror shall obtain stealthily some products which are unique to the country of one of the members. Agents in the guise of merchants shall try to sell them to the other members of the confederacy. Secret agents shall then propagate the [false] idea that these products were, in fact, a present to the conqueror [from the member from whose country they came].

(iii) The conqueror shall release some convicts, sentenced for heinous crimes, give them money and rewards and tell them to kill, with weapon, fire or poison, a member of the confederacy. [In the mean time,] a trusted minister of the conqueror shall [seemingly] desert and take refuge with that member. [To add credence,] the conqueror shall keep the minister's wife and sons in seclusion and announce that they had been killed at night [for the minister's so-called desertion.] The minister shall betray and expose the criminals one by one and thus gain the confidence of the targeted member. Then, he shall warn the member about the danger to his life from the chief of the confederacy. Double agents shall [correspondingly] inform the chief that the targeted member had issued an order for the assassination of the chief.

(iv) The conqueror may send a letter to a powerful and energetic member of the confederacy asking him, in the name of a [non-existent] treaty between them, to seize a particular kingdom. Secret agents shall make it known among the other members.

(v) Agents of the conqueror may destroy the camp, supplies or supporters of one of the members and suggest to him that this was done by those whom he had considered his friends.

(vi) When clandestine agents [of the conqueror] kill or spirit away a brave warrior, elephant or horse of one of the members, secret agents shall blame it on mutual animosity among the members of the confederacy. Then, a [tictitious] letter shall be sent to another member encouraging him to continue such acts [of sabotage] on promise of further reward. Double agents shall make this letter known. When the confederacy is divided, one of them shall be won over.   {from 9.6.28-49}

THE WEAK KING AGAINST AN AGGRESSOR

[The whole of Book 12 is devoted to the consideration of the tactics of a king under attack from a stronger enemy. Where possible, the weaker king should use secret methods to avoid being conquered. Different methods are suggested for different stages of the attack. The enemy king could be killed before he embarks on the expedition, his people could be subverted during an expedition, someone else could be made to begin a counter-attack, chaos could be engineered in the military base camp of the aggressor and he could be assassinated before the battle.]

ASSASSINATING THE AGGRESSOR

[This complicated manoeuvre involves the use of three different types of clandestine agents adopting different disguises.]

An agent, in the guise of a merchant, shall pretend to be in love with an intimate maid of the aggressor's favourite queen, shower wealth on the maid and then abandon her. Then, another agent in the guise of the first one's assistant, shall recommend a third agent, disguised as an ascetic [expert in love potions]. The so-called expert shall give a potion to be rubbed on the body of the object of desire. When this is done [with the help of the attendant-agent] and the merchant-agent 'miraculously' returns to the maid. The same potion shall be recommended to the queen to enable her to retain the love of the aggressor king. Poison shall be substituted and the aggressor killed. {12.2.15-18}

SUBVERSION

SUBVERTING PRINCES

A son of the aggressor, living near the weak king's territory inside his father's fort, shall be instigated by secret agents to revolt. He shall be told that he was ignorant of the fact that though he was better qualified than the Crown Prince to be the king, he had been set aside. He should [be encouraged to] fight and seize the kingdom, before he himself was eliminated by the Crown Prince.

Or, a pretender to the aggressor's throne or a prince in the family's disfavour shall be tempted with money to destroy some of the forces of the aggressor, such as those inside the kingdom or near the frontier.

{12.3.15,16}

SUBVERTING THE HIGHEST LEVEL OFFICIALS (*MAHAMATRAS*)[5]

(i) An agent in the guise of a soothsayer shall gradually gain the confidence of a high official and persuade him that he has all the marks of a king. A mendicant female agent shall [likewise] predict to his wife that she will be the queen and the mother of princes. [The high official will then try to usurp the throne.]

(ii) The wife of a high official may be subverted to become an agent and made to accuse falsely the official's king of wanting to take her away to his harem. She shall produce a [forged] letter and ornaments, as if they had been sent to her by the king through a wandering nun.

(iii) An agent in the guise of a cook or a waiter to a high official shall [falsely] accuse the king of bribing him to poison the high official. An agent, in the guise of a merchant, shall corroborate the story and say that he had sold the poison to the king.

Thus, the weak king shall use one, two or three methods to subvert, one by one, the highest officials of the aggressor and make them either fight their king or desert him. {12.2.19-44}

Or, a secret agent, after gaining the confidence of the aggressor, shall inform the king that a particular high official was in contact with the enemy [i.e. the secret agent's master]. When this is believed, the agent shall present the 'evidence' by producing someone allegedly carrying a letter [from the weak king to the high official accused of treason]. {12.3.12.13}

SUBVERTING THE VICEROY AND
THE CHANCELLOR OF THE STRONG ENEMY

[The *sunyapala* or Viceroy was one of the *mahamatras* put in charge of the capital when the king went away on a military expedition. The *Samahartr* or Chancellor was another *mahamatra* responsible for revenue collection, law and order and the secret service.]

In the fortified towns, secret agents [of the weak king] close to the Viceroy [of the aggressor] shall spread a [false] rumour among the people that the Viceroy had informed the top civil and military officials that their king faced difficulties in his campaign, creating doubt about his coming back alive. The agents shall then give the so-called friendly advice that everyone should look after his own interests by collecting as much wealth as they could and by killing their enemies. When the rumour had become widespread, assassins [of the weak king] shall kill important people and rob citizens at night, proclaiming that these were punishments meted out to those who had disobeyed the Viceroy. The first group of secret agents shall then accuse the Viceroy of murder and pillage.

Similar tactics shall be employed in the countryside against the Chancellor. [The same kind of rumour shall be spread but] the assassins shall, in this case, kill at night officials of the Chancellor's department in the villages and proclaim that they were being punished for their unjust oppression.

After thus maligning the Viceroy or the Chancellor, they shall be got killed by rousing the people against them. Secret agents shall use the opportunity to set fire to the royal palaces, city gates, commodity stores and granaries and to kill the guards; the Viceroy or Chancellor shall be blamed for these acts of wanton destruction. Then, they shall install on the throne a pretender or a prince in disfavour [since such persons will be grateful to the weak king for their enthronement] and call of the attack.

{12.2.25-33}

SUBVERTING ARMY CHIEFS

Brothel keepers shall use young, beautiful women to make the aggressor's army chiefs infatuated with them. When two or three chiefs fall passionately in love the same woman, assassins shall provoke quarrels among them. After a fight, the defeated party shall be induced either to go away [i.e. abandon the attacking king] or help the weak king in his expedition against the aggressor. Or, agents in the guise of ascetics shall administer poison to the infatuated army chiefs on the pretext of giving them love potions which will help them to win over the object of their desire. {12.2.11-14}

Or, the more important among the army chiefs may be bribed with land or wealth to desert or to fight on the side of the weak king.   {12.3.14}

SUBVERTING CHIEF COMMANDERS OF THE DEFENCE CORPS

Secret agents [who had wormed their way] near the aggressor and become his favourites shall subvert the chiefs of the chariot corps, elephant corps, cavalry and infantry as follows. Pretending to disclose a secret out of friendship, the [targeted] official shall be informed that his king was angry with him. When such [false] information had become widespread, assassins shall equip themselves with appropriate night [curfew] passes, go to the houses of some chiefs and bid them to come out in the name of the king. When they do, they shall be killed while shouting that it was the king's message to them. [Other] secret agents shall then point this out to the chiefs who had not been killed [but fed the false information about the king's anger,] and advise them that they should save themselves by abandoning their king.   {12.3.1-4}

OTHERS WHO CAN BE SUBVERTED

[Any one who can be made to be unhappy with his king for one reason or another can be subverted. The three types identified in {12.3.5,7,9} are those who had rendered some service to the king. Kautilya suggests the means for subverting them, irrespective of whether they had received recompense or not and even when they themselves did not expect any! The technique suggested is the same as for defence chiefs: spread false rumours, kill some and frighten the rest.]

Those whose request for recompense for services rendered had been rejected: Secret agents shall tell them that the king had instructed the Viceroy to have them killed because they had gone over to the enemy after having demanded something for which they had no right to ask.

Those who had been recompensed after asking: Secret agents shall tell them that the king had instructed the Viceroy to have them killed because, though they were in league with the enemy, he had given them what they wanted only to make them believe that he trusted them.

Those who had not [even] asked for recompense: Secret agents shall tell them that the king had instructed the Viceroy to have them killed because, by not demanding something which was due to them, they were only displaying the guilt of their own treachery.

All these cases shall be dealt with according to the method suggested for the Chiefs of Defence.   {12.3.5-10}

COUNTER-ATTACKING THE AGGRESSOR

The weak king shall overcome the aggressor by adopting the secret methods [of treachery, use of weapons, poison or fire, or assassination by drawing the enemy out of his camp,][6] choosing the method appropriate to the place where the aggressor may be found. {12.4.29}

PROVOKING AN ATTACK ON THE AGGRESSOR

[For this purpose, the weak king shall use]:
 – in the fortified towns in the aggressor's territory, agents in the guise of merchants;
 – in the villages, agents in the guise of householders; and
 – in the areas [between villages] without permanent settlements, agents in the guise of cowherds or ascetics.[7]

They shall send war material to a neighbouring prince, a jungle chief, a pretender [to the aggressor's throne] or a prince [of the aggressor's family] in disfavour, along with information about a region that could be captured. When their forces arrive at the fort in secret, they shall be rewarded with wealth and honours and shown the weak points of the aggressor. Together, the two groups shall strike at the weak points. {12.4.1-3}

ATTACKING AN AGGRESSOR WITH POISON

[For this stratagem] an agent in the guise of a wine seller or one serving as a chief in the aggressor's army shall be used to poison the army in its camp. The agent shall manufacture an excuse [for offering the wine] by first proclaiming a condemned man as his son and killing him with poison just before the launch of an attack by the aggressor. He shall then distribute poisoned wine liberally as a funeral libation. Or, unadulterated wine may be distributed on the first day and thoroughly poisoned wine the following day. Or, unadulterated wine may first be given to the army chiefs and then, when they are drunk, given thoroughly poisoned wine. {from 12.4.4-7}

Agents in the guise of wine sellers or sellers of cooked meat, rice or cakes shall attract the people in the aggressor's camp by selling high quality food cheaply, ostensibly due to mutual competition. The food or drink shall then be mixed with poison. {from 12.4.8}

Agents in the guise of traders or hawkers shall sell poisoned liquids such as wine, milk, curds, butter or oil.

Or, women and children may buy from the merchants in the camp any liquid product in their own vessels in which they had already put poison. They shall then complain about the quality or the price and pour it back into the merchant's vessel [to be sold unknowingly by the merchant to other customers.]   {from 12.4.9-11}

Elephants and horses in the camp may be poisoned either by agents selling poisoned fodder or water or by agents in the guise of animal attendants mixing it with grass or water.   {12.4.12,13}

CREATING CHAOS IN THE AGGRESSOR'S CAMP ON THE EVE OF AN ATTACK

Chaos shall be created in the aggressor's camp on the eve of an attack by:

(i) agents, who had built up their disguise as cattle traders by long association, letting loose herds of cattle, sheep or goats in places in the camp where they will cause confusion;

(ii) letting loose vicious horses, camels, buffaloes, etc.;

(iii) agents letting loose animals maddened by special herbs;

(iv) agents in the guise of hunters letting loose wild animals from their cages;

(v) snake charmers letting loose poisonous serpents;

(vi) elephant handlers letting loose [wild] elephants;

(vii) arsonists setting fire to the camp;

(viii) secret agents killing from behind the Chief Commanders of Elephants, Chariots, Horses or Infantry;

(ix) agents setting fire to the quarters of the chiefs;

(x) loyal troops of the weak king, who had earlier taken service under the aggressor on the pretext of being deserters, alien forces or jungle troops, attacking in the rear or preventing reinforcements [from reaching the camp];

(xi) troops concealed in the forest luring the aggressor's forces to the edge of the forest and then killing them;

(xii) concealed troops ambushing the supply convoys, reinforcements and foraging parties on a narrow track; or

(xiii) creating a diversion by the weak king's agents in the aggressor's capital blowing trumpets and proclaiming, at a pre-arranged time before a night battle, that the capital had been captured and the kingdom had fallen.   {12.4.14-21}

ASSASSINATING THE AGGRESSOR

The weak king shall arrange the killing of the aggressor by one of the following means:

(i) using the opportunity of a tumult, [assassins] may enter the king's chamber and kill him;

(ii) using the opportunity of the king trying to escape from a tumult, picked fighters of jungle tribes or *mlecchas* may kill him from the shelter of a rampart or by ambushing him;

(iii) using the confusion of an attack, agents in the guise of hunters may assassinate the enemy treacherously;

(iv) [assassins] may use the appropriate method of killing the aggressor depending on the terrain and conditions such as a narrow path, a mountain, a rampart, a marsh or a water course;

(v) [assassins] may drown him by breaching a dam on a river, lake or tank;

(vi) if the aggressor is entrenched in a desert fort, a forest fort or a water fort, assassins may use fire and smoke to destroy him; or

(vii) assassins may kill him with fire if he is in a confined place, with smoke if he is in a desert, with poison if he is in his own place, with crocodiles and other beasts if he is in water and [with weapons] if he tries to escape from a burning building.   {12.4.22-28}

The aggressor may also be killed by mechanical contrivances of the kind described below, when, out of piety, he comes to worship on the occasion of a festival or a frequently visited temple:

(i) by releasing a mechanism causing a wall or a stone to fall on him after he has entered the temple;

(ii) by letting loose a shower of stones from an upper storey;

(iii) by dislodging a door on him;

(iv) by dropping a beam fixed at one end on him;

(v) by firing weapons concealed in the image of the deity at him;

(vi) by poisoning the cowdung spread on the floor or the water used for sprinkling in the places where he stays, sits or moves about;

(vii) by poisoning the flowers and incense offered to him;

(viii) by making him inhale [inside the temple] poisonous fumes concealed by fragrances; or

(ix) by causing him to fall in a spiked pit by the release of a trap door in the floor under his bed or seat.   {12.5.1-8}

> [If all these attempts fail, the aggressor's campaign may result in the weak king becoming besieged. The precautions to be taken by the weak king before the siege, escaping from the besieged fort without surrendering, making peace if necessary, escaping when faced with defeat and taking revenge after defeat are dealt with in XI.xi.]

CONQUEROR BESIEGING AN ENEMY'S FORT

> [The conqueror, who wants to overthrow an enemy who had taken shelter in his own fort, can take a number of steps to minimize the

losses which are inevitable in besieging or storming the fort. One of them is weakening the morale of the people inside the fort before laying siege. This is achieved by making the people believe that the conqueror is in direct communication with the gods.

Another method is to entice the enemy out of the fort and kill him. Presumably, the fort would then capitulate, having lost the king. More than a dozen ways of tricking the enemy to leave the protection of his fort are described in {13.2}. These fall into four broad groups— playing on the gullibility of the enemy's belief in miracles or demons, exploiting his weaknesses such as greed, exploiting his love of elephants, horses or hunting and, lastly, ambushing. A number of the tricks involve agents disguised as ascetics 'with shaven heads or matted locks'; *mundajatila* is an expression which often occurs to describe them. Another set of tricks involves frightening people with agents disguised as demons (*rakshasas*), snake deities (*nagas*), etc. The translation here is a summary of the verses with some inconsequential details left out.]

LOWERING THE MORALE OF THE PEOPLE IN A BESIEGED FORT

[The details of how some of the tricks for making gullible people believe that the besieging conqueror is in direct communication with gods and spirits are actually performed (e.g. fire burning in water) are not clear.]

DEMONSTRATING ASSOCIATION WITH GODS

(i) Agents shall be concealed in tunnels or inside images in temples and fire sanctuaries and the king shall, while worshipping, [ostensibly] carry on a conversation with the deity.

(ii) Agents shall arise out of water, pretending to be *nagas* or the god of water (*varuna*) and the king, while worshipping them, shall engage them in conversation.

(iii) The right chemicals shall be used to demonstrate the [apparently] inexplicable phenomenon of a row of fire burning inside water.

(iv) A concealed raft anchored by bags of stone shall be used to demonstrate the ability to stand on water.

(v) The head of a man shall be shown to be in flames by covering it (except for the nose) in a fire-proof membrane smeared with inflammable oil.

(vi) Women agents familiar with water shall be used to demonstrate the king's ability to talk to mermaids and snake-maidens (*nagakanyas*).

(vii) The trick of emitting fire and smoke from the mouth when angry can also be played. {13.1.3-6}

ENTICING A BESIEGED ENEMY BY TRICKS

AGENTS IN THE GUISE OF ASCETICS AND HOLY MEN

[In all the methods described below, the agent is used to persuade the enemy to live, for a week, with his wives and children outside the fort. This opportunity is to be used for attacking and killing him {13.2.5}.]

An ascetic shall establish himself in a cave near the enemy's city and surround himself with many disciples, who shall claim the ascetic to be four hundred years old. They shall persuade the enemy and his councillors to visit the ascetic, who shall relate the history of ancient kings and kingdoms as if he had seen it all himself. He shall claim to immolate himself after every hundred years and to reappear as a child again. He shall then promise three boons to the enemy, because his fourth immolation is to be honoured by the presence of their king. When the enemy is convinced, he shall be made to spend a week outside the fort in the ascetic's cave to witness the special rites. {13.2.1-4}

An agent shall pretend to be an ascetic and diviner [capable of seeing underground treasures] and prepare a trick purporting to show the presence of gold. A piece of bamboo smeared with goat's blood and gold dust shall be placed in an ant hill, the line of ants attracted by the blood indicating the presence of gold. A cobra shall be placed inside the bamboo and the bamboo be made to look as if it was growing golden leaves. Then a secret agent shall inform the enemy of this miracle. When the king comes to see it, the ascetic shall acknowledge the presence of the treasure and even dig out a bit of gold to prove it. The enemy shall then be persuaded to stay in that place for a week to worship the cobra guarding it so that the treasure may be released. {13.2.6-10}

An agent, pretending to be an ascetic capable of seeing underground treasures, shall stay in an isolated place and, at night, make his body glow by suitable chemicals as if on fire. Secret agents shall convince the enemy that the ascetic could shower unlimited prosperity. When the enemy comes, the ascetic shall promise him whatever he wants on condition that he spends a week doing prayers at that isolated spot. {13.2.11,12}

An agent shall pretend to be a *Naga or Varuna* [gods of water] by painting himself white and showing himself emerging from water by means of a secret entry and exit through a tunnel or underground chamber on the bank. Other agents shall then persuade the enemy of the supposed divinity of the *Naga*, who will grant him whatever he wants, provided he spends a week, etc.   {13.2.16,17}

An agent in the guise of a holy man may convince the enemy of his ability to get, by his magical powers, whatever the king wants and then persuade him to spend a week, etc.   {13.2.13,14}

An agent in the guise of a holy man shall station himself in a popular temple and win over important people by his religious activities and eventually use them to outmanoeuvre the enemy.   {13.2.15}

An agent, in the guise of a holy man, shall station himself on the border between the two countries and invite the enemy to witness black magic performed on the effigy of the conqueror. When the enemy comes to watch the invoking of the conqueror's spirit in the effigy, he shall be killed in an isolated spot.   {from 13.3.18,19}

AGENTS IN THE GUISE OF DEMONS

[In the methods described below, the intention is to frighten the people and convince them that the demons will disappear only when the enemy king himself performs oblations and recite *mantras* every night for seven nights. When thus enticed out of his fort, he shall be attacked and killed. {13.2.34,35}]

The people shall first be terrorized by a manifestation in which alleged demons demand worship threatening otherwise to eat up the [enemy] king and his principal officers. These could be arranged by the following means:

(i) assassins may get into a sacred place at night and shout the warning indistinctly (by speaking through reed into large jars);

(ii) agents in the guise of *nagas* at night may make themselves look like burning by covering themselves with the right oil, stand in the middle of a sacred tank or lake and shout the warning while brandishing their iron clubs and maces;

(iii) agents may dress themselves in bearskins to look like *rakshasas* and go round the city three times anti-clockwise accompanied by baying dogs and jackals shouting the warning while belching smoke and fire from their mouths;

(iv) agents may set fire to the image of a deity by smearing oil on it over a layer of mica and shout the warning;

(v) a rumour that on full or new moon nights *rakshasas* were eating men alive in the cremation ground or a holy place shall first be propagated. Then, an agent in the guise of a *rakshasa* shall demand a human sacrifice.

Any passer-by, brave or otherwise, shall be killed with an iron club and the death blamed on the *rakshasa*.

In all the above cases, secret agents, omen readers and astrologers shall spread the news of devilish manifestations.

People can also be terrorized by contriving animal blood to pour out of images of gods held in reverence. Agents shall interpret this as foretelling defeat as a result of which rivers of blood will flow in the city.

When the people are in the grip of terror, secret agents shall report it to the enemy king. Then, readers of omens and astrologers shall advise the enemy king that unless propitiatory rites are performed, disaster will strike him and his country. When he is convinced, he shall be asked to perform oblations and recite *mantras* at night for seven days. [He shall be killed when thus enticed out of his fort.]

In order to persuade other kings, the conqueror may first have these tricks played on himself and perform the expiatory rites. Then the tricks shall be played on the enemy. {from 13.2.21-37}

EXPLOITING THE ENEMY KING'S WEAKNESSES

Agents, in the guise of horse traders, may offer the enemy a gift of a horse and invite him to inspect it. When he does so, a confusion shall be engineered and the enemy got trampled by horses.

If the enemy king is fond of elephants, guards of elephant forests shall tempt him into a forest by showing him a beautiful animal. When he is inside a dense forest or on a narrow path, he shall be killed or carried off as a prisoner.

The above method can also be adopted if the enemy king is fond of hunting.

If the enemy king is avaricious or fond of women, secret agents shall tempt him using rich widows approaching him to settle a dispute about inheritance or young beautiful women about a pledge or mortgage. When he falls into the trap [of making an assignation at night] the agents shall kill him with weapons or poison. {from 13.2.20,39-43}

AMBUSHING

Assassins may be hidden in underground chambers, tunnels or inside walls in places which the enemy visits frequently like sanctuaries, *stupas*, temples and abodes of holy men and ascetics.

Assassins shall make their way inside with the help of previously placed agents into the places where, because the enemy is unprotected or careless, an opportunity may arise for killing him. After the deed is done, they shall go away by the same means by which they entered the place of ambush.

The occasions suitable for ambush are when:

(i) he goes in person to see performances and shows;

(ii) he is enjoying himself in rest houses on his travels;

(iii) enjoying water sports;

(iv) attending sacred recitals or rituals;

(v) visiting birth ceremonies, funeral rites or the ill;

(vi) in love, sorrow or fear;

(vii) he goes trustingly to a festival of his own people and becomes careless of his security;

(viii) he moves about without a guard;

(ix) it is raining;

(x) he is in the middle of a crowd;

(xi) he has lost his way;

(xii) he enters a place on fire;

(xiii) he goes to a deserted place; or

(xiv) he is dressing, dining, drinking, listening to music, on his bed or seated [alone?]   {from 13.2.44-50}

INFILTRATING A FORCE INSIDE THE ENEMY FORT

[If the efforts at waging psychological warfare, enticing the enemy out of his fort and weakening him (see XI.xi) all fail, the next step for the conqueror is to besiege the fort. The actual taking of the fort will be less costly in terms of men and material, if a part of the besieger's army can be infiltrated inside the fort. This can be done either by tricking the enemy into opening the gates or by gradually building up a clandestine armed unit inside the fort.]

Agents in the guise of hunters shall station themselves outside the gates of the fort and sell meat. They shall make friends with the gate keepers. Twice or thrice, they shall inform the enemy beforehand of attacks by dacoits [made to come true by the conqueror organizing so-called dacoit raids]. When the enemy's confidence has been gained, they shall inform the conqueror who shall divide up his forces into two parts—one part near the villages and the other for making a sudden assault. When the villages are attacked, the agents shall proclaim that a great gang of dacoits was attacking fiercely and that a large army was needed to deal with them. The conqueror shall take over the force sent by the enemy to deal with the dacoits. [In the mean time,] the assault force shall be brought to the gates of the fort. The agents shall then call for the opening of the gates saying that the [enemy's anti-dacoit] force had returned victorious. Or, other agents hidden inside shall open the gates. The assault force can then take the fort [being unprepared and the defending army already depleted].

{13.3.40-43}

Armed agents in the guise of artisans, craftsmen, heretical monks, entertainers and traders shall be sent into the fort. Agents, pretending to be ordinary householders, shall smuggle to them weapons and armour hidden in flags, images of gods or in carts carrying wood, grass, grain or other goods. The armed agents shall [at the appropriate time] create a tumult by blowing conches and beating drums and announce the arrival, at the rear of the fort, of the besieger's army bent on destruction. They shall open the gates [to let the conqueror's army in] disperse the enemy's forces and destroy him. {13.3.44-47}

Or, the conqueror may make peace with the enemy in order to lull him into a false sense of security. Armed forces shall be infiltrated into the enemy's fort using escorts of caravans and trading groups, bridal parties, horse traders, equipment sellers, grain merchants, disguised monks or envoys.

{13.3.48}

[There are a few places in the text where the use of clandestine methods is recommended without actually specifying the method:

(i) when the king needing protection has a choice between two stronger kings, he shall sow dissension between them and then use covert methods to eliminate them one by one {7.2.15}.

(ii) A weak king entering into a treaty with no hostages with a strong king by which he is obliged to move himself and his army elsewhere, shall use covert methods to get himself out of his predicament {7.3.26}.]

IX.v

MAGIC, ILLUSIONS AND THE OCCULT

[The four chapters of Book 14 are a compilation of the techniques of secret practices including the occult and black magic. While a large part of these techniques deal with killing or maiming an enemy by chemicals or by black magic, a few are clearly tricks and do not involve the occult. Chapter {14.4} contains a list of counter-measures and antidotes; a few verses in other chapters deal with the attacker making himself more powerful by becoming invisible or by acquiring the ability to see in darkness.

Chemical preparations can be put to use against the enemy in various ways: causing death immediately or at the end of different periods {14.1.4-8}; killing or blinding with poisonous smoke {14.1.9-15}; making someone unconscious {14.1.16-18}; causing various diseases including madness and leprosy {14.1.19-28, 14.2.11-13}; making someone rabid {14.1.29,30}; poisoning water {14.1.31,32}; and causing disfigurement {14.2.4-10}.

Other uses to which chemicals can be put are: survival without food {14.2.1-3}; changing one's colour {14.2.15-17}; making objects, including parts of the body, burn or glow {14.2.18-26}; walking on fire {14.2.27-29}; performing various tricks with fire {14.2.32-37}; overcoming fatigue {14.2.41-43} and curing leprosy {14.2.14}.

The ingredients used in making these chemicals are a mixture of parts of various animals, insects and plants. Many are unidentifiable. It is impossible to guess at their efficacy.

Some verses in Book 14 deal with tricks which are clearly practicable. Tying burning reeds to the tails of flying birds to simulate meteors {14.2.30} and breathing fire out of the mouth {14.2.4} are examples.

The magical chemicals in {14.3} are mainly concerned with adding to the power of the attacker: ability to see at night {14.3.1-3}; becoming invisible {14.3.4-18}; making people unconscious

{14.3.19-50}; opening locked doors {14.3.51-63}; breaking chains {14.2.39,40} or the ropes of defence machines {14.3.64-66}; protecting oneself against fire {14.2.31,35-39}; overcoming fatigue {14.2.44} and obtaining inexhaustible supplies of food {14.3.79-87}. Some spells are concerned with hurting the victim: causing diseases, blindness or impotence {14.3.67-69,78}; destroying his livelihood {14.3.70,71}; using black magic to invoke disaster on him and his family {14.3.73-77}; killing by magical animals {14.1.33} and invoking uncontrollable fire {14.1.34}. Other verses dealing with magical practices are {1.20.4-8} concerning protection of the Royal Palace against fire, snakes and poisons.

Poisons and poisoning are often mentioned as a means of getting rid of traitors and enemies. One of the types of specialist clandestine agents was the poisoner. Verses {1.21.6,7}, on the security of the king, give a list of how to detect the presence of poison in food and other articles and how to infer the identity of the poisoner from his behaviour.

It is interesting to note that, while the king was advised to use magical spells, occult methods and poisons against his enemies, the common people indulging in these practices were punished!. See {4.4.14-16} on witchcraft, sorcery and black magic and {4.4.17-19} on the detection and punishment of poisoners. Exile was the punishment which could be avoided by paying appropriate compensation.]

The occult and magical practices described in this work are to be used against those who do not follow the *dharma*, in order to protect the four *varnas*.

Mleccha men and women who have gained the confidence of the enemy king shall poison his clothing and other personal articles. The agents shall adopt the language, dress, manners and customs appropriate to the enemy's country and disguise themselves as hunchbacks, dwarfs, *kiratas*, idiots, or as the deaf, dumb or blind.

Clandestine operatives shall kill the enemy with weapons concealed in the enemy's equipment for sports or any other purpose.

Secret agents and arsonists shall set fire [to the enemy's belongings] at night.   {14.1.1-3}

USE OF DECEPTIVE MATERIAL AND TRICKS

Deceptive occult practises shall be used to frighten the enemy. It is also said that these can be used [against one's own people] in case of a revolt in order to protect the kingdom.   {14.2.45}

By means of *mantras*, drugs, illusions and occult practices, one's own people shall be protected and those of the enemy destroyed.   {14.3.88}

The king shall first protect his own troops with the appropriate antidotes and then use poisonous smoke and poisoned water against the enemy.
                                                                 {14.4.14}

Part X

FOREIGN POLICY

'The welfare of a state depends on an active foreign policy.'

{6.2.1}

'The king who understands the interdependence of the six methods of foreign policy plays, as he pleases, with other rulers bound to him by the chains of his intellect.'

{7.18.44}

'The Conqueror shall think of the circle of states as a wheel—himself at the hub and his allies, drawn to him by the spokes though separated by intervening territory, as its rim.'

{6.2.39}

'The enemy, however strong he may be, becomes vulnerable to harassment and destruction when he is squeezed between the conqueror and his allies.'

{6.2.40}

'An enemy's destruction shall be brought about even at the cost of great losses in men, material and wealth.'

{7.13.33}

'When the benefits accruing to kings under a treaty, irrespective of their status as the weaker, equal or stronger king, is fair to each one, peace by agreement shall be the preferred course; if the benefits are to be distributed unfairly, war is preferable.'

{7.8.34}

'A king weak in power shall endeavour to promote the welfare of his people. For power comes from the countryside, which is the source of all activities.'

{7.14.18,19}

X.i

KAUTILYAN FOREIGN POLICY

Though less than a fifth of the *Arthashastra* deals with foreign policy, Kautilya is deservedly known as the great theorist of inter-state relations, because of his unique and unprecedented contribution. Books {7, 11 and 12} together constitute a brilliant, comprehensive, cohesive and logical analysis of all aspects of relations between states. The common understanding is that Kautilya propounded the theory that (i) an immediate neighbouring state is an enemy and (ii) a neighbour's neighbour, separated from oneself by the intervening enemy, is a friend. This is, no doubt, almost always valid. Nevertheless, to reduce Kautilya's theory on foreign policy to just these two observations is to do him a grave injustice. Indeed, the theory deals with not just three states, but with a maximum of twelve. The state is conceived not as a monolithic entity but as one with six internal constituents—the king, the ministers, the fortified city, the countryside, the treasury and the army. The power which a state can bring to bear on promoting its own interests vis-a-vis other states depends on how close to ideal the internal constituents are. Kautilya gives us a detailed theoretical analysis of all possible political situations with recommendations on ways of meeting them.

THEORY AND PRACTICE

In trying to understand Kautilya's analysis, we have to keep in mind the fact that it is essentially theoretical. He does not deal with a particular state in a historical time, but with the state as a concept. Since, in the Kautilyan view, the king encapsulates all the constituents of a state, he has expounded the theory in terms of the king—any king. In other words, what Kautilya calls the 'interest of the king' would nowadays be termed 'national interest'.

For the purposes of enunciating the theory, it is necessary to focus on a particular king, from whose point of view the situation is analysed. Kautilya designated this king as *vijigishu*—the king who wants to win or 'the would-be conqueror'. A neighbouring king is then designated as 'the enemy', and other kings nearby as allies, a Middle King or a Neutral King. The terminology defines only a set of relationships. This needs to be emphasized because the conqueror is not necessarily 'a good king' and, correspondingly, the enemy 'a bad king'. The advice given to the conqueror can equally be applied by the enemy.

We also need to keep in mind the fact that the *Arthashastra* is concerned with the security and foreign policy needs of a small state, in an environment with numerous other small states. This is clear from the map and explanation given earlier in 'The Kautilyan State'. The scope for enlargement of this small state was limited to the Indian subcontinent. 'The area extending from the Himalayas in the north to the sea in the south and a thousand *yojanas* wide from east to west is the area of operation of the King-Emperor' {9.1.17,18}. Territories beyond the subcontinent are not included, probably for the reason that the conqueror is expected to establish in the conquered territories a social order based on the Arya's *dharma, varna* and *ashrama* system. Kautilya perhaps considered the establishment of such a social order outside the limits of India impractical or even undesirable. While some aspects of the treatise can no doubt be applied to large states, the *Arthashastra* does not, in general, deal with the problems of very large states—how centralised or decentralised the government should be, or how to prevent their disintegration.

Kautilya uses four devices to derive practical advice for specific situations from his essentially theoretical concepts. These are: relative power, deviations from the ideal, classification by type of motivation, and the influence of the intangible and the unpredictable.

Throughout the analysis, the distinction about bilateral relations is the power equation; the two kings may be equally strong or one stronger than the other. This usually gives rise to three possibilities from the point of view of the king who initiates a particular action—the other king may be equal in strength, stronger than him or weaker than him. For example, the general policy guidance is that a king shall make peace with an equally powerful king or a stronger king but wage war against a weaker {7.3.2}. However, this is then followed by a series of exceptions, in {7.3.6-20}, when a policy contrary to the general principle is to be followed. A more elaborate analysis of the relationship between power and bargaining power will be found in the analysis of unequal treaties {7.7.7-30}. That the power equation shall make policy is an important Kautilyan contribution.

Power is not a factor which is constant over time. Kautilya frequently warns that both present (short-term) advantages and future (long-term) advantages have to be taken into account. For example, {7.8.5-10} show when to forego short-term advantages, or even any advantage, when concluding treaties.

Another factor which affects the choice of policy is the current condition of the states involved. As mentioned in the Introduction to Part II of this translation, the five chapters of Book 5 are devoted to an examination of calamities, because these might weaken any of the constituent elements of a conqueror's state. Likewise, a calamity afffflicting another king may provide opportunities to the conqueror which would not otherwise have been available. References to the influence of calamities on policy choices will be found throughout the analysis.

In the first exposition of the theory of foreign policy, Kautilya divides states into two broad groups, the first two circles of States—the hostile ones and the friendly ones. This is too broad to be practically useful. We find, therefore, precise subclassifications of types of neighbours {7.18.29}, types of allies {7.9.43-49, 7.18.31-42, 8.5.22-30} and types of vassals {7.16.10-15}. The classification takes into account the characteristics of a particular king, whether he is active or lazy, fickle or steadfast. Further, the motives which prompt another king to adopt a particular course of action are often also examined. An example is the analysis of what to do with an ally who has violated a treaty, gone over to the enemy and then wants to return to the fold {7.6.23-28}.

Lastly, intangible and unpredictable factors affect policy choices. Kautilya does not count power purely in terms of the resources of the state or the size of the army. Greater importance is given to the power of good command, analysis and judgment as well as to following just policies. The word 'mantra' for good counsel, analysis and judgment, also appears in 'mantra yuddha' 'warfare by good counsel', i.e. diplomacy. There are intangible factors dependent on the intellect. Unpredictable factors are Acts of God. 'Events, both human and providential, govern this world;...If an Act of God results in helping the achievement of one's objective, it is good fortune; otherwise, it is misfortune. Any human action which increases one's welfare is a good policy; otherwise it is a bad policy' {6.2.6-12}.

Kautilya's eminently practical approach to foreign policy is shown by his disagreement with earlier teachers on how a weak king should behave. 'One should neither submit spinelessly nor sacrifice oneself in foolhardy valour. It is better to adopt such policies as would enable one to survive and live to fight another day' {7.15.13-20, 12.1.1-9}.

In developing the theory, Kautilya often uses a technique of comparison to indicate the preferred course of action. He visualizes a hypothetical situation of two kings deciding to do similar things; whoever makes a better choice is said to have 'outmanoeuvred' the other. The word 'outmanoeuvring' (*atisamdhi*) occurs whenever it is necessary to indicate an order of preference. This is purely a technique used for elucidation and does not imply that the hypothetical situations of the two king's acting in a similar way occur in reality. It is akin to the form of argument 'If I did this and my enemy did that...'.

It is in the discussion of foreign policy that we see the power of Kautilya's intellect. Being basically a theoretical discussion, there are no descriptive passages and no tiresome lists. The classifications of friendly or hostile kings are there, not for pedantic or superfluous reasons, but because they illuminate the theory and bring it closer to reality. The analysis of renegotiation of treaties is impeccably logical. The step-by-step order used in {7.13} on attacks-in-the-rear, or in Book 12 on the stages of aggression towards the weak king have a remarkably logical precision about them. Notwithstanding the fact that Kautilya wrote this between nineteen hundred to two thousand years ago, the analysis of foreign policy in the *Arthashastra* has a universal and timeless validity.

ABOUT THIS TRANSLATION

Just as the theory of the internal structure of a state is laid down by Kautilya in the first chapter of Book 6, the theoretical basis for its foreign policy is described in {6.2}. This chapter contains the guiding principles of foreign policy and defines the actors, i.e. the circle of states. The other books concerned with foreign policy are the long Book 7 with eighteen chapters, Book 11 on oligarchies in a single chapter and Book 12 on the weak king.

The all-important six methods of foreign policy are described in {7.1.1-19} and these methods are then related to the promotion of the interests of the state. Chapters {7.2 to 7.7} contain a detailed analysis of the six methods. It is in these chapters that Kautilya takes into account practical realities and modifies the application of the theory to real life.

Chapters {7.8 to 7.12} are concerned with joint activities and include an elaborate consideration of the relative merits of various kinds of resources. These constitute, in essence, advice to the conqueror on how to augment his power in order to achieve his objectives of conquest and expansion.

Chapter {7.13 to 7.18} deal with specialised subjects—attacks in the rear, confederacies, the weak king seeking support or shelter, subjugated kingdoms, hostages, and the Middle and Neutral kings.

In the following section (X.ii) of this translation, the elements of the theory of Kautilyan foreign policy have been consolidated. The portions on treaties, scattered in a number of chapters have been brought together in X.iii; this also includes the subject of hostages, an essential part of treaties, given and taken to ensure the observance of the terms of a treaty. The helpers of the conqueror, allies and vassal kings, are covered in X.iv and joint activities in X.v. Planning a military expedition, to which important aspect the whole of Book 9 is devoted, is in X.vi. The next four sections deal with specialised subjects: Middle and Neutral kings in X.vii, attacks in the rear in X.viii, confederacies and oligarchies in X.ix and the weak king in X.x.

Because Kautilya has propounded and developed a unique theory of foreign policy, the use of specialised terminology by him is inevitable. It is quite likely that he invented most of them. The need to categorise different types of kings, treaties and war has led to the terminology becoming quite precise. However, some terms, particularly the words defining the six methods have a variety of nuances. The explanations added at appropriate places will assist in relating this translation to the original text.

Some parts of the text are difficult to understand, let alone translate accurately. Previous translations have differed widely in their interpretations, giving sometimes dramatically opposite meanings, as in {7.7.1}. Some terms like the Middle king 'waiting' to do something are imprecise. The reasons for adopting one interpretation in favour of another in this translation are given in the appropriate Note on Translation.

BASIC PRINCIPLES OF FOREIGN POLICY

The guiding principles which govern the Kautilyan theory of foreign policy are:

(i) a king shall develop his state, i.e. augment its resources and power in order to enable him to embark on a campaign of conquest;

(ii) the enemy shall be eliminated;

(iii) those who help are friends;

(iv) a prudent course shall always be adopted;

(v) peace is to be preferred to war; and

(vi) a king's behaviour, in victory and in defeat, must be just.

The first verse of {6.2}, '*Sama vyayamau yogakshemay-oryonih*'—'The welfare of a state [ensuring the security of the state within its existing boundaries and acquiring new territory to enlarge it] depends on adopting a policy of non-intervention or overt action'—establishes the basis for all foreign policy. While elsewhere in the treatise, '*yogakshema*' is construed as welfare, (as in 'the welfare of the people'), here we have to take into account the meanings implicit in the two words: *yoga*—activity, *kshema*—the enjoyment of the fruit of such activity. The former depends on '*sama*', a word which occurs in only one other verse. In {7.17.1}, it is associated with *samdhi* (peace treaty), *samadhi* (a treaty with hostages). The aim of all three is given in {7.17.2}, as 'means for creating confidence between kings'. In this context, *sama* is better translated as 'non-intervention'.

sanon-intervention, a method designed to build up confidence between kings, is to be understood in a specialized sense. It is not a policy of doing nothing but the deliberate choice of a policy of keeping away from foreign entanglements, in order to enjoy the fruits of past acquisitions by consolidating them. *Vyayama*, (industry or activity) implies an active foreign policy, *Yoga*, the objective of enlargement of one's power and influence, and, through these, one's territory. These are the two stages of policy. Both depend on the state making progress, either materially in terms of its treasury and army or diplomatically in terms of its relations with other states. A state's position is determined by its relative progress or relative decline vis-à-vis other states in the neighbourhood.

The most important of a king's neighbours is the 'enemy'. Among the states surrounding a kingdom, there is always one who is the natural enemy. Presumably, this is the one neighbour who has designs on the king and, in the absence of any action, will be out to attack the king. The other neighbours may be hostile (*aribhavi*), friendly (*mitrabhavi*) or vassal (*bhrityabhavi*). There may also be a small buffer state between the king and the enemy (*antardih*). However, the main target of the conqueror is always the designated natural enemy; 'one cannot make peace with an enemy' {7.13.17}. The reason for many aspects of the analysis of foreign policy being couched in terms of the conqueror outmanoeuvring the enemy, is that the enemy is also the target of the diplomacy of the conqueror. When the conditions are ripe, a military campaign will be undertaken against him.

Allies are important; in fact, allies are described as a 'constituent element of a state' in {6.1.1}, the only external constituent. An alliance is based on giving help. 'The real characteristic of friendship is giving help' {7.9.12}. "A friend is ever a well-wisher" {7.13.17}. 'Even an enemy who helps is fit to be allied with, not an ally who does not act like one' {7.13.27}. Consequently, an ally who violates a treaty, goes over to the enemy and then wants to return to the alliance is to be treated with the utmost circumspection. 'Just as living with a snake is living in constant fear, one who has come from the enemy is always a danger' {7.6.38}. Kautilya gives us a comprehensive analysis of the type of kings with whom an alliance is desirable and the types of allies based on their character and motivation (see X.iv).

Since prudence should always govern choice of policy, Kautilya is against both spineless submission and foolhardy valour. This advice is given twice, in {12.1.1-9} and {7.15.13-20}. Therefore, peace should always be preferred to war: 'When the degree of progress is the same in pursuing peace and waging war, peace is to be preferred. For, in war, there are many disadvantages, such as loss of troops, expenditure and absence from home' {7.2.1,2}. The corollary is that staying quiet is preferable to preparing for war. Similarly, 'When the benefit accruing to kings under a treaty, irrespective of their status as the weaker, equal or stronger party, is fair to each one peace by agreement shall be the preferred course of action. If the benefits are to be distributed unfairly, war is preferable' {7.8.34}. Even a weak king, under threat from an aggressor, may sue for peace at any time, including when the fort where he had taken shelter is about to be taken. (See 'The Weak King' X.x). Peace is also the preferred choice when the relative power equation between a king and his enemy is not likely to change as a result of any action, irrespective of whether both make progress, both decline or both maintain the status quo {7.1.23,27,30,31}. Of the three categories of kings, stronger, equal and weaker, peace is to be made with the first two; war is recommended only against a weaker adversary since it brings gains at least cost {7.3.1-5}.

Even in waging war, Kautilya's advice is that it is better to attack an unrighteous king than a righteous one {7.13.11-12}. Just behaviour also means that a king shall not take land that belongs to his ally, even if it is given to him by somebody else. A king shall also behave in a just manner towards a king whom he has subjugated {7.16.17,19-23,28}.

THE SIX METHODS OF FOREIGN POLICY

The conqueror with his allies and vassals, the enemy with a similar circle of kings, other interested parties like the Middle and Neutral kings—these are the actors in the drama of diplomacy and war. The tools they use are the six methods of foreign policy, defined in {7.1.6-19}. For convenience in elaborating further how these tools are to be used, Kautilya has used a single word to designate each method. However, each word embraces a variety of concepts and nuances. For understanding the comprehensive sweep of Kautilyan foreign policy, it is essential to note the meanings implicit in these six words.

'*Samdhi*', making peace, is defined as entering into an agreement with specific conditions, i.e. concluding a treaty. However, Kautilya also says {7.17.1,2} that 'non-intervention, negotiating a peace treaty and making a peace by giving a hostage, all mean the same thing'. The aim of peace includes a variety of objectives. (i) It enables a king to enjoy the fruits of his own acquisition and promote the welfare and development of his state without intervening in any conflict in his neighbourhood; in other words, he can play the role of the Neutral King. (ii) A king may use a peace treaty to strengthen alliances. (iii) He may purchase peace by giving a hostage and await a favourable opportunity for pursuing his own interests. (iv) He may use it as one arm of a dual policy, as explained later. The techniques of concluding, observing, violating and renegotiating treaties is an integral part of the concept of peace and Kautilya has given a great deal of thought to this aspect, as will be seen from X.iii.

'*Vigraha*', hostilities, is another instrument of foreign policy. It is classified into three kinds: open war, a battle in the normal sense; secret war, attacking the enemy in a variety of ways, taking him by surprise; and undeclared war, clandestine attacks using secret agents and occult practices {7.6.17,40,41}. The term '*mantra yuddha*'—diplomatic offensive—is used in the text, particularly in the context of attacks in the rear and the weak king {7.13.29;12.1.17}. War, in the context of foreign policy thus includes everything from undertaking a diplomatic offensive to fighting a battle. The stages of mobilisation and marching towards a battle are, however, treated as a separate method. It would seem that a declaration of war is actually made only when a military expedition sets up a base camp near the battle field.

'*Asana*', staying quiet, and '*Yana*', preparing for war, are two methods used in connection with both peace and war. These are, in fact, stages in the transition from peace to war and vice versa. Staying quiet is different from the policy of non-intervention mentioned earlier and is actually a pause in implementing a policy of peace or war already initiated. The pause may be of short duration waiting for some improvement, extended if there has to be a longer wait for the right opportunity and deliberate by not choosing to act when one can do so. During the pause after declaring war one may choose to change to a policy of peace if conditions so warrant; it can also be used to change the target of attack from the enemy to the enemy-in-the-rear.

Deciding to undertake a military campaign was a very important, though not totally irrevocable, step for a king. The impression given in the *Arthashastra* is that the king going on a march had to take the army a long way out of the country, leaving the capital city in the hands of a Viceroy. The march meant heavy expenses in mobilisation and transport of the troops as well as a long absence from the capital. A king could mobilise but not actually set out on a campaign; this is implied in the concept of the pause after declaring war. But such pauses also involved expenditure in maintaining an already mobilised army; hence, even mobilisation could not be undertaken without careful consideration. Though it is one of the six methods of foreign policy and, therefore, a part of Book 7, Kautilya has devoted the whole of Book 9 to an analysis of the factors to be taken into account before a decision is made to undertake a military campaign.

The last two of the six methods are special cases which are quite straight-forward. 'Samsraya' is seeking the protection, when threatened, of a stronger king or taking refuge in a fort. 'Dvaidhibhava' is the policy of making peace with a neighbouring king in order to pursue, with his help, the policy of hostility towards another.

The two sets of verses in {7.15.21-30} and {7.16.17-33} make an interesting parallel on the mutual behaviour of the protector and the one who seeks the protection.

THE SPECIAL CASES

The environment envisaged by Kautilya makes provision for some kings who are not directly involved in the conflict between the conqueror and the enemy but can influence the course of that conflict. The Middle king shares a border with the antagonists and is more powerful than both. The Neutral king is even more powerful but does not share a border with any of them. It is not necessary that, in a given situation, these kings be present; if they are, then their potential influence on the course of events has to be taken note of. X.vii deals with this subject.

Since all neighbours are, by definition, hostile and since the enemy's ally is the conqueror's enemy-in-the-rear, guarding the rear is an important part of policy. Any king, therefore, has to be looking constantly over his shoulder, to ensure that his objectives against the enemy are not frustrated by his having to meet a threat from the rear. 'Parshnigraha'—attack in the rear—is an important aspect of foreign policy and can be practised by any king. This is dealt with in X.viii, which has a detailed introductory comment.

Confederacies and oligarchies are two cases of collective leadership and the conqueror needs special techniques to deal with them. One obvious method is to break up such unions by sowing dissension among the leaders, usually by clandestine means or by using secret agents. X.ix deals with these special cases.

THE WEAK KING

Kautilya has designated a king as 'the conqueror' purely for theoretical purposes, to indicate from whose stand-point the analysis is written. This does not mean that the conqueror is successful all the time in enlarging his kingdom by conquest. He may sometimes find himself under attack from a strong king; he may be besieged and even overthrown. A theory of foreign policy which assumes that a king will always win will be an incomplete one. Advice on the policies which a weak king should follow is necessary to complete the analysis of all aspect of foreign policy. Chapter 15 of Book 7 and Book 12 both deal with this aspect. {7.15} is placed in Book 7 because seeking the protection of a stronger king is one of the six methods of foreign policy. Book 12, entitled 'The Weak King' is a brilliant logical presentation of the proper behaviour for a weak king faced with aggression and invasion by a stronger king. The last section, X.x, is devoted to the concept of the weak king.

A king implements the six methods by using all the tools at his disposal. These include not only the resources of his own state such as the treasury and the army but also the troops of his allies, vassals and dependent tribal chiefs, as well as hired persons. In addition, the king can send envoys for his diplomacy. At every stage his clandestine agents can be used to further his interests. Subversion of the enemy is as much a part of foreign policy as anything else. The extensive use of clandestine agents and methods have been translated in Part IX of this translation.

X.ii

DEFINITIONS, PRINCIPLES AND METHODS

[The order in which the verses relating to the delineation of the elements of foreign policy by Kautilya are collated in this section is as follows. We note first that a king may decide either to consolidate his acquisition or to undertake the enlargement of his kingdom. To achieve his aim, he must choose the appropriate method, which may either be a passive or an active one. The chosen policy is implemented using the constituents of his state. If a policy is successful, he will make progress as compared to his enemy; an unsuccessful policy will lead to his relative decline; a continuation of the balance of power is also possible. Acts of God also influence the outcome of policies.

We then proceed to a definition of the terms by designating the role of different participating kings. For convenience, we designate one king as 'the conqueror' and define all other relationships as perceived by him. These relationships are based on the fundamental principle that two states sharing a common border are intrinsically hostile to each other. However, the nature of the hostility may be different for different neighbours; some may deserve only to be weakened while others have to be crushed. Some neighbours may even be friendly and some, after conquest, may become vassals. The basic principle automatically leads to a sequence of enemies and allies. For reasons explained in the previous section, there exist other interested kings in the environment, such as the Middle king and the Neutral king. In {7.13.24}, the concept of the enemy-in-the-rear is amplified and in {7.13.25}, a new concept of an intervening king is introduced to distinguish between the true enemy and a weak king sharing a border with the conqueror.

The complete list of the kings, defined in terms of their relationships to the conqueror is as follows:

ari	- antagonist
shatru	- enemy
mitra	- friend, ally
ari-mitra	- enemy's ally
mitra-mitra	- friend of the ally
ari-mitra-mitra	- enemy's ally's friend
parshnigraha	- enemy-in-the-rear
aakranda	- ally in the rear
parshnigraha-asara	- rear enemy's ally
aakranda-asara	- rear ally's friend
antardhi	- weak intervening king
udhasina	- neutral king
madhyama	- middle king

Every king has his own circle of allies. Since the conqueror, his enemy, the Middle king and the Neutral king are all independent actors, there are four circles. It must, however, be emphasized that the circle of kings is not meant to be imagined geographically as a series of concentric circles, though they may be symbolically represented as such. The nomenclature defines relationships in a dynamic situation, which may create opportunities for some and expose others to danger.

The success of a king's foreign policy initiatives depends on power, which is not to be measured purely in terms of military power. Intellectual power and morale are two other aspects.

By projecting his power by using the appropriate foreign policy, a king makes progress, thus contributing to further increase in his power. There is thus a dynamic relationship between power and progress, mediated by the right policy, executed through the instruments of the circle of states.

The six methods of foreign policy are then defined; the nuances of the terminology used have been explained in the preceding section. Why one policy should be chosen in preference to another depends entirely on whether the chosen method helps the king to make progress. Hence, each of the six methods are evaluated in terms of the situations in which their use will result in progress. The analysis of five of the six methods is clear cut. However, in making peace, there is the special case of the enemy; is there any situation, when peace with the enemy is advisable? Kautilya is of the view that peace can be made with the enemy, purely as a temporary measure, provided that his long-term objective of conquest is thereby facilitated. This is not as

duplicitous as it sounds because the enmity is inherent in the
geography of the situation; by definition, two kings are enemies
when they share a common border. Peace, as explained in
{7.1.32}, is only a stage enabling the conqueror to build up his
strength before attempting to conquer the enemy. We must also
bear in mind that whatever is said about the would-be conqueror
also applies to the enemy, who would think of the 'conqueror'
as his own enemy, whether in front or in the rear. It is assumed
that he too will use the period of peace to increase his strength.

The other part of the dynamic equation is relative power.
The choice of policy is dependent on the power of the king against
whom it is directed. There are three logical possibilities. The
other king may be stronger, weaker or of equal strength. Kautilya
analyses this question thoroughly by stating a general principle
and then modifying it to suit reality.

Kautilya has placed {1.16}, the chapter on envoys in the
first Book, following the chapter on making decisions after due
deliberation. Since envoys are only one of the tools through
which foreign policy is implemented, that chapter has been
included here.]

PROGRESS AND DECLINE

The welfare of a state [ensuring the security of the kingdom within its existing
boundaries and acquiring new territory to enlarge it] depends on [adopting
a foreign policy of] non-intervention or overt action. A policy which helps
in the undisturbed enjoyment of the results of past activities is defined as
non-intervention. An active policy is one which is designed to bring [new]
initiatives to a successful conclusion.   {6.2.1-3}

Active and passive policies both depend on the six methods of foreign
policy [which are described later.]1 The six methods are applied using the
constituent elements of the states involved. Applying these policies may result
in any of the following: <u>decline</u>, <u>progress</u>, or <u>no change in one's position</u>.
                                                          {6.2.4,5; 7.1.1}

A king makes <u>progress</u> by building forts, irrigation works or trade
routes, creating new settlements, elephant forests or productive forests, or
opening new mines. Any activity which harms the progress of the enemy
engaged in similar undertakings is also progress [for the conqueror].
However, a conqueror may ignore an enemy's progress if his own progress
will be quicker or greater [than that of his enemy] or if there is a prospect
of greater future gain.   {7.1.20-22}

A king suffers a <u>decline</u> when his own initiatives are ruined or when the enemy's undertakings prosper. [However,] a king may ignore an enemy's progress if he believes that his own decline will be of shorter duration or lesser extent before progress is resumed and that the converse will apply to his enemy.   {7.1.24-26}

When there is neither progress nor decline, the situation is said to be one of '<u>no change</u>'.[2] A king may [however,] ignore his own [temporary] stagnation if he believes that, after a short period he will make progress while his enemy will take longer to do so.   {7.1.28,29}

From decline a position of no change shall be reached and from that a state of progress; the order of priority may be reversed when there is a special advantage in the future.   {9.7.51,52}

[{7.1.23,27,30-32} contain the advice that if the rate of progress, decline or stagnation is the same for both the conqueror and his enemy, the conqueror shall make peace. See under 'Achieving progress' later in this section.]

It is a decline for the conqueror if the enemy's undertakings flourish; conversely, the decline of an enemy's undertakings is progress for the conqueror. Parity between the two is maintained when both make equal progress.   {7.12.29}

A small gain for a large outlay is decline; the converse is progress. A gain equal to the expenditure on an undertaking means that the conqueror has neither progressed nor declined. Hence a conqueror shall seek to obtain a special advantage by undertaking such works [as building forts] which would produce a large profit for a small expenditure.   {7.12.30,31}

A king may decide to consolidate his recent acquisitions and enjoy the increased prosperity resulting from it or conclude that he is strong and secure enough to undertake further conquests.

A king who is fully conversant with the principles of statecraft shall understand the conditions of progress, decline and no-change [in his own position] and apply the strategic method appropriate to each one in order to weaken or overwhelm the enemy.   {7.18.43}

Events, both human and providential, govern the world [and its affairs]. Acts of God are those which are unforeseeable and whose origin is unknown. If the cause is knowable and, hence, foreseeable, its origin is human. If an Act of God results in [helping] the achievement of one's objective, it is good fortune; otherwise, it is misfortune. [Likewise,] any human action which increases one's welfare is a good policy; otherwise, it is a bad policy.   {6.2.6-12}

DEFINITIONS OF STATES

THE CONQUEROR

A potential conqueror [i.e. a king who wishes to enlarge his territory by conquest] is defined as a king who, having excellent personal qualities, resources and constituents of his state, follows good policies.   {6.2.13}

THE ANTAGONISTS

Any king, whose kingdom shares a common border with that of the conqueror[3] is an antagonist.   {6.2.14}

Neighbouring kings, who are deemed to be antagonists, are of different kinds:

(i) a powerful antagonistic neighbour [having excellent personal qualities, resources and constituents] is an <u>enemy</u>;

ii) one who is afflicted by a calamity [to one or more of his constituents] is a <u>vulnerable adversary</u>;

(iii) one who is weak or without support is a <u>destroyable antagonist</u>; and

(iv) one who has support is an antagonist who can be <u>weakened or harassed</u>.
{6.2.16,17}

Among the kings with contiguous territories, a <u>natural enemy</u> is one who is of the same family or of equally high birth [as the conqueror]; an 'antagonist by intent' is one who is opposed [to the conqueror] or is induced to be so.   {6.2.19}

> [It is better to attack an enemy who suffers from weaknesses in any one of his constituents, including his own personal weaknesses.]

An enemy who has [any of] the following characteristics is easily defeated: one not born of a royal family, greedy, vicious or whimsical, without energy or enthusiasm, trusting in fate, with a habit of behaving unjustly, always doing harm to others, with a mean*mantriparishad*, with unhappy subjects, powerless, or helpless.   {6.1.13,14}

THE GROUP OF FRIENDS

A king whose territory has a common boundary with that of an antagonist [i.e. one whose territory has no common border with that of the conqueror] is an ally.[4]   {6.2.15}

[Like enemies, allies are also of different kinds.] A '<u>natural ally</u>' is one who is of equally noble birth or is [closely] related to the conqueror on the father's or mother's side; an 'ally by intent' is one who needs [the conqueror's help] for wealth or personal safety. {6.2.20}

> [Thus, kinship can be the source of either enmity or friendship. Common interests may bring two kings together; opposing interests make them antagonists.]

THE SEQUENCE OF ENEMIES AND ALLIES

Thus, in front [i.e. the direction of the conqueror's target for conquest] lie the enemy, the [conqueror's] ally, the enemy's ally, the ally's ally, the enemy's ally's ally [and so on], depending on the contiguity of territories. Likewise, behind lie the enemy in the rear, the ally in the rear, the rear enemy's ally, the rear ally's ally [and so on]. {6.2.18}

TYPES OF NEIGHBOURS

> [Though all neighbours having territories contiguous to that of the conqueror are, by definition, enemies, three types of neighbours can be identified.]

<u>Inimical neighbours are:</u>
    - the soulless enemy always intent on harming the conqueror;
    - the enemy-in-the-rear allied with the enemy in the front;
    - one who has suffered a calamity and is, therefore, vulnerable to an attack by the conqueror; and
    - one attacking the conqueror taking advantage of the latter's calamity.
<u>Friendly neighbours are:</u>
    - one undertaking a campaign simultaneously with the conqueror with the same objective;
    - one undertaking a simultaneous campaign for an objective different from that of the conqueror;
    - one who joins his forces with those of the conqueror for a joint campaign;
    - one who starts a campaign after concluding a treaty with the conqueror;
    - one who undertakes an independent campaign which helps the conqueror;
    - one who revolts along with the conqueror;
    - one buying troops from or selling troops to the conqueror; and
    - one who pursues a dual policy [of friendship with the conqueror while fighting some other enemy.]
<u>Vassal neighbours</u> are those under the control of the conqueror such as:

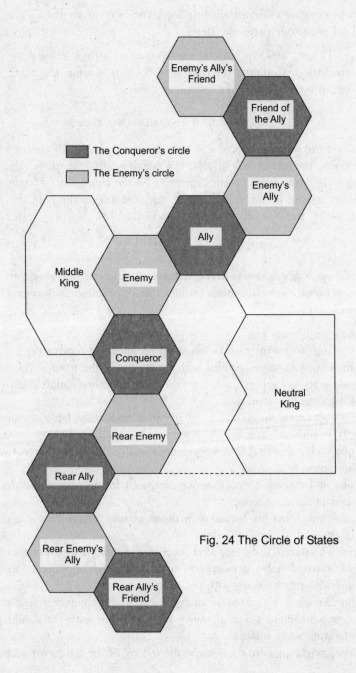

Fig. 24 The Circle of States

- a neighbour with territory intervening between the conqueror and the enemy who is under threat of attack from a strong king;
- kings who are on the two flanks or the rear of the enemy and thus able to threaten an attack on him;
- the [vulnerable] enemy-in-the-rear of a strong king;
- a king who has subjugated himself voluntarily; and
- a king who has been subjugated by force of arms.   {7.18.29}

TYPES OF ALLIES

Likewise, allies, whose territory and that of the conqueror are separated by a [enemy] kingdom, can also be classified into different types.

{7.18.30}

[The way of dealing with different kinds of allies is in {7.18.31-41}; see X.iv]

[Two other powerful rulers, the Middle king and the Neutral king can influence the balance of power between the two groups—the conqueror and his friends on the one hand and the enemy and his friends on the other.[5]]

THE MIDDLE KING

A Middle King is one whose territory is contiguous to those of the conqueror and the conqueror's enemy, who is powerful enough to help them whether they are united or not or to destroy them individually when they are disunited.

{6.2.21}

THE NEUTRAL KING

A Neutral king is one (i) whose territory is not contiguous with those of the conqueror, the conqueror's enemy or the Middle king [i.e. to-tally outside the area of hostilities], (ii) who is stronger than these three and (iii) who is powerful enough to help any of the three, whether they are united or not, or to destroy them individually when they are disunited.   {6.2.22}

THE CIRCLE OF KINGS

The would-be conqueror, the ally and the friend of the ally are the three [basic] constituents of the [first] circle of kings. They, along with the other constituent elements of their states [the ministers, the countryside, the fortified cities, the treasuries and the armies] together make up the eighteen elements of this circle.

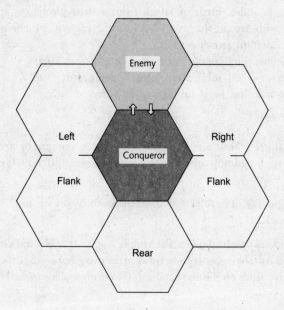

Fig. 25 Types of Enemies-in-the-Rear

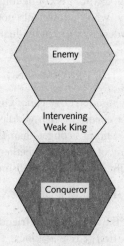

Fig. 26 The Intervening King

Likewise, the enemy, the Middle and the Neutral kings have each a circle of eighteen elements.

Thus, there are four circles, with seventy-two[6] constituents, made up of twelve kings, and sixty other elements [five for each king]. Each of the seventy-two elements has its own strength [and may be weakened due to a calamity].   {6.2.24-29}

TYPES OF ENEMIES-IN-THE REAR

It is necessary to note that kings capable of harassing the conqueror in the rear and impeding his movements are of three kinds: the group of his neighbours behind him and the two groups on either side of him.

{7.13.24}

THE INTERVENING KING

A weak king situated between the conqueror and the enemy is called the intervening king. He becomes an impediment to the strong [only] when he can seek refuge in a fort or in the forest.   {7.13.25}

POWER AND ITS OBJECTIVES

Strength is power; happiness is the objective [of using power].

[Power and success are interrelated.] Power is of three kinds; so is the success resulting from its use. Intellectual strength provides the power of [good] counsel; a prosperous treasury and a strong army provide physical power and valour is the basis for [morale and] energetic action. The success resulting from each one is, correspondingly, intellectual, physical and [psychological].   {6.2.30-34}

To the extent a conqueror is better endowed than his enemy in the three kinds of power, to that extent he will be [stronger and more] successful. If he is less well endowed, he will be weaker. Two kings of commensurate power are equal.

Hence, the conqueror shall [always] endeavour to add to his own power and increase his own happiness. If he is unable to improve his own qualities, he shall endeavour to increase the power of the [human] constituents of his state, keeping in mind their integrity as well as their importance to the work about to be undertaken. He shall [also] endeavour to reduce the power of [his] traitors and enemies.   {6.2.35-37}

[There are, however, five situations when it may be of advantage to the conqueror to permit even the enemy to increase his power and attain his objectives. The first three concern cases when the increase in the enemy's power becomes a liability to him later, due to his own faults. A powerful enemy may so ill-treat his subjects that he becomes easy to conquer;[7] or, the enemy, having consolidated his power, may so weaken himself with uncontrolled enjoyment and dissipation as to be easily overpowered;[8] or, he may adopt wrong tactics such as isolating himself with all his forces in a place that is easily attacked. The other two cases deal with situations when there is a powerful third king. If the plan of the third power is to subjugate the conqueror's enemy first and then to attack the conqueror himself, it is better to have a powerful enemy who may better resist the third power. Alternatively, the conqueror himself may wish to play the role of a Middle king between the other two.]

If the conqueror perceives [that it will be of advantage to him] he may [in the following situations] wish power and happiness even to his enemy. If a powerful enemy is likely to antagonise his subjects by harming them verbally or physically or destroying their property or if an enemy enjoying his success is to become negligent or weak due to [excessive] indulgence in hunting, gambling, women or drink, it will be easy to overpower him. If an enemy, when attacked, is likely to be found with all his troops in one place other than his fort, he will be easily overpowered, being friendless and unprotected by his fort. If a powerful third king plans on subduing the enemy first and then attacking the conqueror, the enemy may be prepared to come to the help of the conqueror even when the latter is unprepared [to launch his own attack]; or, the conqueror may be [able to play the role of] the Middle king between the other two. {6.2.38}

USE OF CIRCLE OF STATES BY THE CONQUEROR

The conqueror shall think of the circle of states as a wheel—himself at the hub and his allies, drawn to him by the spokes though separated by intervening territory, as its rim. {6.2.39}

The enemy, however strong he may be, becomes vulnerable to harassment and destruction, when he is squeezed between the conqueror and his allies. {6.2.40}

In order to further his own interests, the conqueror shall establish, both in the front and in the rear, a circle of kings made up of excellent allies. {7.13.42}

He shall always station envoys and clandestine agents in all states of the circle. These shall cultivate those acting against the interests of the conqueror and, while maintaining their own secrecy, destroy repeatedly such inimical persons. {7.13.43}

He who cannot maintain secrecy will undoubtedly find his efforts destroyed like a broken boat in the sea, even if [temporarily] there are some appearances of success. {7.13.44}

The conqueror may find himself in the role of a frontal attacker, an attacker in the rear, or a victim of aggression;[9] how each situation should be dealt with is given below.

When the conqueror initiates his attack, he shall make:

in the rear

(i) his ally-in-the-rear to engage his enemy-in-the-rear;

(ii) his rear ally's friend to engage the rear enemy's ally;

in the front;

(iii) his ally to engage the enemy's ally; and

(iv) the friend of the ally to engage the enemy's ally's friend.

> [The above is to ensure that the enemy's friends in the front and in the rear are kept occupied by the conqueror's friends and prevented from going to the enemy's help.]

When the conqueror plays the role of an attacker in the rear, he shall first make his own ally in the rear to engage his own enemy-in-the-rear [in order to safeguard his own rear]. He shall then go to the help of his ally by attacking in the rear the enemy.

When the conqueror finds himself under attack, he shall get his ally to attack the rear of the enemy and the friend of his ally to attack the rear of the enemy's ally in the rear. {7.13.37-41}

> [While the conqueror's aim is to expand his own territory by conquest, he may find himself attacked by a stronger king. In this situation, {12.1.10-16} Kautilya identifies three types of aggressors— the righteous aggressor who only wants submission, the greedy aggressor who wants land and goods and the monstrous aggressor who, on top of seizing land, goods, wives and sons, is satisfied only by taking the life of his victim. See X.x]

THE SIX METHODS AND WHEN TO USE THEM

The would-be conqueror shall apply the six methods of foreign policy [as appropriate] to the various constituent elements of his Circle of States with the aim of progressing from a state of decline to one of neither decline nor progress and from this state to one of progress. {7.1.38}

The king who understands the interdependence of the six methods of foreign policy, as explained in this treatise, will bind other rulers by the chains of his intellect and can play with them as he pleases. {7.18.44}

THE SIX METHODS

Some teachers say that the six methods are: making peace, waging war, doing neither,[10] preparing for war,[11] seeking protection,[12] and adopting a dual policy. Vatavyadhi [however,] says that there are only two methods—waging war and making peace, because the others are only derivatives of these two.[13] Kautilya agrees [with the view] that there are indeed six different methods because each one is applicable in a different set of circumstances.   {7.1.2-5}

1. Making peace is entering into an agreement with specific conditions [i.e. concluding a treaty]. A king shall make peace when he finds himself in relative decline compared to his enemy.

2. Active hostilities is waging war. A king superior to his enemy in power shall attack him.

3. Being indifferent to a situation is staying quiet. When a king considers that neither he nor his enemy can harm the other, he shall remain quiet.

4. Augmenting one's own power is preparing for war. A king with special advantages shall make preparations for war.

5. Getting the protection of another is seeking support. A king depleted in power shall seek help.

6. Dual policy is making peace with one king and war with another. A king whose aim can be achieved [only] with the help of another shall pursue a dual policy.   {7.1.6-19}

ACHIEVING PROGRESS

BY MAKING PEACE

A king shall make peace with the enemy when:

    (i) he and the enemy both achieve equal progress in equal time;

    (ii) both decline equally in equal time; or

    (iii) there is no change in their respective situations during the same period of time.[14]   {7.1.23,27,30,31}

The king can achieve progress by making peace with his enemy if he thinks that [he can use the period of peace so that]:

    (i) his gain through productive undertakings would be so great as to enable him to destroy those of the enemy;

    (ii) he can enjoy the additional gain (a) from his own works [not spent in waging war], (b) those arising from works undertaken by the enemy and (c) those accruing from the confidence generated by the peace;

    (iii) he can ruin the enemy's undertakings by using secret methods or occult practices;

(iv) he can entice away the people implementing the enemy's projects by offering them higher remuneration, favours or remissions of taxes;

(v) the enemy, being allied with a much stronger king, will undergo a decline;

(vi) he can manage to prolong the war between the enemy and another king , because of which the enemy had made the peace [with the conqueror];

(vii) he can harass the countryside of another of his enemies;

(viii) he can acquire [parts] of the enemy's territory attacked by another and thereby gain the profits of the enemy's undertakings;

(ix) he can be safe from attack by the enemy who finds himself in a difficult situation due to the destruction of his undertakings;

(x) he can expect to improve his situation to start profitable undertakings elsewhere with another king;

(xi) he can sow dissension between the enemy and the enemy's allies and make them his own allies; and

(xii) he can, by judicious use of favours and punishments, make the enemy's own allies turn against him and [eventually] destroy him.

{7.1.32}

THROUGH WAR

A king can achieve progress by waging war if:

(i) he is confident of repelling an enemy attack because of having (a) [superior forces such as] martial races and fighting guilds or (b) [impregnable defences such as] a mountain, forest or river fort with only one approach;

(ii) he can destroy the enemy's undertakings from the security of an impregnable fort on the border of his kingdom;

(iii) the enemy's undertakings are on the verge of collapse, having been weakened by a calamity; or

(iv) [a part of] the enemy's country can be absorbed while he is busy fighting elsewhere.　　　　　　　　　　　　　　　　　{7.1.33}

BY DOING NEITHER

A king can achieve progress without waging war or suing for peace if:
(i) neither the king nor his enemy can ruin each other's undertakings; or

(ii) the enemy is involved in a calamity or a life and death struggle[15] permitting the king to concentrate on augmenting his own resources.

{7.1.34}

BY PREPARING FOR WAR

A king can make progress while preparing for war when he can bring about the ruin of the enemy's undertakings after making sure that his own will be well-protected.   {7.1.35}

BY SEEKING PROTECTION

If a king is unable to ruin the enemy's undertakings and is also unable to protect his own from the enemy's attacks, he shall seek the help of a stronger king. [Under this protection] he shall first avert his decline and then move towards progress.   {7.1.36}

BY DUAL POLICY

A king shall adopt a dual policy if he can promote his own undertakings by having peace with one [enemy] and [at the same time] ruin those of another by waging war.   {7.1.37}

COMPARATIVE MERITS OF THE SIX METHODS

When the degree of progress is the same in pursuing peace and waging war, peace is to be preferred. For, in war, there are disadvantages such as losses, expenses and absence from home.

For the same reason, a policy of neither peace nor war is to be preferred to making preparations for war.

As between adopting a dual policy and seeking the protection [of a stronger king], the dual policy is to be preferred. For, in adopting the dual policy, one gives importance to one's own undertakings and, thereby, promotes one's own interests. One who seeks the protection of another serves only the other's interests, not his own.   {7.2.1-5}

THE SIX METHODS APPLIED TO STRONGER, EQUALLY STRONG OR WEAK KINGS.

GENERAL PRINCIPLES

The would-be conqueror shall apply the six methods with due regard to his power.

He shall make peace with an equally powerful or stronger king; he shall wage war against a weaker king.

[He shall not wage war against a stronger king] because he who fights against a stronger king is crushed like a foot soldier fighting an elephant. A fight with an equal brings losses to both sides, just like the destruction of two unbaked mudpots hitting each other.

Like a stone striking a mudpot, a more powerful king gains decisive victory over a weaker one. {7.3.1-5}

EXCEPTIONS

[The general principle of attacking a weaker king but not an equally strong or stronger one, cannot be followed slavishly. A contrary policy may be indicated in exceptional circumstances.]

(i) When a peace offer is rejected:

A king, whose offer of peace is rejected by a more powerful king, shall adopt the policies recommended either for one surrendering his troops or for a weaker king.[16]

A king, whose offer of peace is rejected by an equally powerful king, shall harass the other to the same extent that he is harassed. Just as unheated pieces of iron cannot be welded together, there can be no union without heat [brought about by friction]. {7.3.6-9}

(ii) Making peace with a weaker king:

Peace shall be made with a weaker king who is submissive in all respects. For, [if he is ill-treated] anger and resentment will make him fight [bravely] like a forest fire; he will also be supported by his circle of kings.

When a king at war with another finds that the enemy's principal constituents, though greedy, impoverished and rebellious, still do not come over to his side for fear of the war, he shall make peace, even if he is the stronger of the two; he shall at least reduce the intensity of the war.

When two kings are both afflicted by calamities, the more powerful shall make peace if his troubles are greater and if the other is likely to get over his lighter troubles easily and thus is in a position to launch an attack. {7.3.10-12,14,15}

(iii) Waging war though weaker:

When two kings are at peace with each other, [even] a weaker king shall go to war [against the stronger] if he finds that the enemy's principal constituents, though greedy, impoverished and rebellious, are afraid of coming over to his side for fear of being handed back to their king. {7.3.13}

(iv) Neither making peace nor waging war:

Even a powerful king shall refrain from any peacemaking or warlike activity, if by taking action there will neither be an increase in his own strength nor a decrease in that of the enemy. {7.3.16}

(v) Weaker king preparing for war:

Even a weak king shall make preparations for war, if the enemy is afflicted by irremediable calamities. {7.3.17}

(vi) Powerful king seeking protection:

Even a powerful king shall seek protection, if he faces an immediate danger or an irremediable calamity.   {7.3.18}

(vii) Powerful king adopting dual policy:

Even a powerful king shall adopt the dual policy, if he can obtain his objective by making peace on one side and waging war on the other.

{7.3.19}

(viii) The last four methods towards an equal king:

A king shall adopt the four policies [of inaction, preparing for war, seeking help and dual policy] towards an equally powerful king in circumstances similar to the four mentioned immediately above [namely, no advantage, calamity to the other king, calamity to oneself and specific advantages].   {7.3.20}

ASPECTS OF THE SIX METHODS

[Only those aspects of the six methods which are of general application are dealt with here. Treaties, as an instrument of peace, are in X.iii, joint campaigns in X.v, mobilisation for war in X.vi, seeking protection in X.x. and war in Part XI.]

PEACE

The four aspects of making peace [by treaty] are: wanting to make peace where none exists, respecting the provisions of a treaty already concluded, violating a treaty and renegotiating a broken treaty.

Desire to make peace: Examining (i) the prospects of a new treaty keeping in mind the methods of conciliation, etc. (ii) the consequences [of such a treaty] and (iii) the provisions determining the obligations of equal, stronger and weaker parties according to their strength are aspects of the desire to make peace.

Respecting a treaty means (i) the observance, on both sides, of the spirit of the treaty on the basis of mutual respect and advantage (ii) the implementation of the provisions of the treaty as agreed upon and (iii) the protection of the alliance by ensuring that no dissension creeps in between the parties.

Violation of a treaty is breaking it, after establishing, through spies and secret agents, that the other party is not respecting it.

A treaty is renegotiated when there is a reconciliation with a vassal or ally who had, through some fault, violated a treaty.   {7.6.16,19-22}

When the benefit accruing to kings under a treaty, irrespective of their status as the weaker, equal or stronger king, is fair to each one, peace by the agreement shall be the preferred course of action; if the benefits are to be unfairly distributed, war is preferable.   {7.8.34}

WAR

The three kinds of war are; open war, secret war and [undeclared war].
                                                                {7.6.17}

Open war is fighting at a specified time and place.[17]

Secret war is—terrorizing, sudden assault, threatening in one direction while attacking in another, sudden assault without specifying time or place,[18] attacking an enemy when he makes a mistake or is suffering from a calamity, and appearing to yield in one place but attacking suddenly in another.

Undeclared war is using secret agents and occult practices against the enemy.[19]   {7.6.17,40,41}

PAUSE AFTER DECLARING WAR OR MAKING PEACE

TYPES OF PAUSES

Prolonged inaction, inaction for a specific purpose and deliberately not taking action are three similar types of neither waging war nor making peace.

> [*Sthana*—'settled' with the nuance of not actively pursuing preparations for war or peace;
> *Asana*—'sitting' as if ready to jump up when the conditions are ripe; *Upekshana*—ignoring one's ability to act.]

The difference between them: [prolonged] inaction is [necessary] when waiting for one of the constituents of the king's state, which is not at its best, to recover. Inaction for a purpose is waiting for the right opportunity. When a king does not use the means available to him [for peace or for war], it is a case of deliberately not taking action.   {7.4.2,3}

When the conqueror and the enemy are both incapable of harming each other though each may want to conquer the other, [the best policy is] to pause after declaring war or offering peace [and not actively pursue it].
                                                                {7.4.4}

A king shall declare war and then pause when he finds that:

(i) with his own troops, or with those of the ally or by using jungle tribes he can weaken a king equal in strength to him or one more powerful; he shall, however, [first] ensure the safety of the frontier and the interior;

(ii) his own subjects are brave, united and prosperous, able to carry on their work without hindrance and capable of harming those of the enemy;

(iii) the enemy's subjects will come over to his side voluntarily or after instigation because they are greedy, impoverished, rebellious or harassed by the enemy's troops, robbers or jungle tribes;

(iv) while his own economy is prosperous, that of the enemy is miserable and, therefore, the enemy's people are likely to come over to his side when afflicted by famine;

(v) while the enemy's economy is prosperous, his own is miserable and his subjects are likely to go over to the enemy unless there is a war and he can promise them the plunder of the enemy's grain, cattle and gold;

(vi) he can prevent the import into his country of the enemy's goods which harm his economy;

(vii) because of the war, he can divert to his own country the valuable goods now going to the enemy by a trade route, or

(viii) because of the war, the enemy will be unable to suppress the traitors, enemies or jungle tribes in his territories or be compelled to deal with them while fighting the war.

> [Another reason for declaring war is to prevent the enemy overturning a true ally of the king].

[There may arise a situation] when the enemy sets out on an expedition against a true ally of the king, because the enemy would in a short time be able to get abundant wealth or seize very productive land at little cost to himself. Alternatively, the enemy may have to be stopped because he has mobilised all his troops and is ready to start on the expedition against the ally, ignoring the king. In such cases, the king shall declare war and wait in order to prevent the enemy's advance and to proclaim his own valour [in coming to the aid of a true friend]. Some teachers say that [this would be dangerous because] the enemy might turn around, and overwhelm the king himself. Kautilya disagrees. When a king proclaims war and then waits, all that is aimed at is the weakening of an enemy who otherwise is free from troubles. Otherwise, the enemy would enrich himself, first by war against the ally, now saved from losses, will later come to the king's help. Therefore, the king shall mobilize his forces, declare war, and then wait.   {7.4.5-12}

If [for reasons contrary to those given above] the consequences of waiting after proclaiming war are unfavourable, the king shall make peace and wait.[20]
{7.4.13}

SETTING OUT ON A CAMPAIGN

SETTING OUT ON A CAMPAIGN AFTER A PERIOD OF WAITING

After the king has [adequately] increased his strength [during a period of waiting after declaring war] he shall set out on a campaign against the enemy, choosing a time when the enemy does not have all his forces fully mobilized. {7.4.14}

He shall set out on a campaign when he finds that:

(i) the enemy is suffering from a calamity;

(ii) the enemy's troubles with one constituent of his state cannot be compensated by the other constituents;

(iii) the enemy's subjects have become impoverished, discouraged or disunited due to oppression by the troops or ill-treatment by their monarch and thus have become susceptible to enticement to desert; or

(iv) the enemy's draught animals, men, stores and fortifications have been weakened due to fire, floods, disease, epidemics or famine. {7.4.15}

The king shall set out on campaign when his ally and ally in the rear have brave, devoted and prosperous subjects but the enemy, the enemy-in-the-rear and the enemy's ally have the opposite. Thus, while he fights the enemy, his ally can engage the enemy's ally and the ally in the rear can engage the enemy in the rear. Or, if he could tackle them single-handed within a short time, he shall first declare war against the enemy in the rear and the enemy's ally and then set out on a campaign against the enemy. [If he can neither subdue the enemy's allies in a short time nor can get his allies to fight them] he shall first make peace with them and then start on his campaign against the enemy. {7.4.16-18}

JOINT CAMPAIGNS

When a king finds that he cannot set out on a campaign single-handed but nevertheless finds it necessary to start it, he shall do so by joining forces with weaker, equally strong or stronger kings.

If the objective of the campaign is the seizure of a specified object [fort, territory, etc.], the shares shall be fixed beforehand. If the objectives are many or complex, the shares shall be left unspecified.

If there is no agreement on a joint campaign, the king may ask the others to provide troops in return for a fixed payment. Troops can also be hired to go on a campaign with the king's own forces. In such a case, the hired troops shall be promised a specified share of the gain if quantifiable; if not, the share shall be left undetermined.

[When shares are specified before the start of the campaign] it is normal to base them on the proportion of troops contributed; [however], fixing the shares on the basis of the efforts made by each one [during the campaign] is the best type. Shares can also be based on the money contributed by each one or the plunder seized.   {7.4.19-22}

WHOM TO ATTACK

[The state against which a military campaign is initiated has to be chosen with care. In addition to the natural enemy, another state may become vulnerable due to calamities or disgruntled populations. Kautilya's general advice is that the natural enemy shall be the target of attack irrespective of how seriously afflicted by calamities another neighbouring king may be. Further, it is always better to attack kings who are unlikely to have the support of their subjects.]

(i) Between two kings equally affected by calamities:
Between two neighbouring kings equally affected by calamities, should one attack one who has become vulnerable or one who has been unfriendly? The unfriendly king shall be attacked first and after defeating him, the other shall be attacked. [The reasoning is:] the unfriendly king will never help in attacking the other whereas the vulnerable one may help in defeating the enemy.

(ii) Between two kings unequally affected:
Between a neighbouring king seriously affected [but not very hostile] and a hostile one much less affected, who should be attacked first? Some teachers say that the one seriously affected should be attacked first because he will be the easier target. Kautilya disagrees. The hostile king, even if he is less affected shall be attacked first because even his light trouble will be exacerbated by the attack. It is true that the serious troubles of the other will also become much more serious when attacked. However, by not attacking him, the hostile king with a less serious trouble will happily get over it and go to the help of the other or mount his own attack with the help of the [conquered] enemy in the rear.   {7.5.1-8}

(iii) Just and unjust kings with disaffected subjects:
Between a just king seriously affected and an unjust king with disgruntled subjects but lightly affected, who should be attacked first? When a just king is attacked, even if he suffers from a serious calamity, his subjects will help him. [On the other hand,] the subjects of an unjust king will be indifferent to the troubles of their ruler; if they are very dissatisfied, they can bring down even a strong king. Therefore, the king with dissatisfied subjects shall be attacked first.   {7.5.9-11}

(iv) Impoverished and rebellious subjects:

Between a king with greedy and impoverished subjects and one with rebellious subjects who should be attacked first? Some teachers say that the one with greedy, impoverished subjects shall be attacked first, because such people can easily be won over by instigation or coercion whereas the king with rebellious subjects can subdue them by suppressing the leaders [of the rebellion]. Kautilya disagrees. Where there is love, one sees all the virtues in the beloved. Therefore, even impoverished and greedy subjects will remain steadfastly loyal to the king they love, work for his welfare and defeat all instigations. Therefore, the king with rebellious subjects shall be attacked first. {7.5.12-15}

(v) Strong and weak kings:

Between a strong but unjust king and a weak but just king who should be attacked first? When a strong and unjust king is attacked, his subjects will not come to his help but will either topple him or go over to the attacker. [On the other hand] when a weak but just king is attacked, his subjects will not only come to his help but also follow him until death. Therefore, the strong but unjust king shall be attacked first. {7.5.16-18}

SEEKING HELP

GENERAL PRINCIPLES

Amity with a more powerful monarch carries great danger for kings, except when one is actually at war with an enemy. {7.2.8}

A king shall seek the protection of one who is stronger than the neighbouring enemy. {7.2.6}

Should a king seek the help of a king who loves him or a king who is loved by him? The best alliance is that made with one who loves him.

{7.2.25}

EXCEPTIONS

(i) Making peace [even] with the enemy:

If there is no strong king whose protection can be sought [against the enemy], it is better to make peace with the enemy.

[In such a case], the enemy can be helped with money, forces or territory but the king himself should stay away.

If this [keeping away] is impossible, the king shall behave like one surrendering his troops.[21] And when the time is ripe for his own advancement (such as the enemy suffering from a fatal illness, facing internal rebellion, growing powers of the enemy's enemy or his allies being weakened by calamities) the king shall go away under the pretext of some illness or the need to perform religious rites.

If the king is near such an enemy [and cannot get away] he shall attack the weak points of the enemy.

If the king is in his own kingdom he shall not go near an enemy in difficulties.   {7.2.7,9-12}

(ii) Choosing between two strong kings:

If there are two strong kings whose protection can be sought, a king shall choose the one more capable or the one for whom he is a buffer[22] or both. If allied with both, the king shall plead penury [and help neither] but sow dissension between them by carrying tales that each was plotting to deprive the other of his patrimony. When they are divided, he shall promote discord between them and then eliminate them one by one by covert methods.   {7.2.13-15}

(iii) Near two strong kings:

A king situated near [but not between] two strong kings, shall first protect himself against any immediate danger. Or, he may take shelter in a strong fort and follow a dual policy [of peace with one and hostility to another]. Or, he may act after analyzing the causes and consequences of peace and war.[23]

He shall support the traitors, enemies and forest chiefs of both and, going over to one of them, weaken the other using traitors, etc.

If the king is pressured by both, he shall seek the help of his circle of kings, the Middle king or the Neutral king. With such help, he shall support one and destroy the other, or destroy both.

If the two strong kings join together to destroy the kingdom, the [dispossessed] king shall seek shelter with a righteous monarch among the Middle or Neutral kings or any king belonging to their camps. If there are many, equally righteous, to choose from, he shall select one (i) whose subjects will give him happiness, (ii) who will assist him in recovering his lost position, (iii) with whom his forefathers had close connections and exchange of visits, (iv) in whose courts he may find many friends or powerful friends.   {7.2.16-24}

DUAL POLICY[24]

The conqueror shall outmanoeuvre the second element of the Circle of Kings [i.e. the enemy] as follows. He shall induce a neighbouring ruler to undertake a simultaneous expedition, each attacking the enemy from a different direction, [on the understanding that] the spoils will be divided equally. If the neighbour agrees to equal division, a treaty shall be concluded; if he does not, he shall be treated as hostile.   {7.6.1-3}

The conqueror may take the help of the second member of the circle of kings [i.e. the natural enemy] in order to attack another neighbouring king if he considers that:

(i) there is no danger of an attack by the enemy in the rear;

(ii) the conqueror will have twice the number of troops at his disposal; or if the second king will

(iii) prevent an attack by the enemy in the rear;

(iv) not go to the help of the [third] king being attacked;

(v) provide supplies and reinforcements to the conqueror while denying them to the third king;

(vi) help remove the impediments and dangers[25] coming in the way of the expedition;

(vii) use his army against the forts and forest refuges of the king under attack;

(viii) place the king under attack in mortal peril or force him to sue for peace;

(ix) help to create confidence among other enemies, as a result of being rewarded for his services. {7.7.1,2}

ON ENVOYS

When, after due deliberation, a decision [to pursue a particular course of action] has been taken, envoys shall be appointed. {1.16.1}

The conqueror shall entrust to his envoys the various duties specified below. He shall also keep a watch over the [activities of] envoys sent to him by others using spies, visible and invisible guards as well as by sending counter-envoys. {1.16.35}

APPOINTMENT OF ENVOYS

The qualifications necessary for appointment as a plenipotentiary envoy [i.e. one with full powers to negotiate] are the same as for appointment as a counsellor (*amatya*)[26]. One with three quarters of the qualities shall be appointed to carry out a limited mission. One with half the qualifications shall [only] be used as a message carrier. {1.16.2-4}

DUTIES OF AN ENVOY

The duties of an envoy are: sending information to his king, ensuring maintenance of the terms of a treaty, upholding his king's honour, acquiring allies, instigating dissension among the friends of the enemy, conveying secret agents and troops [into the enemy territory], suborning the kinsmen of the enemy to his own king's side, acquiring clandestinely gems and other valuable material for his own king, ascertaining secret information and showing valour in liberating hostages [held by the enemy]. [The envoys shall resort to clandestine methods where necessary]. [The envoy shall ever be diligent in the performance of his duties].[27]   {1.16.33,34}

PREPARATION

[The envoy shall prepare himself physically and mentally.]

He shall start [on the travel to the court of the king where he is sent] after making arrangements, in a well-organised manner, for vehicles, draught animals and a retinue of servants.

He shall [mentally] prepare himself by thinking about how he will phrase the message to be delivered, what the other king is likely to say, what his own reply should be and how the other king is to be outmanoeuvred.

{1.16.5,6}

[In {5.3.19}, translated in VI.iii, the travelling allowance rates for a middle grade envoy is specified as 10 panas per 15 km for journeys up to 150 km, and 20 panas per km for journeys between 150 to 1500 km.]

ON THE WAY

On the way to the place of his mission, the envoy shall:

(i) establish good contacts with jungle chiefs, frontier officers, chief officers of the cities and the countryside;

(ii) observe, both in the territory of his own king and that of the other king, the places suitable for stationing troops, fighting, support facilities and fall-back positions; and

(iii) find out the size and extent of the other king's territory and forts, the strength of the economy, and the strong and weak points in its defences.

{1.16.7-9}

AT THE COURT OF HIS MISSION

He shall present himself before the other king, [only] after he is given permission to do so and he shall deliver the message exactly as given to him, even if he apprehends danger to his life.

[The envoy shall then note whether the king is pleased or displeased with the message received].

The envoy shall note that the other king is pleased by: [during the first audience] the king's graciousness in speech, demeanour and expression, the attention and respect shown to his words, the enquiries about his [comfort and] desires, and the description of the virtues [of his king]; [during subsequent stay] by his being given a seat near the king, by being treated respectfully, by the king remembering him on pleasant occasions and by showing that the king trusts him.

Behaviour contrary to the above will indicate that the king is displeased. To such a king the envoy shall point out that, just as his own envoy was his mouthpiece, so it was with other kings. Envoys, therefore speak as they are instructed to, even if weapons are raised against them. [The *shastras* say that] even if an envoy is an outcast, he shall not be killed. It goes without saying that a Brahmin envoy shall never be harmed. The duty of envoys is but to repeat the words of his master. {1.16.10-17}

[An envoy shall not leave the court of his mission, unless he is permitted to do so].

After delivering an unpleasant message, the envoy may leave [the territory] even without permission if he fears imprisonment or death.

[An envoy who brings an unwelcome message and does not leave] shall be kept under restraint. {1.16.32}

STAY IN THE OTHER KINGDOM

If the envoy stays on because he has not been given permission to leave, he shall (i) not allow the honours shown to him go to his head, (ii) not do anything rash in the foreign court, relying on his own king's power [to save him], (iii) put up with disagreeable speech (iv) avoid women and liquor and (v) sleep alone. [He must remember that] people reveal their intentions while asleep or intoxicated. {1.16.18-23}

He shall employ double agents in the guise of merchants, ascetics, their disciples, physicians or heretics to find out:

(i) how to instigate the treacherous elements in the other court;

(ii) how to subvert loyal elements;

(iii) loyalty or disloyalty of the subjects towards their king; and

(iv) the weak points of the kingdom.

If he is unable to gather information directly by talking to the people of the country, he shall collect intelligence [on the loyalty of the people] by listening to the talk of beggars, drunks, madmen or those babbling in their sleep as well as from paintings, writings and signs in temples and holy places.

He shall use the intelligence gathered to foment trouble.

He shall never reveal the strengths and weaknesses of the constituents of his own king, even when asked by the other. He shall either side-step the question[28] or give whatever reply will promote his king's interests.

{1.16.24-28}

ENFORCED STAY

If the envoy is not permitted to leave even if his mission has failed, he shall analyse the motives of the other king in detaining him. The possible motives are [that the other king]:

(i) anticipates that a calamity will afflict the envoy's king;

(ii) wants to take remedial measures to correct his own weaknesses;

(iii) wants to incite an attack against the envoy's king by the enemy-in-the-rear, the rear enemy's ally or a jungle chief or [foment] internal rebellion;

(iv) wants to obstruct the activities of the ally, or the ally in the rear of the envoy's king;

(v) wants to counteract an attack by his enemy, a jungle chief or an internal rebellion;

(vi) hopes to make the envoy's king miss the season for an expedition for which he is fully prepared;

(vii) wants to strengthen his defences by collecting grains, commodities and forest produce, by improving the fortifications or by raising troops;

(viii) is awaiting the right time and place to attack with his own troops;

(ix) is just careless or contemptuous; or

(x) wants to continue his association with the envoy's king [though rejecting the message received].

Depending on the motive, the envoy shall stay or leave as appropriate, or he may demand from the other king some action considered desirable in the circumstances.   {1.16.29-31}

X.iii

TREATIES

[All verses dealing with agreements between kings have been collected together in this section, starting with the nature of treaties. A brief description of the contents of this section is given below. Further explanations are given in appropriate places. Kautilya prefers agreements based solely on honour though the most common type seems to have been treaties whose observance was guaranteed by the weaker party giving a hostage. The sanction for violation of the treaty was forfeiture of the life of the hostage.

Treaties are of different kinds depending on whether they are made with a neighbour, an ally, or a king who becomes a vassal after conquest. A special case is of an ally or vassal who violates a treaty, goes over to the enemy and then wants to come back; the renegotiation involves careful analysis of the motives of the king both for his leaving and for his return.

The principles of what should be the give and take in treaties is dealt with very comprehensively and logically by Kautilya in {7.7}. The interaction between the conditions prevalent at the time of making the treaty and the terms of the treaty is a clear exposition of the influence of bargaining power in treaty making.

Kautilya is not concerned merely with the immediate benefits flowing from a treaty. In 'Present and Future Gain', he lays down the principles of when to accept small immediate return for the sake of a large future benefit and even when to forego any gain whatsoever.

Sometimes, both the conqueror and the enemy may both want to conclude a treaty with the same king, who may be an ally, the Middle king or the Neutral king. The principle in such cases is that whoever gets a more reliable ally would have outmanoeuvred the other.

Treaties by the weaker king who, when under attack, has to seek the protection of another, is a special case, which has a precise classification of the types of such treaties.

Lastly, the subject of giving and liberating hostages, an important aspect of treaty making, is dealt with comprehensively by Kautilya.]

THE NATURE OF AGREEMENTS

Non-intervention, negotiating a peace treaty and making peace by giving a hostage—all mean the same thing, since the aim of all three is to create confidence between two kings.   {7.17.1,2}

Some teachers say that an agreement made on the word of honour or by swearing an oath is an unstable peace whereas one backed by a surety or a hostage is more stable.

Kautilya disagrees. An agreement made on oath or on word of honour is stable in this world and the next [i.e. breaking it has consequences in life and after death]. An agreement which depends on a surety or a hostage is valid only in this world since its observance depends on the relative strength [of the parties making it]. Kings of old, who were always true to their word, made a pact by [just] verbal agreement. If there was any doubt they swore by [touching] fire, water, a ploughed furrow, a wall of the fort, the shoulder of an elephant, the back of a horse, the seat on a chariot, a weapon, a gem, seeds, a perfume, liquor, gold or money declaring that these would destroy or desert him, if he violated the agreement.[1]

If there was any doubt about the swearer being true to his oath, the pact was made with great men, ascetics or the chiefs standing as surety [guaranteeing its observance]. In such a case, whoever obtained the guarantees of persons capable of controlling the enemy outmanoeuvred the other.[2]

An agreement made on condition that a high official or a relative is kept as a hostage is a 'treaty with hostages'.   {7.17.3-11}

TYPES OF TREATIES

There are two kinds of treaties—those without specific conditions and those with [specific] obligations.   {7.6.4}

TREATIES WITHOUT CONDITIONS

The king, who wants to outmanoeuvre a wicked, hasty, lazy or short-sighted enemy, shall [falsely] create a sense of confidence by making a treaty without any conditions about territory, period or objective and merely an affirmation of alliance. [Under cover of the treaty] the king shall find out the weak points of the enemy and then strike.   {7.6.13}

TREATIES WITH OBLIGATIONS

In this connection, it is said: 'A wise king will make one neighbouring king fight another neighbour and having thus prevented the neighbours from getting together, proceed to overrun the territory of his own enemy'.
                                                          {7.6.14,15}

There are seven types of treaties, according to the nature of the obligations [with three variables of place, time and objective—all three together, any two, or any one]: place, time and objective; place and time; time and objective; place and objective; place alone; time alone; objective alone.

{7.6.11}

A treaty about place is one in which the signatories agree beforehand that each one will attack a different [specified] region. Such a treaty shall be entered into when the other king has to face a campaign in uncongenial territory while the expedition of the king will be in a more favourable territory. An unfavourable territory is one (i) [well-protected by] mountain, jungle, or river forts; (ii) surrounded by forests; (iii) with unreliable supplies of grains, men, fodder, fuel and water [for the attacking force]; (iv) which is uncharted and far away or strange; or (v) with terrain unsuitable for military operations. {from 7.6.5,8}

A treaty about time is one in which the signatories agree beforehand that each one will conduct his campaign for a specified duration. Such a treaty shall be entered into when the other king has to face a campaign at an unfavourable time while the [attacking] king will fight at a more favourable time. An unfavourable time for operations is one when (i) there is too much rain, heat or cold; (ii) many fall ill; (iii) there is a shortage of foodstuffs and other articles; (iv) it is unsuitable for military operations; or (v) there is too much or too little time for the task in hand.

{from 7.6.6,9}

A treaty about objectives is one in which the signatories agree beforehand that each one will conduct his campaign for a specified objective. Such a treaty shall be entered into when the other king's gains will have adverse consequences for him while those of the king will be more permanent. Adverse consequences are: (i) any gains made are easily recovered; (ii) the operation enrages the people; (iii) takes too long; (iv) involves heavy losses or expenses; (v) results in paltry gains; (vi) creates more trouble in the future; (vii) is unwholesome; (viii) is based on *adharma* (unrighteousness); (ix) antagonizes the Neutral or Middle king; or (x) ruins his own ally.[3]

{from 7.6.7,10}

In all cases of treaties with obligations, the conqueror shall start his undertakings well in time, get them established and also obstruct the enemy's undertakings. {7.6.12}

[See also 'unconcealed' treaty, one concluded with no hidden motives of outmanoeuvring the other signatory, {7.11.42} in X.v.]

RESPONSE OF THE ENEMY

The vulnerable enemy who is the target of the proposed treaty between the conqueror and a common neighbour shall offer twice the benefit to one of the parties, with a view to switching the treaty or removing the profit motive. He shall describe to the neighbour thus approached the losses, expenses, absences from home, the benefits to his enemies and the personal hardships likely to result [from a treaty with the conqueror]. If the neighbour agrees, the amount promised shall be paid; or, at least, enmity shall be created between the neighbour and the conqueror and their treaty frustrated. {7.8.1-4}

RENEGOTIATION OF TREATIES

REASONS FOR VIOLATING A TREATY

Some teachers say that a vassal or ally violates a treaty for [any of] the following reasons: (i) seeing the results of his efforts [on behalf of the king] destroyed; (ii) loss of power; (iii) desire to sell his knowledge [to a higher bidder]; (iv) feeling of hopelessness; (v) eagerness to see other countries; (vi) lack of trust [in the king]; or (vii) conflict with a powerful person.

Kautilya disagrees. Fear, lack of employment and resentment are the [only] reasons why a vassal or ally leaves the king. {7.6.30,31}

ASPECTS OF RENEGOTIATION

[It is assumed that renegotiation takes place because a vassal or ally who had left the king, in violation of a treaty, wants to come back to the fold. Normally, a vassal who violates a treaty has to be attacked and defeated; see {7.16.1,2} in X.iv. below]

There are four classes of treaty-violators returning:

(i) <u>One who leaves for good reasons and also returns for good reasons</u>: The good reasons for leaving are the fault of the king or the virtues of the enemy, and the good reasons for coming back are the virtues of the king or the faults of the enemy.

(ii) <u>One who leaves and also returns for no reason</u>: A fickle person who ignores the virtues of both the king and the enemy and leaves or returns for his own ignoble reasons.

(iii) <u>One who leaves for good reasons but returns for no reason</u>: one who leaves because of some fault of the king but returns for his own reasons [on behalf of the enemy, to seek revenge, due to fear or for the sake of old loyalty].

(iv) <u>One who leaves for no reason but returns for good reasons</u>: Returning because of the enemy's faults is coming back for a good reason.

{from 7.6.23-28}

ANALYSIS OF THE SITUATIONS

The king shall make peace [and renegotiate a treaty] with one (i) who left for good reasons and also returns for good reasons and (ii) who has harmed the enemy.

The king shall refuse to renegotiate with one (i) who left and returns for no reason and (ii) who has harmed the king.

The king shall analyse carefully the motives of one who has harmed both [the king and the enemy] and who left for good reasons but returns for his own reasons. Does he come back at the enemy's behest or of his own accord to create mischief against the king? Does he come back because of fear of the king's reprisals, knowing that he is planning to exterminate the enemy? Or, does he come back out of compassion for the king, abandoning the enemy who is planning to exterminate him? A returnee, whose intentions are found to be benevolent, shall be welcomed back with honours; otherwise he shall be kept at a distance.

> [Likewise] the king shall analyse the motives of one who has harmed both and who left for no reason but returns for good reasons. Will he help to compensate for weaknesses thus making his stay here useful? Are his people, being friends of my allies, unhappy at the enemy's place? Has he quarrelled with the king's enemies? Is he afraid of the greed or cruelty of the enemy or the friends of the enemy? Depending on the nature of the intentions, the returnee may be allowed to stay [or be kept at a distance]. {from 7.6.24-29,32}

RENEGOTIATION WHEN NOT ADVISABLE TO DO SO

Just as living with a snake is living in constant fear, one who has come from the enemy is always a danger, because of his long association with the enemy. Just as the *plaksha* seeds dropped by a pigeon nesting in a *salmali* tree eventually take root and smother the *salmali*, one who has come from the enemy must always be feared as posing a danger even in the future. {7.6.38-39}

In case it becomes absolutely necessary to renegotiate a treaty when, in principle, it is inadvisable to do so, the king shall take precautions keeping in mind the particular strength [money, forces, etc.] of the returnee.

One who is suspected of belonging to the enemy's side but has been given favours for coming over, shall be kept at a distance and well-guarded until the end of his life; or he shall be made to fight against the enemy.

If the returnee's actions can be controlled, he may be sent, at the head of an army, to fight hostile jungle tribes or guard a frontier.

Whether the returnee's actions can be controlled or not, he may be sold back to the enemy for a price; or, when it is necessary to make peace with the enemy, the returnee may be falsely accused of conspiring against the enemy [and handed over].

Or, in the interests of the future, the returnee may be killed by secret means. If the returnee is suspected of trying to kill the king, he shall be executed publicly.   {7.6.33-37}

EQUAL AND UNEQUAL TREATIES

BARGAINING POWER

[This sub-section, based on {7.7}, is concerned with the bargaining between a king ('the bidder') who accepts or rejects such an treaty. Theoretically there are four possibilities: offer of troops for money, offer of money for troops, demand of troops for money and demand of money for troops. Since the principles are the same, Kautilya has developed the arguments for the case of obtaining troops on payment. What kind of offer is to be made and whether it is to be accepted or not depends primarily on the inherent bargaining power of the two kings.

The argument is a difficult one to understand because Kautilya has, as in the case of the forty ways of cheating the public, put in this chapter every logical possibility. As in {2.8.21}, the analysis is symmetric. Though the argument is developed in connection with dual policy, this is a general discussion on treaties.

The two kings may be of equal power or strength or one may be stronger and the other weaker. However, there is a clear distinction between whether the weaker or the stronger king makes the first move. Thus, we have three basic types—bargaining between equals, the weaker king making the offer and the stronger king making the offer.

The column under 'conditions' shows how the relative bargaining power is affected by calamities or weaknesses, or by special considerations. In general, the advice is to conclude an 'unequal treaty' if the parties are mutually convinced of good intentions. If there is no such confidence, the acceptor has to treat the offer as one made with hostile intent. In the discussion on bargaining between kings, the bidder is designated as king 1 and the acceptor as king 2.

The general principle stated in verse {7.7.4} is that a king of equal strength should be compensated commensurate with his contribution, the weaker king 'less than the value' and a stronger king 'more'. In other words, if a king of equal strength receives a certain amount of money for a given number of troops, a weaker king should get less for the same number of troops and a stronger king more. This is an expression of 'pure' bargaining power, i.e. a king receives less or more according to his own position in the hierarchy of kings, not strictly in accordance with the size of his contribution. There is no fairness in this concept of exercise of power.

The general principle is applicable only in theory. In actual practice, the circumstances in a given situation may make it necessary for a king to make an offer—and another king to accept—recompense not strictly in accordance with the 'payment according to power' formula. It follows, therefore, that an 'equal treaty' is one in which the contributions and payment are based on the 'payment according to power' formula. An 'unequal treaty' can either be simply unequal or disproportionately unequal; in the first case, the acceptor gets less than his 'normal' share and in the second, very much less. Kautilya distinguishes between a variety of types of 'unequal treaties'. For convenience, the various cases are set out in a tabular form.]

When the conqueror adopts the dual policy, he shall make peace with one neighbouring king while fighting the enemy. From the neighbouring king he shall try to get armed forces in return for money or supply his own forces for payment. {7.7.3}

An equal treaty is one in which the stronger king gets a greater share, an equally powerful king an equal share and a weaker king a smaller share.

An unequal treaty is one in which a strong, equal or weak king does not get a share according to his power.

An exceptionally unequal treaty[4] is one in which one of the signatories gets a disproportionately large share. {7.7.4-6}

When the benefit accruing to kings under a treaty, irrespective of their status as the weaker, equal or stronger party, is fair to each one, peace by agreement shall be the preferred course of action; if the benefits are to be distributed unfairly, war is preferable. {7.8.34}

A king may enter into an equal treaty with another of equal strength for the loan of forces (i) expert in fighting the kind of forces which the enemy, the enemy's ally or jungle tribes might use (ii) conversant with the unfavourable terrain of the enemy's country or (iii) to protect his base or rear. A neighbour thus approached may agree to the loan of troops if he is convinced of the honourable intentions of the proposer; otherwise the proposer shall be considered hostile.   {7.7.16,17}

Both the king who proposes the treaty and the king approached shall consider the reasons which prompted the proposal. Then, after analysing the consequences of peace and hostility, the course of action more conducive to one's well-being shall be adopted.   {7.7.31}

UNEQUAL TREATIES

[See the table on the next six pages.]

PRESENT AND FUTURE GAIN

[The gain from a negotiation, whether it be the payment received for troops supplied or the quality and quantity of troops obtained for a given amount, cannot be computed simply as a mathematical calculation. Kautilya suggests that one should take into account the overall benefit which includes the immediate gain as well as the potential future gain. Sometimes, it may even be advisable to forgo any apparent benefits. These aspects, as well as when to demand the payment, are covered in verses {7.8.5-10}. 'Labha' is translated both as 'gain' and 'benefit'.

The target of the conqueror's activities towards negotiating a treaty with a common neighbour is, as always, the 'enemy'. How the enemy should respond is given in verses {7.8.1-4}]

SMALL PRESENT BENEFIT, LARGE FUTURE BENEFIT

Even when a king is facing financial difficulties or when he distrusts the other partner in the negotiations, he may accept a small immediate gain for the sake of a large future benefit, when he wants:

(i) to make the enemy, whose undertakings had not started well, suffer further losses or expenses;

(ii) to prevent the success of the enemy's undertakings, which had started well;

(iii) to attack the enemy's base camp, heartland or expedition; or

(iv) to extract more benefit later after making a treaty with the enemy of the other partner.   {7.8.5}

[See also {7.9.50-52} in X.v in relation to acquisition of wealth by joint activity.]

UNEQUAL TREATIES

Proposer		Acceptor		Verse Nos.
Nature of offer	Conditions	Status	Conditions for acceptance	
Weaker king contributing, stronger recompensing				
1. Weaker	Equal to the [normal] value of his contribution [i.e. more than he is entitled to get].	When stronger king is (i) suffering from a calamity (ii) cornered or (iii) under threat from his own people or enemies.	Stronger	Treat proposer as hostile if capable of hurting him; if not, accept proposal.	7,8
2. Weaker	More than the [normal] value of his contribution [i.e. much more than he is entitled to get].	Same situation of stronger king as above and weaker king needs additional payment, (i) to recoup his diminished power or forces; or	Stronger	Grant the increased demand, if convinced of the good intentions of the proposer; otherwise, treat proposer as hostile.	9,10

| Proposer | | Acceptor | | Verse Nos. |
Nature of offer	Conditions	Status	Conditions for acceptance	
	(ii) to guard his territory and rear while going after an easily achieved object.	Stronger	Treat as hostile if capable of hurting proposer; otherwise, accept proposal.	11,12
3. Weaker	Less than the [normal] value of his contribution	When the weaker king, entrenched in a fort or supported by an ally wants to		
		(i) undertake a quick [limited] expedition (ii) expects to achieve an objective without a fight or, (iii) is sure of securing an objective; and when the stronger king		
		(i) is suffering from a calamity (ii) has weak support among his subjects or (iii) is under threat.		

Stronger or equal king contributing, weaker recompensing (special case)

	Proposer		Acceptor		Verse Nos.
	Nature of offer	Conditions	Status	Conditions for acceptance	
4. Stronger or equal	Less than the [normal] value of the contribution	Even when proposer has no weakness; if use of weaker king's forces results in (i) greater loss and expenses to enemy who had started an ill-thought out undertaking (ii) elimination of the proposer's own treacherous forces (iii) subversion of enemy's treacherous forces (iv) weaker king's forces helping to harass or liquidate the enemy's tottering forces or (v) peace on honourable terms.	Weaker	Accept the offer if made with honourable intentions [i.e. the smaller amount asked for is not a trick].	13, 14, 15

| Proposer | | Acceptor | | Verse Nos. |
Nature of offer	Conditions	Status	Conditions for acceptance	
Equal kings negotiating				
5. King 1 Less than the [normal] value of his contribution	If King 2 (i) is suffering from a calamity (ii) has a weakness in the support among his subjects or (iii) is opposed by many kings and if King 1 can get help from another source.	King 2	Treat King 1 as hostile if capable of harming King 2; otherwise accept proposal.	11,12
6. King 1 More than the [normal] value of his contribution	If King 2 (i) is suffering from a calamity (ii) has a weakness in the support among his subjects (iii) is opposed by many kings (iv) is dependent on King 1 (v) has to build up his strength.	King 2	Grant the increased demand is convinced of King 1; if not, treat him as hostile.	20,21

	Proposer		Acceptor		
	Nature of offer	Conditions	Status	Conditions for acceptance	Verse Nos.
Stronger king paying, weaker contributing					
7. Stronger	Pay more than the equal value of the contribution [much more than he is entitled to get].	When the stronger king wants to (i) control the weaker on the pretext of undertaking a campaign (ii) eliminate the enemy first and then the weaker king or (iii) recover the excess payment later.	Weaker	Accept if the stronger king can hurt the weaker; if not treat offer as hostile. Or, make an alliance with the enemy of the stronger king or contribute [unreliable] forces such as treacherous troops or jungle tribes.	24, 25 26
8. Stronger	Pay equal to the value of the contribution [i.e. more than he is entitled to get].	When the stronger king (i) suffers from a calamity or (ii) has a weakness in the support of his subjects.	Weaker	Accept if the stronger king can hurt the weaker; if not treat offer as hostile.	27, 28

| Proposer | | Acceptor | | Verse |
Nature of offer	Conditions	Status	Conditions for acceptance	Nos.
9. Stronger	Pay less than the value of the contribution [i.e. even less than he is entitled to get].	When the stronger king suffers from a calamity or (i) suffers from a calamity or (ii) has a weakness in the support of his subjects.		Accept if the stronger king can hurt the weaker; if not treat offer as hostile.	29,30

General Case - Demanding more payment after treaty is negotiated

10. Any king	More than compensation already agreed upon	If the king who demands (i) wants to suppress the other party because the latter has suffered a calamity or a weakness has developed in his support (ii) wants to destroy an undertaking of the other party which has begun well or is sure to succeed (iii) intends to strike at the other party at his own base or (iv) can get more from the enemy against whom the other party has started a campaign.	Stronger, weaker or equal	May pay more if (i) his forces can be safeguarded by destroying, with the hired forces, his enemy's impregnable forts, or the forces of the enemy's ally or jungle tribes (ii) the hired forces will make the enemy suffer losses or a prolon-ged and distant campaign (iii) he intends to increase his own strength in order to destroy the proposer later or (iv) he wants to absorb the hired forces as his own.	22,23

LITTLE PRESENT BENEFIT, SMALL FUTURE BENEFIT

A king may agree to forego a large immediate gain and seek [only] a small future benefit if:

(i) the transaction helps his ally and harms his enemy while maintaining his own advantage; or

(ii) if he intends to use again the partner who is being helped [by asking for very little benefit].   {7.8.6}

SEEKING NO BENEFIT NOW OR IN THE FUTURE

A king may not seek any benefit in the present or in the future if:

(i) he wants to save another engaged in a war with traitors or enemies or with a stronger king threatening his heartland;

(ii) if he wants the other king to come to his help in similar circumstances, or

(iii) if he takes into account a special relationship with the other king.
{7.8.7}

DEMANDING AGREED PAYMENT OR MORE

A king may demand immediate payment of the amount as agreed upon or even more, if he:

(i) wants to break the treaty;

(ii) wants to [weaken his own enemy by utilising an opportunity to] harass the enemy's people or break up an alliance between the enemy and his friend; or

(iii) apprehends an attack on him by the enemy.   {7.8.8}

RESPONSE OF THE OTHER NEGOTIANT

In all the above cases, the second party to the negotiation shall analyse his own present and future benefit [before accepting or rejecting].
{7.8.9,10}

HELPING THE ALLY, THE MIDDLE KING OR THE NEUTRAL KING

[The cases dealt with are (i) when both the enemy and the conqueror try to negotiate a treaty of assistance with the same common neighbour and (ii) when there is the danger of both the conqueror and the enemy competing for the friendship of the Middle or Neutral king, neither of whom is directly involved in the fight between the two].

HELPING AN ALLY

For both the conqueror and the enemy, the ally to be specially helped is one who:

(i) is able, i.e. starts a work he can complete;

(ii) is sound, i.e. starts a work free from defects;

(iii) is productive, i.e. starts a work producing good results;

(iv) is resolute, i.e. works without stopping until it is completed; or

(v) has devoted subjects who help him to finish the work, even with a little outside assistance.

Such allies, once they have achieved their objective, gladly give abundant assistance in return.

Allies who are not able, sound, productive, or resolute or without devoted subjects shall not be helped.   {7.8.11-16}

BOTH CONQUEROR AND ENEMY HELPING SAME NEIGHBOUR, MIDDLE OR NEUTRAL KING

If both the conqueror and the enemy give help to the same neighbour, the Middle king or the Neutral king, whoever is a friend (or a better friend) of the king helped, is to be considered to have outmanoeuvred the other, for, he who helps a friend, promotes his own interests. The other, helping one less friendly, not only reaps losses, expenses, absences from home and gains to his enemies but is all the more hated for having been a benefactor.[5]

When a Middle king, after getting help from the conqueror turns hostile, the enemy is said to have outmanoeuvred the conqueror. For having exerted himself with the Middle king, all that the conqueror has achieved is to make the Middle king hostile and drive him into the arms of the enemy.

The same also applies to competition for the friendship of the Neutral king.
{from 7.8.17-24}

In case both the conqueror and the enemy provide forces to the Middle or Neutral king, he who gives troops that are brave, loyal, having endurance or skilled in the use of arms is said to outmanoeuvre the other.
{7.8.25,26}

When the troops [hired to the Middle or Neutral king] are capable of achieving not only the immediate objective but others as well and when the place and time are clearly specified, the donor can [afford to] give main formations such as the standing army, the territorial army, organised militia, friendly troops and tribal forces:[6] if the campaign is far away or at some time in the future, [only] unfriendly troops or jungle tribes shall be given.   {7.8.27}

DOUBTFUL CASES

If a king believes that the one to whom troops are lent will, after achieving the objective for which they were hired, appropriate them himself, send them to hostile lands or jungles, or, in some fashion make them useless, the forces shall not be lent, using the pretext that they are needed elsewhere.

If, however, he is obliged to lend his troops, they shall be lent only for the [limited] period of that campaign, on condition that they shall stay and fight together and be protected from all dangers till the end of the campaign; as soon as the campaign is over, they shall be withdrawn on some pretext. Alternatively, only unreliable or unfriendly forces and jungle tribes may be lent; or, he shall try to outmanoeuvre the king [of doubtful bonafides] by coming to an agreement with that king's enemy.

{7.8.28-33}

TREATIES BY THE WEAKER KING

[A weak king, when attacked by a stronger king, is advised to seek the protection of a powerful king or an impregnable fort. This involves the weaker king entering into a treaty with the king giving the protection. Kautilya classifies the treaties made by the weaker king into three groups, depending on whether the army, treasury or land is placed at the disposal of the stronger king. Each group is further subdivided into specific types. Though four groups are mentioned in {7.3.22}, submitting himself as a hostage is treated as a special case of surrendering with troops. Other aspects of the policy for the weaker king are given in X.x].

A weak king, attacked by a stronger king whose armies had already started moving against him, shall quickly submit and sue for peace with the offer of himself, his army, treasury or territory. {7.3.22}

The three kinds of treaties [recommended below] are to be used by the weaker king, at the proper place and at the correct time, in accordance with his analysis of his situation. {7.3.36}

1. SURRENDERING HIMSELF OR HIS ARMY

(i) A treaty with self as hostage is one which requires that the king present himself with a specified number or proportion of his troops.

(ii) A treaty with another as hostage is one which requires that the Chief of Defence or the Crown Prince present himself [with the specified troops]. This type has the advantage that the king saves himself.

(iii) <u>A treaty with no hostages</u> is one which requires that the king himself or the army should go away to another designated place. This type has the advantage that the king and the army chiefs are saved.

In the first two cases, the king shall arrange the marriage of one of his important people [e.g. the Crown Prince or Chief of Defence] with a woman of the stronger king's family. In the third case the king shall employ secret means [against the stronger king].   {7.3.23-26}

2. SURRENDERING THE TREASURY

(i) <u>A buying-off treaty</u> is one where the release of the rest of the constituents is obtained by handing over the treasury [either immediately or when convenient].

(ii) <u>A treaty of tribute</u> is one in which (a) payment is made in instalments[7] over a period of time or (b) the [payment demanded as] punishment is limited to time and place [i.e. so many instalments of specified products].

(iii) <u>A golden treaty</u> is one which promotes unity through mutual confidence because the demand is for reasonable payments in the future. Being bearable, such a treaty is even better than the one based on a marriage alliance.

(iv) The opposite of (iii) is the <u>beggaring treaty</u>; it is so-called because of the excessive demands [for immediate payment as against payment in future].

In the first two cases, the tribute shall be made in the form of forest produce or poisoned elephants and horses.[8] In the third case, the payment shall be made as agreed upon. In the last case, payment shall be delayed on the grounds of penury.   {7.3.27-31}

3. SURRENDERING TERRITORY

(i) <u>A treaty of cession</u> is one where the rest of the constituents are saved by surrendering a part of the territory; this is preferable when the ceded territory is infested with secret agents and robbers.

(ii) <u>A scorched earth treaty</u> is one when all wealth has been removed from the ceded territory, except for the [weak] king's own base. This is to be preferred by a king who wants to involve his enemy in calamities.

(iii) <u>A lease treaty</u> is one where the land is saved by payment of the produce from it.

(iv) <u>A ruinous treaty</u> is one when the payment demanded is more than the land can produce.

In the first two cases the weak king shall wait for an opportune time [to regain the land]. In the latter two cases, he shall keep the produce for himself and act according to the recommendations for the weaker king.[9]

                                    {7.3.32-35}

ON GIVING AND LIBERATING HOSTAGES

[As mentioned above, Kautilya considers that a treaty, the observance of which is backed by the giving and receiving of a hostage, the least satisfactory form of treaties. At best, a treaty should be based on word of honour or, second best, on swearing a oath. Even a treaty guaranteed by a surety is preferable to one with a hostage. Notwithstanding the preference for a treaty based on *dharma*, the fact that Kautilya devotes a whole chapter to hostages indicates that the giving and taking of hostages must have been a common practice. Kautilya also devotes half the chapter to liberating the hostage by a variety of underhand methods, implying that the treaty-maker giving a hostage always has in mind the possibility of violating the treaty by liberating the hostage.

The part of Chapter {7.17} dealing with the question of who should be given as a hostage, follows the practice of other chapters of Book 7 of phrasing it as a comparison in the form of who outmanoeuvres whom—in this case, between the hostage giver and the hostage receiver. In effect, an order of preference is prescribed, giving reasons as to why one type of hostage is better, from the hostage-giver's point of view, than another. The list starts with a treacherous minister who is, in fact, intended to be a victim; since the hostage giver does not care what happens to the hostage, he can break the treaty when it suits him! The last person who shall be offered as a hostage is the treaty-maker himself.

The major part of the analysis concerns what type of son shall be given as a hostage. Clearly, the most valued hostage was a son of the hostage giver, daughters being more expendable. The principle behind this is that the continuation of the royal line was the most important consideration. The qualities of the sons considered are legitimacy of birth, wisdom, bravery, and expertise in arms. The question of only sons is also examined.

{7.17.32-61} contain a list of methods by which a hostage can be liberated in order that the hostage giver may have a free hand in observing or violating the treaty.]

GENERAL

An agreement made on condition that a high official or a relative is kept as a hostage is a treaty with hostage.   {7.17.11}

When [the hostage giver has] grown in strength, he shall have the hostage liberated.   {7.17.32}

CHOICE OF HOSTAGE

He who gives a treacherous minister or a treacherous son or daughter as a hostage outmanoeuvres the other [the receiver]. The receiver is outmanoeuvred because the giver will strike without compunction at the weak point—i.e. the trust that the receiver has that the giver will not let the hostage come to harm.

When giving a son or daughter as hostage, it is better to give a daughter; for, a daughter is not an heir, is useful only to others [her husband and his family when she gets married] and costs more to the receiver.

{7.17.12-17}

SONS AS HOSTAGES

It is better to give a son who is illegitimate, less wise, less brave and less expert in the use of arms because:

(i) neither an illegitimate son nor his progeny can be heirs [to the throne];

(ii) an unwise son lacks the power of deliberation and judgment;

(iii) a less brave son lacks enthusiasm and energy; and

(iv) one less skilled in arms cannot fight as well [as one more skilled].

When there is a choice between a legitimate but less wise son and an illegitimate wise son, it is better to give the illegitimate one, though he may have better judgment. For, a legitimate son commands loyalty and can improve his judgment by associating with [and listening to the advice of] elders.

When there is a choice between a wise son and a brave son, it is better to give the brave son, who, though valorous, lacks wisdom. For, a wise son, though timid, uses his intelligence in his endeavours; like the hunter outwitting the elephant, the intelligent outwit the brave.

When there is choice between a brave son and one who is expert in the use of arms, it is better to give the expert son who, though trained in weapons, may not fight as bravely. For a brave son, even if he be not expert in the use of weapons, will fight better due to his steadfastness, quick thinking and alertness.

{7.17.18-26}

ONLY SON

It is better to give one among many sons, rather than an only son. For, all expectations [for the continuance of the royal line] are concentrated on an only son. On the other hand, the hostage giver giving one among many sons is still supported by the rest and can violate the treaty.

If one is obliged to give as hostage his only son, he who can beget a son is better placed. In this situation, he who can beget more sons [from different queens?] is even better placed. He to whom a child is about to be born is in the best situation. {7.17.27-30}

GIVING ONESELF AS A HOSTAGE

A king shall offer himself rather than an only son as a hostage if he himself can no longer beget children and when the only son is capable [of saving the kingdom]. {7.17.31}

LIBERATING THE HOSTAGE

[The hostage referred to as *kumara*, 'the son', shall either liberate himself by his own efforts or be helped to escape by clandestine agents adopting various disguises. {7.17.33-52} are summarised, not in textual order but according to the type of method used. {7.17.53-58} give instructions on how to evade recapture, {7.17.59} on how to act when caught and {7.17.60-61} on how the hostage giver should react to the recapture].

WITH THE HELP OF OTHERS

<u>Using clandestine agents</u>
Agents shall:

(i) disguise themselves as artisans or craftsmen, take up employment near the hostage and liberate him by digging a subterranean passage at night;

(ii) disguise themselves as tradesmen and sell poisoned food or drink to the guards of the hostage;

(iii) disguise themselves as citizens, minstrels, doctors or bakers and set fire at night [as a diversion] to houses of the rich or of the guards; or, disguised as traders, set fire to the market place; or

(iv) carry away the hostage as if he is a corpse [taken for cremation].
{7.17.33,43,45,46,51}

<u>Using entertainers</u>

(i) Entertainers (such as actors, dancers, singers, musicians, storytellers, acrobats and conjurers) stationed beforehand in the hostage receiver's territory, shall take service with the king and also, one by one, entertain the hostage. When they have acquired the right of unrestricted entry, exit or stay in the hostage's quarters, he shall leave disguised as one of them, on a suitable night.

(ii) The hostage can also go out posing as an attendant of the entertainer, carrying musical instruments or other tools of the trade.

(iii) Likewise, a courtesan or a woman shall pose as the wife of the hostage to gain unrestricted access, enabling the hostage to leave disguised as her.   {7.17.34-39}

Using attendants

(i) The hostage may be carried out by an attendant (such as a cook, bath attendant, shampooer, bed maker, barber, valet and water carrier) concealed in a box of commodities, clothes, vessels, bed linen, or furniture.
                                                       {7.17.40}

HOSTAGE'S OWN EFFORTS

(i) He shall escape when it is dark, disguised as a servant, carrying something with him;

(ii) on the pretext of having to offer a night oblation, escape either through a tunnel or get into a watertank [as if for a bath], and swim submerged and emerge far away;

(iii) he may, on the occasions of offering to gods, ancestors or other festivals give poisoned food or drink to the guards and escape;

(iv) the guards may be bribed;

(v) he may set fire to his residence, throw a body inside in order to prevent pursuit [by making the guards think that he had perished in the fire] and escape through a channel or a tunnel or by breaking through a wall;

(vi) he may disguise himself as a porter carrying pots or heavy goods on a shoulder pole and escape at night;

(vii) he may enter a camp of ascetics with shaven or matted hair, and escape disguised as one of them;

(viii) he may change his appearance by suitably disfiguring himself, showing ostensible symptoms of a horrible disease, dressing up as a jungle dweller or similar methods;

(ix) he may disguise himself as a woman and follow a funeral procession [and thus get out of the city gates].   {7.17.41,42,44,47-50,52}

AVOIDING RECAPTURE

[When the hostage succeeds in escaping] agents disguised as foresters shall lead the pursuers in one direction when the hostage himself goes in another: or, he shall hide himself among carts or carters [in a caravan].

If pursuit is close on his heels he shall hide himself and ambush the pursuers. If there is no suitable place for an ambush, he shall scatter gold or poisoned food on both sides of one road and himself take another.
                                                    {7.17.53-58}

WHEN RECAPTURED

If recaptured, the hostage shall try to win over the pursuers by conciliation or any of the other methods; or he may poison his captors.

Alternatively, he may murder the captors secretly at night with a concealed weapon and escape quickly by horse along with his secret agents.

The hostage giver may show another body killed in a fire or drowned and accuse the hostage receiver of murdering his son and mount an attack.

{7.17.59-61}

X.iv

ALLIES AND VASSAL KINGS

[Allies and vassal kings are rulers who have a special relationship with the conqueror. The former are kings who either have close ties with the conqueror or share a common interest. One of the common interests is, of course, having a common enemy, with whom both have common borders. Vassal kings are those who after having been defeated by the conqueror, have been treated so justly as to remain loyal.

The most important characteristic of an alliance is giving help. 'The real characteristic of friendship is giving help' {7.9.12}, and 'help given to a friend in difficulties cements the friendship' {7.9.8}. In the previous section, it was mentioned that the ally to be helped specially was one who was able, sound, productive and resolute, and had devoted subjects {7.8.11-16}.

Kautilya prescribes different criteria for choosing an ally. Various types of allies are also defined according to their characteristics and their ability to help. Using the method of a choice between two alternatives, Kautilya suggests that the desirable qualities in an ally are, in decreasing order: controllability, constancy, ability to mobilise quietly and having troops concentrated in one place. Giving land is the best help, followed by giving money or troops. What kind of help is to be given to allies, ranging from the steadfast to the perfidious, is also clearly specified.

Two special points are made by Kautilya in his analysis of attitudes towards subjugated kingdoms. Antagonists, i.e. neighbouring kings, can be placated with gifts of land; but the land given should be useless, one way or another.

{7.16.17-33} are verses dealing with just behaviour by the conqueror towards a subjugated king. Disloyal ones are to be eliminated, secretly or openly. However, an honourable treatment must be given to not only a king who surrenders but to his family as well. Loyal vassals shall be treated with honour. These verses are a mirror of the advice given to a weak king who had taken shelter under a strong king {7.15.21-20} in X.x—The Weak King. Together these constitute a code of conduct for vassal and protector].

ALLIES

GOOD AND BAD ALLIES

DANGEROUS ALLIES

The following are categories of kings with whom it is difficult to conclude an alliance; even when one is concluded, they quickly become dissatisfied [and cease to be allies]:

– one who has attacked an ally either by joining forces with or under the influence of others;

– one who has deserted an alliance for the sake of another or due to weakness or greed;

– one who has sold himself [for a price] to the enemy and has withdrawn himself from fighting [for the alliance];

– one who, after agreeing to the dual policy of making peace with one and attacking another, goes off in some other direction and attacks another enemy [and not the one agreed upon];

– one who, having inspired confidence in an ally, joins a different expedition or undertakes an expedition on his own;

– one who does not come to his ally's help in times of calamities due to fear, contempt or laziness;

– one who is forcibly kept out of his own place or has left his country out of fear;

– one who has been humiliated by having his possessions snatched away, by being refused what is due to him or by being given unwelcome things;

– one who has been forced to pay tribute or who voluntarily pays an excessive tribute;

– one who goes over to the enemy, being broken in the attempt to do something which proved to be too much for him;

– one who has been ignored, having been [earlier] considered weak

– or one who ignores entreaties for an alliance.   {8.5.22–27}

WORTHY ALLIES

Alliances with the following are easy to make and, when made, [endure because] they remain loyal:

– one who has exerted himself on behalf of the alliance;

– one who is worthy of respect;

– one who is estranged [from the alliance] due to a misunderstanding or due to the actions of traitors;

– one who has not been honoured adequately [by the enemy];

– one who has been prevented [by the enemy] from becoming stronger;

– one who is apprehensive because of a harm done to his friend [by the enemy] or

–one who is frightened of [the possibility] of his enemies forming an alliance [against him].

A wise king shall not allow any situation to arise as would cause harm to his allies. When they do arise, he shall alleviate them by appropriate counter-measures.   {8.5.28-30}

THE BEST ALLY

[The verses {7.9.38-49} are traditional, since they are introduced with the words 'it is said'.]

The best ally is one who has the following six qualities: an ally of the family for a long time,1 constant, amenable to control, powerful in his support, sharing a common interest, able to mobilise [his forces] quickly and not a man who betrays [his friends].   {7.9.37,38; 6.1.1-2}

TYPES OF ALLIES

A true friend is one who shares [with the king] a common objective, is helpful, never changes and never double crosses even when the king is in trouble.

A steadfast ally is one who has the qualities of a true friend [as above].

A fickle ally is one who sides [from time] with the king and the king's enemy.

An indifferent ally is one who has no [real] interest in the king or the enemy and who is friendly to both.   {7.9.43,44}

An ally who has extensive and fertile territory, is contented and strong but is lazy will also be indifferent to the conqueror who suffers from a calamity.   {7.9.47}

A weak ally, who derives benefit from the prosperity of the conqueror and the enemy and who incurs the displeasure of neither is called 'friendly to both'.   {7.9.48}

An unhelpful ally is one who is intrinsically the conqueror's enemy, has become an ally because he is caught between two strong kings and is either incapable of providing any help or is under no obligation to repay past help given to him.   {7.9.45}

An inimical ally is one who helps the conqueror through he is dear to the enemy who protects or honours him or has close relations with him.
                                                                    {7.9.46}

Dangerous allies

He who disregards [the dangers from] an ally who deserts the alliance with or without reason and then returns with or without reason courts his own death. {7.9.49}

UTILITY OF ALLIES

An ally of diverse utility is one who helps in many ways with the products of his ports, villages, mines, herds, forests and elephant forests (namely: gems, articles of high and low value, forest produce, riding animals and transport vehicles).

An ally of great utility is one who gives substantial help with forces or the treasury.

An ally of all-round help is one who helps with troops, treasury and land.

An ally who resists the [conqueror's] enemy is an ally on one side. He who resists both the enemy and the enemy's ally is an ally on two sides.

He who resists the enemy, the enemy's ally, his own neighbour and jungle tribes is an ally on all sides. {7.9.40; 7.16.10-15}

CONSTANCY AND CONTROL

That friend whose friendship has endured since earlier times and who protects and is in turn protected out of love and not for mercenary reasons is called a constant ally. {7.9.39}

Allies who are amenable to control can be classified into two types (according to the type of assistance or the degree of protection), each with three categories.

An ally (whether giving or receiving help) who constantly harasses the [conqueror's] enemy but has [his own] fort or forest retreat is a constant ally not amenable to control. {7.9.41}

An ally is said to be amenable to control but not constant when he becomes an ally because he is under attack or is suffering from some small misfortune. {7.9.42}

CHOICE OF ALLIES

When there is a choice between two possible allies, both in difficulties, of whom one is constant but not amenable to control and the other is temporary but controllable, which one should be preferred? Some teachers say that the constant friend, though not controllable is to be preferred because, even if he cannot help, he can do no harm. Kautilya disagrees. The one amenable to control, though a temporary ally, is preferable because he remains an ally [only] as long as he helps. The real characteristic of friendship is giving help.[2]   {7.9.9-12}

When there is a choice between two possible allies, both amenable to control, of whom one can give substantial but temporary help and the other a constant help but only a little, which one should be preferred? Some teachers say that a temporary friend giving substantial help shall be chosen because such a friend by giving a lot of help in a short time helps to meet a large outlay. Kautilya disagrees. The constant ally giving smaller help shall be preferred. The temporary friend giving substantial help is likely to withdraw for fear of having to give more or, even if he actually provides the help, will expect it to be repaid. The constant ally, giving a small help continuously, does, in fact, give great help over a period of time.   {7.9.13-17}

Who is better—a mighty ally mobilising slowly or a less mighty one mobilising quickly? Some teachers say that a mighty ally is to be preferred because he adds prestige to the venture and, once he has mobilised, helps to accomplish the task quickly. Kautilya disagrees. An ally mobilising quickly, even if he is less mighty, is preferable because he does not allow the opportune time for action to pass and, being weaker, can be used according to the wishes of the conqueror; a mighty friend with extensive territory is less easy to control.   {7.9.18-21}

Who is better—an ally with scattered troops or one whose troops [are together but] not amenable to control? Some teachers say that, because troops more under control can be brought together again, the scattered controllable troops are better. Kautilya disagrees. Troops which are in one place can be brought under control by conciliation and other means; it is difficult to collect in one place scattered troops, each unit being engaged in its own task.   {7.9.22-25}

Who is better—an ally who assists with manpower or one who gives money? Some teachers say that assistance with manpower is preferable because this adds prestige and, once mobilised, helps to accomplish the task quickly. Kautilya disagrees. An ally who helps monetarily is preferable because one can always use money but troops only sometimes; and with money one can acquire troops and anything else one wants. {7.9.26-30}

Who is better—an ally giving money or giving land? Some teachers say that money, being movable property, is better because it enables one to meet all kinds of expenditure. Kautilya disagrees. It has been said in this work before that both money and allies can be got by land.[3] Therefore, an ally giving land is preferable.   {7.9.31-34}

When, among a group of allies, many give equal help in terms of manpower, it is specially advantageous to get the troops from one whose troops are valorous, able to tolerate hardship, loyal and versatile.

{7.9.35}

When equal monetary help is given, it is specially advantageous to get it from one who readily complies with requests, is generous, gives continuously and without too much effort. {7.9.36}

ATTITUDE TO ALLIES

[The conqueror shall treat each ally according to his special characteristics. Kautilya discusses ten types, from the reliable to the perfidious. The principles are that the ally should be prevented from going over to the enemy but, at the same time, neither should be allowed to grow in power nor become too weak. An ally shall not undertake independent operations which are not in consonance with the objectives of the conqueror. All perfidious allies shall be crushed.]

An ally who identifies himself with the conqueror in enmity towards the [conqueror's] enemy shall be helped to increase his power so that he may withstand the enemy.

An ally who is likely to grow in power after defeating the enemy and thus become uncontrollable shall be embroiled in a conflict with his own neighbour and his own ally; or, a pretender in his family or an unjustly treated prince shall be encouraged to seize the throne; or such actions shall be taken as would oblige the ally to remain obedient, in return for help received.

A very weak ally who may either be incapable of helping the conqueror or go over to the enemy shall be so maintained that he neither becomes too weak nor too strong.

An inconstant or fickle ally, who enters into a treaty with the conqueror for his own reasons, shall be prevented from leaving the alliance by removing the causes which may prompt him to do so.

A perfidious ally, who is an ally of both the conqueror and the enemy, shall first be separated from the enemy, then crushed before the enemy himself is crushed.

An indifferent ally shall be made to incur the wrath of his neighbours and, when he is in trouble due to fighting with them, shall be helped so that he is placed under an obligation.

A weak ally who seeks help from the conqueror and the enemy shall be helped with troops [by the conqueror] so that he does not turn to the enemy;

or, he shall be removed from his territory and settled elsewhere and the territory given to another ally who had helped the conqueror with troops.

An unscrupulous ally who refuses to give [the conqueror] in need the help he can or who might do the conqueror harm must be crushed when he comes near the conqueror in good faith.

An ally in a calamity subjected to an unrestrained attack by the enemy shall be helped to overcome the enemy by himself with the conqueror providing whatever help is necessary to overcome the adverse consequences of the calamity.

An ally attacking the enemy affected by a calamity [independently of the conqueror] may become alienated from the conqueror but this will be resolved when the enemy, freed from his calamity, subdues his attacker.

{7.18.31-42}

SUBJUGATED KINGDOMS

[If the conqueror follows the principles of just behaviour and the methods set out herein for dealing with different types of subjugated kings,] such kings, sustained in their own kingdoms by conciliatory methods, will remain loyal to the conqueror and his descendants. {7.16.29,33}

THE USE OF THE FOUR METHODS

The conqueror shall control the members of his circle of kings, (the antagonists with contiguous territory and the allies with non-contiguous territory) using the four methods [*sama, dana, bheda,* or *danda*], in accordance with the principles of restriction, option or combination.[4]

The weak shall be controlled by *sama* [conciliation] and *dana* [placating with gifts], and the strong by *bheda* [sowing dissension] and *danda* [force].

Conciliation, in this context, means the following policies: protecting the people living in villages and forests, cattle herds and trade routes; handing back [to the subjugated king] those who had displeased him, run away from him or done him harm.

Placating with gifts involves the giving away of land, wealth and girls and the promise of security, [freedom from fear of overthrow].

Dissension is sown by demanding wealth, troops, land or inheritance [from the subjugated king] on behalf of a neighbouring king, a jungle chief, a protector or an unjustly treated prince [of the subjugated king's family].

Use of force is capturing the enemy by means of open, deceptive or secret war or by using the methods suggested for capturing a fort.[5]

{7.16.3-8}

TYPES OF SUBJUGATED KINGS

[The same terminology, used to classify allies and subjugated kings, is defined in {7.16.13-15} and referred to in {7.9.40} regarding allies.]

A subjugated king is of
  <u>diverse utility</u>: one who helps in many ways with diverse products;
  <u>great utility</u>: one who helps with forces or treasury;
  <u>all-round utility</u>: one who helps with troops, treasury and land;
  <u>one-sided utility</u>: one who resists the only [protector's] enemy;
  <u>two-sided utility</u>: one who resists the [protector's] enemy and the enemy's ally;
  <u>all-sided utility</u>: one who resists the enemy, the enemy's ally, his own neighbour and jungle tribes.   {from 7.16.10-15; 7.9.40}
  Of these, the kings who are energetic and enthusiastic shall be so placed as to help the army, those who are rich and powerful to help the treasury and the wise kings to help [govern] the land.   {7.16.9}

NEUTRALISING ANTAGONISTS

[Antagonists can be neutralised by a gift of land; however, the type of land gifted shall be chosen carefully according to the nature of the recipient. The basic principle is that, since the recipients are inherently untrustworthy, the land gifted shall be such as not to make them powerful by capitalising on their advantages].

If an antagonist can be neutralised by the gift of land, the conqueror shall win support by giving an appropriate type of land as below:

enemies in the rear, such as jungle chiefs, the enemy-in-the-rear himself, or his high officials	<u>useless land;</u>
one entrenched in a fort	<u>land not connected</u> to that of the conqueror;
a forest chief	<u>land not yielding a livelihood;</u>
a pretender of the antagonist's family	<u>land that can be recovered:</u>
an unjustly treated prince of the antagonist's family	<u>land snatched from the enemy;</u>
a guild of troops	<u>land always threatened</u> by hostile forces;

a union of [private] armies	land <u>next to</u> the territory of <u>a</u> <u>powerful king</u>;
one opposing the conqueror in war	<u>land always threatened</u> by hostile forces and next to a powerful king;
an energetic and enthusiastic king	<u>land not conducive to military</u> <u>exercises</u>;
a supporter of the enemy	<u>waste land</u>;
one enticed from the conqueror	<u>impoverished land</u>;
a deserter who has returned	land which can be <u>settled</u> <u>only</u> <u>with heavy losses and</u> <u>expenses</u>;
one who deserts the enemy	land <u>affording no shelter</u>.

The conqueror shall appropriate for himself any land that cannot be occupied by someone else. {7.16.16}

TREATY VIOLATORS

When a strong king wants to conquer a subject king, who causes harassment by violating the [terms of the] treaty previously agreed upon, the strong king shall choose the direction of attack such that (i) the terrain, season and provisioning are suitable to his own troops and (ii) the treaty violator has no forts for refuge and no supporters in the rear.

In case the above conditions are not satisfied, the strong king shall commence the attack only after taking adequate precautionary measures against any weaknesses. {7.16.1,2}

JUST BEHAVIOUR TOWARDS THE CONQUERED

Towards loyal subjugated kings

Among the subjugated kings, the conqueror shall permit that king who is most helpful and of unchanging loyalty to continue to enjoy [his kingdoms and privileges]. He shall assist, to the best of his ability, any one who helps him by bestowing rewards and honours as befitting the help received and by giving aid in calamities. Those who call on the conqueror voluntarily shall be received with honour and granted an audience when they want it. The conqueror shall not use contemptuous, threatening, insulting or reproachful words towards them. He shall protect, like a father, those who are promised freedom from fear. The son of one killed in action [fighting for the conqueror] shall be installed on the [dead king's] throne. {7.16.17,19-23,28}

TOWARDS DISLOYAL KINGS

Among the subjugated kings, those who are unhelpful or disloyal shall be got rid of secretly. Anyone causing harm shall be publicly condemned and executed; however, if there is a danger of this exciting the enemy, the disloyal king shall be suppressed using clandestine methods.[6]

[Though the disloyal king is to be punished, openly or secretly], the conqueror shall not only not covet the slain king's land, wealth, sons or wives but give the members of his family appropriate positions.

{7.16.18,24-27}

The conqueror who kills or imprisons a king who surrenders or who covets the land, prosperity, sons or wives of the surrendering king will provoke the [kings of the] circle of states to revolt. And the counsellors [of the ill-treated surrendering king] who remain in the territory will also be provoked into seeking refuge with the circle of states, or to seek to take the conqueror's kingdom or life.

{7.16.30-32}

X.v

JOINT ACTIVITIES

[The purpose of concluding treaties and acquiring allies or vassals is to enable the conqueror to increase his power. This can be achieved either peacefully or by force. The choice of method and of the king to be allied with for the joint activity have to be made taking into account the strength of the partner.

The analysis of the question by Kautilya is, in effect, a discussion on the relative merits of the various types of resources—land, wealth, mines, forests, etc. The argument is on the usual pattern of comparing the alternatives on the basis of who outmanoeuvres whom.

The most valuable acquisition is land. This is normally done by conquest, though purchase is also possible. Acquiring wealth is next in the order of priority and acquiring an ally last. If settled land is acquired, whoever wrests it from a more powerful king or a foolish king outmanoeuvres the other. Such land should be nearby, free from troubles, and defensible from the point of view of the attacker. A land fort is easiest to take, a river fort more difficult and a mountain fort most difficult. From the point of view of the besieged, the reverse order applies, the mountain fort being the best. This is in fact spelt out in {7.12.2}.

As regards virgin land useful for settlement, the criteria are its potential for development, both physical and human. 'The value of land is what man makes of it' {7.11.9} and 'It is the people who constitute a kingdom; like a barren cow, a kingdom without people yields nothing' {7.11.25}. Good land for settlement is that which has a river, and is suitable for cultivation, especially grains. However, if there is greater need for minerals, land with mines is preferable. Likewise, land with elephant forests is preferable to land with productive forests and land with land routes for trade to land with water routes. Land which is difficult to settle should be sold to someone who is bound to fail in his attempt to settle it; it should then be reacquired, probably cheaply, with whatever infrastructural improvements that have been made in the failed attempts.

{7.12.1-28} are a description of the good qualities to look for in forts, irrigation works, productive forests, elephant forests, mine and trade routes; the last one being particularly noteworthy.

The choice of the joint activity partner having been made on the basis of relative strength, {7.5.45-49} indicate how a king should terminate prudently the arrangement, in such a manner that he preserves his independence and power.]

BEFORE UNDERTAKING THE JOINT ACTIVITY

Before undertaking a combined operation [with the forces of other rulers] the king shall carefully consider the reasons for waging war or making peace and join forces with powerful and upright rulers. A powerful ruler is one who can attack the king's enemy in the rear and can give [material] help to the campaign. An upright ruler is one who does what he has promised, irrespective of good or bad results.

As between joining forces with a ruler who is stronger than the king or with two rulers of strength equal to the king, it is better to join two equal kings. For with one ruler, the stronger ruler will have the upper hand during the campaign, whereas with two equals the king can keep control. If one of them turns treacherous, it will be easy for the other two to suppress him and make him suffer the consequences of the dissent.

As between joining forces with one equal or two weaker rulers, it is better to join with the weaker ones since the king can delegate two different tasks to them and keep them under control. {7.5.38-44}

OBJECTIVES OF JOINT CAMPAIGNS

The objective of a joint campaign [after a treaty with another king or kings] is to acquire an ally, wealth or land; gaining one later in the list is preferable to one earlier. For, money and allies can be obtained by land and an ally can be obtained with money. However, it is preferable to obtain any of the three, so long as it is a means of getting the other two. {7.9.1-3}

A king shall enter into a treaty and undertake a joint campaign always keeping in mind his own objective, and after analysing the clear and definite benefit or part benefit that will accrue to him. {7.9.53}

The king who, acting according to the policies set out in this *Arthashastra*, seizes land from others, gains a special advantage over his own confederates and his enemies. {7.10.38}

The king who, acting according to the policies of this *shastra* acquires allies, money, populated land or unsettled land, outmanoeuvres his confederates.   {7.11.45}

A king obtains a special advantage when he acquires undertakings such as forts [water works, productive forests, elephant forests, mines, trade routes, parks and roads] at small cost and large benefit.{7.12.31}

A <u>similar treaty</u>[1] is one in which the signatories to a treaty for a joint campaign acquire the same objective [both allies, both money or both land]; when each party gets a different kind of benefit, it is a <u>dissimilar</u> treaty. Any signatory who gains a special advantage is said to outmanoeuvre the others.   {7.9.4-6}

In a similar treaty, whoever obtains an ally with all the [six] qualities[2] or relieves an old friend in difficulties is said to outmanoeuvre the others,[3] for help given to a friend in difficulties cements the friendship firmly.
                                                 {7.9.7,8}

WEALTH

Which is preferable—an immediate small gain or a large gain in the future? Some teachers say that an immediate small gain is preferable because it is opportune in terms of time, place and the nature of the task in hand. Kautilya disagrees. [The choice is not so clear cut]. A large gain in the future is preferable if it is like a seed [yielding fruit in the future] and if it is not likely to disappear [before fruition]. Otherwise, [if there is no growth and if there is a danger of it not fructifying] the small immediate gain is preferable.   {7.9.50-52}

LAND IN GENERAL

Among the signatories to a treaty for a joint campaign, he who acquires land [whether settled land or virgin land] with [the maximum number of] ideal qualities[4] and with many developed productive facilities outmanoeuvres the others.   {7.10.2; 7.11.2}

SETTLED LAND

Between two kings who acquire equally good land, he who acquires it after overcoming the stronger enemy outmanoeuvres the other. For, he not only acquires land [but also] weakens a stronger enemy and adds to his own prestige. It is true that it is easy to wrest land from a weaker king; but the land acquired will also be poor and the neighbour, who was an ally, will become an enemy.

In case the strength [of the kings overcome by the signatories to a treaty for a joint campaign] is equal, he who acquires land after defeating an enemy entrenched in a fort, outmanoeuvres the other. For, the acquisition of a fort enables one to protect one's own territory and to repulse enemies and jungle tribes.

Regarding the acquisition of land from a mobile enemy [not entrenched in a fort], land near a weak neighbour has a special advantage. For, it is easier to safeguard the security and welfare of land near a weak king; on the other hand, it costs a great deal in men and money to protect land near a strong neighbour.

Which is better—a rich land with permanent enemies or poor land without permanent enemies? (A land with permanent enemies is defined as one on whose frontiers there are a number of forests giving shelter to robber bands, *mlecchas*, or jungle tribes). Some teachers say that, because a rich land enables one to get wealth and an army with which to destroy the enemies, a rich land with permanent enemies is preferable. Kautilya disagrees. In acquiring land with such enemies, one only adds to one's number of enemies; and an enemy remains an enemy whether he is helped or harmed: on the other hand, a temporary enemy can be made to be quiet through favours or [at least] by not harming him.

Between a small piece of land nearby and a large tract far away, a small piece nearby is preferable because it is easy to obtain, protect and defend. It is the contrary with land far away.

As between two tracts of land, both far away, one which can be defended with its own resources and one which requires for its defence an army to be stationed there, the former is preferable, since it can be held by the wealth and army produced within itself. [In the other case, there is not only the cost of stationing an army but the unavailability of troops located far away for other purposes].

As between taking land from a wise king and foolish king, the latter is preferable because it is easy to obtain and protect and cannot be taken back. The opposite is the case with land from a wise king because his subjects will be loyal to him.

As between a king who can be harassed and one who can be overthrown, it is better to take the land of the latter. For, when such a king is attacked, he will have little or no help and would only wish to run away taking his treasury and army with him; his subjects will desert him. On the other hand a king who cannot be overthrown but only harassed will still have the protection of his forts and friends.

As between a king entrenched in a land-fort and one in river-fort, seizing the land from the former is preferable. A land-fort is more easily besieged, stormed and captured along with the enemy in it. Capturing a river-fort is doubly difficult—the besieger has to cross the water while the besieged gets water and other necessities from it.

As between a king entrenched in a river-fort and one in a mountain fort, seizing the land from the former is preferable. A river fort can be assaulted using elephants, wooden bridges, earthworks or boats; a river does not have deep water all the year round and the water in it can be diverted. On the other hand, a mountain fort is protected by the mountain itself and, therefore, not easy to breach or ascend; even if one part is breached, everyone inside is not destroyed; and there is great loss to the besieger due to the rocks and trees thrown from above.

As between those fighting on the river and those fighting on land, seizing land from the former is better. River fighters are circumscribed by time and place of fighting; land fighters can do so any where at any time.

As between warriors in trenches and fighters in the open, seizing land from the former is better. Fighters in the open have only their weapons but trench fighters use both trenches and weapons [and are less effective when they do not have time to dig them]. {7.10.3-37}

VIRGIN TERRITORY

Economic potential

As between land dependent on rain and land with flowing water [i.e. a river], a smaller tract with flowing water is preferable to a larger drier one because with flowing water, which is always available, the production of crops is assured.

As between two rain-fed tracts, that which is conducive to the growth of both early and late crops and which requires less labour and less rain for cultivation is preferable.

As between two irrigated tracts, one on which cereals can be grown is preferable. [However], if one of them is larger, the larger one unsuitable to the cultivation of cereals is preferable to the smaller one which is suitable. For, not only can different types of wet crops, dry crops and medicinal plants be grown in [different parts of] a large area but also many forts and defensive works can be built. The value of land is what man makes of it.

As between cultivable land and land with mines, cultivable land is preferable. For, mines [only] fill the treasury while grains fill both the treasury [with taxes] and the storehouses [with produce]. To begin construction of forts and other defensive works, grains are a prerequisite.

However, land with mines is superior when the products of the mines are in great demand.

Some teachers say that land with productive forests is preferable to land with elephant forests, because a productive forest is the source of a variety of materials for many undertakings while the elephant forests supply only elephants. Kautilya disagrees. One can create productive forests on many types of land but not elephant forests. For one depends on elephants for the destruction of an enemy's forces.

As between a land with water routes and one with land routes, one with routes on land is preferable because it is always available for trade.

{7.11.3-17}

Population

As between land with people united in guilds and land not so united, the latter is preferable because they are easier to control, less susceptible to the intrigues of enemies and less able to bear hardships [for a cause]. It is the contrary with people united in guilds, and they pose great dangers when enraged.

When it comes to settling people in virgin territory, it is preferable to induct the [three] lower *varnas* [practicing the three main areas of economic activity] because of the variety of benefits which flow from them. Farmers are dependable and productive; cowherds make agriculture and other activities possible [by opening up pasture lands]; and rich traders are a source of goods and loans [of money].

{7.11.18-21}

Defence

Of all the qualities of land, the best is affording shelter.

As between land providing the protection of forts and one providing the support of people, the latter is preferable for it is the people who constitute a kingdom. Like a barren cow, a kingdom without people yields nothing.

{7.11.22-25}

SALE OF VIRGIN TERRITORY

When a king is asked by a strong king to sell land which has excellent qualities or which can [easily] be seized by the strong king, he shall agree to the sale and conclude an 'unconcealed' treaty [i.e. one with no hidden motives of outmanoeuvring the stronger king].

When asked by an equal or weaker king to sell land [of excellent quality or easily seizable], a king shall analyse the situation. He shall agree to the sale [only] if (i) the land would continue to be under his control or can later be recovered or (ii) the purchaser could be brought under control because of being tied to it or (iii) the sale would bring in allies or wealth, thereby helping him to achieve his objectives.

{7.11.41-44}

LAND DIFFICULT TO SETTLE

If settlement of a tract is likely to entail heavy losses or expenditure, a king shall first sell the land, with the intention of reacquiring it, to one who will fail in the attempt at settlement. Such agreements shall remain verbal. The buyers likely to fail are the following:

(i) a weak king, though of royal blood, will perish along with his loyal subjects because of the heavy losses and expenses of settlement;

(ii) a king not of royal blood, even if he is strong, will fail, because the people, not being as loyal [as they would be to true royalty] will desert him for fear of losses and expenses;

(iii) An apathetic king [one without energy or enthusiasm] will not use force even if he has the means to do so and the heavy losses and expenses will destroy him and his forces;

(iv) one without support [among his people] even if he has wealth, will fail because all his expenses will come to nothing without benefiting anyone;

(v) a king who is unjust or vicious lays waste even settled land; there is no hope of such a one succeeding in settling virgin land;

(vi) a king who trusts in fate and does not believe in human effort will fail because such a king never begins a work and never achieves anything;

(vii) a wilful king, who does whatever he pleases, never achieves anything and is the worst of all. Some teachers do not agree that a wilful king is the worst on the grounds that even such a king may perchance find a weak point on the conqueror. Kautilya believes that, even if he finds accidently a weak point, he will also provide opportunities for his own destruction by his wilfulness.

If the conqueror cannot find a purchaser of any of the types mentioned above, he shall settle territory on accordance with the principles mentioned in 'neutralising antagonists'.[5]

{7.11.26-40}

JOINT UNDERTAKINGS

An agreement to build a fort [or irrigation works, or to exploit productive forests, elephant forests, mines or trade routes] is an 'agreement for a joint undertaking'.

{7.12.1}

FORTS

Among forts of different types—a land-fort, a river fort or a mountain fort[6]—
one later in the list is preferable to one earlier [i.e. order of ascending importance].

Whoever gets an impregnable fort built on a place best suited for it at
less cost and labour is said to outmanoeuvre the other. {7.12.2-3}

WATER WORKS

Dams built to store water from a flowing source [such as a river] are preferable
to those built to store water brought by canals [i.e. dug for that purpose].

Among reservoirs built by damming rivers, the one which irrigates a
larger area is better. {7.12.4,5}

PRODUCTIVE FORESTS

Whoever plants [for exploiting the timber resources] a large forest, near
the border of his country, watered by a river and yielding material of high
value is said to outmanoeuvre the others. A forest watered by a river is
self-sustaining and provides shelter in times of calamities. {7.12.6,7}

ELEPHANT FORESTS

Whoever creates an elephant forest near the border of his country, near a
weak neighbour, stocked with many brave animals and capable of harassing
the enemy is said to outmanoeuvre the others. Some teachers say that a forest
with a few brave elephants is preferable to one with a large number of dull
ones, on the grounds that, since [success in] war depends on the brave, a few
animals can rout many cowardly ones and the defeated ones [turn around
and] destroy their own army. Kautilya disagrees. It is better to have many
dull elephants [than just a few brave ones]; they can be made to do many
things in the army camp, provide protection to the troops and terrify the
enemy troops by their numbers. It is also possible to make the many dull
elephants valorous by [suitable] training. But the few, however brave, can
never be made many. {7.12.8-12}

MINES

Whoever opens up a mine yielding valuable minerals, with easy
communications and exploitable with less cost is said to outmanoeuvre
the other. Some teachers say that a small production of high value minerals
is preferable [to a large production of inferior products] because valuable
products (such as diamonds, precious stones, pearls, corals, gold and silver)
are worth much more than a large amount of inferior products. Kautilya

disagrees. Buyers of high-valued products are rare and are found ónly after a long search; there are many buyers and a steady demand for products of small value.   {7.12.13-16}

TRADE ROUTES

As in the case of mines, many inferior routes are preferable to a few important ones.

Some teachers say that a trade-route by water is preferable to one on land because water routes can be used to transport a large quantity of goods at less expense and exertion. Kautilya disagrees. A water route is not usable at all times, accessible at only a few places, full of dangers and indefensible in contrast to land routes.

Among water routes, a coastal route is better than one on the high sea because there are a large number of ports [along any coast]. A river route is also good because it poses less serious dangers and is more constantly in use.

As regards land routes, some teachers say that a trade route to the north in the direction of the Himalayas is better than a route to the south, because the [northern] products, such as elephants, horses, perfumery, ivory, hides and skins, silver and gold are all of high value. Kautilya disagrees. Apart from [woollen] blankets, hides and skins and horses, the rest are available in the south; besides, conchshells, diamonds, precious stones, pearls and gold, are more plentiful in the south.

Among the southern (or eastern or western) trade routes, it is better to choose either (i) a well-established route with many mines producing goods of high value and requiring less expenditure and exertion or (ii) one used for goods of low value but in great quantities.

A route usable by carts is preferable to a foot path [for men and animals only] because of the larger quantities that can be transported on carts. Depending on the circumstances (of place and reason) baths traversable by donkeys, camels and porters (carrying goods on their shoulders), are also good.   {7.12.17-28}

WHEN THE TASK IS ACCOMPLISHED

ALLIED WITH A STRONGER RULER

If the stronger ruler is not upright, the king shall quickly withdraw under some pretext, when the work has been done. If the stronger ruler is upright, the king shall wait until he is given permission to leave. The king shall make all efforts to move away from a dangerous situation, after ensuring the safety of the Queen.

Even if the king receives a small share, or even no share, from the stronger king, he shall go away with a [seemingly?] content look. Later, when the stronger king comes under the king's power [for any reason] twice the loss shall be exacted. {7.5.45,46,48}

ALLIED WITH AN EQUAL KING

The king may face dangers even from a trusted king of equal power, when the latter has achieved his objective.

Even a equally powerful king tends to become stronger after the task is accomplished and, when his power has increased, becomes untrustworthy. Prosperity changes peoples' minds. {7.5.46,47}

KING AS LEADER

The king, when he himself has led the allies to victory, shall let the others go, after giving them their due shares. He should, if necessary, forgo his own share and not deprive them of theirs. It is thus that a king will win the affection of his Circle of States. {7.5.49}

X.vi

PLANNING A CAMPAIGN

['Yana', literally 'going', is usually translated as 'marching'. Book 9, 'The activity of one setting out on a journey' deals with the factors to be taken into account before a king decides that it is in his interest to set out on a military campaign. Kautilya lists eight different factors, each of which has a bearing on its success or failure. If, after giving due weight to the different factors, the king concludes that he is superior to the enemy about to be attacked, he shall make preparations for war.

The first factor, power, is the most important; one does not foolishly attack a stronger adversary. But power, for Kautilya, is not just military might or the economic strength backing it. Intellectual power which enables a king make an objective analysis and arrive at the correct judgment is the most important. Intellectual power, military might, enthusiasm and morale—these are the three constituents of power, in decreasing order of importance.

The next two factors to be taken into account are place and time—the nature of the terrain where the battle will be waged and two aspects of time. In this context, time means the season when battle is likely and the expected duration of the battle itself.

The first three factors are interdependent. Only when a king is sure that he is superior in power, space and time, shall he proceed to a consideration of the other factors. Equally, when a king finds himself superior, he shall not waste time. 'One should proceed against one's enemy whenever, by so doing, the enemy can be weakened or crushed' {9.1.44}.

The two next stages of the preparation are deciding on the right kind of troops to be mobilised and on the right season for setting out. But these steps should not be undertaken unless the king has considered the next factor—the danger of a revolt against him in his own kingdom when he is away. The categorical advice is that the king shall not absent himself if there is even a remote possibility of an internal rebellion. When a king has to undertake a campaign against an enemy in spite of there being the danger of rebellion, it is better for the king to stay behind and make the Crown Prince or the Chief of

Defence lead the expedition. The details of how to tackle revolts and rebellions have been given in III.iv.

After deciding on the right kind of troops to mobilise and the right season for setting out, the king shall calculate what he hopes to achieve by the campaign, taking into account the nature of his gains and the extent of his losses. The analysis suggested by Kautilya is very logical and precise. After defining the various types of gains, the special situation of when to try to get what type of gain is explained.

The last factor to take into account is the possibility of treachery—either internal or external or a mixture of both. Reference is made in this connection to the danger of an ally defecting ; how to deal with confederacies is also explained. When to use the four methods of conciliation etc is spelt out {9.3.1-8} in X.vi.

When taking a decision to set out on a campaign, Kautilya emphasizes the importance of the king and his counsellors acting together. If the king and the counsellors do not agree on the course of action, it spells future trouble, irrespective of whether the venture is crowned with success or ends in failure. In {9.4.25-27}, Kautilya also warns against the king exhibiting irresolution, other-worldliness, misplaced kindness and similar weak qualities. Once a decision is made to go on a military campaign, it must be pursued steadfastly. It is not in the stars that success lies but in using one's resources to gain more.

It is to be noted that the soldiers mobilised for an expedition were supplied all goods free at the start on condition that double the quantities were repaid when the expedition was over. This took care of interest and a share of the war gains!

Special case: Once a king is aware of the eight factors and analyses them giving due weight to their relative importance, a correct judgment is possible. However, there is a special case of an expedition gaining some advantage not only for the king but also for the enemy. These are cases where the campaign is directed against some king other than the enemy. In such cases, if the enemy gains more than the conqueror, the power balance between them will tilt in the enemy's favour thus making the ultimate objective of defeating the enemy more difficult to achieve. A complex analysis of the factors is required before a king embarks on a campaign of this nature. The chapter which deals with this, {9.7}, is difficult to understand and translate because of the special terminology and the intricate classification. '*Artha*' is used in this chapter in a very special sense, always combined with an adjective— '*aapadartha*', a risky return or acquisition and '*anartha*', a debacle in the sense of a wrong acquisition. A risky acquisition is one which carries the danger of a risk in the future and a wrong acquisition is one which provokes either an internal rebellion or external wrath.

Naturally, there is a third case of doubt about whether the acquisition will be just risky or totally wrong. These three types become six when long-term effects are also taken into account. Kautilya then adds a further complication about whether these effects will be on only one side or on all sides; i.e., whether these will affect all neighbours or only some. Many verses in the set {9.7.23-53} are tautological definitions; it is possible to reduce the analysis to nine distinct situations. In verses {9.7.46-53} Kautilya sets out succinctly how a king faced with losses on most sides should save the best of his resources. If the situation is even worse, the king shall save himself to live to fight another day {9.7.35,36}. Verses {9.7.54-66} provide advice on the timing; i.e. when to undertake campaigns whose effects will be problematic. {9.7} is an outstanding example of the logical completeness of Kautilya's analytical powers.]

FACTORS INVOLVED IN PLANNING A CAMPAIGN

The would-be conqueror shall judge the relative strengths and weaknesses of the following aspects [of waging a war], as applicable to him and to his enemy, before starting on a military expedition:
- power;
- the place [of operations];
- the time [of the military engagement];
- the season for marching [towards the battle ground];
- when to mobilise different types of forces;
- the possibility of revolts and rebellions in the rear;
- the likely losses, expenses and gains and
- the likely dangers.

If, [on balance, after giving due weight to the different factors as explained below], the conqueror is superior, the campaign shall be undertaken; otherwise not.[1]   {9.1.1}

ON POWER

[The three constituents of power are: counsel and correct judgment; might, i.e. the actual strength of the fighting forces; enthusiasm and energy. The three are not equally important. Sheer military strength is more important than enthusiasm (enthusiasm does not compensate for lack of military strength) and power of judgement is superior to might. After discussing place and time, Kautilya holds that power, place and time have to be considered as interdependent.]

Some teachers hold enthusiasm to be more important than might. [They argue:] so long as a king is himself brave, strong, healthy and expert in the use of weapons, he can defeat, with only the army to help him,[2] even a mightier king.

Kautilya disagrees. A mighty king, by his very might, can overpower an energetic one; for, a mighty army, richly endowed with horses, elephants, chariots and instruments of war, can move unhindered anywhere. Further, a mighty king can get the help of another energetic one or he can hire or buy heroic fighters. [It is known that] even women, children, the lame and the blind have conquered the world after winning over or buying heroic fighters with their might. {9.1.2-9}

Some teachers hold might to be more important then the power of good counsel and judgment. [They argue:] however good a king's analysis and judgment, he thinks but empty thoughts if he has no power. Just as a drought dries out the planted seeds, good judgment without power produces no fruit.

Kautilya disagrees. The power of good counsel, [good analysis and good judgment] is superior [to sheer military strength]. Intelligence and [knowledge of] the science of politics are the two eyes [of a king]. Using these, a king can, with a little effort, arrive at the best judgment on the means, [the four methods of conciliation, sowing dissension, etc.] as well as the various tricks, stratagems, clandestine practices and occult means [described in this treatise) to overwhelm even kings who are mighty and energetic. {9.1.10-15}

Thus, the three components of power,—enthusiasm, military might and the power of counsel—are in ascending order of importance. Hence, a king who is superior, as compared to his enemy, in an item later in the list, outmanoeuvres his adversary. {9.1.16}

PLACE

The area extending from the Himalayas in the north to the sea [in the south] and a thousand *yojanas* wide from east to west is the area of operation of the King-Emperor. Within this, there are different types of terrain; the more important ones are: forests, villages, mountains, watery land, dry land, plains and uneven land. From the conqueror's point of view, the best land is one which is suitable for the operations of his own army and unsuitable for that of his enemy; the converse the worst for him; and if the terrain is equally suitable to both, average. On each type of land, the conqueror shall undertake such works as would increase his power. {9.1.17-21}

TIME

By time is meant the climate—heat, cold and rain—as well as the time or duration of the campaign (night, day, fortnight, month, season, half a year, one year and five years). From the conqueror's point of view, the best time is one which is suitable for the operations of his own army and unsuitable for that of his enemy, the converse is the worst for him, and, if equally suitable, average. In each period, he shall undertake such works as would increase his own power.   {9.1.22-25}

OF POWER, PLACE AND TIME

Some teachers say that, as among power, place and time, power is the most important because a powerful king can overcome the difficulties of dry or wet terrain and the effects of heat, cold or rain. Some others hold that the place is the most important; [quoting as an example] a dog on land can pull a crocodile while [on water?] a crocodile can pull in a dog. Some others hold time to be the most important; [quoting as an example] a crow can kill an owl in day-time while an owl can kill a crow at night.

Kautilya disagrees. Power, place and time are interdependent.

{9.1.26-33}

THE RIGHT SEASON FOR THE CAMPAIGN

<u>General</u>

A conqueror, having assured himself about his superiority in power, place and time, shall first leave behind a third or a quarter of his army to protect his capital, the rear, the forest regions and the borders; he shall then march towards the enemy taking with him enough wealth and forces to help him achieve his objective.   {from 9.1.34}

In general, [most] teachers advise that a king shall march against an enemy who is suffering from adversities and calamities. Kautilya disagrees. One cannot be certain when a calamity will strike the enemy or what its effects would be. It is better to march when one has acquired sufficient power, [without waiting for something to happen to the enemy]. One should proceed against one's enemy whenever, by so doing, the enemy can be weakened or crushed.   {9.1.42-44}

The duration of the different stages of the expedition shall be regulated in accordance with the nature of the terrain, (even or uneven and with or without water) and the nature of the task (short duration for tasks easily accomplished and longer duration for difficult ones).

Condition	Period	Reason
Enemy's situation		
1. Food stocks exhausted, new stocks not yet collected, fort in disrepair	Month of *Margasirsha* (Nov./Dec.)	To destroy the enemy's rainy season crops and to prevent winter sowing.
2. (Same as above?)	Month of *Chaitra* (March/April)	To destroy the enemy's winter crops and to prevent spring sowing.
3. Fodder, timber and water exhausted, fort in disrepair	Month of *Jyeshta* (May/June)	To destroy the enemy's spring crops and to prevent rainy season sowing.
Nature of the region		
4. Very hot, with little fodder, fuel or water	Spring (March to May)	
5. Frosty or with snow falls; terrain with deep valleys; densely wooded	Summer (May to July)	
6. Terrain suitable for own army and unsuitable for that of the enemy	Rainy Season (July to September)	
Duration of the expedition		
7. Long	Begin in the winter (between November and January)	
8. Medium	Begin in Spring (between March and May)	
9. Short	Begin in Summer (between May and July)	
10. When the enemy is affected by a calamity, irrespective of duration.	Any season	Conditions explained in {7.4.5-12}

{9.1.34-41}

The need for having to camp in enemy territory during the rainy season shall also be taken into account. {9.1.51-52}

The best season for an expedition against an enemy, keeping in mind the enemy's situation, the nature of the country and the duration are as given below, for the reasons indicated.

Since very hot weather makes elephants sweat and become leprous and since they become slow and dull-witted when they cannot drink or bathe, an army consisting mostly of elephants shall be used only when the hot season is over, when it rains, or in regions where there is plenty of water. In places of little rain and muddy water, donkeys, camels and horses shall be used. In deserts, one may use all four arms in the expedition when it rains.   {9.1.45-50}

TROOP MOBILISATION

The occasions when different kinds of troops—the standing army, the territorial army, the militias, friendly forces, alien forces and tribal forces[3]— are to be mobilised are described below. It is better to mobilise the force mentioned earlier than one later. The mobilisation shall take into account the kind of troops the enemy has and the forces necessary to counteract them.
{9.2.1,13,25,30}

The standing army shall be mobilised when:

(i) there is a surplus over and above what is required for the defence of the base [i.e. the king's own country and capital];

(ii) there is no danger of them creating trouble at the base, because of the presence of many traitors;

(iii) the enemy has a strong, loyal standing army and it becomes necessary to fight with troops well-trained in military operations;

(iv) the king considers that, because of the duration or difficulty of marching, the regular army would be better able to withstand the hardships (losses and expenses);

(v) the king distrusts the other types of troops (such as the territorial army) for fear that they might succumb to the instigations of large numbers of men loyal to the enemy mixing with them during the march; or

(vi) the king does not have any other type of force to fall back upon.
{9.2.2}

The territorial army shall be mobilised when:

(i) the territorial army is much larger than the standing army;

(ii) the enemy's regular army is small or apathetic and his territorial army is weak or insignificant;

(iii) it is necessary to manage the conflict with diplomacy and little actual fighting;

(iv) the march, being of short duration or short distance, involves only small costs;

(v) the territorial army is loyal, with no traitors and able to withstand the enemy's instigations; or

(vi) the force is needed only to put down a small enemy incursion.

{9.2.3}

<u>The militias</u> are to be mobilised when:

(i) there is a large force of militias which could be used both to defend the base and on the campaign;

(ii) the march is over a short distance and the enemy army is mainly of militias;

(iii) it is judged that the enemy intends to conduct a diplomatic offensive with [only limited] military operations; or

(iv) it is more a law and order problem. {9.2.4}

<u>Friendly forces</u> are to be mobilised when:

(i) there is a large allied force which could be used both to defend the base and on a campaign;

(ii) the march is over a short distance and a diplomatic offensive is better than actual war;

(iii) the intention is to use the friendly force to attack first jungle tribes, the cities or the ally of the enemy and then engage him directly with own forces;

(iv) he and the ally have the same objective;

(v) his own success depends on the ally;

(vi) the ally, being close, deserves to be favoured; or

(vii) the campaign helps to get rid of traitors in the army of the ally.

{9.2.5}

<u>Alien troops and jungle tribes</u> must be used when there is a gain to the king, whether they win or lose in fighting the enemy—just as a *chandala* stands to benefit when a wild dog fights a wild boar. When such untrustworthy troops become too large, they shall be kept near the king for fear of revolt except in cases when such proximity poses the danger of a revolt in the interior being helped by them.[4]

Such troops shall be mobilised when:

(i) there is a large force of alien [or jungle] troops which could be used to attack the cities or the jungle tribes of the enemy;

(ii) the campaign helps to get rid of the traitors in the alien or jungle troops; or

(iii) the suitable time for battle for the king is later and the enemy had started earlier because it suited him [and has to be kept at bay in the meantime].

In addition, jungle troops shall be mobilised when they:

(i) are useful for showing the way;

(ii) are suited to the terrain of the enemy;

(iii) are specially suited to counteract the enemy's tactics;

(iv) the enemy force has mostly jungle troops [and has to be counteracted with the same kind, as in the saying] 'a *Bilva* can be destroyed only by another'; or

(v) the force is needed only to put down a small enemy incursion.

Alien or jungle troops shall be paid either in forest produce or given a share of the plunder. {9.2.6-8,10}

GENERAL

An <u>energetic</u> army is one which is composed of many units raised from different areas and which is ready to fight, whether ordered to or not, for the sake of plunder.

A <u>mighty</u> army is one which fights [even] without food and wages, which labours with valour in adversity, which the enemies cannot divide and which is made up of men from the same region, caste or profession.

When the enemy tries to mobilise his own troops, the king shall obstruct the mobilisation divert the potential recruits elsewhere or render the mobilisation ineffective. Or, the king may recruit troops first [to protect them joining the enemy] and, when the time is ripe, disband them.

The king shall obstruct the mobilisation of forces by the enemy while safeguarding his own. {9.2.9,11,12}

Having decided to undertake a military expedition, the army shall be mobilised. Then, secret agents in the guise of merchants shall supply all the necessary goods to the soldiers on condition of repayment of double the quantity when the expedition was over. Thus, two objectives are achieved: the sale of Crown goods and the recovery of [double] the wages paid. By taking care of expenditure and income in this manner, the king avoids a calamity to either the army or the treasury. {5.4.42-45}

REVOLTS AND REBELLIONS IN THE REAR

[Since a king is likely to be away from his country and capital for a long time when he undertakes a military campaign, it is essential that he is absolutely certain of the security of his kingdom. There shall be no possibility of a revolt behind him (*paschatkopa*), which could be exacerbated into a conflagration by enemies, internal and external. However tempting the large gain by conquest may be, it should be resisted if there is even the slightest chance of a revolt in the rear].

A small revolt in the rear outweighs a large gain in the front; for, when the king is not there, a small revolt in the rear may be worsened by the anger of the people or by traitors, enemies and jungle tribes. If this happens, a large gain in front, even if actually obtained, will be eaten up by the subjects, allies, losses and expenses. Therefore, a king shall not undertake a campaign when the gain in front is [less than] a thousand times the likely loss due to a revolt in the rear or, at best, a hundred times the loss.[5] A well-known proverb is: 'Misfortunes are, [in the beginning] no longer than the point of a needle.'

If a revolt arises in the rear, it shall be resolved by using all the four methods—conciliation, placating with gifts, sowing dissension and use of force. If necessary, the king shall stay behind and make the Crown Prince or the Chief of Defence lead the campaign. Only if the king is so strong that he can suppress the revolt in the rear [and lead the campaign], may he assume command. {9.3.1-8}

[The types of internal rebellion and how to tackle them, in {9.3.9-42}, have been dealt with in III.v. on 'Revolts, Rebellions, Conspiracies and Treason'].

LOSSES, EXPENSES AND GAINS

The king shall undertake a march when the expected gain outweighs the losses and expenses. {9.4.3}

Definitions

Loss (*kshaya*) [in this context] means loss of trained men [and animals]. Expense (*vyaya*) means reduction in wealth and grains. Gain (*labha*) is net gain after losses and expenses.

The various aspects of gain can be classified as follows:

- [the contrasting ones of] that which is <u>easily captured</u> and that which is <u>easily retaken</u>. A gain which is easy to obtain and protect and difficult for the enemy to recapture is 'easily captured'. The converse is 'easily retaken'.

– [the contrasting ones of] that which <u>pleases</u> and that which <u>enrages</u>: a gain obtained by a righteous king from an unrighteous one pleases both one's own people and others; the converse is one which enrages [all].

– that which <u>requires a short time</u>; a gain obtainable by just going to where it is;

– that which <u>entails small losses</u> is a gain by diplomacy [rather than by war];

– that which <u>requires little expenditure</u> is a gain which needs only disbursement of food;

– a <u>great gain</u> is a substantial gain available immediately;

– a <u>growing gain</u> is one which is productive of further profits;

– a <u>safe gain</u> is one free from dangers;

– a <u>righteous (*dharmic*) gain</u> is one whose manner of acquisition is praiseworthy;

– a <u>permanent gain</u> is one where the king's share is not limited by confederates.   {9.4.1,2,4-6,10,11,16-23}

<u>An easily retaken gain</u>

A conqueror who captures something easily recaptured by the enemy or stays on land easily retaken only courts destruction.

He may, however, seize even [land] which can be easily recaptured by the enemy when he can:

(i) weaken the enemy's treasury, army, stores or fortifications;

(ii) exploit all the wealth of the enemy's mines, productive forests, elephant forests, waterworks or trade-routes;

(iii) impoverish the enemy's people or relocate them;

(iv) please the people by suitable means so that when the enemy recaptures the territory his rule would enrage them;

(v) sell the gain to the enemy's enemy;

(vi) give it away to an ally or to a disgruntled prince of the enemy's family;

(vii) use it to get rid of harassment by robbers and enemies in his own or an ally's territory;

(viii) use it to drive a wedge between the enemy and his ally or vassal king so that these [supporters] will turn to kinsmen of the enemy; or

(ix) improve the land and then return it so that he may gain a longlasting ally bound to him [by gratitude].   {9.4.7,8}

<u>Gains which enrage or please</u>

The king becomes angry [and the counsellors afraid] when a campaign, undertaken on the advice of the counsellors, fails to produce the gain predicted by them, but leads to losses and expenses. [Counsellors frightened of punishment may rebel.]

When the king gains from a campaign, disregarding the advice of traitorous counsellors, then too the king becomes angry and the counsellors afraid that the successful king will kill them for giving wrong advice. [This too may make them rebel.]

When a campaign undertaken on the advice of trustworthy counsellors achieves the objective or when a campaign undertaken disregarding the advice of untrustworthy counsellors fails,—in both cases, the net result pleases all.   {9.4.12-14}

<u>Comparison of Gains</u>

When the gains [from two campaigns] are equal, the king shall compare the following qualities and choose that one which has more good points:

– place and time;
– the power and the means [required to acquire it],
– the pleasure or displeasure [caused by it];
– the speed or slowness [of getting it];
– the proximity or distance;
– the immediate and future consequences;
– its high value or constant worth;[6] and
– its abundance or variety. {9.4.24}

Obstacles to achieving the gain

These are: passion, anger, timidity, compassion [leading to aversion to fighting], recoiling from awarding deserved punishment, baseness (not acting like an Arya), haughtiness, a forgiving nature, thinking of the next world, being too pious, meanness, abjectness, jealousy, contempt for what one has, wickedness, distrust, fear, negligence, inability to withstand harsh climate (cold, heat or rain) and faith in the auspiciousness of stars and days. {9.4.25}

Wealth will slip away from that childish man who constantly consults the stars: the only [guiding] star of wealth is itself; what can the stars of the sky do? {9.4.26}

Man, without wealth, does not get it even after a hundred attempts.

Just as elephants are needed to catch elephants, so does wealth capture more wealth. {9.4.27}

LIKELY DANGERS

OF INTERNAL TREACHERY

[The two types of internal treachery, mixed and unmixed, and the methods for tackling them have been placed in III.v under Revolts, Rebellions, Treason and Conspiracies {9.6.1-5,8-10,56-61 and 9.7.68,69}].

OF EXTERNAL TREACHERY

Unmixed danger

In the case of direct treachery by the enemy [uncomplicated by conspiracy with allies], the conqueror shall adopt the four methods [of conciliation, etc.] as appropriate against the enemy himself or his subordinate, as the case may be. {9.6.6,7}

Mixed danger—with collusion

Danger from the enemy becomes complicated when the enemy and a friend find common ground. [To avoid this danger] success [should be sought] through the friend. For it is easy to make peace with a friend but not with an enemy.

If the friend does not want to make peace, he shall be solicited often. Secret agents shall separate him from the enemy and win him over to the king's side.

He shall win over the ruler on the border of a confederacy of allies.

For, when those on the edge are won over, those in the middle become divided. Or, he shall win over one in the centre; for, when the centre is won over, those in the edges cannot remain united. He shall use the appropriate methods to make the vassals of the confederacy defect [to the king's side].   {9.6.11-20}

USE OF THE FOUR METHODS

CONCILIATION

The king shall pacify a pious ruler by praising his birth, family, learning and conduct, by pointing out the relationship between the ancestors and, at all times, by providing help to him and refraining from harming him.

The king shall conciliate by displays of good will the following: one who has become dispirited, one weary of war, one who has failed in his efforts, one suffering from losses, expenses or the hardship of a campaign, one who seeks a friend in good faith, one who is suspicious of another, or one who attaches importance to friendship.   {9.6.21,22}

PLACATING WITH GIFTS

A greedy or weakened king shall be placated with gifts, provided an ascetic or a chief stands as surety.[7]   {9.6.23}

SOWING DISSENSION

Ways of sowing dissension among leaders of an oligarchy have been explained elsewhere.[8]

The advice given here about sowing dissension among kings also applies to commanders of armies such as Crown Princes and Chiefs of Defence.
                                                                    {9.6.51,50}

The king shall try to sow dissension among the members of a confederacy of kings, even before they get together to attack him. In particular, he shall frequently send envoys and well-known personalities with presents to the court of one of the kings, while they are still in their own territories. They shall urge the [targeted] king either to make a treaty or to kill another confederate. [Even] if he does not agree, the conclusion of a treaty shall be announced and double agents shall make propaganda about the treachery among other members of the confederacy.

If any member of the confederacy bears a grudge or enmity towards another, dissension shall be sown between them. One of them shall be told [falsely] that the other was trying to make peace with the king [opposed to the confederacy] and that it is in his interests to make peace quickly with the king himself before he is outmanoeuvred.

Or, he may arrange marriages of princes and princesses with the daughters and sons of one of the kings of the confederacy with a view to separating him from others with whom he has no such connection.

{9.6.63-70}

When a group of kings start attacking the king, he shall sow dissension between two rulers who are mutually hostile, who hate each other, who covet each other's land or who are suspicious of each other of any reason. The more timid of the two shall be intimidated by saying that the other has already sent an ally to make peace leaving him out and, after peace is made, he himself will come under attack. When divided, one of them shall be won over. {9.6.26,27,49,62}

[{9.6.28-49} describe a number of methods using secret agents for sowing dissension among members of a confederacy; translations are given in IX.iv.]

USE OF FORCE

Secret persons shall conceal themselves in the fort of a keen, energetic enemy suffering from a calamity; one of them shall murder him with weapons, fire or poison when it is easy to do so. For a single assassin can achieve more than a fully mobilised army can. {9.6.53-55}

The conqueror shall cause their kingdoms to be destroyed by neighbouring kings, jungle tribes, pretenders or unjustly treated princes. He shall destroy their caravans, herds, forests and troops reinforcements. Clans, mutually supporting each other, shall be made to strike at the weak points. Secret persons shall strike with weapons, fire or poison.

{9.6.71,72}

When the conqueror is under attack from a confederacy he shall kill his enemies by deceit after lulling them into trust, just as a fowler does with his decoys and baits. {9.6.73}

WHEN THE CAMPAIGN ALSO BENEFITS THE ENEMY

The pursuit of wrong policies provokes external enemies; immoderation provokes anger in one's own people; both are diabolic practices. {9.7.1,2}

THE THREE TYPES

There are three kinds of cases where progress for the conqueror may also lead to progress for the enemy—risky acquisition, wrong acquisition and doubt about whether it is risky or wrong.   {9.7.4}

Risky acquisition is of three kinds—[gain of] wealth, [gain of] *dharma* and [gain of] pleasure. Of these, it is better to achieve one mentioned earlier in the list than one later.[9]   {9.7.60,61}

Wealth is like a tree; its roots are *dharma* and the fruit is pleasure. Achieving that kind of wealth which further promotes *dharma*, produces more wealth and gives more pleasure is the achievement of all gains (*sarvarthasiddhi*).   {9.7.81}

Wrong acquisition is [also] of three kinds—[loss of] wealth, *adharma* and misery. Of these, it is better to counteract one mentioned earlier in the list than one later.   {9.7.62,63}

Doubt is [also] of three kinds—are the consequences of an action [e.g. a campaign] gain or loss of wealth, gain or loss of *dharma*, pleasure or misery? In each case, it is better to avoid the latter alternative and achieve the earlier.   {9.7.64,65}

The types of <u>risky acquisition</u>, with examples for each one, are as given below:

Type	Example
An acquisition which helps the enemy if it is not captured first [by the conqueror].	When one neighbour is in a calamity and all other neighbours covert his wealth, [the enemy may seize it if the conqueror does not do so.]
An acquisition which can be retaken by enemies.	That which an enemy wants and, by its very nature, is easily acquired by him.
An acquisition which involves and expenses.	When a gain acquired in the front losses prompts an [interior] revolt in the rear or an attack by the enemy in the rear; or when a gain, acquired by sacrificing an ally or breaking atreaty, angers the Circle of States. {9.7.5,6}

<u>Wrong acquisition</u> is that which gives rise to fear [of danger] from one's own people or from enemies.   {9.7.7}

Doubt

The types of <u>doubtful cases</u>, with examples for each one, are as given below:

Type	Example
Is it a risky acquisition or not?	Encouraging a friend of the enemy.
Is it a wrong acquisition or not?	Inciting enemy troops with money and honours.
Is it a risky acquisition or a wrong acquisition?	Seizing the land of a strong neighbour.
Is it a wrong acquisition or a risky acquisition?	Going on a joint campaign by merging forces with those of a more powerful king.

In these cases, the conqueror shall choose that course of action which favours risky acquisition. {9.7.8-13}

IMMEDIATE AND FUTURE CONSEQUENCES

[Both risky acquisition and wrong acquisition can either have long-term consequences or none; the long-term consequences can either be risky acquisition or wrong acquisition. Thus, there are six possibilities. The different types, with examples for each one, are as given in page 642. These are listed in order of importance, i.e. an earlier one is better than a later one.]

THE GEOGRAPHICAL SITUATION

[The geographical situation could be such that, in the simplest cases, there is gain on all sides or gain on the flanks only; likewise there may be loss on all sides or on the flanks only. There are four possibilities. These could be modified by an enemy or an ally introducing an element of doubt, making the number of possibilities eight. In more complex cases, there could be gain, loss or uncertainty on one side paired with these three on another side; this gives rise to six more possibilities. However, as the course of action suggested is the same for two or more cases, the total number is reduced by Kautilya to nine. The different types, along with the procedure for dealing with them, are given in pages 643 and 644.]

THE TIME FACTOR

At the start and during an expedition:

Because the effects of risky acquisition, wrong acquisition or uncertainty are apparent immediately during the course of an expedition, it is better to obtain the gain at the start or in the middle of the expedition. They [the gains] become useful for overcoming the enemy-in-the-rear, and the rear enemy's ally, for recouping the losses, expenses and the rigours of the march and for protecting the base. Likewise, a wrong acquisition or a doubtful venture becomes more easily bearable to one staying in one's country [before setting out].

However, at the end of a campaign, after achieving the objective of weakening or destroying an enemy, it is better to act [only] to achieve fortune and not wrong acquisition or uncertainty, because of the dangers arising from an enemy.

However, it is better for one who is not a leader in a joint expedition to meet with wrong acquisition or uncertainty in the middle or at the end, because the other members are not likely to be affected similarly.

{from 9.7.54-59}

IMMEDIATE AND FUTURE CONSEQUENCES

Immediate consequence	Future consequence	Example
	Risky acquisition..... >	Destruction of the enemy in the front resulting in ability seize the enemy-in-the-rear.
Risky acquisition...... >	None...................... >	Helping the Neutral king with forces in return for payment.
	Wrong acquisition... >	Destroying the buffer state [between the conqueror and the enemy; for it brings the conqueror face to face with the enemy.]
	Risky acquisition.... >	Helping a neighbour on the flank of the enemy with money or troops [without asking for payment; immediate loss of money or troops but long-term gain].
Wrong acquisition..... >	None......... >	Doing nothing after encouraging a weak king.

Wrong acquisition... >	Doing nothing after encouraging a king stronger than the conqueror.

{9.7.14.22}

THE GEOGRAPHICAL SITUATION

Types	Procedure
Risky acquisition on all sides or on both sides:	The campaign shall be directed towards acquiring that gain with the best qualities [See above—comparison of gains]
Risky acquisition on all sides, made doubtful by the hostility of an enemy-in-the-rear:	Take the help of the ally and the rear ally.
Risky acquisition on both sides:	If the gains on both sides are equal, direct the campaign towards the gain which is pre-eminent, near, urgent or fulfils a need.
Wrong acquisition on all sides due to danger from enemies or on both sides:	Take the help of allies.
Wrong acquisition on all sides mitigated by support from the ally	Tackle the mobile enemy [one without a fort]; take the help of the rear ally; adopt the measures (see above) for mixed 'danger with collusion'.
Wrong acquisition on all sides or both sides, with no allies to help	If wrong acquisition on two sides, attack the weaker enemy. If wrong acquisition on more than two sides, attack the stronger enemy.
	If wrong acquisition on all sides, protect the base; if this is not possible, abandon everything and go away; for, the cases of *Suyatha* and *Vyadana* prove that he who lives can regain his throne.

Risky acquisition and wrong acquisition on all sides, or, risky acquisition on one side and wrong acquisition, on the other, i.e. attack on the kingdom

Direct the campaign towards risky fortune if it will avert the attack; if not, meet the attack.

Wrong acquisition and uncertainty on all sides or wrong aquisition on one side and uncertainty on the other

First overcome the wrong acquisition; then go after the doubtful case.

Risky acquisition and uncertainty of wrong acquisition on all sides, or risky acquisition on one side and uncertainty of wrong acquisition on the other

Save the constituents of the state one by one, in order of their importance, from the uncertainty of wrong acquisition; for, it is better that the ally remain in danger but not the army; likewise the army but not the treasury. If the constituents as a whole cannot be saved, at least parts shall be rescued; i.e. in the case of the army save the more numerous or loyal troops, leaving out the sharp and the greedy; in the case of the treasury, save the most valuable or most useful. The less important one shall be saved by peace, inactivity or the dual policy and the more important ones by other means. From decline, a position of no change shall be reached and from that, a state of progress except that the order of priority may be reversed when there is a special advantage in the future.

{from 9.7.23-53}

X.vii

MIDDLE AND NEUTRAL KINGS

[The Middle king and the Neutral king are both outside the immediate circles of the conqueror and the enemy but powerful enough to influence the interaction between the two. It is also likely that, once the conqueror has subjugated his enemy, the Middle king may become the natural enemy, because of the common border. It is, therefore, in the conqueror's interest not to let the Middle king become too powerful. By and large the Neutral king is to be treated in the same way as the Middle king except for the fact that since he has no common borders with any, he is a bit remote from the scene of action. However, he is even more powerful than the conqueror, the enemy and the Middle king.

Seven different situations are analysed. The cases covered in verses {7.18.5-11,12-13} and 14-17} are difficult to understand with different translators giving different explanations. See Notes on Translation No.11.]

GENERAL

The policies to be adopted [by the conqueror] towards the Neutral king are similar to those [described below] for the Middle king. {7.18.26}

In the following analysis about the Middle king, the first refers to the conqueror and the third and the fifth [i.e. the ally and the friend of the ally] are the constituents friendly to the conqueror. The second, fourth and sixth [the enemy, the enemy's ally and the enemy's ally's friend] are the constituents of the circle of states unfriendly to the conqueror.

{7.18.1,2}

[If the Middle king does not take sides as between the two groups, he may help both or neither.]

If the Middle king helps both groups, the conqueror shall maintain friendly relations with him; if he helps neither, the conqueror shall [continue to be] friendly to the first group. {7.18.3,4}

AIM

The conqueror, having strengthened himself by adopting the policies described below, shall weaken his enemy and strengthen his ally.

{7.18.28}

REACTING TO THE POLICIES OF THE MIDDLE KING

1. Towards a true friend of the conqueror

[In this case, the Middle king may seek to separate a true ally from the conqueror and make him his own ally or to subjugate the ally in order to increase his own power. There are different ways of dealing with this, depending on the strength of the Middle king or the support that the conqueror gets from his Circle of States].

(i) The conqueror shall preserve the alliance [with the true ally] by (a) making his own friends and the ally's friends rise up against the Middle king and (b) sowing dissension between the Middle king and his own allies.

(ii) Or, the conqueror shall incite the kings of his Circle of States to rise against the Middle king by pointing out that, with the rise in power of the Middle king, destruction of the whole circle is likely and that it is necessary to mount a joint campaign to frustrate the Middle king's designs. If the Circle agrees, the conqueror shall increase his own power by suppressing the Middle king.

(iii) If the kings of the Circle of States do not all agree, the conqueror shall [proceed step by step as follows:] first help the [targeted] ally with men and money, and then win over, with conciliation of gifts, one of the many kings who are hostile to the Middle king. (Such kings may be of different kinds: they may be a group of small kings who help each other in resisting the Middle king; they may be a group who do not rise against the Middle king because they are afraid of each other; or they may be such that if one of them is won over, others will follow). It is better to choose a leading king or one whose territory is adjacent to that of the Middle king. Having doubled his power by winning over one of these kings, the conqueror shall try to triple it by winning over another and so on. When he has accumulated enough power, he shall suppress the Middle king.

(iv) When the conditions [time and place] are not suitable the conqueror shall make peace with the Middle king while helping the ally.

(v) The conqueror may also try to [undermine the Middle king and] enter into a treaty with the traitors in the Middle king's court.

{7.18.5-11}

2.Towards an ally who deserves to be weakened

[In this case, the conqueror's interest lies in cutting down to size an ally who is likely to grow to strong[1] while, at the same time, making sure that the Middle king, who attacks the ally, does not gain an advantage].

The conqueror, in order to avoid the ally being overrun by the Middle king, shall keep on promising to save the ally but do so only when he has been weakened enough. {7.18.12-13}

3.Towards an ally who deserves to be crushed

[As in the previous case, the conqueror's interest lies in not letting the Middle king grow too strong while dealing with a perfidious or unscrupulous ally.[2]]

In order to prevent the Middle king from increasing his power, the conqueror may [even] give protection to an unscrupulous or perfidious ally, after he is weakened. Alternatively, he shall be brought under control, by granting him some other land when he is driven out of his own; this is to prevent him from seeking his shelter elsewhere [e.g. with the enemy].

{7.18.14-15}

4.Towards unreliable allies who help the Middle king

[There are two possibilities. If the Middle king is more powerful, then the conqueror has no interest in protecting the unscrupulous or perfidious ally from whatever designs the Middle king may have on him. It is better to make peace with the Middle king. On the other hand, if the perfidious allies are more powerful, it is better to make peace with them].

If any of the unscrupulous or perfidious allies of the conqueror help the Middle king, the conqueror shall make peace with the Middle king, [even] by giving a hostage such as the Crown Prince or the Chief of Defence.

If these [unreliable] allies are powerful enough to subdue the conqueror, it is better to make peace with them. {7.18.16-17}

5.Towards the conqueror's enemy

[This is a clear case of the interests of the Middle king and the conqueror coinciding].

The conqueror shall make peace with the Middle king when he proceeds against the conqueror's enemy, thus gaining his own ends while pleasing the Middle king. {7.18.18-19}

6.Towards the Middle king's own true ally

[The conqueror has no direct interest when the Middle king proceeds against his own true ally other than to make peace between them].

If the Middle king were to attack his own true ally the conqueror shall (i) promote peace between them, by the ally giving a Crown Prince or Chief of Defence as hostage, (ii) use his influence to dissuade the Middle king by pointing out how unworthy it is to attack one's own ally, or (iii) remain indifferent if he thinks that the Middle king's Circle of States would, in any case, get angry with him for destroying his own side.

{7.18.20-22}

7.Towards the Middle king's own enemy

If the Middle king wants to proceed against his own enemy, the conqueror shall provide help with men and money, in a covert manner [in order to put the Middle king under an obligation while not antagonising the other king].   {7.18.23}

MIDDLE AND NEUTRAL KINGS

Between the Middle and Neutral kings, the conqueror shall lean towards that king who is liked by his Circle of kings.   {7.18.25}

If the Middle king is to proceed against the Neutral king, the conqueror shall help the Middle king with a view to sowing dissension between the two.   {7.18.24}

If the Neutral king were to proceed against the Middle king, the conqueror shall side with the one who helps him to outmanoeuvre his own enemy, who helps his ally, or who helps him with troops.   {7.18.27}

[The marginal preference for the Middle king is due to the fact of there being a common boundary between him and the conqueror and none between the conqueror and the Neutral king].

X.viii

ON ATTACKS IN THE REAR

[As mentioned in the introduction to this Part, *parshnigraha* is a very important concept. The word represents both the concept of attacking another king in the rear and the king doing the attacking. The analysis is based on the conqueror and the enemy being faced with the identical sitation and is described using the technique of who outmanoeuvres whom. It must be noted that the terms used are relative; for example, a king who attacks someone else in the rear could himself be attacked in the rear. The concept simply means that when one king is fighting another, a third king attacks the first one from a different direction. Since the discussion is theoretical and is based on a hypothetical situation, chapter {7.13} has been interpreted in a variety of ways.

Let us envisage a situation where both the conqueror and his natural enemy have an opportunity of increasing their power by attacking their respective enemies in the rear, because these latter two are, in turn, engaged in fighting their own enemies. This basic situation, described in {7.13.1}, is shown in the diagram; it is easier to visualise if it is shown as two figures, one from the conqueror's point of view and the other from the enemy's point of view.

For convenience, the different relationships in the diagram can be tabulated as follows.

From the point of view of	Frontal Enemy	Enemy in the rear	Ally
A, the conqueror	B	C	D
B, the enemy	A	F or H	G
C	D	A or E	B
C	E	A or D	B
F	G	B or H	A
F	H	B or G	A

In the diagrams and table, A is the conqueror, B his natural enemy and C, the conqueror's enemy in the rear. C could be engaged in his own fight with D while, correspondingly, F (the enemy's enemy in the rear) could be engaged in his own fight with G. In this parallel situation, when A attacks C and B attacks F, who does better?

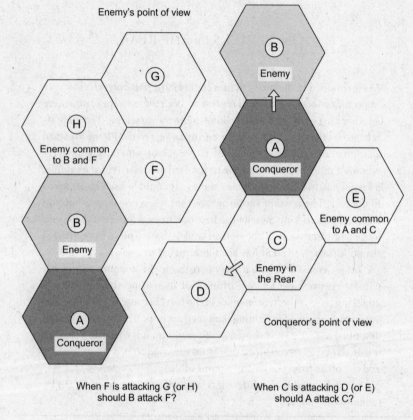

When F is attacking G (or H) should B attack F?

When C is attacking D (or E) should A attack C?

Fig. 27 Attacking Enemies-in-the Rear

This is the problem analysed in verses {7.13.1-10}. The analysis is in terms of four successive logical levels: the first is if, of the kings attacked in the rear by the conqueror and the enemy, one is more powerful than the other; the second is if both are equally powerful, the king who has mobilized more extensively; the third is, in case of equal mobilization, the one who uses all his resources for the attack; and the last, when the first three are all equal is, he who attacks one entrenched in a fort. The purpose of this step-by-step analysis is to show that, when the conqueror and the enemy both attack different kings in the rear, he who chooses a more difficult adversary will eventually emerge stronger, because of having eliminated a stronger threat to his own rear. {7.13.11-13} state the principle that, as between the conqueror and the enemy, whoever attacks a more unpopular king will do better.

A different situation exists when C is fighting D (an ally of the conqueror) but F is attacking H (an enemy common to B and F); this situation is analysed in {7.13.14-19}. The importance of going to the help of threatened allies is stressed.

{7.13.20-23} consider the situation after the attack in the rear. Obviously, whoever gains more, either materially or strategically, comes out better.

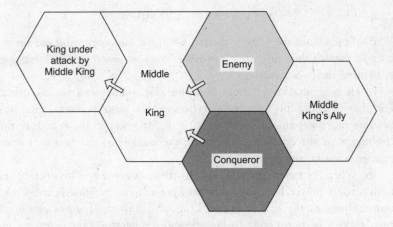

Fig. 28 Attacking the Middle King in the Rear

{7.13.26,28} are special cases of both the conqueror and the enemy attacking the Middle or Neutral king. We must recall that both the Middle and Neutral kings are bigger than both the conqueror and the enemy and can influence both.

The situation analysed is one when the Middle or Neutral king is engaged in a fight with someone else and the conqueror or his enemy can utilise this opportunity to attack in the rear the Middle or Neutral king, as the case may be, with a view to reducing his power. Who comes out better out of this operation, may depend on the third king attacked by the Middle or Neutral king since the third king may become a friend as a result of the help given by the rear attack. Alternatively, the relations between the Middle or Neutral king and his own ally may become strained due to the ally not doing anything to prevent the attack in the rear. In short, an attack-in-the-rear on the Middle or Neutral king is worth making only if it wins an ally.

{7.13.29-36} contain advice to the king who is himself attacked in the rear. Such an attack should never be ignored. The Kautilyan dictum is that 'an enemy's destruction shall be brought about even at the cost of great losses and expenses'. For fighting the attacker-in-the-rear, unreliable troops should be used, thus killing two birds with one stone-warding off the attack while getting rid of treacherous troops.]

MOUNTING AN ATTACK-IN-THE REAR

ATTACKED KINGS UNEQUAL

[The following are the relative merits] when the conqueror and the enemy intend to attack their respective enemies-in-the-rear, when these are engaged in fighting their own enemies:

(i) He who attacks the more powerful king, outmanoeuvres the other. For after defeating his own [primary] enemy the more powerful king will become more capable of dealing with the attacker-in-the-rear [i.e. the conqueror or the conqueror's enemy]; the weaker of the two may even emerge without any gain.

(ii) When the two kings attacked [by the conqueror and his enemy] are both equal in power, he who attacks the king who has mobilised extensively, outmanoeuvres the other. For, a king who has made more extensive preparations is more likely to become more powerful after defeating his own enemy and thus more capable of dealing with his attacker-in-the-rear. The weaker of the two might end up with his army bogged down [for lack of preparation.]

(iii) If the two kings attacked [are not only equal in power but have also mobilised to the same extent,] he who attacks the king attacking [his own enemy] with all his resources outmanoeuvres the other. For, it is easier to overpower a king whose base is left undefended than one who goes on a campaign with a part of his troops, after having made arrangements to defend his rear.

(iv) If the two kings attacked utilise the same number of troops [for attack and for defence of the rear,] he who attacks the king fighting against a mobile enemy not entrenched in a fort, outmanoeuvres the other. For, one fighting against an unentrenched enemy can win more easily than the one fighting an entrenched enemy and [after winning] be able to tackle the king [i.e. the conqueror or his enemy] who had attacked him in the rear. The king fighting against an entrenched enemy, even if he is repulsed by the fort and turns against the attacker-in-the-rear, is still threatened by the enemy in the fort. This [aspect of entrenchment in a fort] also applies to the earlier cases.   {7.13.1-10}

OTHER CASES

UNPOPULARITY OF ATTACKED KING

(i) <u>Righteousness:</u> If the two kings are equal [in all respects,] he who attacks the king fighting a righteous king, outmanoeuvres the other. For, he who attacks a righteous king will be hated by his own people and by others [and an attack in the rear on the attacker will, therefore, be welcomed.] Conversely, one who attacks an unrighteous king will be liked by all [and an attack in the rear on such a king will promote hostility.]
{7.13.11,12}

(ii) <u>Prodigal or miserly kings:</u> For similar reasons, whoever [conqueror or enemy] attacks in the rear a king fighting a prodigal, spendthrift or miserly[1] ruler, loses popular sympathy.   {7.13.13}

ALLIES AND ENEMIES

(i) Likewise, whoever goes to the help of an ally by attacking in the rear the ally's enemy is appreciated.   {7.13.14}

(ii) If one of the two kings attacks an ally [of, say, the conqueror] and the other attacks an enemy [of, say, the enemy] he who attacks in the rear the attacker of an ally outmanoeuvres the other. For, one attacking an ally may easily overpower him and then turn round on the enemy-in-the-rear. One cannot make peace with an enemy and a friend is ever a well-wisher.
{7.13.15-17}

(iii) If one of the two kings is about to destroy his own ally and the other is about to destroy his own enemy, he who attacks in the rear the destroyer of his own enemy outmanoeuvres the other. For, a king who has destroyed an enemy will become more powerful and may then turn round and attack his enemy-in-the-rear. Conversely, the other only weakens his own side.   {7.13.18,19}

AFTER THE ATTACK

MATERIAL GAIN

(i) If the two kings fighting their respective enemies come out of their fights with no gains, whoever [conqueror or enemy] had attacked in the rear that king who had lost the prospects of a greater gain or had suffered heavy losses and expenses outmanoeuvres the other.

(ii) If the two kings fighting their respective enemies come out of their fights with gains, whoever [conqueror or enemy] had attacked in the rear that king who had gained less outmanoeuvres the other. Alternatively, the outmanoeuvrer is the one who had attacked in the rear a king who had attacked another king capable of doing him greater harm in the war.

{7.13.20,21}

STRATEGIC GAIN

(iii) As between the conqueror and the enemy, each of them attacking in the rear a [different] king, the outmanoeuvrer is the one who (a) is better at raising [sufficient] troops to succeed in the campaign, (b) attacks a king entrenched in a fort or (c) attacks a king situated on his flank. For, a king situated on the flank [of the conqueror] can both attack the base of the conqueror and go to the help of the other king under attack in the rear from the conqueror. A king situated in the rear can only attack the base [and cannot go to the help of the other, being too far away.]

{7.13.22,23}

ATTACKING THE MIDDLE OR NEUTRAL KING IN THE REAR

When the conqueror and the enemy both contemplate an attack in the rear on the Middle or Neutral king with a view to reducing his power, whoever, at the end of the campaign, succeeds in separating the Middle (or Neutral) king and his ally or converts a former enemy into his own ally, is said to outmanoeuvre the other. Even an enemy who helps is fit to be allied with, not an ally who does not act like one.   {7.13.26-28}

ON DEALING WITH AN ATTACK IN THE REAR

Some teachers say that when a king, about to go on a campaign against his enemy, is attacked in the rear, it is better for him to adopt the measures of *mantrayuddha*,[2] a diplomatic offensive to persuade the attacker-in-the-rear not to do so. [The reason is:] in an actual war with troops, both parties suffer a decline because of losses and expenses; even the winner, with depleted treasury and army, will be a loser.

Kautilya disagrees. An enemy's destruction shall be brought about even at the cost of great losses and expenses.

When the conqueror and the enemy both fight their respective rear enemies and both suffer equal losses, whoever gets his untrustworthy troops destroyed by making them face the attacker first and then, freed of traitors, fights with reliable troops outmanoeuvres the other.

Even when both get their untrustworthy troops destroyed, whoever succeeds in eliminating more powerful, very treacherous or a larger number of troops, outmanoeuvres the other.

The above also applies to attacks by other hostile forces and by jungle tribes.   {7.13.29-36}

X.ix

AGAINST CONFEDERACIES AND OLIGARCHIES

AGAINST AN ATTACKING CONFEDERACY

[{7.14} deals with the situation when a king is beset by a confederacy of allies and needs to recoup his powers and build up his strength. The first step is to break up the unity of the confederacy. Kautilya distinguishes two cases and suggests courses of action when there is a clearly defined leader in the confederacy {7.14.1-9} and another when there is no such leader {7.14.10,11}. When the king under attack cannot afford the time needed to sow dissension among the members of the confederacy, Kautilya advises that it is best to make peace by making concessions; with the time bought by peace, he shall try to remedy his weaknesses. What to do to remedy each type of weakness is given in {7.14.14-28}.]

GENERAL

When the king under attack is assailed by a confederacy of kings he shall try to [prevent them from attacking him and use the time gained to] augment his group of allies, powers of analysis and judgment, wealth and military forces with a view to escaping the clutches of his enemies. {7.14.1,29}

WHEN THE CONFEDERACY HAS A LEADER

The king under attack shall offer to the leader of the confederacy both money and [a treaty of] alliance and point out that he is doubly benefited by money and friendship. He shall point out that the others in the confederacy are taking advantage of him while masquerading as his friends and, when they have grown at his expense, will overthrow him.

Or, he may try to sow dissension by pointing out that, just as he himself who had done no harm to anyone was being attacked by the confederacy, so could they, with their combined force, also attack the leader, irrespective of whether the leader was free or beset by calamities. [He shall point out that] since power corrupts minds, it is better to prevent the other members from becoming too powerful. When the king succeeds in sowing dissension within the confederacy, he shall adopt whichever course best suits his own interests—either set the leader against the weaker members of the confederacy or assist the weaker ones to fight the leader. [In any case,] he shall bring in such enmity among the members of the confederacy that it breaks up.

Or, the king under attack may make a separate agreement with the leader, offering him more than he would have got from the confederacy. Then double agents shall poison the minds of the other confederates by showing how they had been cheated by their leader who makes greater profit by the separate treaty. When their minds are duly poisoned, some of them shall be made to break the confederacy agreement. Double agents shall again use this as further proof of disunity within the confederacy and sow more dissension. When the confederacy is divided, the king under attack shall support one of the groups and plan his actions accordingly.[1]

{7.14.1-9}

WHEN THE CONFEDERACY HAS NO LEADER

When there is no clear leader among the confederates, the king under attack shall select one according to the following criteria and win him over by the method described below. Ones later in the list shall be selected before the one earlier [i.e. the list is in descending order of difficulty of bringing about the break-up of the confederacy].

(i) the inciter: by surrendering himself;

(ii) the resolute: by conciliation and obsequiousness;

(iii) one with loyal subjects; by marriage alliances;

(iv) one who joins the confederacy out of greed: by offering him double what he expects to get out of joining it;

(v) one who joins out of fear: by offering money and forces;

(vi) one afraid of the king under attack: by creating confidence with the offer of a hostage;

(vii) one with blood ties to the king under attack: by offering even closer ties of unity;

(viii) an ally: both by doing what is mutually beneficial and by the king under attack sacrificing some gain in favour of the ally;

(ix) a fickle enemy: both by dropping hostile activities against him and by offering help.

The conqueror shall adopt any means as appropriate—the four methods of conciliation, placating with gifts, sowing dissension and the use of force or any of the methods explained [earlier] under Revolts and Rebellions[2] in order to win over the members of the confederacy.   {7.14.10,11}

WHEN IT IS NECESSARY TO GAIN TIME

When, because of a calamity, the conqueror is under attack [and does not have the time to implement the techniques of sowing dissension] he shall enter into a treaty [with the confederacy], offering the use of his wealth or his forces and specifying the terms (the time, the place and the nature of the work).

After concluding the treaty, he shall set about remedying his own weaknesses [which may be (i) lack of support or protection, (ii) inadequate analysis and judgment, (iii) insufficient material resources or (iv) unenthusiastic troops].

If he lacks support, he shall create a group of supporters from among his friends and kinsmen. If he lacks [physical] protection, he shall build an impregnable fort. For, he who is defended by forts and allies is respected by his own people and by others.

If he lacks the power of good counsel, he shall recruit wise men into his service and surround himself with old men learned in the sciences. This will benefit him immediately.

If he lacks power, he shall endeavour to promote the welfare of his people. For, power comes from the countryside, which is the source of all activities.

[The means of augmenting one's resources and power are:]

In times of trouble, the fort provides a haven to the people and the king himself. Water works [dams, embankments, etc.] are the source of crops; the best results are obtained from a good rainfall when the water is continuously made available by means of storage reservoirs. Trade routes are the means of outmanoeuvring the enemy; for it is through these routes that armies and secret agents are sent, weapons, armour, carriages and draught animals are bought, and travel facilitated. Mines are the source of war material. Productive forests are the source of materials for building forts, carriages and chariots. Elephant forests provide elephants. Animal herds provide cattle, horses, donkeys and camels.

In case the resources are not available [in his own territory] he shall obtain them from allies and kinsmen.

If his forces lack enthusiasm and energy, he shall recruit, to the [greatest] extent possible, brave men from the guilds, robber bands, jungle tribes, *mlecchas* and agents trained in doing harm to enemies.

He shall employ either the methods suggested for dealing with mixed treason [internal treachery and treachery by the enemy] or those suggested for the weaker king.[3]   {7.14.12-28}

ON CONTROLLING OLIGARCHIES

[The whole of Book 11, with its single chapter, is devoted to how the conqueror can control *samghas*, normally translated as 'oligarchies'. The *Arthashastra*, for the most part, deals with states as if they were synonymous with their single, absolute rulers; as mentioned in {8.2.1}, a king encapsulates all the constituents of a state. However, at least one other type of government, 'the oligarchy', existed. Though in some *samghas*, the rulers called themselves *rajas*, or kings, the oligarchies were characterised by the collective leadership of a council of leaders.

In {11.1.4,5} are listed the states with oligarchic rule in Kautilya's time. For details see Notes on Translation 12.

Except for a few verses, Book 11 is concerned with how the conqueror can sow dissension among the members of the ruling oligarchy and to kill some of them in order to bring them under control.

Kautilya also cautions the oligarchies against falling into the traps set by the conqueror.

The use of clandestine agents and methods to sow dissension among the chiefs of an oligarchy {11.1.6-14,20-29,31-52} have been included in IX.iv.]

ON OLIGARCHIES

Because oligarchies are cohesive entities, enemies cannot break them [easily].
                                                                {11.1.2}

The chief of an oligarchy shall endear himself to his people by just behaviour, being self-controlled and diligent in pursuing activities which are liked by the people and are of benefit to them.   {11.1.56}

The oligarchies shall protect themselves from the deceitful tricks of the single king.   {11.1.55}

ON CONTROLLING OLIGARCHIES

GENERAL

Among gaining an oligarchy, an army or an ally, gaining an oligarchy is the best, because of its unassailable cohesiveness.

The conqueror shall win over those favourably disposed towards him with conciliation and gifts and sow dissension or use force against those hostile to him. {11.1.1,3}

When the oligarchy has been divided by sowing dissension, the conqueror shall remove the weaker parties from their own territory and settle them together somewhere else; or, [better still] they shall be settled as agriculturists in groups of five or ten families. For if settled together they may become an armed group. [When settled in a dispersed manner] any attempt by them to get together shall be made a punishable offence.

In all cases of strife among the members of an oligarchy, whether they arise by themselves or are incited by assassins, the conqueror shall assist the weaker party with money and arms, make them fight the hostile group and urge them to kill their rivals. {11.1.15-19,53}

SOWING DISSENSION

(i) Sowing the seeds of dissension

In all cases, secret agents placed close to the chiefs of an oligarchy shall find out the causes of quarrel such as mutual jealousy, hatred or enmity and shall sow the seeds of discord by systematically getting each one to believe that someone else was slandering him.

When resentment has thus been built up between two groups, agents in the guise of teachers shall stir up quarrels [even] among the children using their rivalry in learning, skill, gambling or sports. [These quarrels shall then be used as follows]. {11.1.6,7}

(ii) Using class conflicts

[Agents may] excite the ambitions of sons of chiefs of lower status to aspire to high status. Then while urging those of lower status to dine at the same table with those of higher status or to marry a girl of higher status, the agents shall persuade the chiefs of higher status not to agree to inter-dining or inter-marriage. Or, they may encourage the sons from the families of the lowest status to seek equality in matters of family, valour or social precedence. In case any agreement is reached [among the contending parties] on settling their questions, the agents shall have it nullified by establishing the grounds for a contrary agreement.

{11.1.9-13}

(iii) Using assassins

Assassins shall start quarrels among the supporters of the chiefs, in brothels and taverns, by praising their opponents—or by supporting the treacherous elements among them.

When there is a legal dispute, assassins may create fights by creating a provocation at night such as damaging objects or killing animals or men.

{11.1.8,14}

(iv) <u>By putting up a pretender</u>

The conqueror may install as a prince a young man, born of a noble family, but one who has been ignored or cast out by those calling themselves kings. Soothsayers and readers of omens shall proclaim to the oligarchy that the young man has characteristics of royalty and instigate the just chiefs to acknowledge the nobility of his descent. The conqueror shall send men and money to those who agree in order to strengthen the traitors [to the unity of the oligarchy]. When a fight develops between the two groups, agents in the guise of vintners shall liberally offer liquor spiked with special juices using some excuse such as the birth of a son, a marriage or a death. {11.1.20-24}

(v) <u>By false accusations of treachery</u>

Secret agents shall place at the gates of sanctuaries, temples or in fortified places [of one of the chiefs of the oligarchy], bags of gold with [identifiable] seals or vessels with coins, as if they were payments after an [alleged] agreement. When other chiefs appear, the agents shall proclaim that the payment was made by the conqueror [as a bribe]. [Having created dissension,] a fight shall be provoked.

Or, the conqueror may borrow vehicles or gold from the oligarchy, and he shall then give back the best known to one of the chiefs. When the oligarchy demands the return of the borrowed items, they shall be informed that they had been returned to a chief [giving the impression that he was cheating the others]. {11.1.25-29}

X.x

THE WEAK KING

[The analysis of foreign policy in this part, until now, has been from the point of view of the conqueror and, sometimes, of the conqueror and his enemy, as initiators of the action. The concept of the weak king is, however, quite different; he is the king who is the target of aggression by a stronger king. That a king cannot always make the first move in conquest is recognised by including 'seeking shelter' as one of the six methods of foreign policy. This is discussed in {7.15}, which covers both seeking the protection of a stronger king and taking shelter in a fort. Book 12 covers all aspects of the aggression against a weak king who has taken refuge in a fort. Of the five chapters, most of {12.2} and {12.3} and the whole of {12.4} contain a description of clandestine methods to be used against the aggressor.

The general advice to a weak king, under threat from an aggressor, is given in {12.1.1-9,32} and {7.15.13-20}. Kautilya eschews the extreme positions of earlier teachers and cautions both against spineless submission and foolhardy valour. It is better to give up what is sure to be taken by force and live to fight another day. Only if the circumstances are not conducive to peace shall he fight. The attitude to be adopted towards the aggressor also depends on the character of the aggressor, whether he is righteous, greedy or monstrous.

A weak king can either seek shelter in a fort or with another king. If the protection of another king is sought, the preference shall be for a strong king who is immune to the diplomatic machinations of the aggressor, has sound advisers, comparable military strength and has mobilised. In the absence of such a strong king, protection of kings weaker than the aggressor can be sought, so long as they have these good qualities and also have terrain and time suitable for fighting.

If no protector can be found, the weak king may seek refuge in an impregnable fort with a strong body of men to defend it. While sheltered in the fort, the weak king shall do whatever is possible to improve his position, as indicated in detail in {7.15.12}.

The last resort is surrendering, with honour, to the aggressor. Verses {7.15.21-29} prescribe the submissive code of conduct of the surrender. It is presumed that a righteous aggressor will treat the subjugated king fairly, as described in {7.16.17,19-23,28} in X.iv.

Book 12 is a strictly logical exposition of advice to the weak king for dealing with different stages of the aggression. The stages are:

(i) when the aggressor is getting ready to attack;

(ii) when he starts the military campaign by marching towards the fort;

(iii) when he starts the siege;

(iv) when defeat is imminent; and

(v) after the defeat.

A weak king may try to reduce his losses by suing for peace during most of the stages. Equally, he can employ clandestine methods to kill or weaken the aggressor. What, in all prudence, he should do will depend on the circumstances of each case.

In the first stage, when the aggressor is mobilising for an attack, the weak king may sue for peace, try diplomacy or wage clandestine warfare, as described later {12.1.17-22}.

Peace can be sought even after the aggressor starts on his campaign but by offering useless things {12.1.24-31}. If this fails, an envoy can be sent to dissuade the aggressor from continuing his campaign {12.2.15-18}. If this is also useless, the aggressor can be killed or undermined by provoking rebellions and attacks {12.2.8-10}. Or, he can be assassinated {12.2.2-7}; clandestine methods can be used to subvert his princes {12.3.15-16}, high officials {12.2.19-24; 12.3.12,13}, the Viceroy and the Chancellor {12.2.25-33}, army chiefs {12.2.11-14;12.3.14}, the Chief Commanders of the four wings {12.3.1-4}; and others {12.3.5-10}. Translations of the verses referred to above will be found in IX.iv. Other kings may be approached for assistance {12.3.18-21}. {12.4} contains a series of clandestine methods for counteracting the aggressor.

Eventually the aggressor may besiege the fort itself. The weak king can take a number of precautions {12.5.9-15} to be better able to withstand the siege. The use of tunnels as a means of both attack and defence is an interesting aspect {12.5.16-20}. It is also possible for the weak king to escape, leaving the fort in the hands of a trusted relative {12.5.21,22}. Tricks may be played on the aggressor in order to obtain his stores or massacre his troops {12.5.23-30}. The weak king may, even at this stage, sue for peace {12.5.31-34}.

When the weak king can no longer defend the fort, he can either mount a night attack and escape, or escape through a tunnel {12.5.35-42}.

If he cannot escape, he may hide himself in a secret place and when the aggressor is installed in the kingdom, wreak vengeance on him {12.5.43-51}.]

ATTITUDE TOWARDS A STRONGER KING

Bharadvaja says that a weak king, when attacked by a stronger king, shall bend like a reed and surrender his all. For he who submits to a strong king bows to Indra.

[On the other hand] Vishalaksha says that a weak king shall fight with all his resources, for only with valour can one surmount calamities. It is the *dharma* of a *kshatriya* to fight, whether he wins or loses.

Kautilya disagrees [with both]. He who surrenders all lives only a life of despair, like a sheep that has strayed from its herd. [On the other hand,] one fighting with a tiny army perishes like one trying to cross the ocean without a boat. It is better to seek the protection of a powerful king or an impregnable fort.   {12.1.1-9}

The weaker king shall offer, by one means or another, that which the other will, in any case, take by force. It is life that is worth preserving not wealth which, being impermanent, can be given up with out regrets.
{12.1.32}

TYPES OF AGGRESSORS

There are three types of aggressors:

(i) The <u>righteous aggressor</u> is satisfied with submission. The weak shall yield to him, particularly when there is danger from another enemy.

(ii) The <u>greedy aggressor</u> is satisfied with seizing land and goods. The weak king shall give up wealth to him.

(iii) The <u>monstrous aggressor</u> is satisfied only when he takes the land, goods, wives, sons and [even the] life of the defeated. A weak king may give up land and goods but shall not let himself be taken. {12.1.10-16}

SEEKING PROTECTION WHEN ATTACKED

PROTECTION OF OTHER KINGS

When attacked by a strong king, a weak king shall seek the protection of a king who is stronger than the aggressor and who cannot be swayed by the diplomacy[1] of the aggressor trying to outmanoeuvre the weak king.

Where there is a choice between kings equally immune to the diplomacy of the aggressor, the weak king shall seek the protection of one who has better councillors[2] and who surrounds himself with [wise] elders.

If there is no king stronger than the aggressor, the weak king shall join forces with a king who has the same military strength or the same number of troops as the aggressor; such a king shall be one who is immune to the aggressor's efforts to outmanoeuvre the weak king with his [diplomatic] intrigues and his might.

When there is a choice between kings equally immune to the diplomacy and might of the aggressor, the one who has made more extensive preparations [for war] shall be preferred.

If there is no king [even] of strength equal to that of the aggressor, the weak king shall join forces with kings who, though less powerful than the aggressor, are upright, energetic and opposed to the aggressor; they shall be immune to the aggressor's efforts, using his diplomacy, might and enthusiasm to outmanoeuvre the weak king.

When there is a choice between kings equally immune to the diplomacy, might and energy of the aggressor, he who has battlefields favourable to him shall be preferred; among those having equally favourable battlefields, he who can fight at a time suitable to him shall be preferred; among those equal in place and time of war, he who has better weapons and armour shall be preferred.   {7.15.1-8}

PROTECTION OF FORTS

If a weak king cannot find any other king to protect him, he shall seek shelter in a fort; it shall be such that the aggressor, even with a large force, cannot cut off supplies of food, fodder, fuel and water and [shall be so impregnable that the aggressor] will suffer heavy losses and expenses [if he tries to take it].

When there is a choice of forts, [some teachers think that] one with a better stock of materials shall be preferred. Kautilya is of the view that a fort with men, as well as stocks, is preferable.   {7.15.9-11}

[Seeking shelter in a fort is not an end in itself; the aim is to utilise the protection to defeat the aggressor].

The weak king shall entrench himself in a fort in order to:

(i) win over the enemy-in-the-rear, the rear enemy's ally, the Middle king, or the Neutral king to his side and against the aggressor;

(ii) have the aggressor's kingdom captured or destroyed by one of the following: a neighbour, a jungle chief, a pretender of his family or an unjustly treated prince;

(iii) instigate a revolt in the aggressor's fort, country or camp with the help of a group of traitors;

(iv) kill the aggressor, when he is near, by means of a weapon, fire, poison or clandestine methods and as and when the entrenched king chooses;

(v) make the aggressor suffer heavy losses and expenses by operations conducted by the king himself or through his clandestine agents;

(vi) gradually sow dissension among the aggressor's allies or army when these suffer from heavy losses, expenses or long marches;

(vii) capture the aggressor's camp by cutting off the supplies going to it and by destroying the foraging parties;

(viii) strike at the aggressor with all one's forces mobilised after creating a weak point in his forces by a secret [diversionary] attack;

(ix) compel the aggressor when he is disheartened to make peace with the entrenched king on his own terms;

(x) keep the aggressor engaged while insurrections rise all round him;

(xi) get the forces allies or jungle tribes to devastate the denuded base of the aggressor;

(xii) safeguard, from the safety of the fort, the welfare of his own vast territory;

(xiii) collect together, by staying in one place, an invincible army made up of one's own dispersed forces and those of allies;

(xiv) free one's own army who are expert in fighting on water from trenches or at night, tired from the rigours of a long march, for a battle when the aggressor comes near the fort;

(xv) render the attack ineffective by making the aggressor lay siege to the fort at a wrong time and in inhospitable terrain after suffering heavy losses and expenses in getting there;

(xvi) ensure that the aggressor suffers heavy losses and expenses in getting to the inaccessible fort, having had to contend with forts and forests along the way; or

(xvii) ensure the destruction of the aggressor, by being made to pass through regions full of sickness and with no suitable places for military operations; he will arrive, if at all, in distress and even if he arrives, will never return. {7.15.12}

PEACE OR RESISTANCE?

Some teachers say that, if none of the above mentioned aims are achievable or if the aggressor is of very much greater strength, the weak king has only two choices. He can either leave the fort and run away; or, he can fight [the much superior force of] the enemy and perish like a moth in a flame. [Even a desperate fight has some value]. For to one who has given up all hope there is success one way or the other—either victory or death. {7.15.13-15}

Kautilya disagrees. If the weak king finds that the circumstances are conducive to peace between him and the aggressor, he shall sue for peace by sending an envoy. If the aggressor sends an envoy, the weak king shall greet the envoy with money and honour and surrender himself and his kingdom while offering gifts to the envoy's king from himself and to the queen and princes from his queen and princes.   {7.15.16,17,19,20}

If the circumstances are not conducive for peace, the weak king shall first fight and then by his valour seek peace or asylum.[3]   {7.15.18}

CONDUCT OF A KING GIVEN PROTECTION

When a weak king has been afforded protection, he shall behave towards his protector like a courtier taking service with a king.[4]   {7.15.21}

A king surrendering with his forces shall serve the strong king by merging his own forces with those of the protector and by avoiding the company of undesirable people such as those suspected [of treachery to the strong king].
{7.15.30}

He shall undertake the following activities only when permitted by the protector: build a fort or other defensive works; arrange the marriages of princes and princesses; install the heir-apparent as Crown Prince; trade in horses; capture elephants; go on pilgrimages or pleasure trips.

He shall also obtain his protector's permission before doing anything in his own territory, such as giving instructions to ministers and officials or punishing deserters.

If anyone in his cities and countryside becomes hostile, he shall get rid of them by using clandestine methods suggested elsewhere for dealing with traitors or ask his protector to give some other land with well-behaved people. In any case, he shall not accept any land, however suitable, offered to him out of the territory of an ally.

When he cannot get an audience with the protector, he may see the protector's counsellor, *purohita*, Chief of Defence or Crown Prince, and show them favours to the extent possible.

On all occasions of worshipping gods or recitations of blessings he shall make his people pray for the long life of the protector.

Everywhere, he shall proclaim the benefits to him of his protector, [so as not to display any disaffection on his part].   {7.15.22-29}

WHEN THE AGGRESSOR IS GETTING READY TO ATTACK

When an aggressor is on the point of attacking, the weak king [has three choices]: he can make peace [with the aggressor], try to avert the attack [by diplomacy—*mantrayuddha*] or wage secret warfare.[5] He shall [try to] win over the sections favourable to him in the aggressor's camp by means of conciliation and gifts and prevent treachery in his own camp by sowing dissension and use of force.   {12.1.17,18}

[At this stage] the weak king may make peace without taking any action to harm the aggressor.   {12.1.23}

[If, however, he wants to weaken the aggressor first] he may send an envoy after taking any of the following actions:

(i) using clandestine agents to destroy, with weapons, poison or fire, the aggressor's fort, country or camp;

(ii) harassing the aggressor's rear from all sides;

(iii) making jungle tribes devastate the aggressor's country; or

(iv) helping a pretender or an unjustly treated prince to seize the throne.
                    {12.1.19-22}

AFTER THE AGGRESSOR HAS STARTED ON HIS MARCH

If the aggressor sets out in spite of efforts to avert the attack, the weaker king shall sue for peace.   {from 12.1.24}

SUING FOR PEACE

In negotiating for peace the weak king shall [successively] offer a quarter more of money and arms each day [until the offer is accepted].
                    {12.1.24}

> [Since the intention is to avert the attack at the lowest possible cost, the weak king shall first make a low offer, wait for a day to see whether it is accepted, increase the offer by a quarter and so on. The specification of a quarter or delay of a day need not be taken literally].

If the weak king seeks peace on condition of surrendering a portion of his forces [and the offer is accepted], he shall give dull and cowardly elephants and horses; if he has to give active and energetic animals, a long-acting poison[6] shall be administered to them.

If peace is sought on condition of surrendering a portion of his men, the weak king shall give:

(i) treacherous, foreign or jungle tribes under the command of a trusted officer who will arrange the destruction of both the strong king's troops and the troops supplied; or

(ii) [temperamental and] hot-headed troops who are likely to revolt when feeling insulted; or

(iii) loyal troops of the standing army who will strike [on behalf of the weak king] when the strong king is in difficulty.

If peace is sought on condition of paying money, the weak king shall give articles of high value for which there are no buyers, or forest produce that is unfit for use in war.

If the condition is surrender of land, the weak king shall give land that can be easily recovered, which has permanent enemies,[7] which provides no shelter or which can only be settled with heavy losses and expenses.

[In extreme cases] the weak king may make peace by offering to surrender everything, except his capital city.   {12.1.25-31}

AVERTING AN ATTACK

If the aggressor declines to conclude a peace treaty, the weak king shall [try to persuade him to do so by reasoning with him]. The arguments to be used are that the strong king (i) was being misled by friends in name but enemies in reality, (ii) frightening all his allies, (iii) promoting the interests of his enemies, and (iv) [because of all this] risking his wealth and his life.

[The envoy, speaking for the weak king shall point out that] in times past kings had perished because they fell prey to one or other of the six vices (lust, anger, greed, conceit, arrogance and foolhardiness)[8] and that the aggressor was in danger of following these kings who had no self-control. It was better to pay heed to spiritual and material well-being (*dharma and artha*). Those who advised him to behave rashly, in violation of the principles of *dharma* and *artha*, were friends only in name but were really his enemies. It was rash to fight brave men, who cared not for their own lives; it was a violation of *dharma* to cause the death of many on both sides; it was a violation of *artha* to sacrifice one's existing wealth and one's blameless ally [i.e. the weak king himself].

[The envoy, shall also point out the following]. The weak king, who had many allies, would get many more with the things [forces, men, wealth or land] rejected by the strong king: together they could attack the strong king from all sides. While the weak king still enjoyed the support of his own circle of kings, the Middle king and the Neutral king, all these had abandoned the strong aggressor. For they were just waiting for him to start the war, incur heavy losses and expenses, be cut off from his allies and lose his control over his stronghold; then they would strike and overwhelm him.   {12.2.2-7}

UNDERMINING THE AGGRESSOR

If, in spite of the efforts to avert an attack, the aggressor actually starts his campaign, the weak king shall adopt the following measures:

(i) provoke a revolt among the subjects of the strong king, using the methods suggested for dealing with oligarchies;[9]

(ii) draw out and assassinate the strong king using the methods suggested elsewhere;[10]

(iii) use assassins and poisoners to attack those points of protection which have been specified in the section on 'The king's personal security'[11]; and

(iv) win over jungle chiefs to his side, by giving them wealth and honour and use them to devastate the aggressor's country.

{12.2.8-10;12.3.17}

[For clandestine methods of assassinating the aggressor and subverting the princes, high officials, Viceroy, Chancellor, Chief Commanders of Corps and others see IX.iv]

USING THE CIRCLE OF KINGS

The aggressor's enemy in the rear shall be persuaded to attack the aggressor in the rear on the grounds that, after destroying the weak king, the aggressor was bound to turn against his enemy in the rear. This king shall be promised that, in case the aggressor turns on him first, the weak king will himself attack in the rear the aggressor [i.e. promise corresponding help].

The aggressor's own allies shall be persuaded to join him in a combined campaign on the grounds that, without the weak king acting as a dam, they were all in danger of being overwhelmed by the aggressor.

All kings, whether allied or not shall be cautioned that, after destroying the weak king, the aggressor would turn against them and that it was in their own interest to help the weak king.

The Middle king or the Neutral king, whoever is nearer, may be appealed to, even by offering to surrender everything, for the sake of deliverance [from the aggressor].   {12.3.18-21}

COUNTER ATTACK

[For clandestine methods of counter-attacking the aggressor, provoking an attack on him by others, attacking him with poison, creating chaos in his camp and attempting to kill him when his expedition is approaching the fort for the siege, see IX.iv.]

WHEN BESIEGED BY THE AGGRESSOR

The reasons why a weak king should seek the protection of a fort have been explained earlier. {12.5.12}

PRECAUTIONS

The weak king shall take the following precautions as the aggressor approaches to lay a siege:

(i) move those people who can [help him to] resist the siege into the fort from the countryside;

(ii) move those incapable of withstanding the siege out of the fort;

(iii) send out of the fort things easily replaceable or things which help the enemy;

(iv) concentrate the rest of the population of the countryside in a mountain, forest or river fort or in an inaccessible place in the middle of a forest and place these under the charge of a son or a brother [i.e. a reliable member of the family];

(v) burn all grass and wood for a distance of one *yojana* around the fort [to improve visibility and deny the enemy any cover];

(vi) spoil or divert all [nearby] water works; and

(vii) lay traps such as deep well-like holes, concealed pits and thorny obstructions. {12.5.9-11,13-15}

USE OF TUNNELS

(i) The besieged king shall cause a tunnel to be dug [from the fort] with many openings into the aggressor's camp and carry away stores, leaders or even the besieger himself;

(ii) If the besieger digs a tunnel, it shall be flooded either by deepening the moat or by digging a well outside the fort walls;

(iii) Precautions shall be taken for finding out whether the besieger was digging a tunnel by placing water pots and bronze vessels in places where digging is suspected;

(iv) When the aggressor is discovered to be digging a tunnel, a counter-tunnel shall be dug, the enemy's tunnel broken into and flooded with water or filled with smoke. {12.5.16-20}

LEAVING THE FORT WITHOUT SURRENDERING

The besieged king may make arrangements for the defence of the fort, appoint a kinsman in charge and himself go away in a direction away from the path of the aggressor. He shall go to such a place where:

(i) he may join up with allies, kinsmen, jungle chiefs or great enemies or traitors of the aggressor;

(ii) by his presence, he may be able to sow dissension between the enemy and the enemy's allies, mount an attack on the enemy's rear, capture the enemy's kingdom, obstruct the enemy's supplies and reinforcements or harass the enemy by trickery;

(iii) he may be able to protect his kingdom;

(iv) he can strengthen his standing army; or

(v) he can sue for peace on his own terms from where he is.

{12.5.21,22}

DEPRIVING BESIEGER OF MONEY OR TROOPS BY DECEPTION

Those accompanying the king [pretending to be traitors] may ask the besieger to send money or troops (as if for trade or barter) on receipt of which they would either kill the king or hand him over bound. When the aggressor sends money or troops, the [weak] king shall appropriate them.

Or, a frontier governor shall pretend to surrender the fort, invite the enemy's troops in to take it over and kill them when they come inside trusting the governor.

Or, the enemy's troops may be invited to massacre the civilian population concentrated in one place. When they come trustingly to the fort or inaccessible region, they shall be killed.

An agent posing as a friend of the besieger shall [mis] inform him that the supplies (such as grains, oil, sugar or salt) inside the fort having been exhausted, new supplies were expected at a specified time and place; the besieger shall be invited to seize them. Then, poisoned supplies shall be sent along with treacherous troops, jungle forces or condemned persons [thus poisoning the enemy's troops while getting rid of undesirables in his own forces]. Similar tactics can be employed with all types of supplies [and reinforcements].   {12.5.23-30}

MAKING PEACE

The weak king may make a peace treaty [agreeing to pay tribute]. [Only] a part of the tribute shall be paid [immediately] and the rest after a long delay. Payment can be delayed by bribing the aggressor's associates who come to collect it. The time gained shall be used to weaken the defences of the aggressor or the clandestine methods of fire, weapon or poison may be used.   {12.5.31-34}

[For the type of treaties made by the weaker king surrendering himself, his army, treasury, or territory, see above {7.3.22-36}, in 'Treaties', X.iii above]

WHEN FACING DEFEAT

[When the resources of the weak king are totally exhausted and defeat is imminent, he can escape unseen by the besieger or make a surprise night attack to break out of the siege; and, if the attack fails, he can leave in disguise. Even then, he can mount a counter-attack.]

When the besieged king's resources are totally exhausted, he shall abandon the fort and escape, by a [secret] tunnel, by digging a new passage or by breaching a wall of the fort.

Alternatively, he may mount a [surprise] night attack. If it succeeds, he may continue to hold on to the fort. If the attack fails [and the enemy troops pour into the fort] he shall escape using one of the following disguises: an ascetic with a small retinue; a corpse carried by clandestine agents; or a woman following a funeral cortege. Before leaving, he shall poison the food and drink likely to be used as offerings for gods, funeral rites or festivals.

He may also instigate treacherous troops and strike with a concealed army.[12]

{12.5.35-42}

IF UNABLE TO ESCAPE /REVENGE AFTER DEFEAT

[If the fort is taken while the besieged king is still in it, he can hide himself in it and await a suitable opportunity to kill the enemy and the occupying troops.]

If the fort is taken, the king shall hide himself in a sanctuary where plenty of food has been stored; he may conceal himself inside an image, in a hollow wall, in an underground chamber, or hidden behind an image. He shall lie low until the victorious occupier forgets him [and becomes careless]. Then the victor shall be killed while sleeping by entering his bedchamber at night through a tunnel; by dropping a heavy weight released by a mechanism; by setting fire to a house [previously] prepared with a poisonous or ignitable mixture when he is sleeping in it; while he is enjoying himself carelessly in a park or a leisure area; by assassins gaining access through underground chambers, tunnels or hollow walls; by clandestine agents poisoning him; or by secret women agents killing him with snakes, poison, fire or smoke while he is asleep in a secluded place.

Or, whenever an opportunity occurs, the concealed king shall move about the palace secretly and do whatever he can to harm the occupier. He shall then return secretly to his hiding place after conveying signals to his own agents.

[Once the occupying enemy is killed,] he shall sound the trumpet to summon his agents in the palace [such as door-keepers and old retainers] and have the rest of the occupier's people killed.   {12.5.43-51}

Part XI

DEFENCE AND WAR

"To be in accordance with *dharma*, the place and time of battle must be specified beforehand."

{10.3.26}

"An archer letting off an arrow may or may not kill a single man, but a wise man using his intellect can kill even reaching unto the very womb."

{10.6.51}

"In the territories acquired by him, the conqueror shall continue the practice of all customs which are in accordance with *dharma*, and shall introduce those which had not been observed before. Likewise, he shall stop the practise of any custom not in accordance with *dharma* and shall also refrain from introducing them."

{13.5.24}

XI.i

KAUTILYA ON WAR

[A king had two responsibilities to his state, one internal and one external, for which he needed an army. As mentioned in the Introduction to this translation, one of the three internal duties of the king was *raksha* or protection of the state from external aggression. The other responsibility was the enlargement of the territory by conquest. The references to the defence of the realm are scattered throughout the text. Conquest by war is mainly in Books 10 and 13.

War against an enemy is defined broadly by Kautilya and not limited to only physical warfare. Four kinds of war are mentioned. *Mantrayuddha*, 'war by counsel', means the exercise of diplomacy; this applies mainly when a king finds himself in a weaker position and considers it unwise to engage in battle. *Prakasayuddha* is open warfare, specifying time and place—i.e. a set-piece battle. *Kutayuddha* is concealed warfare and refers primarily to *upajapa*, psychological warfare including instigation of treachery in the enemy camp. *Gudayuddha*, 'clandestine war', is using covert methods to achieve the objective without actually waging a battle, usually by assassinating the enemy. In waging clandestine war, the king used not only his own agents and double agents, but also allies, vassal kings, tribal chiefs and the suborned friends and supporters of the enemy.

The defence of the realm, a constant preoccupation for the king, consisted not only of the physical defence of the kingdom but also the prevention of treachery, revolts and rebellion. The physical defensive measures were the frontier posts to prevent the entry of undesirable aliens {2.1.5} and forts in various parts of the country. Four different types of forts—mountain, river, jungle and desert—are mentioned in {2.3.1,2} in IV.i. The details of fortifications are shown in this translation as diagrams in IV.i. A list of ordnance, including weapons, armour and siege machines is given in Appendix 12.

The king maintained control over his army by a variety of means. The Chiefs of the army were paid well so that they would not be tempted by the bribes of the enemy and could afford to pay their men well. Their integrity was tested, particularly to weed out the cowardly {1.10.9-12}. They were kept under constant surveillance through clandestine agents, especially to see that they did not succumb to the instigations of the enemy. For the same reason, each of the four wings of the army were placed under the control of more than one chief, so that mutual suspicion and fear would ensure their loyalty. Those suspected of treachery were posted to remote areas while their families were kept in the capital as hostages. Sometimes, they were secretly eliminated.

An item in the accounting of government revenues and expenditure {2.6.21, 2.15.10} refers to the money saved from demobilisation, implying that, in peace time, only sufficient forces were kept for defence and additional forces were raised for conquest. From {5.3.26}, it is seen that these were mainly the forces guarding the forts and royal property. The officers commanding such forces were in permanent service but were often transferred. A special type of force, also never disbanded, was the *antarvamsikasainya*, the 'King's Own Guards'. When the forces raised for a conquest were demobilised, the king is advised to disperse them in his own country and not in that of an ally, so that the army can easily be collected together again.

The rations for elephants, horses and men {2.15.42, 2.31.12-17, and 2.30.8-10,18-24} will be found in Appendix 4. The prescribed rations appear to have been based on different 'work months'—32 days for infantry, 35 for horses and 40 for elephants {2.20.51-53}. The responsibility for payment of rations and wages rested with the battalion commander, in charge of a hundred units and the divisional commander in charge of a thousand units {5.3.25}.

When a force was recruited for a campaign, the king sold Crown goods on credit through his own agents, disguised as traders; double the price of the goods, given to the men for the maintenance of their families while they were away, was recovered from them on return from the campaign. Thus the king not only managed to dispose of his stores but also recovered more than their original price {5.3.42-44}.

The military forces described in the *Arthashastra* conform to the classical Indian pattern of four wings—elephants, chariots, horses and infantry. However, in battle, each warrior on horseback was surrounded by six foot soldiers and elephants and chariots by five horse units. Infantry had archers as well as soldiers equipped with swords, spears and lances for hand-to-hand combat. References to fighters on water are found in {2.33.8, 7.10.34,35 and 10.4.2} and fighting from trenches in {7.10.36,37}. In recruiting, Kautilya prefers an army of trained *kshatriyas* or a large force composed of *Sudras* and *Vaishyas*; in his view, an enemy was likely to disarm Brahmin troops by prostrating himself before them {9.2.21-24}.

The classification of troops into different types—the standing army, the territorial army, the militias, allied troops, alien forces and tribal forces - is fully explained in {9.2.14-19}; this classification is referred to elsewhere {2.33.8, 7.8.27, 9.2.2-11} because the nature of the force is relevant to when it was mobilised and how it was used.

In the text, the characteristics of an ideal army are described using the method of contrasting qualities, under calamities in Book 8. The structure of the army and the responsibilities of high defence officials are described in various chapters of Book 2 such as {2.2, 2.18. 2.30-33} since that long book contains the duties of all heads of departments, both civil and military. Chapter 9.2, with the definition of the classification of troops into different types, and the use of the right kind of force is found under 'Planning for Battle', because these are relevant to deciding on when to go on a campaign. In this translation, all these subjects have been brought together in the next section (XI.ii), in the interests of consolidating all verses relating to defence and war.

'*Yana*', one of the six methods of foreign policy, refers to 'marching' on a military campaign. This march ended with the setting up of a base camp nearer the chosen site of the battle. This camp was near a fort in the king's own country, to be used as a place of refuge in case of defeat; see XI.iv below. The plan of the base camp resembles that of the city, as will be seen by comparing Fig. 15 and Fig. 33. There was a further march from the base camp to the battle ground (XI.v). On reaching the battle camp near the site of the battle, the king could choose to either engage the enemy in an open battle or, if a frontal attack was not advisable, use tactics like hit-and-run, harassment of enemy forces or ambushing (XI.vi). Preparing oneself for the battle and building up the morale of the troops were the tasks for the night before the battle (XI.vii). The battle tactics were decided then, particularly the choice of battle arrays and formations. This technical subject is explained by Kautilya in {10.5} and {10.6} in XI.viii. The order of attack is given in 'The Battle' (XI.ix). When a king wins, he is advised to sue for peace with an inherently stronger king, accept a peace offer from a king equally strong but destroy a weaker king. However, a defeated army should never be harassed to the point of making it so desperate that it will return to the fight with reckless vehemence.

The conqueror may go to war against another king for a variety of reasons—to neutralise an enemy-in-the-rear, to help an ally or to subdue a small state. The ultimate objective is always the destruction of the natural enemy, i.e. the king who is the main obstacle to the conqueror's ambition. It is a symmetric situation; if the conqueror does not eliminate the enemy, the enemy will eliminate him. This is how the relationship is defined.

The enemy could be destroyed by clandestine methods; or he could be defeated in battle and killed. Or, after defeat, his territory could be absorbed and he himself made a vassal in a different part of the enlarged kingdom. The various options have been fully analysed in X.ix on the conduct of the weak king. One option open to the defeated enemy was for him to take refuge in a fort. For the conqueror, the besieging and capturing of the fort was the final vital step in the crushing of the enemy. Chapters {13.1 to 13.4} deal with the siege in a systematic manner (XI.x). The last chapter of Book 13 is the culmination of the purpose of the whole work—how to consolidate the newly acquired territory so that the king can embark on further conquests.]

XI.ii

MILITARY ORGANIZATION

[Verses relating to the following subjects have been brought together in this section: the characteristics of an ideal army; the six types of troops, ranging from the loyal standing army to the unreliable alien and jungle forces; the organizational structure; and the duties and responsibilities of the officials concerned with war.]

THE IDEAL ARMY

[A calamity, as used in the *Arthashastra*, means anything that weakens a constituent of a state. As in the case of calamities affecting other constituents, those affecting the army and the fort are also found in Book 8. {8.5.2-20}, in effect, describe the qualities of an ideal army.

Kautilya examines thirty-four different calamities which can affect the fighting capacity of the army. Unlike the discussion of the adversities which affect the other constituents of the state (see II.iii, II.iv), which are arranged in order of seriousness, those affecting the army are examined in pairs. In each case, the calamity stated earlier is a remediable one.

A study of the comparisons brings out what an ideal army should be like. It should be well paid, honoured and kept up to strength. It should not have any traitors or dissension within its ranks. It should not be scattered but kept together. Even if demobilised, the soldiers should be kept in one's own country, in case it is necessary to collect the army together again. In war, it should never be abandoned, left leaderless or totally merged into someone else's army. It should always have adequate reinforcements. It should not be allowed to become too tired by long marches. The terrain most suited to the type of force should be chosen for the battle. It is better to allow it to withdraw than perish in a frontal battle. It should not be allowed to be sandwiched between a frontal enemy and an enemy-in-the-rear nor be completely encircled.

In view of the importance of the fort in defence as a place of refuge, {8.4.48} specifies 'obstruction', internal or external, as a calamity to it.]

The calamities which affect adversely [the efficient functioning of] the army are:
- not given due honours;
- not paid;
- not healthy;
- tired after a long march;
- exhausted after a battle;
- depleted in strength;
- having suffered a setback;
- after defeat in a frontal battle;
- having to fight in an unsuitable terrain;
- having to fight in an unsuitable season;
- low in morale;
- abandoned by its commander;
- having women in it;
- with traitors in it;
- an angry one;
- a disunited one;
- one which has run away [from battle];
- a dispersed one;
- one fighting alongside another;
- one absorbed in another force;
- one obstructed;
- one encircled;
- one cut off from supplies;
- one cut off from reinforcements;
- one demobilised and dispersed;
- one threatened [also] by an army in the rear;
- one whose base has been weakened; and
- one without leaders.   {from 8.5.1}

An <u>unhonoured army</u> will fight if honoured with money; not so a <u>dishonoured army</u> which holds resentment in its heart.

An <u>unpaid army</u> will fight if paid immediately, but not so a <u>sick army</u>, which is unfit to fight.

An <u>army newly arrived</u> in a region will fight if, mixed with experienced troops, it learns about the region from others; not so an <u>army tired after a long march</u>.

An <u>exhausted army</u> will fight after refreshing itself by bathing, eating and sleeping but not so a <u>depleted army</u>, having been reduced in fighting men and draught animals.

An <u>army repulsed</u> will fight if rallied by heroic men; not so an <u>army defeated after a frontal attack</u> since it would have lost many of its brave men.

An army [made to fight] in an <u>unsuitable season</u> will do so if provided with suitable vehicles, weapons and armour. An army cannot fight in <u>unsuitable terrain</u> because its movement will be impeded and it cannot undertake raids.

A <u>despondent army</u> will fight if its hopes are fulfilled, but not an <u>army abandoned</u> by its chief.

An <u>army with women</u> [accompanying it] will fight if the women are separated from it; not so an <u>army with traitors</u> and enemies in it.

An <u>angry army</u> [whose officers are provoked for some reason] will fight if their resentment is overcome by conciliation and similar means; not so a <u>disunited army</u> whose members are estranged from each other.

[A defeated army may take refuge in one state or be scattered in many states.] An <u>army staying together</u> and taking refuge with an ally or in a fortress will fight if persuaded by diplomatic and conciliatory tactics. It is more dangerous to try to collect together a <u>scattered army</u>.

[In the case of a joint expedition, one's own army may be encamped near another and fight alongside or may be merged completely into another.] An <u>army fighting alongside</u> can fight the enemy separately because it will have its own positions and possibilities of mounting independent attacks. An <u>army completely integrated with another</u> has no independence of movement.

An <u>obstructed army</u> can fight the [enemy] obstruction by choosing another direction for attack; not so an <u>encircled army</u>, being obstructed on all sides.

An <u>army with its supply of grain cut off</u> can fight if grain is brought in from elsewhere; it can also subsist on [locally available] animals and vegetables. But an <u>army cut off from reserves of men</u> cannot fight, being bereft of reinforcements.

An <u>army kept dispersed in one's own land</u> can be collected together in case of trouble, being disbanded in one's own territory; not so an <u>army dispersed in the land of an ally</u>, being far removed in place and [requiring] time [to collect and move it.]

An <u>army full of traitors</u> will [still] fight if officered by trustworthy commanders who can isolate the traitorous units; not so an <u>army with a hostile army in the rear</u> being frightened of an attack from behind.

An <u>army with a denuded capital city behind it</u> will fight after it is fully mobilised with the support of the citizens; not so an <u>army cut off from its leaders</u> being without king or commander.

An <u>army whose commander is dead</u> will fight under a new commander; not so a <u>blind [leaderless] army</u>.

The means of preventing calamities to an army are: removal of vices and defects, reinforcement with fresh troops, entrenching oneself in a strong [defensible] place, reaching over the enemy [to secure allies or to attack him from the rear] and making a treaty with one who can help [in counteracting the calamity].

The king shall always guard his army carefully against troubles caused by enemies and strike at the weak points of the enemy's army.

{8.5.2-20}

EXCELLENT ARMIES

The best infantry is that which consists of men of the same qualities as described for the army [as a whole].

[See {6.1.11} in II.ii—the soldiers shall be men of tested loyalty, strong, obedient, not averse to a long expeditions, skilled in handling all weapons, possessed of endurance and with the experience of many battles].

The best horses and elephants are those with good pedigree, strength, youthfulness, vitality, loftiness, speed, mettle, good training, stamina, a lofty mien, obedience, auspicious marks and good conduct.

{10.5.41,42}

CALAMITIES TO THE FORT

Calamities to the fort can either be internal, such as obstruction by chiefs inside the fort or external, i.e. obstruction to (army) movements by an enemy or by unsubdued tribes.

{8.4.48}

TYPES OF TROOPS

[The expression *maula-bhrita-sreni-mitra-amitra-atavi* (sometimes without *amitra*) occurs, as a description of the type of troops, in {2.33.8}, {7.8.27} and {9.2.1}. These are not clearly defined in the text, perhaps because they were commonly used in such works and Kautilya did not impute any special meanings to them. However, we can deduce the nature of these troops, partly from the words themselves and partly from the comparisons made between then in {9.2.14-19}. For, example, *maula* is derived from *mula*, a word often used in the text to describe the 'base' of the king; this usually signifies the capital fort and, by extension, the original country of the king. Likewise, *bhrita*—

territorial subjects; *sreni*—guild; *mitra*—friendly; *amitra*—inimical, therefore, alien; *atavi*—jungle. Though *maula* is generally translated as 'hereditary', a more accurate translation will be 'regular standing army'; *sreni*, usually translated as 'banded' or 'corporate' troops, is better rendered as a 'militia'. Of the six, only the first three were raised from the citizens of the country. When the different types of troops should be mobilised is explained in {9.2.2-8} in X.vi. The list below is in decreasing order of importance].

Maula—regular standing army—composed of natives of the country, dependent on the king, sharing his interests, constantly trained [owing loyalty hereditarily to the royal family, honoured by the king.[1]]

[A special part of the regular army is the *antarvamsikasainya*, or the 'King's Own Guards', which was never disbanded.]

Bhrita—territorial army—raised from natives of the country for a particular campaign; can be easily mobilised and are more obedient [than the other types described hereafter].

Sreni—organised militias—native militias, acting as a group, having the same interest as the king.

Mitra—friendly troops—those of an ally, or those hired or bought from other kings under a treaty; available to the king at any time for use anywhere and with interests similar to those of the king.

Amitra—alien forces—who happen to fight with the king for their own reasons.

Atavi—Jungle tribal forces; commanded by their own chiefs.

COMPARISON

It is better to mobilise a force earlier in the list than one later.

Because the standing army depends on the king for its existence and because it is constantly under training, it is better than a territorial army.

Because a territorial army is nearby, more easily mobilised and more obedient, it is better than organised militias.

Because the militias are part of the population of the country, the members have a common objective and because they have the same feelings of rivalry, resentment and expectations of success and gain, they are better than friendly [non-native] forces.

Because friendly forces have interests similar to those of the king and because they are available for use anywhere and at any time, they are better than alien forces.

Alien troops and jungle tribal forces both have plunder as their objective. [They are both equally untrustworthy]. When there is no plunder or when there is a calamity, they are as dangerous as a viper in one's bosom. [Nevertheless] alien troops commanded by Aryas are better than tribal forces [commanded by *mlecchas* and others outside the pale].

{from 9.2.13-20}

VARNA COMPOSITION

Some teachers say that among *Brahmin, Kshatriya, Vaishya,* and *Sudra* troops, a higher varna force shall be mobilised before a lower one because the higher the varna the more the spirit.

Kautilya disagrees. An enemy may win over *Brahmin* troops by prostrating himself before them. It is better to have either an army composed of *Kshatriyas* trained in the use of weapons or a *Vaishya* or *Sudra* army with a large number of men.   {9.2.21-24}

ORGANIZATIONAL STRUCTURE

[The officers of the armed forces mentioned in Books 1 and 2 of the text are: the Chief of Defence (*senapati*) (See Notes on Translation No. 13), the Chiefs of the four wings (chariots, elephants, horses and men) and the Chief of Ordnance. The chiefs of the four wings were subordinates of the Chief of Defence. Under the Chief Commanders, there were Divisional Commanders. There were other officers such as Camp Superintendents who were given specific functions during the march to battle.

The structure of the Defence forces at the highest level was as shown below.

The salaries of the officials are given in {5.3} (see IV.ii). The *senapati* was paid a princely 48,000 panas per year, 'to prevent him from succumbing to the temptations of the enemy or rising up in revolt'. The Commanders of the four wings were paid 8000 panas per year so that 'they could carry their men with them'. Divisional Commanders were paid 4000 panas a year and specialist soldiers such as commandos were paid 500 panas a year.

The structure below the level of Divisional Commanders is specified in connection with battles. The use of *senapati* for both the battalion commander and the Chief of Defence is confusing.]

Every ten units [e.g. a chariot unit with its own chariot, horses and men] shall be placed under a company commander, *patika*. For every ten *patikas* there shall be a battalion commander, *senapati*, and for every ten *senapatis*, a divisional commander, *nayaka*.   {10.6.45}

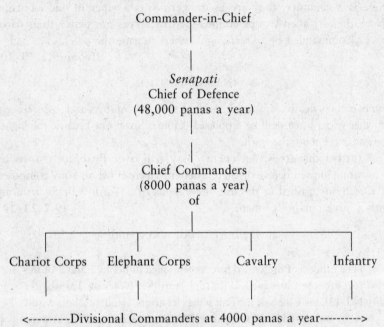

Commander-in-Chief

Senapati
Chief of Defence
(48,000 panas a year)

Chief Commanders
(8000 panas a year)
of

Chariot Corps   Elephant Corps   Cavalry   Infantry

<----------Divisional Commanders at 4000 panas a year---------->

Every division of the formation shall have its own distinguishing trumpet sound, flags and banners, These shall be used to signal the commands to that division—dividing themselves [into sections], joining together, halting, advancing, turning and attacking.   {10.6.46}

Battalion commanders and divisional commanders shall be responsible for moblisation and demoblisation; they shall also be responsible for the payment of wages and rations to the men under their command.

{5.3.25}

The units guarding royal property, the city and the countryside shall never be demobilised. The commanding officers of such units shall be made permanent but frequently transferred [from one duty to another].

{5.3.26,27}

Secret agents, prostitutes, artists and artisans, and retired military officers shall vigilantly watch over the loyalty or otherwise of soldiers.

{5.3.47}

DUTIES OF DEFENCE OFFICIALS

THE CHIEF OF DEFENCE

QUALIFICATIONS

The Chief of Defence shall be:

(a) an expert in the use of all kinds of weapons used in warfare;

(b) renowned for his ability to ride elephants, horses and chariots; and

(c) conversant with the relative strengths of the four wings of the army and how to deploy them in battle. {2.33.9}

RESPONSIBILITIES

The Chief of Defence shall:
Discipline in the armed forces:

(i) be conscious [at all times] of the maintenance of discipline in the army, whether the army is camping, marching on an expedition or fighting a battle;
Formations:

(ii) [give different identities to and] distinguish between different formations by allotting them different trumpet calls, standards and flags;
Strategy and tactics:

(iii) choose the best time to start on an [offensive] expedition;

(iv) choose the best terrain and the best season for fighting;

(v) arrange the disposition of his own forces [in the light of the enemy's array];

(vi) plan the breaking up of the enemy's ranks;

(vii) regroup his own broken arrays;

(viii) organize the breaking up of [the enemy's] close order formations;

(ix) destroy [the enemy's] scattered troops; and

(x) [besiege and] destroy [enemy] forts. {2.33.10,11}

[For the role of the Chief of Defence just before the battle commenced, see {10.3.45,46} in XI.vii below.]

CHIEF COMMANDERS

[Of the four Chief Commanders, the duties of the Chief of Elephants are described separately and extensively. The duties of the Chiefs of Chariots and Infantry are, however, said to resemble those of the Chief of Horses. To this list, one must also add the post of the Chief Elephant Forester, described in {2.2}, since the purpose of maintaining elephant forests was to catch the elephants for use in war.]

THE CHIEF COMMANDER OF ELEPHANT CORPS

[Elephants occupied an important place in the army. In {2.2.13}, Kautilya says that a King's victory depends mainly on elephants. Since elephants were captured and not bred, elephant forests had to be demarcated and set aside when determining the land use of the country. The Chief of Elephants was responsible for all aspects of work relating to them, including capture and training. The Chief Elephant Forester was his subordinate. All details about types of elephants, rules for catching them, their training, their accoutrements and daily routine will be found in the Appendix 13 'On Elephants'. The rations prescribed and details of construction of elephant stables will be found in the appropriate appendices.]

RESPONSIBILITIES

(i) The Chief Commander of Elephant Corps shall be responsible for all types of elephants—male, female, the young, those under training and those which have completed their training.

(ii) He shall also be responsible for:

(a) the protection of elephant forests [see below]

(b) the [construction and maintenance of] stables, stalls and places for them to lie down;

(c) the proper distribution of their rations;

(d) their training;

(e) the assigning of tasks to them;

(f) the maintenance of implements, ornaments and equipment for war; and

(g) the supervision of the work of veterinary doctors, trainers and all attendants.   {2.31.1}

(iii) Elephant Stables

There shall be an elephant stable for keeping them at night and a place for them, inside or outside the fort, for the daytime.

The elephant stable shall be built facing north or east and shall have a breadth and height double the length of the animal.[2] The stables shall have stalls for each [male] elephant, additional [separate] stables for females and an entrance hall. The stables shall be strong with many [pillars and beams].

The stall for each elephant shall be square, with each side the length of the animal and shall have smooth plank flooring, a tying post and facilities for removal or dung and urine. The back half, the place for the elephant to lie down, shall have a platform half the height of the animal for it to lean on.

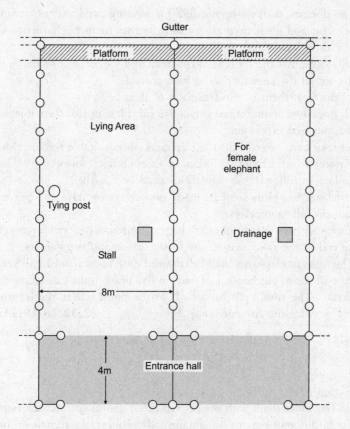

Fig. 30 Elephant Stables
{2.31.2-3}

[When not in the stalls] elephants used in war and for riding shall be kept inside the fort and those that are being tamed and rogue elephants outside it.

(iv) Maintenance and upkeep:

The following shall be employed: veterinary doctors, trainers, expert riders along with their helpers, mahouts, attendants to groom and decorate the animals, cooks and fodder givers, attendants to tether the animals, stable cleaners and night guards.

The doctor, the stall cleaner and the cook shall be given free rations of one *prastha* boiled rice, salt, a handful of oil and two *palas* of sugar. All the above, except the doctors, shall be given, in addition, ten *palas* of meat.

The doctors shall be responsible for treating aged and sick animals, those in rut and those tired after a long journey or through overwork.

The other attendants shall:

(a) ensure that the stalls are kept clean and fodder is collected in time;

(b) not let the animals rest on bare ground;

(c) not beat them in sensitive parts of their bodies;

(d) not allow unauthorized persons to ride them or ride them themselves at unauthorized times; and

(e) take care not to lead the elephants on unsuitable terrain, through deep water which cannot be forded or through thick forests.

Failure to follow these regulations shall be punished.

Offerings to spirits shall be made on new moon days and prayers to *Senani*[3] on full moon days.

Expiatory rites (lustration) shall be performed once every four months— at the end of the rainy season, the frosty season and the summer.

The tusks of elephants shall be trimmed once in two and a half years in the case of plains elephants, and once in five years in the case of mountain elephants. The tusk shall be cut off at the point where the length left behind is twice the circumference.   {2.32.16-19,21,22}

THE CHIEF ELEPHANT FORESTER

RESPONSIBILITIES

Protection:

(i) The Chief shall, with the help of forest guards, protect the elephant forests in different regions (mountains, river banks, lake regions or marshy lands). He shall be knowledgeable about their boundaries, the entrances and the exits.

Recording:

(ii) The Chief shall maintain a record of every [wild] elephant whether it is part of a herd or lone, whether it is a leader of a herd or one driven out of it and [in case of lone animals] whether it is a wild one, in rut, a young adult or one escaped from captivity.

Tracking:

(iii) Wild elephants shall be tracked by following footprints, sleeping places, dung and damage to river banks. They shall be tracked by forest guards, with the help of mahouts, tetherers, border guards, trackers and attendants as well as a group of five or seven female elephants as decoys. They shall hide their presence by covering themselves with elephant dung and urine and use hideouts made of branches.

CHAU

NAV

xxxxxx06-2

Exp: 7/15/2023

Item: 0010105830813
320.954 K16A 199

Printed: Saturday, July 8, 2023

Capture:

(iv) Elephant trainers shall judge, from the physical characteristics and behaviour of wild elephants, which ones are to be captured. Only those animals judged to be excellent shall be caught.

Rewards:

(v) Anyone who brings in a pair of tusks of a [wild] elephant dying naturally shall be paid a reward of 4 1/4 panas.   {2.2.7,9-42}

PUNISHMENTS

Killing a wild elephant	Death	{2.2.8}
Failure to obey the regulations	Deduction from	{2.32.20}
mentioned in {2.32.19} [such as	rations or wages	
lack of cleanliness, maltreatment		
of animals, etc.]		

CHIEF COMMANDERS OF THE OTHER WINGS

[The duties and responsibilities common to these three would be:
    – knowing about the different types of equipment needed for his wing and the use of such equipment in war;
    – giving the appropriate training;
    – keeping accurate accounts of equipment and animals under his charge;
    – maintaining their equipment in good condition and repairing them when necessary;
    – supervising the work of all those employed by him;
    – maintaining discipline; and
    – reporting to the king on the state of readiness of his troops.]

THE CHIEF COMMANDER OF CAVALRY

[Horses were bred and trained for use in war as cavalry, chariot horses and pack animals. Horses were also bred in the Crown stables for sale to the citizenry. Details about different types of horses and the various gaits of horses, given in {2,30.14-16, 29, 32-41}, have not been translated.]

QUALIFICATION

The Chief Commander of Cavalry shall be conversant with:
    (a) the facial and bodily characteristics of the best, medium and lowest types of horses;

(b) the characteristics of horses from the different regions of India and abroad;[4]

(c) the type of training to be given, depending on the temperament of the horse and its purpose; and

(d) the work different horses are capable of doing.

{from   2.30.14-17,29,30,39}

RESPONSIBILITIES

The Chief Commander of Cavalry shall be responsible for the following.

(i) <u>Construction and maintenance of stables:</u>

The stable, the floors of which shall be made of smooth planks, shall be square, each side being equal to the length of a horse. A receptacle for fodder and others for dung and urine shall be provided for each one.

(ii) <u>Accounting:</u>

The Chief shall keep a register of all the horses under his charge, showing the following: breed, age, colour, distinguishing marks, type, origin and method of acquisition. The last item shall be indicated under one of the following categories: received as a gift, bought, captured in war, bred in the stables, borrowed, received in return for help rendered and received as treaty payment.

He shall make a report to the king about animals which have become unserviceable due to illness, broken legs or other causes.{2.30.1,2}

(iii) <u>Upkeep:</u>

The following shall be appointed [as required] to look after the horses: a Superintendent for each stable, trainers, veterinary doctors, grooms, saddlers (or yokers of horses to chariots), cooks, stall cleaners, trimmers [of manes and tails] and specialists in curing poisons.

{from   2.30.4-7}

The stable-in-charge shall be issued the monthly[5] rations [for each horse] from the Treasury and the store houses and shall be responsible for maintaining the animals under his charge.

The rations prescribed for mares which have given birth, foals and mature horses shall be strictly followed.[6]

The cook, the groom and the veterinary doctor shall taste the food [before it is given to the horses].

Horses incapacitated due to injury in war, old age or sickness shall be maintained with appropriate rations.

Veterinary doctors shall be responsible for adjusting the rations so that horses do not become either too fat or too thin and shall also vary the diet according to the season.

The horses shall be bathed twice a day and decorated with garlands and perfumes.

Offerings to spirits shall be made on new moon days and auspicious verses shall be recited on full moon days.

Expiatory (lustration) rites shall be performed on the ninth day of *Asvayuja* (September/October), when an animal is sick and at the beginning and end of expeditions. {2.30.2,3,8-13,26,27,42-44,50,51}

(iv) <u>Training:</u>

The purpose of training a horse is for its use in war. {2.30.31}

Trainers shall also be responsible for supervising the manufacture of straps and fastenings; likewise, charioteers for the accoutrements of horses yoked in chariots. {2.30.42}

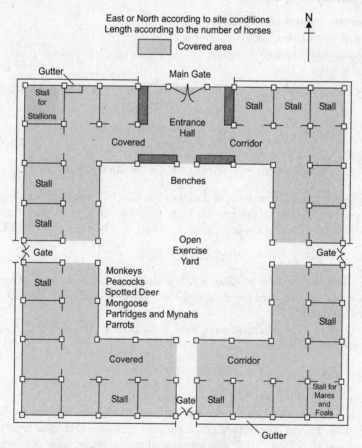

Fig. 31 Horse Stables

Riding horses shall be trained to gallop, canter, trot and jump in response to signals. Pack horses shall be trained to walk steadily [over long distances] or walk fast [over short distances] with and without loads. Chariot horses shall be trained to stride, gallop, jump and run at fast and moderately fast speeds. War-horses shall also be trained in cavalry formations.

{2.32.32,40,41}

PUNISHMENTS

Any attendant (groom, saddler, etc.) failing to perform his duty	Deduction of that day's wages	{2.30.45}
Riding a horse that is kept isolated for treatment or for expiatory rite	12 panas	{2.20.46}

When the condition of a sick horse becomes worse either due to the carelessness or wrong treatment of the veterinary doctor:

If the horse is cured	Twice the cost of treatment	{2.20.47}
If the horse dies	The value of the horse	{2.20.48}

THE CHIEF COMMANDER OF CHARIOT CORPS

The [special] qualifications and duties of the Chief Commander of Chariot Corps, in addition to the general responsibilities similar to those of the Chief Commander of Cavalry, shall be as set out below. {2.33.1}

QUALIFICATIONS

The Chief Commander of Chariot Corps shall know the use, in warfare, of bows and arrows, striking weapons [like maces and clubs], armour and other equipment.

He shall also be conversant with the duties of charioteers, chariot attendants and chariot horses. {2.33.6}

RESPONSIBILITIES

The Chief Commander of Chariot Corps shall:

(i) establish factories for the manufacture of chariots of various sizes, including chariots for temples, and for special occasions such as coronations and royal weddings, battle chariots, travelling carriages, chariots used in storming an enemy fort and chariots used for training.

(ii) be responsible for the distribution of rations and wages to all those working under him, whether permanently or temporarily employed. He shall ensure that they are well trained and shall safeguard their welfare by appropriate gifts and honours.   {2.33.2,5,6}

THE CHIEF COMMANDER OF INFANTRY

The special qualifications of the Chief Commander of Infantry shall be as set out below. His responsibilities are similar to those of the Chief Commander of Cavalry.   {2.33.7}

QUALIFICATION

The Chief Commander of Infantry shall know:

(i) the [relative] strengths and weaknesses of the standing army, the territorial army, organised militias, friendly troops, alien troops and tribal forces;

(ii) the tactics to be used for fighting—in valleys or on high ground, of open and covert attacks, trench fighting or fighting from above and by day or night;[7]

(iii) how to keep control over the fitness or otherwise of troops in battle and in peacetime.   {2.33.8}

CHIEF OF ORDNANCE

(Salary—as for a Head of Department)

[The qualifications required for appointment to this post are not given separately. It is also not clear whether he was considered a civilian official, like the other Heads of Departments in charge of industries, or as a defence service official. From his responsibilities it is clear that he was fully conversant with the manufacture and correct storage of all types of offensive and defensive weapons, armour and material required for secret warfare.

There is an exhaustive list of ordnance material, including weapons, armour and siege machines. The list is in Appendix 12.]

RESPONSIBILITIES

Manufacture:

(i) The Chief of Ordnance shall establish factories staffed with craftsmen expert in their respective fields for the manufacture of machines for attacking in battles as well as for attacking enemy forts, machines for defending one's own forts, weapons, armour and accoutrements [for horses and elephants]. He shall determine the time to be allowed for making each of these and the wages to be paid.   {2.18.1}

Storage

(ii) All equipment brought into the armoury shall be stamped with the king's seal.   {5.3.37}

All ordnance material shall be stored in places suitably prepared for each one.

They shall be frequently moved and exposed to sun and wind [to prevent deterioration]. Special precautions shall be taken in case of material likely to be damaged by heat, moisture or insects.

The Chief of Ordnance shall be responsible for the safety of the equipment and shall keep an account of the weapons destroyed. He shall be fined double the value of whatever is lost or destroyed [through negligence].

{5.3.39,40}

Inspection:

(iii) All material shall be inspected periodically with reference to their class, appearance, characteristics, quantity, place of manufacture, cost of manufacture and method of storage.

Control:

(iv) The Chief of Ordnance shall [at all times] know precisely the demand for [each type of] weapon, the supply available, the distribution [to different units], wear and tear or loss in battle and the cost of replenishment.

{2.18.1-4,20}

XI.iii

THE FOUR WINGS

[The specific uses to which each of the four wings of the army are to be put are listed in this section. Though labour was not a fighting arm, a contingent of workers always accompanied the army to set up the camp and to do support jobs. Depending on the function, the different modes of fighting are also given in the *Arthashastra*. When to use a particular type of force in battle also depended on the nature of the opposing force. Lastly, the ground chosen for camping or for battle must also be suitable for the type of force used.]

CHARIOTS

<u>Their functions are:</u> protecting the army; repelling attacks by any of the four wings; capturing and liberating [battle positions]; reuniting [one's own] broken ranks and breaking up [the enemy's] unbroken ranks; causing terror [in the enemy's army] and adding magnificence [to one's own]; and making an awesome noise.   {10.4.15}

A king who has few horses may use bullocks, as well as horses, in his chariots.   {10.4.18}

TYPES OF CHARIOTS

The biggest chariot shall be ten *purushas* (7 1/2 feet) in height and twelve *purushas* (9 feet) long. There are successively smaller sizes, each one *purushas* (nine inches) less in length.   {2.33.3,4}

[The lengths are: 9', 8'3", 7'6", 6'9", 5'3" and 4'6". It is to be assumed that the width of all chariots was the same.]

ELEPHANTS

A king relies mainly on elephants for achieving victory in battles. With their very large bodies, they are able to do things in war which are dangerous for other arms of the forces; they can be used to crush the enemy's foot soldiers, battle arrays, forts and encampments.   {2.2.13,14}

<u>Their functions are</u>: marching in front; making new roads, camping grounds and fords; protecting the flanks; helping to cross water and climb or descend from mountains; entering difficult or crowded places; starting fires or extinguishing them; using elephants alone for victory; reuniting [one's own] broken ranks and breaking up the [enemy's] unbroken ranks; protecting against dangers; trampling the [enemy's] army; frightening [by mere presence]; causing terror [in the enemy's army by action]; adding magnificence; capturing and liberating [battle positions]; destroying ramparts, gates and towers; and bringing [one's own] and carrying away [captured] wealth.   {10.4.14}

[{9.1.45-48} in X.vi on 'Preparations for a campaign') contain the advice that an army composed mostly of elephants should be used only when the hot season is over, when it rains or in places where there is plenty of water.]

A king who has few elephants, may constitute his centre out of carts [drawn by] camels or donkeys.   {10.4.18}

HORSES

<u>Their functions are</u>: reconnoitring battle grounds, camping sites and forests; securing level ground, water supply sources, fording places and positions favourable with regard to the sun and the wind; destroying [the enemy's] or protecting [one's own] supplies and reinforcements; maintaining the discipline of the army; extending the range of raids; protecting the flanks; making the initial attack; penetrating or breaking through [enemy ranks]; providing respite [to one's own forces]; capturing prisoners; liberating prisoners [held by the enemy]; diverting a pursuing army; carrying off the treasury and princes [one's own or the enemy's]; attacking the enemy in the rear or at the extremities; pursuing the weak; marching with [one's own] troops [to guard them]; and rallying the troops.   {10.4.13}

INFANTRY

The <u>functions</u> of the infantry are to bear arms in all places and at all seasons and fighting.   {10.4.16}

[From the verse on choosing the best battle ground {10.4.2}, it is seen that some types of infantry were better suited for fighting in deserts, some in forests and others in water-logged areas. Some were trained to fight on open ground and others from trenches. There were fighters by day and night fighters. From {7.10.34}, it is seen that, while troops trained for fighting on rivers were more circumscribed, fighters on land could be used anywhere and at any time. Likewise, fighters from trenches were more difficult adversaries than fighters in the open {7.10.35}.]

LABOUR

The functions are: maintaining camps, roads, embankments, wells and fording places; carrying machines, weapons, armour, implements and provisions; and removing weapons, armour and the wounded from the battlefield. {10.4.17}

MODES OF FIGHTING

HORSES

Horses shall be used to: rush forward, around, beyond or back; hold enemy forces at bay after an attack; surround enemy forces by a pincer movement; moving zig-zag (like cow's urine); encircle [enemy forces after cutting them off]; scatter enemy forces; first retreat and then renew the attack; protect [one's own] broken ranks in the front, rear or flanks; and pursue [the enemy's] broken army. {10.5.53}

ELEPHANTS

Elephants shall be used in the same manner as horses, except for scattering enemy forces; [i.e. rush forward, around, beyond and back; hold enemy forces at bay after an attack; surround enemy forces by a pincer movement; move in a zig-zag; encircle [enemy forces after cutting them off]; first retreat and then renew the attack; protect [one's own] forces broken ranks in the front, rear or flanks; and pursue [the enemy's] broken army.

In addition, elephants shall be used to: destroy the four constituents of the enemy's forces whether combined or separate; trampling the centre, flanks or wings; making surprise attacks, e.g. when the troops are asleep. {10.5.53,54}

CHARIOTS

Chariots can be used like elephants except for holding enemy forces at bay and, in addition, for fighting on land suitable to them, while going forward, going backward or remaining stationary. {10.5.55}

INFANTRY

Foot soldiers can be used to attack at all times in all places and for silent [surprise] attacks. {10.5.56}

TRAINING AND CONTROL

TRAINING

Infantry, cavalry, chariots and elephants shall have their training outside the city at sunrise every day except on days of conjunction of planets. The king shall take a personal interest in the training and make frequent inspections.

{5.3.35,36}

CONTROL

Secret agents, prostitutes, artisans, entertainers and military personnel with long service shall keep a diligent watch over the honesty and loyalty of soldiers.   {5.3.47}

THE RIGHT KIND OF FORCE

Against elephant divisions	Elephants, machines and wheeled vehicles at the centre; infantry armed with lances, javelins, tridents, staves, maces, bows and arrows;
Against chariot divisions, cavalry, armoured elephants and horses	As above; infantry also equipped with stones, clubs, shields and hooked weapons;
Against an army with all four divisions	Armoured chariots and mailed infantry.

{9.2.26-29}

BATTLE AND CAMPING GROUNDS

GENERAL

The ground and time suitable for fighting for the following types of troops shall be chosen according to their special qualities:
  - infantry when fighting in deserts, forests or water-logged areas;
  - infantry when fighting from trenches or open ground;
  - infantry when fighting by day or by night;
  - elephants and horses according to where they were bred
  - land with rivers, mountains, marshes and lakes.

For elephants, horses and chariots both even and uneven ground is suitable for camping and as battle ground; [not so, for chariots].

{10.4.1-3}

CHARIOTS

Ground suitable for chariots is that which [gives them free unobstructed run, i.e.] - is level, firm, clear, has nothing which will make wheels, hooves or axles get stuck, free of trees, plants, creepers, tree trunks, water-logging, pits, ant-hills, sand, mud and fissures.

If, [in addition], the ground also has water-reservoirs and shelters and is suitable for chariots to turn around, it is excellent.

{from 10.4.3,10}

ELEPHANTS

Ground suitable for elephants is that which, though hilly, watery or even, can be traversed by elephants, which has uprootable trees and creepers that can be torn out, and is muddy and free of fissures.

If, [in addition] the ground has dust, mud, water, reeds and rushes, is free of thorns (called 'dog's teeth') and is free of obstruction from branches of big trees, it is excellent.

{from 10.4.6,9}

HORSES

Ground suitable for horses is that which has small stones and trees, small pits which horses can easily jump over, and is pitted with small fissures.

If, [in addition] the ground is also doubly wide for turning, free of mud, water, bogs and small pebbles, it is excellent.

{from 10.4.4,8}

INFANTRY

Ground suitable for infantry is that which may contain big tree trunks, stones, trees, creepers, ant-hills and thickets.

If, [in addition] the ground is free of thorns, not too uneven and has room for the infantry to manoeuvre, it is excellent.

{from 10.4.5,7}

CHOICE OF BATTLE GROUND

The battle ground shall be surveyed for evenness in the front, on the flanks and in the rear.

The army shall be arrayed in a favourable position, not facing the south, but with the sun behind its back and the wind favourable.

If the ground is not suitable, cavalry shall be used [to secure favourable ground].

When the army is on ground that is neither suitable for standing firm nor for moving quickly, it will be defeated whether it stands and fights or moves away. On favourable ground, however, it can fight or change positions.

The types of arrays to be used are:

on level ground—arrays of the type 'truncheon' or 'circle';

on uneven ground—arrays of the type 'snake' or 'dispersed';

on mixed ground—mixed arrays.   {10.3.48-53}

[For explanation of these arrays, see under 'Modes of attack' in XI.viii.]

XI.iv

THE BASE CAMP

[The base camp was a fortified area set up near the war zone, far away from the capital of the conqueror. The base camp, being a semi-permanent establishment, resembled the town plan of the capital city, with fortifications such as a moat, towers, ramparts, parapets and gates. {10.1.1}. Like the city, the camp was also divided by roads into sectors with the king in the innermost sector, protected by his own bodyguards. {10.1.2,3}. The additional fortification in the base camp was from obstacle-fences made up of carts, thorny branches and a parapet. {10.1.5}. This divided the camp into five concentric areas. From the centre outwards, each succeeding sector was occupied by less important officials and less trustworthy troops. In the innermost sector, around the king's quarters, were the audience chamber, the treasury, the communication centre (i.e. the place from where orders were issued) and the king's personal elephant, horse and chariot. In the next circle were the counsellors, the *purohita*, the armoury and warehouses. The more reliable troops, i.e. the standing army and the territorial army occupied the next circle, which also housed the Chief of Defence, horses and chariots. Militias, elephants and the Camp Superintendent occupied the next. The non-native forces (allied, alien and jungle) and the labour corps were placed in the outermost circle. Merchants and courtesans were placed alongside the main roads. {10.1.4,6-10}. Traps were laid outside the perimeter where the outcast helpers like dog-handlers and hunters were stationed, equipped with drums (for warning) and fire. {10.1.11,12}. Secret agents and sentinels were also stationed outside. Two diagrams illustrate the camp plan; only a few other important verses are translated below.]

The conqueror shall make secure a mountain or forest fort at the rear in his own country as a refuge and a place for recoupment, and then establish a base camp for fighting the battle. {10.2.20}

The Camp Superintendent shall march ahead with carpenters and labourers and make arrangements for protection [like clearing and driving away wild animals] and for water. {10.1.17}

On a site chosen by experts in the science of building, and at a time chosen by astrologers, the commander[1] shall make carpenters set up a camp, in order that the army may halt, safe from attack [by the enemy]. The base camp may be circular, square, rectangular or according to the shape of the terrain. {10.1.1}

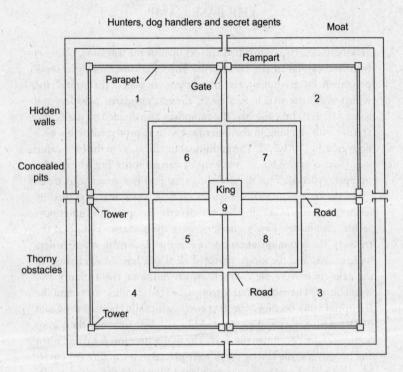

Fig. 32 The Base Camp-General Plan
{10.1.1, 11,12}

The king's quarters shall be 100 *dhanus* (about 200 metres) long and 50 *dhanus* (100 metres) wide, situated in the ninth part [just] north of the centre and have palace guards stationed around it. The king's personal quarters shall be on the western half. {from 10.1.2,3}

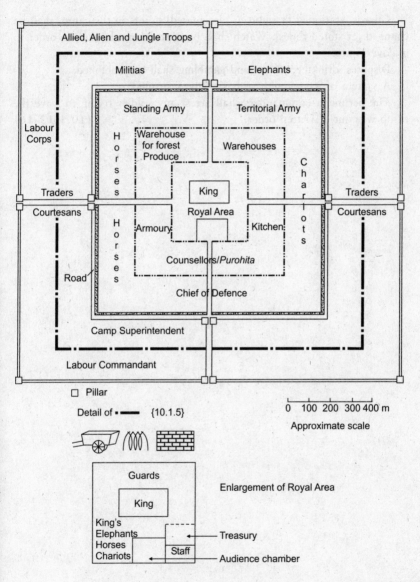

□ Pillar

Detail of ▪━━ {10.1.5}

0 100 200 300 400 m
Approximate scale

Enlargement of Royal Area

Fig. 33 The Base Camp-Disposition
{10.1.2-10}

PROTECTION AND DISCIPLINE

Guards, stationed at eighteen [designated] points in the camp, shall be changed [at stated times]. Watch shall be kept during the day, in order to uncover spies.

Disputes, drinking, parties and gambling shall be prohibited.

A system of passes with seals shall be instituted.

The perimeter-commander[2] shall arrest any soldier trying to leave the camp without a written order.   {10.1.13-16}

XI.v

BASE CAMP TO BATTLE GROUND

[The base camp had necessarily to be set up at some distance from the war zone since it had to be near a place of refuge in the king's own territory, secure and capable of being provisioned and reinforced. The actual war zone could still have been a few days or weeks march away. This section deals with the various aspects of this all-important march taking the army to the battle ground. Verses {10.2.5-8} have been omitted since these contain obvious definitions, likely to have crept into the text from some commentary.[1]]

PROVISIONING

The march of the army [from the base camp to the battle ground] shall be determined taking into account the rate of march, the programme of extended stay, short stay and marching and the ability of villages and forests on the way to supply fodder, fuel and water. Twice the amount of food and equipment needed shall be carried. If this is not possible, the troops shall themselves transport it or it may be stored beforehand at intervals along the route. {10.2.1-3}

CHOICE OF ROUTES

If there is a choice of routes, the one most suitable for one's own army shall be chosen. For, those who fight from suitable terrain will be superior in battle to those who fight from unsuitable terrain. {10.2.10,11}

ORDER OF MARCH

The order of march shall be: the commander in front, the king and women in the middle, horses and bodyguards on the flanks, elephants and reinforcements at the end and finally the Chief of Defence. The same shall be the order of encampment. {10.2.4}

MARCH ARRAY

The type of array used shall depend on the circumstances:

If an attack is anticipated

In the front	*makara*	Crocodile
In the rear	*sakata*	Cart
On the two flanks	*vajra*	Thunder-bolt
On all sides	*sarvato badra*	Uniformly circular

If the path is narrow
permitting only single file   *suchi*   Needle

{10.2.9}

RATE OF MARCH

One *yojana* (9 miles/15 km) [per day] is the slowest rate of march; one
and a half *yojanas* (22.5 km) per day is middling and two *yojanas* (30 km)
per day is the best. The rate can be varied according to circumstances.
The rate of march shall be slowed down in the following cases:

(i) When steps have to be taken to counteract the enemy-in-the-rear,
the enemy's rear ally, the Middle king or the Neutral king, any of whom
may provide refuge [to the enemy] or [use the opportunity to] attack the rich
lands [of the conqueror];

(ii) when a difficult path has to be cleared;

(iii) when awaiting a suitable season or the arrival of the treasury,
reinforcements, allied troops, alien troops or jungle forces;

(iv) when expecting a deterioration in the enemy's fortifications, stores,
precautionary measures or the morale of his mercenary or allied troops;

(v) when his secret agents have been slow in their task [of inducing
treachery in the enemy camp]; or

(vi) when the enemy himself will do something to help the conqueror.

In the absence of any such reason, the march shall be speeded up.

{10.2.12,13}

OBSTACLES

The army shall cross water by means of elephants, pillar bridges, causeways,
boats, wood and bamboo rafts, gourds, baskets covered with hide, canoes,
tree stems and ropes. If the crossing point has been seized by the enemy,
the army shall cross the water at another point at night and then ambush
the enemy [from his rear].

In waterless regions, animals and carts shall carry as much water as
they can in accordance with the duration of the march [in the region].

{10.2.14-16}

PROTECTION

Arrangements shall be made for protecting the army when any of the following affect its [fighting] strength:

(i)   a long march in a waterless region:

(ii)   running short of fodder, fuel or water;

(iii)   having to march over a difficult route;

(iv)   harassment by enemy attacks;

(v)   hunger, thirst or the rigours of a long march;

(vi)   crossing rivers in mud or deep water;

(vii)   climbing or descending hills;

(viii) many marching in single file through mountainous terrain or in narrow paths;

(ix)   suffering from lack of equipment during the march or halts;

(x)   eating, exhausted or sleeping;

(xi)   [marching through regions] afflicted by diseases, epidemics or famine;

(xii)   the infantry, cavalry or elephants falling ill; or

(xiii) marching on unsuitable terrain.

[Conversely] the conqueror shall destroy the enemy's troops when they suffer from any of the above.

The enemy can ascertain the strength of the conqueror's army by counting it when they march in single file or from the quantity of fodder, food and bedding, or from the number of cooking fires, banners and weapons [the army carries]. Therefore, all of these shall be kept well hidden.

{10.2.17-19}

XI.vi

OPEN AND DECEPTIVE BATTLES

In order to be strictly in accordance with *dharma* the place and time of battle must be specified beforehand.   {10.3.26}

OPEN BATTLES

A king shall engage in a [declared] open fight when (i) his army is superior, (ii) his instigations [in the enemy's camp] have been successful, (iii) all precautions against dangers have been taken and (iv) the terrain is suitable to him.   {10.3.1}

DECEPTIVE BATTLES

If the above conditions are not satisfied, he shall use deception, as described below.   {10.3.2}

The enemy shall be attacked when (i) his forces are suffering from a calamity, (ii) his forces are unprotected,[1] and (iii) he is on less suitable terrain compared to the attacker.

The enemy may be attacked even if he is on suitable terrain, provided that the attacker has the support of all the constituents [of his state?]. [In such a case], the attacker shall lure the enemy on to unsuitable terrain by pretending that his own unreliable, alien or jungle forces have suffered a rout. He shall [first] break the compact battle array of the [pursuing] enemy using elephants and then attack with his own unbroken army.

{from 10.3.3-6}

Or, the enemy's army may be attacked in the front [with a part of the forces] and when it is staggering or has turned its back, attacked in the rear with elephants and horses. Or, the enemy's army may be attacked in the rear [with a part of the forces] and when it is staggering or has turned its back, attacked with the best of the forces. Similar tactics may also be employed for the two flanks. The attack may also be directed towards where the enemy's forces are weak or unreliable.   {from 10.3.7-10}

[The general principle is:] if frontal attack is unfavourable, the attack shall be from the rear and vice versa; similarly, if attack on one flank is unfavourable, it shall be made from the other.   {from 10.3.11-13}

The enemy's forces shall be made tired by attacking with unreliable, alien or jungle troops and then attacked by the conqueror with his own fresh troops.

The enemy may be made to believe that he has won by a seeming defeat of [the conqueror's] unreliable troops, then his forces shall be ambushed by the conqueror's [reliable] forces from safe positions.

A vigilant conqueror may strike at an enemy who is negligent [about protection] while his forces are plundering a caravan, animal herds, a camp or transport.

Alternatively, the conqueror may conceal a strong force behind a weak force and when the weak force has penetrated the enemy ranks, reinforce the attack with the strong one.

The enemy's warriors may be lured into an ambush by tempting them with cattle [for seizure] or wild animals [for hunting].

The enemy's warriors may be kept awake by night forays and then attacked during the day when they are drowsy or asleep.

The enemy's sleeping warriors can also be attacked with elephants, whose feet have been covered in leather [to make their passage silent or as protection against dogs].

If the enemy forces are tired after making preparations for the battle in the forenoon, they shall be attacked in the afternoon.

The ranks of the enemy's horses and elephants may be broken by letting loose frightened cattle, buffaloes or camels, which are made to run helter-skelter with contraptions which make a lot of noise tied to their backs.[2] The conqueror shall make sure his own ranks are not broken.

Any force which has to fight facing the sun or wind shall be attacked.

It has been mentioned earlier that the conqueror shall attack the enemy when he suffers from any of the difficulties against which he should have taken appropriate protective measures.[3] These are also the occasions for using deceptive tactics.   {10.3.14-23,25}

OPPORTUNITES FOR AN AMBUSH

A desert, forest, narrow path, marsh, mountain, valley, uneven ground, boat, cattle, cart-array of the army, mist and night are opportunities for ambushes.   {10.3.24}

XI.vii

PREPARATIONS FOR BATTLE

EXHORTATION OF TROOPS

The conqueror shall collect his forces together and say to them: 'I am as much a servant [of the State] as you are; we shall share the wealth of this state. Attack these, mine enemies.'   {10.3.27}

[Verses {10.3.28-31} have been omitted. See Notes on Translation No. 14.]

Counsellors and the *Purohita* shall encourage the troops by pointing out the excellent qualities of [the army and] the chosen battle formation.

Astrologers and similar professionals shall inspire the troops by proclaiming the king to be omniscient and divinely aided and shall fill the enemy troops with dread.   {10.3.32,33}

THE NIGHT BEFORE THE BATTLE

The king shall observe a fast the night before the battle and sleep beside his chariot and weapons. He shall make oblations in the fire according to the *Atharva Veda*. He shall have prayers said for victory in battle and for attainment of heaven [by those who fall]. He shall entrust himself to Brahmins.   {10.3.34-37}

THE DAY OF BATTLE

Troops which are brave, skilful, of noble birth, loyal and not unhappy with the wealth and honours bestowed on them shall be placed in the centre of the forces. [Among them] the king shall take his place, bare of flags and distinguishing features and surrounded by warrior kinsmen [paternal relatives, brothers and sons]. He shall [normally] ride a chariot or an elephant and be guarded by cavalry; or he may ride whatever is preponderant in his army or in which he is proficient. A double shall impersonate the king at the head of the battle formation.   {10.3.38-42}

Bards and praise-singers shall describe the heaven that awaits the brave and the hell that shall be the lot of cowards. They shall extol the clan, group, family, deeds and conduct of the warriors.

Assistants of the *Purohita* shall speak of the spells and incantations they have used against the enemy, technicians and carpenters of the machines they have built and astrologers of the good omens for their side and the bad ones for the enemy. {10.3.43,44}

The Chief of Defence shall make the troops happy with wealth and honours and announce the following rewards—a hundred thousand panas for killing the enemy king, fifty thousand for a prince or the Army Chief, ten thousand for a division chief, five thousand for an elephant or chariot warrior, thousand for a horse, one hundred for an infantry section leader, twenty for a soldier, as well as double normal wages and whatever booty they seize. These rewards shall be made known to the leaders of groups of ten [i.e the company, battalion and divisional commanders].

{10.3.45,46}

The following shall be stationed in the rear: Physicians with surgical instruments, equipment, medicines, oils and bandages; women with cooked food and beverages and women to encourage the men to fight.

{10.3.47}

XI.viii

BATTLE ARRAYS AND FORMATIONS

[Kautilya gives an exhaustive description of how to arrange the forces for a set-piece battle, starting with positioning of reinforcements made up of the best forces at about a kilometre behind the battle ground.

<u>Basic units:</u> The description starts with defining a basic 'unit' for the cavalry (warriors on horses), elephants and chariots. These never fought alone. A warrior on a horse was accompanied by six soldiers as shown in Fig. 34.

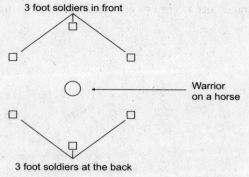

Fig. 34 Basic Unit for Cavalry
{10.5.9-11}

Both the chariot unit and the elephant unit had five cavalry units surrounding it, as shown in Figure 35.

<u>Close and open orders:</u> The forces could be arrayed in a densely packed close order or in a more spread out open order. The choice, no doubt, depended on the nature of the terrain, the type of forces available and the type of forces fielded by the enemy. In the close order for infantry, equipped with only swords, spears or lances, the soldiers

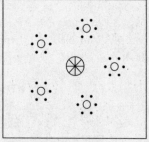

Fig. 35 Basic Unit for
Elephants and Chariots
{9.7.5, 6}

in a row were separated from each other by only 26.5 cm, presumably measured with their arms outstretched. However, archers were arranged in a more open fashion, with the distance between two in a row being 225 cm. This is described as a 'bow's length' (*dhanus*) for arrays, longer by one-fifth compared to the normal measure of *dhanus*.[1] The wider distance between archers must have been due to their not being involved in hand-to-hand fighting but firing from a distance behind the other soldiers. The two types are illustrated in Figure 36. The distance between two rows of soldiers is not given in the text.

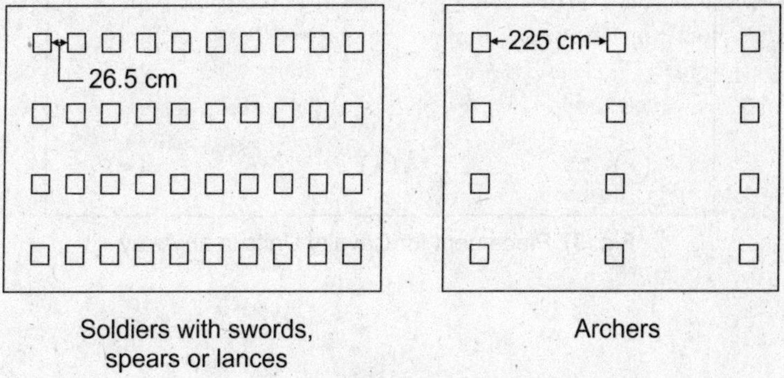

Soldiers with swords,   Archers
spears or lances

Fig. 36 Infantry Placement
{10.5.3, 6, 7}

The distance separating two soldiers is only an indication of the minimum; this could be doubled or trebled. The soldiers should never be so closely packed as to overcrowd them and impede their fighting ability.

The placement of horses, elephants and chariots was a multiple (3 times for cavalry and 5 times for elephants and chariots) of the distance for foot soldiers, as shown in Figures 37 and 38.

Arrays: Out of these basic units, arrays were formed. The arrays for chariots and elephants were identical, with the minimum number in an array being nine, arranged in three rows of three each as shown in Fig 38. Since each chariot was supported by five cavalry units (each with one mounted warrior and six foot soldiers), the minimum array consisted of nine chariots, forty-five mounted warriors and two hundred and seventy foot soldiers.

The number of chariots in each row could be increased by two, up to 21 in each row; the number of rows was always three. Thus, an array could consist of 9, 15, 21, 27, 33, 39, 45, 51, 57 or 63 chariots.

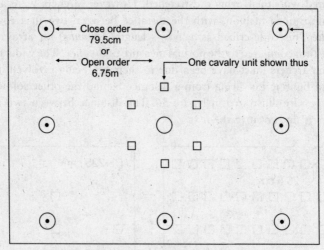

Fig. 37 Placement for Cavalry Units in an Array

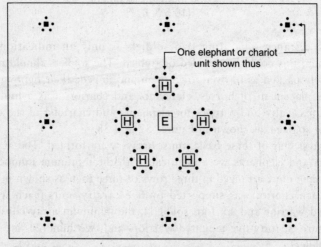

Fig. 38 Placement of Elephant and Chariot Units in an array
{10.5.3, 7}

Formations: Arrays were put together in a formation by placing one array in the centre, two in the flanks and two in the wings. The distance separating the arrays in given as five *dhanus* or 11.25 metres {10.5.8}. See Figure 39.

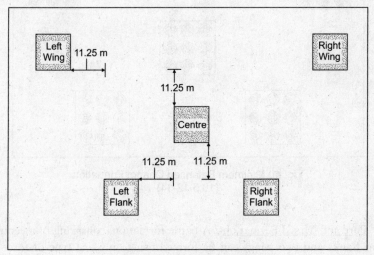

Fig. 39 Battle Formation
{10.5.12}

When the five arrays of a formation are all of equal size, it is called 'balanced'. Another possibility is that the arrays in the wings and the flanks could have two more chariots (or elephants) as compared to the central array. Such formations are called 'unbalanced'.

Figures 40 and 41 illustrate the minimum balanced formation and one example of an unbalanced formation with five chariots in the central array and seven each in the wings and flanks.

The number of chariots (or elephants), horses and men in each of the possible combinations of with 21 chariots in each row of each array was indeed very large; there were 315 chariots, 1575 mounted warriors and nearly 10,000 foot soldiers.

Surpluses and strengthening; After allocating the available forces to forming the units and arrays, some forces may still be available. Rules for distributing them to strengthen the wings, flanks and centre are given.

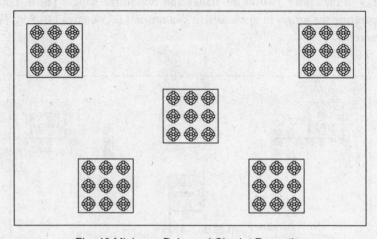

Fig. 40 Minimum Balanced Chariot Formation
{10.5.12-14}

<u>Pure and Mixed Formations:</u> A battle formation, consisting of a centre, two flanks and two wings can be formed using only one type of force—only foot soldiers, only cavalry units or only chariot or elephant units. These are defined as 'pure' formations.

A 'mixed' formation consisted of more than one type of force. Horse units, elephants and chariots could be used together; all four wings could also be used. The placement of forces in mixed formations is also given.

<u>Modes of Attack:</u> The different arrays in a formation could attack the enemy forces in a variety of ways. There are four basic types—a straight line, a snake, a circle or dispersed. In the straight line or 'truncheon', the centre, flanks and wings advanced evenly, in the snake, unevenly in a sinuous manner, in the circle, radiating outwards and in the dispersed, independently of each other. Kautilya gives a list of the sub-types of the basic four. There are eighteen sub-types under 'the truncheon' including the basic type, four under 'the snake', three under 'the circle' and seven under 'the dispersed'—a total of thirty-two! The text contains only brief indications of how each one differed from the basic type. There are hints that a wing or a flank may have advanced or retreated in a different fashion. The names given to the sub-types are not of much help since often they are simply called 'victorious', 'invincible', 'irresistible', etc. In some cases, a hint is given of the shape of the formation. For example, if the

centre remained stationary and the wings moved forward, the formation was stretched out like a 'bow'. The 'snake' formation is said to be either 'moving like a serpent' or 'like cows' urine'; the subtle distinction seems to be that, in the former, the troops move together closely and continuously, while, in the latter, they may be separated and of different sizes. As is

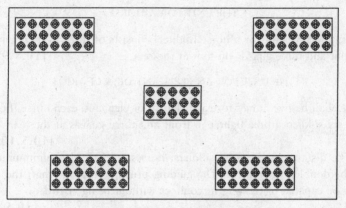

Fig. 41 Unbalanced 5/7 Formation
{10.5.17-19}

usual with Kautilya, there is some attempt, particularly in the sub-types of the truncheon, to find symmetrical counter-types. One cannot be sure whether these sub-types were introduced for the sake of logical completeness or whether they were actually practicable on the battlefield. {10.6.42} (not translated) gives a list of formations to be used against others. Since the subject of battle formations in such detail will be of interest only to military historians of classical Indian warfare, the verses {10.6.9-23,25-29,31-33,35-38 and 42} are not translated here. Kautilya thinks that any formation can be successfully countered by the one called 'the invincible', a sub-type of the truncheon].

BEFORE MAKING THE BATTLE FORMATION

A fortified area shall be set up [approximately 1000 yards or 900 metres] behind the battle ground, depending on the nature of the terrain. The best parts of the army shall be detached and kept out of sight of the enemy. The battalion and divisional commanders shall then arrange the army in a battle formation.   {10.5.1,2}

Battle formations of different kinds shall be arranged according to the rules given below, so that the strength of the four constituents of the force are used appropriately.   {10.5.57}

BASIC UNITS

THE UNIT FOR A HORSE

The supporting unit for a horse [fighter] consists of three soldiers on foot in front and three guards on foot at the rear.   {10.5.9,11}

THE UNIT FOR AN ELEPHANT OR A CHARIOT

There shall be five horses for each chariot or elephant, each horse [fighter] with six soldiers [three fighter in front and three guards at the rear].
{10.5.10,11}

The distances separating soldiers, horses, etc. are the minimum; they can be doubled or trebled. [The guiding principle shall be that] the army must be capable of fighting in comfort without being crowded.
{10.5.4,5}

CHARIOT AND ELEPHANT ARRAYS

The arrays for chariots and elephants are identical.
{10.5.30}

BATTLE FORMATIONS

Ushanas says that a battle formation shall consist of two wings, a centre and reserves; but according to Brihaspati, it shall have two wings, two flanks, a centre and reserves.   {10.6.1,2}

[Kautilya seems to agree with both dispositions, according to 15.1.42 in I.i which quotes the view of Ushanas as indicating agreement with it. The text generally follows the second type recommended by Brihaspati, with two flanks added].

When the battle formations of the conqueror and the enemy are equally matched, he who has better terrain, time and troops, wins.   {10.6.47}

The separation between arrays in a formation shall be 11.25 metres.
{10.5.8}

BALANCED FORMATION

The minimum array [for a chariot or elephant formation] is nine chariot-units in the centre, each flank and each wing, arranged in three rows of three each. [Since each chariot or elephants has its own attendant five horses and thirty men,] a formation consists of a minimum of 45 chariots, 225 horses and 1350 men.

The number of chariot units in each row can be 5,7,9,...up to 21.

There are thus ten possible combinations

- 3,5,7,9,11,13,15,17,19, or 21 chariots per row, the smallest formation having 45 chariots units and the largest, 315.   {10.5.12-16}

UNBALANCED FORMATIONS

The array is said to be unbalanced when the wings and flanks have two more chariot-units than the centre. [For example, the centre could have three rows of 7 chariot units and each flank and wing three rows of 9 units].

There are ten possible unbalanced arrays, with the centre having 1,3,5....up to 21 units.[2]   {10.5.17-19}

SURPLUSES AND STRENGTHENING

Any troops left over after making the formation shall be used to strengthen it by inserting the surplus.   {10.5.20}
Strengthening by insertion is of four kinds:

   proper insertion—addition of surplus chariots, horses and men in the right proportion;

   improper insertion—addition of only foot soldiers;

   unitary insertion—addition of only chariots or only horses;

   counter-productive insertion—addition of unreliable troops.
          {10.5.25-28}

Out of the surplus chariots units, elephants or horses, two third shall be distributed to the outer parts [wings and flanks] and one-third placed at the centre. The insertion shall be made so as not to cause over-crowding among the horses, chariots or elephants. The conqueror may strengthen his formations by up to four times the number of chariots/elephants inserted by the enemy and up to eight times the number of men inserted by him.
          {10.5.21-24,29}

PURE FORMATIONS

Elephant arrays

In an array consisting only of elephants, war elephants shall be placed at the centre, riding elephants at the rear and vicious elephants at the extremities.

Horse arrays

The placement in an array of only horses is: armoured horses at the centre and unarmoured ones at the flanks and wings.

Infantry

Men with armour shall be at the front and archers at the back.

{10.5.34-37}

MIXED FORMATIONS

A formation may be made by combining chariots, elephants and horses as follows:

[Normal]: Chariot units in the centre, horses on the flanks, elephant units at the extremities.   {10.5.31}

To break the enemy's centre: Elephant units in the centre, chariot units on the flanks; horses on the wings.   {10.5.32}

To break the enemy's ends: Horses inthe centre, elephant units on the flanks, chariot units on the wings.   {10.5.33}

[The horses referred to do not include those used to support chariots or elephants.]

When the formation also includes infantry, the placement shall be: infantry on the wings, horses at the flanks, elephants in the front and chariots in the rear.

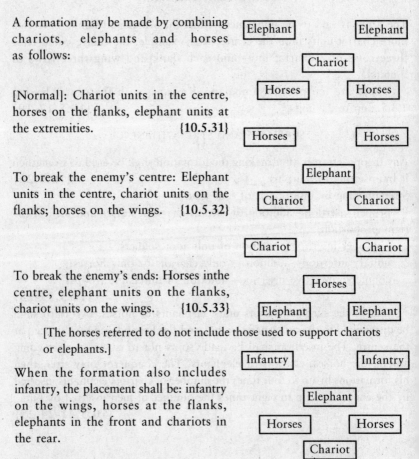

This placement can be varied according to the enemy formation.

The four forces can also be arranged in three arms. for example:

Infantry		Infantry
Chariot	Elephant	Chariot
Infantry		Infantry

{10.5.38-40}

PLACEMENT ACCORDING TO QUALITY

One-third of the best among the infantry, cavalry, elephants and chariots shall be placed in the centre and the other two-third in the wings and flanks.

All forces—best, middling and weak—shall be used.

[This can be done in a number of ways, depending on the conditions.]

The normal order is the best forces in the front and the second-best behind. Placing the third-best behind the best is not usual.

Putting the worst forces in front is abnormal order.

Placing the weakest forces at the extremities may help to dampen the vehemence of the enemy attack.

An order good for resisting an enemy attack is the best troops in front, the second-best at the extremities, the third best at the rear and the weakest in the middle.   {10.5.43-47}

MODES OF ATTACK

According to both [Ushanas and Brihaspati—and Kautilya who does not disagree], there are four basic types:

(i) the truncheon (*danda*) - one in which the wing, flank and centre arrays advance evenly abreast;

(ii) the snake (*bhoga*)—in which they advance unevenly in a sinuous manner, one after the other;

(iii) the circle (*mandala*)—in which the wings, flanks and the centre become one and the advance is in all directions [simultaneously];

(iv) the dispersed (*asamhata*)—in which the wings, flanks and the centre advance independently of each other, irrespective of their original positions in the formation.   {10.6.3-8,24,30,34}

If, in the straight (truncheon) formation, the arrays move one behind the other, it is called 'the needle'. If there are two such [parallel] columns, it is 'the bracelet'. Four such is 'the invincible'. An octagonal formation, [a form of the circle] is [also] called 'the invincible'.

Any kind of formation [of the enemy] can be successfully countered by 'the invincible'.   {from 10.6.20-23,32,43}

ORDER OF THE FOUR CONSTITUENTS

The <u>benevolent</u>—Chariots at the centre, elephants on the flanks, horses in the rear [and infantry on the wings?]

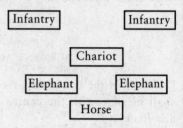

The <u>immovable</u>—Infantry, cavalry, chariots and elephants in that order, one behind the other.

| Infantry |
| Horses |
| Chariots |
| Elephants |

The <u>unrepulsable</u>—Elephants, horses, chariots and infantry, one behind the other.

| Elephants |
| Horses |
| Chariots |
| Infantry |

{10.6.39-41}

XI.ix

THE BATTLE

THE ATTACK

The conqueror shall not attack without having reinforcements in the rear, since these are essential for rallying broken ranks. He himself shall remain, with the reinforcements, at a distance of [approximately] 360 metres [behind the main troops]. {10.5.58}

After setting up the battle formation, the enemy shall be attacked with one or two of the groups in the array—the centre, the wings or the flanks. The rest shall [be kept in reserve] for supporting the attack.

A large part of the best troops shall be used to attack that part of the enemy forces which have weak units, no elephants or horses, unreliable troops or have been [previously] seduced.

When the enemy's army is strongest, the attack shall be made with twice the number of the best troops.

That part of the attacking force which has few of the best troops shall be reinforced by a larger number.

The reinforcements shall be directed to where the enemy forces are weak or from where a danger [of defeat or counter-attack] is apprehended. {10.5.48-52}

Infantry shall be attacked by horses; horses by chariots and chariots by elephants.

An enemy force weak in one constituent shall be attacked by a stronger force [of the same constituent]. {10.6.44}

[During the battle] the conqueror shall strike terror in the enemy forces by various means such as:

Use of machines, occult practices, assassins killing those busy doing something, witchcraft, proclamation of the conqueror's association with gods,[1] using carts or elephants or herds of cattle to frighten, inciting traitors, setting fire to the [enemy] camp, and killing the ends and the rear [supporters and camp followers?]. Agents in the guise of messengers may also create panic by spreading false information such as the burning or capture of the enemy's fort, the revolt of a kinsman or the rebellion of a jungle chief in his territory.   {10.6.48-50}

AFTER THE BATTLE

After routing the enemy's army, the conqueror shall:

(i) sue for peace if the enemy force was more powerful;

(ii) agree to peace if sought by an enemy of equal power; and

(iii) destroy an enemy of inferior power, except when he has reached [the sanctuary of] his own territory or is ready to sacrifice his life.

The fury of a desperate king returning to battle with no thought for his own life is irresistible; therefore, a routed army shall not be further harassed [to the extent of provoking it to fight until annihilation]. {10.3.54-57}

XI.x

THE SIEGE

[When an enemy defeated in battle takes shelter in a fort, his overthrow has to be achieved by besieging and capturing it. The siege was a costly exercise; in Kautilya's words, it entailed losses of men, heavy expenditure and long absence from home. The absence from home was as important as the other two; when the king was away, there was a greater likelihood in his own kingdom of internal rebellion, palace coups, intrigue and treachery. It was therefore essential for the aggressor to capture the fort in the shortest possible time at minimum cost to himself. Kautilya describes a variety of methods in logical order. At each stage, the successful use of the recommended method obviated the need for the use of a more expensive method of the next stage.

Before laying the siege, the aggressor may wage psychological war (*upajapa*) in {13.1} with the aim of frightening the people inside the fort and boosting the morale of his own people, subverting the enemy's high officials or depopulating the territory of the enemy.

If this does not succeed, the aggressor shall try to draw out the enemy from the protection of the fort by various clandestine methods and kill him (*yogavamana*) in {13.2}. The presumption is that with the high officials subverted or the leader dead, the fort would fall into the aggressor's hands without a fight. These tricks have been translated in IX.iv of this translation.

If the enemy is intelligent and as much a student of Kautilya as the aggressor, it is unlikely that he will fall for any of the tricks. Indeed, Kautilya implies that those who know how to manipulate these tricks also know how to counteract them {13.2.36}. If the attempts at killing the enemy prove to be impracticable or if they fail, the conqueror shall set about weakening the enemy (*apasarpa*) {13.3}. The methods suggested include a trusted subordinate of the conqueror gaining the enemy's confidence and then betraying him and using allies or the enemy's enemy.

The next possibility is for the aggressor to infiltrate his own forces into the fort, so that it can be taken from the inside.

Laying siege (*paryupasana*) and taking the fort by direct assault (*avamardha*) is the last resort, both in {13.4}. However, there still some steps which could be taken to emasculate the enemy before the siege is actually laid. Removing the civilian population from around the siege and fort area is one; however, Kautilya is categorical that there shall be no permanent loss of population from the area which will, after victory, become that of the conqueror. For, 'there cannot be a country without people and there is no kingdom without a country.' {13.4.5}. Reducing the supplies available to the enemy for withstanding the siege is another precaution.

The aggressor shall then strengthen his own siege camp and lay the siege at the right time. While carrying out activities like undermining ramparts and breaching the walls, the besieger shall try to avoid further bloodshed and get the enemy to surrender by using the four methods of conciliation, gifts, sowing dissension and force {13.4.13}. Setting fire to the fort by various means {13.4.14-21} is a possibility but this is not recommended for there is little to be gained by conquering ashes. {13.4.22-24}

Even when the enemy's strength is depleted, there are alternatives to direct assault. The enemy can be tricked into coming out of the fort by pretending to withdraw the siege and convincing him by using different types of people that it is safe for him to come out. He shall then be killed.

When all else fails, there is no option but to take the fort by storming it. The rules for the assault also specify that those inside the fort who surrender or do not take part in its defence shall be spared.

When the fort is taken, it shall be cleared of all supporters of the enemy and suitable precautions taken to eliminate the possibility of secret attacks. For example, as mentioned in X.x on the weak king, the defeated enemy may hide himself in the fort and try to assassinate the conqueror. Only when the conqueror is absolutely sure of security, shall he enter the fort as the victor.]

The five means of taking a fort are: psychological warfare, enticing the enemy out, weakening him, besieging him and taking the fort by direct assault.   {13.4.63}

The conqueror who wants to absorb the enemy's territory shall terrify the enemy and fill his own side with enthusiasm by demonstrating his omniscience and his close association with the gods.   {13.1.1}

PSYCHOLOGICAL WARFARE

DEMONSTRATING OMNISCIENCE

The conqueror shall demonstrate his pervasive knowledge by:

(i) letting his chiefs know that he is aware of their domestic affairs and secret activities [having found out about them through secret agents];

(ii) unmasking traitors, having first found them out through secret agents employed for that purpose;

(iii) revealing that someone was about to make a request for a favour having ascertained that through unnoticed contacts, prior knowledge or signals; and

(iv) revealing knowledge about foreign countries before it becomes public, having got [from agents] a secret sealed communication through homing pigeons.   {13.1.2}

DEMONSTRATING ASSOCIATION WITH GODS

[The conqueror shall make gullible people believe that he is in direct contact with gods by various tricks; some of the ones mentioned are not clear. For details see {13.1.3-6} in IX.iv.]

PROPAGANDA

Soothsayers, readers of omens, astrologers, reciters of *Puranas*, intuitionists, clandestine agents, those who helped the king perform the tricks and those who had witnessed them shall advertise them inside his own territory. In the enemy's territory, they shall advertise, in particular, the appearance of gods and his receiving army and treasury from divine sources. Whenever there is an opportunity, (e.g. when interpreting questions to gods (*devaprasna*) [e.g. oracles], omens, the cawing of crows, body-language, dreams, bird-calls and animal noises) they shall proclaim the meaning to be victory for the conqueror and defeat for the enemy. Any appearance of a meteor in the constellation of stars of the enemy's birth shall be proclaimed by a beat of drums [as an omen of the imminent defeat of the enemy].

{13.1.7-10}

AGAINST THE ENEMY'S CHIEFS

Agents, in the guise of envoys pretending to be motivated by friendliness, shall tell the chief principals of the enemy of the high regard the conqueror has for them, of the strength of his side and of the deterioration in the enemy's side. The principals, both civilians and soldiers, shall be promised that they will not lose [i.e. have the same rewards and honours when the conqueror absorbs the territory]. The principals shall be looked after if they encounter calamities and be treated as a father would treat his children.

{13.1.11-13}

An agent, in the guise of a holy man shall take refuge in a popular temple of the city and by his performances of magical tricks gradually win over the principals and use them to outmanoeuvre the enemy.

{13.2.15}

[The methods for subverting the principals of the enemy are described not only in {13.1.16} but also in {1.14}. For translation see IX.iv.]

When the population in the enemy territory suffers from famine or depredations of jungle tribes, secret agents shall encourage them to seek the conqueror's protection, and persuade them that, even if they do not get that protection, they should go elsewhere [thus ensuring depopulation of the enemy territory.] If the people agree to move, they shall be given grains and money.   {13.1.20,21}

ENTICING THE ENEMY OUT OF THE FORT BY TRICKS

[See IX iv.]

WEAKENING THE ENEMY

USING ONE'S OWN TRUSTED OFFICERS

[The methods described below involve ostensibly dismissing or banishing a trusted official and sending him over to the enemy to win the enemy's confidence with a view to betraying him at an opportune time. The intention is to weaken the enemy and thus reduce the losses and expenses of taking the fort].

A trustworthy counsellor, jungle chief or militia chief,[1] [ostensibly] dismissed from his post, shall seek shelter with the enemy and gradually bring over his own men on the grounds of protecting his people. He shall then, with the help of spies, attack a treacherous town of the conqueror, or an unreliable and weak force of the conqueror or an unreliable rear-ally of the conqueror.[2] Alternatively, the planted official may increase his own strength by winning over the militias or tribal forces in a part of the enemy's territory. When the traitor has earned the full confidence of the enemy, word shall be sent to the conqueror, who, pretending to go to catch elephants or put down tribal rebels, shall attack the enemy without warning, [the planted official revealing his true colours at that time.]   {from 13.3.1-7}

The conqueror shall first make peace with the enemy[3] and then ostensibly dismiss some counsellors, who are then to appeal to the enemy for help in reconciling them with their master. Any envoy sent by the enemy for this purpose shall be insulted. Whereupon one of the dismissed counsellors shall seek shelter with the enemy and gain his confidence by recommending treacherous spies [who have betrayed the conqueror], the disgruntled, the unreliable, the weak, robbers or jungle chiefs who harass both. [Again, the choice is to be made so as to please the enemy while ridding the conqueror of harassment]. He shall then falsely betray important officers of the enemy, such as frontier officers, tribal chiefs or army chiefs accusing them of being in league with the conqueror. So-called proof shall be provided by letters carried by the condemned men. [Thus important officials providing valuable support shall be eliminated, thereby weakening the enemy].   {from 13.3.8-14}

The conqueror shall ostensibly banish a chief official of a fort, province or army accusing him of treachery. The banished official shall [take shelter with the enemy and] use the opportunity of a battle, a sudden assault, a siege or a calamity to outmanoeuvre the enemy. [While waiting for an opportunity] he shall set about sowing dissension among the supporters of the enemy. In this also, they shall use letters carried by condemned men.
{from 13.3.36-39}

WEAKENING THE ENEMY BY USING OTHER KINGS OF THE CIRCLE

[This series of methods makes use of the enemy's enemy, the conqueror's ally or the enemy's ally. An important set of methods suggests that the conqueror shall invite an attack on himself, call upon the enemy for help and then adopt an appropriate one among a variety of measures to kill the enemy. These are, in fact, a graphic example of Kautilya's basic advice: the conqueror shall clearly identify the main aims (i.e. the elimination of the enemy) and then use short-term stratagems to achieve the main aims].

The enemy can also be destroyed with methods involving the use of armed forces.   {13.3.15}

The conqueror shall contrive a situation whereby the enemy is invited to come with armed forces to his help.

[This can be done using the enemy's enemy, the conqueror's ally or the enemy himself.]

[In the first case,] the enemy's enemy [in theory, a friend] shall, by secret methods, be made [to appear] to do harm to the conqueror, who shall then [pretend to] mount an attack against the ally in retaliation. The enemy shall then be invited to join in it on the promise of a share of land or gold [captured on the expedition].

[In the second case,] the conqueror shall make a treaty with the ally for sharing the enemy's land. When the ally attacks the enemy, he shall [appear to] do harm to the conqueror, who shall then [pretend to] mount an attack in retaliation and invite the enemy to join in an attack on an ally of the conqueror, promising a share of the land.

[The enemy may or may not trust the conqueror. The methods of destroying the enemy depends on his reaction.]

If the enemy trusts the conqueror and agrees to a joint campaign:	The enemy shall be killed in an ambush or an open battle with the supposed target of the expedition. [If this is not possible], the enemy shall be invited to the court of the conqueror on some plausible pretext [gift of land, installation of the Crown Prince or grant of protection] and then imprisoned. [If this is also not possible], the enemy shall be done away with by secret means.
If the enemy only provides his army but does not accompany it himself:	The target of the campaign shall be made to destroy the [enemy's] army.
If the enemy leads his forces separately and not with the conqueror:	He shall be destroyed by being squeezed between the two forces [of the conqueror and that of the king used as bait].
If the enemy is distrustful and engages in the campaign on his own or if he wants to attack a different part of the territory:	He shall be killed by the target of the campaign or the conqueror shall do so, mobilising all his forces.
When the enemy is actually fighting the targeted king:	The conqueror shall seize the base [i.e. the fort] of the enemy by sending a different force.

In the case of the enemy undertaking a campaign against the conqueror's ally:	The enemy shall first be helped with troops and when he is engaged in battle, he shall be outmanoeuvred by the conqueror.

{from 13.3.16-28}

The conqueror may, after taking suitable precautions, pretend to be suffering from a calamity and make his ally encourage the enemy to attack. When the enemy does so, he shall be squeezed between the two forces [of the conqueror and the ally]. The enemy may be killed or, if caught alive, released in exchange for his kingdom.   {13.3.29,30}

If the enemy becomes unassailable through being protected by his friend, his neighbours shall be encouraged to lay waste enemy territory. If the enemy relies on the army of the ally to save his fort, that army must be destroyed. If the enemy and his ally are united, the conqueror shall openly bargain with each one for the other's land. Then double agents or agents pretending to be the friend of the enemy or the ally shall sow mistrust. When one of them gets angry or suspicious of the other, the conqueror shall divide them and eliminate them one by one.   {13.3.31-35}

INFILTRATING A FORCE INSIDE THE FORT

[A part of the conqueror's army can be infiltrated into the fort either by tricking the enemy into opening the gates or by building up gradually a clandestine armed force inside. Verses {13.3.40-48} have been included in IX.iv.]

LAYING THE SIEGE

DEPLETING THE ENEMY'S RESOURCES BEFORE THE SIEGE

The work of laying a siege shall be preceded by actions designed to deplete the resources of the enemy. These are: destroying his sowings and crops, cutting off his supplies and foraging raids, making his people run away and killing the leaders secretly.

The countryside around the fort shall be protected from fear. Favours and [tax] exemptions shall be granted to those who desire to move [to get away from the fighting] to persuade them to settle elsewhere. Those who actually move shall be made to settle on land away from the battle field or move together to a different place. Kautilya says: 'There cannot be a country without people and there is no kingdom without a country.'

The sowings or the crops of the enemy entrenched in the fort shall be destroyed, his supplies cut off and foraging raids foiled.   {13.4.1-7}

TIME FOR BESIEGING

The enemy's fort shall be besieged when:

(i) the attacker's troops are supplied abundantly with high quality grains, forest produce, machines, army, armour, labour, ropes and other equipment;

(ii) the climate is favourable to the conqueror and unfavourable to the enemy; and

(iii) the enemy suffers from disease, famine, depletion of stores, deterioration of fortifications and the weariness of his mercenary and allied troops.   {13.4.8}

BESIEGING

The besieger shall first make sure of the protection of his own camp, transport, supplies, reinforcements and roads. The fort shall then be encircled along the moat and ramparts of the fort. Drinking water supply [for the fort from outside] shall be defiled. The moat shall be emptied or filled up [with earth]. The ramparts shall be undermined by tunnels or by breaking [the foundations?] and breached by armoured elephants. Uneven places shall be filled with earth. Any place defended by many men shall be destroyed by machines. Enemy troops emerging from concealed exits shall be hunted down by horses.

In between these activities, the attacker shall try to achieve success [i.e. the surrender of the enemy] by using the four methods in restriction, option or combination.[4]   {13.4.9-13}

USE OF FIRE

When a fort can be captured by fighting, fire shall not be used at all. For fire is a divine calamity whose effects are unpredictable; it is a destroyer of uncountable numbers of people as well as grains, animals, wealth, forest produce and other goods. Even when captured, a fort whose stores are all burnt down only gives rise to further losses.   {13.4.22-24}
The following are the methods of setting fire to the fort:

(i) Birds (like hawks, crows, pheasants, kites, parrots, mynahs, owls and pigeons) which have their nests in the forts, shall be caught, fire brands tied to their tails and then released to fly back to the fort;

(ii) If the camp is at a distance from the fort and if there is an elevated part with protection for the archers of the besieging army, fire arrows can be used;

(iii) [The attacker's] secret agents serving as guards inside the fort may tie fire brands to the tails of mongoose, monkeys, cats or dogs and let them loose over thatches, [wooden] fortifications and houses;

(iv) A piece of burning charcoal may be hidden inside dried fish or meat to be picked up by crows [and dropped on houses inside the fort].

{13.4.14-17}

[{13.4.18-21} which give recipes for making fireballs, fire arrows etc., have not been translated because the names of the different ingredients are not clear].

PRETENDED WITHDRAWAL OF THE SIEGE

[It is not clear whether the methods in {13.4.27-49} are to be used as alternatives to storming the citadel or because the siege is ineffective. Most of them are tricks, many using people posing as friends of the besieged; even a true friend or supporter of the besieged king can be tricked into joining the attacker, then killed and the murder blamed on the besieged. A few verses are inconsistent with the intent of the sequence. {13.4.41} recommending the use of secret agents entering the fort with forged passes and taking it from inside is interpolated between two tricks both involving people pretending to be supporters of the besieged. {13.4.48,49} recommending that the aggressor make a treaty with the besieged and then destroy the country, not the enemy, is quite inconsistent with the rest of Kautilya's philosophy of distinguishing between the people and the king as enemy. These verses are probably holdovers from other texts.

In the translation below, trick 1 does not use anyone; trick 2 is to be used by someone pretending to be either an ally or supporter (*mitra-aasaravyanjana*); trick 3 is a variation for use by a vassal king or a tribal chief. The fourth trick is for one posing as a friend and the fifth and sixth by one posing as a supporter. The seventh uses the true ally or friendly jungle chief of the besieged].

1. Lifting the siege

The attacker may abandon his siege camp, hide himself in a forest and kill the enemy when he emerges from the fort. {13.4.27}

The attacker may send in secret agents with [forged] passes on the pretext of seeing friends or relatives inside and then capture it while inside.

{13.4.41}

2. So-called friends or supporters

A king, pretending to be a good ally or supporter, shall befriend the besieged and send a condemned man as messenger ostensibly with information about traitors in the fort who are sources of danger or traitors in the besieger's camp who could be exploited. When the so-called friend returns from the fort with another messenger, the conqueror shall [pretend to] arrest him, try him for conspiracy and banish him. The siege shall be lifted. The so-called friend shall then send a message to the besieged calling for his help for protection or for jointly attacking the conqueror. When the besieged responds, he shall be squeezed between the two forces [the conqueror's and the so-called friend's], and killed; or he shall be let off in return for surrendering his kingdom; his fort may be razed to the ground, or his best forces called out and destroyed.   {13.4.28-33}

3. Using a vassal king or tribal chief

A vassal king, who has surrendered with his troops to the conqueror or a tribal chief can be used to [pretend that they are dissatisfied with the conqueror and] suggest to the besieged king that the conqueror is suffering from some calamity—e.g. that he is ill, he is being attacked by an enemy-in-the-rear, there is a revolt in his army, or that he is lifting the siege and going elsewhere. When the besieged is convinced of this, the conqueror shall lift the siege, set fire to his camp and go away. Then the vassal or jungle chief shall send word to the besieged calling for help. The rest of this trick is the same as the last one.

While abandoning the siege, the conqueror may also outmanoeuvre the enemy by leaving behind his stores having first laced them with poison.
                {13.4.34-38}

4. The so-called friend

A greedy ally of the besieged may be persuaded [on the promise of his keeping the territory] to use his friendship to divide the king and his brave warriors and have the warriors killed.   {13.4.46,47}

5. and 6. The so-called supporter

A false supporter of the besieged may send a envoy with the [false] information that he himself had mounted an attack against the besieger and that the besieged should come out and join it. When he does so, he shall be squeezed between the two forces [as in trick 2].   {13.4.39,40}

Alternatively, the false supporter may intimate that he will attack the besieger at a specified time and place and invite the besieged to join. When the besieger agrees, a lot of noise shall be made as if attack was in progress and as the besieged comes out of the fort at night he shall be killed.
                {13.4.42,43}

7. Ally or friendly tribal chief of the besieged

An ally or friendly tribal chief [of the besieged] shall be suborned to fight against the besieged on the promise of letting him keep the territory. When he does so, he shall be killed by poison, by treacherous chiefs or the people. The besieged shall be discredited by casting the blame on him for killing his own ally.   {13.4.44,45}

STORMING THE FORT

THE RIGHT CONDITION

The best opportunity to storm the fort is when:

(i) the conqueror is fully equipped with all implements and labourers;

(ii) the enemy is ill;

(iii) the enemy's principal officials are unhappy through being subjected to secret tests [of loyalty];[5]

(iv) the enemy's fortifications are incomplete, stores depleted and reinforcements unavailable; or

(v) the enemy is likely to make a treaty with an ally to provide reinforcements before the assault.

{13.4.25}

THE RIGHT TIME

The right time for storming the fort is when

(i) there is an accidental fire in the fort or when it has been intentionally set alight;

(ii) the people are participating in a festival or watching a show;

(iii) there is a drunken quarrel among the troops [inside the fort];

(iv) the enemy troops are tired after constant fighting;

(v) the enemy troops have suffered many casualties after heavy fighting;

(vi) the people are tired after being kept awake [for many nights] or when they are asleep; or

(vii) it is cloudy, raining, flooded or foggy.

{13.4.26}

THE ASSAULT

The conqueror shall first mount a diversionary attack with his own unreliable troops or tribal forces so that a part of the enemy forces are drawn out against them.

The attack shall be led by the conqueror's unreliable, alien or tribal forces as well as by those who hate the enemy and deserters from the fort, who had been rewarded and honoured by the conqueror. The attackers shall be provided with suitable signs and signals [for coordination].

The following shall not be harmed when the enemy for or camp is attacked:

(i) anyone falling down in the fight;

(ii) those turning their backs;

(iii) anyone surrendering;

(iv) anyone who unties his hair [as a symbol of surrender?] or throws his weapons down;

(v) anyone contorted by fear; or

(vi) anyone who does not fight.

After capturing the fort, it shall be cleared of the enemy's supporters and precautions shall be taken, both inside and out, against secret attackers or tricks.

Only then shall the conqueror enter the fort.   {13.4.50-53}

XI.xi

PEACEFUL RULE OF ACQUIRED TERRITORY

There are three ways by which a conqueror can acquire territory—by inheritance, reacquisition and conquest. The acquisition may be of two kinds—extensive, including forests and other types of land, or a single city, fort or village. {13.5.1,2}

INHERITED TERRITORY

The conqueror shall avoid the mistakes of his father and emulate his virtues.

Among the customs and practices in vogue when the kingdom is inherited, those in accordance with *dharma* shall be continued and those against discontinued. Likewise, only those customs and practices which are in accordance with *dharma* shall be introduced and not those which do not conform to it. {13.5.23,24}

REACQUIRED TERRITORY

In the case of territory which was originally his and had been reacquired, the conqueror shall avoid the mistakes—his own or those of the constituents of his state—which led to the territory being lost and strengthen those qualities through which he regained it. {13.5.22}

NEW TERRITORY, ACQUIRED BY CONQUEST

Having acquired new territory, the conqueror shall substitute his virtues for the enemy's vices and where the enemy was good, he shall be twice as good.

He shall follow policies which are pleasing and beneficial to the constituents by acting according to his *dharma* and by granting favours and [tax] exemptions, giving gifts and bestowing honours.

He shall reward, as promised, those who were traitors to the enemy for his sake; if they had exerted themselves more [than required], they shall be rewarded more than promised. For he who does not keep his promises or acts against the interests of the people, becomes unworthy of the trust of his own and other people.

He shall adopt the way of life, dress, language and customs of the people [of the acquired territory], show the same devotion to the gods of the territory [as to his own gods] and participate in the people's festivals and amusements.

He shall please the chiefs of the country, towns, castes and guilds by looking after their customary rights, tax exemptions and safety. Secret agents shall tell the chiefs often of the misdeeds of the enemy [their former king], the [present] king's high regard for them, his devotion to their interests, and how he considers it a great good fortune to have them in his kingdom.

He shall ensure that devotions are held regularly in all the temples and *ashrams*.

He shall grant land, money and tax exemptions to the men distinguished for their learning, speech, *dharma* or bravery.

All prisoners shall be released [on a special amnesty].

The ill, the helpless and the distressed shall be helped. Slaughter of animals shall be prohibited during one fortnight in each month of *chaturmasya* [the four-month period set apart for devotions], for four days around the full moon day and for a day on the birth star of the king or country. The slaughter of females and young animals as well as castration of male animals shall also be prohibited.

All practices which are not in accordance with *dharma* or which affect the treasury or the army shall be discontinued and replaced by those in accordance with *dharma*.

Thieves and *mlecchas* shall be removed from their usual places of residence and dispersed. Chiefs of the fort, army and police, ministers and *purohitas* who were supporters of the enemy shall be dispersed to different parts on the frontier regions of the territory. Those who conspire against or can cause harm to the conqueror shall be put down secretly. The posts previously occupied by the enemy's men shall be filled by the conqueror's own people or those who were in disfavour with the enemy.

A pretender from the enemy's family who can recover the territory or a noble in the frontier forests who can harass the conqueror shall be tackled by giving him sterile land or land which is, at best, one-quarter fertile. The grant shall be made subject to payment of an exorbitant tribute in money and troops, so that its payment will make the citizens in the towns and countryside revolt and kill the prince or noble.

Any official who incurs the displeasure of the people shall either be removed from his post or transferred to a dangerous region.

{13.5.3-21}

EPILOGUE

[As mentioned in {6.2.3}, after conquering an enemy, a king may adopt a policy of enjoying his acquisition peacefully. He may also embark on further conquests, either immediately or later. One important result of the victory is that alignments will have changed, because borders will have changed. Old allies may become new enemies. New states acquire the roles of Middle or Neutral kings. He himself may play one of these roles. There will be four new sets of Circles of States and a new natural enemy. This enemy may even be the one who was the Middle king before the conquest, because, by definition, his kingdom and the conqueror's share a common border. After the conquest and acquisition, the conqueror may have acquired strength commensurate with that of the Middle king. The cycle of acquisition by conquest thus recommences. Once the Middle king is subdued, the conqueror will have enough power to tackle the Neutral king. This is one possible scenario. There are three others, all suggesting different kings as targets for conquest. The eventual objective is *Chakravartikshetram*—the area of operation of the King-Emperor. This area, according to Kautilya, is the whole of *Bharatavarsha*, i.e. the Indian sub-continent. The last verse in this translation, reiterates that the King-Emperor shall rule in accordance with *dharma*.]

The area extending from the Himalayas in the north to the sea [in the south] and a thousand *yojanas* wide from east to west is the area of operation of the King-Emperor (*chakravartikshetram*).   {9.1.18}
There are four ways of conquering the world:

1. After conquering the enemy, the conqueror shall direct his attention to the king who is the Middle king; then he shall turn to the Neutral king.

2. If there are no Middle or Neutral kings, the conqueror shall win over the constituents of the enemy by his excellent qualities and [having thus consolidated his position] tackle the other members of his Circle of States.

3. If there is no circle, the conqueror shall squeeze an enemy between himself and an ally or squeeze an ally between himself and an enemy.

4. The fourth way is to overcome a weak neighbour without allies; having become doubly powerful, overcome another neighbour and with the increased power a third one and so on.

And, having conquered the world characterised by the different *varnas* and stages of life, the conqueror shall enjoy it according to the precepts of the *dharma* for kings.   {13.4.54-62}

Notes

Introduction

1. The Cultural Heritage of India, Vol.II, p. 601, The Ramakrishna Mission Institute of Culture, Calcutta, 1962.

2. R.P. Kangle, *The Kautiliya Arthasastra*, in three parts:

Part I - A critical Edition with glossary; 1st ed. (1960); 2nd ed. (1969)

Part II - An English Translation with critical and explanatory notes; 1st ed. (1963); 2nd ed. (1972)

Part III - A Study; 1965, University of Bombay. This reference-Part III, p.3.

3. Not the Manu of the *Manusmriti* (the Code of Manu) which is a codification a few centuries after Kautilya, judging by the nature of the Hindu society described in it, especially on the role of women, widows' right to remarry, etc.

4. Most of the details on Chandragupta Maurya in this section are taken from Radha Kumud Mookerji: *Chandragupta Maurya and His Times*, Motilal Banarsidas, Delhi 1988. See, in particular, Appendices I and II on Chanakya and Chandragupta traditions from Buddhist and Jaina sources.

5. The primordial ancestor of the family being the sage *kutila*.

6. Ibid., App. 1, p. 229. The quotation is from the *Mahavamsatika*.

7. Ibid., p. 5

8. Kangle, op.cit., Part III, pp. 61–98.

9. T.R. Trautmann, *The Structure and Composition of the Kautilya Arthasastra*, Ph.D. Thesis, University of Iowa, 1968.

10. MLBD Newsletter, Vol. XI, No. 10, October 1989, p.8; Motilal Banarsidas, Delhi.

11. Kangle, op. cit., Part III, p. 104.

12. Ibid., p. 106.

13. Ibid., p.98.

14. R. Shamasastry, *Arthasastra of Kautilya*, University of Mysore, Oriental Library Publications:

Text: 1st ed. - 1908; 2nd ed. - 1919

Translation: 1st ed. - 1915; 3rd ed. - 1929; 8th ed. - 1967

Index Verborum: Part I - A to N - 1924

Part II - T to Y - 1925

Part III - R to H - 1925

15. Kangle, Part III, pp. 21–25.

16. Ibid. p. 19, 20.

17. R.K. Mookerji, op.cit., p. 80.

18. R.C. Majumdar, *Corporate Life in Ancient India*, referred to in Kangle, op.cit., Part III, p. 135.

19. Kangle, op. cit., pp. 135-138

20. Kangle III, p.239

21. Shamasastry, op.cit., p. 223.

22. Kangle II, note to {11.1.42}, p.457.

23. Prabhati Mukherjee; *Beyond the Four Varnas: The Untouchables in India,* Motilal Banarsidas, Delhi, 1988. p. 14 and note 2 on p. 105.

24. Kangle, op.cit., Part III, p.30.

25. V.K. Gupta,'*Kautilyan Jurisprudence*', B.D. Gupta, Delhi, 1987. It is a pity that there is not a word of acknowledgment to Kangle, from whose work this is a scissors and paste exercise. Gupta's classification is different in:criminal breach of trust {3.20.16, 4.10.7, 4.1.28, 29}; cheating {2.5.9, 4.1.27, 4.4.20-23, 4.10.9}.

26. Aradhana Parmar, *Techniques of Statecraft: A Study of Kautilya's Arthasastra*, Atma Ram & Sons, Delhi, 1987.

27. Vaivasvata Manu. Three different Manus are, in fact, known as teachers—the Svayambu (self-generated), the Prachetasa (the ancient) and the Vaivasvata (son of Vivasvat).

28. Kangle, op.cit., Vol.III, p.191.

29. Ibid, p. 186.

30. Ibid., p.274.

31. Parmar, op.cit., p. 5.

32. Kangle, op.cit., Part III, p. 283.

The Kautilyan State and Society

1. For the political situation in the sub-continent, I am indebted to R.K. Mookerji, *Chandragupta Maurya and his Times;* U.N. Ghosal, 'Political Organization: The Monarchical States' and 'Political Organization: Republics and Mixed Constitutions' in the *Cultural History of India*, Vol. II, The Ramakrishna Mission Institute of Culture, Calcutta, Second Ed., 1962 and Romila Thapar, *A History of India*, Vol. I, Pelican, first published 1966.

2. The map is made up from two maps (p. 61 and pp. 80-81) in Romila Thapar, op.cit.

3. Kangle, Part II, notes on pp. 277, 282 and 285.

4. Prabhati Mukherjee, *Beyond the Four Varnas*, Motilal Banarsidass, Delhi, 1988.

5. Aparajita, Apratihata, Jayanta and Vijayanta—Kangle—All different names for spirits of victory; Meyer—Forms of Kumara or Skanda; Malayalam commentary and R.K. Mukerjee—'They are, respectively, Durga, Vishnu, Subrahmanya and Indra';

Commentary of Bhikshu Prabhamati-Vishnu, Indra, son of Indra and Skanda. (See Kangle, Part II, note on p. 70 and Mukerjee).

6. Kangle, op. cit., Part III, p. 159.

I.i

1. Another example is given in the methods which could be used by a king about to attack an enemy {9.7.73-76}.

II.i

1. See Kangle, Vol. III, pp. 117,118.

2. Ibid, pp. 133,134.

II.ii

1. See Notes on Translation No. 3.

2. Also often *mahajanapada*. See: for settlements - {7.11.3-5}; administrative structure - {2.35.1}; revenue centre - {2.3.3}; ideal - {6.1.8}; relative importance of *janapada* and city - {8.1.29-32}; enemy *janapada* - {7.11.18-20} and {13.4.1-5}; see also under Chancellor in IV.iv.

3. For details of how to evaluate the qualities of persons considered for appointment as ministers, etc. see IV.ii.

4. For details on different kinds of allies and how to deal with them see X.iv.

II.iii

1. A good minister can take effective counter-measures against man-made or natural calamities which affect the people. If the minister himself is afflicted, there will be no one to look after them. Hence, a calamity affecting the minister is more serious than one affecting the *janapada*.

II.iv

1. In {9.7.82} referred to as 'Satanic' instead of divine.

2. List given in {2.36.18}—water pots, a big jar, a trough, a ladder, an axe for chopping down pillars and beams, a winnowing basket for fanning away the fire, a hook for pulling away burning objects, a hooked rake for pulling away thatch and a skin bag; there are only nine articles in this list.

3. The punishment for not restraining dogs does not apply to forest guards.

II.v

1. {1.20.14-17} See III.iv, 'The King's Security'.

2. In both cases, there is a collective leadership of a number of chiefs or kings; see X.ix.

III.i

1. For definition, given in {1.5.14}, see I.ii.

III.ii

1. The stories are well known and many are found in the *Ramayana* and the *Mahabharata*. See Kangle, II, notes on pp. 12,13.

III.iii

1. Verses 7 and 8 give the lengths of the shadow of the gnomon of a sundial which mark each of the four periods before and after middday. The measurement of time during night is not given in the text. See Appendix 1.

III.iv

1. See Fig. 17, Treasury - Cross section in IV.iv.
2. See the Training of a Prince above in III.i.

III.v

1. All verses relating to clandestine methods are in Part IX of this translation.
2. See X.vi.

3. Use of secret agents against a disgruntled prince; see III.vi.

4. {13.1}, deals mainly with psychological warfare with a view to intimidating the enemy's people and boosting the morale of one's own people. See XI.x.

III.vi

1. Primordial male ancestor.
2. See {13.1} in XI.x.
3. See {9.5} in III.v.
4. See {5.1} - Three methods: Using kinsmen, entrapment, playing one against the other. see IX.iii.
5. See, 'The Weak King', X.x.
6. *Rajyasri:* the kingdom as the goddess of wealth; hence, figuratively, a woman.

IV.i

1. 1 *krosa* = 2 1/4 miles or 3.66 km.
2. Literally, 'playing with money'.
3. According to {5.3.32}, 'all salaries in settlements on virgin lands shall be paid in cash; no land shall be allotted, as part of the salary, until the village is fully established.'
4. Wasteland, used for settlement, is state property and, therefore, reverts to the Crown on the death of the holder.

5. Such grants are to be made to any new settlement even in times of financial difficulties. See {5.2.4} in V.ii.

6. *Goruta* is another name for *krosa*; see note 1 above.

7. The translation is a compromise between Kangle ('The king should enforce discipline on slaves, etc.') and Shamasastry ('Those who do not heed the claims of slaves....shall be taught their duty.')

8. The unit for measuring the width of roads (*a dhanus*) was 6' 9" as against the standard *dandaldhanus* which was 6'; see Appendix 2 on Weights and Measures.

9. See Appendix 14 for list.

10. Explained in VIII.vii on Loans, deposits, etc.

IV.ii

1. See Kangle, vol. III, p.134.

IV.iv

1. *Sasana* has two meanings—'to control' and 'to administer'.

2. {2.10.13-21} on the basic principles of Sanskrit grammar (number of letters in the alphabet, parts of speech, etc.) are not translated.

3. '*Iti*'—'Thus'.

4. For details of commodities and products classified under these names see Appendix 2.

5. For details of revenue, budgeting and maintenance of accounts see V.iii.

6. For the type of spies and the cover to be used by them, see IX.ii.

7. For the methods to be used by secret agents to expose each type, see IX.iii.

8. For explanation of transaction tax (*vyaji*) and its collection by use of different weights and measures see V.ii on Sources of Revenue and Appendix 1 on Weights and Measures.

9. Expenditure relating to allies: treaty receipts, tributes paid or received. Expenditure relating to enemies: espionage, war.

10. The thirteenth month inserted to harmonize the lunar year with the solar year.

11. Inspectors shall not be friends or close relatives of the king or other powerful people. For punishments for loss of revenue caused by negligent or fraudulent inspectors see VI.iv.

12. See also {8.4.34-36} in II.iv for Kautilya's view that harassment by the population by merchants is worse than harassment by frontier officers.

13. Of clean, new grain in full measure.

14. Of corresponding goods of specified quality.

15. For punishments for violation of curfew offences see. VII.vii.

IV.v

1. 'Lost' for inanimate things and 'driven away' for animals and slaves.

IV.vi

1. Their own clothes shall be marked with the sign of a mace or club.
2. See {3.19.12-14} in VIII.xiii.

V.iii

1. The date was recorded according to the lunar calendar, with some fortnights having 14 days and others 15, with an intercalary month and with the years numbered according the number of years since the beginning of that king's reign. Thus, the date entry will show the king's regnal year, the month, the fortnight (waxing or waning of the moon) and the day. For details of the method of recording time see Appendix 1.
2. For example, the type of daily account to be kept by the Chief Controller of Alcoholic Beverages {2.25.40}.

VI.i

1. Literally: 'Departments of Government shall have many temporary heads.'
2. See {1.9.1,2} in II.ii.

VI.ii

1. Enough for four meals for one Arya male; see {2.15.43}.
2. Approximately 9 miles or 15 km; see Appendix 1 on Weights and Measures.

VII.i

1. Kangle Vol.III, p. 194.

VII.ii

1. Whether loose gems or set in jewellery, whether dressed or undressed furs and skins, etc.
2. See V.ii on 'Sources of Revenue'. Such contributions, perhaps in the form of rice, oil and salt, do not seem to have been a fixed tax but levied as and when the army was sent to a region at their request.
3. Such as those paid by someone for damage done by his cattle.
4. See under conversion ratios in Appendix 1 on commodities.
5. For rations see Appendix 4.

VII.iii

1. See under agriculture in IV.v 'Aspects of the Economy'.
2. Details, as above.
3. See Appendix 3 for lists of types of cattle.

4. Of aged cows, milch cows, pregnant cows, heifers and calves.

5. Death due to age, illness, drowning, falling from a precipice or river bank, being swallowed up in quagmire, falling off a tree or rock, being struck by lightning, attack by a tiger, snake or crocodile or in a forest fire.

6. In the form of the skin with identification mark for a cow or a buffalo, the ear with the mark for goats and sheep, the skin and tail for a horse, donkey or camel.

7. See Appendix 3.

8. For example, putting a rope through the nose, breaking in and training to the yoke.

VII.iv

1. For the various kinds of ores mentioned by Kautilya and some details on smelting of metals see Appendix 5 on Metallurgy.

2. {2.15.14,15}; for list see Appendix 1.

3. Four different rooms probably for different types of work such as (i) purifying, hardening and softening metals, (ii) gold plating and enamelling, (iii) making beads and hollow-ware, and (iv) making jewellery.

4. There will thus be 17 standards ranging from 64 carat pure gold down to 48 carat gold.

VII.v

1. For the responsibility of merchants if stolen goods are found in their possession, see VIII.viii on lost property.

VII.vi

1. Prof. Kangle points out (note on p. 154 of Vol. II) that if the sale price was higher, the vintner was likely to pocket the difference and, if lower, he was likely to adulterate the products.

2. For details of transaction tax (*vyaji*), *manavayaji*, sticking allowance (*manasrava*) and countervailing duty (*vaidharana*) see respectively—{2.19.29}, {2.16.10}, {2.19.44} and {2.25.40}—all in Sources of Revenue (V.iii).

3. See Samahartr (Chancellor) in IV.iv; see also use against oligarchies {11.1.34-39}.

4. Literally, annual payment to be double the [average] monthly earnings.

5. The whole of {3.20.9} applies only to gambling masters because heavier punishments are prescribed in {4.10.9} for the same offences when committed by the players.

VII.vii

1. See also {2.29.21} in VII.iii on grazing herds in land which had been cleared of thieves, tigers and other predators.

VII.x

1. See Kangle, Part II, notes on pp.223 and 224 to verses {3.10.16, 21, 22}.

2. See also Animal Welfare in VII.iii.

3. For punishment, see VIII.viii.

4. Part of verse {3.10.44}, most likely a later marginal gloss which has crept into the text, not translated.

VII.xi

1. In the text 'forty families'.

VIII.ii

1. In the text: 'feet'; i.e. foundations.

VIII.iii

1. Headquarters of 10, 400 or 800 villages.

VIII.iv

1. The year, the month, the fortnight and the day.

2. The region, the village, the caste, the family, the name and occupation.

3. Such as being involved in a lengthy religious ritual.

4. See also {3.1.12} persons who are not competent to enter into ransactions.

5. Plaintiff gets less than he deserved to the extent of one-fifth of the excess claim; this acts as a disincentive to making unreasonable claims.

6. Authenticity of last sentence {3.1.37} is doubtful.

VIII.v

1. See footnote to {3.2.1}, p. 196 of Kangle, Vol. II, where Meyer's discussion on the arrangement is cited.

2. For a table of 'Inter-*varna* marriages and their progenies', see Prabhati Mukherjee, *Beyond the Four Varnas*, pp.44–50.

3. The names of the different forms of marriage—of the Supreme Being (*Brahma*), of the Primordial Begetter (*Prajapati*), of the sages (*rishis*), of the gods (*devas*), of the celestial attendants (*gandharvas*), of the non-gods (*asuras*), of the demons (*rakshasas*) and of the evil spirits (*paisachas*)—are indicative of the degree of goodness and *dharma* associated with each one. The order and nomenclature are traditional.

4. The word '*vritti*' has been translated as 'support' in a general sense; maintenance' is used in this translation in the specialised sense of the amount of alimony or other kind of support provided to divorced or separated women.

5. The text is ambiguous.

6. See village/village headman {3.10.18} in VII.ix.

VIII.vi

1. Every Arya had the obligation to perform an annual oblatory *pinda* sacrifice for his father in which offerings were made to the father, the paternal grandfather and great grandfather.

2. See VIII.v: Marital life, 'widows who remarry'.

3. Giving away 'with water'.

VIII.vii

1. Kangle II, note to {3.11}, p. 226.

2. For example, a surety for the repayment of a debt shall be restricted only to its repayment and not to producing the debtor in person.

3. In the text: 'loss of chariot troops'.

4. In the text, interest rates are given per month. Since interest cannot be added to principal, there cannot be interest on interest and the annual rate is, therefore, a simple multiple of the monthly rate. If the rate is to be compounded, the APR (Annual Percentage Rate) for the four categories in the table will respectively be: 16%, 79.6%, 213.8% and 791.6%. The last two, even for trade transactions of high risk, are unlikely.

5. See {4.2.36}, on future stocks.

VIII.viii

1. E.g. cultivating a field abandoned by its owner.

2. The term 'forty neighbouring families' need not be taken to be a strict numerical condition but as a description of witnesses likely to be knowledgeable about the property and the seller.

3. See IV.i for widths of different types of roads.

4. *Sulkasthana*, a place where *sulka* or tolls and duties were collected. Since the customs house near the city gates is called *ghatikasthana* in {2.21.5}, Lost Property Offices could be set up in any number of places including the capital city, wherever there was an official authorized to collect duties, tolls and octroi.

5. By favourites of the king, etc. see {8.4.23} in II.iv.

VIII.ix

1. Compulsory purchase or take-over in public interest.

VIII.x

1. For a detailed discussion see Kangle Vol. III, pp. 185–188.

2. Mookerjee, *Chandragupta Maurya and his Times*, p.195. A more detailed extract from Arrian is in Kangle III, p. 187: 'All the Indians are free and not one of them is a slave...the Indians do not even use aliens as slaves, much less countrymen of their own.'

3. In most translations, the distinction made in the *Arthasastra* between *dasa, ahitaka* and *udaradasa* is not rigorously maintained and the term 'slave' is used indiscriminately. In this translation, *dasa* is always translated as 'slave', *ahitaka* as 'bonded labour' and *udaradasa* as 'working for maintenance'.

4. Translations of this part of the verse are contradictory. For example: 'Those who do not heed the claims of slaves etc., shall be taught their duty'—(Shamasastry) and 'The

King should enforce discipline on slaves...' - (Kangle). Is the King to protect the interests of the slaves or their masters?

5. The word used in this verse is *dasa* though the context is bonded labour. The meaning is not clear and the verse could be an interpolation.

6. 'Leavings of food', after eating; considered ritually polluted.

7. 'Cultivating for half the produce'.

8. 'made known to neighbours'.

VIII.xi

1. The exact stages, which are specified in the text, are only of specialised interest and are not translated here.

2. The organiser, sponsor, supplicant or beneficiary of the ritual and, sometimes, the actual performer, under the guidance of the priests.

3.'Not tending to the sacred fire, though owner of 100 cows'; 'not performing ritual sacrifices though owner of 1000 cows'.

VIII.xii

1. Though this verse follows immediately after the reference to the Chief Controller of Private Trade, it is more likely that the interrogation would have been conducted by a law officer.

2. '*vipralapantam*'—'bewailing' may mean either protesting one's innocence or falsely confessing for fear of torture.

3. The reference is to a story in the *Mahabharata* in which the sage refused to declare his innocence because he did not want to break his vow of silence.

4. Both meanings are possible.

5. {4.8.22} is somewhat obscure. It is not clear whether the eighteen include the four in {4.8.21} and, if so, what exactly are the fourteen in {4.8.22}. Here, the fourteen have been made up by considering the tying of leg and head and the tying of hand and foot as two separate items each.

6. See {3.12.38-51} above.

VIII.xiii

1. See note to these verses in Kangle II, p. 248 and note in Shamasastry p. 223.

2. The text also includes the offence of 'violating the sanctity of a Brahmin's kitchen'. This is considered by scholars to be an interpolation. See Kangle II p.285 note to {4.11.21}.

VIII.xv

1. Verses {4.12.36-40}, the first two being in prose form and later three in verse, are almost identical in content and have been amalgamated.

2. Such lenient punishment because they must have been 'mad' (i.e. taken leave of their senses) to do such a thing? '*Anatmanam*'—one without a soul or sense?

VIII.xvi

1. See similar punishments for guards who misbehave with women during curfew hours.

VIII.xvii

1. This verse occurs in the chapter on courtesans but may be of general applicability as well.

2. The three stages in the life of the twice-born (excepting the stage of a householder) when he does not own any property.

3. For soldiers, Highest SP.

4. Five different kinds of cruel murder are spelt out but the meanings are not clear.

5. Impaling on a stake is a special form of capital punishment which involves slow torture.

6. If the woman is pregnant, the sentence was executed a month after delivery of the baby.

7. Perhaps an interpolation, derived from the *Apasthambha Sutra*.

8. See {4.10.1}.

IX.ii

1. See 'Testing the Integrity of Ministers' in IV.ii. For details of the methods of testing, see next section.

2. A commentator says that ascetics with shaven heads were *shakyas* (Buddhists and Ajivikas) and those belonging to sects like the *pashupatas* had matted hair.

3 See below {4.4.3}.

4. These are spelt out in greater detail as follows: (i) and (ii) in IX.iii and (iii) and (iv) in IX.iv.

IX.iii

1. See courtesans employed on such duties in {2.27.4} in VII.vi.

2. See Notes on Translation No. 7.

3. For methods of dealing with discontent see III.v, Revolts and Rebellions.

4. Probably a god of importance to robbers and one in whose honour wine was offered generously.

IX.iv

1. For the system of *parokta* see {3.1.20,21} in VIII.iv.

2. See {5.1.15-18} in IX.iii for a similar trick.

3. See above {5.1.19}.

4. From what follows it is clear that the condemned man was dispensable. He may go free if the ruse succeeded and, if it failed, his life was forfeit.

5. See IV.iv for the eighteen *mahamatras*.

6. Similar to the methods recommended for drawing an enemy out of his fort in {13.2} in this section.

7. See also above {1.12.22} in IX.ii for a slightly different recomendation.

X.i

1. Arrian, the Greek historian, says: '... a sense of justice, they say, prevented any Indian king from attempting conquest beyond the limits of India'—see Kangle Vol.III, p.3.

X.ii

1. cf. {7.1.2} below.

2. Stable condition, stagnation, invariant condition are other equivalent meanings.

3. Literally 'with territory adjacent to that of the conqueror, [anywhere] on the boundary'.

4. Since contiguity is a source of enmity, two states having common borders with an intervening state, but no common border between them, are natural allies.

5. See Kangle, Vol. II, note to {6.2.21}.

6. Kangle (Vol. III, p.248, also Vol.II, note under {6.2.24}) considers that there are two variants of the theory of the circle of states. There is no need to postulate two different theories because {6.3.13-22} are just definitions. See {6.2.23}: 'Thus the elements (defined).' See also Notes on Translation No. 8.

7. See {8.3.2}, vices due to anger, causing verbal or physical injury, or destroying property. Same words used in both verses.

8. See {8.3.38}—vices from excessive desire for hunting, gambling, women or drink.

9 'One marched against'—i.e. against whom another king had started a campaign; see 'The Weak King', X.ix.

10. Literally, 'sitting'. Staying quiet and observing neutrality are other nuances. It also includes a pause after declaring war or making peace, as expalined in {7.4.2,3}.

11. Literally, 'marching'—i.e. going on a military expedition. Also includes mobilisation for war.

12. Seeking shelter, joining another king, forming an alliance.

13. This is logically impeccable. If war and peace are two policies, doing both and doing neither are also logical options implicit in them; making preparations for war is only a prior step to actually waging it; seeking help to preserve the peace or to assist in war is a corollary. Nevertheless, in the realm of practical politics, it is more convenient to treat the six as separate methods.

14. (iii) is atrributed to 'some teachers' in the text. Kautilya agrees with this view in {7.1.31}.

15. Literally, 'as in a fight between a wild dog and a boar'.

16. For surrendering with troops, see below {7.15.21ff}; also 'The Weak King'.

17. cf {10.3.26}.

18. See *Kutayuddha* {10.3}.

19. See Part IX.

20. For example, if proclaiming war alerts the enemy to dangers and is likely to make him more powerful during the waiting period; the king's own subjects are likely to become more restive; the economy is likely to suffer under mobilization; the advantages of trade lie more with peace than war.

21. See below {7.15.21ff}.

22. As defined in {7.13.25}.

23. See {7.1.32,33}.

24. See Notes on Translation No. 9.

25. Literally 'thorns'.

26. cf.modern usage: Envoy Extraordinary and Minister Plenipotentiary. See {1.9.1}.

27. The sentence *Yogasyachasrayah* can be interpreted either as resorting to clandestine practices or as being diligent in the performance of duties.

28. E.g. 'You know everything'.

X.iii

1. He will suffer the appropriate consequence by touching: fire or water—destruction; elephants, horses, chariots, forts and articles of war - being left defenceless; furrows, seeds, etc.— being denuded of prosperity.

2. This verse reverts to the usual technique of making a point by comparison of alternatives as between the conqueror and the enemy.

3. The terms used are defined in {9.4.5,6,16-22}.

4. In the text, *atisamdhi*, overreaching or outmanoeuvring treaty, with a nuance of trickery.

5. {7.8.17-18,20-21.24} are all similar and are merged here.

6. For explanations of these terms, see.XI.ii.

7. In the text 'in shoulder loads', i.e. in parts.

8. cf. {12.1.25}.

9. cf. Book 12, X x.below.

X.iv

1. 'From the times of the father and the grandfather'.

2. See {7.9.7,8} in X.v—Joint Activities—'Help given to a friend in difficulties cements the friendship firmly'.

3. cf. {7.9.2} in X.v.

4. The terms 'antagonist' and 'ally' in terms of contiguity of territory have been defined in {6.2.14,15}; the principles of using the four methods unequally, alternatively or in combination are described in {9.7.73-76} in I.iii.

5. See above; also {10.3, 12.4, 12.5 and 13}.

6. As described in {5.1}.

X.v

1. The word used in the text for this type of treaty, *sama*, is the same as the one for equal treaties, in the sense of equal bargaining power (see Treaties, X.iii). Nevertheless, to avoid confusion, we shall use 'similar' to distinguish it from the other type.

2. See {6.1.12, 7.9.38}.

3. For a detailed discussion of qualities of allies see.X.iv.

4. See {6.1.8} in II.ii.

5. {7.16.16} above in X.iv—'subjugated kingdoms'.

6. See {2.3.1,2}.

X.vi

1. 'Stay put'—i.e. staying quiet, one of the six options of foreign policy.

2. May lack other support such as an adequate treasury. His own prowess will make even a small army win successes. However mighty his army may be, a king without energy and enthusiasm will perish when confronted by a valiant enemy.

3.For definitions of different types of troops, see XI.II, Military Organization.

4. See {9.3.12} in III.v.

5. 'Thousand' and 'hundred' need not be be taken literally. The meaning is that even a manifold gain is not worth having if there is a danger of a revolt in the rear.

6. For definition of *saratva* (high value) and *satatya* (constant worth), see {7.12.16}.

7. cf. {7.17.8} on agreements with sureties.

8. See X.ix.

9. It is not clear why, in the context of a military expedition, *artha* is ranked higher than *dharma*.

X.vii

1. See {7.18.32,33} in X.iv.

2. See {7.18.36,40} in X.iv.

X.viii

1. cf. {2.9.21-23}; the definitions are given there in connection with servants of the state.

2. See {12.2.1-7}.

X.ix

1. The various steps of the method suggested for sowing dissension are not very clear. The starting point is to bribe the leader of the confederation. This is then to be used to create distrust between the leader and other members.

2. See {9.5 to 9.7} in Part IX and X.vi.

3. For compounded treason see {9.6.11 ff} in X.vi; also' The Weak King'.

X.x

1. '*Mantra*', usually good counsel in the sense of good advice, analysis and judgment, is here translated as 'diplomacy'. In this context, the word has the meaning of counsel, persuasion or instigation with the nuance of intrigue.

2. Text read as *anamatya sampada* instead of *ayatta sampada* as suggested by Kangle, note to {7.15.2,} Vol. II, p. 369.

3. The implication is that, in Kautilya's view, it is senseless to destroy oneself. A weak king, faced with overwhelming odds, shall seek peace immediately or do so after a fight. In any case, he must live to fight another day.

4. See chapter {5.5}, of the text in VI.iii on service with a king, particularly the section on survival.

5. *Mantrayuddha* is literally 'waging war by counsel'; however as {12.2.1} shows this method is a means of averting the attack by diplomacy. *Kutayuddha*—secret warfare— is of two types—{12.2.2-5}, and {10.3}.

6. One which kills in a fortnight or a month; recipe given in {14.1.6-8} [not translated].

7. For definition of permanent enemies and the relative merits of various types of land see X.v.

8. See {7.6.1,2,4-12} in III.ii 'Self-Control'.

9. Book 11 is primarily concerned with sowing dissension among the chiefs of an oligarchy (see X.ix), and there is no description of provoking internal rebellion.

10. See {13.2} in IX.iv.

11. See {1.21} in III.iv.

12. {12.5.42} is obscure; whether the attack is to be made before or after escaping, whose treacherous troops are to be instigated and how the army is to be kept concealed—none of these is clear. For one plausible explanation, see note to this verse, Kangle, Vol. II, p.473.

XI.ii

1. The phrases within square brackets are due to possible alternative readings of the text.

2. Assuming a length of 7 *aratnis*, or 10 1/2 ft, for a high quality elephant, the breadth and height will be 21 ft].

3. Skanda or Kartikeya.

4. Arabia, Bactria and Persia.

5. A month of 35 days—see the Appendix on Time, verse {2.20.52}.

6. For prescribed rations see Appendix 4.

7. See {7.10.34-37; 10.4.2}.

XI.iv

1. *Nayaka* (the City Commander), is mentioned in {5.3.8} in the salary list. The same designation is used for the Camp Superintendent probably because their duties, in the city and in the military camp, were similar.

2. Though the designation '*antapala*' is also used for a frontier governor, the context makes it clear that here the special responsibility of the officer in charge of the camp perimeter is meant.

XI.v

1. See Kangle Vol. I, p.234 note on verses {10.2.4-12} and Vol.II, note on p.435.

XI.vi

1. See {10.2.17} in XI.v.
2. Sacks of dry skins with pebbles in them.
3. As in 1 above, {10.2.17}.

XI.viii

1. {10.5.6}. See also {2.20.18} in Appendix 1.
2. {10.5.19} is ambiguous: 'thus the odd numbers make the ten unbalanced arrays'. Since Kautilya's arithmetic of permutations and combinations is always accurate, the ten can be made up only by assuming that the centre had only three chariots, one behind the other or that the wings and flanks could have 23 chariots, instead of the maximum 21. In any case, we cannot assume (i) that the wing and the flank has different numbers or (ii) that any combination of odd numbers (centre 9, wings 15) was possible; both of these will give rise to many more than 10 combinations.

XI.ix

1. How to do it is given in {13.1.3} in connection with laying a siege to capture the enemy's fort; see IX.iv.

XI.x

1. See also {9.6.35-41} in IX.iv.
2. The choice is made so as to please the enemy by seemingly attacking the conqueror while, at the same time, helping his true master by removing unreliable chiefs, towns or forces.
3. See also {9.6.35-41}.
4. See I.iii
5. See {1.10} in IX.iii.

APPENDICES

List of Appendices

Appendix 1

WEIGHTS, MEASURES AND TIME

[The degree of centralization of the Kautilyan state is apparent from the standardization of weights and measures. That such standardization should have been thought of nearly 2000 years ago is astonishing.]

LINEAR MEASURE

The basic linear measure is the '*angula*', though Kautilya gives subdivisions right down to the '*anu*'. The *angula* is defined, in {2.20.7}, as the middle-most joint of the middle finger of a man of average height and girth. It is generally accepted that the *angula* is three-quarters of an inch or about 19mm. In the conversion table below, only approximate equivalents in round figures in FPS and metric system are given; the <u>inter se</u> equivalence between the two modern systems is not mathematically accurate. Sometimes, a measure of the same name has different dimensions, depending on the use to which it is put. These are separately listed as 'Special measures of length'.

SUBDIVISIONS OF THE *ANGULA*: {2.20.2-6}

8 *anus*	1 chariot wheel particle
8 particles	1 *liksha* (nit)
8 *likshas*	1 *yuka* (louse)
8 *yukas*	1 barley middle
	(width of a grain of barley
	at its widest)
8 barley middles	1 *angula*.

Therefore, 1 *angula* = 32,768 *anus*.

MULTIPLES OF THE *ANGULA*: {2.20.8-10,12,18}

	1 *angula*	=3/4 in	=1.9cm
4 *angulas*	1 *dharnurgraha* (bow grip)	=3 in	=7.5cm

8 *angulas*	1 *dhanurmushti* (fist with thumb raised)	=6 in	=15.0 cm
12 *angulas*	1 *vitasti* (span - distance between the tips of a person's thumb and little finger when stretched out)	=9 in	=23 cm
2 *vitastis*	1 *aratni* (cubit) (also called *hasta*)	=18 in	=45 cm
4 *aratnis*	1 *danda* or 1 *dhanus* or 1 *nalika* or 1 *paurusha*	=6 ft	=180 cm

MEASURES FOR LONG DISTANCES: {2.20.21,22,25,26}

10 *dandas*	1 *rajju*	=60 ft	=18.25 m
2 rajjus	1 *paridesa*	=120 ft	=36.5 m
2000 *dhanus*	1 *goruta* (also called *krosa* in in {2.1.2})	=4000 yds or 2 1/4 miles	=3.66 km
4 *gorutas*	1 *yojana*	=9 miles	= nearly 15 km

[A possible reading is 1 *goruta* = 1000 *dhanus*, making a *Yojana* 4.5 miles or 7.5 km].

SPECIAL MEASURES OF LENGTH: {2.20.11,13-17,19,20}

sama, sala, pariraya, pada	*sama* used in battle arrays {10.5.3.4}. Use of others not known.	=10.5"	=26.5 cm
hasta (lengthened)	For balances and cubic measures and for surveying pastures	= 21"	= 52.5 cm
	For surveying timber forests	=40.5"	=103 cm
kisku or *kamsa*		=24"	=60 cm
kisku	For carpenter's sawing, for forts, camps and royal property	=31.5"	=80 cm
vyama	For ropes, surveying, digging of	=43"	=160 cm

paurusha	moats	=43"	=160 cm
dhanus	For roads and city walls	=6'9"	=2.05 m
	For placing archers in battle	7'6"	=2.25 m
paurusha	arrays		
	For sacrificial altars	=6'9"	=2.05 m
danda	For making gifts to	=12 ft.	=3.60 m
	Brahmins and guests		
	(=6 *kamsas*)		

SQUARE MEASURES: {2.20.23,24}

1 *nivartana*	A square of sides	32,400 sq ft or	3000 sq metres
	3 *rajjus*	3600 sq yds or 3/4 of an acre	or 0.3 hectares
1 *bahu*	a square of sides	4096 sq yds or	3425 sq metres
	32 *dandas*	0.85 acres	or 0.35 hectares

MEASURES OF CAPACITY

[As in the case of weights, measures of capacity were also made in four different standards. This was to enable the collection of the *Vyaji* (transaction tax) in kind without having to measure out the tax separately. Each successive measure was 6.25% smaller than the previous one, the highest being the measure for receipts into the Treasury and the lowest for payments towards royal personal expenditure. For explatnation, see V.ii, Sources of Revenue.

Revenue measure = the standard for receiving payments into the Treasury.

Trade measure = 6.25% less than the above (or 93.75% of the standard measure).

Payment measure = For payments out of the Treasury 12.5% less than the standard (i.e. 87.5 % of the standard).

Palace measure = For payments for royal expenditure 18.75% less than the standard (i.e. 81.25% of the standard).]

The standard measure, the revenue *drona*, is defined as the measure which will hold 200 *palas* of *masha* beans. {2.19.29}

[It is difficult to find modern equivalents of these measures since the volume is derived from the weight of beans. The weight of one bean is half that of a *gunja* berry, whose weight has been differently by different authors: Shamasastry—1 5/16 grains (op.cit., p. 115); Kangle—2 grains; Fleet—1.80 grains and Hemmy—1.8295 grains (Kangle, Vol. II, note to {2.19.2}, p. 134).]

The sub-division and multiples of the drona are:

4 *kudubas*	= 1 *prastha*
4 *prasthas*	= 1 *adhaka*
4 *adhakas*	= 1 *drona*
16 *dronas*	= 1 *khari*
20 *dronas*	= 1 *kumbha*
10 *kumbhas*	= 1 *vaha* (cartload)

{2.19.30-33}

The Chief Controller of Weights and Measures shall have standard capacity measures made for the above as well as for one-eighth *kuduba*, one-quarter *kuduba* and half a *kuduba*.   {2.19.45}

SPECIAL PROVISIONS

In the case of liquids, wine, flowers, fruits, husk, charcoal and lime, one quarter shall be given in addition to the measure (e.g. making 5 *kudubas* to a *prastha*, etc).   {2.19.35}

SPECIAL PROVISIONS FOR OIL AND GHEE

Measures

Ghee	21 *kudubas*	= 1 *ghatika*
	4 *ghatikas*	= 1 *varaka*
Oil	16 *kudubas*	= 1 *ghatika*
	4 *ghatikas*	= 1 *varaka*

{2.19.46}

Since ghee and oil have to be heated in order to facilitate measuring and pouring] the following extra quantites shall be paid out to compensate for heating loss

– for ghee, one thirty-second part
– for oil, one sixty-fourth part.

[Since some quantity of oil or ghee is likely to stick to the measure] an additional quantity of 1/50th shall also be paid out.

The compensations apply to sale by merchants to the public and to payments into the Treasury.   {2.19.43-44}

WEIGHTS

TROY WEIGHTS: {2.19.2-7}

	Gold	Silver	Diamonds
10 *masha* beans or 5 *gunja* berries	= 1 *mashaka*		
88 white mustard seeds		= 1 *mashaka*	
20 rice grains			= 1 *dharana*
16 *mashakas*	= 1 *Suvarna* or 1 *Karsha*	= 1 *dharana*	
4 *karshas*	= 1 *Pala*		

[Though *dharana* and *mashaka* are weights applicable to gold, silver and precious stones, they are not all the same, e.g. a silver *mashaka* is 2/5ths of a gold *mashaka*. See Kangle, Vol. II, note to {2.19.5,6}, p. 134.]

AVOIRDUPOIS WEIGHT: {2.19.19,20}

(For all goods except precious metals and stones)

[The basic weight is a *dharana*, which is the weight of 640 black (*masha*) beans, 320 *gunja* berries or 14,080 white mustard seeds. A rough estimate is that one *dharana* is equivalent to 3.5 grams.]

10 *dharanas*	= 1 *pala*	= 1 1/4 oz.	= 35 gm.
100 *palas*	= 1 *tula*	= 7 3/4 lbs.	= 3.5 kilos
20 *tulas*	= 1 *bhara*	= 154 lbs	= 70 kilos

STANDARD WEIGHTS

The Chief Controller of Weights and Measures shall have the following series of weights made:

1/2, 1, 2, 4 and 8 *mashakas* (for gold and silver)

1, 4, 8, 10, 20, 30, 40 and 100 *suvarnas* and *dharanas*.   {2.19.8,9}

COMPENSATION FOR USE OF PAN-LESS BALANCES

In the case of use of the steel-yard with movable fulcrum, an additional 5% shall be given for all commodities except meat, metals, salt and gems (to compensate for inaccuracies).   {2.19.24}

DIFFERENT WEIGHT SYSTEMS: {2.19.21,22}

[As in the case of measures, different weights were used for automatic collection of the transaction tax. Each successive weight was 5% less than the previous one. See table below. For the different balances used for each system, see under weighting machines later in this Appendix.]

	Objects weighed in	
	Tulas	Palas
Revenue - *Ayamani*	100 *palas*	10 *dharanas*
Trade	95 *palas*	9 1/2 *dharanas*
Payment	90 *palas*	9 *dharanas*
Palace expenditure	85 *palas*	8 1/2 *dharanas*

WEIGHING MACHINES

[Kautilya describes two different types of weighing instruments: (i) a balance with two pans and (ii) a movable-fulcrum steel-yard. The scales with two pans were no doubt similar to modern ones, a pointer indicating when the beam was level. The Kautilyan steel-yard was, however different from the modern steel-yard which works on the basis of a beam with unequal arms and a fixed fulcrum with the object to be weighed suspended at the end of the shorter arm and a counterpoise moved along a graduated scale. In the steel-yard described in the *Arthashastra* a fixed weight was suspended at one end, the object to be weighed at the other and the fulcrum moved along the graduated beam until it was level.]

Since standard officially stamped weights were in subdivisions of a *pala* and multiples of *palas* (1,2,3,4 and 10), the scales with two pans could only used to weigh quantities up to 10 *palas*. A steel-yard was used for weighing higher quantities.

To weigh different quantities, Kautilya specifies a total of 19 machines—ten sizes of two-scale balances, two different sizes of steel-yards (each in four categories depending on use) and a large wooden one for weighing very large quantities (e.g. firewood)]

<u>*Tula* - Balance with 2 scales with a pointer to indicate level beam</u>

(To weigh up to 10 *palas*)   {2.19.11}

Number	Weight of beam in *palas*	Length		
1	1	6 *ang*	= 4 1/2 in	= 11.5 cm
2	2	14 *ang*	10 1/2 in	= 27 cm
3	3	22 *ang*	= 16 1/2 in	= 42 cm
.	.	.	.	.
		and so on, + 8 *angulas,* or 6 in. or 15 cm each step.		
10	10	78 *ang*	= 58 1/2 in	= 150 cm

Samavritta - Moving fulcrum steel-yard   {2.19.12-16}
Metal beam to weigh from 1/4 *pala* to 100 *palas*
A counterweigh of 5 *palas* suspended at one end.

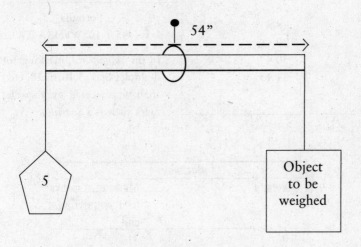

54"

5

Object to be weighed

Fig. 42 Movable Fulcrum Steel Yard
{2.19.17,18}

Metal Beam, with a counterweigh of 5 *palas*, to weigh from 100–200 *palas*.

BEAM MARKINGS FOR REVENUE MEASURE

[See Table next page.]

Samavritta		*Samavritta*	
Weight	Marking at inches from counterpoise end	Weight	Marking at inches from counterpoise end
0	21	20	36.5
1/4	21.36	30	39.9
1/2	21.71	40	42.1
3/4	22	50	43.75
1	22.4	60	45
2	24.7	70	46
3	24.9	80	46.75
4	26	90	47.4
5	27	100	47.9
6	28		
7	28.8		
8	29.6		
9	30.4		
10	31.15		

Formula

$$x=(945 + 108W)/(45 + 2W)$$

In the *samavritta*, markings of multiples of 5 (5,10,15,20, etc.) shall be indicated by a special mark such as a *Svastika*.

Parimani	
Weight	Marking at inches from counterpoise end
0	31.5
100	60.4
120	61.875
150	63.5
200	65.25

Wooden Weighing Machine {2.19.25}

Beam made of hardwood, of length - 12 ft or 3.60 m. Shall be provided with different sets of counterpoises and corresponding markings. It shall be supported on 'peacock's feet' (two posts, set 1 to 2 ft apart, with a top beam from which the balancing beam is to be suspended. See Figure 43.

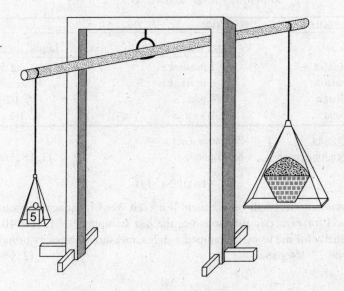

Fig. 43 Wooden Weighing Machine

WEIGHING MACHINE FOR DIFFERENT WEIGHT SYSTEMS {2.19.23}

In the case of the *Samavritta* and the *Parimani*, different weighing machines shall be made, corresponding to the purpose of weighing and using the appropriate set of weights.

	Samavritta				*Parimani*			
	Length			Weight of beam	Length			Weight of beam
	ang.	*in.*	*cm*	*Pala*	*ang.*	*in.*	*cm*	*Pala*
Revenue	72	54	137	35	96	72	183	70
Trade	66	49 1/2	126	33	[88	66	168	66
Payments	60	45	114	31	80	60	152	62
Palace	54	40 1/2	103	29	72	54	137	58]

[It may be noted that for the same length, the *Parimani* used a heavier (thicker) beam, since it was used for heavy weights of up to 200 *palas*].

PRICES OF STAMPED WEIGHTS,
MEASURES AND WEIGHING MACHINES

Capacity	Price	
	Dry measures	Liquid measures
kuduba	= 1 mashaka	2 mashakas
prastha	= 6 mashakas	12 mashakas
adhaka	3/4 pana	1 1/2 pana
drona	1 1/4 pana	2 1/4 panas
Weights	20 panas a set	
Weighing machines	6 2/3 panas	{2.19.36-39}

STAMPING FEE

The stamping fee shall be 1 *kakani* [for each weight, capacity measure or balance] for each day [of use] since the last stamping(?).   {2.19.40,42}

Penalty for use using unstamped weights, measure of capacity or balance shall be 27 1/4 panas.   {2.19.41}

TIME

NALIKA

The basic unit of time is a *nalika*, defined {2.20.35} as the time it takes for one *adhaka* (1.87 kg or litres) of water to flow out of a pot through a hole of the same diameter as that of a wire 4 *angulas* long made out of 4 *mashas* of gold. This would be a hole approximately 0.6 mm diameter (23 or 24 gauge wire).

Kangle gives the definition 'Two *nalikas* make a *muhurta*' while Shamasastry gives twelve *nalikas* as a *muhurta* making a *nalika* either 24 minutes or 4 minutes. We shall follow Kangle.

SUBDIVISIONS OF A NALIKA

	1 *Tuta*	= 6/100ths of a second
2 *Tutas*	= 1 *lava*	= 12/100ths of a second
2 *lavas*	= 1 *nimesha*	= 24/100ths of a second
5 *nimeshas*	= 1 *Kashta*	= 1.2 seconds
30 *Kashtas*	= 1 *Kala*	= 36 seconds
40 *Kalas*	= 1 *nalika*	= 24 minutes
2 *nalikas*	= 1 *muhurta*	= 48 minutes
15 *muhurtas*	= (a day or a night)	= 12 hours

{2.20.29-34,36}

LENGTH OF DAYS AND NIGHTS

Day and night of equal length (15 *muhurtas* each) occur in the month of *Chaitra* (vernal equinox) and *Asvayuja* (autumnal equinox).

The increase and decrease of daytime is as follows:

From the vernal equinox daytime increases for 3 months to summer solstice (the longest day—18 *muhurtas*—14 hrs 24 minutes)

From the summer solstice daytime decreases for 3 months to autumnal equinox (equal day of 15 *muhurtas*, 12 hours)

From the autumnal equinox, daytime further decreases for 3 months to the winter solstice (the shortest day, 12 *muhurtas*, 9 hrs 36 minutes)

From the winter solstice, daytime increases for 3 months to the vernal equinox.   {2.20.37,38}

MEASURING TIME

During the day, time was measured by a sundial with a gnomon (central rod casting the shadow) of length 12 *angulas* (9"). No shadow indicated noon. Lengths of the shadow of 27", 9", 3" before and after mid-day, divided the day into eight parts.   {1.19.7,8}

In the month of *Asadha*, the gnomon does not cast a shadow at midday. From then on, the shadow at midday increases by 2 *angulas* (1 1/2' ') a month during the six monthly period *Sravana* to *Pausha*. From *Magha* to *Ashada*, the midday shadow decreases by 2 *angulas* each month.

{2.20.10,41,42,39,40}

CALENDAR

15 days (and nights)	=	*Sukla* fortnight (waning moon)
		Bakula fortnight (waxing moon)
2 fortnights	=	1 month
		Special categories of months:
		Work month = 30 days and nights
		Solar month = 30 1/2 days and 30 nights
		Lunar month = 29 1/2 days and 30 nights
		Sidereal month = 27 days and nights
		Work month for the infantry = 32 days and nights
		Work month for the cavalry = 35 days and nights
		Work month for the elephant corps = 40 days and nights

2 months	=	1 Season
	=	*Dakshinayana*

Varsha (rainy) - *Sravana* (July/Aug.) and
Praushtapada (Aug./Sep.)
Sharat (autumn) - *Asvayuja* (Sep./Oct.)
and *Kartika* (Oct./Nov.)
Hemanta (winter) - *Marghasirsha* (Nov./
Dec.) and *Pausha* (Dec./Jan.)
Uttarayana
Sisira (frosty) - *Magha* (Jan./Feb.) and
Phalguna (Feb./Mar.)
Vasantha (spring) - *Caitra* (Mar./Apr.)
and *Vaishaka* (Apr./May)
Grishma (summer) - *Jyeshtamulya*
(May/June) and *Ashada* (June/July)

3 seasons		1 *ayana*	
2 *ayanas*	=	1 year	
5 years	=	1 *Yuga*	{2.20.43-64}

CALENDAR ADJUSTMENT

The solar day is longer than the standard day by 1/60th; thus every two months, there is a loss of one day. Likewise, the lunar day is shorter than the standard day by 1/30th, causing a loss of one day every two months.

Thus every two and a half years (30 months) an intercalary month has to be added, the first in the summer and the second at the end of the five year period.   {2.20.65-66}

Appendix 2

COMMODITIES

{2.11} contains the most comprehensive list of commodities, particularly three of the four types mentioned in I.iii—precious stones, high valued commodities and those of low value. These lists are not translated in full in this Appendix partly because they are mainly classifications indicating the quality of the product from different regions and partly becauese the meaning is often not clear. The same applies to the comprehensive list of forest products, particularly varieties of timber in {2.17}; those interested may consult Shamasastry, who has given the botanical names for most of these. Agricultural products are found in {2.15} and livestock products in {2.29}.

RATNA, SARA, PHALGU AND *KUPYA*

RATNA AND *SARA*

Ratna (gems and precious stones)		Sara (articles of high value)	
Diamonds	2.11.37-41	Sandal wood	2.11.43-56
Pearls	2.11.2-5	Aloe	2.11.57-60
Gems in general	2.11.28,33,34	Incense, camphor and oil additives	2.11.61-71
Rubies	2.11.29		
Beryl	2.11.30		
Sapphire	2.11.31		
Pure crystal	2.11.32		
Coral	2.11.42		

{2.11.6-27}
Jewellery of various types; varieties of pearl strings in necklaces, headbands, bracelets, waistbands and anklets, with or without gems, strung with gold.

A <u>good diamond</u> is one which is big, heavy, hard (does not shatter when hit), regular in shape, capable of scratching a vessel and reflecting light brilliantly in all directions. That without sharp edges, is uneven and asymmetric is bad. **{2.11.40,41}**

A good pearl is big, round, without a flat surface, lustrous, white, heavy, smooth and properly perforated. The following are bad pearls: lentil shaped, triangular, shaped like a tortoise (with a flat side), semi-spherical, with more than one layer on the surface, doubled, scratched, with a rough surface, spotted, shaped like a gourd, dark brown, blue or badly perforated.   {2.11.4,5}

Good gems are hexagonal, rectangular or circular in shape, pure in colour, easily settable in jewellery, unblemished, smooth, heavy, lustrous, transparent and reflecting light from inside. Any gem of faint colour, lacking lustre, grainy, blemished, with holes in it, cut badly or scratched is bad.   {2.11.33,34}

The best sandal wood is light, smooth, moist, oily like ghee, with a pleasant smell, absorbed by the skin, not overpowering, not fading in colour, cooling and pleasant to the touch.   {2.11.56}

Good aloe is heavy, smooth, of pleasant long lasting smell, burning slowly without a thick smoke, of uniform fragrance and not friable (i.e. not easily removed by rubbing).   {2.11.60}

Good incense, camphor and mixing substances have qualities similar to those of good sandal wood and aloe, retain their qualities when mixed with their substances and give a long lasting fragrance even when formed into a paste, boiled or burnt.   {2.11.71,72}

PHALGU

Articles of low value
Skins and furs   {2.11.73-95}
The best are soft, smooth and hairy.   {2.11.96}
Woollen articles
Blankets (both natural and dyed), head scarfs, blankets for horses and elephants, saddle cloth, bedspreads, undershirts for armour, floor covering.

May be white, all red, partly red or undyed; may be woven, knotted in piles or strings sown together.

The best are soft, shiny (like a wet surface) and made of fine yarn.

The ones from Nepal are water-proof.

Woollen cloth can also be made of hair other than lambswool or wool from sheep.   {2.11.97-106}
Silk and silk fabrics   {2.11.107-114}
Cotton fabrics   {2.11.115}

KUPYA—FOREST PRODUCTS

<u>Timber</u> like Teak, Mimosa, Pine, hardwoods and Sal. Twenty varieties are listed in {2.17.4}, for most of which botanical names are given by Shamasastry.

<u>Varieties of Bamboos and reeds</u> including types of bamboo for making bows and flutes and reeds of large diameter are listed in {2.17.5}.

<u>Creepers</u>—{2.17.6}

<u>Fibrous plants</u>—e.g. hemp, listed in {2.17.7}.

<u>Rope-making material</u>—{2.17.8}.

<u>Leaves used for writing</u>—{2.17.9}.

<u>Flowers for extracting colouring material</u>—{2.17.10}.

<u>Medicinal plants</u>—{2.17.11}.

<u>Poisonous plants</u>—{2.17.12}.

ANIMAL PRODUCTS

<u>Poisons</u>—particularly snakes and poisonous insects—{2.17.12}.

<u>Useful products</u>—skins, bones, bile, tendons, eyes, teeth, horns, hooves and tails—{2.17.13}.

<u>Metals</u>—Iron, copper, *Vritta* (?), bronze, lead, tin, *Vaikrantaka* (?) and brass—{2.17.14}.

<u>Containers</u> - Vessels made of bamboo, cane or clay - {2.17.15}.

<u>By-products</u>—Charcoal, husks and ashes—{2.17.16}.

CULTIVATED CROPS
[List compiled from {2.15}]

<u>Grains</u>	*Sali* rice, *Vrihi* rice.
	Wheat
	Barley
	Kodrava
	Priyangu (millet)
<u>Lentils and Beans</u>	*Mudga, Masha, Saibya, Udaraka, Varaka, Kulutha*
<u>Oil seeds</u>	Sesame, safflower, linseed, mustard
<u>Creeper plants</u>	Pepper, Grapes, Pumpkins
<u>Vegetables</u>	Vegetables, bulbous roots, other edible roots
<u>Others</u>	Perfumery plants
	Medicinal plants and herbs, *Usira* (?),
	Hribera (?), *Pindaluka* (?)
<u>Green plants for fodder</u>	
<u>spices</u>	Long pepper, black pepper, ginger, cumin seed, White mustard, coriander, anise. {**2.15.20**}

PROCESSED PRODUCTS

Dried fish and meat		{2.15.21}
Oils:	Butter, ghee, edible oil	{2.15.13}
Sugars:	Treacle, molasses, jaggery, powdered sugar, sugar candy	{2.15.14}
Salts:	Rock salt, sea-salt, muriate of soda, muriate of lime; salt petre, borax, salt from saline water.	{2.15.16}
Honey:	Bees honey, grape juice.	{2.15.16}
Vinegar:	Made from sugarcane juice, jaggery, honey, grape juice, molasses and sour fruits infused with a decoction of myrobalan extract and kept for a month, six months or a year.	{2.15.17}
Sour fruit juices:	Made from tamarind, lemon, pomegranate, myrobalan, lime and similar material.	{2.15.18}
Sour liquids:	Yoghurt, sour gruel, etc.	{2.15.19}

CONVERSION RATIOS

GRAINS AND PULSES

Type	Yield when dehusked or hulled	Yield when cleaned and pounded into flour	Yield when cooked
Rice			
Sali	3/8	1 1/2 times	5 times
Kodava	1/2	"	3 times
Vrihi	1/2	"	4 times
Varaka	2/3	"	3 times
All varieties		Parboiling 1 1/2 times	Fried rice double
Wheat	No change	1 1/5	Fried 1 1/5
Millets			
Priyangu	11/18		3 times
Udaraka	No change		3 times

Barley	No change	Double When half cooked for animals, 1 1/2 times	Fried - double
Cleaned Sesame	No change		
Beans	No change	7/8	Soaked - double sprouted - 3 times
Peas		3/4	
Legumes		1/2	
Lentils		2/3	Flour (*sattu*) 1 1/2 times

OIL EXTRACTION

Oilseed	Yield
Linseed	1/2
Sesame and similar	1/4
All others	1/5

SPINNING

Cotton and flax—yield of yarn is 1/5th.   {2.15.25-41}

BY-PRODUCTS

Charcoal and husks to be used in metal workshops and for plastering walls.

Broken grain to be given to labourers, broth makers and cooked food vendors.   {2.15.60,61}

Appendix 3

DOMESTICATED AND WILD ANIMALS

CATTLE

COWS		BULLS	
Dhenu	Milch cow	*Pungava*	Male
Pashtauhi	Cow in season	*Vatsa*	Calf
Garbini	Pregnant	*Vatsatara*	Weaned calf ?
Vatsika	Calf	*Damya*	Young bulls, tameable
Vatsatari			
Tara	Heifer	*Vahija*	Draught bullock
Aprajata	Not yet borne a calf	*Vrsha Ukshana*	Stud bulls
Vandhya	Sterile?		
Jaradgu	Aged cow		

Mahisha—buffaloes		Other domesticated animals
Yugavahana	Yoked draught	Horses
Sakatavaha	Cart puller	Camels
Vrishaba	Stud	Donkeys
Sunamahisha	Slaughtered for meat	Sheep and goats
Prishtaskand-avahina	Load carriers	

{2.29.4,8}

ANIMAL PRODUCTS

Ghee

Normal yield of ghee from 1 drona of milk:

Cow's milk	1 prastha
Buffaloes milk	1 1/5 prastha
Goat and sheep's milk	1 1/2 prastha

Other products

Kurchika—Cheese (to be supplied to the army)

Kilata—Whey (mixed with oil cake, used as animal feed)

Butter—removed buttermilk—Not for human consumption, to be fed to dogs and pigs.

Wool: Of sheep and goats   {2.29.27-29,41}

In all cases, the actual yield shall be ascertained by tests, because the quantity of milk obtained and its butter content are determined by the nature of the soil and the quality of the grass and water. {2.29.35,37}

WILD ANIMALS

Dvipi	Leopard	*Gavaya*	Gayal
Riksha	Bear	*Srimara*	Deer
Simha	Lion	*Seraka*	Dolphins?
Vyaghra	Tiger	*Simsumara*	Porpoise ?
Khanga	Rhinoceros	*Godha*	Alligator ?
Gomriga	Bison	*Chamara*	?

{2.17.13}

By-products, such as hair, skin, bladder, bile, tendons, teeth, hooves and horns, of the following animals are classified as useful products from the forest.   {2.29.25}

Appendix 4

RATIONS

CIVILIANS

An Arya male	One *prastha* rice, one quarter *prastha* broth, one *kuduba* butter or oil, one quarter *kuduba* salt
A non-Arya male	One *prastha* rice, one-sixth *prastha* broth, half a *kuduba* oil, one quarter *kuduba* salt
Women	three-quarters of the ration for the corresponding male
Children	half the ration for the corresponding male {2.15.43-46}

DEFENCE SERVICES

People

Infantry men	8 *adhakas*
Chiefs	7 *adhakas*
Queens and princes	6 *adhakas*
Kings	5 *adhakas* or 1 *prastha* of unbroken cleaned rice grains

{2.15.42}

Ingredients for cooking

For 20 palas of fresh meat	Half a *kuduba* oil, one *pala* salt, one *pala* sugar, two *dharanas* spices and half a *prastha* yoghurt
For vegetables	One and half times above quantities
For dried meat	Double the above.

{2.15.47-49}

Elephants

12 *adhakas* of cleaned rice are obtained from 5 *dronas* or 20 *adhakas* of paddy.

Young elephants	12 *adhakas*
Vicious elephants	11 *adhakas*

Riding elephants	10 *adhakas*
War elephants	9 *adhakas*

Rations for elephants are calculated by multiplying its winter rations by its height. For example, an elephant of seven *aratnis* (10 1/2 ft or 3.15 m) will need seven units.

Unit ration per month

Food

Rice grains	1 *drona*
Oil	1/2 *adhaka*
Ghee	3 *prasthas*
Salt	10 *palas*
Meat(?) fruit pulps(?)	50 *palas*
For wetting the food	1 *adhaka* of juice or
	2 *adhakas* of curds
Green fodder	2 *bharas*
Dry grass	2 1/2 bharas
leaves, plants	As much as they will eat
Invigorating drink	1 *adhaka* liquor and
	10 *palas* sugar, or 2
	adhakas milk

Other items

Oil for smearing on limbs	1 *prastha*
Oil for the head and for the lamp	1/8 *prastha*

Special Provisions

An elephant which is beyond the stage of rutting shall be given the same rations as the normal rations of an elephant one *aratni* shorter.

The above are for top quality elephants. An elephant of middling quality shall have ration three-quarters of the above and one of low quality, half.

{2.31.12-15}

Cubs shall be fed milk and green fodder. {2.31.16}

Rations for elephant attendants

The doctor, the stall cleaner and the cook shall be given free [daily?] ration of 1 *prastha* boiled rice, salt, a cupful of oil and 2 *palas* of sugar. All, except the doctor, shall be given, in addition, 10 *palas* of meat.

{2.32.17}

<u>Horses (standard rations per month)</u>

Sali rice, *Vrihi* rice, barley or *priyangu* (soaked or parboiled)	2 *dronas*
Fat	1 *prastha*
Salt	5 *palas*
Meat (?) fruit pulp (?)	50 *palas*
For wetting the food	1 *adhaka* of juice or 2 *adhakas* or curds
Sugar	5 *palas*
Liquor (or milk)	1 *prastha*

{2.30.18}

Proportions for different types

Standard rations	3/4 standard rations	1/2 standard rations
Best types of riding horse; chariot horses; stallions of medium	Medium type of riding horses and stallions of lowest type	Lowest type

{2.30.20-22}

3/4 of each for mares and mules	{2.30.23}
1/2 of each for foals	{2.30.24}

<u>Special rations</u>

To make tired horses eat after a long journey or bearing heavy loads		1 *prastha* of fat as enema *kuduba* of fat for the nose 1/2 *bhara* of green fodder or 1 *bhara* of grass (or a horse to be bedded down on grass six *aratnis* (in circumference). {2.30.19}
For mares giving birth:	First 3 days after giving birth	1 *prastha* of ghee
	Next 10 days	1 *prastha* of barley meal Mixture of ghee and medicine
	After 13 days	Boiled barley or beans, fodder according to season.
Foals	After 10 days up to 6 months	1 *kuduba* barley meal 1/4 *kuduba* ghee 1 *prastha* milk

After six months	1 *prastha* of barley
up to 3 years	for 1 month, 1 1/2 *prasthas*
	next month and so on.
Fourth year	1 *drona* of barley, etc.
In fourth or fifth	
year shall be treated	
as an adult horse.	{2.30.11-13}

DOMESTICATED ANIMALS

Bullocks	1 drona of *masha* beans or *pulaka* (cooked barley) and the rest as for horses.	{2.15.51}
	Special Ration: 1 *tula* of oil, or 10 *adhakas* of broken grains and bran.	
Buffaloes and camels	2 *tulas* of oil cake, or 20 *adhakas* of broken grains and bran	{2.15.52,53}

Special rations

Trained bullocks used for pulling carts	In addition to abundant grass and water:
	1/2 *bhara* of green forage, 1 *bhara* of grass, 1 *tula* oil-cake, (or) 10 *adhakas* of broken grains and bran, 5 *palas* rocksalt, (1 *Kuduba* oil for the nose), 1 *prastha* to drink, 1 *tula* fruit pulp, 1 *adhaka* yoghurt, 1 *drona* of barley or cooked beans, 2 *drona* milk or 1/2 *adhaka* of fermented liquor, 1 *prastha* of fat, 10 *palas* of sugar, 1 *pala* ginger.
Mules, cows, donkeys	3/4 of above
Buffaloes, camels	Double the above

Buffaloes used for ploughs, according to the work done, Cows suckling calves, according to the milk yield.	{2.29.43-47}

OTHER ANIMALS

Donkeys, spotted deer, real deer	1/2 *drona* of *masha* beans or *pulaka*	{2.15.54}
Smaller deer	1 *adhaka* of *masha* beans or *pulaka*	{2.15.55}

Goats, rams, boars	1/2 *adhaka* of above or 1 *adhaka* of broken grain and bran	{2.15.56}
Dogs	1 *prastha* boiled rice	{2.15.57}
Swans, herons, peacocks	1/2 *prastha* of boiled rice	{2.15.58}
For other beasts, birds and wild animals	The Chief Superintendent of Warehouses shall make an estimate from one meal eaten by them.	{2.15.59}

The amount of firewood required for cooking rice is 25 *palas* for every *prastha* of rice.   {2.19.26,27}

Appendix 5

METALLURGY

ORES

The heavier the ore, the greater will be the quality of metal in them.

{2.12.7}

The following ores are mentioned by Kautilya:

(i) <u>Gold-bearing liquids</u> are viscous, clear and heavy. [The colours of such ores are described by numerous examples in {2.12.2}. They spread on the water in a thin film, absorb mud and dirt and can form amalgams with copper or silver, up to hundred times its own weight {2.12.3}.]

(ii) Liquid gold-bearing ores shall not be confused with <u>bitumen</u> which looks similar but has the wrong smell and taste {2.12.4}.

(iii) <u>Solid gold ores</u>, whose colour is described by numerous examples in {2.12.5}, do not shatter when heated but give off lots of smoke and foam. These can also be used for forming amalgams with copper or silver.

(iv) The colour of <u>silver ores</u> is described by examples in {2.12.6}. These ores, [usually] assocated with lead and antimony, smell like raw flesh. When, broken, the silver sparkles as white lines in black or black on white. These too do not split when heated but give off foam and smoke.

(v) <u>Copper ores</u> are heavy, greasy, soft and tawny, green or reddish in colour {2.12.12}.

(vi) <u>Lead ores</u> are black, pigeon-coloured or yellow and smell like raw flesh {2.12.13}.

(vii) <u>Tin ores</u> are either grey or brick-colour {2.12.14}.

(viii) <u>Iron ore</u> is reddish {2.12.15}.

(ix) <u>*Vaikrantaka* ore (?)</u> {2.12.16}

(x) <u>Gem ore</u> is hard, cold, light coloured, smooth, clear, lustrous and makes a sound when struck {2.12.17}.

METALLURGY

Verses {2.12.8,9} give details of chemicals to be used in smelting ores.

Verses {2.12.10,11} provide details of softening and hardening metals.

The sources and qualities of <u>gold</u> are given in {2.13.3-4,25-27}, its purification in {2.13.5,6} and softening in {2.13.7-9}.

When gold is cut, if the cut section is of uniform colours, it is pure gold. If it is veined blue or black, it is impure. When heated, if the colour is uniform inside and out, it is pure {2.13.25-27}.

The sources and qualities of <u>silver</u> are given in {2.13.10-12,14} and its purification, by adding one-fourth part lead, in {2.13.13}.

<u>Purifying gold:</u> Impure gold shall be purified by repeatedly smelting with lead, using four times as much lead as the [suspected] impurity. If too much lead has been added and the gold becomes brittle, the lead shall be removed by smelting with dried cowdung. If the gold is brittle due to other impurities, it shall be annealed by quenching it in sesame oil {2.13.6-8}.

The sources and qualities of <u>touchstones</u> are given in {2.13.20,21}.

Coloured precious metal:

<u>White Silver {2.13.49}:</u> After purifying 17 times insert 1/64 to 1/8 in silver as colouring agent {2.13.51-57}.

<u>Ornamental gold:</u> of different colours {2.14.51-57}.

Precious metal work:

Setting, stringing with beads and making solid or hollow objects are ways of working with precious metals {2.13.37-40}.

<u>Jewellery:</u> A good ornament is one which is uniform in colour, symmetrical, with solid beads, strongly made, well-polished, not artificially gilded, well-proportioned, pleasant to wear, not gaudy, full of lustre, beautifully shaped, even and captivating to the eye and the mind {2.13.60,61}.

<u>Setting:</u> the amount of metal in the base of the setting shall be twice that used for the side {2.13.38,41}.

Substituting one-quarter of the silver by copper is one way of cheating by goldsmiths and silversmiths {2.13.42}.

<u>Gold plating:</u> Copper is to be plated with equal amounts of gold; silver with half the amount or with a quarter of the amount using a chemical solution (of vermilion) {2.13.44-46}.

<u>Enamelling:</u> On gold (colours blue, yellow, white, green, parrot feather and black) {2.13.47,48}.

Appendix 6

PROFESSIONS

Over one hundred and twenty separate professions are listed in the *Arthashastra*, some categories being more detailed than others. For example, the lists of entertainers, personal attendants and elephant attendants are much longer than other categories. In fact, the lists of entertainers and personal attendants and elephant attendants are much longer than other categories. In fact, the lists of entertainers and personal attendants often appear as almost identical strings, for the reason that these were not only true professions but were also used as cover by clandestine agents. The number of times a profession is mentioned in the text is no indication of its numerical strength in the population. Farmers, who must have been the most numerous, are mentioned only five times in the text. Labourers are called *karmaka* or *karmanta* in general but the category also included *vishti*, those providing their labour free in lieu of fines. *Karu* (artisan) {2.35.4} and *karushilpi* (artisans and craftsmen) {3.13.30 and 5.3.16} are also general terms. Experts in any profession are termed *tajjata* {e.g. 2.11.1, 2.12.1}. *Kushala* is used in the special sense of an expert acting as arbitrator in {4.1.21}. The term *vaidehaka* for trader or merchant, occurs in many places, both for a genuine trader and for a clandestine agent disguised as one.

ARTISANS, CRAFTSMEN AND PROFESSIONAL SERVICES

Artist/sculptor	*Shilpi*	{1.18.12}
Barber	*Napita*	
Basketmaker	*Medaka*	{2.24.3}
Carpenter	*Kuttaka*	{2.24.3}
Engineers	*Vardhaki*	{5.3.12,, 10.1.1,17}
Goldsmith	*Suvarnakara, kanchanakaru*	
Leather worker	*Charmakara*	{2.13.3, 4.1.26, 5.2.48}
Potter	*Ayaskara*	
Rope maker	*Rajjuvartaka*	{2.24.3}

Smith/blacksmith	*Karmara*	{2.24.3}
Tailor	*Tunnavaya*	{4.1.25}
Maker of straps and bindings	*Varmakara*	{4.1.14-18}
Washerman	*Rajaka*	{4.1.8-13}
Weaver	*Tantuvaya*	

ENTERTAINERS

Lists (*nata-nartaka-gayana-vadaka-vagjivana-kushilava-plavaka-saubika-charana*) are in {2.27.25} and {1.12.9} (up to *kushilava*).
    Entertainers in general - *kushilava* - {1.18.12, ,2.27.25, 3.13.30, 4.1.58}.
    Actresses, in general - *rangopajivi*
    Independent prostitute? - *rupajivi*, one who lives by her beauty.
    Where verse reference is not given in the third column of the table below, see {1.12.9} or {2.27.25}.

Acrobat	*Plavaka*	
Actor/actress	*Nata*	
Bard/praise singer	*Sutamagadha*	{5.3.13}
Conjurer	*Saubhika*	
Dancer	*Nartaka*	
Dancer?	*Talavacara*	{3.4.22}
Juggler/clown	*Kuhaka*	{4.1.65}
Musician	*Vadaka*	
Prostitute/courtesan	*Ganika*	{2.27}
Prostitute under a courtesan	*Ganikadasi*	{2.27}
Reciter of *Puranas*	*Pauranika*	13.1.7
Singer	*Gayana*	
Story teller	*Vagjivana, kathavaka*	{1.18.12, 3.13.30, 4.8.15}
Trumpeter	*Turyakara*	{5.3.15}
Wandering minstrel	*Charana*	{3.4.22, 4.1.62, 3.13.30}

AGRICULTURE, FISHERIES AND ANIMAL HUSBANDRY
{2.35.4}

Buffalo herdsman	*Pindaraka*	{2.29.2}
Churner	*Manthaka*	{2.29.2}
Conch/pearl fishermen	*Sanka, mukta grahinah*	{2.28.5}
Cowherd	*Gorakshaka, gopala, gopalaka*	{2.35.4, 3.4.22, 3.13.28, 4.5.15}

Farmer	*Karshaka*	{2.35.4, 3.13.28}
Fishermen	*Matsyabandhaka*	{3.4.22}
Flower garden watchman	*Shandapala*	{2.24.28}
Hunter guard	*Lubdhaka*	{2.29.2, 3.4.22}
Milker	*Dohaka*	{2.29.2}
Orchard watchman	*Vatapala*	{2.24.28}

JEWELLERS AND THEIR ASSISTANTS

Beadmakers	*Prishtakaru*	{2.13.33}
Blowers	*Dhamayaka*	{2.13.33}
Enamellers	*Tapaniyakaru*	{2.13.33}
Gemsetters	*Kanchanakaru*	{2.13.33}
Gilders, platers	*Tvashtrakaru*	{2.13.33}

ASTROLOGERS, ETC.

{mainly in 5.3.13; 13.1.7}

Astrologer	*Mauhurtika*	also in {10.1.1, 10.3.44,
Intuitionist	*Ikshanika*	13.1.7}
Reader of omens	*Naimittika*	
Soothsayer	*Kartantika*	
Attendants of above	*Sachivyakara*	

DOCTORS/MIDWIFES

Physician	*Chikitsaka*
Midwife	*Sutika*

SHIPPING
{2.28.13}

Bailer	*Utsechaka*
Captain	*Sasaka*
Steersman	*Niryamaka*
Rope and hook handler	*Dhattarasmigrahaka*

WORKERS IN STOREHOUSES
{2.15.63}

Accountants	*Salakapratigrahaka*
Labourer	*Karmaka*
Measurers	*Mayaka/mapaka*
Slave	*Dasa*
Supervisors of receipts and deliveries	*Dayaka/dapaka*
Sweeper	*Marjaka*
Watchman	*Rakshaka*
Weighman	*Dharaka*

ELEPHANT HANDLERS
{2.32.16-18, 2.2.10}

Attendants	*Parikarmika*
Attendants to riders	*Adhorana*
Border guards	*Sainika*
Cook	*Vidyapachaka*
Elephant forest guard	*Nagavanapala*
Expert riders	*Arohaka*
Feeder	*Yavashika*
Grooms, decorators	*Aupacharika*
Mahout	*Hastipaka*
Night guard	*Aupasyaka*
Stable cleaner	*Kutirakshaka*
Tetherer	*Padapashika*
Tracker	*Vanacharika*
Trainer	*Ankastha*
Veterinary doctor (elephant)	*Chikitsaka*

HANDLERS OF HORSES
{2.30,42-44}

Cook	*Vidhapachaka*
Expert in poison antidotes	*Jangulividha*
Feeder	*Yavashika*
Groom	*Sutragrahaka*
Mane trimmer	*Keshakara*
Saddler/yoker of horse to chariot	*Ashvabandhaka*
Stable superintendent	*Ashvavaha*
Stall cleaner (maintenance man)	*Sthanapalaka*
Trainer	*Yogyacharya*
Veterinary (horse) doctor	*Chikitsaka*

FOOD VENDORS
{2.36.8}

Baker	*Aapupika*
Cooked meat seller	*Pakvamamsika*
Drinking hall attendant	*Prapavika*
Rice vendor	*Audanika*
Wine seller	*Soundika*

ATTENDANTS {3.13.30}		KING'S ATTENDANTS {5.3.12,13,17}	
Attendants (Aupasthayika) in {2.32.16}.	in general	Animal breeder Attendant	Yoniposhaka Parikarmaka
Barber	Kalpaka	Bodyguard	Palaka
Bath attendant	Snapaka	Charioteer	Rathika
Bed maker	Astharaka	Deputy to purohita	Purohitapur- usha
Cleaner	Charaka	Horse trainer	Asvamadhaka
Cook	Paricharaka	King's mahout	Aryayukta-
Cook; waiter	Sudaralika	Labour foreman	Vishtibandh-
Shampooer	Samvahaka	Miner	Sailakanaka
Sweeper	Pamsudhavaka	Trainer	Anikasthaka
Valet	Prasathaka	Valet	Aupashayika
Water bearer	Udakaparich- araka	Valet	Aupasthayika

HUNTERS AND FOWLERS

Hunter	Lubhaka	{3.4.22,10.1.11, etc.}
Hunter with hounds	Svaganina, Vyadha	{4.5.15}
Snake catcher	Sarpagraha	{2.24.3}

WHITE COLLAR WORKERS
{5.3.14}

Accountant	Sankhyayaka	{5.3.14}
Clerk	Lekhaka	{5.3.14}

Yukta, upayukta, tatpurusha, mahamatras, adhyakshas, accountants, auditors, etc. are explained in the main body of the translation.

DEFENCE SERVICES

Armed personnel	Ayudhiya	
Army doctor	Chikitsaka	{10.3.47}
Technician	Yantrika	
Warrior	Yodha	{10.3.43}

APPENDIX 7

NOMENCLATURE OF HOLDERS OF STATE OFFICE

Designation	No.	Kangle {1.12.6}	Kangle {5.3}	No.	Shamasastry {1.12.6}	Shamasastry {5.3}	R.K. Mookerji {5.3}	No.	This Translation Throughout
Ritvik		Sacrificial Priest			Sacrificial Priest				Officiating Priest
Acharya			Preceptor			Teacher			King's Guru
Mantri Amatya	1	Councillor	Minister	1	Minister	Minister	Prime Minister	1	Councillor
Purohita	2	Chaplain		2	Priest		Chief Priest	2	Purohita
Senapati	3	Commander-in-Chief		3	Commander of the Army		Commander-in-Chief	3	Chief of Defence
Yuvaraja	4	Crown Prince		4	Heir Apparent (Prince)		Crown Prince	4	Crown Prince
Dauvarika	5	Chief Palace Usher		5	Door Keeper		Warden of the Palace	5	King's Chamberlain
Antarvamsika	6	Chief of Palace Guards		6	Officer in charge / Superintendent of the Harem			6	Overseer of the Harem
Prasastr	7	Director (Labour		7	Magistrate	Commandant	Officer in charge of munitions	7	Prasastr

Designation	Kangle			Shamasastry			R.K. Mookerji	This Translation	
Samahartr	8	Administrator		8	Collector General		Collector-General	8	The Chancellor
Samnidhatr	9	Director of stores		9	Chamberlain		Treasurer-General	9	The Treasurer
Pradestr	10	(*Pradestranayaka*)		10	Commissioner			10	*Pradestr*
Nayaka		Magistrate Commandant		11	Chief Constable			11	City Commandant
Paura-Vyava-harika	11	Commandant	City Judge	12 13	Officer in charge of the city Superintendent Superintendent of transactions of law or commerce		City Prefect	12	City Administrator
?	12	City Judge							
Karmantika	13	Officer in charge of Factories	Director of Factories	14	Superintendent of Manufactories		Superintendent of Agriculture and Forests	13	Head of Manufacturing establishments
Mantripari-shad	14	The Council of Ministers		15	Assembly of Councillors	Council of Ministers	Members of the Council	14	Ministers

Designation	Kangle	Shamasastry	R.K. Mookerji	This Translation
Adhyaksha	15 Superintendent	16 Head of Department		15 Chief Official of a Department (Chief Controller, etc.)
Dandapala	16 Chief of Staff Army	17 Comissary-general		16 Dandapala
Rashtrapala	Provincial officer	Superintendent of country parts	Provincial Governor	Provincial Governor
Durgapala	17 Commander of the fort	18 Officers in charge of fortifications, boundaries and wild tracts / Superintendent of boundaries		17 Commander of the fort
Antapala	18 Commander of the frontier forts / Frontier officer		Warden of the Frontiers	18 Governor of frontier region

For explanation see Notes on Translation No. 2

Appendix 8

SOURCES OF REVENUE

The various lists used to consolidate sources of revenue are brought together in this Appendix as they appear in the text. The numbers listed against each refer to the verses where more details may be found.

Verse {2.6.9} states that the source of revenue are those given in verses {2.6.2-8}.

From the fortified towns *(durgam)* - {2.6.2}

Sulka	Customs duties	{2.21.1-2,22,23,31}
		{2.22.3-8}}
Danda	Fines	[throughout]
Pautavam	Charges regarding standard weights and measures	{2.19.36-42}
Nagarika	Revenue collected by the Governor-General of the City	{2.36}
Lakshanadhyaksha	Revenue collected by the Chief Master of the Mint	{2.12.24}
Mudradhyaksha	Fees collected by Chief passport Officer	{2.34.1}
Sura	Revenue collected by the Chief Controller of Alcoholic beverages	{2.25.1-2,39,40}
Suna	Revenue collected by the Chief Controller of Animal Slaughter	{2.26.3}
Sutram	Revenue collected by the Chief Textile Commissioner	{2.23}
Tailam	Oil [sale of]	

Gritam	Ghee [sale of]	{2.29.5-7,30,41}
Kshara	Sugar [sale of]	
Sauvarnika	Revenue from Chief Superintendent of Precious Metals and Jewellery	{2.14}
Panyasamstha	Revenue from trade and marketing	{2.16}
Vesya	Revenue from Controller of Entertainers and Courtesans	{2.17}
Dhyutam	Revenue collected by Chief Controller of Betting and Gambling	{3.20.10}
Vastukam	Revenue from real estate transactions	{3.8; 3.9}
Karushilpigana	Revenue from artisans and craftsmen	
Devatadhyaksha	Revenue from Controller of Temples and Holy Places	{5.2.38}
Dwarabahiri-kadeya	Octroi and similar levies at the city gates and from foreigners	{2.22.8;2.4.32}

From the countryside (*rashtram*){2.6.3}

Sita	Revenue from crown lands	{2.24.16-18}
Bhaga	Production Share; lease rent	{2.15.3}
Bali	Special levies	{5.2}
Kara	Taxes	
Vanik	Revenue from merchants	
Nadipala	Revenue from river guards	
Tara	Ferry charges	{2.28.21,25}
Nava	Boats and shipping	{2.28.2-5,11}
Patthanam	Port dues	{2.28.7}
Vivitam	Revenue from pasture	{2.34.12}
Vartani	Road cess	{2.21.24}
Rajju	Revenue from land survey	
Chorarajju	Recovery from thieves in unpoliced lands	

From mines (*khani*) - {2.6.4}

Suvarna	Gold
Rajata	Silver
Vajra	Diamonds
Mani	Gems
Muktha	Pearls
Pravala	Corals
Sankha	Conch
Loha	Metals
Lavana	Salt
Bhumiprastar	Other ores
a-rasa-ghatava-khani	and minerals

From irrigation works (*setu*) - {2.6.5}

Pushpa	Flowers
Phala	Fruits
Vatshanda-kedara	Vegetable garden
Mulavapa	Root crops

From forests (*vana*)-{2.6.6}

Pasuvana	Deer forest
Mrigavana	Game forest
Dravyavana	Productive forest
Hastivana	Elephant forest

From animal husbandry (*vraja*)-{2.6.7}

Go	Cows
Mahisha	Buffaloes
Ajavika	Goats
Kharoshta	Camels
Asva	Horses
Asvatara	Mules

From trade (*vanikpatha*) - {2.6.8}

Sthalapatha	Land routes
Varipatha	Water routes

From form of accounting (*ayamukham* - Heads of Income) {2.6.10}

Mulya	Cost price	{2.12.35}
Bhaga	Share	
Parigha	Monopoly taxes	{2.12.35}
Kliptham	Fixed charges	{2.28.2}
Rupikam	Manufacturing charges	{2.12.26}
Athyaya	Fines and penalties	
Vyaji	Transaction tax	{2.6.22; 2.7.2; 2.12.26,35,36; 2.15.11; 2.16.10}

From the Chief Superintendent of Warehouses - {2.15.1-11}		Vyayaprathyaya {2.6.21 and 2.15.10} (Savings from Expenditure)	
Sita	Revenue from Crown lands	*Vikshepa*	Savings due to demobilisation of part of the army
Rashtram	See below		

Krayima	Cash transactions (including interest received in kind)	*Vyadhitantar-arambha*	Works abandoned before completion
Parivartika	Barter	*Arambhasesha*	Economies made
Pramityaka	Received as aid		in actual invest-
Pamityaka	Borrowed		ment compared
Samhanika	Labour in lieu of taxes		to original budget estimate
		Rashtram	{2.15.3}
Anyajatha	Unforeseen income	*Pindakara*	Taxes paid in kind by whole villages
Vyayaprathyaya	Savings from expenditure (see below)	*Shadbhaga* *Senabhaktham*	1/6th share Contributions from people for maintenance of the army
Upasthanam	Changes in stock		
Prarjitam	Receipt of outs-tanding arrears already written off	*Bali*	Special levies
		Kara	Taxes (generally paid in cash)
		Utsangha	Presents from the people on festive occasions
		Parsvam	Surcharge
		Parihinikam	Compensatory payments
		Aupayanikam	Gifts to the king
		Kaushteyakam	Income from water reservoirs, parks.
Miscellaneous Income	{2.6.20}	<u>From revenue collection by the Chancellor</u>	{2.35.1}
Nashta-prasmatham	Recovery of debts and dues earlier written off	*Ayudhiyam*	Supply of soldiers in lieu of tax

Ayukthadanda	Fines paid by government servants	<u>Pratikara -</u> <u>Taxes collected</u> <u>in kind</u>	{2.35.1}
Parsvam	Surcharge	*Dhanya*	Grains
Parihinikam	Compensatory payments	*Pasu Hiranya*	Cattle Gold
Aupayanikam	Gifts to the king	*Kupya*	Forest produce
Damara-gatakasvam	Confiscated property	<u>From {2.35.12}</u> *Vishti*	Labour
Aputrakam	Intestate property	*Sulka* *Vartani*	Duty Road cess
Nidhi	Treasure trove	*Ativahikam*	Escort charges
<u>From Chief</u> <u>Controller of</u> <u>Mining</u>	{2.12.35,36}	*Gulma* *Taradeya*	Dues payable at military stations Ferry charges
Mulya	Cost price	*Bhaga*	Share
Bhaga	Share	*Bhakttha*	Subsistence
Vyaji	Transaction tax		allowance
Parigham	Monopoly tax		
Athyaya	Fines and penalties		
Sulka	Customs duty/Octroi		
Vaidharana	Countervailing duty		
Danda	Punishment		
Rupam	Inspection fee		
Rupikam	Manufacturing charge		
From {2.35.8} and {2.35.3}	{2.35.3}	{2.35.8}	
Taxes Exemptions	*Karada* *Bhoga*	*Aakarada* *Parihara*	
<u>Confiscation</u> *Ubhaya-paroktam*	Disputed landed property, all claims over which have been rejected by village elders	{3.9.17}	

Pranashta-swamikam	Landed property whose owner has disappeared	{3.9.17}
Parokta	Fines for loss of suit	{3.1.20,21,31}
<u>Miscellaneous</u>		
-	Revenue from salt	{2.12.28}
-	Poll-tax	{2.6.2}
-	Tax on liquor not manufactured by the state	{2.25.39}
Vaidharanam	State monopoly products (e.g. liquor)	{2.12.31}
-	Confisction for non-cultivation	{2.1.12}
- -	Excess of sale price over called-out price at customs post or in sale of buildings	{2.21.9; 3.9.5}
-	Difference between [larger] amount proved in court and actual amount claimed by plaintiff	{3.1.42}

Appendix 9

CUSTOMS TARIFFS

TARIFF SCHEDULE

IMPORT DUTY	{2.12.3,29}
On edible salt	one-sixth in kind + countervailing duty
All other goods	20% ad valorem

EXPORT DUTY	{2.22.4-7}

Live animals:

		Medicines, Spices and Perfumery:	
Quadrupeds and bipeds	4% or 5% in cash	Spices; perfumery such as sandalwood and aloe	1/10th or 1/15th in cash 1/15th in cash

Food:

Grains, fats, sugar, salt	4% or 5% in cash	Perfumes n.e.s Medicines	4% or 5% in cash "

Fresh produce:

Flowers, fruits, vegetables, root, vegetables, fruits of creepers, seeds	one-sixth in kind	Cotton Ivory; skins Timber, bamboo, bark	4% or 5% in cash 1/10th or 1/15th in cash 4% or 5% in cash

Raw material:

Preserved food:

Dried fish or meat	one-sixth in kind	Pigments and colouring material	1/10th or 1/15th in cash
Cooked food	4% or 5% in cash	in cash	

Liquor:

Wine	4% or 5% in cash
Fermented liquor	1/10th or 1/15th in cash

Manufactures:

Garments of cotton and similar in cash fibres; leather garments; silk yarn; covering material such as bedspreads; carpets; wool and woollen goods	1/10th or 1/15th in cash
Cotton yarn; garments n.e.s; leather goods n.e.s; earthenware.	4% or 5% in cash

Gems and jewellery:

Conch shells; diamonds; precious stones; pearl necklaces; coral.	20% of basic cost (price less value added) in cash; experts to evaluate value added.

Appendix 10

ALCOHOLIC BEVERAGES

LIQUORS MADE FROM *KINVA*

Kinva   1 part rice to 3 parts beans with added spices; for example:
1 *drona* of pulp of raw or cooked masha beans.
1/3 *drona* of rice.
1*karsha* of each of the six mixed spices.

Medaka   2 parts rice to 3 parts ferment and 16 parts water; for example:
Rice-wine - 3 *prasthas* of *kinva*
1/2 *adhaka* of rice
1 *drona* of water

Prasanna Flour wine (white)
2 parts rice to 3 parts ferment and 16 parts water; for example:
5 *prasthas kinva*
12 *adhakas* flour
24 *dronas* of water
Back and fruit of *kramuka* (?)

Addition to *Medaba* and *Prasanna*

5 *karshas* each of the following: *patha, lodha, tejuvati,* cardamom, *valuka,* liquorice, grape juice, *priyangu, daruharidra* (turmeric?), black pepper and long pepper.

Clarifying agent for *Medaka* and *Prasanna*

A decoction of liquorice and jaggery.

Varieties of *Prasanna*

Mahasura - White liquor and mango juice, replacing in part the spice mixture given above. This is to be clarified with a handful of mixed spice, burnt jaggery and pulp of herbs, like *partha,* etc. The liquor can be made sweeter by adding 5 *palas* of jaggery.   {2.25.17,18,26-28,31-34}

OTHER LIQUORS

Asava   (for 8 *tulas* of water)
1 *tula* wood apple
5 *tulas* treacle
1 *prastha* honey

This is for average quality; for superior quality add one quarter more of each of the three ingredients and for lower quality less.

Spices to be added—1 *karsha* each of cinnamon, *chitraka*, *vilanga*, quarter of the quantity of each of these is to be kept in the liquor (tied up in a piece of cloth).   {2.25.19,20,29,30}

Maireya

A decoction of the bark of the *meshashringi* with jaggery; spices to be added: long pepper and black pepper or tripala (nutmeg, arecanut and cloves).   {2.25.22,23}

Madhu

Grape wine—*Kapishayana* imported from Afghanistan.

Harahuraka—imported from Arachosia.   {2.25.24,25}

APPENDIX 11

FOREIGN POLICY METHODS

Term	Verse No.	Kangle	Shamasastry	Konow	CHI	Others	This Translation
Samdhi	{7.1.6}	Peace; Entering into a treaty; Policy of peace, Making a treaty containing conditions or terms.	Peace; Agreement with pledges	Agreement	Peace (Policy of Peace)		Making peace; Entering into an agreement with specific conditions.
Vigraha	{7.1.7}	War; Doing injury; Policy of hostility.	War; Offensive operation.	Harming; War	War		Waging war; Active hostilities; Declaring war
Aasana	{7.1.8}	Staying quiet; Remaining indifferent; Policy of remaining quiet	Observing neutrality; Indifference.	Sitting; Overlooking; Disregarding	Neutrality Halt.	Cold war (G)	Doing neither; Pause; Being indifferent to a situation.

(Table continued)

Term	Verse No.	Kangle	Shamasastry	Konow	CHI	Others	This Translation
Yana	{7.1.9}	Marching; Augmentation (of power); Marching on an expedition.	Marching; Making preparations.	Going; Marching; Increase of one's own resources.	Expedition	Marching on an expedition; Set out on a campaign of conquest (P)	Expedition; (Preparing for War); Augmenting one's own power, i.e. mobilising.
Samsraya	{7.1.10}	Seeking shelter; Submitting to another; Seeking shelter with another king.	Alliance; Seeking the protection of another.	Leaguing; Joining; Entrusting onself to to another.	Alliance	Umbrella (G)	Seeking protection Geeting the protection of another.
Dvaidhi bhava	{7.1.11}	Dual policy; Resorting to peace with one and war with another; The double policy of *samdhi* with one king and *vigraha* with another at the same time.	Making peace with one and waging war with another.	Duplicity; Adopting agreement and fight.	Dubious attitudes		Adopting a dual policy; Making peace with one and war with another.
Aasana	{7.4.1}	Staying quiet	Neutrality			Not planning to march on an expedition; Condition of armed neutrality (P)	

(Table continued)

Term	Verse No.	Kangle	Shamasastry	Konow	CHI	Others	This Translation
Sthana	[7.4.2]	Remaining still	Keeping quiet				Prolonged inaction
Aasana	[7.4.2]	Staying quiet	Withdrawal				Inaction for a purpose
Upeksbma	[7.4.2]	Remaining indifferent	Negligence				Deliberately not taking action
Sama	[7.17.2]	Peace	Quiet				Non-intervention
Samdhi	[7.17.2]	Treaty	Agreement for peace				Peace Treaty
Samadhi	[7.17.2]	Hostage	Reconcilement				Treaty with hostage
Sapatha	[7.17.5]	Plighting one's	Honesty troth				Agreement made on oath: or word of honour
Pratibhu	[7.17.5]	Surety	Security				Agreement guaranteed by a
Pratigraha	[7.17.5]	Hostage	Hostage				Agreement with a hostage

<u>Notes:</u> CHI:Cultural History of India, Vol.II, p.457, The Ramakrishna Mission Institute of Culture, Calcutta, 1962; Konow: Konow, Sven, Kautilya Studies, Oslo, 1945; G: Gupta, V.K., Kautilyan Jurisprudence, p. 218; P: Parmar, A Study of Kautilya's *Arthashastra*, p.205.

Appendix 12

WAR MATERIAL

FIXED MACHINES {2.18.5}		WEAPONS WITH SHARP POINTS {2.18.7}	
Sarvatobhadra	A machine like a cart-wheel for throwing stones	Sakthi	4 *hastas* long, with a leaf-shaped tip
		Prasa	Two feet long, double handed
Jamadagnya	A machine to shoot arrows	Kunta	A long sharp weapon for horse riders
Bahumukha	A tower for archers (with many holes to shoot from)	Hataka	Three-pointed weapon
Visvasaghatin	A beam, released by a mechanism, so as to fall on attackers	Bhindipala	A broad-bladed weapon for horse riders
Samghatika	A machine with long poles to set fire to attacking mobile turrets	Sula	Spear
		Tomara	Four to five *hastas* long with an arrow-shaped tip
Yanaka	A rotating machine to throw logs	Varahakarna	Spear with a tip like a boar's ear
Parjanyaka	An engine to pump water to put out fire	Kanaya	A throwing weapon, about two feet long, with

Bahu	Two pillars, released by a mechanism, to fall towards each other and block a passage or kill animals		triangular points at either end and with a grip in the middle
		Karpana	Arrow-like throwing weapon
		Trasika	A two-handed weapon like the *prasa* but with a tail (?)
Urdhvabahu	A heavy pillar released by a mechanism		
Ardhabahu	A smaller version, half the length of the above		

MOBILE MACHINES
{2.18.6}

Panchalika	A wooden plank studded with nails and placed in the moat
Devadanda	A beam, with or without nails, placed on top of the fort wall
Sukarika	A leather bag filled with cotton or wool placed around turrets
Musalayashti	Pike
Hastivaraka	A pike with multiple points for use against elephants
Talavrinta	A machine to raise wind dust

BOWS AND ARROWS
{2.18.8-11}

Bows can be made of palmyra, bamboo, wood, bone or horn. The diffe-rent types are: *karmuka, kodanda, druna* and *dhanus*. Bow strings can be made of *murva, arka,* hemp, *gavedhu,* bamboo, bark of the sinews of animals.

Types of arrows are: *venu, sara, dandasana* and *naraca.* Arrow heads shall be made of iron, wood or bone so as to cut, pierce or tear.

SWORDS {2.18.12,13}

Nishtrimsa (with a curved tip), *mandalagra* (straight with a rounded tip) and *asiyashti* (long and thin) are types of swords. The hilts shall be made of rhinoceros horn, buffalo horn, elephant tusk, wood or the root of bamboo.

Mudgara	Hammer (thrown by machines?)
Gada	Mace (thrown by machines?)
Spriktala	Mace with sharp nails
Kuddala	Spade (?)
Asphatima	A catapult
Utpatima	A machine to pull down pillars
Udhghatima	A machine to pull down towers
Satagni	A movable pillar studded with nails
Trisula	Trident
Chakra	Discus

CUTTING WEAPONS {2.18.14}

Parasu two feet	A scimitar, long
Kutara	Kind of axe
Pattasa	An axe with a trident at one or both ends
Khanitra	Saw
Kuddala	Axe (?)
Chakra	Discus
Kandach-hedana	A big axe

STONE WEAPONS {2.18.15}

Stones can be thrown by machines, catapults or by hand. Millstones are also weapons.

ARMOUR {2.18.16,17}

Lohajalika	(A coat made of) metal rings
Pattajalika	(Armour made of) sheet metal
Sutrakankata	(Made of fabric stuffed [with cotton, wool or hair]

Skin, hooves and horns of dolphins, rhinoceros, bisons, elephants or bulls can also be used.

Types and parts of Personal Armour

Sirastrana	Helmet
Kantatrana	Neck guard
Kurpasa	Cuirass (breast plate and back plate)

OTHER PROTECTIVE DEVICES

Peti	Protective box or camouflage of creepers
Charma	Protector made of leather
Hastikarna	Board used as a cover
Talamula	Shield shaped like the root of a palm tree
Dhamanika	Blown-up leather bags
Kapata	Hinged wooden board
Kitika	Cover made of leather, bamboo or cane
Apratihara	Device to deter elephants
Balahakanta	Same as above but with metal tips

Kanchuka	Hauberk (coat of mail up to the Knees)
Varavana	Coat of woollen cloth reaching to the ankles; see {2.11.98}
Patta	Sleeveless armour not made of metal
Nagodarika	Tasset (thigh guard) or Gauntlet (glove)

ACCESSORIES AND ACCOUTREMENTS {2.18.18}

Ornaments for horses, elephants and chariots. Goads, hooks and other implements used to train elephants and horses and lead them into battle.

EQUIPMENT FOR DEFENCE OF FORTS {2.3.33-35}

Stored in pits along the ramparts: stones, spades, axes, arrows and implements for sharpening them, choppers, clubs, hammers, sticks, chakras, machines, weapons of mass destruction, pikes and bamboos with sharp points, long-necked vessels for pouring hot oil as well as various kinds of forest produce necessary for defence.

SECRET WORK {2.18.19}

Secret work is of two kinds—those which delude by creating illusions and those which destroy.

Appendix 13

ON ELEPHANTS

CATCHING ELEPHANTS:

Only those elephants whose physical characteristics and behaviour are judged excellent by elephant trainers shall be caught.

Summer is the time to catch them.

Twenty-year-old elephants shall be caught.

The physical characteristics of a good elephant are: red patches, evenly fleshed, of even sides and rounded girth, with a curved backbone and well covered with flesh.

A suckling cub, one with no tusks or undeveloped tusks, a diseased one or a pregnant or suckling female shall not be captured.

A cub may be caught to play with.   {2.2.12; 2.31.8-11,16,17}

TYPES OF ELEPHANTS:

Elephants are classified into four kinds, (under training, war elephant, riding elephant and untrainable ones) each with its own method of training and handling. The types of work for which they are trained and the methods of doing so are given below.

Type	Work	Treatment/training
Preliminary training	Getting the elephant used to: (i) a man on its shoulders; (ii) being tied to a post; (iii) being taken to watering places; (iv) hilly terrain; (v) strange elephants.	During this period the elephant shall be treated with as much care as a cub elephant.
Training for war	(i) stationary drill, including standing still, rising, bending and jumping over obstacles [on command];	Binding with girths, putting on collars and making them work with trained troupes of elephants

	(ii) movement drill, including stopping, lying down and jumping over obstacles [on command]; (iii) advancing and marching in straight, transverse, zigzag or circular movements; (iv) trampling and killing horses, chariots or men; (v) fighting with other elephants; (vi) assaulting forts; (vii) fighting with infantry, cavalry or chariots in war.	[are the stages of training].
Training for riding	(i) raising fore or hind limbs [to let rider mount]; (ii) leading a [wild] elephant with a man on its own back; (iii) trotting; (iv) running at different gaits; (v) obeying the stick; (vi) obeying the goad; (vii) obeying without stick or goad; (viii) getting used to hunting.	Keeping the animal fit, giving it adequate exercise and training it to obey commands.
Rogue elephants	Cannot be trained to do useful work because they are frightened, obstinate, perverse, wilful, in rut or mad. Such elephants can be genuinely mad, clever enough to feign madness, mischievous or vicious.	These have to be kept in solitary confinement.

{2.32.1-10}

The training of each elephant shall be modified according to the seasons and shall take into account the animal's physical capacity, intelligence and a mixture of other characteristics.

{2.31.18}

ACCOUTREMENTS

The equipment for tying up and other purposes [for each elephant] shall be as indicated by the trainers [and shall include:]

<u>Tying equipment:</u> Tethering posts, neck collars, girths, bridles, leg chains and upper chains.

<u>Implements:</u> Goad, bamboo staff and machines.

<u>Ornaments:</u> Garlands, necklaces, covering for the back and similar decorations.

<u>War material:</u> Armour, clubs, quivers for arrows and war machines.

{2.32.11,15}

DAILY ROUTINE:

Dividing the day into eight parts:

First part	Bath
Second part	Feeding
Third and fourth parts	Exercise
Fifth and sixth parts	Rest or displays
Seventh part	Bath
Eighth part	Feeding

The elephant sleeps two-third of the night and spends one-third of the time sometimes getting up and sometimes lying down.   {2.31.5-7}

RATIONS

The best kind of elephant measures seven *aratnis* (10 1/2 feet) high, nine *aratnis* (13 1/2 feet) in length and ten *aratnis* (15 feet) in girth, when it is 40 years old.

The medium kind at age 40, (and the best kind at age 30), measure six *aratnis* (9 feet) in height and the lowest kind at age 40 (and the best kind at age 25), measures five *aratnis* (7 1/2 feet) in height [and other measurements proportionately].

The ration for the medium type is three quarters of the standard ration and that for the lowest, one half.   {2.31.11,12,15}

For details of the actual quantities of rations prescribed, see Appendix 4 on 'Rations'.

Appendix 14

NOTES ON TRANSLATION

1. OTHER SCHOOLS OF *ARTHASHASTRA*

Attempts have been made (see Kangle, Part III, pp. 43, 44, 46) to guess at what the teachings of the older schools were. But the very few references to these schools in Kautilya's *Arthashastra* are insufficient to build up a complete picture of each school, even if we assume that they shared many ideas. For example, even Ushanas and Bharadvaja, the ones quoted more often than others, are mentioned only seven times each. The other teachers referred to by name are: Brihaspati, Vishalaksha and Parasara (6 times each), Prachetasa Manu, Vatavyadhi and Pisuna (5 times each), Kaunapadanta (4) and Bahudantiputra and Ambhi (once each). The unidentified teachers are referred to by Kangle as 'teachers' and by Shamasastry as 'my teacher'; it is better to render the word *acharyah* as 'some teachers'. The location in this translation of the various views is given in the index. The subjects on which Kautilya disagrees with earlier teachers are not many: the nature of the sciences, the number of ministers, the process of deliberation, fines for erring officials, the punishments for perjury and robbery, and calamities, including the discussion on anger and lust, are the more important ones. Most of the disagreements with the unidentified teachers are concentrated in the books on calamities and foreign policy.

2. TECHNICAL TERMS

All Sanskrit words are given an immediate translation. Some of the more important technical terms are given in lists in the relevant sections: high officials (IV.iv); sources of revenue (V.ii and Appendix 8); heads of departments (VII.i); loans, deposits, etc. (VIII. vii); the Circle of Kings (X.ii); measurements (Appendix 1); domesticated and wild animals (Appendix 3); professions (Appendix 6) and defence equipment (Appendix 12).

3. AMATYA IN II.i

An examination of all the places in the text where *amatya*, *mantri* and *mantriparishad* occur shows that *amatya* and *mantri* are often used interchangeably. Apart from the salary list {5.3.7}, *mantriparishad* (Council of Ministers) is used only in one specialised portion of the text, i.e. on the king taking advice {1.15.47-50}. *Amatya* occurs as a general term in criteria for appointment {1.8.1-29; 1.10.13,4}; as a minister {1.9.1,2}, Head of a Department {2.9.1}, judge {3.1.1} or magistrate {4.1.1}. A very wide definition of the duties of *amatyas* is given in {8.1.8, 23}. In {1.8.29} it is clearly stated that suitable people should be appointed as *amatya*, allotting work to them according to their ability and rank, but not as *mantrin*, implying that a *mantri* held a superior position. However, in two places, the position of the *amatya* is shown as being very important—in {1.7.8} where he was as important as the king's teacher in advising the king to follow the right path and in 5.6 where he is expected to play a crucial role in organizing the succession to a dying or dead king. The chapter on taking advice (*mantra*), particularly verses {1.15.34-44}, indicates that those who advised the King—the *mantrin*—were very few in number and were superior to the general run of ministers and heads of departments. Further, a revolt by a *mantri* was as dangerous as those of the *purohita*, the Chief of Defence or the Crown Prince {9.3.12}. It is clear that the very few close advisers held the rank of councillors; there were many ministers, heads of departments, judges and magistrates. Depending on the context, the advisers closest to the king are referred to in this translation as Councillors and the others by their function.

4. THE *MAHAMATRAS* IN IV.iv

Verse {1.1.20} makes it clear that there were eighteen designated high officials, collectively known as the *mahamatras* and referred to as such throughout the treatise. The list in {1.12.20} has to be read with the salary list in {5.3}. One problem is to understand the two lists in such a way as to produce eighteen designations. R.K. Mookerjee does not attempt this. While most designations are clear, two are ambiguous. Is *pradeshtranayaka* one official or two, *pradeshtr* and *nayaka*? Likewise, is *pauravyavaharika*, one official or two (*paura* and *vyavaharika*)? After considering all the translations, it seems best to treat *pauravyavaharika* as one official, particularly as the only two references in the text use the combined word. But, *pradeshtr* and *nayaka* are two separate officials. This judgment is based on the facts that (i) *pradeshta* (magistrate) is used widely, particularly in Book 4 and (ii) *nayaka*, as a military designation, is used in Book 10.

As for the translation of the designations, the official *prasastr* is mentioned only in the two lists and his duties are not spelt out anywhere. It is possible that this designation is a retention from earlier texts and, in the *Arthashastra*, is used only to represent a higher grade for salary and honorific purposes. The same argument applies to *dandapala*. If *pradeshtr* is to be deemed to be different from the posts of magistrates, then a precise translation of this designation is also not possible. The reasons for the specific translations of *dauvarika* and *antarvamsika* are given in IV.iv. The translation of *samahartr* as Chancellor (of Administration of the countryside) and *samnidhatr* as Treasurer are obvious from the nature of their duties. For translating *mantri* as councillor, see Note 1 above. For reasons explained in Note 10 below, *senapati* is translated as Chief of Defence.

5. SIMPLE DEFAMATION OF CHARACTER {3.18.7,8} in VIII.xiii

It is very difficult to construct a rational table of penalties to fit in with the two conditions. The method suggested by Kangle (II, p. 247, note to verse 3.18.7) is a scale of fines of 12, 9, 6 and 3 panas if an outcast defames a Brahmin, Kshatriya, etc. and a fine of 8, 6, 4 and 2 panas if a Brahmin defames a Kshatriya, Vaishya, etc. This leads to two anomalies: (i) there is no punishment at all if a person defames another of the same *varna* and (ii) the fine for a Brahmin defaming a Kshatriya is greater than the one for a Kshatriya defaming a Brahmin. The anomalies arise because Kangle has assumed that 'over 3 panas' means 'stages of 3 panas' and that 'below 2 panas' also means 'stages of 2 panas upwards'. An alternative logical set of fines is given below.

Defamer	Person defamed				
	Brahmin	Kshatriya	Vaishya	Sudra	Outcast
Brahmin	3	2	1 1/2	1	1/2
Kshatriya	4	3	2	1 1/2	1
Vaishya	5	4	3	2	1 1/2
Sudra	6	5	4	3	2
Outcast	7	6	5	4	3

In this table, when the defamer and defamed are both of the same *varna*, the fine is always 3 panas and the two conditions are filled around the diagonal.

6. COVERT ACTIVITIES IN IX.i

Kangle (Vol. III, p. 208) considers that the established spies definitely worked for Chancellor and hence all agents were under his control. This is based on a misunderstanding; just because the king's agents and the Chancellor's agents both adopted similar covers (householder, trader, etc.) it does not follow that they were the same persons. It is unlikely that the vital area of the secret service would have been left to a subordinate, however highly placed he might have been. It is clearly stated in {1.12.6} that the duty of the king's agents was spying on the *mahamatras*, of whom the Chancellor was one. An agent working under and reporting to the Chancellor could hardly report on his master. Secondly, the functions of the king's agents were quite different from those of the Chancellor's agents. Thirdly, there is no indication in the text that the Chancellor had anything to do with foreign policy, in which areas the secret service was widely used. Lastly, from {1.19.13}, we see that the king personally received, every morning, reports from his spies.

7. THE ORIGIN OF KINGSHIP {1.13.5-10} IN IX.iii

Verses {1.13.5-10} contain a more elaborate counter-argument including the theory of the origin of kings and kingship. 'When there was no order in society and only the law of the jungle prevailed, people [were unhappy and being desirous of order] made Manu, the son of *Vivasvat*, their king; and they assigned to the king one-sixth part of the grains grown by them, one-tenth of other commodities and money. The king then used these to safeguard the welfare of his subjects. Those who do not pay fines and taxes take on themselves the sins of kings, while kings who do not look after the welfare of the people take on themselves the sins of their subjects. Therefore, even those who live in forests [*vanaprasthas* and *sanyasins* who do not own any property] offer to the king one-sixth of the grain gleaned by them as the [legitimate] share of one who protects them. The king, who disperses both favours and punishments is both Indra [the god who rewards] and Yama [the god who punishes].'

8. THE CIRCLE OF KINGS IN X.II

Kangle's conjecture that Kautilya had propounded two theories of the Circle of Kings is probably due to the similarity in the number of kings in the circle—twelve are defined in {6.2.17-22} and twelve are mentioned in {6.2.24-27}. Verses {6.2.17-22} are just definitions of the terms used in developing the theory, as clearly emphasized in {6.2.23}. Out of the twelve kings defined, two are the Middle and Neutral kings. The other ten are formed out of two groups of six, counting the conqueror and the enemy twice. The first group are the six kings in front of the conqueror—himself and his two allies and the enemy and *his* two allies. The mirror image are the six at the rear. For theoretical purposes, the actual direction is immaterial, serving only to define the direction of the attack. Supposing the conqueror attacks the enemy (northward in the diagram), the kings concerned are: the conqueror, the enemy, the Middle king and the Neutral king, each with two allies. This is the circle referred to in {6.2.24-29}. In this context, the rear-enemy is the *parshnigraha*, and his role is analysed separately.

9. VERSES {7.6.1, 2} AND {7.7.1} IN X.ii

{7.6.1} and {7.7.1} give rise to difficulties because they envisage the conqueror entering into a treaty with his primary enemy. Most translators consider that there is no likelihood at all of the conqueror entering into a treaty with his enemy. See, for example, Kangle, Part II, note to {7.13.1}. This is not so. A treaty with an enemy was possible in exceptional circumstances, so long as it was intended to outmanoeuvre him, i.e. the treaty was used to gain advantages. Such a treaty is envisaged in {7.6.13}, as a treaty without stipulation. In this translation, {7.6.1, 2} are treated as explaining dual policy. This judgment is based on the similarity with the opening verses of the previous chapters. For example, {7.2.1-5} compares the relative merits of the six policies, {7.3.1-5} deal with peace and war in relation to the balance of power, and {7.4.1-4} define aspects of doing nothing. There are significant differences between {7.6.1} and {7.6.2} and between {7.6.1} and {7.7.1}. While {7.6.1} refers to the second element of the Circle of States, which is always the enemy, the second refers only to *samantha* (neighbour), without specifying that it is the *ari*, the enemy. Though all neighbours, in principle, are enemies, every one of them need not be treated as the main one at a given time; only one of the neighbours is the main enemy. The other difference is that, in {7.6.1}, the enemy is to be outmanoeuvred but in {7.7.1} a neighbour's help is to be accepted.

10. HOSTAGES IN X.III

Two words are used in the text to describe a hostage. *Samadhi*, as Kangle points out, is related to *adhi*, a pledge and can be literally translated as a 'pledge for peace', hence, hostage. That this word means the person held as hostage is shown by the title of {7.17} *samadhimoksha*, 'liberation of the hostage'. The second word, used in {7.17.11}, is *pratigraha*, 'got in exchange'. This emphasizes the conditionality aspect of keeping a hostage in exchange for good behaviour by the hostage giver.

11. MIDDLE AND NEUTRAL KINGS {7.18.1-28} IN X.vii

Shamasastry's translation of this chapter is, on the whole, unsatisfactory since he assumes that the analysis is from the point of view of the Middle king. As pointed out by Kangle in his note to {7.18.1} on page 380 of Vol. II, Kautilya's discussion on foreign policy is always from the point of view of the conqueror. Another problem in translating this chapter is that the text uses repeatedly the phrase 'the Middle king wants', without explaining what exactly it is. Kangle assumes that it is always to 'seize' while Shamasastry substitutes different objectives ranging from 'securing the friendship' to 'routing out'. In this translation, different objectives are attributed to the Middle king, depending on the context. For example, it is clear that the Middle king may plan to subvert an ally of the conqueror. Since the Middle king shares a common border with both the conqueror and the enemy, the conqueror's relations with his allies are bound to be complex, depending on the quality of the ally. The meaning of different verses depends on how to construe the words describing an ally—friendly, one who deserves to be weakened and one who deserves to be crushed. The conqueror cannot adopt the same policy towards an unreliable ally as he would towards a true ally. If we assume that {7.18.28} specifies the basic principle, then the conqueror's aim, at all times, is to support a true ally and take appropriate action against those allies who are less true.

12. OLIGARCHIES {11.1.4,5} IN X.IX

Some of the oligarchic states listed in the *Arthashastra* are also known from other sources such as the Greek historians, Buddhist literature and the Hindu epics. For details, see the note to this verse in Kangle, Vol.II p. 454. Of these, the Kambojas, Surashtras, Kshatriyas (the Xathroi of the Greek historians) and the Srenis (the Greek Sinae?) 'had their livelihood in economic activity and the profession of arms', i.e. they practised agriculture, cattle-rearing and trade but were also trained troops ready to take up arms when necessary. Kautilya mentions a second group in {11.1.5}—the Licchavikas, Vrjikas, Mallakas, Madrakas, Kukuras, Kurus and the Panchalas—who used 'the title of rajas', implying that all members of the collective leadership called themselves kings. Jayaswal (in Hindu Polity) has pointed that the first five of the second group were more likely to have been political groups based in a region while the latter two were probably tribes. Kangle also points out that most of the oligarchies mentioned belong to the north and north-west of India.

13. SENAPATI IN XI.II

Senapati is usually translated as Commander-in-Chief; this does not seem right. The king encapsulated in himself all the constituents of his state. He had supreme authority over all aspects of the governance of the country. It is clear from the text that normally it was the king who led the troops into battle; only exceptionally was the Crown Prince or the Chief of Defence made battle commander. Therefore, only the king could have been the Commander-in-Chief. The *senapati* occupied a post similar to that of the Chairman of the Joint Chiefs of Defence Staff. The designation 'Chief of Defence' is used in some countries even now.

14. VERSES {10.3.28-31} IN XI.vii

For reasons explained by Kangle in note to {10.3.28-31}, p. 440 of Vol. II, these verses would seem to be a marginal gloss that has entered the text. The substance of {10.3.28} is: 'Even in the Vedas it is said that brave men who fall in battle attain the same heavenly rewards as those who do their *yajna* properly and completely.' Two other verses, said to be in common currency, are then quoted. {10.3.30}: 'The brave who sacrifice their lives in battle obtain immediately heavenly rewards which even Brahmins cannot get after performing any number of *yajnas* or doing penance.' {10.3.31}: 'One who will not fight for a master whose salt he had eaten will go to hell, being unworthy to receive the sacred oblations.'

Appendix 15

NOTE ON BIBLIOGRAPHY

This Note is not meant to be an exhaustive bibliography on all works related to Kautilya's *Arthashastra* but is intended to be only a general guide to interested readers on where to look for more material on the text, translations, commentaries and studies.

TEXTS OF THE *ARTHASHASTRA*

R.P. Kangle's *The Kautilyan Arthashastra*, Part I: A Critical Edition with a Glossary, (2nd Ed., University of Bombay, 1969) has been used as the authoritative text for this translation. In his detailed Introduction to this volume, Kangle has described all the available manuscripts that he had used in preparing the authoritative text. These include: (i) a fragmentary (Book 1 and a part of Book 2) palm leaf manuscript in Devanagari, discovered in a Jain library in Patan; this is the only text available from North India and is thought to be as old as the 12th century; (ii) a palm leaf manuscript with the entire text in Malayalam characters, about 300 years old; (iii) the entire text in a palm leaf manuscript, in the Grantha script, about a century old; (iv) a transcript of the above in Devanagari script made in 1907; (v) another similar transcript made in 1905; (vi) a copy of (ii) made a century ago; and (vii) an incomplete transcript made in 1906. Though there are references to some other manuscripts, these are now not traceable and must be presumed lost. After an exhaustive comparison, Kangle has concluded that there are, apart from the very old North Indian fragment, there are only two original complete manuscripts, the two mentioned as (ii) and (iii) above. The reasons why some verses are considered to be interpolations, why some passages are marginal comments which had become incorporated into the text and why one variant reading is preferred to another, have been fully explained by Kangle in both Part I (Text) and Part II (Translation).

COMMENTARIES

There are some very old commentaries which helped Kangle in determining the text. He has referred to: (i) *Bhashavyakhyana*, about the 12th century

AD, with the text in Malayalam; (ii) a fragmentary (up to 3.1, with gaps) Sanskrit commentary containing two separate commentaries, the *Chanakyatika* of Bhikshu Prabhamati and the *Jayamangala* of Shankararya: (iii) the *Nayachandrika*, a Sanskrit commentary by Madhavayajvan of the segment {7.7} to {12.4.12} some gaps: (iv) a small fragment of a Sanskrit commentary, the *Nitinimiti* of Yogghama, discovered along with the manuscript in Patan and (v) the commentary, from {2.8.5} to the end of Book 3, called the *Pratipadapanchika* by Bhattasvamin.

In modern times, T. Ganapati Sastri has published, along with the text, a commentary in Sanskrit, the *Srimula*.

TRANSLATIONS

The earliest translation in English is Shamasastry's. The translation in German by J.J. Meyer contains exhaustive notes. B. Breloer's three-volume study is also important. In the very detailed footnotes to each verse in Part II of his work, Kangle has referred to the different interpretations in the above works. There are a number of translations in Indian languages listed in pages 285 and 286 of Kangle's Part III *The Kautaliya Arthashastra:A Study*. I have consulted the one in Tamil (Annamalai University, 1980); unfortunately this is couched in literary Tamil and is barely comprehensible.

All these translations follow the textual order. The only work I know of which has attempted a partial reorganization is V.K. Gupta's *Kautilyan Jurisprudence* (B.D. Gupta, Delhi, 1987); this is only a selection from Kangle's translation with the original text cut and pasted and a few passages from Shamasastry, without a word of acknowledgment to the debt owed to either author.

STUDIES ON THE *ARTHASHASTRA*

The range of studies on the *Arthashastra*, both books and articles, is extensive. A comprehensive list will be found in pages 287 to 290 of Kangle's study. Attention is also invited to the list in page 17, notes 57 to 65 in pages 20 and 21 and the Bibliography in pages 265 to 276 in Aradhana Parmar's *Techniques of Statecraft: A Study of Kautilya's Arthashastra*, Atma Ram and Sons, Delhi, 1987). To these lists, one may add Sven Konow's *Kautilya Studies* (Oslo, 1945). T.R. Trautmann's *Kautilya and Arthashastra: A Statistical Investigation of Authorship and Evolution of the Text* (E.J. Brill, Leiden, 1971) has been consulted by me in its 1968 Ph.D. thesis form at the School of Oriental and African Studies, University of London.

A recent bilingual (Hindi and English) selection of articles is *Kautilya's Arthashastra: An Appraisal*, edited by Pushpendra Kumar (Nag Publications, Delhi, 1989). *Kautilya on Crime and Punishment* by Krishna Mohan Agrawal (Shree Almora Book Depot, Almora, 1990) is a good compilation on this topic.

Among the background books I have found useful are: (i) *The Cultural History of India*, Vol.II, Second Ed., (The Ramakrishna Mission Institute of Culture, Calcutta, 1962); (ii) *The History and Culture of the Indian People, Vol. II—The Age of Imperial Unity* (Bharatiya Vidya Bhavan, Bombay, 5th Ed., 1980); (iii) Romila Thapar, *A History of India*, Vol. I (Penguin Books, 1966) and (iv) Radha Kumud Mookerji, *Chandragupta Maurya and his Times* (Motilal Banarsidas, Delhi, Fourth Edition, 1988).

Maps, Charts and Figures

Index of Verses—By Textual Order

The index is meant to assist in finding out in which Part and Section a particular verse of the text has been included. Verses which have been omitted because they are either superfluous (e.g. 'By this is explained...') or interpolations are not included. Verses which are either summarized or shown as charts or diagrams are shown as fully translated I.0 indicates the title page of part I.

Index